A CHECKLIST of AMERICAN IMPRINTS for 1827

Items 27762 - 31874

Compiled by

Richard H. Shoemaker

assisted by

Gayle Cooper

The Scarecrow Press, Inc.

Metuchen, N.J. 1970

ISBN 0-8108-0336-4

Preface

Volumes Seven and Eight, 1826 and 1827

In 1969, the National Endowment for the Humanities made an offer of a matching grant to the compiler of these volumes and the Scarecrow Press, Inc. matched the offer. As a result, this _Check list_ has the best financial support in its history.

The grant has enabled the compiler to secure the services as a research assistant of Miss Gayle Cooper who for several years has worked at the Library Company of Philadelphia, with its great wealth of Americana. It is expected that these volumes, Seven and Eight, for 1826 and 1827, will be followed before the end of 1970 by volumes Nine, Ten and Eleven, covering the years through 1830. After that, the compiler intends to publish additions and corrections, and then author and title indexes to the _Checklist_ from 1820 through 1830. Corrections and additions are earnestly requested from the users of this set. They should be sent to the compiler at the Graduate School of Library Service, Rutgers University, New Brunswick, New Jersey, 08903.

The compiler gratefully acknowledges the help of two student assistants from the Graduate School of Library Service, Judith Ann Valcho and Bronwen Umberger, who worked on the project in the Spring term of 1969. Mr. William J. Crowe, Jr., a staff member of the Boston Public Library and a Rutgers Library School graduate, has given generously of his spare time in searching in several Boston libraries for solutions to bibliographical puzzles.

Additional sources, first used in these two volumes, are:

Bell, Mathew J. _A Check List of Worcester, Mass. imprints from 1826-1833._ Catholic University of America thesis, 1966.

Cale, William E. _Checklist of Hartford, Conn. imprints from 1826 to 1828._ Catholic University of America thesis, 1966.

Dion, D. E. A checklist of Hartford, Conn. imprints from 1828-1829. Catholic University of America thesis, 1967

Dunn, B. B. A checklist of Charleston, S. C. imprints for the years 1826-1830. Catholic University of America thesis, 1967.

Kansas University. Chronological shelf list of the Rare Book Department.

McMurtrie, Douglas C. Unpublished checklist of Rochester, N. Y. imprints, 1816-1850. At Rochester Public Library.

Thomson, Peter G. A bibliography of the state of Ohio. Argonaut Press 1966, 2 vol.

Whitelock, M. M. A checklist of Princeton, N. J. imprints in the years 1826-1845. Catholic University of America thesis. 1967.

Williams College. Library. Card catalogue of Williamstown imprints, 1827-30.

Woolery, Rosemary J. Check list of Maine imprints, 1826-30 Catholic University of America thesis, 1951.

Wright, Lyle H. American fiction, 1774-1850: second revised ed. The Huntington Library, 1969.

New Brunswick, New Jersey
January, 1970

1827

A

Abbeville District. South Carolina
The memorial with resolutions adopted at the Anti-tariff meeting, held at Abbeville Court House, S. C. Monday 3d Sept. 1827. [Charleston] A. E. Miller, 1827. 22 p. ScC. 27762

Abbot, Abiel, 1770-1828
Ecclesiastical peace recommended. A discourse delivered before the annual convention of the Congregational Ministers of Massachusetts in Boston, May 31, 1827. Boston, Bowles & Dearborn, I. R. Butts and Co., prs., 1827. 20 p. CSmH; DLC; ICMe; MBAt; MBC; MH; MHi; MWA; MeB; NNUT; NjPT; RPB. 27763

---- Example of the first preachers of the gospel considered. A sermon at the installation of the Rev. Abiel Abbott, as pastor of the Congregational Church in Peterborough, N. H. Boston, Bowles & Dearborn, 1827. 16 p. CtSoP; MB; MH; MWA; MiD-B; NN; Nh-Hi; RPB. 27764

An abstract of the census of Alabama, taken in 1827. 1 p. DLC. 27765

Academy of Natural Sciences of Philadelphia
Report of the transactions of the Academy of Natural Sciences of Philadelphia, during the years 1825 & 1826. Submitted by S. G. Morton, M. D. Recording Secretary. Philadelphia, Pr. by Solomon W. Conrad, 1827. 14 [1] p. CU; DLC; MBAt; MH-Z; NBLiHi; NNNAM; PPL. 27766

Account of the dinner given to Professor List, by the Pennsylvania Society for the Encouragement of Manufactures and the Mechanic Arts, at the Mansion House, Philadelphia, Nov. 3, 1827. 15 p. DLC; MB. 27767

An account of the trial of the conspirators. On an indictment for carrying away William Morgan, from the jail of Ontario county, on the evening of Sept. 12, 1826. To which is added, Judge Throop's address... [Canandaigua, 1827] 12 p. Rep. with additions from the Ontario repository of Jan. 10, 1827. CSmH. 27768

An account of the visit of General Lafayette to the United States, from his arrival in August, 1824, to his embarkation on board the Brandywine frigate; return to France, reception & retirement to La Grange. Philadelphia, J. P. Ayres [1827] [2], [361]-507 p. (Cap. title: Appendix. Chapter IX.) Ct; IEN; Nj; PHi. 27769

Adair, John
Letters of Gen. Adair & Gen. Jackson, relative to the charge of cowardice, made by the latter against Kentucky troops at New Orleans. [Lexington, Thomas Smith, 1827] 63 p. ICU; KyU; OCHP; PPiU. 27770

Adam, Alexander, 1741-1809
Adam's Latin grammar... Boston, Hilliard, Gray, Little & Wilkins, etc., 1827. 299 p. CtHT-W; InU; MB; MH; MeB; MiD-B;

NNC; NcA-S; OMC; PPL. 27771

---- ---- New-York, E. Duyckinck, Collins & Co. [etc.] 1827. viii, 232 p. CFS; CSt; DLC; ICU; IaHi; KyLoF; MBC; NBuU. 27772

---- ----, simplified by means of an introduction: Designed to facilitate the study of Latin grammar... 3d ed., from the 2d ed., rev. and corr. New York, Pub. and sold by White, Gallaher, & White. Stereotyped by A. Chandler, 1827. 190, 16 p. CtW; IC; MB; MH; MoSpD; NNC; NjP. 27773

Adams, Daniel, 1773-1864

Geography; or, A description of the Earth... Accompanied by an atlas. 10th ed. Boston, Pr. and pub. by Lincoln & Edmonds, 1827. 323 p. CtY; DLC; IU; MnHi; MoSW; NNC; NjR; PLFM; TxU; ViU. 27774

---- Adams's new arithmetic. Arithmetic, in which the principles of operating by numbers are analytically explained, and synthetically applied... Keene, N. H., Pub. by John Prentiss, 1827. 264 p. CSmH; INS; IaHA; InGrD; KyOwK; MHolliHi; Mi; MnU; MoK; NIC; NNE; NRHi; NjR; OClWHi; PMA; RPB; TxDaM; TxU; WHi. 27775

---- ---- Keene, N. H., J. W. Prentiss [1827] 254 p. KU. 27776

---- The scholar's arithmetic; or Federal accountant... Stereotype ed., rev. and corr., with add. Keene, N. H., Pr. by John Prentiss, 1827. 224 p. Nh. 27776a

Adams, Jasper

An inaugural discourse delivered in Trinity Church, Geneva, New York, August 1, 1827. Geneva, Pr. by James Bogert, Sept. 1827. 56 p. CSmH; CtY; MB; MH; NGH; NHi; NN; PPL. 27777

Adams, Thomas, 1792-1881

A sermon on intemperance. Hallowell, Pr. by Glazier & Co., 1827. 24 p. CSmH; ICN; MH; MWA; MeHi; MeLB; N. 27778

Adams Female Academy, Derry, N. H.

Catalogue of the officers and members of the Adams Female Academy, 1824, 1825, 1826. Concord, Pr. by Jacob B. Moore, 1827. 11, [1] p. MShM. 27779

Address from a meeting of Democratic citizens. See National Republican Party, Philadelphia.

An address from the administration committee of Hamilton County. See National Republican Party, Ohio.

An address of a bank director to his constituents. Bog-Town, Md., July 4th, 1827. [Baltimore? 1827?] 16 p. MdBP. 27780

Address of the administration convention. See National Republican Party, North Carolina.

Address of the convention of 27th June, 1827, to their fellow citizens of Pennsylvania. [Harrisburg] 1827. 12 p. NN; PPULC. 27781

Address to the freemen of Kentucky. See National Republican Party, Kentucky.

An address to the guardians of the Washington Asylum, and the members of the board of Aldermen and common council. By a physician. Washington City, 1827. 16 p. (Signed, "Medicus.") DNLM; MBAt; NNNAM; OC; PPL. 27782

An address to the members of the Methodist Episcopal Church, on the subject of reform in their government. Philadelphia, Clark

& Raser, prs. 1827. [5], 31 p. CBDP; MdHi; MsJMC; PHi; WHi. 27783

An address to the pewholders & congregation of St. Mary's Church (signed, A Worshipper at St. Mary's.) [Philadelphia, 1827] 7 p. PHi. 27784

Address to the young men of the County of Essex. Newark, Dec. 20, 1827. 1 p. DLC. 27785

An address to young people attending Sabbath schools. Philadelphia, American Sunday School Union, 1827. 33 p. MNF. 27786

Adelaide, or The rainy evening, a moral tale. Boston, Pub. at the Christian Register office, 1827. 34 p. DLC; MB; MH. 27787

Administration convention. See National Republic Party, Kentucky.

Adventures of a French serjeant. See Barbaroux, Charles Ogé.

AEsopus

Fables of Aesop, and others, tr. into English. With instructive applications: and a print before each fable. Philadelphia, S. Probasco, 1827. 335 p. MdBP. 27788

African colonization. See Maryland Colonization Society.

Agricola, P., pseud.

The New-York gardener, or Twelve letters from a farmer to his son, in which he describes the method of laying out and managing the kitchen-garden. By P. Agricola [pseud.] White Creek [N. Y.] Pub. by A. Crosby. G. M. Davison, pr., Saratoga Springs, 1827. 95, [1] p. CSmH; MB; MBH; N; NNBG. 27789

The agricultural almanack for 1828. By John Armstrong. Blairsville, James F. M'Carty; Zanesville, Wm. Davis [1827] 18 l. MWA; PHi. 27790

Agricultural Society of Hamilton County, O.

Constitution of the Agricultural Society of Hamilton County, Ohio: adopted at Cincinnati, June 9th, 1827. Cincinnati, Pr. at the office of the Western Tiller, 1827. 8 p. OCHP. 27791

Aikin, Samuel Clark, 1790-1879

An address, delivered in Utica, before the Sunday School Societies on the fifty-first anniversary of American independence... Utica, Western Sunday School Union, J. Colwell, pr., 1827. 12 p. CSmH; DLC; PPL. 27792

Aires, Littleton

Tables of discount, or interest on every cent from one to one hundred, from one month to ten years; and on every dollar, from one to one thousand, and on every hundred from one to six thousand... Baltimore, Pub. by the author, Wm. Woody, pr., 1827. 92 p. CSmH; DLC; MdBL; MdBP; MdHi. 27793

Alabama (State)

Acts passed at the eighth annual session of the General Assembly of the state of Alabama, begun and held in the town of Tuscaloosa, on the third Monday in November, one thousand eight hundred and twenty-six. Tuscaloosa, Pr. by Grantland & Robinson, state prs., 1827. 124 p. AB; AU-L; DLC; ICLaw; In-SC; MH-L; MiU-L; NNB; NNLI; Nj; OClW; RPL; BrMus. 27794

---- Journal of the House of Representatives of the state of Alabama, begun and held at the town of Tuskaloosa, on the third

Monday in November, 1826,... Tuskaloosa, Pr. by Grantland & Robinson, state prs., 1827. 279 p. Alabama Supreme Court Library, Montgomery. BrMus. 27795

---- Journal of the Senate of the state of Alabama. Begun and held at the town of Tuskaloosa, on the third Monday in November, 1826, ...Tuskaloosa, Pr. by Grantland & Robinson, state prs., 1827. 156 p. Alabama Supreme Court Library, Montgomery. BrMus. 27796

---- Report of the committee appointed to examine the state bank. Jan. 8th, 1827. 1 p. DLC. 27797

Albany and Schenectady Railroad Co.

Petition of the president and directors of the Mohawk and Hudson Rail Road Company. To the honourable the Legislature of the state of New York. [New York? 1827] 2 p. NN. 27798

Albany Medical Seminary

Circular... with a catalogue of students attending the course of instruction for 1827. Albany, 1827. 6 p. MBCo; N. 27799

Albemarle, George Thomas Keppel, 6th earl of, 1799-1891

Personal narrative of a journey from India to England, by Bussorah, Bagdad, the ruins of Babylon, Curdistan, the court of Persia the western shore of the Caspian Sea, Astrakhan, Nishney Novogorod, Moscow, and St. Petersburgh: In the year 1824. By Captain the Hon. George Keppel. Philadelphia, Carey, Lea, & Carey, 1827. [Griggs & Dickinson, prs., Whitehall] 344 p. CU; DLC; ICMcC; KyLx; LNHT; MB; MBAt; MWA; MnS; NCH; NNEC; NcWsS; NhD; NjP; OC; OCl; PPL; PU; RPB; Vi. 27800

Alden, Timothy, 1771-1839

An account of sundry missions performed among the Senecas and Munsees in a series of letters. With an appendix. New-York, Pr. by J. Seymour, 1827. 180 p. CSmH; CtY; DLC; IC; ICN; MA; MB; MBAt; MH; MHi; MdBE; MiD-B; NN; NhD; NjP; NjR; OMC; PHi; PPL; PU; WHi. 27801

Alexandria, Va.

Charter, with the revised code of laws. [Alexandria, D. C., 1827?] v. p. IU. 27802

Alleine [Mrs.] Theodosia

Memoirs of the life of Joseph Alleine, author of "An alarm to the unconverted," including a narrative written by his widow, Mrs. Theodosia Alleine... Philadelphia, Uriah Hunt, stereotyped by L. Johnson, 1827. 172 p. IaHi; MBNEH; NNUT; ScCoT. 27803

Allen, Benjamin, 1789-1829

Letter to the Right Reverend John Henry Hobart, D. D. Bishop of the Protestant Episcopal Church in the diocese of New York. Philadelphia, Russell and Martien, prs., 1827. 32, lxiv p. CSmH; CtHT; MWA; MdBS; MiD-B; NBLiHi; NIC; NNG; NjP; PHi; PPAmP; PPL; TxDaM. 27804

---- Second letter to the Right Reverend John Henry Hobart, D. D. Bishop of the Protestant Episcopal Church in the diocese of New York. Philadelphia, Russell & Martien, prs., 1827. 70, [1] p. DLC; MB; MiD-B; NN; NNG; NjP; PPAmP; PPL; TxDaM. 27805

Allen, Joseph, 1790-1873

Easy lessons in geography and history, by question and answer. Designed for the use of the younger classes in the New England schools. 2d ed., rev. and improved. Boston, Hilliard, Gray,

Little and Wilkins, 1827. 54 p. DLC; MB; MH; NRHi; TxU; BrMus. 27806

Allen, Morrill
An address delivered at Pembroke, in presence of the school committee... January 6, 1827. Plymouth, Pr. by Allen Danforth, 1827. 24 p. CtY; MB; MH; NN; RPB; BrMus. 27807

Allen, Stephen, 1767-1852
Observations in opposition to the project of prohibiting, or greatly augmenting the duties on foreign manufactured articles. New York, Pr. by J. & J. Harper, 1827. 104 p. InHi; MH; NHi; NN. 27808

[----] Observations on penitentiary discipline, addressed to Wm. Roscoe esq. of Liverpool, England. New York, J. C. Totten, 1827. 87 p. DLC; DNLM; MB; MH; NN. 27809

Allen, William
Thoughts on the importance of religion. By William Allen. Also a definition of religion, from Elizabeth Smith's fragments in prose and verse. Philadelphia, Pub. by Kimber & Sharpless. 1827. 16 p. PHC. 27810

Allen M'Leod. See Tonna, Mrs. Charlotte Elizabeth (Browne) Phelen.

Almack's, a novel. See Hudson, Marianne Spencer (Stanhope).

Almanach de la Louisiane pour 1828. Nouvelle-Orleans, Francis Bouvain [1827] 16 l. AU. 27811

Almanack for 1828. By David Young. Auburn, U. F. Doubleday [1827] 18 l. DLC; MWA. 27812

---- ---- Ithaca, Mack & Andrus [1827] 18 l. MWA; NBuG; NIC; NSyOHi. 27813

---- ---- Ithaca, A. P. Searing, [1827] 18 l. MWA; NHi; NIC; WHi. 27814

Alnwick castle. See Halleck, Fitz-Greene.

Alspach, S.
Schuylkill Canal navigator... Philadelphia, Pr. by Joseph Rakestraw, for the author, 1827. 8 p. CSmH; MH; P; PHi; PPL. 27815

Althans, Henry, 1783-1855
Scripture natural history of birds, insects, etc. with reflections designed for the young. 1st Amer. ed. Hartford, D. F. Robinson, 1827. 2 v. MHa; MdBS; NGH. 27816

Always happy: or, Anecdotes of Felix and his sister Serena... By a mother. Boston, Pr. by Isaac R. Butts and Co., Pub. by Bowles & Dearborn, 1827. 142 p. MWey. 27817

America, or, A general survey. See Everett, Alexander Hill.

American Academy of the Fine Arts. See New York. American Academy of the Fine Arts.

The American almanack for 1828. By E. R. Lambert. New-Haven [1827] 12 l. MWA. 27818

---- By Ephraim A. Lambert. New-Haven [1827] 12 l. CLU; Ct; CtY; MWA. 27819

The American annual register for the years 1825-6... New-York, Pub. by G. & C. Carvill, 1827. 380, 250, [4] p. CSmH; DLC; KU; MWA; NjR; PPL; PU. 27820

American Asylum for the Deaf and Dumb, Hartford. See American School for the Deaf, Hartford.

American Bible Society
Eleventh anniversary of the American Bible Society... May, 1827. [New York, 1827] p.[41]-67. MiD-B; PPL. 27821

---- Eleventh report of the American Bible Society, presented May 10, 1827, with an appendix, containing extracts of correspondence, &c. &c. New-York, Pr. for the Society, by Abraham Paul, 1827. 96 p. DLC; MeBaT; MiD-B; PPL; WBB. 27822

American Board of Commissioners for Foreign Missions
Missionary paper, No. 2. 6th ed. November 1827. [Boston, Crocker & Brewster, 1827] 11, 4 p. MiD-B. 27823

---- Missionary paper, no. 7. Containing, a brief memoir of Asaad Shidiak; an Arab young man, of the Maronite Roman Catholic Church in Syria. Oct. 1827. The mission to Western Asia... [Boston, Crocker & Brewster, 1827] 47 p. WHi. 27824

---- Report of the American Board of Commissioners for Foreign Missions, compiled from documents laid before the board at the eighteenth annual meeting, which was held in the city of New York, Oct. 10, 11, 12, 13 & 15, 1827. Boston, Crocker & Brewster, 1827. 126, [2], xxvii, [3] p. CBPac; IEdS; KWiU; MA; MeB; MeBat; NSchU; RP. 27825

The American Chesterfield, or, Way to wealth, honour and distinction; being selections from the letters of Lord Chesterfield to his son... Philadelphia, J. Grigg, 1827. iv, 272 p. CSmH; CtY; DLC; ICHi; KU; MB; MH; MdBS-P; PP; RPB; ViLC. 27826

American Colonization Society

By-laws of the Board of managers of the American Colonization Society. Adopted 25th Jan., 1827. [Washington, D. C. 1827] 1 p. DLC. 27827

American Colonization Society. Controversy between Caius Gracchus and Opimius. See Caius Gracchus, pseud.

---- The tenth annual report of the American Society for Colonizing the Free People of Colour of the United States... Washington, Way & Gideon, prs., 1827. 101, [1] p. AB; CSt; DLC; GDC; KHi; MA; MdHi; NbU; NjPT; PPL; TxHuT. 27828

American Education Society
Eleventh annual report of the directors of the American Education Society, for the year ending May, 1827. Andover, Pr. by Flagg and Gould, 1827. 76 p. CtW; ICMcC; MA; MeHi; NRAB; NcMHi; NjR; PPL; WBB. 27829

---- Conn. Branch
First annual report of the directors of the Connecticut Branch of the American Education Society; exhibited at Stratford, June 20, 1827. With an appendix. New Haven, Treadway and Adams, 1827. 76 p. CBPac; Ct. 27830

---- New Hampshire Branch
Annual report of the New Hampshire Branch of the American Education Society. Hanover, Thomas Mann, pr., 1827. 23, [1] p. CSmH; MH; MHi; NjR. 27831

---- Constitution of the New Hampshire Branch of the American Education Society with an address of the directors. [Concord, N. H., Pr. at the Repository and observer Office, 1827] 11 p. CtSoP; M; NhHi. 27832

---- Northwestern Branch
The seventh report of the directors, presented to the Society at their annual meeting at Orwell, January 10, 1827. Middlebury, Pr. by J.W. Copeland, 1827. 16 p. MBC. 27833

American farmers' almanac for 1828. By Charles F. Egelmann. Hagers-Town, John Gruber and Daniel May [1827] 15 l. MWA; MdBE; PPL; PYHi; ViU. 27834

American Home Missionary Society
The first report of the American Home Missionary Society, presented by the executive committee at the anniversary meeting, May 9, 1827, with an appendix... New York, Pr. by D. Fanshaw, 1827. 119 [1] p. CSmH; Ct; CtSoP; GDC; ICN; ICU; M; MA; MB; MBAt; MeB; MnHi; OMC; PHi; PPL; PPPrHi; TxU. 27835

American Literary, Scientific, and Military Academy. See Norwich University, Northfield, Vt.

American Lyceum of Science and the Arts composed of associations for mutual instruction and designed for the general diffusion of useful and practical knowledge. Worcester, Pr. by Samuel H. Colton and Co., Apr., 1827. 7 p. DLC; MWA. 27836

An American physician, pseud. See Dispensatories eclectic and general.

American popular lessons. See Robbins, Eliza, 1786-1853.

American School for the Deaf, Hartford.
Eleventh report of the directors of the American Asylum at Hartford for the Education and Instruction of the Deaf and Dumb; exhibited to the Asylum, May 12, 1827. Hartford, W. Hudson and L. Skinner, prs., 1827. 34 p. CtY; KHi; Mi; MiU. 27837

The American shooter's manual, comprising such plain and simple rules, as are necessary to introduce the inexperienced into a full knowledge of all that relates to the dog, and the correct use of the gun... by a gentleman of Philadelphia county. Philadelphia, Carey, Lea & Carey, 1827. 249, [2] p. CSmH; DNAL; MWA; MnSM; MoSHi; NWM; NcWsW; PHi; PU; WyU. 27838

American Society for Colonizing the Free People of Colour. See American Colonization Society.

American Sunday School Union
The Sunday school hymn book; 19th ed. Philadelphia, American Sunday School Union; J. Johnson, stereotyper, 1827. 128 p. NjPT. 27839

---- The third report of the American Sunday School Union; read at their annual meeting held in the city of Philadelphia, on Tuesday afternoon, May 22, 1827. Philadelphia, Pr. for the American Sunday School Union, by I. Ashmead & Co., 1827. 19 p. CtHT; MA; MeB; NRAB; P; PPL. 27840

---- ---- Philadelphia, Pr. for the American Sunday School Union, by I. Ashmead, 1827. xxvii, 120 p. PPL. 27841

---- The Union spelling and reading book. Philadelphia, American Sunday School Union, 1827. CtHT-W; MWA. 27842

American taxation. [36 quatrains of verse] Printing of all kinds done with accuracy and despatch, by S.H. Salisbury, Black Rock. [1827?] Bdsd. in 2 columns.

CSmH. 27843

The American toilet. See Murray, Hannah Lindley.

American Tract Society, Boston
Thirteenth annual report of the American Tract Society, Boston, read May 30, 1827... Boston, T. R. Marvin, pr., 1827. 47, [1] p. DLC; MeBaT. 27844

---- New York
Doctrines and duties of the Christian religion, stated in the language of the Bible. New York, Pub. by the American Tract Society [Fanshaw, pr., 1827?] 20 p. WHi. 27845

---- Second annual report of the American Tract Society, instituted at New-York, 1825. With lists of auxiliaries and benefactors, the publications of the society, &c. Printed at the Society's house, New-York, by Daniel Fanshaw, 1827. 64 p. CtHT-W; ICMcC; IHi; MWA; MeB; MiD-B; NNS; PPL; TNJ. 27846

American Unitarian Association
Causes of the progress of liberal Christianity in New England. 2d ed. No. 9. American Unitarian Association. Boston, Bowles & Dearborn, 1827. Isaac R. Butts & Co., prs. 16 p. CBPac; GAGTh; ICMe; MH-AH; MMeT; MeB; MeBat. 27847

---- On experimental religion... Boston, Bowles & Dearborn [Isaac R. Butts, prs.] 1827. 19 p. CBPac; CtSoP; ICMe; MH-AH; MMeT; MNF; MeB; NjPT; ScCC. 27848

---- The faith once delivered to the saints. Printed for the American Unitarian Association. Boston, Bowles & Dearborn, 1827. 24 p. CBPac; GAGTh; ICMe; MDovC; MH; WKenHi. 27849

---- One hundred scriptural arguments for the Unitarian faith. Printed for the American Unitarian Association... Boston, Bowles & Dearborn, [Isaac R. Butts & Co., prs.] 1827. [3], 16 p. CBPac; CtHC; ICMe; IEG; MDovC; MH; MNF. 27850

---- Review of tracts published by the American Unitarian Association. First printed in the Christian magazine. Boston, T. R. Marvin, pr., 1827. 62 p. CBPac; CLU; ICN; MB; MH; MHi; MWA; MeHi; NNUT; OO; PLT. 27851

---- Second annual report of the American Unitarian Association. With an appendix. Boston, Isaac R. Butts, prs., 1827. 84 p. CBPac; Ct; MNF; MWA; MiD-B. 27852

---- Tracts of the American Unitarian Association. First series ...Vol. 1. Containing Numbers 1 to 12. Boston, Bowles & Dearborn, [Press of Isaac R. Butts & Co.] General Depository, 1827. CBPac; ICMe; MBAt; MH; MNF; MW; MdBP; NbO; RP; WHi. 27853

Americanischer Stadt und Land Calender auf 1828. Philadelphia, Conrad Zentler [1827] 18 l. CLU; CtY; DLC; MWA; NjP; NjR; PHi; PPL; RPB. 27854

Der Amerikanisch-Teutsche Hausfreund und Baltimore Calender auf 1828. Baltimore, Johann T. Hanzsche [1827] 18 l. DLC; MWA; MdBE; MdHi. 27855

Amherst Academy
Amherst Academy. Catalogue of the trustees, instructers and students. For the term ending August 22, 1827. Amherst, Mass. John S. and C. Adams, prs., [1827] 7, [1] p. MA. 27856

---- Catalogue of the trustees, instructors and students. For the term ending Nov. 20, 1827. Amherst, J. S. and C. Adams, prs. [1827] 8 p. MA; MAJ. 27857

---- Laws of Amherst Academy, for the use of the students. Amherst, John S. and C. Adams, prs., 1827. 7 p. MA. 27858

---- Franklin Society
Amherst Academy. Order of exercises at the exhibition of the Franklin Society. Thursday evening, (7 o'clock) Feb. 20, 1827... Carter and Adams, prs., Amherst, Mass. [1827] Bdsd. MA. 27859

---- Platonic Society
Amherst Academy. Exhibition of the Platonic Society. Feb. 19, 1827. .. Carter and Adams, prs. Amherst, Mass. [1827] Bdsd. MA. 27860

Amherst College
Catalogue of books belonging to the library of Amherst College. [Amherst] J. S. & C. Adams, prs. [1827] 38 p. DLC; IU; MA; MH; MWA; N. 27861

---- Catalogue of the corporation, faculty and students... 1827. Amherst, Mass., J. S. and C. Adams, prs. [1827] 16 p. CU; CtHT-W; MBC; MH; MeHi; NN. 27862

---- Outline of the system of instruction recently adopted in the college at Amherst, Mass. 1827. Amherst, Carter & Adams, prs. [1827] 8 p. CtHT-W; DHEW; MA; MBAt; MH; MWA; OO. 27863

---- The substance of two reports of the faculty of Amherst College, to the Board of trustees, with the doings of the Board thereon. Amherst, Carter & Adams, prs., 1827. 22 p. CLU; CSmH; Ct; DLC; MA; MB; MBAt; MBC; MH; MWA; MeB; NN; NNC-T; OClWHi; OO; PPL; RPB. 27864

---- Alexandrian Society
Amherst College. Exhibition of the Alexandrian Society. 7 o' clock, P. M. July 4, 1827. [Amherst] J. S. and C. Adams, prs. [1827] 4 p. MA. 27865

---- Order of exercises at the exhibition of the Alexandrian Society, in Amherst College. Wednesday evening, 7 o'clock, March 7, 1827. Amherst, Mass. Carter and Adams, prs. [1827] 4 p. MA. 27866

Amherst, Mass. Second Congregational Church
Articles of faith and form of covenant, revised and adopted by the Second Church in Amherst. March 1, 1827. [Amherst] J. S. & C. Adams, prs. [1827] 7 p. MA; MAJ. 27867

Amica Religionis, pseud. See Dodge, Mrs. H. M.

Amis, John D.
The celebrated horse, Sir Archie, will stand the ensuing season at my stable, in Northampton County, North-Carolina. Raleigh, Lawrence & Lemay, prs. 1827. [1] p. NcU. 27868

Amusements of Westernheath. See Penrose, Elizabeth (Cartwright).

Analysis of the Seneca language. See Hyde, Jabez Backus.

Anderson, Rufus
Memoir of Catherine Brown, a Christian Indian of the Cherokee Nation. 3d ed. Cincinnati, Morgan, Fisher & L'Hommedieu, 1827. 143 p. ICN; IHi; MHi; Me; NN; NcMHi; OCHP; PPPrHi. 27869

Andover Theological Seminary
General catalogue of the Theological Seminary. Andover, Pr. by Flagg & Gould, 1827. 21 p. MNtcA; RPB; BrMus. 27870

---- Laws of the Theological Institution in Andover. Andover, Pr. by Flagg & Gould, 1827. 32 p. CSmH; CoU; Ct; GDC; M; MAnP; MB; MHi; NNC; NNUT; PPPrHi; RPB. 27871

---- Order of exercise at the anniversary of the Theological Seminary, Andover, 26th of September, 1827. 3 p. MNtcA; MeHi. 27872

Anecdotes for little boys. Philadelphia, American Sunday School Union Depository, 1827. 8 p. CtY; BrMus. 27873

Angell, Joseph Kinnicut, 1794-1857
An essay on the right of a state to tax a body corporate, considered in relation to the present bank tax in Rhode-Island. Boston, Hilliard, Gray, Little & Wilkins, 1827. 44 p. CtY; IU; MH-L; MWA; MiD-B; PPB. 27874

---- An inquiry into the rule of law which creates a right to an incorporeal hereditament, by an adverse enjoyment of twenty years. With remarks, on the application of the rule to light, and in certain cases to a water privilege. Boston, Hilliard, Gray, Little and Wilkins, 1827. 117 p. CLL; CSf; CU-Law; DLC; ICLaw; IaU-L; MBS; MH-L; MWCL; NIC-L; NNC-L; NNLI; NcD; OCLaw; PPB; PU-L; PPiAL; RPB; WMM; BrMus. 27875

Ann and her little book. Philadelphia, American Sunday School Union, 1827. 7 p. BrMus. 27876

Anna Ross. See Kennedy, Grace.

Another candid address. See Plain Truth, Jr., pseud.

An answer to nine objections made by an anonymous writer against the doctrines of the Catholic Church, by a Catholic clergyman of Chambersburg, Franklin County, Pennsylvania. Chambersburg, Pa., Pr. for the author by G. K. Harper, 1827. 57 p. CSmH. 27877

Anthem for Thanksgiving. Boston, Pub. by Richardson & Lord, 1827. 8 p. IaHi. 27878

The Anti-Masonic almanack for 1828. By Edward Giddins. Rochester, Edwin Scrantom [1827] 14 l. CSmH; InU; MB; MWA; NIC; NRHi; NRU; NUt. 27879

---- ---- Rochester, Edwin Scrantom [1827] (5th ed.) 14 l. N; NR; NRU. 27880

An appeal to the lay members of the Protestant Episcopal Church in Pennsylvania. [Philadelphia?] April, 1827. 19 p. (Signed, An Episcopalian.) NNG; PPL; WHi. 27881

Appendix, No. IV. Colbert-No. 1. See Carey, Mathew.

Arabian Nights
The Arabian nights, entertainments consisting of one thousand and one stories... 9th Amer. from the 18th English ed., trans. from the Arabian mss. Exeter, Pub. by J. & B. Williams, 1827. 2 v. MH; PAtM; PU; RJa; RPB; WGrNM. 27882

---- New Arabian nights entertainments, selected from the Oriental mss... trans. into English by the Rev. George Lamb. Philadelphia, R. W. Pomeroy, 1827. 2 v. MH; PPL. 27883

Archbold, John Frederick, 1785-1870
The practice of the Court of Kings bench in personal actions and ejectments, 2nd Amer. ed., from the 2d London ed. with considerable additions and alterations. New York, Edward E. Gould; Geo. F. Hopkins, pr., 1827. 2 v. CSdCL; CoGuW; In-SC; MH-L; Md; MiDU-L; N-L; Nj; NjR; ViU. 27884

Arden, the unfortunate stranger, who was tried for the murder of Miss Harriet Finch... To which is added, Glenwar, the Scottish bandit, a tale of former times interspersed with original poetry by an Etonian... Philadelphia, Pub. by Freeman Scott, 1827. 72 p. CtY; ICN; RPB; ViU. 27885

The argument of Domesticus. See Gunn, Alexander.

Aristides, pseud. See Van Ness, William Peter.

Arithmetical tables, rules and definitions, for the use of schools ... Philadelphia, Pub. by John Simmons, 1827. 24 p. NNC-T. 27886

Arkansas (Territory)
Journals of the fifth session of the General Assembly of the Territory of Arkansas, begun and held at Little Rock, in said Territory, Oct. 1, 1827. Little Rock, Pr. by William E. Woodruff, pr. to the Territory, 1827. 119 p. ArU. 27887

Armstrong, John, 1758-1843
A key to the Western calculator, containing the solution of all the examples and questions for exercise, with reference to the page where they stand. 2d ed., rev. and corr. Pittsburgh, Pr. and pub. by Johnston & Stockton, 1827. 139 p. InU; OClWHi; OO. 27888

Arndt, Johann, 1555-1621
Wahres Christenthum. Mit 63 schenen sinnbildlichen Stichen. Samt dem Paradies-Gartlein. (True Christianity. With 63 beautiful symbolic etchings. Together with the Paradise-Garden.) Harrisburg, Pr. by Wm. Boyer u. J. Baab, 1827. Seidensticker p. 233, not loc. 27889

Arnold, Samuel
The substance of two discourses on the mode of baptism, delivered at Hebron and Bristol, in New Hampshire in the months of September and December, 1826... Concord, Pr. at the Repository and Observer office, 1827. 40, 7 p. CBPac; CSmH; CtY; ICU; MBAt; MH; MWA; MiD-B; MoSpD; NNUT; NRAB; NhD; NjPT; NjR; PPPrHi; RPB; BrMus. 27890

Arnold, Thomas D.
Arnold's review (of Jackson) To the freemen of the counties of Cocke, Sevier, Blount, Jefferson, Grainger, Claiborne and Knox. [Knoxville, 1827] 31 p. T. 27891

---- Thomas D. Arnold to the freemen of the counties of Cocke, Sevier, Blount, Jefferson, Grainger, Claiborne and Knox. Friends and fellow-citizens: [Knoxville, 1827] 22 p. DLC. 27892

The artist and tradesman's guide. See Shepard, John.

Ashe, Simeon, d. 1662
Primitive divinity: a treatise on divine contentment... London, Pub. with notes, by Stephen Gerrish, No. 2 Charter street. 3d Amer. ed. Boston, Pr. by E. G. House, 1827. 216 p. MBC; ODW; WGr. 27893

Associate-Reformed Church of North America
The constitution and standards of the Associate-Reformed Church of North America. Pittsburgh, Pr. by Johnston and Stockton, 1827. 589, [1] p. IEG; NcD; ODW; PPiPT; ScCliJ; TJaU. 27894

---- ---- Salem, N. Y., Dodd & Stevenson [etc.] 1827. 488 p. [1] l. CSmH; CtHT-W; NCaS; NNUT; NcMHi; PPPrHi; PPiPT. 27895

---- Proceedings of the convention of delegates of the different synods of the Associate Reformed Church of North America, held in Pittsburgh, Sept. 12, 1827. Pittsburgh, D. & M. Maclean, 1827. 40 p. NcMHi; PPPrHi; PPiPT. 27896

---- Synod of the West
Extracts from the minutes of the proceedings of the Associate-Reformed Synod of the West, held in Cadiz, the 25th day of April, 1827, and continued by adjournment, by the committee. Cadiz, 1827. 30 p. ICMcC; NN. 27897

Association for the Relief of Respectable Aged Indigent Females, New York
The fourteenth annual report of the Association for the Relief of Respectable, Aged, Indigent Females, established in New-York, Feb. 7, 1814, presented at the annual meeting of the Society, Nov. 29, 1827... New-York, Pr. by J. Seymour, 1827. 12 p. NNG. 27898

An astronomical diary for 1828. The New-York almanack, for the year of our Lord and Saviour 1828... by Thomas Spofford... New York, Pub. by David Felt [1827] 16 l. MB. 27899

An astronomical ephemeris, or Almanack for 1828. By Joel Sanford. Bridgeport, J. B. & L. Baldwin [1827] 12 l. CtB; CtY; MWA. 27900

Asylum for the Relief of Persons Deprived of the Use of their Reason. See Philadelphia. Friends Asylum for the Insane.

At a meeting of Salt Manufacturers, convened at New-Bedford, on the 18th of 12th mo. (Dec.) 1827, to take into consideration the subject of the reduction of the present duty on imported salt, introduced before the Senate of the United States, at their present session. [New Bedford, (Mass.), B. T. Congdon, pr., 1827] 7, [1] p. MH; MHi; MNBedf. 27901

At a very numerous* and respectable meeting of farmers and manufactures... of the city and county of Philadelphia... May 31, 1827... the following resolutions were presented. Resolutions. [Philadelphia, 1827] 4 p. PU. 27902

The Atlantic souvenir, a Christmas and New Year's offering, 1828. Philadelphia, Carey, Lea & Carey [1827] xii, 384 p. DLC; KU; MB; MWA; NNC. 27903

Atterly, Joseph, pseud. See Tucker, George.

Atticus, pseud. See Clayton, Augustin Smith.

Atwater, Caleb, 1778-1867
The general character, present and future prospects of the people of Ohio. An address delivered at the United States' court house, during the term of the United States' circuit court, in Columbus, Ohio, December, 1826. Columbus, Pr. by P. H. Olmsted & co., 1827. 21, [1] p. DLC; MWA. 27904

Auburn Theological Seminary
Catalogue of the officers and students of the Theological Seminary at Auburn [New York] January, 1827. Auburn, Pr. by Richard Oliphant, 1827. 8 p. MBC; MH; N; NAuT. 27905

Aunt Mary's tales. See Hughes, Mrs. Mary (Robson).

Austin, Arthur, pseud. See Wilson, John.

Auxiliary Foreign Mission Society, Boston
Proceedings at the sixteenth anniversary of the Auxiliary Foreign Mission Society of Boston and vicinity. May 31, 1827. Boston, T. R. Marvin, pr., 1827. 38 p. DLC; M; MLow. 27906

Auxiliary Foreign Mission Society in the Eastern District of Fairfield County
Third annual report of the Auxiliary Foreign Mission Society, in the Eastern District of Fairfield County; at a meeting in Brookfield, Oct. 4, 1827. New-Haven, Pr. by Nathan Whiting, 1827. 24 p. Ct; CtY. 27907

Auxiliary Foreign Mission Society in the Eastern District of New Haven County
Annual report of the... September 26, 1826. New-Haven, Pr. at the Intelligencer Office, 1827. 24 p. CtHi. 27908

---- Annual report... Oct. 2, 1827. [New Haven? 1827?] 12 p. CtY, cannot loc., 1969. 27909

Auxiliary Foreign Mission Society of Brookfield Association, Brookfield, Mass.
Proceedings... fourth annual meeting... Brookfield, E. and G. Merriam, 1827. 31 p. CSmH; NNMAI. 27910

Auxiliary Foreign Mission Society of Cincinnati
The first annual report of the Auxiliary Foreign Mission Society of Cincinnati. Presented January 4th, 1827. Cincinnati, Pr. by Samuel S. Brooks, 1827. 20 p. PPPrHi. 27911

Auxiliary Foreign Mission Society of Essex County
Proceedings at the first anniversary of the Auxiliary Foreign Mission Society of Essex County, held at Newburyport, April 10, 1827. Newburyport, Pr. at the Herald Office, 1827. 24 p. MBC; MWA; MeB; MiD-B; WHi. 27912

Auxiliary Foreign Mission Society of Franklin County, Mass.
Fifteenth annual report of the Auxiliary Foreign Mission Society, of Franklin County, at a meeting in Conway, October 10, 1827. Greenfield, Mass., Phelps & Clark, prs., 1827. 16 p. N. 27913

Auxiliary Foreign Mission Society of New Haven, West
The annual report of the Auxiliary Missionary Society, of New-Haven, West, at a meeting holden in Milford, Oct. 5, 1826. New-Haven, Pr. at the Journal Office, 1827. 24 p. Ct; MiD-B. 27914

Auxiliary Foreign Mission Society of Worcester
Report of the executive committee; and proceedings of the Auxiliary Foreign Mission Society of Worcester, North Vicinity, at their fourth annual meeting in Westminster, Oct. 5, 1827. Boston, T. R. Marvin, pr., 1827. 11, [1] p. MBC; MWA. 27915

Auxiliary Mission Society at Barnstable County, West
Report of the Auxiliary Missionary Society at Barnstable

County, West, holden at Sandwich, April 25, 1827; with remarks on some objections to Missionary report. Plymouth, Allen Danforth, 1827. MWA. 27916

Auxiliary Missionary Society of New Haven, West
The seventh annual report... October 3, 1827. New Haven, Treadway and Adams, prs., 1827. CtY, not loc. 1969. 27917

Auxiliary New York Bible and Common Prayer Book Society
The twelfth annual report of the board of managers of the Auxiliary New-York Bible and Common Prayer Book Society. New-York, Pr. by T. & J. Swords, 1827. 16 p. PPL. 27918

Ayton, Richard, 1786-1823
The rendezvous; an operetta, in one act. Philadelphia, C. Neal, Mifflin & Perry, prs., 1827. 32 p. CSmH; MH; PPL. 27919

B

[Bache, Richard]
Notes on Colombia, taken in the years 1822-3. With an itinerary of the route from Caracas to Bogota; and an appendix. By an officer of the United States Army. Philadelphia, H. C. Carey & I. Lea, 1827. 303 p. CtY; ICN; KyLx; MB; MBAt; MH; MWA; MdBE; MeB; NIC; NN; NcD; NhD; OU; PPAmP; PHi; PPL; PU; RPB; ScC; TxU; Vi. 27920

Bacon, Henry, attorney.
Lessee D. M'Arthur vs. John Reynolds. Letter from Henry Bacon Esq. council for the plaintiff, containing a brief exposition of the proceedings of the above action of ejectment, in the Court of Common Pleas, for the county of Champaign, Ohio, with his argument in support of the same. [Dayton? 1827?] 16 p. CtY. 27921

Bacon, W.
Relation of the fearful state of Francis Spira, after he turned apostate from the Protestant Church to Popery... Wilmington, Pr. by P. Brynberg for J. Thompson [1827] 57 p. DLC. 27922

Bacon, William
Salvation made sure or An attempt to show, first - that all Christians do not obtain the full assurance of hope... Revised ed. Albany, Stereotyped by G. J. Loomis, 1827. 156 p. CtY; LNB; MBC; NjP; NjPT; NN; PPPrHi; PPL; ViRUT. 27923

Badger & Porter
...Stage register; containing a full account of the principal lines of stages, steamboats and canal packets, in the New England states and the state of New-York; their hours of departure and arrival... Boston, James F. Howe, pr., 1827. 24 p. CtHi; MH. 27924

Bailey's Franklin almanac for 1828. By Joshua Sharp. Philadelphia, Lydia R. Bailey [1827] 18 l. CLU; DLC; MWA; NjR; PHi; PPL. 27925

---- ---- Philadelphia, Thomas Desilver; Lydia R. Bailey, pr. [1827] 18 l. Ct; CtY; MWA; NCH. 27926

Bailey's Washington almanac for 1828. By Joshua Sharp. Philadelphia, Lydia R. Bailey [1827] 18 l. CtY; DLC; MWA; NCH; NN; PHi; PPL. 27927

Baird, H. L.
An address, delivered at a public installation of the officers of Menominie Lodge, at Green-Bay, Michigan. Dec. 27, A. L. 5826.

Detroit, Pr. by Sheldon and Wells, 1827. 18 p. NCH; NN; WHi. 27928

Baker, Daniel, 1791-1857
A scriptural view of Baptism ... [Washington, 1827] 23 p. DLC; TxAuPT. 27929

---- ---- [Large paper edition. Washington, 1827?] 16 p. DLC; TxAuPT. 27930

Baker, Pacificus
The Lenten monitor, or Moral reflections and devout aspirations on the Gospels, for each day from Ash-Wednesday to Easter Sunday ... Baltimore, Pub. by P. Blenkinsop, at his Catholic Book Warehouse, Matchett, pr., 1827. 259 p. DGU; DLC; IU; MBAt; MBtS; MdBL; MdBS; MdW; MiDSH. 27931

Bakewell, S. R.
A letter, addressed to the citizens of Baltimore, generally and exporting merchants and mechanics in particular... Baltimore, Pr. for the author, 1827. 12 p. MdToH, not loc. 1969. 27932

[Baldwin, Charles N.]
A universal biographical dictionary, containing the lives of the most celebrated characters of every age and nation; abridged from Lempriere's Biographical dictionary... Hartford, D. F. Robinson, 1827. 444 p. CSaT; CtHC; CtHT; CtY; DAU; ICU; KWiU; MH; MWA; MdBE; MiDSH; MnU; NIC; NT; NcA-S; NcGuG; NcU; NhPoA; ODaML; OSW; PPL; RPB; TxGR; TxU. 27933

Baldwin, Henry, 1780-1844
An oration, delivered by Honorable Henry Baldwin, at the request of the Jackson Democratic Republicans of this city, July 4, 1827. Pittsburgh, Pub. by committee of arrangement. Pr. by Cramer & Spear, 1827. 16 p. NBuG; NN; OClWHi; PHi; PPi. 27934

Baldwin, Thomas, 1753-1825
A catechism; or compendium of Christian doctrine and practice. 7 ed. Boston, Lincoln & Edmands, 1827. 34, [2] p. KU; NN; NRAB. 27935

Balfour, Walter, 1776-1852
An inquiry into the Scriptural doctrine concerning the devil and Satan; and into the extent of duration expressed by the terms olim, aion, and aionios, rendered everlasting, forever, &c., in the common version and especially when applied to punishment. 2d ed. Charlestown, [Ms.], Davidson, pr., 1827. 359 p. DLC; GDC; ICMe; MMeT-Hi; MiD; NIC; TxH; ViU. 27936

Ball, Lemuel
Tanning and currying in their various branches, explained and made easy, from actual experience. Sangerfield, Pr. by Joseph Tenny, 1827. 29 p. NNE. 27937

[Ballard, William] 1780-1827
A sketch of the history of Framingham... Boston, Pr. for the publisher, 1827. 70, [1] p. MB; MBAt; MFm;MH; MWA; MnHi; WHi. 27938

Ballmer, Daniel
A collection of new receipts and approved cures for man and beast. Made by Daniel Ballmer, near Chambersburg, A. D. 1826. Shellsburg, Pa., Pr. by Frederick Goeb, 1827. 35 p. CSmH; DLC. 27939

---- Eine Sammlung von neuen Recepten und bewahrten Curen... Schellsburg [Pa.] Gedruckt bey Friedrich Goeb, 1827. 40 p. CSmH; NNNAM; PHi; PPL. 27940

Ballou, Adin
An oration delivered July 4th,

A. D. 1827, before the Republican citizens of Milford, and the neighbouring towns at the Universalist meeting house, in said Milford. Boston, True & Greene, prs., 1827. 35 p. MBC; MMeT-Hi; MWHi; MiD-B; Nh; BrMus. 27941

Ballou, Hosea, 1771-1852
The child's Scriptural catechism. 4th ed. Boston, Henry Bowen, 1827. 24 p. MWA. 27942

---- Orthodoxy unmasked. A sermon, delivered in the Second Universalist Meeting in Boston, on Sabbath morning, June 24, 1827, in which some notice is taken of Professor Stuart's election sermon. Boston, Pub. by Henry Bowen, 1827. 15 p. DLC; MB; MBC; MH; MMeT-Hi; MWA; WHi; BrMus. 27943

---- A sermon delivered at the ordination of the Rev. John Samuel Thompson, as pastor of the First Universalist Society in Charlestown, Mass. on Wednesday, July 11, 1827. Boston, Henry Bowen, 1827. 16 p. M; NN; RPB; BrMus. 27944

Baltimore (City)
The ordinances of the Mayor and City Council of Baltimore, passed at the extra sessions in 1826, and at the January session 1827. Baltimore, Pr. by John D. Toy, 1827. 68, xxx p. MH-L; MdHi; PPL. 27945

---- Proceedings of sundry citizens of Baltimore, convened for the purpose of devising the most efficient means of improving the intercourse between that city and the western states. Baltimore, Pr. by William Wooddy, 1827. 38 p. CtY; DLC; MBAt; MWA; MdBE; MdBJ; MdHi; MnHi; NNC; NNE; NRU; OMC; PPAmP; PPF; PPL; WU; BrMus. 27946

---- Report and resolution relative to internal improvement: and the Susquehanna canal report. Adopted January 5th, 1827. Baltimore, P. Edes, 1827. 29 p. MdBE; MdBP; MdHi; PHi. 27947

---- Report of the trustees of the alms-house, for Baltimore City and County--1827. [Baltimore, 1827] 7 p., 10 l. PHi; PPL. 27948

---- Standing rules for conducting business in the first and second branches of the city council of the city of Baltimore... Baltimore, Pr. by Benjamin Edes, 1827. 11 p. PPL. 27949

Baltimore and Ohio Rail Road Company
An act to incorporate the Baltimore and Ohio Rail Road Company. [Baltimore, Wm. Wooddy, 1827] 12 p. CtY; DBRE; PPL. 27950

---- By-laws. [Baltimore, 1827] 2 p. MBAt; NN. 27951

---- First annual report of the Directors to the stockholders of the Baltimore & Ohio Railroad Co., [Baltimore? 1827?] 4 p. CSmH; CtY; DBRE; IU; MH-BA; MdBJ; MdBP; MdHi; NN; NjP; WU. 27952

---- Regulations for the engineer department. Organization of the engineer department of the Baltimore and Ohio Rail Road Company, providing a system for the government of the same; and for securing a strict accountabilily [sic] in the fiscal operations of the Baltimore and Ohio Rail Road Company, and economy in the disbursement of its funds. [Baltimore, Wm. Wooddy, pr., 1827?] 8 p. NN. 27953

---- Report of the committee appointed by the Baltimore and Ohio

Rail Road Company, to examine the Mauch Chunck & Quincy Rail Roads. [Baltimore, Wm. Wooddy, pr., 1827] 8 p. CtY; DBRE; DLC; MBAt; MCM; MdBJ; MdHi; NN; NNE; OClWHi; PHi. 27954

Baltimore Athenaeum
Catalogue of books belonging to the library of the Baltimore Athenaeum. Baltimore, Pr. by Edes and Leakin, 1827. MdBP (impf.) 27955

Baltimore Patriot Office. See ...Mr. Clay and General Jackson.

Bancroft, Aaron, 1755-1839
A discourse delivered before the Second Congregational Society in Worcester, on the eighth day of April, 1827, the Lord's Day following the ordination of Rev. Alonzo Hill. Worcester, Charles Griffin, pr., 1827. 20 p. CSmH; CtSoP; ICN; IEG; KWiU; MBAt; MBC; MH; MHi; MWA; MiD-B; NCH; NIC; NN; NNUT; NjPT; OO; PPAmP; RPB; WHi. 27956

Bancroft's agricultural almanack for 1828. By Luther S. Bancroft. Boston, Hilliard, Gray, Little & Wilkins [1827] 24 l. DLC; MH; MHi; MWA. 27957

Bangor Theological Seminary, Bangor, Me.
General catalogue of the Theological Seminary, Bangor, Dec., 1827. Bangor, Burton & Carton, prs. [1827] 5 p. DLC; MBC. 27958

[Banim, John] 1798-1842
Tales by the O'Hara family. 2d ser. Comprising the Nowlaus, and Peter of the Castle... Philadelphia, H. C. Carey & I. Lea, 1827. 2 v. CtY; MBAt; MH; NN. 27959

Bank of Hamilton, Ohio
Report, read to the stockholders of the Bank of Hamilton, at a meeting in January, 1824. Since corrected, so as to exhibit the situation of the institution, to July, 1827. Hamilton, O., Pr. by J. B. Camron & T. Webster, 1827. 31 p. OCHP. 27960

Bank of North America, Philadelphia
Act of incorporation of the Bank of North America... together with the by-laws. Philadelphia, Pr. by Conrad Zentler, 1827. 36 p. MH-BA; NNC; PHi; PPL; PU. 27961

Banks, Henry, fl. 1781-1826
Frankfort, February 5th, 1827. Sir, The enclosed memorial is submitted to your consideration ...Henry Banks. Secretary of the State of the United States. Printer omitted. Bdsd. DNA. 27962

---- A memorial to Congress of the U. States, relating to revolutionary events... Frankfort, Ky., Pr. by A. G. Hodges, 1827. 71 p. CtHT; DLC; MBAt; MdHi; NN; WHi. 27963

---- A reply & Remarks of Philo-Jackson on the castigations of Shelbyville & Co. Frankfort, Pr. for the author, 1827. 12 p. NcD; OCHP. 27964

Banks of the Irvine... See Pollock, Robert.

Baptist General Tract Society
Proceedings of the Baptist General Tract Society, at its third annual meeting, held in Philadelphia, Jan. 3, 1827; with the constitution. Philadelphia, Pub. by the Society, J. Rakestraw, pr., 1827. 28, 448 p. MeBat. 27965

Baptists. Ala. Bethlehem Assoc.
Minutes of the Bethlehem Baptist Association convened at the Olive-Branch Church, Conecuh County... 1827. Claiborne [Ala.]

Thomas Eastin, pr., 1827. 8 p. A-Ar. 27966

---- ---- Cahawba Association.
Minutes of the ninth annual session, of the Cahawba Baptist Association: convened at Shoal Creek Meeting House, Shelby County, Alabama. From the 21st to 24th October, inclusive, 1826. Greensborough, Pr. at the office of James Hillhouse, 1827. 8 p. NRAB. 27967

---- ---- State Convention.
Fourth anniversary of the Baptist State Convention in Alabama. Montgomery, Pr. at the Alabama Journal Office, Aug. 1827. 15 p. Owen, p. 808, accounts for the third meeting as being held at Greensborough, in 1826; and the second at Tuscaloosa, in 1825. Owen does not locate copies of these minutes. 27968

---- Arkansas. Little Rock Association.
Minutes for 1826 and 1827. Minutes of the Regular Baptists, of the Little Rock Association, held at Arkansas Church, Marion, Conway County, Arkansas Territory, the first Saturday in November, 1826. Also minutes of the Regular Baptists of the Little Rock Association, held at Little Flock Church, Crawford Court House, Arkansas Territory, on the first Saturday in November, 1827. Little Rock, A. T.: Wm. E. Woodruff, pr. [1827?] 12 p. Caption title. Riley. 27969

---- Connecticut. Hartford Association.
Minutes of the thirty-eighth anniversary of the Hartford Baptist Association, held in the meeting-house of the First Baptist Church in Colebrook, October third and fourth, 1827. [Hartford? 1827?] 12 p. NRAB. 27970

---- ---- New Haven Association.
Minutes of the second anniversary of the New-Haven Baptist Association, held in the Baptist meeting-house, in New Haven, August 8th and 9th, 1827. New-Haven, Treadway & Adams, prs. 1827. 11 p. NRAB. 27971

---- ---- New London Association.
Minutes of the tenth anniversary of the New London Association, held in the Baptist meeting house of the second church in Montville (Chesterfield), N. London Co., Conn. September 26th and 27th, 1827. [J. Dunham, pr. Chelsea] 8 p. NRAB. 27972

---- ---- Stonington Union Association.
Minutes of the 10th anniversary of the Stonington Union Baptist Association; held in Stonington Borough, June 20th and 21st, 1827. Stonington, W. Stover, Jun., pr., 1827. 8 p. NRAB; RWe. 27973

---- Delaware. Delaware Association.
Minutes of the Delaware Baptist Association, held at the Baptist meeting house of the Welch Tract Church, the 2d, 3d and 4th of June, 1827. Wilmington, Pr. at the Gazette office [1827] 10 p. NRAB. 27974

---- Illinois. Friends to Humanity.
Minutes of the annual meeting of the Friends to Humanity, held at New Design, Monroe County, Illinois, September the 20th, 1827 and the two succeeding days. St. Louis, Pr. by Edward Charless, 1827. 7 p. ISB. 27975

---- ---- Illinois Association.
Minutes of the Illinois United Baptist Association, held at the house of Dr. Alexander Conlee, Ridge Prairie, Madison County,

Illinois, on the 22d, 23d & 24th September, 1827. [Edwardsville, R. K. Fleming, pr., 1827] Bdsd. ISB; NRAB. 27976

---- Indiana. Coffee Creek Association.

Minutes of a Baptist Association held at Coffee Creek meeting-house, 3d Saturday in August, 1827. [C. P. J. Arion, pr., Madison, (Ia.)] 4 p. InFrlC; TxDaHi. 27977

---- ---- Indianapolis Association.

Minutes of the Indianapolis Association, begun and held at Indianapolis on Friday before the 4th Saturday in August 1827. [Indianapolis, John Douglass, 1827] 8 p. NRAB. 27978

---- ---- Laughery Association.

Minutes of the tenth annual meeting of the Laughery Association of Baptists, held at Bear-Creek, Dearborn County, Ind. commencing the 3d Friday in September, 1827. 4 p. NRAB. 27979

---- ---- Lost River Association.

Minutes of the Lost-River Association, held at Sharon meeting house, in Washington county, Indiana, commencing the first Saturday in September, Sunday and Monday succeeding in 1827. 4 p. InFrlC; TxDaHi. 27980

---- ---- Silver Creek Association.

Minutes of the Silver Creek Association, begun and held at Silver Creek meeting house Clark county, Ia. commencing the fourth Saturday in August, Lord's day, and Monday successively, 1827. [Madison? 1827] 6 p. In. 27981

---- ---- Union Association.

Minutes of the Union Association of Baptists, held at Mount Vernon meeting house, Daviess county, Indiana, on the 15th, 16th, and 17th of September, 1827. [From the Press of Elihu Stout, Vincennes, Ia.] [4] p. In; InFrlC. 27982

---- ---- Wabash Association

Minutes of the Wabash Baptist Association, held at Glady Fork Church, Lawrence County, Illinois October 6th, 1827, and days following. [Vincennes, Elihu Stout, 1827] 4 p. ISB. 27983

---- ---- Whitewater Association.

Minutes of the White-Water Baptist Association; held at New Bethel, Fayette county, Ind.; on the 10th, 11th, and 12th of August, 1827. 2, [1] p. NRAB. 27984

---- Kentucky, Bethel Association.

Minutes of the third Bethel Baptist Association, held at Pleasant-Grove meeting house. In Logan County, Kentucky, the 22nd, 23rd and 24th days of Sept. 1827. Russellville, Rhea and Atchison, prs., 1827. [2] p. LNB. 27985

---- ---- Boon's Creek Association.

Minutes of the Boon's Creek Association, begun and held at Mount Gilead meeting house, Fayette County, Ky. on the 15th, 16th, and 17th days of September, 1827. [T. Smith, pr., Lexington] 4 p. KyLoS. 27986

---- ---- Elkhorn Association.

Minutes of the Elkhorn Association, begun and held at David's Fork meeting house, on Saturday the 11th day of August, 1827. 6 p. ICU (film). 27987

---- ---- Gasper River Association.

Minutes of the sixteenth Gasper's River Baptist Association, held at Antioch meeting house, in Todd County, Kentucky, on Saturday preceding the fourth Lord's day in August 1827, and days following. Russellville, Pr. by Rhea & Atchison, 1827. [4] p. NRAB. 27988

---- ---- Green River Association.

Minutes of the twenty-eighth Green River Baptist Association, holden at Green River Church, in Hart County, on the second Saturday in August, 1827... 4 p. NRAB. 27989

---- ---- Kentucky Association

Minutes of the Baptist Association, at a meeting held at Salt River Meeting-House, in Anderson County, commencing on the first Saturday in October, 1827. Frankfort, Pr. by A. G. Hodges--Commentator office, 1827. 8 p. NRAB. 27990

---- ---- Licking Association.

Minutes of the Licking Association of Particular Baptists, held at East Hickman meeting-house, Jessamine County, on the 2d Saturday and two succeeding days in September, 1827. 7 p. NRAB. 27991

---- ---- Long Run Association.

Minutes of the Long Run Association, met at Flat Rock, on the first Friday in September, 1827. 6 p. ICU; NRAB. 27992

---- ---- Russell's Creek Association.

Minutes of the twenty-third Russel's Creek Association of Baptists, held at Mount Pleasant meeting-house, Adair County, Ky. on the 15th of September, 1827- and days following. 4 p. NRAB. 27993

---- ---- South District Association.

Minutes of the South District Association of Baptists, convened at Sugar Creek Meeting-house, Garrard County, Ky. on the 3rd Saturday in August, 1827. 4 p. ICU. 27994

---- Maine. Cumberland Association.

Minutes of the Cumberland Baptist Association, held at the Baptist meeting house, in Portland, Me., Oct. 3d and 4th, 1827, together with the circular and corresponding letters. Portland, Pr. by James Adams, Jun., 1827. 24 p. MeHi; NRAB. 27995

---- ---- Eastern Maine Association.

Minutes of the Eastern Maine Association, holden with the First Baptist Church in Sullivan, on Wednesday and Thursday, September 12 and 13, 1827. Ellsworth, Pr. at the Courier Office, 1827. 12 p. MNtcA; NRAB. 27996

---- ---- Penobscot Association.

Minutes of the Penobscot Association, held at Dexter, Sept. 5-6, 1827, together with their circular and corresponding letters. Bangor, Me., Pr. by Burton & Carter, 1827. 12 p. MeBat. 27997

---- Mass. Boston Association.

Minutes... meeting at Charlestown. Boston, Lincoln & Edmands, 1827. 21 p. MHi; MNtcA; MiD-B. 27998

---- ---- Old Colony Association.

Minutes... in Marshfield, Mass., Oct. 3rd and 4th, 1827. Plymouth, Allen Danforth [1827] 15 p. MiD-B; NRAB. 27999

---- ---- Worcester Association.

Minutes of the Worcester Baptist Association, held in Worcester, August 15 and 16, 1827. Worcester, Pr. by S. H. Colton and Co., 1827. 15 p. MB; MWA. 28000

---- Mississippi. State Convention.

The fifth annual report of the Mississippi Baptist State Convention. Held at Mars-Hill meeting-house, in the county of Amite, state of Mississippi, on the 2nd, 3rd and 4th days of November, 1827. Natchez, Pr. by Wm. C. Grissam and Co., 1827. 12 p. LNB (reported by Imprints Inventory; but copy could not be found there in March 1943, for more detailed description). McMurtrie, 217. 28001

---- ---- Union Association.
Minutes of the Union Baptist Association. Held at the meeting-house of Hephzibah Church, in the county of Copiah, state of Mississippi, on the 5th and 6th of October, 1827. Natchez, Pr. by William C. Grissam & Co., 1827. 8 p. MWA. 28002

---- Missouri. Mount Pleasant Association.
Minutes of the Mount Pleasant Baptist Association, [held at the Mount Pleasant meeting house, Howard county, Missouri, on the 8th, 9th, and 10th days of September, 1827] ... Fayette, Pr. at the office of the Western Monitor [1827] 8 p. MoHi. 28003

---- ---- Salem Association.
Minutes of the proceedings of a convention, formed of delegates from the Baptist churches herein named, and held at Cedar Creek meeting house. Callaway county, Missouri, for the purpose of forming a constitution for a new association, on the 20th, 21st, and 22nd of October, 1827. Fayette, Pr. by Nathaniel Patten, [1827] 8 p. MoHi. 28004

---- New Hampshire. Domestic Mission Society.
Eighth annual report of the trustees of the New Hampshire Baptist Domestic Mission Society, presented and read at the meeting of the society, held in Salisburg, June 26, 1827. Published by order of the Society. Concord, Pr. by George Hough, for the Society, 1827. 11 p. NRAB. 28005

---- ---- Dublin Baptist Association.
Minutes of the Dublin Baptist Association, held in Mason, N. H. Sept. 5 and 6, 1827. Published for the Association. Keene, N. H. Pr. by John Prentiss, 1827. 8 p. WMBC. 28006

---- ---- State Convention.
Minutes of the proceedings of the New Hampshire Baptist Convention, held in Concord, June 6, 1827. Published by order of the Convention. Concord, Pr. by George Hough, for the convention, 1827. 15 p. NRAB. 28007

---- New Jersey. New Jersey Association.
Minutes of the New-Jersey Baptist Association, held by appointment with our sister church at Cohansey, in their meeting house at Rhoadstown, Sept. 4th, 5th & 6th, A. D. 1827. 12 p. NjR. 28008

---- New York. Education Society.
Tenth annual meeting of the Baptist Education Society, of the state of New-York, held at Hamilton, June 7, 1827. Utica, Pr. by Northway & Bennett, 1827. 23, [1] p. ICU; MB; MWA; NRAB; TxFS. 28009

---- ---- Franklin Association.
Minutes of the Franklin Baptist Association, convened at the Baptist meeting-house in Middlefield, Otsego county, June 20, and 21, 1827. Also an account of collections for missions, with their circular & corresponding letters. Cooperstown, Pr. by J. H. Prentiss, 1827. 12 p. NRAB. 28010

---- ---- Hudson River Association.
The twelfth anniversary of the

Hudson River Baptist Association ...held in the Meeting House of the Baptist Church, Catskill, Aug. 1 & 2, 1827. New York, Pr. by Gray & Bunce, 1827. 20 p. NRAB. 28011

---- ---- Madison Baptist Association.

Minutes of the Madison Baptist Association, held at Cazenovia, (Woodstock) on the 12th & 13th of September, 1827, together with their circular and corresponding letters. Salina, N. Y., Pr. by Benj. F. Brigham, 1827. 12 p. NRAB; WMBC. 28012

---- ---- New York Association.

Minutes of the New-York Baptist Association, held in the meeting house of the First Baptist Church, in the city of New-York, May 29, 30, and 31, 1827. New York, Pr. by J. & J. Harper, 1827. 18 p. NRAB. 28013

---- ---- Oneida Association.

Minutes of the Oneida Baptist Association, held in the meeting-house of the Baptist Church, Vernon, Aug. 29th & 30th, 1827. Utica, Pr. by Northway & Bennett, 1827. 12 p. NRAB. 28014

---- ---- ---- Pastoral letter of the ministers of the Oneida Association, to the churches under their care, on the subject of revivals of religion. Utica, Pr. by Ariel Works, 1827. 22 p. CBPac; CSmH; CtY-D; MBC; MH; MWA; MeBaT; NNUT; NRAB; NUtHi; Nh; NjR; TxDaM; WHi. 28015

-------- St. Lawrence Association.

Minutes...held at Hopkinton on Wednesday and Thursday, September 13th and 14th, 1827. [Ogdensburgh, N. Y., Pr. by Spafford & Barter, 1827] 8 p. CSmH; DLC; NRAB; NRCR. 28016

---- ---- ---- Minutes...held at Madrid, on Wednesday and Thursday, Jan. 17th and 18th, 1827. [Utica, Northway & Bennett, 1827] 8 p. NRAB. 28017

---- ---- Washington Association.

Minutes of the first session of the Washington Baptist Association convened at Adamsville, N. Y. on the 13th and 14th of June, 1827, containing their circular and corresponding letters. [Sandy Hill, J. Wright, pr., 1827] 12 p. WMBC. 28018

---- Ohio. Columbus Association.

Minutes of the Columbus Baptist Association, held by appointment, at Johnstown, Licking Co., Ohio, Aug. 31, & Sept. 1, 2, 1827. Delaware, Ohio, Pr. at the office of the People's Press, 1827. 8 p. NRAB; OClWHi. 28019

---- ---- Eagle Creek Association.

The Eagle Creek Baptist Association; begun and held agreeable to appointment, at the Bethel meeting house, Clermont County, Ohio, Sept. the 15th and 17th, 1827. Opened by public worship. [1827] 5, [1] p. OClWHi. 28020

---- ---- East Fork of the Little Miami Association.

Minutes of the East Fork of the Little Miami Baptist Association, held at Second Ten Mile meeting house, Clermont county, Ohio, on the 1st, 2nd and 3d of September, 1827. Cincinnati, Pr. by Morgan, Fisher, and L'Hommedieu [1827] 8 p. NRAB; OClWHi. 28021

---- ---- Huron Association.

Minutes of the Huron Baptist Association, at their session at Eldridge, Aug. 29 & 30, 1827. Norwalk, Ohio, Pr. by M'Adrle

[sic] & Buckingham, 1827. 10 p. NRAB; OClWHi. 28022

---- ---- Mahoning Association.
Minutes of the Mahoning Baptist Association, convened at New Lisbon, Ohio, Aug. 23, 1827. [New Lisbon? 1827] 4 p. OClWHi. 28023

---- ---- Meigs Creek Association.
Minutes of the Meigs Creek (O.) Baptist Association. Held at Marietta, May 18th, 19th, & 20th, A. D. 1827. [Marietta, R. Prentiss, 1827] 8 p. NRAB; OClWHi. 28024

---- ---- Miami Association.
Minutes of the Miami Baptist Association, held at Pleasant Run, Hamilton county Ohio, September the 7th, 8th and 9th A. D. 1827. [1827] 8 p. OClWHi. 28025

---- ---- Salem Association.
Minutes of the Salem Baptist Association. Saturday, October 6, 1827. [Mirror Office, Athens, Ohio] 16 p. NRAB. 28026

---- Pennsylvania. General Association.
Origin, constitution, and proceedings of the Baptist General Association of Pennsylvania, for missionary purposes. Philadelphia, Pub. by Shadrach Taylor, P. M. Lafourcade, pr., 1827. 8 p. ICN; NRAB. 28027

---- ---- Juniata Association.
Minutes of the Juniata Baptist Association, held in the meeting-house of the Huntingdon Church, at Trough Creek, Huntingdon co. Pa. Oct. 18, 19, & 20, 1827. Milton, Pa., Pr. at the office of the State's Advocate by W. Tweed & E. H. Kincaid, 1827. 20 p. NRAB. 28028

---- ---- Philadelphia Association.
A confession of faith, put forth by the elders and brethren of many congregations of Christians, (baptised upon profession of their faith) in London and the country. Adopted by the Baptists association, met at Philadelphia, Sept. 25, 1742. With two additional articles... West-Chester, Penn., Pub. by Simeon Siegfried, 1827. 108 p. CSmH; ICU; NNUT; NRAB; PRHi; PWcHi. 28029

---- ---- ---- Minutes of the Philadelphia Baptist Association convened in the meeting house of the Third Baptist Church, in Philadelphia, Oct. 2d, A. D. 1827. 16 p. NRAB. 28030

---- Rhode Island. Warren Association.
Sixtieth anniversary. Minutes of the Warren Baptist Association, held at the First Baptist Meeting House, in Providence, Tuesday and Wednesday, Sept. 11, and 12, 1827. Providence, H. H. Brown, pr., 1827. 16 p. NRAB; RHi. 28031

---- Tennessee. Concord Association.
Minutes of the Concord Association of Baptists, held at Drake's Creek, Sumner county, Sept. 1st, 1827. Nashville, Pr. at the Whig and Banner Press, 1827. 8 p. MWA. 28032

---- Vermont. Barre Association.
Minutes of the Barre Baptist Association, held at Bethel Baptist Meeting-house, Sept. 12 and 13, 1827. Royalton, Pr. by W. Spooner [1827?] 8 p. NRAB. 28033

---- ---- Fairfield Association.
Minutes of the Fairfield Baptist Association, held at Swanton, Sept. 19th and 20th, 1827. Burlington, Pr. by E. & T. Mills, 1827. 11 p. NRAB. 28034

---- ---- Leyden Association.
Minutes of the Leyden Baptist Association, held in the Baptist meeting house, in Marlboro, Vt., on Wednesday and Thursday, October 10th and 11th, 1827. Greenfield, Mass., Phelps & Clark, prs., 1827. 12 p. NRAB. 28035

---- ---- Vermont Association.
Minutes of the Vermont Baptist Association, holden at Orwell, Oct. 3 and 4, 1827. Rutland, Pr. by Wm. Fay, 1827. 11 p. NRAB. 28036

---- ---- Woodstock Association.
Minutes of the Woodstock Baptist Association, held at Jamica and Townsend, Vt., Sept. 26 and 27, 1827. Windsor, Pr. by Simeon Ide, 1827. 8 p. MNtcA; NRAB. 28037

---- Virginia. Albemarle Association.
Minutes of the Baptist Association of the Albemarle District, held at Blue-Run Church, Orange county, Virginia, on the 13th of August, 1827. Lexington, Pr. by Valentine M. Mason, 1827. 15 p. ViRU. 28038

---- ---- Appomattox Association.
Minutes of the Appomattox Baptist Association, held at Mulberry Grove meeting house, in the county of Buckingham, Aug. 10th, and the three days succeeding. Lynchburg, Pr. at the Virginian Office, 1827. 8 p. CSmH; ViRU. 28039

---- ---- Dover Association.
Minutes of the Dover Baptist Association, held at Mathews meeting-house, in Mathews county, Oct. 13, 14, & 15, 1827. 16 p. DLC. 28040

---- ---- General Association.
Minutes of the Baptist General Association of Virginia, held in Cartersville, June 2, 3, 4, 1827. Lynchburg, Pr. at the Office of the Virginian, 1827. 15 p. NRAB; ViRU; Wv. 28041

---- ---- Goshen Association.
Minutes of the Baptist Association, in the district of Goshen: held at Elk-Creek meeting-house, Louisa county, Virginia: commencing on the first Saturday in October, 1827. Pr. at the Herald Office, Fredericksburg, Va. 16 p. ViRU. 28042

---- ---- Ketocton Association.
Minutes of the Ketocton Baptist Association, held by appointment at Broad Run, Fauquier County, Va. Aug. 16, 17, & 18, 1827. [Pr. by S. H. Davis, Winchester, 1827] 8 p. ViRU. 28043

---- ---- Meherrin Association.
Minutes of the Meherrin Baptist Association, held at Wilson's meeting house, Mecklenburg county, Va. on Saturday, 21st April 1827, and on the two following days... Petersburg, Pr. by Edward Pescud, at the Republican Office, 1827. 8 p. ViRU. 28044

---- ---- Mission Society.
Proceedings of the fourteenth annual meeting of the Baptist Mission Society of Virginia, held at the First Baptist Church, in the city of Richmond, Dec. 30th, 1826, with extracts from the reports of the board of managers. Richmond, Pr. by Thomas W. White, 1827. 11 p. ViRU. 28045

---- ---- Strawberry Association.
Minutes of the Strawberry District Baptist Association, convened at Mill-Creek meeting house, in the county of Botetourt, Sept. 30th, 1826... and likewise the minutes of the same Association, convened at Blue-Ridge meeting house, in the county of Botetourt,

on the 26th day of May, 1827... Lynchburg, Pr. at the office of the Virginian, 1827. 8 p. ViRU. 28046

---- ---- Union Baptist Association.

Minutes of the Union Baptist Association, held at Union meeting house in Harrison county, Virginia, Aug. 23rd, 24th, 25th, and 26th, 1827. Clarksburg, Va., Pr. by Joseph Israel, 1827. 8 p. NRAB. 28047

[Barbaroux, Charles Ogé] 1792-1867.

Adventures of a French sergeant, during his campaigns in Italy, Spain, Germany, Russia, &c. from 1805 to 1823. Philadelphia, Pub. by J. J. Woodward, 1827. 300 p. MsWJ; NHuntHi; PPL; TNJ; ViL. 28048

Barbauld, Mrs. Anna Letitia (Aikin) 1743-1825

A discourse on being born again. Printed for the American Unitarian Association. Boston, Bowles & Dearborn, 1827. 12 p. CBPac; ICMe; ICT; IEG; MBC; MWA; MeB. 28049

---- Hymns in prose; for little children... New Haven, S. Babcock, 1827. 16 p. CtHi. 28050

Barber, Daniel, 1756-1834

The history of my own times. Washington city, Pr. for the author, by S. C. Ustick, 1827-32. 3 v. CtHT; DGU; DLC; ICN; InNd; MWA; MdBS; MdW; NN; PPCHi; PPL; WHi. 28051

[Barber, John Warner] 1798-1885

Historical scenes in the United States; or, A selection of important and interesting events in the history of the United States... New Haven, Monson & Co., [Treadway & Adams, prs.] 1827. 120 p. CtY; MB; MiD-B; NNU-W. 28052

Barclay, Robert, 1648-1690

An apology for the true Christian divinity. 1st stereotype ed. from the 8th London ed. New York, Pr. by Samuel Wood & Sons, 1827. [2], 8, xii, 587 p. CBPac; CtSoP; DLC; KWiU; MB; MH; MWA; MeBat; MeHi; MeLB; NGH; NN; NRAB; PHC; PPF; PSC-Hi; RPB. 28053

---- A confession of faith... first published in the year 1673, and reprinted by the Society at various times; to which is added an extract from the letter of George Fox and others to the governor and council of Barbadoes... Philadelphia, Pr. by Joseph R. A. Skerrett, 1827. 24 p. NN; NjR; PHC; PHi; PSC-Hi. 28054

Barker, Jacob, 1779-1871

Jacob Barker's letters, developing the conspiracy formed in 1826 for his ruin. (Letters 1-6, only.) [New York, 1827] 48 p. CSmH;NN. 28055

---- ---- [New York, 1827] 93 p. DLC; ICU; MH-BA; MWA; NN. 28056

---- ---- Eighth letter. [New York, 1827] 8 p. PPL. 28057

---- The speeches of Mr. Jacob Barker and his counsel, on the trials for conspiracy, with documents relating thereto, Pt. i-ii. New York, W. A. Mercein, 1827. p. [155]-324. DLC; MB; MH; NN; PPAmP. 28058

Barker, James Nelson, 1784-1858

Sketches of the primitive settlements on the river Delaware. A discourse delivered before the Society for the Commemoration of the Landing of William Penn, on the 24th of October, 1827.

Pub. by request of the Society. Philadelphia, Carey, Lea, and Carey, Mifflin & Parry, prs., 1827. 62 p. CSmH; CtSoP; DLC; MiU-C; NN; NSy; OClWHi; PHC; PHi; PP; PPAmP; PPL; PSC-Hi; RPB; BrMus. 28059

Barksdale, W. J.
Land, Negroes, stock, &c. for sale... W. J. Barksdale, Haw-Branch, Amelia, Nov. 6, 1827. 1 p. DLC. 28060

Barnes, Albert, 1798-1870
An address delivered July 4th, 1827, at the Presbyterian Church in Morristown. Morristown, N. J., Mann, 1827. 30 p. PPPrHi. 28061

[Barringer, Daniel Laurens]
To the freemen of the congressional district, composed of the counties of Orange, Person, and Wake. [Wake county, Mar. 14, 1827] 3 p. NcU. 28062

Barrington, Sir Jonah, 1760-1834
Personal sketches of his own time... Philadelphia, Carey, Lea and Carey, 1827. 2 v. in 1. CL; CtW; DeWI; MBAt; MBL; MH; MWA; NIC-L; NWM; NcWsS; NjP; PPL; PU; ScC; ViAlTh. 28063

Barry, William Taylor, 1785-1835
Speech of W. T. Barry, esq. at the great dinner given by the citizens of Fayette county, in honor of Gen. Jackson and the people's rights, July 21st, 1827. [Louisville, Ky., Penn, pr., 1827] 12 p. ICU. 28064

Bartlett, Benjamin D.
An address delivered at Brunswick, before the Medical Society of Maine, at their annual meeting, Sept. 4, 1827. Bath, Joseph G. Torrey, 1827. 17 p. MeB; MeLB; PU. 28065

Bartlett, Montgomery Robert
The common school manual; a regular and connected course of elementary studies, embracing the necessary and useful branches of a common education. In four parts. [Part I] Utica, Pub. by William Williams; Northway & Bennett, prs. 1827. 84 p. DAU; DLC; NUt; BrMus. 28066

---- ---- Part II. Utica, Pr. and pub. by Northway and Bennett, 1827. [85]-345, [3] p. DLC; MH; NNC-T; NUt. 28067

Barton, Benjamin Smith, 1766-1815
Elements of botany: or, Outlines of the natural history of vegetables... 3d ed., cor. and greatly enl. Philadelphia, R. Desilver, 1827. 2 v. DLC; ICF; KU; MBCo; MH; MSaP; MdBP; MiU; MoSW-M; NNNBG; NcU; PPAN; PPAmP; PPF; ViRM. 28068

Barton, David, 1785-1837
Speech of Mr. Barton of Missouri, in the Senate U. S. on Tuesday, Jan. 9, 1827. on the subject of public lands. [Washington, 1827] 12 p. DLC. 28069

Barton, John Rhea
On the treatment of anchylosis, by the formation of artificial joints. Philadelphia, J. Harding, pr., 1827. 17 p. DNLM; MdBJ; NBM; NNNAM; OC; PPL. 28070

Barton, William Paul Crillon, 1787-1856
Outlines of lectures on materia medica and botany, delivered in Jefferson Medical College, Philadelphia... Philadelphia, J. G. Auner, 1827. 2 v. (V. 1 pr. by T. Town, v. 2 by Lydia R. Bailey.) DLC; DNLM; ICJ; KU; MBH; MH-A; MdBM; MoSU; NNNAM; OCLloyd; PHi; PPC; PPL; PU; RPB; ViRM;

WU-M. 28071

The basket-makers. Philadelphia, American Sunday School Union, 1827. 32 p. MB. 28072

Batchelder, John Putnam
Memoir on the fracture of the lower extremity of the radius. Pittsfield, Argus office, 1827. 4 p. DNLM; MBCo; NNNAM. 28073

The battle of Aughrium, or The fall of Monsieur St. Ruth: with Ireland preserved, or The siege of Londonderry, To which is added, The deserted village, written by Dr. Goldsmith, 1st American from the 20th Dublin ed. Rochester, Pr. by Edwin Scrantom, 1827. 45, 94, 16, 7, 14 p. NRHi; PPL. 28074

Baxter, Richard, 1615-1691
A call to the unconverted. 2d Princeton ed. Princeton, D. A. Borrenstein, 1827. 112 p. OO. 28075

Beach, Lazarus
Jonathan Postfree, or The honest Yankee. A musical farce, in three acts. Philadelphia, Pub. by C. Neal, Mifflin & Parry, prs., 1827. 32 p. CSmH; CtY; ICU; IaU; MB; MBAt; MH; MWA; RPB. 28076

[Beaconsfield, Benjamin Disraeli] 1st earl of, 1804-1881
Vivian Grey... Philadelphia, Carey, Lea and Carey, 1827. Vol. 1, pt. 1, 3d Amer. ed; vol. 1, pt. 2, vol 2, pt. 2, 2nd Amer. ed. CtY; ViU. 28077

Beard, Ithamar A.
An address delivered before the Middlesex Mechanic Association, at their anniversary, Oct. 4, 1827... Lowell, Pr. at the Journal office, 1827. 10 p. MB. 28078

Beattie, Francis S.
The following facts in relation to J. Kunkle, deceased, (the patient) and Dr. George M'Clellan, (the surgeon)... Philadelphia, Sept. 21st, 1827. 6 p. PHi; PPL. 28079

The beauties of Sir Walter Scott, and Thomas Moore, Esquire; selected from their works; with historical and explanatory notes. By a Gentleman of Philadelphia. 2d ed., corr. and imp. Philadelphia, Towar & Hogan, and T. Desilver, 1827. ix, 204 p. MBC; MdHi. 28080

The beautiful grape vine... Boston, James Loring, 1827. 35 p. CtY. 28081

Beazley, Samuel, 1786-1851
My uncle; a farce, in one act. New-York, E. Dunigan, 1827. 32 p. DLC; MH. 28082

[Beck, Nicholas F.]
Considerations in favour of the construction of a great road, from Lake Erie to the Hudson river, by a citizen of New-York. Albany, Websters & Skinners, pr. 1827. 48 p. CSmH; DLC; MB; N; NBu; NN; NjR; WHi. 28083

Bedell, Gregory Townsend, 1793-1834
The cause of the Greeks. A discourse, delivered in St. Paul's Church... Philadelphia, W. Stavely, 1827. 40 p. DLC; MBAt; MBC; MWA; MiD-B; NN; NNG; NjPT; NjR; PHi; PPAmP; PPL. 28084

---- Sequel to the Evangelical Rambler; a series of tracts published in London. Revised by the Rev. G. T. Bedell... Philadelphia, Pub. by Wm. Stavely, 1827. 305 p. PHi; VtU. 28085

Beebe, Stuart
The time and lunar register,

referring to the year, month, days of month and week, from the advent of our Saviour to the close of the nineteenth century... Hartford, Pr. by R. Canfield for the author, 1827. 55 p. CtHi; CtSoP; DLC; MWA. 28086

Beecher, Lyman, 1775-1863

The Bible a code of laws. A sermon, delivered in Park Street Church, Boston, Sept. 3, 1817, at the ordination of Mr. Sereno Edwards Dwight, as pastor of that church; and of Messrs. Elisha P. Swift, Allen Graves, John Nichols, Levi Parsons, & Daniel Buttrick, as missionaries to the heathen. Andover, Pub. by Mark Newman [Flagg & Gould, prs.] 1827. 43 p. CSmH; CoU; DLC; ICN; MB; MH; MWA; MeB; MiD-B; MoSpD; NCH; NNUT; NjR; PPL; PPPrHi; BrMus. 28087

---- A comparison of the apostolic age with the present in respect to facilities for conducting missionary operations, from a speech at the annual meeting of the Auxiliary Foreign Missionary Society of Boston and vicinity, June 1, 1826. [Boston, Crocker & Brewster] 1827. 24 p. (American Board of Commissioners for Foreign Missions. Missionary paper no. 5.) WHi. 28088

---- The government of God desirable. A sermon delivered at Newark, N. J., Oct. 1808. During the session of the Synod of New York and New Jersey. 7th ed. Boston, T. R. Marvin, 1827. 27, [1] p. CBPac; CtY; ICT; MB; MH; MNtcA; MWA; MeBat; NjPT; PPPrHi; BrMus. 28089

---- Resources of the adversary and means of their destruction. A sermon preached Oct. 12, 1827. Boston, Pr. by Crocker & Brewster, 1827. 35 p. CtHi; CtY; DLC; ICMe; ICN; MBAt; MBC; MH; MWA; MiD-B; NBLiHi; NCH; Nh; OClWHi; OO; PLT; PPL; PPPrHi; RPB; VtMiM; BrMus. 28090

---- A sermon preached at the funeral of the Hon. Tapping Reeve, late chief justice of the state of Connecticut, who died Dec. 13, 1823, in the eightieth year of his age; with explanatory notes. Litchfield, Conn. [Pr. by S. S. Smith] 1827. 20 p. CSmH; CtHi; CtSoP; CtY; MWA; MiD-B; MiU-L; NjR; PPPrHi; RPB; WHi; BrMus. 28091

---- A sermon preached Oct. 12, 1827, before the American Board of Missions at New York. Boston, Pr. by Crocker & Brewster, 1827. 35 p. CtHT; IC; MA; MNtcA; MeBat; MeLB; PPL; ViRU. 28092

---- Six sermons on the nature, occasions, signs, evils, and remedy of intemperance. Boston, Pr. by T. R. Marvin, sold by Crocker & Brewster, and J. Leavitt, New York, 1827. 107 p. CBPac; CtY; MA; MB; MMeT-Hi; MNF; MWA; NBLiHi; NhD; NjPT; PPPrHi; TxDaM; VtMiM. 28093

---- To the Congregational ministers and churches of Connecticut. Copy of a letter from the Rev. Dr. Beecher, to the editor of the Christian Spectator. Boston, Dec. 18th, 1827. 4 p. CtY. 28094

---- ---- Boston, Dec. 18th, 1827. 22 p. OCHP. 28095

Beers' Louisiana and Mississippi almanack for 1828. By William Collom. Natchez, Henry Moss & Co. [1827] 18 l. Ms-Ar. 28095a

---- By Elijah Middlebrook. Natchez, Wm. C. Grissam; W. C. Grissam & Co., prs. [1827]

18 l. NbO; PHi. 28096

Belchertown, Mass., Congregational Church
Articles of faith and covenant... Sentinel and Journal office, 1827. 15 p. MiD-B. 28097

Bell, John, 1763-1820
The anatomy and physiology of the human body. By John and Charles Bell. The whole more perfectly systematized and corrected by Charles Bell... The 5th Amer. ed. (repr. from the 6th London ed. of 1826). The text revised... by John D. Goodman... New York, Collins & co., 1827. 2 v. CSt-L; CU; DLC; DNLM; KU; KyLxT; KyU; LU-Med; MB; MBCo; MdBJ; MdU-H; MoSW-M; MsU; NBM; NIC; NNC-M; NNNAM; NbHi; OO; OU; PPC; PU; RPM; TNJ; ViRM; VtU; WaSK. 28098

Benjamin, Asher, 1773-1845
The American builder's companion; or, A system of architecture particularly adapted to the present style of building... illustrated with seventy [sic] copperplate engravings... 6th ed. corr. and enl. Boston, R. P. & C. Williams, 1827. 114 p. 67 plates. CSmH; MA; MBMu; MH; NN; NNC; OO; VtU. 28099

Bennet & Walton's almanack for 1828. By Jos. Cramer. Philadelphia, D. &S. Neall [1827] 18 l. (variant of 28103a) DLC; MWA; NjR; PHi. 28100

Bennett, Cephas
A dictionary of the New Testament, for the use of Sabbath schools... Utica, Pr. and pub. by Northway & Bennett, 1827. v, 123 p. NRAB. 28101

Bennett, John
Letters to a young lady, on a variety of interesting subjects, calculated to improve the heart, to form the manners, and enlighten the understanding... 9th American ed., corr. New York, Long, 1827. 288 p. CtW; NN. 28102

Bennett, Titus
Revised impression of the New system of practical arithmetic, particularly calculated for the use of schools in the United States... Philadelphia, Bennett & Walton, 1827. v. p. PU not loc., 1969. 28103

Bennett & Walton's almanack for 1828. By Joseph Cramer. Philadelphia, D. & S. Neall [1827] 18 l. (variant of 28100. CtY; InU; MWA; N; NjR; PHi; PPL; WHi. 28103a

Benson, Joseph
Hymns for young persons and children, or the principal truths and duties of religion and morality. Selected from various authors, and arranged in a natural and systematic order. 4th Amer. ed. New York, N. Bangs and J. Emory, 1827. 160 p. RPB. 28104

Bentz, Michael
The new harmony; or, A new collection of church music... Gettysburg, Pa., Pr. for the author, at the press of the Theological Seminary... [c1827] xvi, 152, 16 [1] p. PPeSchw. 28105

Berard, Claudius, 1786-1848
Leçons françaises á l'usage des commençans, et surtout des cadets de l'Académie militaire des Etats-Unis à West-Point. 2e édition, augmentée. New York, Berard & Mondon, 1827. 247, iii p. MB; MH. 28106

The Berkshire agricultural almanack for 1828. By Henry K. Strong. Pittsfield, M. Spooner [1827] 12 l. DLC; MHi; MWA. 28107

Bernard, Simon
An estimate of the revenue

which may be derived from the Morris Canal; extracted from a report made in 1823, to the War Department of the United States, by General Bernard, and Colonel Totten, of the Engineer Corps. With notes. New-York, Wm. Davis, jr., pr., 1827. 10 p. NNC. 28108

Bernard, Stephen

A treatise on the French verbs, regular, irregular, defective, &c. Richmond, Va., Pr. by Samuel Shepherd & Co., 1827. 95 [1] p. CSmH; DLC; MoS; Vi; ViU. 28109

Berquin, Arnaud, 1749-1791

The beauties of the children's friend; being a selection of interesting pieces from that celebrated author, M. Berquin... Boston, Lincoln & Edmands, 1827. 252 p. DLC; MH; PU; RPB; TxU-T. 28110

Bible

An amended version of the Book of Job, with an introduction, and notes chiefly explanatory. By George R. Noyes. Pub. by Hilliard & Brown: Cambridge [From the University Press--By Hilliard, Metcalf & Co., Cambridge] 1827. [xi] 116 p. CtW; GMM; IEG; LNHT; MA; MB; MBAt; MH-AH; MHi; MoSpD; NNAB; NjP; BrMus. 28111

---- Die Bibel, oder die ganze heilige Schrift des Alten und Neuen Testaments, nach der Deutschen Uebersetzung D. Martin Luthers. Philadelphia, in der Deutsch Europäischen Buch und Kunst Handlung von J. G. Ritter ... 1827. vi, 1557, [3] 454, [8] p. PRHi; ViU. 28112

---- The gospel according to Saint Luke, trans. into the Mohawk tongue, by H. A. Hill. New York, Pr. for the American Bible Society, A. Hoyt, pr., 1827. [Mohawk title page on left hand side facing English title.] 157 p. CtHT-W; NhD; PU; WGrNM; BrMus. 28113

---- The Holy Bible, containing the Old and New Testaments according to the authorized version; with explanatory notes, practical observations, and copious marginal references, by Thomas Scott... Stereotype ed., from the 5th London ed., with the author's last corr. and imp. Boston, S. T. Armstrong [etc.] 1827. 6 v. CU; CtHT; GAU; GMM; ICU; MCE; MWA; MnU; NNAB; NR; NbOU; OClW; PPDrop; PU; RNHi; ScCoT; TC; ViU; WvED. 28114

---- The Holy Bible... with Canne's marginal notes and references. Together with the Apocrypha... Stereotyped by B. & J. Collins. J. H. A. Frost, pr., pub. by C. Ewer and T. Bedlington, Boston, 1827. MBU-T. 28115

---- The Holy Bible, containing the Old and New Testaments... Brattleboro, Holbrook & Fessenden, 1827. 684 p. MA; MWiW; NN. 28116

---- ---- Cooperstown [N. Y.] Stereotyped, pr. and pub. by H. & E. Phinney, 1827. 768 p. CtY; MWA; NbOP; ScCMu. 28117

---- ---- Hartford, S. Andrus, stereotyped by B. & J. Collins, N. Y., 1827. 640, 208 p. CtHT-W; VtMiS; WHi. 28118

---- ---- Hartford, S. Andrus, Stereotyped by J. Howe, Philadelphia, 1827. 660 p. KyLo; NNG; NRAB; OClWHi. 28119

---- ---- Hartford, H. Hudson, 1827. (unpaged) NN. 28120

---- The Holy Bible... Canne's

marginal notes and references... Index... Tables... Stereotyped by James Conner, New-York... Azor Hoyt, pr., N. Bangs and J. Emory, for the Methodist Episcopal Church... New-York, 1827. [iv] [642] [92] [200] [12] [4] [47] p. CaOTP. 28121

---- Daniel D. Smith's stereotype ed. The Holy Bible, containing the Old and New Testaments: together with the Apocryphia... Stereotyped by E. White, New York. New York, Pub. & sold by Daniel D. Smith, 1827. 878 p. NjP. 28122

---- The Holy Bible... with Canne's marginal notes and references and a concise table of contents of the books of the Old and New Testaments. Stereotyped by J. Howe, Philadelphia. New York, Daniel D. Smith, 1827. 2 v. 811 p. NNAB; NNUT. 28123

---- ---- stereotyped for The American Bible Society by D. & G. Bruce, A. Paul, Pr., New York, 1827. 837 p. MH; MH-AH; MWA. 28124

---- ---- With a commentary and critical notes designed as a help to a better understanding of the sacred writings... New York, Pub. by N. Bangs & J. Emory for the Methodist Episcopal Church [Azor Hoyt, pr.] 1827-1828. 6 vols. GHi; MdBS; TNT; ViU (vols. I-IV only, all dated 1827) 28125

---- ---- Stereotype ed. New-York, Stereotyped by A. Chandler, for the American Bible Society, 1827. 824, 251 p. MB. 28126

---- ---- Printed by A. Paul, 1827. 824, 251 p. NN. 28127

---- ---- to which are annexed, an extensive introduction... By the late Rev. John Brown. New York, Pr. and pub. by T. Kinnersley, 1827. 1222 [1] p. DLC; NNUT; NRAB; NcD; PHi; PPi. 28128

---- ---- 3d stereotyped ed. New York, Pub. by White, Gallaher & White, 1827. 704, 216 p. IObB; MB; MnSM; NN; Nh; TWcW. 28129

---- ---- Philadelphia, Pub. by Eugene Cummiskey, 1827. 335, 444, 191 p. DGU. 28130

---- ---- Stereotyped by E. White, New-York. Philadelphia, Pub. and sold by Kimber & Sharpless, 1827. 4, [6], 5-570, 112, [4] p., 1 l., 573-770, 54 p. CSmH. 28131

---- ---- Stereotyped by J. Howe ... Philadelphia, Pub. by H. Holdship. Sold also by R. Patterson, agent and by Johnston & Stockton... Pittsburgh, 1827. 743, 238 p. NNAB. 28132

---- ---- Utica, New York, Pub. by Wm. Williams, 1827. O'Callaghan. 28133

---- Die kleine Lieder Sammlung, oder Auszug aus dem Psalterspiel der Kinder Zions, zum Dienst inniger heilsuchender Seelen... Zweyte Auflage. Ephrata, Joseph Bauman, 1827. 216 p. P; PHi. 28134

---- Last wills and testaments of thirteen patriarchs, and Gospel of Nicodemus, the believing Jew. Trans. from the German prints for the benefit of English readers. By the Rev. Moses Henkle, of Clark County, Ohio. Urbana, O., Pr. by Evans Banes, Jr. 1827. 67, [1], 40 p. OClWHi. 28135

---- Das Neue Testament unsers Herrn und Heilandes Jesu Christi. Nach der deutschen Uebersetzung von Dr. Martin Luther... Achte mit stereotypen gedruckte Auflage. Carlisle (Pa.) Moser und Peters, 1827. 511, 5 p. CU; DLC; MA; MiU-C; P; PP; PPL. 28136

---- The New Testament ... [Stereotype ed.] G. J. Loomis, Albany, 1827. 276 p. (Leaves pr. on one side only.) NN 28137

---- ---- Stereotyped by David Hills. Boston, Pr. by F. Ingraham, and J. Putnam, 1827. 500 p. GDC; MB; MH; NjMD; NN; NNAB. 28138

---- ---- 2d ed. rev. and imp. Boston, Hilliard, Gray, Little & Wilkins, 1827. 308 p. CtW; MB; MWA; NN; PPF; PPL. 28139

---- ---- with references and a key sheet of questions... 12th ed. By Hervey Wilbur, Boston, Pub. by Hilliard, Gray, Little & Wilkins... Pr. at Treadwell's Power Press, 1827. 324, 36, [4] p. MBC; MoSU; NN; PPL. 28140

---- ---- 1st Amer. stereotype ed. Boston, Richardson & Lord, 1827. 312 p. NNUT. 28141

---- ---- Pub. by Holbrook & Fessenden, Brattleborough, Vt. [1827?] 335 p. NN 28142

---- ---- Concord, N. H., Pub. by John M. Putnam, 1827. 283 p. Nh; Nh-Hi; PPeSchw. 28143

---- ---- Stereotype ed. Cooperstown [N. Y.] H. & E. Phinney, 1827. 324 p. MiU. 28144

---- ---- Stereotyped by Hammond Wallis, New York. Elizabeth-Town, N. J., James Sanderson, 1827. 200 p. CoU; DLC. 28145

---- ---- Pub. by J. & B. Williams: Exeter, N. H., 1827. 299 p. O'Callaghan, p. 187. 28146

---- ---- Hartford, S. Andrus, Stereotyped by A. Chandler, 1827. 251 p. DLC; MBD; NN; NbOU. 28147

---- ---- Hartford, Pub. by Silas Andrus, 1827. 288 p. DLC. 28148

---- ---- Lowell, Mass., Pub. by Thomas Billings, 1827. 350 p. MB; MLow; NN; NNAB. 28149

---- ---- Lunenburg, Mass., Pub. by Edmund Cushing, 1827. 310 p. CSmH; NN; NNAB. 28150

---- ---- By James Nourse. New York, Pub. by G. & C. Carvill, 1827. 373, xxiii p. DLC; MH; NN; NjPT; PPPrHi; ViU; BrMus. 28151

---- ---- 3d ed. New York, White, Gallaher & White, 1827. 216 p. MWA; NNAB; NjPT; OkEnS. 28152

---- ---- New York, Abraham Paul, 1827. 315 p. ICartC; MWA; RPB. 28153

---- ---- Boston & New York, Pr. for the American Bible Society, by Abraham Paul, stereotyped by Baker & Greele, 1827. 315 p. GHi; NN; NNAB. 28154

---- ---- Stereotyped by Baker & Greele, Boston. New-York, Pr. for the American Bible Society, by D. Fanshaw, 1827. 315 p. MB. 28155

---- ---- Stereotyped by J. Howe, Philadelphia. New York, Pub. by E. Bliss, 1827. 252 p. CBPac; ICN; MWA; MoSU; NN; OC. 28156

---- ---- Stereotyped ed. New York, Stereotyped by James Conner for "The American Bible Society." 1827. 237 p. NNAB; NPotU. 28157

---- ---- [Stereotyped by J. Conner] ... A Hoyt, pr. ... Pub. by N. Bangs and J. Emory, for the Methodist Episcopal Church, New-York, 1827. 237 p. NNAB. 28158

---- ---- Stereotyped by J. Howe, New York. Newark, N. J., Olds, 1827. 286 p. NjP; OClW. 28159

---- ---- Philadelphia, Pub. by Joseph McDowell, and Kimber & Sharpless, Stereotyped by J. Howe, 1827. 269 p. PWerv. 28160

---- ---- Woodstock, Pr. by Nahum Haskell, 1827. Gilman, p. 33, not loc. 28161

---- A new translation of the Epistle to the Hebrews, by M. Stuart. [Andover] Flagg & Gould [1827] [24] p. MH; PPPrHi. 28162

---- ... Novum testamentum graecum. Ad exemplar Roberti Stephani accuratissime editum. Cura P. Wilson. Hartfordiae, O. D. Cooke, stereotypis H. Wallis, 1827. 369 p. CO; MdW; NN. 28163

---- Psalms carefully suited to the Christian worship in the United States of America. New York, White, Gallaher & White, 1827. 274 p. NCanHi; OO. 28164

---- ---- By Isaac Watts... A new ed., corr. Edited by Joel Barlow. Princeton, N. J., D. A. Borrenstein, 1827. 316 p. NNUT; PPPrHi. 28165

---- The Psalms of David, imitated in the language of the New Testament, and applied to the Christian use and worship... A new ed., in which the Psalms omitted by Dr. Watts are versified, local passages are altered, and a number of Psalms are versified anew, in proper metres. By Timothy Dwight. [Hartford] Pr. for Hudson & Goodwin. From Sidney's press, 1827. 505 p. DLC; MdBJ. 28166

---- The Psalms of David, imitated in the language of the New Testament and applied to the Christian state and worship... Hartford, S. Andurs, pub., 1827. 322, 282 p. MDeeP; PWaybu. 28167

---- ---- A new ed., in which the Psalms omitted by Dr. Watts are versified, local passages are altered, and a number of Psalms are versified anew in proper metres. By Timothy Dwight, DD. New Haven, N. Whiting. Stereotyped by A. Chandler, 1827. 506 p. CSmH; Ct; CtHi; CtW; DLC; ICN; MWiW; MeBat; NBuDD; NN; NjPT; OO; RPB. 28168

---- ---- (Stereotype ed.) Philadelphia, Pub. by L. B. Clarke, 1827. 589 p. CSmH. 28169

---- Der Psalter des Königs und Propheten Davids, verdeutscht von Dr. Martin Luther... Die vierte Auflage. Reading, Gedruckt und zu haben bey Johann Ritter u. Co., 1827. 251, [1] p. PPL; PPeSchw. 28170

---- The reference Bible, containing an accurate copy of the common English version of the Old and New Testaments, by Henry Wilbur. 6th ed. Boston, Hillard, Gray, Little, Wilkins, Crocker & Brewster, pub., 1827. Treadwells Press, prs. 1012, 324, 100 p. IaGG; WHi. 28171

Bible atlas... New-Haven, Pub. by N. & S. S. Jocelyn, 1827. 1 p. l., 9 col. maps, 2 l. (Cover title: Bible Atlas; Consisting of nine maps, with explanations: illustrative of scripture history. Designed for the use of children and youth.) CtHT-W; CtY. 28172

---- Philadelphia, American Sunday School Union, 1827. 9 maps. CtHi; MH; PPL; PPAmS. 28173

---- Philadelphia, American Sunday School Union, 1827. 9 maps. (Has Scripture questions, adapted to the Bible atlas.) CtHi. 28174

The bible boy; being the history of a lad who was reputed to have got the whole Bible by heart. By a minister. Author of the "Missionary Week." Concord, Pub. by Jacob B. Moore, 1827. 21 p. Nh-Hi. 28175

Bible history. Wendell, Mass. J. Metcalf, pr., 1827. 16 p. DLC. 28176

The Bible recommended to young people. Revised by the Committee of Publication. Philadelphia, American Sunday School Union, 1827. 31 p. BrMus. 28177

Bible Society of Philadelphia
Address of the managers of the Philadelphia Bible Society, to the inhabitants, of the state of Pennsylvania. Philadelphia, Pr. by Clark & Raser, 1827. 15 p. MBAt; MHi; MdHi; PPPrHi. 28178

---- The nineteenth report... read before the Society, May 2, 1827. Philadelphia, Pr. by order of the Society, by John W. Allen, 1827. 31, [1] p. PPL. 28179

---- Zuschrift der Verwalter der Bibelgesellschaft von Philadelphia an die Einwohner des Staates Pennsylvanien. Philadelphia, Pr. by Conrad Zentler, 1827. 16 p. PHi. 28180

Bichat, Xavier, i.e. Marie François Xavier, 1771-1802
Pathological anatomy. The last course of Xavier Bichat, from an autographic manuscript of P.A. Béclard; with an account of the life and labors of Bichat, by F.G. Boisseau... Trans. from the French by Joseph Togno... Philadelphia, J. Grigg, 1827. 232 p. CU; CtY; DLC; DNLM; GEU-M; ICU; KU; KyLxT; LNT-M; MB; MBCo; MWA; MdBJ; MeB; MiDW-M; MoSW-M; NBM; NcD; NcU; OU; PPAmP; PPC; PPL; RPM; ScCMu; TxU; ViRM; ViU; BrMus. 28181

---- Physiological researches on life and death, by Xavier Bichat; tr. from the French, by F. Gold. With notes, by F. Magendie... The notes tr. by Geo. Hayward, M.D. Boston, Richardson & Lord, J.H.A. Frost, pr., 1827. 334 p. ArU-M; CSt-L; GHi; ICJ; KU; MA; MBCo; MH; MdBJ; MdUM; MeB; MoSW-M; NIC-M; NRU; OC; PPC; PPL; PU; ScCM; TxU; ViRUT. 28182

Biddle, Nicholas, 1786-1844
Eulogium on Thomas Jefferson, delivered before the American Philosophical Society, on the eleventh day of April, 1827. Philadelphia, R.H. Small, 1827. 55 p. DLC; ICHi; ICN; MB; MBAt; MH; MHi; MWA; MiU; MoSHi; NIC; NjPT; PHi; PPAmP; PPL; PU; RPB; ViU; BrMus. 28183

Bigelow, Andrew
The Bible the Christian's text-book; and the theory of original sin examined. Two sermons preached at Chelsea on Lord's Day, Oct. 21, 1827. Boston, Bowles & Dearborn [Boston, Press of Isaac R. Butts & Co.] 1827. 40 p. MB; MBAt; MBC; MH; MWA; MiD-B; PPAmP; RPB; BrMus. 28184

Bingham, Caleb, 1757-1817
The Columbian orator: containing a variety of original and selected pieces... Stereotype ed. Boston, Pr. and pub. by J. H. A. Frost, 1827. 300 p. CSmH; CtW; CtY. 28185

Binney, Horace, 1780-1875
An eulogium upon the Hon. William Tilghman, late Chief Justice of Pennsylvania. Philadelphia, Philip H. Nicklin; Mifflin & Parry prs. 1827. 46 p. CSmH; DLC; ICN; ICU; MBC; MH; MWA; MdBP; MdHi; MiD-B; MnU; NjP; PHC; PHi; PP; PPL; PPPrHi; PPiU-L; PU-L; RPB. 28186

---- Union Canal Company. Opinion from Horace Binney, esq. [Philadelphia, 1827] 8 p. PPL. 28187

Binns, John, 1772-1860
Office of the Democratic Press, Philadelphia. Dec. 6, 1827. Supplement. To the public. 8 p. DLC; MBAt; PHi; PPL; RPB. 28188

A biographical memoir of Richard Jordan, a minister of the Gospel in the Society of Friends; late of Newton, in Gloucester County, New Jersey... Philadelphia, Pr. by Joseph R. A. Skerrett, 1827. 38 p. MBAt; MH; MWA; OClWHi; PHC; PHi; PPL; PSC-Hi; WHi; BrMus. 28189

[Bishop, Abraham] 1763-1844?
Farmington canal. To the citizens of New-Haven. [New-Haven? 1827] 14 p. CtSoP. 28190

Bishop, Henry Rowley
The marriage of Fiagaro; an opera in three acts. New York, Pub. by E. M. Murden, 1827. 52 p. MH; NN. 28191

Black, John, 1768-1849
A sermon on national righteousness and sin, delivered in the First Presbyterian Church, April 3, 1827, before a large assembly, convened for the purpose of adopting resolutions against duelling. Pittsburgh, Pittsburgh Recorder, 1827. 16 p. CSmH; NjPT; NjR; PPPrHi; BrMus. 28192

The blackbird; consisting of a complete collection of the most admired modern songs. New York, J. McCleland, 1827. 140, [4] p. RPB. 28193

Blackstone, Sir William, 1723-1780
Commentaries on the laws of England; by the late Sir W. Blackstone, to which is added an analysis by Barron Field, Esq. A new ed., with practical notes, by Christian, Archbold, and Chitty; together with additional notes and references, by a gentleman of the New York Bar. In two volumes. New York, Pub. by E. Duyckinck, G. Long, Collins & Hannay, Collins & Co., and O. A. Roorback, and John Grigg, Philadelphia: W. E. Dean, pr., 1827. 2 v. CtY; DLC; ICHi; ICLaw; LNT-L; MH-L; NIC-L; NNC-L; NjP; OWoC; OkHi; PPL; PU; PU-L; WaU-L. 28194

Blair, David, pseud. See Phillips, Sir Richard.

Blair, Hugh
An abridgment of lectures on rhetorick... Greatly improved by the addition, to each page, of appropriate questions. By Rev. J. L. Blake. Concord, Pub. by Jacob B. Moore, 1827. 342 p. CtHT-W; KyLoS; MH; MoSW; Nh; NRHi; OO. 28195

Blair, John, d. 1782
Blair's outlines of ancient history; on a new plan, embracing biographical notices of illustrious persons, general views of the geography, population, politics, re-

ligion, military and naval affairs, arts, literature, manners, customs and society of ancient nations: A chronological table and a dictionary of proper names that occur in the work. Boston, S. G. Goodrich, Pr. by I. R. Butts & Co., 1827. 408 p. CtHT-W; GAM; MA; MAnHi; NbCrD; OOxM; OkOkU. 28196

Blake, John Lauris, 1788-1857
Conversations on natural philosophy... also by illustrative notes, and a dictionary of philosophical terms. 8th Amer. ed. Boston, Pr. and pub. by Lincoln & Edmands. Stereotyped by T. H. Carter & co., Boston. 1827. 252, 11, [1] p. CtHT; LNL; MH; MWHi; MeBa; NNC; RPB; WaU. 28197

---- The historical reader designed for the use of schools and families, on a new plan... Concord, Pr. and pub. by Manahan, Hoag & co. [Stereotyped by T. H. Carter & Co., Boston] 1827. 372 p. CtHT-W; MB; Nh; OCl. 28198

---- ---- On a new plan. By Rev. J. L. Blake... Rochester, N. Y., Pr. by E. Peck & co., [stereotyped by T. H. Carter & co., Boston] 1827. 372 p. CSmH; DLC; NRHi; NRMA; NRU. 28199

---- The juvenile companion, being an introduction to the historical reader. Boston, Bowles & Dearborn, Isaac R. Butts and Co. prs. 1827. 300 p. KU; MBevHi; MH; MWbor; Nh; Nh-Hi; RPB; BrMus. 28200

Blanchard, Charles
A sermon preached at Sanford, May 9, 1826, at the funeral of Mr. Joseph Butler. Kennebunk, James K. Remich, 1827. 14 p. Williamson: 1121. 28201

Bledsoe, Jesse
Hon. J. Bledsoe's introductory lecture on law. Delivered at Nashville, Tenn. on the fifth November, 1827. Nashville, Pr. at the Office of the Republican Gazette, 1827. 11 p. MH-L; TKL. 28202

---- Speech of Jesse Bledsoe, esq. on the resolutions, proposed by him concerning banks. Delivered in the Senate of Kentucky, at the annual session of 1818. Trenton, Repr. by Wm. L. Prall, 1827. 39 p. PHi. 28203

Bliss, George, 1793-1873
An address to the members of the bar of the counties of Hampshire, Franklin and Hampden, at their annual meeting at Northampton, Sept. 1826. Springfield [Mass.] Tannatt & co., prs., 1827. 85 p. CSmH; DLC; MAJ; MBAt; MBS; MH-L; MHi; MNF; MWA; MnU; NN; NNUT; NjPT; OCLaw; PHi; WHi; BrMus. 28204

Blunt, Edmund M.
The American coast pilot... By Edmund M. Blunt. 11th ed. New York, Pub. by Edmund & George W. Blunt. Gray & Bunce, prs., 1827. xvi, 676 p. CSmH; CtW; MBAt; NNA; NjP; NjR; PHi. 28205

Blunt's edition of the nautical almanac, and astronomical epehmeris, for the year 1829. Published by order of the commissioners of longitude, London, and examined by E. C. Ward, professor of nautical science at the U. S. naval school, Brooklyn. New-York, Repub. by Edmund M. Blunt, John Gray & co., prs., Feb. 1827. 237 p., 40 p. of advs. MsWJ; TNJ. 28206

Boaden, James, 1762-1839
Memoirs of Mrs. Siddons. Interspersed with anecdotes of authors and actors. Philadelphia,

H. C. Carey & I. Lea, and E. Littell. New York, G. & C. Carvill. Wm. Brown, pr., 1827. 382 p. CLU; CtY; MA; MBAt; MH; MWA; NN; NNS; NWM; NjP; NjR; OO; OU; PPAmP; PPL; PU; RPA; Vi; VtU; WHi. 28207

A boat to Richmond. See Mant, Alicia Catherine.

Bogota
Exposicion de los sentimientos de los funcionarios publicos asi nacionales como departamentales y municipales y demas habitantes de la ciudad de Bogota hecha para ser presentada al libertador presidente de la republic. New York, 1827. 26 p. MWA; PPAmP; TxU. 28208

Boieldieu, François Adrien, 1775-1834
La dame Blanche. Rondo from the celebrated chorus of Highlanders. Arranged for the pianoforte, by C. Thibault. New York, Dubois & Stodart, 1827. 6 p. DLC; MB. 28209

---- ---- New York, E. M. Murden & A. Ming, 1827. 57 p. DLC; MB; PHi; PPL; PPULC. 28210

Bolles, William
A spelling book; containing exercises in orthography, pronunciation, and reading. 2d ed. New-London, S. Green for William Bolles, 1827. 78 l. PP. 28211

Bolmar, A.
Key to a selection of Perrin's Fables. By A. Bolmar, professor of the French language at the High School of Philadelphia. Philadelphia, Pr. by P. M. Lafourcade, 1827. 227 p. OO; PHi; PPFM. 28212

---- Key to the first eight books of the Adventures of Telemachus, the son of Ulysses. Philadelphia, Pr. by P. M. Lafourcade, 1827. 273 p. PPeSchw; WBB. 28213

Bolton, A. M.
The whore of Babylon unmasked; or, A cure for orthodoxy; being a letter addressed to Richard Mott, of New York. Philadelphia, 1827. 36 p. DLC; ICN; MWiW; OClWHi; PHC. 28214

Bonaparte, Charles [Lucien Jules Laurent] prince de Canino, 1803-1857
On the distinction of two species of Icterus, hitherto confounded under the specific name of icterocephalus. Read Feb. 28, 1826. [Philadelphia, 1827] [4] p. DLC. 28215

Bond, Alvan, 1793-1882
A sermon, preached Oct. 2, 1827, before the Auxiliary Foreign Mission Society of Brookfield Association, at their fourth annual meeting. Brookfield [Mass.] E. & G. Merriam, prs., 1827. 18 p. CSmH. 28216

Bond, Thomas Emerson, 1782-1856
An appeal to the Methodists, in opposition to the changes proposed in their church government. Baltimore, Pub. by Armstrong & Plaskitt, William Wooddy, pr., 1827. 69 p. CSmH; DLC; IEG; MBAt; MH; MdBBC; MdBE; MdHi; MsJMC; PPL. 28217

---- ---- 2d ed. Baltimore, Pub. by Armstrong & Plaskitt, J. D. Toy, pr., 1827. 69 p. MHi; MdHi; PPL. 28218

---- ---- Cincinnati, Pr. by Morgan, Fisher, and L'Hommedieu, 1827. 52 p. KyLx; MiD. 28219

Bonnycastle, John
An introduction to Algebra: With notes and observations. 3rd New York, from the last London

ed., rev., corr. and enl. New York, Pub. by Evert Duyckinck & O.H. Roorbach [W. E. Dean, pr.,] 1827. 312 p. MA; MH; MoS; NCH; NNC; PHC; WaPS. 28220

---- Introduction to mensuration & practical geometry... 4th Amer. ed. from 10th London ed. enl. Philadelphia, Kimber & Sharpless, 1827. 252 p. MChiA; PU. 28221

Boston, Thomas, 1676-1732
A view of the covenant of grace from the sacred records. Philadelphia, Pub. by Towar & Hogan, J.H. Cunningham, pr., 1827. 2 v. CSaT; KyDC; LNB; MNtcA; MWiW; NNUT; NcMHi; NjPT; OMC; OO; PLT; PPPrHi; ScDuE. 28222

Boston
At a meeting of the Directors of the House of Industry, held at said house, on Thursday, 3d May, 1827, the following report of their committee was read... [Boston, 1827] 35 p. MBAt; PPL. 28223

---- The charter of the city of Boston and ordinances made and established by the mayor, aldermen, and Common council... Boston, True & Greene, city prs., 1827. 260, xv p. DLC; ICJ; IU; MB; MBAt; MH-L; MHi; MeB; NNC. 28224

---- City of Boston. In common council, June 25, 1827. Ordered, that the terms on which the city agreed to accept the Free Bridge from Sea Street to the newly made land at South Boston, be printed for the use of the members... [Boston, 1827] 15 p. M; MB. 28225

----- ----- The committee of the city council on the subject of the lands lying north of the county court-house, and of the vacated parts of Faneuil Hall, and the lands lying in that vicinity, respectfully report... [Boston, May 1, 1827] 12 p. MBAt; MHi. 28226

---- ---- The committee, to whom was referred the consideration of the expedience of introducting [!] the system of monitorial instruction into the primary schools, respectfully report... [Boston, April, 1827] 16 p. CtHT-W; MBAt; MHi. 28227

---- Common Council, March 5, 1827. Report [on the reduction of the city debt.] Boston, 1827. 14 p. MBAt. 28228

---- Fifteenth annual report of the receipts & expenditures of the city of Boston, and county of Suffolk, May 1, 1827. Boston, True & Greene, prs., 1827. 47 p. DLC; MBAt; MBB; MiD-B; PPL. 28229

---- General return [of the Boston Fire Department] 1827. (Boston, True & Green, prs., 1827) Bdsd. MBAt. 28230

---- List of persons, co-partnerships, and corporations, who were taxed $25 and upwards, in the city of Boston, in the year 1827 ... [Boston?] From Hale's Press ... City printer [1827?] MBAt; MBB; MHi. 28231

---- Notification. The inhabitants of the city of Boston, qualified as the law directs, are hereby notified that the meeting which was held at Faneuil Hall on the 12th inst. stands adjourned to meet at the same place on Thursday the 26th day of April instant... to give in their ballots for or against the acceptance of the following act of the Legislature... Boston, April 16, 1827. Bdsd. MB. 28232

---- Regulations of the school committee of the City of Boston

Boston, Pr. by Nathan Hale, 1827. 30 p. CtHT-W; MB; MH; MiD-B; P. 28233

---- Report on the money necessary for the ensuing year. Boston, 1827. 19 p. MBAt. 28234

---- Rules and orders of the Common Council of the city of Boston. Pub. by order of the Board. Boston, Hilliard, Gray, Little & Wilkins. Pr. at the University Press, 1827. 52 p. NbU. 28235

Boston Athenaeum

Catalogue of books in the Boston Atheneum[!]; to which are added the by-laws of the institution... Boston, Pr. by William L. Lewis, 1827. 356 p. CtY; ICN; MA; MB; MBAt; MH; MnU; MoSpD; NBu; NCH; NNS; NcU; NhD; OClWHi; PPAmP; PPL; PU; RNR; BrMus. 28236

---- A catalogue of the first exhibition of paintings, in the Athenaeum gallery: consisting of specimens, by American artists... Boston, From the press of W. W. Clapp, 1827. 8 p. CtY; MB; MBAt; MBB; MBMu; MH; MiD-B; RPD. 28237

Boston. Citizens.

A memorial to Congress against an increase of duties on importations, by citizens of Boston and vicinity. Boston, Dutton & Wentworth, prs., 1827. 15 p. CU; DNA; MH; MiD-B; NIC; PHi; PPAmP; RPB; WHi; BrMus. 28238

---- Report of a committee of the citizens of Boston and vicinity, opposed to a further increase of duties on importations. Boston, From the press of Nathan Hale, 1827. 196 p. CSmH; CU; CtHT; CtY; DLC; ICU; MB; MBAt; MH; MWA; MdHi; MiD-B; NNS; NcD; Nh; NjR; PHi; PPAmP; RPB; ScU; TxH; Vi; WHi; BrMus. 28239

Boston Daily Advertiser

Address of the carrier of the Boston Daily Advertiser, to his patrons. January 1, 1827. [Boston, 1827] Bdsd. MB. 28240

The Boston directory. Boston, Pub. by Hunt & Stimpson, and John H. A. Frost... John H. A. Frost, pr., 1827. [24], 336 p. DLC; MB; MBAt; MHi; MWA; NIC; NN. 28241

Boston Fatherless and Widows' Society

Constitution of the Fatherless and Widows' Society. Including the report for 1827. Boston, Wm. L. Lewis, pr., 1827. 8 p. MH; MHi; MWA. 28242

Boston Female Asylum

Order of services at the twenty seventh anniversary of the Boston Female Asylum, celebrated in the First Church, Chauncy Place, October 26, 1827. [Boston] Isaac R. Butts & Co., prs., [1827] Bdsd. MB. 28243

Boston. High School for Girls.

Regulation of the High School for Girls, Boston... Boston, Pr. by T. B. Wait & son, 1827. 16 p. CtHT-W; CtY; DLC; MB; MBAt; MH; MHi; WHi. 28244

Boston Mechanics Institution

The constitution of the Boston Mechanics' Institution. Boston, Pr. by Moore and Sevey, 1827. 7 p. MBAt; MBB; MH-BA; MHi. 28245

Boston News-letter and City Record.

New-year's address, Jan. 1, 1827. [Boston, 1827] Bdsd. MBAt. 28246

Boston. Public Latin School

A catalogue of the scholars in

the Public Latin School... September, 1827. Boston, Pr. by Munroe & Francis, 1827. 8 p. DLC; MBAt; MH. 28247

Boston. Second Baptist Church of Christ
A summary declaration of the faith and practice of the Second Baptist Church of Christ, in Boston... revised 1821, and reprinted by a vote of the Church, 1827. Boston, True & Green, prs. [1827] 24 p. IHi; MiD-B. 28248

Boston Society for the Moral and Religious Instruction of the Poor.
Eleventh annual report of the directors of the Boston Society for the Religious and Moral Instruction of the Poor. Read and accepted, Nov. 21, 1827. Boston, Pr. by Crocker & Brewster, 1827. 28 p. MB; MeBat. 28249

Boston. Sunday School Society
Constitution of the Boston Sunday School Society. Formed Apr. 18th, A. D. 1827. Boston, T. B. Wait, 1827. 10 p. CBPac; MHi. 28250

[Boston] Theatre
For the benefit of Mr. Finn, Paul Pry... [Play bill] April 6, 1827. [Boston] True & Greene, prs. Bdsd. MB. 28251

[----] Last night of Woodstock [Play bill] Jan. 18, 1827. [Boston] True & Greene, prs. Bdsd. MB. 28252

---- The last night of Woodstock, and The lady of the lake [Play bill] Jan. 25, 1827. Boston, True & Greene, prs. Bdsd. MB. 28253

[----] Mr. Macready's last night but two, positively [Play bill] Mar. 12, 1827. [Boston] True & Greene, prs. Bdsd. MB. 28254

Boston. Tremont Theatre.
The act of incorporation, and by-laws of the Tremont Theatre ... Boston, Beals and Homer, prs., 1827. 16 p. MB. 28255

A Bostonian, pseud. See Poe, Edgar Allan.

The botanical garden. Boston, Bowles & Dearborn, Isaac R. Butts & Co., prs., 1827. 8 p. MB. 28256

[Boudinot, Elias] 1740-1821
Memoirs of the life of the Rev. William Tennent... Philadelphia, F. Scott, 1827. 72 p. ICMcC; MBC; NjP; PPC. 28257

Bowdler, Jane
Poems and essays... Printed from the 16th English ed. Boston, Wells & Lilly, 1827. 268 p. ICMe; KyLx; MB; MBAt; MH; MdBJ; RPB; TBriK. 28258

Bowdoin College, Brunswick, Me.
Catalogue of the officers and students of Bowdoin College, and the Medical School of Maine, February, 1827. Brunswick, Jos. Griffin, 1827. 16 p. MeB; MeHi. 28259

---- Order of exercises for commencement, Sept. 5, 1827. Brunswick, 1827. 4 p. MHi. 28260

Bowen, E.
A sermon delivered at Wilkesbarre, before the Genesee Annual Conference, on moral agency; 1827. Utica, Pr. by Dauby & Maynard, 1827. 28 p. CSaT; MWA; N; PPL. 28261

Bowring, John
Matins and vespers; with hymns and occasional devotional pieces. 1st Amer. from the 2d London ed. Boston, Hilliard, Gray, Little & Wilkins, 1827. Cambridge, University Press. Hilliard, Metcalf & Co. 251 p. CBPac;

CtHT-W; ICN; KyBB; MB; MBC; MDeeP; MH; MiD; MPB; MsJMC; NGH; NIC; NNUT; NjMD; PPLT. 28262

Boyer, Abel
Boyer's French dictionary; comprising all the additions and improvements of the latest Paris and London editions... Sterotyped by T. H. Carter & co., Boston. Boston, T. Bedlington and Bradford & Peaslee, 1827. 2 v. IaDuU; LNHT; MB; MH; MeBat; MnHi; NCH; NCaS; NjP; OMC; VtU; WBB; WHi. 28263

Boykin, John
To the freemen of Kershaw district. Fellow Citizens!--The great excitement which was produced by candidates canvassing for popular favor is now allayed; and the mind can freely act and adjudge, independent of the strifes, the prejudices and calumnies, which foment political heat and discussion... [1827] 2 p. DLC. 28264

Bradford Academy, Bradford, Mass.
Catalogue of the officers and students. July, 1827. Bradford, A. W. Thayer, pr. [1827?] Bdsd. MShM. 28265

Bradstreet, Martha
An offering at the altar of truth, dedicated to the good sense of a free people... New York, Pr. for the author, 1827. 79 p. MB; MBAt; NUt; OClWHi. 28266

[Brainard, John Gardiner Calkins] 1796-1828
Fort Braddock letters; or, A tale of the French and Indian wars, in America, at the beginning of the eighteenth century. Worcester [Mass.] Dorr & Howland, 1827. 98 p. CSmH; CtHi; DLC; IEN; IU; IaGG; MH; MWA; MeBa; MiD-B; NN; OC; OClWHi; PPi; PU. 28267

Braman, Milton Palmer, b. 1799
A sermon preached at Danvers on the day of annual thanksgiving, Nov. 30, 1826... Salem, Pr. at the office of the Essex Register, 1827. 19 p. MBAt; MBC; MHi; MeBat; MiD-B; NcU; NjPT; NjR; PHi; RPB; WHi. 28268

Brantly, William Theophilus, 1816-1882
Additional hymns, intended as an appendix to Watts and Rippon. Selected by W. T. Brantly. Philadelphia, Pub. and for sale by David Clark, 1827. 38 p. NNG; PPAmS; PPPrHi; PPL. 28269

Bray, John, 1782-1822
The tooth-ache; or, Mistakes of a morning. A petit comedy in one act. A free translation from the French... Philadelphia, Pub. by C. Neal; Mifflin & Parry, prs., 1827. 31 p. CSmH; RPB. 28270

Braynard, Selden
Copy of the record of the trial of Selden Braynard in the Municipal Court of Boston. With some explanatory remarks, to correct impressions made by inaccurate reports in the newspapers... Boston, Beals & Homer, prs., 1827. 17 p. MB; MBAt; MH-L; MHi; MiD-B; PP; PPB. 28271

Bread the staff of life. Revised by the Committee of Publication. Philadelphia, American Sunday School Union, 1827. 16 p. BrMus. 28272

[Brice, James Frisby]
Castler Crosier. A romance. By an American. Annapolis, Pr. by W. M. M'Neir, 1827. 79 p. DLC; MnU. 28273

[----] Democedes, an interlude in one act. 2d ed., (rev.) with the addition of a third scene.

Performed with unbounded applause in Annapolis, (Md.) on the 16th of August 1827, by Messrs. Mestayer & Company. [Annapolis] Pr. by J. Green, Nov. 1827. 8 p. MH; MWA. 28274

A brief account of the life of Emanuel Swedenborg, a servant of the Lord and the messenger of the New-Jerusalem dispensation. Taken from the New Jerusalem Magazine, published in London. Cincinnati, Pr. by Looker & Reynolds, 1827. 72 p. OUrC. 28275

A brief account of the origin and progress of the divisions in the First Presbyterian Church in the city of Troy; containing, also, strictures upon the new doctrines broached by the Rev. C. G. Finney of N. S. Beman, with a summary relation of the trial of the latter before the Troy Presbytery... Troy, N. Y., Pr. by Tuttle & Richards, 1827. 47 p. DLC; MH; NIC; WHi. 28276

Brief memoir of Solomon Underhill, late of Westbury, Long Island: Including an address to the members of the quarterly meeting of Westbury. Philadelphia, Pr. by Jos. R. A. Skerrett, 1827. 16 p. InRE; NN; OClWHi; PHC; PSC-Hi. 28277

A brief memoir of the life and conversion of Mahomed Ali Bey, a learned Persian of Derbent. Philadelphia, American Sunday School Union, 1827. 125 p. ICMcC; BrMus. 28278

A brief sketch of the occurrences on board the Brig Crawford, on her voyage from Matansas to New York; together with an account of the trial of the three Spaniards, Jose Hilario Casares, Felix Barbeito, and Jose Morandó, in the circuit court of Richmond, before Chief Justice Marshall, for piracy and murder... By a member of the bar. Richmond, Pr. by Samuel Shepherd & Co., 1827. 51 p. CSmH; DLC; MBAt; MH-L; MdHi; NNNAM; PP; PPAmP; ViU. 28279

A brief sketch of the property belonging to the North American Coal Company; with some general remarks on the subject of coal and coal mines. New-York, Pr. by G. F. Hopkins, 1827. 23 p. DLC. 28280

Brigham, Juan C.
  Nuevo sistema de geografia, antique y moderna, con diez y ocho laminas y custro mapes. Nueva York, La Publican los Srs. White, Gallaher, y White, Imprenta de Elliot y Palmer, 1827. 520 p. C-S; DLC. 28281

British Charitable Society, Boston, Mass.
  For the years 1826, and 1827. Report of the British Charitable Society... Boston, Lincoln & Edmands, 1827. 24, [2] p. ICMe. 28282

Brockway, Josephus
  Mr. Brockway's apology to the Rev. Nathan S. S. Beman, with the facts in the case... Troy [N. Y.] Pr. for the author, at the office of the Troy Sentinel, 1827. 55 p. CSmH. 28283

---- A delineation of the characteristic features of a revival of religion in Troy in 1826 and 1827 ... Troy, Pr. by Francis Adancourt, 1827. 64 p. CSmH; DLC. 28284

Bronson, A.
  A masonic address, delivered at Carmel, (Red-Mills) on the anniversary of John the Evangelist, December 27, 1826. Peekskill, Pr. by Wm. Marks, 1827. 31 p. NAuT. 28285

[Bronson, Isaac]
New-York, January 18th, 1827. Micah Sterling Esq., executor of Ethel Bronson, Esq., deceased. Dear Sir, On a review of your letters and those of Isaac H. Bronson, I have not been able to discover a sentence in either which contains the semblance of argument, or a single reason in support of your claims... [New York, 1827] 2 l. NN. 28286

Brooklyn, N. Y.
An act to reduce the law incorporating the village of Brooklyn, and the several acts amendatory thereof into one act, and to amend the same. Passed April 3, 1827. Brooklyn, Pr. by A. Spooner, 1827. NB; NBLiHi; NJQ; NN. 28287

Brooklyn. First Reformed Church. Young Men's Missionary Society.
The first report of the Young Men's Missionary Society, of the Reformed Dutch Church in Brooklyn, presented 6th Feb. 1827. [Brooklyn] A. Spooner, pr., 1827. 11 p. NBLiHi. 28288

Brooklyn Sabbath Union School Society.
The constitution, by-laws and rules, of the Brooklyn Sabbath Union School Society and school auxiliary to the Sunday School Union of the Methodist Episcopal Church, formed, July 16, 1821, for the promotion of Sabbath schools. 2d ed. rev. and amended, with add. resolutions of the Society, to Sept. 24, 1827. Pr. by George L. Birch, Brooklyn (L. I.) 1827. 16 p. NBLiHi. 28289

Brown, Aaron Venable
Supplement to the Nashville Banner. Nashville, Nov. 9, 1827. Resolutions, and accompanying argument, offered by Mr. Brown, of the Senate, in favor of amending the United States' Constitution arraigning the conduct of the President and Secretary of State condemning the measures of the present administration, and recommending for the presidency General Andrew Jackson, with a portion of the discussion thereon, together with the resolution offered by Mr. Rogers, of the House of Representatives, in favor of an impeachment of the President, with a portion of the debate thereon. [Nashville, 1827] 21 p. DLC; OCHP; T. 28290

[Brown, Bartholomew]
Templi carmina; songs of the temple [a collection of sacred music] 17th ed. Boston, Richardson & Lord, 1827. 337 p. ICN. 28291

Brown, Charles Brockden, 1771-1810
The novels of Charles Brockden Brown; Wieland, Arthur Mervyn, Ormond, Edgar Huntly, Jane Talbot, and Clara Howard. With a memoir of the author. Boston, Pub. by S. G. Goodrich, sold by Bowles and Dearborn, Boston; G. & C. Carvill, New York; and H. C. Carey & I. Lea, Philadelphia [Isaac R. Butts & Co., prs.] 1827. CtY; DLC; InU; MB; MBAt; MWA; MnU; NN; PPL; PU. 28292

Brown, Erastus
The trial of Cain, the first murderer, in poetry, by rule of court... Boston, Pr. for the purchaser, 1827. 36 p. CtY; DLC; ICU; MH; MWA; MWH; N-L; PU; RPB; BrMus. 28293

Brown, Goold, 1791-1857
A catechism of English grammar; with parsing exercises... New York, Pub. by Samuel Wood & sons [1827] 72 p. CtHT-W; NNC. 28294

---- ... The child's first book; being a new primer, for the use of families and schools. [M. Day's 6th ed.] New York, M. Day, 1827. 35 p. DLC. 28295

---- The institutes of English grammar, methodically arranged; with examples for parsing... 3d ed. New York, S. Wood & sons, 1827. 304 p. CtHT-W; CtY; MH; NNC; NRHi; PPL. 28296

No entry. 28297

---- An obituary memoir of Robert F. Mott; read before two literary societies to which he belonged... New York, Pub. by Samuel Wood & sons, and Richard Wood, 1827. 30, [1] p. InRE; MBAt; MBNEH; MH; MWA; MiU-C; NBLiHi; NjR; PHC; PHi; PPL; PSC-Hi; RPB. 28298

Brown, John

The Christian pastor's manual: a selection of tracts on the duties, difficulties, and encouragements of the Christian ministry. Philadelphia, J. Whetham, J. L. Powell, pr., 1827. 420 p. GMiW. 28299

Brown, John, 1722-1787

A brief concordance to the Holy Scriptures of the Old and New Testaments... revised and corr. Stereotyped by B. & J. Collins. Pub. by C. Ewer, & T. Bedlington. Boston, 1827. 56 p. NjPT. 28300

---- ---- Miniature ed. Stereotyped by James Conner. New York, Pub. for the Methodist Episcopal Church, by N. Bangs and J. Emory, 1827. 239 p. GEU-T. 28301

---- Gospel truth accurately stated and illustrated, by the Rev. Messrs. James Hog, Thomas Boston, Ebenezer and Ralph Erskine, and others; occasioned by the republication of the marrow of modern divinity. Collected by John Brown... 1st Amer. ed. Canonsburg, Pub. by Andrew Munro. [Pittsburgh, Johnston & Stockton, prs.] 1827. 375 p. CSmH; NbOP; PPPrHi; PPiPT. 28302

Brown, John Thompson

To the people of Harrison county. [Clarksburg, Pr. at the office of the Clarksburg Intelligencer, A. G. M'Rae, pr., 1827] 19 p. ViW. 28303

Brown, Josiah

Poems written on various subjects. Woodstock, Pr. by David Watson, 1827. 71 p. RPB; Vt. 28304

Brown, Paul, fl. 1827

Twelve months in New-Harmony; presenting a faithful account of the principal occurrences which have taken place there within that period; interspersed with remarks. Cincinnati, Pr. and pub. by Wm. Hill Woodward, 1827. 128 p. DLC; InHi; MB; OC; OCHP; OClWHi; WHi. 28305

Brown, Thomas, 1778-1820

A treatise on the philosophy of the human mind... Cambridge, Mass., Pub. by Hilliard & Brown, 1827. Cambridge, University Press, Hilliard, Metcalf & Co., 2 v. CtB; CtY; GEU; GU; ICMe; IEG; MA; MB; MBC; MBedf; MC; MDeeP; MH; MMeT; MNS; MeB; MiDU; MoK; NCH; NjP; NmU; OClW; OMC; OU; PV; RPB; ScCC. 28306

Brown University

Catalogue Senatus Academici, eorum qui munero et officia gesserunt, quique alicujus gradus laurea donati sunt in Universitate Brownensi, Providentia. Providentiae, Typis H.H. Brown, 1827. 28 p. MeHi. 28307

---- The laws of Brown University in Providence, Rhode Island, enacted by the corporation, March, 1827. Providence, Pr. by Walter R. Danforth, Microcosm Office, 1827. 20 p. DLC; M; MH; PU; TxU. 28308

Browne, E.
Map of the states of Missouri and Illinois and territory of Arkansas, taken from recent surveys in the office of the surveyor general, by E. Browne and E. Barcroft. Engraved by John Warr, Jr., St. Louis, 1827 [c1825] 145x98 cm. RPB. 28309

Browne, Peter Arrell, 1782-1860
Memorial. To the honourable the Senate and House of Representatives of the Commonwealth of Pennsylvania. [contains proposals for making a geological survey of Pennsylvania]. [Philadelphia, 1827?] 20 p. DLC; N; P. 28310

Brownlee, William Craig, 1784-1860
On the loftiest and most important branch of all sciences. An oration... before the two literary societies of Rutgers College... New Brunswick, Rutgers Press, Terhune & Letson, prs., 1827. 32 p. CSmH; MB; MH; MnHi; NNG; NjPT; NjR; PLT; PPAmP; PPPrHi. 28311

Bruce, Nathaniel F.
Messiah's advent; a Christmas eve's sermon, delivered on Sunday evening, December 24, 1826, in the Protestant Episcopal Church, Meridan, Connecticut. Hartford, P.B. Goodsell, pr., 1827. 13 p. CSmH; CtMer; MBD; NcU; RPB. 28312

Brun, Conrad Malte. See Malte-Brun, Conrad.

Brutus, pseud. See Turnbull, Robert James.

Bryan, Thomas
Observations on the tariff, with reference to the printing of silk into handkerchiefs, etc. Addressed to the Secretary of State of the United States. [New York, 1827] 7 p. Sabin 8801 DLC, not loc., 1969. 28313

The buccaneers. See Judah, Samuel Benjamin Herbert.

Buchanan, James, pres. U.S., 1791-1868
Gen. Jackson's letter to Carter Beverley, and Mr. Clay's reply. Mr. Clay's speech at the Lexington dinner. Gen. Jackson's reply to Mr. Clay, in which he gives up James Buchanan, a member of Congress from Pennsylvania, as his authority for his assertions about bribery, corruption, &c. Mr. Buchanan's reply, which effectually prostrates to the earth every imputation against Mr. Clay and his friends. [Portsmouth] Pr. by Miller and Brewster, Portsmouth journal office, 1827. 16 p. CSmH; DLC; ICU; MB; MBAt; MBC; MWA; MH; Nh-Hi; PHi; PPFM; T; WHi; BrMus. 28314

---- Mr. Buchanan's statement. Extract from Gen. Jackson's second letter... Mr. Buchanan's statement to the Editor of the Lancaster Journal... Lancaster, 8th August, 1827. Pr. at the Office of the Wheeling Gazette [1827] 1 p. DLC. 28315

Buel & Wilson
Catalogue of fruit trees, and

of ornamental trees, shrubs, herbaceous and greenhouse plants; cultivated and for sale at the Albany Nursery, by Buel & Wilson. Also garden seeds, raised in their nursery and for sale by S. Moulton & Co. Albany, Pr. by J. B. Van Steenbergh, 1827. 24 p. N; NAl. 28316

Bull, Marcus
Experiments to determine the comparative value of the principal varieties of fuel used in the United States, and also in Europe ... Philadelphia, J. Dobson; New York, G. & C. Carvill [etc.] 1827. x, 103, [1] p. CSt; CtY; DLC; GHi; IU; KSalW; MA; MB; MBAt; MCM; MH; MWA; NNBG; NWM; NjR; OCl; P; PPAN; PPF; PPL; PPi; RPB; BrMus. 28317

Bull-us, Hector, pseud. See Paulding, James Kirke.

Bunn, Matthew
Narrative of the life and adventures of Matthew Bunn (of Providence, R. I.) in an expedition against the Northwestern Indians, in the years, 1791, 2, 3, 4 & 5. Batavia, Pr. for the author, by Adams & Thorp, 1827. 71 p. OClWHi; RP. 28318

Bunyan, John, 1628-1688
The holy war, made by King Shaddai upon Diabolus, for the regaining of the metropolis of the world... Philadelphia, Towar & Hogan, U. Hunt, J. Grigg, and the Sunday School Union, 1827. 278 p. NbLU. 28319

---- ... The Pilgrim's progress from this world to that which is to come, delivered under the similitude of a dream... with copious notes by Newton, Hawker, Burder, and others, to which is prefixed the life of the author. Bridgeport, M. Sherman, 1827. 324 p. CSmH; NbOU; OTifH. 28320

---- ---- Hartford, S. Andrus, pub., 1827. 360 p. CU. 28321

---- ---- Philadelphia, Pub. by Joseph Marot, 1827. 347 p. NN 28322

Burder, Henry Forster
Mental discipline; or, Hints on the cultivation of intellectual and moral habits: addressed particularly to students in theology and young preachers. Andover, Pr. by Flagg & Gould, 1827. 126 p. CBPac; CSaT; ICMe; LNHT; MAnP; MB; MBAt; MH; MMeT; MWA; MoWGT; NCH; NSchU; NbCrD; NhD; NjPT; TWcW; ViRUT. 28323

Burder, John
Elementary discourses; or, Sermons addressed to children. 2d Amer. ed. Boston, Crocker & Brewster, 1827. 212 p. GDC. 28324

Burges, Tristam, 1770-1853
Literary Cadet - Extra. January 11, 1827. Speech of the Hon. Tristam Burges delivered in the House of Representatives of the United States on Thursday, January 4th, on introducing the bill for the settlement of Revolutionary claims. [Providence, 1827] 11 p. DLC; MH; RP; RPB. 28325

---- Speech of the Hon. T. Burges delivered in the House of Representatives of the U. S., Jan. 4., on introducing the bill for the settlement of revolutionary claims. [Providence, 1827] 6 p. NN. 28326

Burhans, Hezekiah
The nomenclature, and expositor of the English language... Philadelphia, U. Hunt, 1827. 212 p. DLC; NCH. 28327

Burns, Robert, 1759-1796

The works of Robert Burns: with an account of his life, and criticism on his writings... From the last London ed. of 1825. Philadelphia, J. Crissy, 1827. 2 v. in 1. DLC. 28328

Burnside, Robert
Remarks on the different sentiments entertained in Christendom relative to the weekly Sabbath. From the 1st London ed. Schenectady, Pub. by Joseph Stillman, Isaac Riggs, pr., 1827. 318, 5 p. ICU; MBC; PPiPT. 28329

Burroughs, Charles, 1787-1868
An address on female education, delivered in Portsmouth, New-Hampshire, October 26, 1827. Portsmouth, Childs and March [1827] 44 p. CSmH; CtHT-W; CtHi; IaU; MB; MBAt; MH; Nh-Hi; NjR; OCHP; PPPrHi. 28330

[Burt, Daniel]
The second book of masonry; containing seven degrees; illustrated with drawings, by a Mason... New York, Pr. for the proprietors, 1827. 74 p. IaCrM. 28331

Burt, Sylvester, d. 1836
Character and work of a gospel minister, illustrated in a discourse delivered at Canton, Conn., December 20, 1826, at the ordination of the Rev. Jarius Burt. Hartford, Roberts & Burr, 1827. 12 p. CtHi; CtSoP; NN. 28332

Busby, Thomas, 1755-1838
A complete dictionary of music. To which is prefixed, a familiar introduction to the first principles of that science. 1st Amer. ed. Philadelphia, G. M. & W. Snider, 1827. xxvii, [272] p. CtHT-W; CtY; DLC; ICN; MdBP. 28333

Bush, George, 1796-1859
Scripture questions designed principally for adult Bible classes ... Princeton, Borrenstein, 1827. 87 p. NjP. 28334

Butler, Charles, 1750-1832
Reminiscences of Charles Butler... Boston, Wells & Lilly, 1827. 284 p. CSaT; CtHT; DLC; GU; ICLaw; IU; InGrD; KyLx; LNHT; LU; MB; MBC; MH; MWA; MdW; MeB; MiDSH; MnHi; MoS; NNG; NNS; NRAL; NRU; Nh-Hi; O; PV; ScC; ViAl; VtU. 28335

Butler, David
A sermon, preached in Saint Paul's Church at Troy, April 1, 1827: being the next Sunday after confirmation was administered in the congregation by the Rt. Rev. Bishop Hobart. Troy [N. Y.] Pr. by Tuttle & Richards, 1827. 15 p. CSmH. 28336

Butler, Frederick
Elements of geography and history combined, in a catechetical form... 3d ed. New York, Pub. by Rossiter Robbins [Johnston & Stockton, pr., Pittsburg] 1827. 407 p. IHi; KyLxT; OClWHi. 28337

---- A history of the United States of America, with a geographical appendix and a chronological table of contents... Philadelphia, Pub. by E. Strong, 1827. 452, [5] p. (Private collection of Dr. J. A. Nietz, University of Pittsburgh.) 28338

---- ---- 3d rev. and imp. ed. Wethersfield [Conn.] Deming & Francis, 1827. 452 p. KyLxT; NBLiHi; Nh-Hi; O; TNJ. 28339

Butler, James, bp., fl. 1774-1791
Butler's catechism. Philadelphia, Pub. by Eugene Cummiskey, 1827. Parsons 923. 28340

Butler, Joseph
The analogy of religion, natur-

al and revealed, to the constitution and course of nature... Cambridge, Pub. by Hilliard and Brown. Boston, Hilliard, Gray, Little, and Wilkins, [Isaac R. Butts & co., pr.] 1827. 348 p. MCE; MH; MMeT-Hi; VtNN. 28341

---- Sermons by Joseph Butler... Cambridge, Pub. by Hilliard & Brown. Boston, Hilliard, Gray, Little, and Wilkins [Press of Isaac R. Butts & co.] 1827. 364 p. KEmC; LNB; MCE; MH; OAU; PPLT; PWW; RBr. 28342

---- The works of Joseph Butler, L. L. D. late Lord Bishop of Durham. To which is prefixed, a life of the author... Cambridge, N. E. Pub. by Hilliard and Brown. Boston, Hilliard, Gray, Little, and Wilkins [Press of Isaac R. Butts & co.] 1827. 2 v. CStoC; CtHT; CtW; M; MMeT-Hi; MdHi; MoSpD; MsJMC; NjP; NjR; OO; RPB; VtU. 28343

---- The works of the Rt. Rev. Father in God, Joseph Butler... New York, R. Carter & bros., [1827] 2 v. in 1. CStoC. 28344

Butler, Samuel
Hudibras, by Samuel Butler, with a life of the author... New York, Pub. by Evert Duyckinck [W. E. Dean, pr.] 1827. 363 p. MWHi; MeB. 28345

Buzzell, John, 1798-1863
The life of Elder Benjamin Randal. Principally taken from documents written by himself... Limerick [Me.] Hobbs, Woodman & co., 1827. 308 p. CSmH; DLC; ICMe; MB; MWA; MeB; MeHi; NRAB; Nh-Hi. 28346

---- Psalms, hymns, and spiritual songs, selected for the use of the United Churches of Christ, commonly called Freewill Baptist and for saints of all denominations. ... 1st New-York ed. Rochester, N. Y., Pr. for David Marks, Jr., by E. Peck, 1827. 350 p. NR; NRU. 28347

Byerly, Stephen
Byerly's new American spelling-book, calculated for the use of schools, in the United States. Philadelphia, M'Carty & Davis, 1827. 167 p. P. 28348

Bynum, Turner
Arlan, or the force of feeling, a poem, with other pieces, Columbia [S. C.] Sweeny & Sims, 1827. 99 p. CtW; NcD; ScU. 28349

Byron, George Gordon Noél Byron, 6th baron
The beauties of Lord Byron, selected from his works, to which is prefixed, a biographical memoir of his life and writings... by a gentleman of Philadelphia. 2d ed., corr. & enl. Philadelphia, T. Desilver and Towar & Hogan, 1827. 11, 204 p. DLC; IObB; MB; NcCQ; NjP; OMC; PP; PU; RPB; WHi. 28350

C

C. Brown's New-York state almanac for 1828. By Poor Richard. New-York, C. Brown [1827] 18 l. MWA; NBuG; NRvS. 28351

---- By Uri Strong. New-York, C. Brown [1827] 18 l. MWA; NN. 28352

The cabinet-maker's guide: or Rules and instructions in the art of varnishing, dying, staining, Japanning, polishing, etc. Concord, Pr. by Jacob B. Moore, 1827. 120 p. MWA. 28353

The cabinet of Momus, a choice selection of humerous poems, from P. Pindar, Freneau, Ladd

... Embellished with six engravings. 6th ed. Philadelphia, R. Desilver, T. Town, pr., 1827. 8, 136 p. DLC; MiU; MnU; PHi; PPL; RPB; TxU. 28354

The cabinet of useful arts and manufactures: designed for the perusal of young persons. New York, Pub. by Caleb Bartlett, 1827. 143 p. DLC; KU; MH; PPL. 28355

Cadalso, Jose
Cartas marruecas y poesias selectas. Preparado, revisado y corregido por F. Sales... Boston, de la imprenta de Munroe y Francis, 1827. 288 p. AU; CSfCW; CtY; MB; MH; MdBE; MdCatS; MeB; Ms-Ar; NbU; NcU; OMC; ViU. 28356

Caesar, Caius Julius
C. Julii Caesaris, quae extant, interpretatione et notis, illustravit. Johannes Godvinus, professor regius in usum Delphini. The notes and interpretations translated and improved. By Thomas Clark. 5th ed. Philadelphia, Pub. by Carey, Lea & Carey, John Grigg, Thomas Desilver, M'Carty and Davis, Bennett & Walton and B. & T. Kite, 1827. 410, [6] p. CtY; IGK; IaHi; MdW; NjP; OClStM; OO; WBB. 28357

Caius Gracchus, pseud.
Controversy between Caius Gracchus and Opimius [pseud.] in reference to the American Society for Colonizing the Free People of Colour of the United States... Georgetown, D. C., J. C. Dunn, 1827. 118 p. DLC; IU; LNHT; MB; MH-AH; MdHi; MeHi; NN; PHC; PHi; PPL; PPPrHi. 28358

Caldwell, Charles
Elements of phrenology. (2d ed. greatly enl.) Lexington, Ky., Pr. by A. G. Meriwether, 1827. viii, 279 p. DLC; ICU; KyLxT; KyU; NcD; OC. 28359

---- Medical and physical memoirs... Lexington, Ky., Pr. by A. G. Meriwether, 1827. 85 p. ICU; KyLxT; MB. 28360

Caldwell, Joseph
Address to the senior class and before the audience assembled at the annual commencement on the 28th of June, 1827. Raleigh, Gales, 1827. 12 p. NcU. 28361

A calm review, of the spirit, means and incidents of the late "Oneida Revival," as exhibited in various Presbyterian societies. Utica, Pr. for the author, by Dauby & Maynard; Pr. by Ariel Works, 1827. 24 p. DLC; ICMe; MH; MNF; WHi. 28362

Calvin and Arminius rectified. See Campbell, Alexander.

Cambridge, Mass. Evangelical Congregational Church
Order of services at the dedication of the Evangelical Congregational meeting-house, and the organization of the Evangelical Congregational Church, in Cambridge-Port, Sept. 20, 1827. [1827] Bdsd. MHi. 28363

Cambridge, Mass. Friendly Fire Society
Regulations of the Friendly Fire Society, instituted at Cambridge, March 17, 1797, as amended to the present time, January 29, 1827. Cambridge, Pr. by Hilliard, Metcalf, and Co., 1827. 11 p. Sabin 10153, not loc. 28364

Cambridge, Mass. Third Church.
Order of services at the dedication of the church at Lechmere Point, erected by the Third Congregational Society in Cambridge. December 25, 1827. True and

Greene, prs. Boston, [1827] Bdsd. MB. 28365

[Cameron, Mrs. Lucy Lyttleton (Butt)] 1781-1858
The kind little boy. By the author of Margaret Whyte, etc. Philadelphia, American Sunday School Union, 1827. BrMus. 28366

[----] Martin and his two little scholars, at a Sunday School. By the author of "The Two Lambs," etc. revised by the Committee of Publication. Philadelphia, American Sunday School Union, 1827. BrMus. 28367

[----] Religion and its image. By the author of "The Two Lambs." etc., etc. Revised by the Committee of Publication. Philadelphia, American Sunday School Union, 1827. 49 p. MH. 28368

[----] The two lambs. An allegorical history. Philadelphia, American Sunday School Union [1827] 32 p. DLC; BrMus. 28369

[Campbell, Alexander] 1788-1866, supposed author.
Calvin and Arminius rectified and reconciled... [Dover, Del., A. M. Schee, pr., 1827] 32 p. CSmH. 28370

Campbell, David
Duty and privilege of Christians to devote their all to spreading the gospel. Amherst, Mass., J. S. and C. Adams, 1827. 15 [1] p. CBPac; DLC; MA; MWA; VtMiM; BrMus. 28371

Campbell, John
The life of Africaner, a Namacqua chief of South Africa... Philadelphia, American Sunday School Union, 1827. 35 p. MH; NSchHi. 28372

Campbell, Thomas, 1777-1844
The poetical works of Thomas Campbell, consisting of the Pleasure of Hope, Gertrude of Wyoming, Theodric, and other poems, written at different periods from 1799 to 1827. Boston, Munroe & Francis, 1827. 300 p. ICMe; MB; MH; NRU; PU; VtU. 28373

---- ---- Philadelphia, J. Crissy and J. Grigg, 1827. 183, 38 p. CtY; KyDC; LNB; LNHT; MB; MNS; MWA; OSW; PP; PPL; PV; RPB; WvC. 28374

[Campe, Joachim Heinrich von] 1746-1818
New Robinson Crusoe; an abridgement of the New Robinson Crusoe... Philadelphia, Pub. by M'Carty & Davis; John Grigg; and Kimber & Sharpless, 1827. 224 p. MWA; PPL. 28375

Canada Company
To emigrants of industrious habits from Europe, & settlers of enterprising character from all parts of America... John Galt, Superintendent for the Canada Company. York, U. C. Dec. 7, 1827. J. Bogert, pr., Geneva, N. Y. Bdsd. NN. 28376

A candid address to the Episcopalians of Pennsylvania. See De Lancey, William Heathcote, bp.

Candid and spiritual reasons. See Coleman, H.

Candid examination of the Episcopal Church. See Strong, Titus.

Canfield, Russell
A candid review of ten letters, containing reasons for not embracing the doctrine of universal salvation, by Rev. Joel Hawes; to which are added thirteen friendly letters to a candidate for the ministry. Hartford, Pr. by and for the author, 1827. 260 p.

CSmH; Ct; CtHi; DLC; ICT; MBC; MMeT; NCaS. 28377

---- The light of truth, and pleasure of light, in four books. Great is truth and it shall prevail. Milledgeville [Ga.] M. Smith, 1827. 292 p. DLC; GU; MB; NR. 28378

The captive in Ceylon. Revised by the Committee of Publication. Philadelphia, American Sunday School Union, 1827. 16 p. DLC. 28379

Cardell, William Samuel, 1780-1828

Elements of English grammar deduced from science and practice adapted to the capacity of learners... 2d ed. Philadelphia, Pub. by Uriah Hunt, Jesper Harding, pr., 1827. xii, 142 p. MFiHi. 28380

---- ---- 3d ed. Hartford, H. & F. J. Huntington, pub.; J. & J. Harper, N. Y., prs., 1827. 135 p. MB; MWHi; NNC; OHi. 28381

---- Philosophic grammar of the English language, in connection with the laws of matter and of thought... Philadelphia, U. Hunt, Mifflin and Parry, prs., 1827. 236, [2] p. DLC; IEG; MB; MH; MdBG; NCaS; NNC; NhD; NjR; OO; PHi; PP; PPL; WU. 28382

---- Story of Jack Halyard, the sailor boy; or, The virtuous family... 6th ed., rev. by the author. Philadelphia, Uriah Hunt, Pub. Stereotyped by L. Johnson, 1827. 224 p. DLC. 28383

Carden, Allen D.

The Missouri harmony, or, A choice collection of psalm tunes, hymns and anthems, selected from the most eminent authors... Cincinnati, Pub. by Drake & Conclin, Morgan, Fisher and L'Hommedieu, prs., 1827. 199 p. MoSHi; RPB. 28384

Cardozo, Isaac N., 1751-1832

A discourse delivered in Charleston [S. C.] before the Reformed Society of Israelites for Promoting True Principles of Judaism. Pr. by James S. Burges, Charleston, 1827. 18 p. ICMe. 28385

Carey, Henry Charles, 1793-1899

A complete historical chronological and geographical American atlas, being a guide to the history of North and South America, and the West Indies... to the year 1826. According to the plan of Le Sage's atlas and intended as a companion to Lavoisne's improvement of that celebrated work. 3d ed., corr. and imp. Philadelphia, H. C. Carey & I. Lea, 1827. 45 maps, 4 charts. C-S; ICU; IU; In; KU; MB; MH; MnU; NIC; NjMoW; OCl; P; PHC; PHi; PP; PPL; TxU; WHi; BrMus. 28386

Carey, H. C. and I. Lea, firm.

On the first of March, 1827, will be published by H. C. Carey & I. Lea, Philadelphia, the first number of The American Quarterly Review. 1 p. DLC. 28387

Carey, Mathew, 1760-1839

Address delivered before the Philadelphia Society for Promoting Agriculture, at its meeting on the twentieth of July, 1824. By Mathew Carey... 5th ed., rev. and cor. Philadelphia, Mifflin and Parry, prs., 1827. 71 p. CSmH; CoCsC; CtY; DLC; ICU; InU; MB; MH-BA; MWA; NN; NNBG; OO; PHi; PPL; PU; ScCleA; ScHi; TxU; Vi; WHi; BrMus. 28388

[----] Appendix, No. IV. Colbert--No. I. 4th ed. April 25, 1827. [Philadelphia, 1827] pp.

[41]-48. MdHi; PU. 28389

---- Circular letter on the system of committing to jail prisoners for trial. Philadelphia, Oct. 8, 1827. 1 p. PHi, not loc. 1969. 28390

[----] ... Colbert--No. I-IV. [March 29, 1827] 3d ed. [Philadelphia, 1827] 16 p. MH-BA; MdHi; PPL; PU. 28391

[----] Colbert - Third series - No. I [-III]. [Philadelphia, 1827] 12 p. PPL. 28392

[----] Philadelphia, May 23, 1827. Colbert - Third series - No. I [-III]. 2d ed. [Philadelphia, 1827] 12 p. (Nos. 2-3 = Third edition, May 24, 1827) MH-BA; PU. 28393

[----] Colbert - Third series - No. II [-III] 2d ed. [May 3 - May 23, 1827] [Philadelphia, 1827] [5]-12 p. PU. 28394

[----] Colbert - Third series - No. IV. To the merchants of the United States. [Philadelphia, June 14, 1827] 5 p. PU. 28395

[----] Essay on free trade from Blackwood's Magazine for May, 1825. Philadelphia, Pr. by Wm. Stavely, 1827. 23, [1] p. CtY; ICJ; ICU; MB; MH-BA; MHi; MWA; NjR; P; ScC; ScHi. 28396

[----] Examination of the Charleston (S. C.) memorial... Philadelphia, July 17, 23, 25, 1827. (Signed: "Jefferson") 7, [17]-22 p. CSmH; DLC; ICU; MB; MBAt; MHi; MWA; MdHi; MiD-B; NHi; PU; ScCC; ScHi. 28397

[----] The Infant School... (signed Howard) [Philadelphia, Dec. 28, 1827] 4 p. PU. 28398

[----] Jefferson - No. III. 2d ed., corrected. [Philadelphia, July 25, 1827] p. [9]-16. PPL. 28399

[----] Letters on religious persecution... 4th ed. imp. To which is annexed, the Declaration of the Catholic bishops, the vicars apostolic and their coadjutors, in Great Britain... Philadelphia, For the Society for the Defence of the Catholic Religion from Calumny and Abuse, 1827. 68 p. DGU; DLC; MH; MWA; MdBS; MdW; NjPT; NjR; PHi; PPAmP; PPL; PU; RPB. 28400

[----] Madam, Without being able to ascertain what degree of attention you may be desposed to pay to the recommendation of a town meeting... [Philadelphia, Dec. 29, 1827] Bdsd. PHi. 28401

[----] Pauperism. Nos. 1-3. To the citizens of Philadelphia, paying poor taxes. [Philadelphia, July 11-20, 1827] 3, 3, 3 p. (signed Howard) PPAmP; PPL. 28401a

[----] Rail-roads. [Statement favoring the building of a rail-road in the state of New Jersey from the Delaware to the Raritan. Signed: Fulton, i. e. Mathew Carey. Philadelphia, Sept. 18, 1827] 4 p. MWA; NN; PHi; PPL; PU. 28402

[----] Philadelphia, July 7, 1827. Sir, As very erroneous impressions prevail on that portion of the proceedings of the convention at Harrisburg... [Philadelphia, 1827] [2] p. PHi. 28403

[----] Sir, On the 4th of May, I received a letter from Lewis Tappan, Esq. suggesting the propriety of a state and general convention, on the subject of the depressed state of the woolen manufacture... [Philadelphia, June 14, 1827] [2] p. PHi. 28404

[----] Sir, The salutary bill for the protection of the woolen manufacture failed... [Philadelphia, March 19, 1827] 4 p. PHi. 28405

[----] Slave labor employed in manufactures. [Philadelphia, 1827] 2 p. DLC; PPPrHi. 28406

---- To the citizens of the commonwealth of Pennsylvania. Internal improvement. [Philadelphia, Mar. 6, 1827] 4 p. MWA; NN-P. 28407

---- ---- [Philadelphia, 1827] 4 p. (At head of title: Third edition--Mar. 17, 1827) MWA; NN. 28408

[----] To the thinking few. Signed Hamilton. Philadelphia, Nov. 20, 1827. Bdsd. CtY; PHi. 28409

[----] Universal emancipation. No. 1-2. [Philadelphia, Nov. 24, 26, 1827] 8 p. (Signed Hamilton.) PPL. 28410

[----] ---- 2d ed. [Philadelphia, Nov. 24, 26, 1827] 8 p. PPL; PU. 28411

Carll, M. M.
A lecture on infant schools, delivered at the hall of the Franklin Institute, Feb. 2, 1827. Philadelphia, Pr. by Thomas S. Manning, 1827. 16 p. PPAmP; PPL; PPPrHi. 28412

Carpenter, George Washington, 1802-1860
Observations and experiments on the pharmaceutical preparations and constituent principals of opium. [Philadelphia, 1827] 16 p. CSt-L; PPL. 28413

Carpenters Company of the City and County of Philadelphia.
An act to incorporate the Carpenters Company... Philadelphia, Pr. by T. Town, 1827. 30 p. PHi; PPCC; WHi. 28414

Carter, Nathaniel Hazeltine, 1787-1830
Address read before the New-York Horticultural Society, at the anniversary celebration, of the 28th of Aug. 1827. New-York, Pub. at the request of the Society. Sleight & George, prs., Jamaica, L. I., 1827. 22 p. CSmH; IC; MBH; NHi; NN; NNMus; PPAmP; BrMus. 28415

---- Letters from Europe. Comprising the journal of a tour through Ireland, England, Scotland, France, Italy and Switzerland, in the years 1825, 1826 and 1827. New York, Pub. by G. & C. Carvill [Sleight & George, prs., Jamaica, L. I.] 1827. 2 v. CSt; CU; CtHT-W; CtW; CtY; DSI; IEN; IU; IaDaM; KTW; MBAt; MHi; MWA; MnU; MoS; NBuG; NNS; NR; NWM; NbFrM; NcD; NcU; Nh-Hi; OC; OO; OkHi; PHC; PPL; PSC; PU; RNR; RPB; WM; BrMus. 28416

The case of the Episcopal Churches in the United States considered. Philadelphia, Pr. by David C. Claypoole. Repr. by Wm. Stavely, 1827. 31 p. ICMe. 28417

Casey, John
Universal peace; being a rational and scriptural vindication, of the establishment of permanent and universal peace; upon the immovable basis of Christian principles. In two vol. Vol. I. Black Rock, Pr. by Smith H. Salisbury, 1827. 216 p. (apparently completed in one vol.) CSmH; NBuG; NBuHi; BrMus. 28418

[Cass, Lewis] 1782-1860
Remarks on the policy and practice of the United States and Great Britain in their treatment of the Indians... Boston, Fred-

erick T. Gray, 1827. 78 p. DLC; ICN; MiD; MiD-B; NN. 28419

Castler Crosier. See Brice, James Frisby.

Catechism for a young child. Selected and arranged for the use of the Sunday schools in the Protestant Episcopal Church... Philadelphia, W. Stavely, 1827. 13 p. PHi. 28420

Catechismus oder kurze unterricht Christlicher lehre... sammt der Haul-Tafel... Philadelphia, 1827. Gedruckt bey Conrad Zentler. 108 p. PLT; PPeSchw. 28421

The catechist: a fragment. Lesson first. Parable of the unjust steward. Revised by the Committee of Publication. Philadelphia, American Sunday School Union, 1827. 36 p. DLC; KU; BrMus. 28422

Catholic Apostolic Church
The Christian liturgy and book of common prayer... of the Apostolic Catholic or Universal Church of Christ. Boston, 1827. IEG, not located, 1969. 28423

Catholic Church
A catechism of the Christian doctrine, wherein the principles of the Roman Catholic religion are explained with morning and evening prayers. By the Rt. Rev. Doctor Henry Conwell, bishop of Philadelphia. For the use of his diocese. Philadelphia, Mifflin & Parry, prs., 1827. 55 p. InNd; MdW. 28424

---- The pocket manual of spiritual exercises; or, Devout vade mecum for Catholics... Philadelphia, Pub. by E. Cummiskey. Stereotyped by L. Johnson, 1827. 192 p. MdW. 28425

A Catholic clergyman of Chambersburg. See An answer to nine objections.

Causes of the progress of liberal Christianity. See American Unitarian Association.

Cervantes Saavedra, Miguel de
Life and exploits of Don Quixote de la mancha. Exeter, J. & B. Williams, 1827. 4 v. MWat; Nh-Hi. 28426

---- Trabajos de Persiles y Sigismunda, historia setentrional ... Precede la vida del autor por D. J. Antonio Pellicer... New York, Lanuza, Mendia y c., 1827. 2 v. C-S; MH; PSC; PU. 28427

Chahta holisso a tukla. See Wright, Alfred.

Challoner, Richard, bp.
The morality of the Bible; extracted from all the canonical books, both of the Old and New Testament... Philadelphia, Peter Fox, 1827. 296 p. ArLSJ; DGU; IaDuMtC; MdW; MiDSH; NjMD; PRosC; PV. 28428

Chambers, Talbot
Remarks and reflections upon the trial of Colonel Talbot Chambers, before a court martial commenced and held at Camp Morgan, in Georgia, on the fifteenth of March, 1826. By himself... Washington, 1827. 23 p. MBAt. 28429

Chandler, Amariah, 1782-1864
The spirit of the gospel essential to a happy result of our religious inquiries. An address to the Society for Religious Inquiry in the University of Vermont, Burlington, Aug. 7, 1827. Burlington, Pr. at the Free Press Office, 1827. 16 p. MAnP; MiD-B; BrMus. 28430

Channing, William Ellery, 1780-1842
A discourse, preached at the dedication of the Second Congregational Unitarian Church. New York, Dec. 7, 1826. 2d ed. New York, Pub. for the Second Congregational Unitarian Church [J. Seymour, pr.] 1827. 57, [1] p. CtHt; DLC; MA; MB; MBAt; MBC; MH; MWA; MiD-B; NjR; NNUT; PHi; PPL; RPB; ScC; TNJ. 28431

---- A discourse, preached at the dedication of the Second Congregational Unitarian Church. New-York, Dec. 7, 1826. 4th ed. New-York, Pub. for the Second Congregational Unitarian Church. By David Felt, 1827. 47, [1] p. MB; MnHi. 28432

[----] Remarks on the character of Napoleon Bonaparte, occasioned by the publication of Scott's life of Napoleon. From the Christian examiner. Vol. IV. no. V. Boston, Bowles & Dearborn, 1827. Stephen Foster, pr. 51 p. CU; CtHT-W; CtY; ICU; IU; MB; MBAt; MH; MHi; MNF; MWA; MdHi; MiD-B; NjR; OCHP; PHi; PPL; RHi; WHi; BrMus. 28433

Chapman, Lebbeus
Tables of interest, calculated according to equitable and legal principles, at the rate of six per cent. per annum. Stereotyped. New York, E. Bliss & E. White, 1827. 384 p. Ct; MH; Vi. 28434

Chapman, Nathaniel
Elements of therapeutics and materia medica... 5th ed. Pub. by Carey, Lea and Carey; Philadelphia, Mifflin & Parry, prs., 1827. 2 v. GEU-M; IU-M; MdBM; MnU; MoKJ; MoSW-M; NBMS; NNNAM; RPM; ViRM. 28435

Chapone, Hester (Mulso)1727-1801
Letters on the improvement of the mind, addressed to a lady, by Mrs. Chapone. A father's legacy to his daughters, by Dr. Gregory. A mother's advice to her absent daughters, with an additional letter on the management and education of infant children, by Lady Pennington. New York, Pr. by Samuel Marks, 1827. 288 p. CSmH; MH; MiD; OCY. 28436

[Chaptal de Chanteloup, Jean Antoine Claude compte] 1756-1832
Essay on import duties, translated from the French. 2d Philadelphia ed. Philadelphia, Pr. by W. Staveley, 1827. 17 p. MWA; PPL; ScCC. 28437

A chapter of Modern chronicles. See Samuel, pseud.

Charless' Missouri almanac for 1828. St. Louis, Edward Charless & Co. [1827] [Rusk from an advertisement in the "Missouri Republican."] 28438

Charleston, S. C.
The memorial of the chamber of commerce, and of the citizens of Charleston, against the tariff on woollen goods proposed at the 2d session of the 19th Congress. Charleston, Pr. by C. C. Sebring, 1827. 16 p. MB; MH; MWA; MiD-B; NcD; NcU; PHi; PPAmP; RPB; ScU; TxU. 28439

Charleston Bethel Union
Fifth annual report of the Charleston Bethel Union... Dec. 11, 1826... Charleston, Pr. by C. C. Sebring, 1827. 24 p. MH. 28440

Charleston, S. C. Female Seminary in Meeting Street
A general prospectus of the course of instruction, laws and government, of the Female Seminary in Meeting Street, No. 236. Samuel W. Doggett, Preceptor...

Charleston, S. C., Pr. by Wm. Riley, 1827. 8 p. MB. 28441

Charleston, S. C. Harbour master.
Masters of vessels as well as others therein concerned, are required to make themselves properly acquainted with, and in all cases to act in due conformity with the following port regulations... Charleston, S. C. [Jan. 24, 1827] 1 p. Bdsd. DLC. 28442

Charleston Port Society for Promoting the Gospel Among Seamen
Fourth annual report of the board of managers of the Charleston Port Society, March, 1827. Charleston, Pr. by C. C. Sebring, 1827. 24 p. MH; PPL. 28443

Charleston Protestant Episcopal Sunday School Society
The eighth annual report of the board of managers of the Charleston Protestant Episcopal Sunday School Society, made at the anniversary of the Society, on Whitsun Tuesday, June 5th, 1827. To which is annexed, a list of the officers and members of the Society. Charleston, Pr. by A. E. Miller, 1827. 27 p. NNG. 28444

Charlotte Elizabeth. See Tonna, Mrs. Charlotte Elizabeth (Browne) Phelen.

Chase, Philander, bp., 1775-1852
A plea for the West. Pub. by Samuel H. Parker, Boston, 1827. 15 p. CtHT-W; DLC; ICMe; IEN-M; IHi; LNHT; MB; MBAt; MBC; MH; MHi; MWA; MiD-B; Nh-Hi; PPPrHi. 28445

Chastellux, François Jean, marquis de, 1734-1788
Travels in North America in the years 1780-81-82 by the Marquis de Chastellux... Trans. from the French, by an English gentleman who resided in America at that period. With notes by the translator. Also a biographical sketch of the author; letters from Gen. Washington to the Marquis de Chastellux; and notes and corrections, by the American editor. New York, White, Gallaher & White [Sleight & George, prs.] 1827. 416 p. CSmH; CSt; CtW; CtY; DLC; GEU; GHi; GU; ICHi; InHi; MB; MBAt; MDeeP; MH; MHi; MWiW; MdHi; MiD-B; NBLiHi; NBu; NHi; NN; NT; NWM; NcD; NjP; OHi; OU; PHi; PU; TKL. 28446

[Cheney, Mrs. Harriet Vaughan (Foster)]
The rivals of Acadia, an old story of the New World. Boston, Wells & Lilly, 1827. 271 p. CSmH; CtY; DLC; ICN; ICU; MB; MH; MdBE; RPB. 28447

Cheney, Martin
A sermon delivered at the installation of the Rev. Lorenzo D. Johnson, as pastor of the Roger Williams Baptist Church and Society, in Providence, Oct. 25, 1827... Providence, H. H. Brown, 1827. 22 p. MiD-B. 28448

Cherokee Nation
Constitution... made and established at a general convention of delegates... at New Echota, July 26, 1827. Pr. for the Cherokee Nation, at the office of the Statesman and Patriot [Milledgeville] Georgia. 16 p. MBAt; NN. 28449

Chesapeake and Delaware Canal Co.
Eighth general report of the president and directors... June 4, 1827. [Philadelphia? 1827] 28 p. PPL. 28450

Chesapeake and Ohio Canal Company
Laws relative to the Chesa-

peake and Ohio Canal. Washington, Pr. by Way & Gideon, 1827. 28 p. DBRE; MH-BA; MiD-B. 28451

Chesapeake and Ohio Canal Convention, Washington
Proceedings of the Chesapeake and Ohio Canal Convention, which assembled in the capitol of the United States, in the city of Washington, on the sixth day of November, 1823, and reassembled in the same city on the sixth day of December, 1826. Prepared and published pursuant to a resolution of the convention. Washington City, Pr. by Way & Gideon, 1827. 112 p. CSmH; DBRE; DLC; ICJ; IU; MH-BA; MdBE; NN; NNE; OClW; P; PPAmP; PPi. 28452

Chester County Auxiliary Colonization Society
Respected friend. By direction of the Board of managers of the Chester County Auxiliary Colonization Society, I enclose their address, together with a copy of the constitution... West Chester, Pa. 12th Mo. 10th, 1827. 1 p. DLC. 28453

Chesterfield, Philip Dormer Stanhope, 4th earl of. See The American Chesterfield.

[Chew, Benjamin] 1758-1844
A sketch of the politics, relations, and statistics of the Western World, and of those characteristics of European policy which most immediately affect its interests: intended to demonstrate the necessity of a grand American Confederation and alliance... Philadelphia, Pub. by R. H. Small [James Kay, Jun., pr.] 1827. 200 p. CU-B; ICJ; ICU; MB; MdBJ; MiU; PHi; PPAmP; PPL; PU; WHi. 28454

[Child, Lydia Maria (Francis)]
Emily Parker, or Impulse, not principle... Boston, Bowles and Dearborn, Isaac R. Butts & Co., prs., 1827. 63 p. MB; MHi. 28455

Children in the Wood.
Children in the wood. New-York, Pr. by Charles Spear, 1827. 18 p. MH. 28456

The childrens' companion; or A manual of short and easy exercises... Boston, Pub. by Samuel Walker [Stereotyped at the Boston Type and Stereotype Foundry] 1827. 192 p. MBtS; MH. 28457

The child's first alphabet of Bible names. Philadelphia, American Sunday School Union, 1827. 15 p. BrMus. 28458

The child's prayer book. See Palfrey, John Gorham.

Chillicothe Colonization Society
Circular, Chillicothe, May 12, 1827. To the Rev. Dear Sir: The board of managers of the Chillicothe Colonization Society, feeling deeply impressed with the importance and magnitude of the cause in which they are associated... [signed] Edward Tiffin, President Samuel Williams, Cor. Sec'ry. [Chillicothe, 1827] Bdsd. ICN. 28459

Chitty, Joseph
A practical treatise on the law of contracts, not under seal; and upon the usual defences to actions thereon. Boston, Wells & Lilly, 1827. xvi, 40, 345 p. CtY; LNB; MB; MnU; NNC-L; NNLI; NcU; PU-L; ViU; WaU; WU-L. 28460

Choice pleasures for youth, recommended, in a series of letters from a father to his son. Boston, Crocker & Brewster, 1827. 123 p. KyLxT. 28461

A choice selection of hymns and spiritual songs. Designed to aid in the devotions of prayer, conference, and camp-meetings. Windsor, Simeon Ide, 1827. 159 p. MBrZ; BrMus. 28462

---- 3d ed. Montpelier, E. P. Walton, 1827. 168 p. RPB. 28463

The Christian almanac for Connecticut and Massachusetts for the year 1828... Hartford, Pub. for the Connecticut Branch of the American Tract Society, [1827] [36] p. CLU; CtHT-W; CtHi; DLC; InU; MWA; N; NjR; OClWHi; P; WHi. 28464

The Christian almanac for Connecticut for 1828. New Haven, Connecticut branch of the American Tract Society [1827] 18 l. CtY. 28465

The Christian almanac for 1828. Charleston, Charleston Religious Tract Society. [1827] 24 l. ScCC. 28466

The Christian almanack for 1828. New-York, American Tract Society; Rochester, Repub. by E. Peck & Co. [1827] 18 l. MiD-B; N; NIC; NR; NRHi; NT; NjP; OClWHi; PU. 28467

The Christian almanac, for Maryland and Virginia for 1828. Baltimore, Baltimore Branch of the American Tract Society; Samuel Young [1827] 18 l. DLC; MWA; MdBE; NHi; PHi. 28468

The Christian almanac for Missouri and Illinois for 1828. [St. Louis] Missouri and Illinois Auxiliary Tract Society [1827] 18 l. MoSHi. 28469

The Christian almanac, for New England for 1828. Boston, Lincoln & Edmands [1827] 20 l. CLU; CtY; DLC; ICU; MH; MWA; NN; NjR; PHi; RPB. 28470

The Christian almanac, for New-York, Connecticut, New-Jersey and Pennsylvania for 1828. New-York, American Tract Society; Fanshaw, pr. [1827] 18 l. CLU; DLC; MH; MWA; NN; NjP; PPL. 28471

The Christian almanac for North Carolina for 1828. Raleigh, American Tract Society [1827] 18 l. NcU. 28472

The Christian almanac, for Ohio, Kentucky, and Indiana for 1828. Cincinnati, Auxiliary Tract Society of Cincinnati [1827] 20 l. IHi; MWA; OCHP. 28473

The Christian almanac, for Pennsylvania & Ohio for the year of our Lord and Savior, Jesus Christ, 1828... Adpated to the meridian of Pittsburgh. Pittsburgh, Pub. for the American Tract Society; and for sale by R. Patterson, agent of the Pittsburgh Auxiliary Tract Society [1827] 38 p. Ia-HA; MWA. 28474

The Christian almanac, for Pennsylvania for 1828. Philadelphia, Philadelphia branch of the American Tract Society; Nicholas Murray [1827] 18 l. DLC; MWA; NjR; PHi; PP; PPL. 28475

The Christian almanac, for the state of New-York for 1828. Albany, American Tract Society, for the New-York State branch; Cornelius Gates [1827] 18 l. N; NNUT. 28476

The Christian almanac, for the United States for 1828. New-York American Tract Society [1827] 24 l. CtY; DLC; NCooHi; NR; NjR; OClWHi; OMC; WHi. 28477

The Christian almanack, for South Carolina and Georgia for

1828. By Robert Grier. Augusta, Georgia Religious Tract Society; Timothy Edwards [1827] 24 l. GEU; NN. 28478

Christian almanack, for the Western District for 1828. Utica, American Tract Society; Western Sunday School Union; J. Colwell, pr. [1827] 18 l. CLU; CtHi; MWA; MiD-B; NIC; NN; PHi; WHi. 28479

The Christian and farmers' almanack for 1828. By Zadock Thompson. Burlington, E. & T. Mills [1827] 24 l. CLU; DLC; MWA; VtU. 28480

The Christian calendar and New-England farmer's almanack for 1828. Boston, Christian Register Office [1827] 24 l. CLU; DLC; InU; MB; MWA; N; NBuG; OMC. 28481

The Christian calendar and New-England farmer's almanck for 1828. Boston, Christian Register Office; Keene, Geo. Tilden [1827] 24 l. MWA. 28482

---- Boston, Christian Register Office, also N. S. Simpkins & Co.; Keene, George Tilden [1827] 24 l. NjR. 28483

Christian Mirror

Address of the carriers of the Christian Mirror, to its patrons. Portland, Jan. 1, 1827. 16 p. (In manuscript on cover of CtSoP copy: By Edward Harris.) CtSoP. 28484

Christian revolutioner. See Romer, John.

Christmas holidays; or, A visit at home. Written for the American Sunday School Union. Philadelphia, American Sunday School Union [1827?] 34 p. DLC; KU; MH. 28485

Christmas tales. Boston, Monroe and Francis. New York, Charles S. Francis, [1827] 288 p. MBMu. 28486

Chronicles of Cannongate. See Scott, Sir Walter.

Church, Aaron Billings, 1797-1857

A sermon on the divinity of Christ. Andover, Pub. by Mark Newman [J. S. & C. Adams, prs., Amherst, Mass.] 1827. 32 p. CBPac; CtSoP; DLC; GDC; IaGG; IU; MBAt; MBC; MiD-B; RPB. 28487

[Church, Benjamin] 1639-1718

History of Philip's war, commonly called the great Indian war, of 1675 and 1676. Also, of the French and Indian wars at the eastward, in 1689, 1690, 1692, 1696, and 1704... 2d ed. Boston, Pr. by J. H. A. Frost, 1827. 360 p. CSmH. 28488

[----] ---- 2d ed. with plates... Boston, Pr. by T. B. Wait and son, 1827. 360 p. CSmH; DLC; KMK; MAnP; MB; MH; MSaP; MWA; MeB; Mi; MiU-C; NIC; NN; OMC; ScDuE; ScRhW; ViU. 28489

[----] ----... With numerous notes... also an appendix... by Samuel G. Drake, 2d ed., with plates... Exeter, N. H., Pub. by J. & B. Williams, 1827. 360 p. CLSR; MNBedf. 28490

Church, John Hubbard

A sermon preached at the formation of the First Congregational Church in Lowell, June 6, 1826. Andover, Pr. by Flagg & Gould, 1827. 30, [2] p. DLC; M; MBC; MH-AH; PPPrHi. 28491

The church catechism broken into short questions and answers. 8th ed. New-York, Pr. and sold by T. & J. Swords, Jan. 1827. 34 p. NNG. 28492

Church Scholarship Society, Hartford
Constitution of the Church Scholarship Society, with an address to the public, from a constitution for auxiliary societies; list of officers, etc. Hartford, P. Canfield, pr., 1827. 16 p. CtHT; NBuU-M. 28493

Cianchettini, P.
I love but thee! Written by Thomas Moore, Esq. Composed by P. Cianchettini. New York, Dubois & Stodart [1827?] 3 p. MB. 28494

Cincinnati. Christ Church
Proceedings of the wardens and vestry, and of the parish of Christ Church, Cincinnati, in relation to the separation of the Rev. Samuel Johnston from said church. Cincinnati, Aug. 1827. Looker & Reynolds, prs. 8 p. OCHP. 28495

Cincinnati Equitable Insurance Company
The act of incorporation, the deed of settlement, and articles of association of the Cincinnati Equitable Insurance Company. [Cincinnati? 1827] 12 p. OCHP. 28496

Cincinnati. Union Association of Journeymen Hatters
The constitution and by-laws of the Union Association of Journeymen Hatters, of the city of Cincinnati, S. J. Browne, pr. Cincinnati, 1827. 18 p. NN. 28497

Circular [Concerning the Rhode Island Coal Co.] See Sedgwick, Henry Dwight.

Circular. To the voters of the senatorial district. See Greene, James I.

A citizen of Baltimore. See Hollins, William.

A citizen of New York. See Beck, Nicholas F.

A citizen of the United States. See Everett, Alexander Hill.

A citizen of the United States. See Niles, John Milton.

Citizens & farmers' almanack for 1828. By Joseph Cramer. Philadelphia, Griggs & Dickinson [1827] 18 l. DLC; MBC; MWA; NjR; PP; PPL. 28498

The citizens' and farmers' little messenger, or, New town and country almanac for 1828. Baltimore, J. T. Hanzsche; R. J. Matchett, pr. [1827] 18 l. DLC. 28499

The citizens' and farmers' yearly messenger, or New town & country almanac for 1828. By Charles F. Egelmann. Baltimore, John T. Hanzsche [1827] 18 l. DLC; MWA; MdBE; PDoBHi; PPi; ViW. 28500

Civis, pseud. See Smith, Francis Ormond Jonathan.

Clarendon, Edward Hyde, 1st earl of, 1609-1674
The history of the rebellion and civil wars in England, to which is added an historical view of the affairs of Ireland. New ed. exhibiting a faithful collation of the original ms. with all the suppressed passages; also the unpublished notes of Bishop Warburton. Oxford, Clarendon press; Repr. Boston, Wells & Lilly, 1827. 6 v. CtHT; CtW; CtY; GU; ICU; LNHT; M; MeB; MiU; NNF; NR; NUtHi; NcGC; NjP; OCY; OClW; PHi; PLFM; PLT; PPF; TCU; TxD-T; ViU; VtU; WvW; BrMus. 28501

Clark, Daniel Atkinson, 1779-1840
The influence of a good taste upon the moral affections, an ad-

dress delivered at Amherst College before the Alexandrian Society, on Tuesday preceding commencement, Aug. 21, 1827. Amherst, J. S. & C. Adams, prs., 1827. 30 p. CSmH; CtHT-W; CtY; ICT; MA; MAJ; MBAt; MBC; MH; MWA; NjP; NjR; NNUT; OClWHi; TNJ. 28502

Clark, John A.
An address delivered to the Masonic fraternity, of Ark Lodge, Geneva, upon the festival of St. John the Baptist, immediately before the dedication of the new hall, June 25, A. L. 5827. Geneva, Pub. by request of the Committee of Arrangements. 1827. 17 p. NN. 28503

Clarke, Adam, 1760?-1832
A collection of discourses on various subjects... New York, Pub. by N. Bangs & J. Emory, for the Methodist Episcopal Church at the Conference Office, A. Hoyt, pr., 1827. 274 p. CSmH; CtW; GEU-T; InGrD; MBNMHi; MH-AH; MoSP; MoStj; NRAB; NcD; TNJ. 28504

Clarke, Dorus
Foundation of Christian hope, a sermon, preached at the ordination of Rev. Tertius S. Clarke, over the Second Congregational Church and parish, in Deerfield, Oct. 3, 1827... Northampton, Mass., Pr. by T. W. Shepard, 1827. 24 p. MNF; OO; RPB; BrMus. 28505

Clarke, James
Circular. To the people of Fayette, Woodford and Clark Counties. Fellow Citizens. The nineteenth Congress having closed its second session, and the term for which I was elected having expired, I feel it my duty... to give a brief detail of its proceedings ... Jas. Clark. Winchester, Ky. March 24, 1827. 2 p. DLC. 28506

Clarkson, Thomas, 1760-1846
Memoirs of the private and public life of William Penn; who settled the state of Pennsylvania and founded the city of Philadelphia. Dover, N. H., Samuel C. Stevens, 1827. 2 v. in 1. CSmH; MA; MBBC; MH; NIC; TNF. 28507

Clay, Henry, 1777-1852
The address of Henry Clay to his constituents, and his speech at the dinner given him at Lewisburg, Va. Louisville, Pr. by W. W. Worsley, 1827. 32 p. ICU; KyLo; KyLoF; MoSHi; PPL. 28508

---- An address of Henry Clay, to the public; containing certain testimony in refutation of the charges against him, made by Gen. Andrew Jackson, touching the last presidential election. Washington, Pr. by P. Force, 1827. 61 p. Az; CSmH; CtY; DLC; MB; MBAt; MDeeP; MH; MHi; MWA; MdHi; MiD-B; MiU; MoSpD; N; NcU; OCHP; OClWHi; OMC; PPAmP; PPL; RPB; TxD-W; BrMus. 28509

[----] [---- Washington, 1827?] p. [3]-66. Variant issue. Completely reset. PPL. 28510

---- ... Mr. Clay's speech, at the dinner at Noble's Inn, near Lexington, Ky., July 12, 1827. [Charlottesville, at the office of the Virginia Advocate, Aug. 15, 1827] Bdsd. ViU. 28511

---- ---- [Lexington? 1827] 14 p. CSmH; DLC; ICU; IU; InHi; KyU; MWA; MiU; NN; NbHi; NbU; OClWHi; PPL; TNJ. 28512

---- ---- [Louisville, Ky., W. W. Worsley, pr. 1827] 8 p. CSmH. 28513

---- Speech of Mr. Henry Clay,

delivered on the 12th July, at the dinner at Noble's Inn, near Lexington, Richmond, Pr. by Thomas W. White, 1827. 19 p. T; ViRVal. 28514

---- Speech of the Hon. Henry Clay, before the American Colonization Society, in the hall of the House of Representatives, January 20, 1827. Washington [D. C.] Pr. at the Columbian office, 1827. 15 p. CSmH; DLC. 28515

---- ---- With an appendix, containing the documents therein referred to. Washington, Pr. at the Columbian office, 1827. 13, 8 p. DLC; PPL. 28516

---- The speeches of Henry Clay, delivered in the Congress of the United States; to which is prefixed a biographical memoir; with an appendix containing his speeches at Lexington and Lewisburgh, and before the Colonization Society at Washington; together with his address to his constituents, on the subject of the late presidential election... Philadelphia, H. C. Carey & I. Lea; New York, G. & C. Carvill; [etc., etc.] 1827. Pr. by James Maxwell. xx, 381 p. DLC; GAU; IEdS; InU; KyDC; LU; MH-BA; MNF; NIC; O; PP; PPAmP; PPL; TNJ; TxU; ViU. 28517

[Clayton, Augustin Smith]
Vindication of the recent and prevailing policy of the state of Georgia in reference to its internal affairs, and its relations with the general government; in two series of essays originally pub. in the Columbian Centinel. Athens, Pub. by O. P. Shaw, 1827. 90 p. CSmH; GU-De; MBat. 28518

[Clement, Samuel]
Truth is no slander; therefore read--enquire--reflect. Natchez, Pr. at the Ariel office, 1827. 72 p. DLC; MBNEH; MWA; PPAmP. 28519

Clericus, pseud. See Gunn, Alexander.

Cleveland, Charles D.
An epitome of Grecian antiquities. For the use of schools. Boston, Hilliard, Gray, Little & Wilkins; and Richardson & Lord. Flagg & Gould, prs., 1827. xi, 177 p. CtW; CtY; InCW; KyDC; KyLxT; LShC; MBAt; MH; MWiW; MeB; MoS; MoSpD; NbCrD; NjR; OCY; OClStM; OMC; PLFM; TNJ; ViU. 28520

Clifton Park, N. Y. Baptist Church
Articles of faith and practice of the Baptist Church in Clifton Park - Halfmoon. Waterford, N. Y. Pr. by N. W. W. Fish, 1827. 8 p. NRAB. 28521

Clopton, Abner Wentworth, 1784-1833
Wisdom's voice to the rising generation; being a selection of the best addresses and sermons on intemperance... Philadelphia, Pub. by the compilers, John Gray, pr. [1827?] 172 p. CSmH. 28522

Clough, Simon
An account of the Christian denominations in the United States. In a letter to the corresponding secretary of the General Baptist assembly of England. Boston, 1827. 12 p. MBAt; MH; MH-AH; NRAB. 28523

---- A discourse, on the nature of the instrumentality which God exercises by his son, in the salvation of the world; delivered at the opening of the Christian meeting-house in Alexandria, New-Jersey, Nov. 28, 1827... New York, Pub. for the congregation of Alexandria [Vanderpool & Cole, prs.] 1827. 24 p. ICMe; MB; MWA; NjPT; NjR; PHi. 28524

---- Three discourses on the faith which was once delivered to the Saints. New-York, Charles S. Francis; Boston, Bowles & Dearborn [Pr. by Vanderpool & Cole] 1827. 71 p. ICMe; MWA; PPL. 28525

Clowes, Timothy
The heart which condemneth not. A sermon preached at Chestertown, Md. on the festival of St. John the Evangelist, 1826 before the Masonic brethren of Clinton Lodge, No. 83... Chestertown, Pr. by Bro. N. Mitchell, 1827. 11 p. MdHi. 28526

Cobb, James, 1756-1818
The haunted tower, a comic opera, in three acts. Baltimore, Pr. and pub. by J. Robinson, 1827. 50 p. MB; MH; MWA; NN. 28527

Cobb, Sylvanus, 1798-1866
A sermon, delivered in the Village Meeting House, Bowdoinham, Sabbath afternoon, Feb. 11, 1827. Waterville, [Me.] Pr. by Wm. Hastings, 1827. 16 p. CSmH. 28528

Cocheco Manufacturing Company
The acts of incorporation, and by-laws of the Cocheco Manufacturing Company. Together with extracts from the statute laws of New Hampshire relative to manufacturing corporations. Boston, Pr. by Beals & Homer, 1827. 26 p. MBAt; MHi. 28529

Cockburn, James
A letter to Thomas Wistar, relating to recent transactions in the monthly meeting of Friends of Philadelphia... Philadelphia, Pr. on the Vertical press by D. & S. Neall, 1827. 11 p. CSmH; MH; OClWHi; PHC; PHi; PPFr; PPL; PSC-Hi. 28530

Coffin, Robert Stevenson, 1797-1827
The eleventh hour, or confession of a consumptive... Boston, Ingraham and Hewes, prs., 1827. 36 p. CSmH; DLC; RPB. 28531

Cogswell, William, 1787-1850
The assistant to the family religion, in six parts... Boston, Crocker & Brewster, 1827. 384 p. CBPac; MDeeP; MoSpD; Nh-Hi. 28532

Colbert. See Carey, Mathew.

Colburn, Samuel W.
A sermon before the Palestine Missionary Society at their sixth annual meeting, held at Braintree, Mass., June 20, 1827... Boston, Pr. by Crocker & Brewster, 1827. 36 p. MBC; MWA; MiD-B; NcD; OC; BrMus. 28533

Colburn, Warren, 1793-1833
Arithmetic upon the inductive method of instruction... Boston, Hilliard, Gray, Little & Wilkins, 1827. 245, [5] p. CtHT-W; DLC; MB; MChB; MH; PPL; PU; RHi; TxU-T; WaPS. 28534

---- Colburn's first lessons. Intellectual arithmetic, upon the inductive method of instruction. Stereotyped at the Boston Type and Stereotype Foundry. Boston, Hilliard, Gray, Little & Wilkins, 1827. 172 p. MH; MWHi; MiU; NNC; NR. 28535

---- ---- Watertown, N.Y., Pub. by Knowlton & Rice, 1827. 178 p. CSmH; MiDSH; N. 28536

---- A key, containing answers to the examples in the sequel to intellectual arithmetic. Boston, Hilliard, Gray, Little and Wilkins,

1827. 70, 24 p. [2nd pagination is for advertisements.] CtHT-W. 28537

---- A key containing the answers to the examples in the introduction to algebra upon the inductive method of instruction. Boston, Hilliard, Gray, Little & Wilkins, 1827. 50 p. CtHT-W; MH; MeB; BrMus. 28538

Colby, John, 1787-1817
The life, experience and travels of John Colby, preacher of the gospel. Written by himself... First New-York ed. Rochester, N. Y., Pr. for David Marks, jr. by E. Peck, 1827. 356 p. CSmH; MWA; NBuG; NRHi; NcD; OHi. 28539

Cole, John
Go it, Jerry, a round for four voices. Baltimore [1827] 2 p. MB. 28540

Cole, John, 1774-1855
The beauties of psalmody, containing a selection of sacred music, calculated for public worship or the use of singing schools. 3d ed. Baltimore, Cole [1827] viii, [88] ICN (imperfect). 28541

---- The seraph; a collection of sacred music: consisting of the most celebrated psalm and hymn tunes, arranged generally in four vocal parts... Baltimore, Pub. by the editor, J. Robinson, pr. [1827] xvi, [160] 32 p. ViU. 28542

Cole, Samuel W., 1796-1851
The muse; or, Flowers of poetry. A choice collection of favorite odes, poems, songs, elegies, dirges, epitaphs, epigrams, elegant extracts, &c. Cornish, Me., Pub. and sold by the author [James Adams, Jr., pr., Portland] 1827. 216 p. CSmH; DLC; IU; MB; MH; MeHi; MnU; NN; PPFM; RPB; TxU. 28543

[Coleman, H.]
Candid and spiritual reasons for not embracing the doctrine of universal salvation. By a lover of the souls of men. Hartford, Pr. for the author, 1827. 24 p. MH-AH. 28544

[Coleridge, Samuel Taylor] 1772-1834
...Rime of the ancient mariner, with other poems... Boston, Pr. by True & Greene, 1827. 2 pl., 49-99 p. CtY; MB. 28545

---- Selections from the Sibylline leaves... By S. T. Coleridge. [Boston, Pr. by True & Greene, 1827] [4], 43 p. (Spirit of contemporary poetry, No. 1) MBAt; MHi; MWA; NjP; RPB. 28546

Collection of facts and documents relating to ecclesiastical affairs in Groton, Mass. Occasioned by the publication of "The result of an Ecclesiastical council convened at Groton, Mass., July 17, 1826 ... Boston, The Christian Examiner [Stephen Foster, pr.] 1827. 44 p. DLC; ICN; MH; MWA; OO; BrMus. 28547

A collection of psalms and hymns, for social and private worship. 2d ed. Stereotyped by E. White, New-York. New York, David Felt, 1827. 420 p. MCE; MH-AH; MPeaHi; TxU. 28548

Colman, George
The iron chest; a play in three acts. Philadelphia, C. Neal, 1827. 92 p. MH. 28549

---- The review, or The wag of Windsor; a comic opera in two acts. Philadelphia, C. Neal, 1827. 36 p. DLC; MH. 28550

Colombo, Christoforo
Personal narrative of the first voyage of Columbus to America.

From a manuscript recently discovered in Spain, trans. from the Spanish. Boston, Pub. by Thomas B. Wait & Son, 1827. 303 p. CSmH; CtHT; CtW; CtY; GU; IaHi; IaU; KSalW; MB; MBAt; MH; MHi; MdAN; MdBE; MeB; MiU-C; MnHi; MoS; Ms; NBLiHi; NNA; NNS; NR; NbO; Nj; OCHP; PPAmP; PPL; PU; RNR; ScC; T; Vi; BrMus. 28551

Columbia County almanack for 1828. By Edwin E. Prentiss. Hudson, Wm. E. Norman [1827] 22 l. Ct; N. 28552

Columbia Institute for the Promotion of Arts and Sciences
[Circular letter from the Columbia Institute dated Washington, October 1, 1827] 3 p. DLC. 28553

Columbia University
Statutes of Columbia College, revised and passed by the board of trustees, Oct. 1827. New York, T. & J. Swords, 1827. 30 p. CSmH; Ct; DLC; MHi; NNUT; RPB. 28554

Columbian almanac for 1828. By William Collom. Philadelphia, Joseph M'Dowell [1827] 18 l. DLC; InU; MWA; N; PDoBHi; PHi. 28555

Columbian Artillery, Boston, Mass.
Constitution of the Columbian Artillery Company. Instituted October, 1798. To which is added the roll of the present members. Revised and adopted, March, 1827. Boston, Dutton & Wentworth, prs., 1827. 12 p. MB. 28556

The Columbian calendar, or New-York and Vermont almanack for 1828. Troy, Francis Adancourt [1827] 24 l. MWA; NN; NHi; NT; OClWHi; VtHi. 28557

Columbian Centinel
Tribute of the muses through the carriers of the Columbian Centinel, to its generous patrons, on the commencement of the New Year 1828. [1827?] 16 p. MH. 28558

The Columbus magazine almanac for 1828. By William Lusk. Columbus, P. H. Olmsted & Co. [1827] 24 l. OClWHi. 28559

Colver, Phinehas
Abrogation of the Jewish Sabbath. A sermon preached in Kingsbury, N. Y. to the Baptist Church, Oct. 22, 1826... Sandy-Hill, Washington Co., N. Y., Pr. at the Sun Office, April, 1827. 37 p. MBAt; MWA; NRAB. 28560

Comly, John, 1773-1850
A new spelling book, adapted to the different classes of pupils ...[Stereotyped by J. Howe] Philadelphia, Pub. by Kimber & Sharpless, 1827. 168 p. MH; ViU. 28561

Compendium of the order of the burial service, and rules for the mournings, &c. New York, 5587. Pr. by S. H. Jackson, 5587 [1827] 12 p. NN. 28562

Comstock, Cyrus
Some Scripture facts and prophecies illustrated in a treatise in answer to three questions ... Williamstown, Pr. by R. Bannister, 1827. 190 p. DLC; I; IaDm; MBC; MH; MWiW; MoSpD. 28563

Comstock, John Lee, 1789-1858
Elements of minerology, adapted to the use of seminaries and private students... Boston, Pub. by S. G. Goodrich, sold by Hilliard, Gray, Little & Wilkins; New York, G. & C. Carvil; Philadelphia, H. C. Carey & I. Lea [Norton and Russell, prs., Hartford] 1827. 338 p. CSmH;

DLC; MB; MHi; MSaP; NjP; OClW; OO; PPF; PPL; WNaE. 28564

[Comstock, W.]
The intolerants, a drama... Three first acts of Things among us; as performed... with more effect than applause... Philadelphia, Pr. and pub. for the purchaser, 1827. 26 p. CtY; ICU; MH; PPL; PSC-Hi; PU. 28565

A concise narrative of Gen. Andrew Jackson's first invasion of Florida. See Van Ness, William Peter.

Concord, N. H. Visiting School Committee
Report of the Visiting School-Committee of Concord, appointed by the town to visit the schools in the several districts, presented and read in town meeting, March 14, 1827... Concord, Pr. by George Hough, 1827. 16 p. DLC; M; MH. 28566

Confirmations-Schein. New-Market: Shenandoah county, Vir. Gedruckt von Pfr. Ambrosius Henkel fuer die confirmirte Iugend. 1827. Bdsd. (In private collection of Mrs. Henry Tusing, New Market, Va.) 28567

Congregational Churches in Connecticut. General Association
Proceedings of the General Association of Connecticut in their session in Stratford, July 1827. Hartford, P. B. Gleason, pr., 1827. 23 p. IEG; NcMHi. 28568

Congregational Churches in Massachusetts. Ecclesiastical Council, Groton, 1826.
The rights of the Congregational churches of Massachusetts. The result of an ecclesiastical council, convened at Groton, Massachusetts, July 17, 1826. Boston, T. R. Marvin, pr., 1827. 63 p. CBPac; CSmH; DLC; MA; MB; MH; MeBa; NN; NjPT; RPB. 28569

---- ---- 2d ed. Boston, Pr. by T. R. Marvin, 1827. 47 p. C; CtW; CtY-D; DLC; ICMe; IU; IaHi; MA; MH; MHi; MWA; MeHi; MiD-B; MtHi; NN; Nh; OC; OO; PPPrHi; VtU. 28570

Congregational Churches in New Hampshire. General Association
Minutes of the proceedings of the General Association of New-Hampshire, at the annual meeting, holden at Rindge, Tuesday, Sept. 4, 1827. Concord, Pr. by George Hough, for the Association, 1827. 16 p. CSmH. 28571

Congregational Churches in New York. Oneida Association
Pastoral letter of the ministers... to the churches under their care, on the subject of revivals of religion. Utica [N. Y.] Pr. by Ariel Works, 1827. 22 p. CSmH. 28572

Congregational Churches in Vermont. General Convention
Extracts from the minutes of the general convention of the Congregational and Presbyterian ministers of Vermont, at their session at Montpelier, Sept. 1827. Castleton, Pub. for the Convention, 1827. 19 p. IEG; MH; MiD-B; OMC; VtMiM. 28573

Congregational Education Society. See American Education Society.

Congregational Home Missionary Society. See American Home Missionary Society.

Connecticut (State)
Message of His Excellency Gideon Tomlinson, Governor, to the General Assembly of the state of Connecticut, May 1827... Hartford, C. Babcock, pr., 1827. 12 p. Ct; NNUT; PHi. 28574

---- The public statute laws of the state of Connecticut, passed at the session of the General Assembly in 1827. Hartford, C. Babcock, pr., 1827. 141-171 p. CSfL; CtW; DLC; IaU-L; MB; MdBB; Mo; NNLI; Nb; OCLaw; W-L; Wa-L. 28575

---- Report of the commissioner of the school fund of the state of Connecticut, submitted to the General Assembly, May session, 1827. Pr. by order of the legislature. Hartford, C. Babcock, 1827. 12 p. OClWHi; P. 28576

---- Report of the commissioners appointed by the Legislature at their last session to build a new state prison... Hartford, C. Babcock, 1827. 15 p. Ct; CtHi; CtSoP. 28577

---- Reports of cases argued and determined in the Supreme Court of Errors of the state of Connecticut, 1823-25. By Thomas Day. Hartford, O. D. Cooke, P. B. Goodsell, pr., 1827. vii, 639 p. MdBB. 28578

The Connecticut annual register, and United States' calendar for 1827-1828. New-London, Samuel Green [1826-7] 84 l. CtSoP; CtY; MB; Nh. 28579

Connecticut Retreat for the Insane. See Hartford, Conn. Retreat for the Insane.

Connecticut Sunday School Union
The annual report of the Connecticut Sunday School Union. Presented at the third annual meeting of the Society, holden in Hartford, Thursday, May 3, 1827. New-Haven, Pr. by Thomas G. Woodward, 1827. 40 p. CtHi. 28580

Conrad, Robert Y.
Orations by Robert Y. Conrad, Esq., and David W. Barton, Esq. Washington, The Columbian office, 1827. 12 p. LNHT. 28581

Considerations in favour of the construction of a great road. See Beck, Nicholas F.

Considerations in support of the memorial of the Delaware & Hudson Canal Company. Albany, Pr. by Croswell & Van Benthuysen, 1827. 16 p. N; NRom. 28582

Consolidated Association of the Planters of Louisiana
An act to incorporate the subscribers to the Consolidated Association of the Planters of Louisiana. New Orleans, Pr. by Buisson & Boimare, 1827. 15 p. LNHT. 28583

---- Acte d'incorporation de l'-Association Consolidée des Cultivateurs de la Louisiane. Nouvelle-Orleans, de l'imprimerie de Buisson & Boimare, 1827. 15, [1] p. LNHT. 28584

---- Ordannances etablissant des reglemens pour l'administation de l'Association Consolidée des Cultivateurs de la Louisiane. Nouvelle-Orleans, 1827. 16 p. LNHT. 28585

The constitution of '76. By a member of the Staunton Convention. [Winchester, 1827?] 64 p. NcU; Vi. 28586

Controversy between Caius Gracchus and Opimius. See Caius Gracchus, pseud.

Convention of Delegates of the State of Pennsylvania. Held for the Promotion of the State Agricultural and Manufacturing Interests, Harrisburg, 1827.
Address of a convention of delegates of the state of Pennsyl-

vania, for the purpose of promoting the state agricultural and manufacturing interests, at Harrisburg: June 27, 1827. [Harrisburg? 1827?] 8 p. MWA; NN; P. 28587

---- Journal of a convention of delegates of the state of Pennsylvania, held for the promotion of the state agricultural and manufacturing interests, at the Capitol in Harrisburg, on Wednesday, the 27th of June, A. D. 1827. [Harrisburg] Atkinson & Alexander, prs., 1827. 16 p. Ct; ICU; N; OCHP. 28588

Conversations on natural philosophy. See Marcet, Mrs. Jane (Haldimand).

Conversations on the Bible. See Hall, Mrs. Sarah (Ewing).

Converse, Amasa, 1795-1872
A discourse delivered before the Amelia Washington Lodge, of Free and Accepted Masons, on the anniversary of St. John, Sunday, June 24, A. L. 5287. Richmond, 1827. 16 p. MBFM; PPPrHi; RBr. 28589

Conway, E. H.
Le maitre de danse; or, The art of dancing cotillons. By which every one may learn to dance them without a master... 2d ed. New York, Pr. by C. Van Winkle, 1827. 43 p. IaU. 28590

Conwell, Henry, bp. See Catholic Church.

Cooke, Charles Turner
Observations on the efficacy of white mustard seed in affections of the liver, internal organs and nervous system... 1st Amer. from the 4th English ed. New York, G. & C. Carvill [etc.] [Sleight & George, prs. Jamaica, L. I.] 1827. 116 p. CSt-L; CtHT-W; DLC; DNLM; ICJ; MB; MBCo; MeB; NIC; NJQ; NNC; NNNAM; OO; PPC; PU. 28591

Cooke, Parsons, 1780-1864
A sermon preached at the dedication of the meeting house belonging to the East Evangelical Church & Society in Ware, Mass. Jan. 24, 1827. Amherst, Carter & Adams, prs., 1827. 22 p. CtY; DLC; MA; MNF; MWA; NjPT; RPB. 28592

Cooley, Ebenezer
A brief exposition of the claim of Ebenezer Cooley of the state of Louisiana, upon the government of the United States... Washington, Pr. by F. S. Myer, 1827. 23 p. DLC; PPL. 28593

Cooper, Edward
The crisis; or, An attempt to show from prophecy, illustrated by the signs of the times, the prospects and duties of the Church of Christ at the present period. 1st Amer. from the 3d London ed. Cincinnati, Pr. by Morgan, Fisher and L'Hommedieu, 1827. 196 p. DLC; ICMcC; ICU; OCHP; OClWHi. 28594

[Cooper, James Fenimore] 1789-1851
The last of the Mohicans, a narrative of 1757. 3d ed. Philadelphia, H. C. Carey & I. Lea, 1827-8. 2 v. CtY; MWA. 28595

[----] Lionel Lincoln; or, The leaguer of Boston... By the author of The pioneers, Pilot, &c. In two vol. 2d ed. Philadelphia, Carey, Lea & Carey, 1827. 2 v. MWA; OASht; TNJ. 28596

[----] The pilot: a tale of the sea by the author of The pioneers &c. &c... 3d ed. Philadelphia, Carey, Lea & Carey, 1827. 2 v. DLC; MdBS; PPL. 28597

[----] The pioneers; or, The sources of the Susquehanna... 4th ed. Philadelphia, Carey, Lea & Carey, 1827. 2 v. DLC; MH. 28598

[----] The prairie: a tale. By the author of the "Pioneers and The last of the Mohicans"... Philadelphia, Carey & Lea, 1827. 2 v. CLU; CSmH; CSt; CtY; DLC; MB; MBAt; MH; MWA; MoSW; MnU; NBuU; NIC; NN; NhD; OCl; ScU; PU. 28599

[----] The Red Rover, a tale. By the author of The pilot, &c. &c. Philadelphia, Carey, Lea & Carey, 1828, '27. 2 v. CSmH; CtY; DLC; ICU; MBAt; MH; MnU; NBuU; NN; NRU; OClW; PJA; PPL; PU; RNH. 28600

[----] The spy: a tale of the neutral ground... 5th ed. Philadelphia, Carey, Lea & Carey, 1827. 2 v. PPL. 28601

[Corbett, Misses]
The odd volume. Printed from the 2d Edinburgh ed. Boston, Wells & Lilly, 1827. 274 p. MB; MBAt; MH. 28602

Corporation for the Relief of Poor and Distressed Presbyterian Ministers and Widows and Children.
Address of the Corporation... to the ministers and congregations of the Presbyterian Church in America. Philadelphia, Pr. by Clark & Raser, 1827. 16 p. PPPrHi. 28603

Corporation for the Relief of the Widows and Children of Clergymen in the Communion of the Protestant Episcopal Church in Maryland.
Charter, laws, and regulations of the Corporation for the Relief of the Widows and Children of the Clergy of the Protestant Episcopal Church in Maryland. Baltimore, J. Robinson, pr., 1827. 12 p. PHi. 28604

The cottage girl; or An account of Ann Edwards. Philadelphia, American Sunday School Union Depository, 1827. 35 p. MB; MH. 28605

The cottage minstrel; or Verses on various subjects. By a female of this city. Philadelphia, Pr. for the authoress, by Joseph Rakestraw, 1827. 120 p. DLC; IObB; ICU; MB; MH; PPL; PSC-Hi; PU; RPB. 28606

Cottin, Marie (Risteau) called Sophie, 1770-1807
Elizabeth; or, The exiles of Siberia... From the French of Madame Cottin. Boston, Hilliard, Gray, Little & Wilkins, 1827. John G. Scobie, pr. v, 184 p. MeB. 28607

---- ---- Providence, Doyle & Hathaway, publishers, 1827. 139 p. MPem. 28608

Cottom's new Virginia & North-Carolina almanack for 1828. By Joseph Cave. Richmond, Peter Cottom. Petersburg, Richard Cottom [1827] 18 l. ViW. 28609

Cottom's Virginia & North Carolina almanack for 1828. By Joseph Cave. Richmond, Peter Cottom [1827] 18 l. DLC; MWA; NcD; NcU. 28610

A country curate, pseud. See Neale, Erskine.

Courtenay, James Carroll, 1803-1835
An inquiry into the propriety of establishing a national observatory. Charleston, Pr. by W. Riley, 1827. 24 p. CSfCW; CtY; DLC; MB; MBAt; MH; NcD; PPL; ScC; ScCC. 28611

Courtney, John
The Christian's pocket companion; being a selection of hymns for social worship... Richmond [Va.] Repr. for the publisher at the Franklin press, 1827. 306 p. CSmH; MeLB. 28612

Cox, John
To the people of Berkeley county... [Candidacy for U. S. Congress] John Cox. March 27, 1827. [Martinsburg] Bdsd. WvU. 28613

Coxe, John Redman, 1773-1864
The American dispensatory... 7th ed. Philadelphia, H. C. Carey, & I. Lea, 1827. iv, 780 p. ICAC; ICJ; ICRM; InLP; MdW; NNC-P; NNNAM; PPC; ScCM; TNJ; ViRM; ViU; WU. 28614

Cramer's magazine almanack for 1828. Pittsburgh, Cramer & Spear [etc.] [1827] 36 l. InU; MWA; OC; PPi. 28615

Cramer's Pittsburgh almanack for 1828. Pittsburgh, Cramer & Spear [1827] 18 l. CLU; ICHi; MWA; OClWHi; PPiU. 28616

Cranch, William, 1769-1855
Memoir of the life, character, and writings of John Adams; read, March 16, 1827, in the capitol, in the city of Washington, at the request of the Columbian Institute, and pub. by their order. Washington, S. A. Eliot, pr., 1827. 70 p., 1 l. CSmH; CtHT-W; DLC; ICMe; MB; MBAt; MH-L; MQ; MWA; MdBE; MdBJ; MdHi; NCH; NIC; NjPT; OCHP; OClWHi; OMC; BrMus. 28617

Crawford, Samuel Wylie
A sermon on creeds and confessions, preached Dec. 31, 1826. Chambersburg, Pa., Pr. by Geo. K. Harper, 1827. 43 p. CSmH; DLC; ICN; ICU; NjPT; PHi; PPPrHi; PU. 28618

[Cresson, Warder]
An humble and affectionate address to the select members of Abington Quarterly Meeting... Philadelphia, Pr. by John Young, 1827. 12 p. PPL. 28619

The crisis. See Turnbull, Robert James.

Croes, John, bp.
The Episcopal Church not Calvinistick, a sermon... New York, Pr. by T. & J. Swords, 1827. 22 p. CtHT; ICU; MWA; NGH; NNG; NjR; PHi; PSC-Hi. 28620

Croker, Thomas Crofton
Fairy legends and traditions of the south of Ireland... Philadelphia, H. C. Carey & I. Lea, 1827. 257 p. FT; InNd; RP. 28621

Croly, George
The Apocalypse of St. John, or prophecy of the rise, progress, and fall of the Church of Rome... Philadelphia, E. Littell and G. & C. Carvill, New-York, 1827. xvi, 319 p. CBDP; CBPac; CtHT; CtW; DLC; IEG; KyLoS; MB; MBC; MDeeP; MH; MNtcA; MdBP; MeBaT; MiD; MiU; NGH; NNS; NSyU; NjPT; OClW; PPLT; PPPCPh; RPB; ViRU. 28622

[Crosby, William George]
Poetical illustrations of the Athenaeum Gallery of paintings. Boston, Pub. by True & Greene, 1827. [4], 39, [1] p. CtY; MB; MBAt; MH; MHi; MWA; MiD-B; TxU. 28623

Cross, James C.
The purse; or, Benevolent tar. A musical drama, in one act. As performed at the New-York theatre. Philadelphia, Pub. by C. Neal. Mifflin and Parry, prs., 1827. 18 p. CSmH; MH; MWA; NN; PU. 28624

Crowell, Robert, 1787-1855
A sermon, delivered November 19, 1827, at the interment of the Rev. Joseph Dana, D. D., senior pastor of the South Church in Ipswich, who died November 16, 1827, aged LXXXV years. Ipswich [Mass.] Pr. by John H. Harris, jr., 1827. 20 p. CSmH; MWA. 28625

[Cruger, Alfred]
A report of the proposed Saugatuck and New-Milford canal. [New York, 1827] 11 p. DLC. 28626

Cruise, William
Digest of the laws of England, respecting real property. 3d Amer., from the last London ed. revised and enl., with notes and references to American decisions. New York, Collins & Hannay [E. & G. Merriam, prs., Brookfield, Mass.] 1827. 7 v. ArU; CtHT; CtW; DLC; ICLaw; KyLxT; MBS; MH-L; Md; MiU-L; NRAL; NjP; PPiAL; PU-L; TxU-L; ViU; WaU. 28627

Cubi y Soler, Mariano, ed.
Estractos de los mas celebres escritores Españoles, en prosa y verso, para el uso del colegio De Sta. Maria. Segunda Edition, revista, corregida y mejorada... Baltimore, En la libreria de F. Lucas, impreso por J. Robinson, 1827. 560 p. CtW; InLP; MB; MH; MdBE; MdHi; MdW; NBuG; NjP. 28628

---- The Latin translator, or, A practical system of translation, applied to the Latin language. Boston, Hilliard [etc.] 1827. 324 p. PPM (library now dispersed). 28629

Cumberland almanac for 1828. By W. L. Willeford. Nashville, John S. Simpson [1827] 18 l. MWA; OClWHi; THi. 28630

Cumberland College, Princeton, Ky.
Laws of Cumberland College, at Princeton, Kentucky... Princeton, A. Brock, pr. [1827?] 19 p. DLC; KyBgW. 28631

Cuming, Francis Higgins
A letter to the parishioners of St. Luke's Church on the subject of the spiritual character of the liturgy of the Episcopal Church. By the Rev. F. H. Cuming. Rochester, Pr. by Edwin Scrantom, 1827. 30 p. CtHT; MWA; NNG; NRHi; NRU. 28632

Cummings, Jacob Abbot, 1773-1820
First lessons in geography and astronomy. Boston, Hilliard, Gray, Little & Wilkins, 1827. 72 p. MH. 28633

---- An introduction to ancient and modern geography, to which are added rules for projecting maps, and the use of globes... 10th ed. Boston, Hilliard, Gray, Little & Wilkins, 1827. iv, 202 p. DLC; MBAt; MHaHi; NGH; OWoC; PPL; PPAmP. 28634

---- The pronouncing spelling book, adapted to Walker's Critical Pronouncing Dictionary... Revised and improved from the 4th ed. Stereotyped. Boston, Hilliard, Gray, Little and Wilkins, 1827. 166 p. MH. 28635

---- ---- Stereotyped at the Boston Type and Stereotype Foundry. Hallowell, Me., Pub. by Glazier & Co., and sold by booksellers generally, 1827. 168 p. MeHi; RPaw. 28636

---- ---- Rev. and imp. from 4th ed. New York, Collins & Hannay, 1827. 166 p. MB; MH; OMC; RPB; ViHal. 28637

---- Questions on the historical parts of the New Testament... 5th ed. Boston, Hilliard, Gray, Little & Wilkins, 1827. 72 p. MB; MH; BrMus. 28638

Cunningham, Allan, 1784-1842
Paul Jones; a romance. Philadelphia, H. C. Carey & I. Lea, 1827. 3 v. CSmH; CtY; MBAt; MH; NCH. 28639

Cunningham, Joseph L., auctioneer.
Catalog of original pictures and engravings... to be sold... on Tuesday, June 19, 1827... Boston, Bellamy & Newell, prs., 1827. 8 p. MB. 28640

---- Catalogue of elegant cabinet furniture, mahogany and fancy chairs... to be sold on Tuesday, March 13, 1827... Boston, E. Bellamy, pr. 8 p. MHi. 28641

Curtis, Henry Barnes
An oration, delivered before the Mansfield Lodge, No. 35, at Mansfield, Ohio, on the anniversary of St. John the Baptist, June 25, 1827... Mansfield [O.], Pr. by J. & J. H. Purdy, 1827. 18 p. OClWHi. 28642

Curtis, Winslow
The confession of Winslow Curtis, alias Sylvester Colson, convicted of murder... of Edward Selfridge... 2d ed. Boston, Dutton & Wentworth, 1827. 15 [1] p. MeHi; PHi. 28643

---- ---- 3d ed. Boston, Dutton, and Wentworth, 1827. 15, [1] p. MH-L; In-SC. 28644

Cusick, David, d. ca. 1840
David Cusick's sketches of ancient history of the Six Nations: --comprising--First--A tale of the foundation of the great island; (now North America,)... Lewiston, Pr. for the author, 1827. 28 p. DLC; ICN; NN. 28645

No entry 28646

D

Dabney, J. P.
A selection of hymns and psalms, for social and private worship. 6th ed. Boston, Pub. by Thomas Wells [Cambridge, University Press, Hilliard, Metcalf, & Co.] 1827. unpaged. MB. 28647

Daboll, Nathan
Corrected stereotype [edition?] Daboll's schoolmaster's assista[nt] improved and enl. Being a plain practical system of arithmetick. Adapted to the United States. Stereotyped ed. With the addition of the Farmers' and mechanicks' best method of book-keeping, designed as a companion to Daboll's arithmetick. Ithaca, Pr. and pub. by Mack & Andrus, by permission of the proprietors, 1827. 240, [12] p. MWA (2 copies, one with the mispprint "Magk" corrected to "Mack"); NIC. 28648

---- Daboll's schoolmaster's assistant improved and enl. being a plain practical system of arithmetic adapted to the United States ... With the addition of the practical accountant or farmers' and mechanics' best method of book-keeping, for the easy instruction of youth designed as a companion to Daboll's arithmetic. New London, Pr. and pub. by Samuel Green, 1827. 250 p. CoCsLTG; IaMp; WHi. 28649

The Dagon of Calvinism, or The Moloch of decrees; a poem in three cantos. To which is annexed A song of reason. [Cincinnati?] Pr. for the publisher, 1827. 95 p. DLC; RPB. 28650

The dainty boy. By the author of "The little girl taught by experience," "The shower," &c. Boston, Bowles & Dearborn, I. R. Butts & Co., prs. 1827. 32 p. MB; MWal. 28651

The dairyman's daughter. See Richmond, Legh.

Dam & Hardy. Private School Boston.
School. Messrs. Dam & Hardy take this method to inform their friends and the public, that their Spring quarter commences on Monday the second day of April, for instructing youth of both sexes, in rooms entirely disconnected with each other... Boston, Mar. 24, 1827. [Boston, 1827] Bdsd. MHi. 28652

Damphoux, Edward
Greek course, comprising extracts calculated to lead the student, progressively, to a classical knowledge of the Greek language... Baltimore, Fielding Lucas, Jun'r, 1827. 344 p. MdBL. 28653

Dana, Joseph, 1742-1827
A discourse, delivered in Ipswich, Mass., on the fourth of July, 1827, being the fifty-first anniversary of the declaration of American independence... Ipswich, Pr. by J. H. Harris, jr., 1827. 15 p. CSmH; DLC. 28654

---- Stereotype ed. Liber primus; or, A first book of Latin exercises; prepared for the use of schools and academies... 5th ed. corr. and imp. Boston, Pr. and pub. by J. H. A. Frost, 1827. 192 p. CtHT-W; DLC; IaDuU; MB; MH; MHi; MeU; NNC; NjP; RP; TNJ; TxD-T; ViU. 28655

Dana, Richard Henry, 1787-1879
Poems. Boston, Bowles and Dearborn [Pr. by I. R. Butts & Co., Boston] 1827. viii, 21, 113 p. CSmH; CtY; DLC; ICN; ICU; MB; MBAt; MH; MNF; MWA; MdW; MeB; NIC; NN; NNC; NbOC;

NcD; OC; PHi; PU; RNR; RPB. 28656

Daniel, Henry, 1786-1873
Speech of Henry Daniel, in the House of Representatives of Kentucky, on an amendment to the resolutions, which originated in the Senate, instructing our senators and requesting our representatives in Congress to submit to that body a proposition to amend the federal Constitution, so as to cause the people to vote for president and vice president, delivered January 1827. [Frankfort? 1827?] 24 p. DLC. 28657

Danvers, Mass. First Unitarian Church
Order of services at the ordination of Mr. Charles C. Sewall ... April 11, 1827. Salem, Foote & Brown, prs. [1827] Bdsd. CSmH. 28658

Da Ponte, Lorenzo
Storia della lingua e letteratura Italiana in New York. New York, Gray e Bunce, stampatori. 1827. 80 p. DLC; MWA; NN. 28659

Darby, John
An entire new work, just published, and lately composed by the author, John Darby, Exeter, Gospel poems, on different heads, which will be found to contain the great truths of the Everlasting Gospel. Exeter, W. C. Pollard, 1827. 36 p. CtY. 28660

Darby, William, 1775-1854
Darby's universal gazetteer; or, A new geographical dictionary ... 2d ed., with ample additions and imp. Philadelphia, Pub. by Bennett & Walton, Wm. Brown, pr., 1827. 892 p. Ct; CtHT-W; CtY; DLC; GDC; GU; ICU; Ia; MH; MWA; MdBP; MeBa; MiU-C; NNUT; NcD; Nh-Hi; OClWHi; PPL; PV; ScU; TNJ; TU; ViU; BrMus. 28661

Dartmouth College
A catalogue of the officers and students of Dartmouth College, October 1827. Windsor, Pr. by Simeon Ide, 1827. 17, [1] p. CtY; DLC; MeB; VtMiM. 28662

---- Medical Department
New Hampshire Medical Institution. [Description] [Hanover, New Hampshire, 1827] 8 p. OC. 28663

Davidson, James, 1732-1809
Davidson's Latin grammar, rev., imp. and enl., by the several additions and amendments... Baltimore, F. Lucas, junr., 1827. 240 p. CtHT-W; CtY; DLC; MH; MdBL; MdBP; MdHi; NNC; NcU. 28664

Davis, Gustavus Fellows
Free-masonry an honorable institution. An address delivered in Haverhill, Mass., before the Northern Association of the second Masonic district, at the festival of John the Baptist, June 25, A. L. 5827. Boston, Lincoln & Edmands, prs., 1827. 16 p. DLC; IaCrM; MH; MNtcA; RPB. 28665

---- The young Christian's companion, being a selection of hymns, particularly adapted to private devotion and conference meetings... 2d ed. Boston, Lincoln & Edmands, 1827. 108 p. DLC; MB; NBuG; PPPrHi. 28666

Davis, John, 1787-1854
Duties on woollens. Speech of Mr. Davis of Mass. in the House of Representatives... [Boston, E. Bellamy, pr., 1827?] 8 p. M. 28667

Davis, Matthew L.
The speech of Matthew L. Davis, on his trial for a conspiracy. Taken in short hand by Nathaniel B. Blunt. New-York, Wm. A. Davis, pr., 1827. 31 p. DLC;

NjR; PPL. 28668

Davis, William M.
To the people of Ohio County. [Frankfort, Ky., 1827] 8 p. NN has photostat of first and last pages of C. P. Everitt copy. 28669

Day, Jeremiah, 1773-1867
An introduction to algebra, being the first part of a course of mathematics, adapted to the method of instruction in the American colleges. 4th ed. Pub. and sold by Hezekiah Howe, New-Haven. Sold also by Collins & Hannay, New-York: and John Grigg, Philadelphia. Hezekiah Howe, pr., 1827. 332 p. CtHT; CtY; MH; MdBL; MiU; TWcW; ViU. 28670

Day's New-York pocket almanac for 1828. New-York, M. Day [1827] 12 l. DLC; MWA; NHi; PHC. 28671

Deane, Samuel
A discourse on the good and evil principles of human nature, delivered before the First Congregational Society in Scituate... Pub. and pr. at the office of the Christian Register. Boston, 1827. 16 p. ICMe; MBNEH; MWA; MScitHi; MiD-B; OMC; PHi; RPB. 28672

Dearborn, Benjamin
A lenient system, for adjusting demands, and collecting debts, without imprisonment; uniting justice with clemency, in coercive measures, for stimulating debtors, to fulfil their contracts. Boston, Pr. and pub. by John H. Eastburn, 1827. 64 p. ICU; IEG; MBAt; MH-L; MWA; BrMus. 28673

Death: an essay in verse. See Engles, William Morrison.

The debates, resolutions, and other proceedings in convention. See Elliott, Jonathan, ed.

Decatur, Susan (Wheeler)
Documents relative to the claim of Mrs. Decatur, with her earnest request that the gentlemen of Congress will do her the favour to read them. Georgetown, D. C., James C. Dunn, pr. 1827. 66 p., 1 l. MB; MWA; N; WHi. 28674

The decision. See Kennedy, Grace.

Dedham, Mass. South Church
The confession of faith, and the covenant of the South Church in Dedham; publickly read on the admission of members. Dedham, Mass., H. & W. H. Mann, 1827. 30 p. M; MH; MHi; MWA. 28675

A defence. See Mumford, Paul M.

A defence of truth, and Free-Masonry exposed... Albany, Pr. at the National Observer Office, 1827. 46 p. MBFM; MiGr; NNFM. 28676

De La Motta, Jacob, 1789-1845
Eulogium to the memory of Dr. Samuel Wilson, April 10, 1827. Charleston, Miller, 1827. 26 p. PPC; RPB. 28677

[De Lancey, William Heathcote] bp. 1797-1865
A candid address to the Episcopalians of Pennsylvania, in relation to the present situation of the affairs of the diocese. By Plain truth. [Philadelphia] April, 1827. 32 p. MWA; NNG; PPL; RPB. 28678

[----] Three letters; one to the Committee of correspondence; one to "Plain truth, junior;" and one to "Plain fact;" in support of the "Candid address"... by Plain

truth. [Philadelphia] May, 1827. 55 p. NNG; PPL. 28679

Delaware (State)
Journal of the House of Representatives of the state of Delaware, at the January session, held at Dover, in the year of our Lord, one thousand, eight hundred and twenty-seven... Dover, Del., Augustus M. Schee, pr., 1827. 330 p. DLC. 28680

---- Journal of the Senate of the state of Delaware, at a session, commenced and held at Dover, agreeably to the direction of an act of the General Assembly, on Tuesday the 2d day of January, in the year of our Lord, one thousand eight hundred and twenty-seven... Dover, Del., Augustus M. Schee, pr., 1827. 182 p. DLC. 28681

---- Laws of the state of Delaware passed at a session of the General Assembly, commenced and held at Dover, on Tuesday the second day of January in the year of our Lord, one thousand eight hundred and twenty seven... Dover, Pr. by J. Robertson, 1827. 159; [1]-56 p. In-SC; MiL; NNLI; Nb; Nj; Nv; OCLaw. 28682

The Delaware and Maryland almanac for 1828. Wilmington, Robert Porter & Son [1827] 18 l. MWA; PHi. 28683

Dell, William, d. 1664
The doctrine of baptism, reduced from its ancient and modern corruptions: and restored to its primitive soundness and integrity... 6th ed. Philadelphia, Pr. by B. Franklin & D. Hall, from the 4th London ed., 1759. Cincinnati, Repr. by Morgan, Fisher, and L'Hommedieu, 1827. 35 p. OCHP; PPL. 28684

---- ---- New York, Samuel Wood & Sons, 1827. 31 p. DLC; MiD-B; NRAB. 28685

Demarest, Cornelius T.
A lamentation over the Rev. Solomon Froeligh... New York, Pr. by Chas. M'Devitt, 1827. 70 p. MB; NjR; PPL. 28686

Deming, E.
An oration, delivered at Oldtown, Ross County, Ohio, on the fifty-first anniversary of American independence. [Chillicothe? 1827] Title from Kyle 244; and Rusk II:202, which cites Western Monthly Review, v. 1, p. 239, August, 1827. 28687

Democedes, an interlude. See Brice, James Frisby.

Democratic Party. Maryland.
Address of the Jackson state convention to the people of Maryland, on the late and approaching election of president. Baltimore, Pr. at the Jackson press, 1827. 19, [1] p. CLU; DLC; MBAt; MdBE; MdBJ; MdHi; NcD; OClWHi. 28688

---- New Hampshire
(Circular) To. Agreeably to the advice of many Democratic Republicans in various parts of the state, a Central committee of consultation and correspondence has been organized, with a view to produce that united effort necessary to the preservation and preponderance of the doctrines and principles of Jefferson... Benjamin Evans. Chairman. Concord, Nov. 8, 1827. 2 p. DLC. 28689

Dennant, John
The Sunday scholar. Revised by the committee of publication. American Sunday School Union, Philadelphia, 1827. 15 p. MH; WHi; BrMus. 28690

Depping, George Bernard, 1784-1853
Evening entertainments; or, Delineations of the manners and customs of various nations. 4th ed. Philadelphia, Towar & Hogan, 1827. 360 p. CtHT; CtW; MB; MBC; NN; Nh; OHi; PAtM; PPPCity. 28691

Description of the four pictures. See Trumbull, John.

Description of the Incas of Peru, with their wives... These elegant figures are now exhibited at No. 44 North Market Street... Boston. [Boston] 1827. 12 p. MH. 28692

A description of the Thames tunnel. New York, Elliott & Palmer [1827?] 9 p. DLC. 28693

Deshia, Joseph
$150 reward, ran away from the subscriber, on the night of the 27th October a negro man named Ben... Joseph Deshia. Frankfort, Ky., Nov. 5th, 1827. 1 p. DLC. 28694

Detroit, Michigan
Charter. An act relative to the city of Detroit. [Detroit? 1827?] 23 p. DNA. 28695

De Vere. See Ward, Robert Plumer.

Dewees, William Potts, 1768-1841
A treatise on diseases of females. 2d ed. Philadelphia, Carey Lea and Carey, 1827. 538 p. PPHa. 28696

[Dewey, Orville] 1794-1882
On religious phraseology. 3d ed. No. 5 Pr. for the American Unitarian Association. Boston, Bowles & Dearborn, 1827. [Isaac R. Butts, pr.] 36 p. CBPac; DLC; ICMe; MB; MH; MMeT-Hi; MeB; MeBat. 28697

---- Two discourses designed to illustrate in some particulars, the original use of the Epistles of the New Testament, compared with their use and application at the present day... Boston, Pub. by the New Bedford Book and Tract Association, Pr. by Isaac R. Butts & co., 1827. 35 p. CBPac; ICMe; MB; MBAt; MHi; MMeT; MWA; NNUT; RPB; WHi; BrMus. 28698

A dialogue between a father and son on the subject of Christian baptism. Portland, A. Shirley, pr. [1827] 35 p. Williamson: 2831. 28699

A dialogue on providence, faith, and prayer. Pr. for the American Unitarian Association. Boston, Bowles & Dearborn, [Isaac R. Butts and Co., prs.] 1827. 24 p. DLC; MWA. 28700

Dibdin, Thomas John
The cabinet; a comic opera, in three acts... As performed at the theatres Covent-Garden, New York, and Baltimore. From the prompt-book by permission. Baltimore, J. Robinson, 1827. 59 p. DLC; MB; MH; MWA; NN; PU. 28701

Dick, Thomas, 1774-1857
The Christian philosopher; or, The connection of science and philosophy with religion. 2d Amer. ed. New York, G. & C. Carvill [Jamaica, L.I.: Sleight & George, prs.] 1827. 399 p. CtY; ICU; MB; MBAt; MBC; MH; NBuDD; NNNAM; NNUT; NjR; PPL. 28702

Dickerson, Mahlon
Speech of Mr. Dickerson, of N.J. on the distribution of revenue, delivered in the Senate of the United States, February 1, 1827. Washington, Pr. by Gales

& Seaton, 1827. 23 p. MWA; PPL. 28703

Dickson, John
The essentials of religion, briefly considered in ten discourses. Charleston, Wm. Riley, 1827. 207 p. CtY; GDC; MBC; NNUT; OMC; PPPrHi; ScC; ScCC. 28704

Dilworth, Thomas
A new guide to the English tongue. New York, Pub. by Daniel D. Smith, 1827. 144 p. MoS. 28705

Dimmick, Luther Fraseur
The influence of truth. A sermon, delivered in Newburyport, March 20, 1827 at the dedication of the New Brick Church in Titcomb Street. Newburyport, Pub. by Charles Whipple, 1827. Pr. at the Herald Office. 32 p. CSaT; CtSoP; DLC; ICN; MB; MBAt; MH-AH; MiD-B; MoSpD; PPPrHi. 28706

Directions for transferring prints to the surface of wood. From the [Boston] Mechanicks Magazine... [Boston, 1827] 8 p. MB. 28707

A directory for the village of Rochester: Containing the names, residence and occupations of all male inhabitants over fifteen years of age, in said village, on the first of January, 1827, to which is added a sketch of the history of the village from 1812 to 1827. Rochester, Pub. by Elisha Ely. Everard Peck, pr., 1827. 141, [1] p. CSmH; DLC; MB; MH; NRHi; OClWHi; PPL; BrMus. 28708

Dispensatories, eclectic and general, comprehending a system of pharmacy, materia medica, etc. By an American physician. Philadelphia, Towar & Hogan, 1827. 627 p. MBCo; MBP; MW; MdBJ-W. 28709

The diverting history of John Bull. See Paulding, James Kirke.

The Divine purpose. See Matthews, John.

[Dix, John Adams] 1798-1879
Sketch of the resources of the city of New-York. With a view of its municipal government, population, &c. &c. from the foundation of the city to the date of the latest statistical accounts. New-York, G. & C. Carvill, 1827. 104 p. CSmH; CtY; DLC; ICU; MA; MB; MH; MWA; MiD-B; NIC; NN; NNC; NNUT; NbU; NcU; Nh; OCHP; OClWHi; OkU; PPL; PU; BrMus. 28710

Dr. J. W.'s last legacy. See Williams, John.

The doctrine of incest stated. See McClelland, Alexander.

Doctrines and duties of the Christian religion. See American Tract Society, New York.

Documents relating to the late election of the professor of surgery. See Harlan, Richard.

Dodd, William
Reflections on death. A new ed. New-York, Pr. by Samuel Marks, 1827. 176 p. DLC; MWA; NN; PPLT. 28711

Dodd, William, 1729-1777
Thoughts in prison; in five parts, viz. the imprisonment, the retrospect, public punishment, the trial, futurity; to which are added his last prayer, written in the night before his death; the convict's address to his unhappy brethren; and other miscellaneous pieces; with some account of the author. New York, Evert Duyckinck, 1827. 222 p. CtHT-W; MBC; MiD; NN; OC; OClW; PPL. 28712

Doddridge, P.
Washington, February 17, 1827. The Hon. Littleton W. Tazewell and John Randolph, Senators from Virginia, in the Congress of the United States. Gentlemen: After mature reflection, and with the advice of others more experienced in such matters, I have determined... to address you... on the subject of the bill now depending before the Senate for quieting certain Virginia militia claims to lands... in the state of Ohio... 4 p. DLC; NN. 28713

Doddridge, Philip, 1702-1751
Poetical lessons for children. Philadelphia, American Sunday School Union, 1827. 32 p. ICU; BrMus. 28714

---- The rise and progress of religion in the soul: illustrated in a course of serious and practical addresses... Princeton, W. D'Hart, 1827. 188, vi p. NjP; NjR. 28715

---- Some remarkable passages in the life of the honourable Col. James Gardiner, who was slain at the battle of Prestonpans, 21st Sept. 1745. Princeton, D. A. Borrenstein, 1827. 208 p. GDC; NjP. 28716

---- Three discourses on the evidences of the Christian religion, designed for the benefit of the young persons. Princeton, N. J., Pub. by D. A. Borrenstein, 1827. 96 p. CtY; NjP; NjPT; OO; PU; TxU. 28717

---- Twelve sermons on the power and grace of Christ and on the evidence of His glorious gospel; preached at Northampton, Pa. Gettysburg, Pa., Pr. by H. C. Neinstedt, 1827. 300 p. CBPac; OSW; OWoC; P; PAtM; PHi; PPiPT; PWW. 28718

[Dodge, Mrs. H. M.]
Heselrigge, or, The death of Lady Wallace. With other poems, by Amica Religionis [pseud.] Utica, Pr. by Hastings and Tracy, 1827. 158 p. ICU; MH; NUtHi; RPB. 28719

[Dodsley, Robert] 1703-1764
The economy of human life. Trans. from an Indian manuscript, written by an ancient Bramin. Cambridge, Hilliard & Brown, 1827. 113 p. MB; MBC; OO; PU-Penn; ViU. 28720

[----] ---- Haushaitungskunst des Menschlichen Lebens. Englisch und Deutsch. Chambersburg, Pa., Pub. by Timotheus Evans, J. Pritts, pr., 1827. 264 p. ICU; PHi; PLF; PP. 28721

Doggett, Simeon, 1765-1852
A discourse, delivered to the First Society in Mendon, at the funeral of Richard George. Boston, True & Greene, 1827. 14 p. MH; MWA; NN; RPB; BrMus. 28722

The domestic physician, and travellers' medical companion. Compiled from the practice of the most eminent physicians and surgeons, viz: Sir Astley Cooper, Sir Henry Halford, Drs. Baillie, Latham, Heberden, Saunders, Babington, Birckbeck, &c. &c. &c. ... By a physician. 1st Amer. from 2d London ed. ... New York, Elam Bliss, 1827. 316, [4] p. [4 p. numbered irregularly as 25, 286, 287, 288]. OCLloyd. 28723

Domesticus, pseud. See McClelland, Alexander.

Dorsey, Clement
Speech of Mr. Dorsey, of Maryland. House of Representatives U. S. February, 1827. [Washington, 1827] 24 p. DLC; NcD. 28724

Dorsey, Dennis B.
A review of an "Address," professing to be a vindication of the Baltimore annual conference; signed by "William Wilkins." Respectfully addressed to the Friends of Truth. To which is added, A reply to the same "Address," by a member of the conference, and an extract of a letter from "Vindex." Baltimore, Matchett, pr., 1827. 24 p. KyLx; MBAt; MH; MdHi; MsJMC. 28725

Dow, Lorenzo, 1777-1834
Progress of light & liberty. I. Historically. II. Geographically. III. Politically. IV. Ecclesiastically. V. Prophetically. VI. Experimentally. 6th ed. Pittsburgh, Pr. at the Statesman office, 1827. 23 p. OClWHi; WHi. 28726

---- A short account of the long travel, with the Beauties of Wesley. 2d ed., imp. Philadelphia, Pr. 1823. Pittsburgh, Repr. at the office of the Statesman, 1827. 59, [1] p. N; OClWHi; WHi. 28727

Doyle, John
John Doyle's catalogue of books, by auction, on Wednesday even'g, Nov. 28, 1827. at his store. No. 237 Broadway, Corner of Park-Place... [New York] E. M. Murden & A. Ming, Jr., prs. [1827] 1 p. DLC; NN. 28728

Drake, Benjamin
Cincinnati in 1826. By B. Drake, and E. D. Mansfield. Cincinnati, Pr. by Morgan, Lodge, and Fisher. Feb. 1827. 100 p. CSmH; CtHT; DLC; ICN; ICU; IHi; IU; InHi; MB; MH; MHi; MMeT; MNtcA; MiD-B; NCH; NN; NNUT; NcD; OC; OCHP; OClWHi; OHi; PHi; PPAmP; PPL; RHi; WHi. 28729

Dramatic exhibition and ball. Order of exercises. A comedy--"The Rivals." Peterborough, November 1827. J. Prentiss, pr. Keene. Bdsd. NhPHi. 28730

Dreadful effects of intemperance. An affecting account of the tragical death of Mrs. Lucy Johnson, who was most inhumanly murdered in Elsington (Ken.) in February last, by her own husband, in presence of their only child, a little daughter but eleven years of age. Annexed is a solemn address to the whole human family, warning them to beware of intemperance... Providence, Pr. for D. White, 1827. 12 p. CSmH; MWA. 28731

Dreadful riot on Negro Hill! O read wid detention de melancholly tale and he send you yelling to your bed. Copy of an intercepted letter from Phillis to her sister in the country, describing the riot on Negro Hill... Boston, 1827. 1 p. DLC. 28732

Drysdale, Isabel.
Scenes in Georgia... Philadelphia, American Sunday School Union, 1827. 83 p. DLC; GU; ICN; IObB; MH; MWA; NN; NSyHi; PU. 28733

Ducamp, Théodore Joseph, 1792?-1823?
A treatise on the retention of urine, caused by strictures in the urethra; and of the means by which obstructions of this canal may be effectually removed... New York, S. Wood & sons, 1827. 219 p. v pl. CSt-L; CU-M; CtY; DLC; GU-M; ICJ; ICU-R; Ia; InU-M; KyLxT; MBCo; MWA; MdBJ; MdBM; MdUM; NBuU-M; NIC-M; NN; OClM; PPC; PU; ScCM. 28734

[DuCange, Victor Henri Joseph Brahain] 1783-1833
Therese, the orphan of Gen-

eva, a drama... New-York, Pub. by Murden & Thomson, at the Museum Circulating Library, May 1827. 1st Amer. ed. NN, 1930, had photostat of t. p. ; not found 1970. 28735

Duer, John
An examination of the controversy between the Greek deputies and two mercantile houses in New York: together with a review of the publication on the subject, by the arbitrators, Messrs. Emmet and Ogden, and Mr. Wm. Bayard. New York, Pr. by J. Seymour, 1827. 179 p. NNC. 28736

Duffield, George
Ministerial qualifications: a sermon delivered Oct. 30th, 1827, at a meeting of the Presbytery of Carlisle, in Harrisburg, Penn., on the occasion of the ordination of Messrs. Den'l McKinley and M'Knight Williamson... Carlisle, Pr. at the "Herald" office, 1827. 25 p. DLC; MH; MiD-B; NjPT; OCHP; OClWHi. 28737

Dufief, Nicholas Gouin, 1776?-1834
Nature displayed in her mode of teaching language to man... 7th ed., corr. Philadelphia, Pr. for the author, 1827. 2 v. CtW; GU; KyDC; PP; PPPCity; Vi. 28738

Du Hausset, Madame, b. ca. 1720
The private memoirs of Madame Du Hausset, lady's maid to Madame de Pompadour. New-York, Pub. by Elam Bliss [Wm. A. Mercein, pr.] 1827. 179 p. CSmH; CtHT; CtY; MH; Mi; NCH; NGH; NN; NNG; NNS; NjPaT. 28739

Dunallan. See Kennedy, Grace.

Dunglison, Robley, 1798-1869
Syllabus of the lectures on medical jurisprudence and on the treatment of poisoning & suspended animation. Delivered in the University of Virginia... Pr. for the use of the students. University of Virginia, Pr. by Clement P. M'Kennie, 1827. 142 p. DLC; MdBJ-W; MdBM; PPC; Vi; ViU. 28740

Dunlop, John Colin, 1785-1842
History of Roman literature, from its earliest period to the Augustan age. From the last London ed. Pub. by E. Littell, Philadelphia. G. & C. Carvill, New York, 1827. 2 v. ArL; CtHT; CtW; CtY; DLC; GU; ICN; ICMcC; InCW; KyU; LNHT; LU; MBAt; MH; MWA; MdAS; MdBJ; MnDu; MoS; MsU; NGH; NN; NNC; NNS; NRU; NSyHi; NbOC; NcRA; NjPT; OC; OClW; OO; PHi; PPL; PU; TNJ; TU; ViRVal; ViU. 28741

Dunstable, Mass. Congregational Church of Christ
Confession of faith, and covenant... Andover, Flagg & Gould, 1827. 8 p. MBC; OCHP. 28742

Dunwody, Samuel
Substance of a sermon, preached June 10, 1827, in the Methodist Chapel, in the city of Savannah. New York, Pr. for the author at the Conference office, 1827. 44 p. GEU; KyU; NjPT. 28743

Du Ponceau, Peter Stephen, 1760-1844
Eulogium in commemoration of the Honourable William Tilghman, LL. D., chief justice of the Supreme court of Pennsylvania, and president of the American Philosophical Society... Delivered before the Society, pursuant to their appointment, at the University, on Thursday, Oct. 11, 1827... Philadelphia, R. H. Small, Russell & Martien, prs., 1827. 46 p. DLC; ICN; MB; MBAt; MH; MHi; MWA; MdHi; MiD-B; NIC; NN; OCHP; PHi; PPAmP; PPL; RPB; WHi; BrMus. 28744

The Dutchess county farmer's almanac for 1828. Poughkeepsie, P. Potter [1827] 18 l. NHi; NP; NjR. 28745

---- By David Young. Poughkeepsie, J. C. Meeks [1827] 18 l. MWA; N; NP. 28746

Dwight, William Theodore, 1795-1865

An oration before the Washington Benevolent Society of Pennsylvania, delivered in the hall of the Musical Fund Society, on the 22nd of February, 1827,... Philadelphia, Pr. by J. Maxwell, 1827. 34 p. CSmH; CtY; DLC; MB; MBAt; MBC; MHi; NjPT; NjR; PHi; PPAmP; PPL; RPB; ScCC. 28747

E

Earle, Thomas

An essay on penal law in Pennsylvania, with reference to its proposed revision and amendment. Philadelphia, Pub. by the Law Academy, Mifflin & Parry, prs., 1827. 34 p. DLC; MBC; MH-L; MWA; MiD-B; MiU-L; OClWHi; PHi; PPL; PU; WHi; WaU-L. 28748

Early piety... Philadelphia, American Sunday School Union, 1827. 60 p. KSalW. 28749

East Windsor, Conn. First Congregational Church

Confession of faith and covenant, adopted since A. D. 1810, by the second church in East-Windsor. [1827] 8 p. Ct. 28750

Eastern Auxiliary Foreign Mission Society of Rockingham County, N. H.

Second annual report of the Eastern Auxiliary Foreign Mission Society... presented at Dover, June 21, 1827. Portsmouth, Pr. by T. H. Miller and C. W. Brewster [1827] 8 p. Nh-Hi. 28751

Eastman, Jacob Weed

A sermon, delivered at the ordination of Rev. David Page Smith, over the First Congregational Church and Society in Sandwich, N. H. May 23, 1827. Concord, Pr. by Jacob B. Moore, 1827. 22 p. MBC; MWA; Nh; Nh-Hi; PPL; RPB. 28752

[Eaton, Charlotte Anne (Waldie)] 1788-1859

Rome in the nineteenth century; containing a complete account of the ruins of the ancient city, the remains of the middle ages, and the monuments of modern times ... New York, Pr. by J. & J. Harper. Pub. by E. Duyckinck, et al. 1827. 2 v. CtHT; CtY; GU; MB; MBAt; MH; MeB; MiDSH; NIC; NNC; NP; NjP; PFaL; PU; ViAl. 28753

[----] ---- In a series of letters written during a residence at Rome, in the year 1817 and 1818. 1st Amer. from the 4th Edinburgh ed. New-York, Pr. for E. Duyckinck, Collins & Hannay, Collins and Co., O. A. Roorbach, E. Bliss and E. White, G. & C. Carvill, A. T. Goodrich, and William B. Gilley, 1827. 2 v. CtY; PU. 28754

Eaton, John Henry

The life of Andrew Jackson, major-general in the service of the United States... Cincinnati, Pub. by Hatch & Nichols. W. M. & O. Farnsworth, Jr., prs., 1827. 454 p. CSmH; GU; IHi; MB; O; OC; OCl; OClWHi; OMC; TC. 28755

Eaton, William

Searsburgh poetry; consisting of beautiful productions of the mind and fancy, in sentiment &

language, aided by the prodigality of genius, a garland of miscellaneous poems, on novel and interesting subjects. Williamstown, Pr. and pub. for the author, 1827. 38 p. MWA; MWiW; TxU. 28756

Eberle, John
Notes of lectures on the theory and practice of medicine delivered in the Jefferson Medical College at Philadelphia. Philadelphia, Pub. by J. G. Auner, Lydia R. Bailey, pr., 1827. 252 p. MBCo; MdBM; NBMS; NBuU-M; NNNAM; NjR; OClM; OsW; PPC; PPHa; RNR. 28757

Ecce homo. See Holbach, Paul Henri Thyri, baron d'.

The eclectic and general dispensatory: comprehending a system of pharmacy, materia medica, the formulae of the London, Edinburgh, and Dublin pharmacopoeias, prescriptions of many eminent physicians, and receipts for the most common empirical medicines: collated from the best authorities, by an American physician. Philadelphia, Towar & Hogan, Mifflin & Parry, prs., 1827. 627 (i.e. 625) p. 7 pl. CSt-L; CtY; DNLM; ICJ; IEN-M; IaU; KyLxT; LNOP; MB; MBCo; MdBJ-W; MeB; MeU; MiDW-M; MnU; NBMS; NNNAM; OC; OClM; PPC; PPL; PU; ViRMC. 28758

The economy of human life. See Dodsley, Robert.

Eddy, Ansel Doane
A discourse, delivered at the dedication of the Brick Church, in Buffalo, N.Y. March 28, 1827. Buffalo, Pr. by Day, Follett & Haskins, 1827. 25 p. NAuT; NBu; NN; RPB; BrMus. 28759

---- A sermon occasioned by the death of Mrs. Beulah Clark, wife of William Clark, esq. of Utica, delivered in the Brick Church, Canandaigua, N.Y., Feb. 18, 1827... New York, Pub. by John P. Haven, Sleight & George, prs., Jamaica, L.I., 1827. 28 p. IU; MBC; MiD-B; NBLiHi; NN; NUtHi; NjPT; PHi; RPB. 28760

Edgeworth, Maria
Early lessons. Philadelphia, Robert Desilver, 1827. 6 v. MWA; PP. 28761

---- Little plays, being an additional volume of the Parent's assistant, published from the manuscript... Philadelphia, R. Wright, printer for Thomas T. Ash, 1827. 59 p. MH; MNBedf. 28762

---- Little plays for children. The grinding organ. Dumb Andy. The Dame school holiday. Being a continuation of The parent's assistant. New York, Pub. by Wm. Burgess, Jr., 1827. 178, [2] p. DLC; KU; MH; NjR; PHi. 28763

---- Parent's assistant; or, Stories for children. New York, William Burgess, F.A. DeVoe, pr., 1827. 2 v. NN; OCo; PU. 28764

Edson, Theodore
Christ the true light. A sermon, preached at the convention of the Protestant Episcopal Church of the Eastern diocese, Sept. 26, 1827. Boston, Pub. at the request of the Convention, by the Committee [Pr. by J. Adams] 1827. 21 p. CtHT; DLC; MB; MBD; MH; MHi; MWA; MdBD; MiD-B; NNG; RPB; BrMus. 28765

Edwards, Charles Lee
An oration, delivered on the 4th of July, 1827, before the Cincinnati & Revolution Societies. Charleston (S.C.), A.E. Miller, 1827. [2], 21 p. CtY; MH; MHi;

NcD. 28766

No entry 28767

Edwards, Justin

A sermon delivered at the installation of Rev. Jacob Scales at Henniker, N.H. January 17, 1827. and at the ordination of the Rev. Daniel Crosby, at Conway, Mass. Jan. 31, 1827... Andover, Pr. by Flagg & Gould, 1827. 21 p. CBPac; CtY; MBC; MH-AH; MMeT-Hi; MWA; MeBa; MiD-B; MnHi; MoSpD; Nh; Nh-Hi; NjR; OO; PPPrHi; BrMus. 28768

---- A sermon delivered at the ordination of Rev. Moses G. Grosvenor as pastor of the church and society in the West Parish, Haverhill, Mass., Dec. 27, 1826. Andover, Flagg & Gould, 1827. 31 p. MBC; MH-AH; MHa; MeBat; Nh; NjR; BrMus. 28769

Eells, James

Conversations on baptism, containing answers to the enquiries of a young convert, respecting the sentiments of those who practise infant baptism. Utica, Pr. by Hastings & Tracy, 1827. 68, [1] p. CSmH; IU; N; NCH; NUt; OO. 28770

Election day written for the American Sunday School Union... Philadelphia, No. 148 Chestnut Street, 1827. 101, 6 p. DLC; BrMus. 28771

Elements of intellectual philosophy. See Upham, Thomas Cogswell.

Elizabeth de Bruce... See Johnstone, Mrs. Christian I. M.

Ellen, pseud.

The minstrel lyre, a collection of metricals... Philadelphia, Atkinson & Alexander, 1827. 162 p. IU; PHi; RPB. 28772

Ellen: or, The disinterested girl. Revised by the committee of publication. American Sunday School Union. Philadelphia, Stereotyped by L. Johnson, 1827. 36 p. DLC. 28773

Elliot, J.

Bounding billows, with variations for the piano forte... Philadelphia, G. Willig [c1827] 4 p. CtY; ICN; MB; ViU. 28774

Elliot, Jonathan, 1784-1846 ed.

The debates, resolutions, and other proceedings, in convention, on the adoption of the federal consitution; as recommended by the general convention at Philadelphia, on the 17th of Sept., 1787; with the yeas and nays on the decision of the main question. Collected and revised from contempory publications... Washington, Pr. by and for the editor, 1827-1830. 4 v. AMob; CLSU; CoCsC; GU; ICLaw; InNd; KHi; LNL; M; MBAt; MiGr; MnM; MoSW; NIC; NcD; O; OClWHi; OM; OU; PPi; PPB; PU; ScC; ScU; T; WHi; BrMus. 28775

---- Diplomatic code of the U.S. of America: embracing a collection of treaties and conventions between the U.S. and foreign powers, from the year 1778 to 1827... Washington, Pr. by J. Elliot, junior, 1827. 668 p. CSfU; CoD; ICLaw; LNHT; MBAt; PPL; RPB; TNJ. 28776

Elliot's annual calendar and congressional directory for 1828-1829. Washington, Jonathan Elliot [1827-8] 28 l. MWA. 28777

Elliot's Washington pocket almanac; or Strangers' manual for 1828.

Washington, S. A. Elliot [1827] 29 l. DWP; MB; MBAt; NCH. 28778

Elliott, Mary (Belson)
The two Edwards; or, Pride and prejudice unmasked. Philadelphia, Thomas T. Ash, 1827. 180 p. MB; PP; BrMus. 28779

Ely, Alfred
A sermon, delivered Feb. 23, 1827, at the interment of the Rev. Henry H. F. Sweet, pastor of the Church of Christ in Palmer. Belchertown, Mass., Pr. at the Sentinel and Journal Office, 1827. 23 p. MBC; MWA; MiU; NjPT. 28780

Elnathan, a narrative, illustrative of the manners of the Ancient Israelites... Philadelphia, American Sunday School Union, 1827. 136 p. NcD; BrMus. 28781

Elwall, Edward, 1676-1744
Triumph of truth, being an account of the trial of Mr. E. Elwall for heresy and blasphemy at Stafford assizes... England, 1726. Philadelphia, The editor, 1827. 24 p. PPAmP. 28782

Emerson, Frederick
Primary lessons in arithmetic ... 3d ed. Boston, Pr. and pub. by Lincoln & Edmands, 1827. 34 p. DLC; MH; NNC. 28783

Emerson, George Barrell, 1797-1881
Address delivered at the opening of Boston Mechanics' Institution, Feb. 7, 1827. Boston, Hilliard, Gray, Little & Wilkins, 1827. 24 p. CLU; CSmH; CtHT-W; ICMe; MBAt; MBC; MH; MH-BA; MHi; MiD-B; MnHi; Nh-Hi; OO; PPL; PPPrHi; RPB; BrMus. 28784

Emerson, Gouverneur, 1796-1874
Biographical memoir of Dr. Samuel Powel Griffitts... Philadelphia, J. Harding, pr., 1827. 22p. CSt-L; ICMe; MWA; PHC; PPAmP; PPC; PPL; PU. 28785

---- Medical statistics: being a series of tables, showing the mortality in Philadelphia, and its causes. [Philadelphia, 1827?] 26 p., 11 tables. PHi; PPL; PU. 28786

Emerson, Joseph, 1777-1833
The evangelical primer, containing a minor doctrinal catechism; and a minor historical catechism to which is added the Westminster Assembly's Shorter catechism... Boston, Crocker & Brester, 1827. 72 p. PU-Penn. 28787

Emerson, Reuben, 1772?-1860
A sermon on the qualifications of a spiritual shepherd, delivered June, 1825, at the installation of Rev. Noah Emerson, to the pastoral care of the Congregational Church & Society, Baldwin, Me. Portland, Pr. at the Mirror Office, 1827. 16 p. MeBat; MeHi. 28788

Emily Parker. See Child, Lydia Maria (Francis).

Emmons, Nathanael, 1745-1840
Sermon on the perdition of Judas. With a review of the same by Rev. David Pickering of Providence, R. I. Providence, Cranston & Marshall, prs. 1827. 52 p. CtHT; CtY; ICMe; MWA; MiD-B; RHi; RPB; BrMus. 28789

---- Sermon, preached Dec. 13, 1826, at the installation of the Rev. Calvin Park, in the First Congregational Church in Stoughton. Boston, Pr. by T. R. Marvin, 1827. 22 p. CBPac; MB; MBAt; MBC; MH; MNe; MWA; MiD-B; MnHi; NjPT; OClWHi; PPL; RPB; BrMus. 28790

[Emmons, Richard] b. 1788
An epick poem in commemoration of Gen. Andrew Jackson's vic-

tory on the eighth of January, 1815. Boston, Pub. for the author, by W. Emmons, 1827. 33 p. CSmH; DLC; RPB. 28791

---- The Fredoniad; or, Independence preserved. An epick poem on the late war of 1812. Boston, Pub. for the author, by W. Emmons, 1827. 4 v. C; CLU; CSmH; CtHT-W; CtY; ICN; ICU; IU; KyBgW; MA; MB; MBAt; MBNEH; MH; MWA; MdAN; MdAS; MdHi; MeB; MnHi; NN; NT; NbOM; NcD; NjP; PU; RNR; RPB; ScU; TxU; BrMus. 28792

Emmons, William

An oration on Bunker Hill Battle, delivered on the battle ground, in Charlestown, 18th of June, 1827. Together with a caucus speech, delivered at Faneuil Hall, May 9th... Boston, Pr. for the author, 1827. 16 p. CSmH; CtHT-W; MBAt; MH; MWA; WHi; BrMus. 28793

Emory, John, bp., 1789-1835

A defence of "our fathers," and of the original organization of the Methodist Episcopal Church against the Rev. Alexander McCaine, and others... New York, Pub. by N. Bangs and J. Emory, Azor Hoyt, pr., 1827. 92 p. CBDP; CSmH; CoDl; DLC; GEU; IU; KSalW; LNHT; MdBS; MsJMC; NNMHi; NcHiC; NjR; OClWHi; PHi; PPAmP; PPL; TxDaM; TNS; BrMus. 28794

[Engles, William Morrison]

Death: an essay in verse... Philadelphia, Mifflin & Parry, prs., 1827. 23 p. ("Advertisement" signed W. M. E.) PPL; PPPrHi. 28795

Enlargement of the Erie Canal. Proposed loan anticipating the canal revenue, for expediting that magnificent work... Rochester, December 31, 1826... Committee of Correspondence. [Rochester, 1827?] Bdsd. NCanHi. 28796

The entertaining and marvellous repository: containing biography, manners, and customs, tales, adventures, essays, poetry, etc. Boston, Baker & Alexander, 1827-30. 3 v. CtY; DLC; IObB. 28797

An epick poem in commemoration of Gen. Andrew Jackson's victory. See Emmons, Richard.

Episcopal Female Tract Society of Philadelphia.

Episcopal Female Tract Society of Philadelphia. An Episcopal tract. The forms of the church opposed to formality. Religious tracts, No. 51. Published by the Episcopal Female Tract Society of Philadelphia for the Society of the Protestant Episcopal Church for the Advancement of Christianity in Pennsylvania. Philadelphia, Pr. by Wm. Stavely, 1827. 12 p. NcD. 28798

An Espiscopalian. See An appeal to the lay members of the Protestant Episcopal Church.

Ernesti, Johann August, 1707-1781

Elements of interpretation, translated from the Latin of J. A. Ernesti, and accompanied by notes with an appendix containing extracts from Morus, Beck and Keil... 3d ed. Andover, Pub. by Mark Newman; Flagg & Gould, prs., 1827. 124 p. ArBaA; CtHT; GDC; GEU; MnU; NjR; OClW; PPLT; PPP; WNaE; WaPS. 28799

Essay on free trade. See Carey, Mathew.

Essay on import duties. See Chaptal de Chanteloup, Jean Antoine Claude.

An essay, on the probation of fallen men. See Wilson, James Patriot.

Essays of Philanthropos. See Ladd, William.

Essays on peace & war. See Ladd, William.

Essays on the present crisis in the condition of the American Indians: First published in The National Intelligencer, under the signature of William Penn. Boston, Pub. by Perkins & Marvin, 1827. 112 p. Nh. 28800

Esther, by the author of Sophia Morton... Boston, Pub. at the Christian Register office, 1827. 32 p. NNC. 28801

The eternal principle of life and light, the only ground of the perfectibility of man:... Philadelphia, Pr. by Atkinson & Alexander, 1827. 32 p. MB; PPL. 28802

Evangelical Lutheran Ministerium of Pennsylvania and adjacent states.

Principles of the Christian religion, in questions and answers, designed for the instruction of youth in Evangelical Churches. 3d ed. Harrisburg, Pr. by J. S. Wiestling, 1827. 47 p. P. 28803

---- Verhandlungen der Deutschen Evangelisch- Lutherischen Synode von Pennsylvanien, gehalten zu Easton in der Trinitatis- Woche, 1827. Easton [Pa.] Gedruckt bey H. und W. Hütter, 1827. 28 p. DLC; ICN; PAtM; PPL. 28804

Evangelical Lutheran Ministerium of the state of New York and adjacent states and counties.

Extracts from the minutes of the XXXII session of the synod and ministerium of the Evangelical Lutheran Church, in the state of New York and adjacent parts... Troy, N. Y., Pr. by Tuttle & Richards, 1827. 37 p. PPL. 28805

Evangelical Lutheran Joint Synod of Ohio and Other States.

Proceedings of the tenth Evangelical Lutheran Synod of Ohio and the adjacent states; begun and held at Columbus, Ohio, in Trinity week (June 10th, 1827) [Columbus, O., 1827] 11 p. CSmH. 28806

Evangelical Lutheran Synod of West Pennsylvania

Minutes of the Evangelical Lutheran Synod of West Pennsylvania. Convened at Mifflin, Mifflin County, Pa. on Sept. the 30th and the succeeding days. A. D. 1827. Gettysburg, Pr. at the press of the Theological Seminary, H. C. Neinstedt, pr., 1827. 30 p. PPLT. 28807

---- Minutes of the proceedings of the Evangelical Lutheran Synod of West Pennsylvania, convened at Gettysburg, Pa., Oct. 26, 1827. Gettysburg, Pa., Pr. by H. C. Neinstedt. 1827. 31 p. PHi; PPLT; PPPrHi; WKenC. 28808

---- Verhandlungen der Deutsch-Evangelisch- Lutherischen Synode von West-Pennsylvanien. Gehalten zu Mifflin, Mifflin County, am 30sten September 1827... Gettysburg, Gedruckt in der Druckerey des Theol. Seminars, H. C. Neinstedt, Drucker, 1827. 30 p. PPLT. 28809

---- Verhandlungen der Deutsch-Evangelisch-Luth. Synode von West-Pennsylvanien, gehalten zu Berlin, Somerset Co. am 10ten Sept. 1826... Gedruckt zu Yorktaun, 1827. 20, 4 p. PPL; PPLT. 28810

Evangelical Lutheran Tennessee Synod.
Bericht von den Verrichtungen der Evangelisch-Lutherischen Tennessee Synode, während ihrer achten Sitzung vom dritten bis zum achten September, 1827, gehalten in der Zions Kirche, Sulivan Caunty, Tennessee. Neu-Market: Gedruckt in Salomon Henkel's Druckerey, 1827. 49 p. PPLT; ViNmM; ViNmT. 28811

Evans, Hugh Davey, 1792-1868
An essay on pleading with a view to an improved system. Baltimore, Pub. by Edward J. Coale. Benjamin Edes, pr., 1827. 318 p. CSmH; ICLaw; KyBgW; KyLoU-L; KyLxT; LNT-L; MB; MH-L; Md; MdBB; MdBE; MdBP; MdLR; NIC; NNLI; NNU; NRAL; PP; PPB; ViU. 28812

[Evarts, Jeremiah] 1781-1831
An examination of charges against the American missionaries at the Sandwich Islands as alleged in the voyage of the ship Blonde and in the London Quarterly Review. Cambridge, Hilliard, Metcalf & Co., prs. to the University, 1827. 67 p. C; CBPac; CU; MB; MBC; MH-AH; MWA; NBLiHi; NNG; NUtHi; Nh-Hi; PPAmP; PPL; VtMiM; BrMus. 28813

Evening hours. [no. 106] Boston, Munroe and Francis [1827] 2 v. DLC; MB; NNCoLi. 28814

Evenings in Boston... Boston, Bowles & Dearborn [Press of I. R. Butts & Co.] 1827. 120 p., 1 l. MB; MH; NNC. 28815

[Everett, Alexander Hill] 1790-1847
America: or, A general survey of the political situation of the several powers of the western continent, with conjectures on their future prospects... By a citizen of the United States... Philadelphia, H. C. Carey & I. Lea, 1827. 2, 1., [9]-346 p. CL; CLU; CSmH; CSt; CU; CoFcS; Ct; CtHT; CtW; CtY; GU; IC; ICN; In; InCW; InHi; KU; KyLx; LU; MB; MBAt; MBC; MDeeP; MH; MS; MWA; Md; MdBE; MdBJ; MdBP; MiD-B; MiU; MnDu; MoSHi; MoSM; NBLiHi; NIC; NNC; NNS; NNUT; NWM; NbU; NcD; Nh; Nh-Hi; NjP; OCHP; OClW; OU; PHi; PPAmP; PPL; PU; RNR; RPJCB; ScC; TNJ; TxU; Vi; ViU; Vt; VtMiS; WHi; Wv; BrMus. 28816

Everett, Edward
Address delivered before the Adelphic Union Society of Williams College, Aug. 16, 1827. Boston, Dutton & Wentworth, prs., 1827. 36 p. MNF. 28817

---- Discurso pronunciado en Plymouth, Decembre 22, de 1824 ... Boston, Lo publica N. Hale-G. L. Lewis, impresor, 1827. 28 p. MB; MHi; MWA; PPL. 28818

Everett, Linus S.
A review, of a pamphlet, entitled, Universalism, or, the rich man and Lazarus; a sermon, by Thomas Lounsbury, A. B. Pastor of the First Congreation in Ovid. Black Rock, Pr. by S. H. Salisbury, 1827. 24 p. CSmH. 28819

Every man his own lawyer. See Potter, Paraclete.

[Ewell, James] 1773-1832
The medical companion, or family physician: treating of the diseases of the United States, with their symptoms, causes, cure, and means of prevention... [7th ed. Philadelphia, 1827] xxxix, 852 p. TxU-M [title page defective]. 28820

---- ---- 7th ed., rev., enl. and very considerably improved.

Washington, Pr. for the proprietors, 1827. 862 p. GHi; NNF; OCLloyd; PPC; ScCMe; ViU; WU. 28821

Ewing, Finis
A series of lectures on the most important subjects in divinity. Fayetteville, Tenn., For the Cumberland Presbyterian Synod by E. and J. B. Hill, 1827. 222 p. CSansS; CSmH; KyLxT; KyU; LNB; MoHi; NcMHi; PPPrHi; T; TKL; WKenC. 28822

Ewing, John
A refutation of certain calumnies, published in John Laws handbill, addressed to the citizens of Knox, Daviess and Martin counties. Vincennes, 1827. 12 p. In. 28823

An examination of charges against the American missionaries. See Evarts, Jeremiah.

An examination of the charge, prepared by Gen. Jackson against Mr. Adams and Mr. Clay. First published in the National Intelligencer, over the signature of "Hampden." ... Washington, 1827. 43 p. DLC; MA; NN; OClW; PHi; PPL. 28824

Examination of the Charleston (S. C.) Memorial. See Carey, Mathew.

An examination of the question "Whether a man may marry his deceased wife's sister?" with some remarks on the essay of "Domesticus," and others. By a layman. Philadelphia, Pr. on the Vertical Press by D. & S. Neall [May, 1827] 24 p. PPPrHi. 28825

An examination of the reasons alleged by a Protestant, for protesting against the doctrine of the Catholic Church: or, An answer to objections, Under the title of: "Protestantism and Popery," Made by an anonymous writer. By a Catholic. Philadelphia, Pub. for the use of Catholics and others, who wish to know what the Catholic religion is, rather than what it is represented to be. Thomas Town, pr., 1827. 40 p. ICMcC; MdW; MoSU; PPAmP. 28826

Excerpta quaedem scriptoribus Latinus. See Wells, William.

The experienced American housekeeper. See Rundell, Maria Eliza (Ketelby).

An exposition of the political character and principles of John Quincy Adams. See Ingham, Samuel Delucenna.

An exposition of the practicability of constructing a great central canal, from Lake Erie to the Hudson, through the southern tier of counties in the state of New-York: being a series of numbers originally published in the Western star, under the signature of Hercules. Westfield, N. Y., Pr. by Harvey Newcome, 1827. 31 p. CSmH; MiU-T; NBu. 28827

An exposition of the principles on which the system of infant education is conducted. Philadelphia, Dec. 1, 1827. 19 p. PPL. 28828

---- 2d Philadelphia ed. Philadelphia, 1827. 20 p. CtY; OClWHi; PHi. 28829

Extracts from legal opinions, showing that the Rev. Henry U. Onderdonk... has not been elected assistant bishop. Philadelphia, 1827. 8 p. CtHT; MiD-B. 28830

The extraordinary life and adventures of Robin Hood. See Robin Hood.

F

Facts and observations in relation to the origin and completion of the Erie Canal. 2d ed. Providence, F. Y. Carlisle and H. H. Brown, 1827. 32 p. DLC; MB; MWo; Vi. 28831

Facts are the theme; our country's good the aim... being plain statements, addressed to all men ... [New Brunswick, 1827] 15 p. NjR, not loc. 1969. 28832

Facts relating to the improvement of Connecticut River... [Boston? 1827] 4 p. MH-BA. 28833

Fair Lucretia's garland... Hudson, Pr. by Ashbel Stoddard, 1827. 8 p. NN. 28834

Fairfield, Sumner Lincoln
The cities of the plain. A scripture poem. Boston, Pub. by Charles G. Greene, 1827. 58 p. CSmH; DLC; MB; MWeA; RPB. 28835

Fairfield Literary and Theological Seminary. Bond County.
Circular. Plan of the Fairfield Literary and Theological Seminary, located in Bond County, Illinois. Bond County, Ill., Aug. 1827. Bdsd. MHi. 28836

The faith once delivered to the saints. See American Unitarian Association.

The faithful dog. New-York, Pr. for the booksellers, 1827. 8 p. MH. 28837

The faithful little girl. A story for children. Boston, Munroe & Francis, and C. S. Francis, New York. 1827. 70 p. IObB. 28837a

Falconer, William, 1732-1769
The shipwreck, and other poems... New York, W. Borradaile, 1827. 172 p. CtY; MWA. 28838

Farmers almanac for 1828... by John Armstrong. Blairsville, Pa., James F. McCarty, pub. [1827] 38 p. IaHA; PHi. 28839

The farmer's almanack for 1828. By Robert B. Thomas. Boston, Richardson & Lord; J. H. A. Frost, pr. [1827] 24 l. CU; CtHT-W; DLC; MB; MWA; NN; NNC; PHi. 28840

---- By Zadock Thompson. Burlington, E. & T. Mills [1827] 12 l. DLC; MWA; N; NRMA. 28841

---- By James W. Palmer. Lexington, James W. Palmer [1827] 12 l. KyLoF; KyLx; MoHi; NCH. 28842

---- ---- Lexington, James W. Palmer [1827] 13 l. ICU; PPiU. 28843

---- By John Ward. Philadelphia, M'Carty & Davis [1827] 18 l. CLU; CtY; ICU; MWA; PHi; PPL. 28844

---- By Robert B. Thomas. Portland, Wm. Hyde [1827] 24 l. Me; MeP; MeWC; MiD-B. 28845

---- New-York, C. Brown [1827] 18 l. DLC; NB; NCooHi. 28846

---- By David Young. New-York, James A. Burtis [1827] 18 l. F; MWA; N. 28847

---- By David Young. New-York, John Montgomery [1827] 18 l. NN. 28848

---- By David Young. Newburgh, Ward M. Gazlay [1827] 18 l. NHi. 28849

The farmers' and planters' almanac for 1828. Salem, J. C. Blum [1827] Drake 8957. 28850

Farmer's calendar or Utica almanac for 1828. Utica, William Williams [1827] Drake 6920. 28851

Farmers' calendar, or Western almanack for 1828. Fredonia, James Hull [1827] 18 l. NRU. 28852

---- Fredonia, Hull & Snow [1827] 18 l. DLC; ICHi; MWA. 28853

The farmers' diary, or Ontario almanack for 1828. By Oliver Loud. Canandaigua, Bemis, Morse & Ward [1827] 18 l. DLC; MWA; NCanHi; NN; NRMA. 28854

The farmer's, mechanics and gentleman's almanck for 1828. By Nathan Wild. Wendell, J. Metcalf [1827] 24 l. DLC; MAJ; MHi; MWA; N; NN; Nh-Hi. 28855

Farmington canal. To the citizens of New Haven. See Bishop, Abraham.

Farrar, John, 1779-1853

An elementary treatise on astronomy, adapted to the present improved state of the science, being the fourth part of a course of natural philosophy, compiled for the use of the students of the university at Cambridge, New England. Cambridge, N. E., Pr. by Hilliard, Metcalf and co., at the University press, 1827. vii, 420 p. CU; CtHT; GU-M; IGK; InCW; MA; MB; MBAt; MH; MHi; MWA; MWiW; NCH; NNG; NRU; NWM; NhD; NjP; NjPT; OC; OHi; PHC; PP; PPL; PU; RPB; TNJ; ViU; VtMiM; VtU; BrMus. 28856

Father Clement. See Kennedy, Grace.

A father's reasons for Christianity, in conversations on paganism, Mahometanism, Judaism, & Christianity. Revised by the Committee of publication. Philadelphia, American Sunday School Union, 1827. 102 p. Ct; MB. 28857

A fellow-labourer, pseud. See Heighton, William, 1800-1873

Felt, Joseph Barlow, 1789-1869

The annals of Salem, from its first settlement. Salem, W. & S. B. Ives, 1827. 611 p. CSmH; DLC; IaGG; M; MBAt; MBNEH; MH; MHa; MHi; MSa; MWA; MeHi; NBLiHi; NNS; Nh; Nh-Hi; OClWHi; OO; RHi; RPJCB; TNJ; BrMus. 28858

Feltus, Henry J.

Address upon the ceremony of dedicating the new Masonic hall in the city of New York... together with the proceedings of the Grand Lodge of the state of New-York on that occasion. New York, Pr. by Bro. Wm. A. Mercein, 5827 [1827] 28 p. N; NNFM; PPFM. 28859

Female Bible, Missionary, and Tract Society

Second annual report of the Female Bible, Missionary and Tract Society, of New-Utrecht, Feb. 1st, 1827. A. Spooner, pr., Brooklyn. 11 p. NBliHi. 28860

Female Missionary Society of the Western District, N. Y.

The eleventh annual report... 1827. Utica, Pr. by Hastings & Tracy, 1827. 22 p. NUtHi; BrMus. 28861

Female Tract Society of New York

Fifth annual report of the Female Tract Society of the City of New-York, auxiliary to the American Tract Society. New York, Pr. by Daniel Fanshaw, American Tract Society House, 1827. 19 p. M; NjR; PHi; TNJ; WHi. 28862

[Fendall, Phillip Richard] 1794-1868

An argument on the duties of the Vice-President of the U. States, as president of the Senate, and on the manner in which they were discharged, during the first session of the 19th Congress, by the Honourable John C. Calhoun. By Patrick Henry [pseud.]... Washington, P. Force, pr., 1827. 56 p. CSmH; DLC; MH; MWA. 28863

[----] An argument on the powers, duties, and conduct of the Hon. John C. Calhoun, a vice president of the United States, and president of the Senate. By Patrick Henry [pseud.] .. Washington, Pr. by P. Force, 1827. 56 p. DLC; MH; N; NjR; OCHP; PPL. 28864

Fénelon, François de Salignac de la Mothe

Les adventures de Télemaque, fils d'Ulysse, par Fénelon. From the last and best Paris ed. Philadelphia, Pr. by P. M. Lafourcade, and to be had at the bookstore of J. Laval, 1827. [2], ii, 355 p. IU; MB; MWA; NBuU; NRU; NbCrD; OO; PSC; TNL; WS; WU. 28865

---- Les aventures de Télemaque, fils d'Ulysse... Nouvelle ed. D'après l'édition de M. Charles LeBrun. Philadelphia, Ballantine, 1827. 420 p. NjP. 28866

---- Extracts from the writings of Francis Fenelon, Archbishop of Cambray. By John Kendall. Boston, Pr. & Pub. by Lincoln & Edmands, 1827. 162, [2] p. ICU; MoSU. 28867

Fenning, Daniel

A new and easy guide to the use of the globes; to which is added, a plain method of constructing maps. Illustrated with plates. 1st Amer. ed., rev. and corr. by Jos. Walker, Sr. and Jos. Walker, Jr. Baltimore, Pub. by Fielding Lucas, Jr., 1827. 244 p. CtHT-W; CtW; DGU; MWH; MdBE; MdBL; OSW. 28868

Fenwick, E.

Infantine [sic] stories; in words of one, two and three syllables. Boston, Munroe & Francis, 1827. 104 p. ScCliTO. 28869

Ferguson, Walter

My early days. Boston, Bowles & Dearborn, 1827. 8, 144 p. CtSoP; MH; MHi; MPiB; MWA; WHi. 28870

Fessenden, William Pitt, 1806-1869

An oration delivered before the young men of Portland, July 4, 1827. Portland, Pr. & pub. by James Adams, Jr., 1827. 31 p. CSmH; DLC; MWA; MeHi; MiD-B; NCH; Nh-Hi; OCLaw. 28871

A few plain and candid objections. See Kesley, William.

Field, Jacob T.

Farewell sermon of Rev. Jacob T. Field... at Pompton... Paterson, N. J., Pr. by Day & Burnett, at the office of the "Paterson Intelligencer," 1827. 32 p. NjR. 28872

Finley, Anthony, pub.

[American Atlas] Philadelphia, Pub. by Anthony Finley [1827] 2 l., 15 colored maps of North and South America. InHi; MnDu. 28873

---- Atlas classica; or Select maps of ancient geography, both sacred and profane... Philadelphia Pub. by Anthony Finley, Wm. Fry, pr., 1827. 3 p. l. (2 fold) 10 col. maps (2 double). CLU; NWM; OrP. 28874

---- A new general atlas, comprising a complete set of maps, representing the grand divisions of the globe, together with the several empires, kingdoms and states in the world. Compiled from the best authorities, and corrected by the most recent discoveries. Philadelphia, A. Finley, 1827. 58 col. maps. (With this is bound the author's: Atlas classica, or, Select maps of ancient geography, both sacred and profane, 1827.) CLU; InCW; MiD-B; MiU; NIC; NSyHi; NT; NbHi; PPi; WHi. 28875

Finney, Charles Grandison, 1792-1875

A sermon preached in the Presbyterian Church at Troy, March 4, 1827. Philadelphia, Pr. by Wm. F. Geddes, 1827. 16 p. CtY; IEG; IU; MH; MWA; OO; NjR; PHi; PLT; PPPrHi; TxH. 28876

---- ---- Troy, N.Y., Pr. by Tuttle and Richards, 1827. 16 p. CSmH; DLC; KyLo. 28877

Fireside stories; or, Recollections of my school fellows... New York, Wm. Burgess, Jun. [Pr. by Vanderpool & Cole] 1827. 223 p. CSmH; IObB; PPL; ScCMu. 28878

The first day of the week. Revised by the Committee of publication. American Sunday School Union. Philadelphia, American Sunday School Union, 1827. 108 p. DLC; KU; BrMus. 28879

The first of April. Written for the American Sunday School Union. American Sunday School Union. Philadelphia, 1827. 72 p. IObB; ViRUT; BrMus. 28880

Fischer, Ernst Gottfried, 1754-1831

Elements of natural philosophy, by E. S. [!] Fischer... Trans. into French with notes and additions by M. Biot... and now trans. from the French into English for the use of colleges and schools in the United States. Boston, Hilliard, Gray, Little and Wilkins, Pr. by Hilliard, Metcalf & Co., printers to the University, 1827. 346 p. CSt; CtHT; CtY; GU; InCW; KBB; MB; MH; MdAN; MdBS; MiD; MoU; NCH; NNC; NNF; NRU; NhD; Nj; OC; OMC; OO; OkU; PPC; PU; TNJ; ViU; BrMus. 28881

Fisher, Jonathan, 1768-1847

Short poems: including a sketch of the Scriptures to the book of Ruth; Satan's great devise, or Lines on intemperance... Portland [Me.] A. Shirley, pr., 1827. 143, [1] p. CSmH; DLC; ICN; MB; MBC; MWA; MeBat; NNC; OO; PU; RPB; TxU. 28882

Fisk, Elisha, 1769-1851

A sermon, occasioned by the sudden death of Mrs. A. Fisher, wife of David Fisher, esq. of Wrentham. Preached Feb. 18, 1827. the next Lord's day after her interment. Providence, Miller & Hammond, prs. 1827. 18 p. Ct; MB; MH; MWA. 28883

Fisk, Theophilus

Lecture sermon, No. 1, delivered at the Lombard Street Church, Philadelphia... Dec. 2, 1827. [New York? 1827?] 8 p. MChiA; PPL. 28884

---- Truth teller, No. 1. entitled Jonah and the Devil! Together with some thoughts on being willing to be damned! Discourse. Smith H. Salisbury, pr. Black Rock, N.Y. [1827?] 12 p. MMeT-Hi; NBuHi; NN. 28885

Fisk, Wilbur, 1792-1839

A discourse, delivered before the Legislature of Vermont, on the day of general election at

Montpelier, Oct. 12, 1826. 2d ed. Woodstock, Pr. by Rufus Colton, 1827. 22 p. CtW; MBNMHi; MiD-B; PPPrHi. 28886

Fitch, Charles, 1804-1843
View of Holliston in its first century. A century sermon, delivered in Holliston, Mass., Dec. 4, 1826. Dedham, H. & W. H. Mann, 1827. 36 p. CtY; DLC; ICN; MB; MBAt; MBC; MH; MHi; MHolliHi; MMeT-Hi; MWA; MeHi; MiD-B; MiU-C; MnHi; NBLiHi; Nh-Hi; OClWHi; RPB; WHI; BrMus. 28887

Fitch, Eleazar Thompson, 1791-1871
An inquiry into the nature of sin: in which the views advanced in "Two Discourses on the Nature of Sin," are pursued; and vindicated from objections, stated in the Christian Advocate. New-Haven, Pub. by A. H. Maltby, Treadway and Adams, pr., 1827. 95 p. CSansS; CSmH; Ct; CtHT-W; CtHi; CtY; ICN; ICU; IU; MA; MAnP; MB; MH; MWA; MeB; MiU; N; NCH; NNG; NcU; Nh; NjPT; NjR; OCHP; OO; PPPrHi; VtU; BrMus. 28888

Fletcher, Ebenezer, 1761-1831
A narrative of the captivity & sufferings of Ebenezer Fletcher, of New-Ipswich, who was severely wounded and taken prisoner at the battle of Hubbardston, Vt. in the year 1777, by the British and Indians, at the age of 16 years... Written by himself... 4th ed., rev. and enl. New Ipswich, N. H., Pr. by S. Wilder, 1827. 24 p. CSmH; DLC; ICN; MWA; NhD; WHi. 28889

Fletcher, Nathaniel Hill, 1769-1834
A discourse delivered at Kennebunk, May 6th, 1827, on the following subject: How far unanimity in religious opinions is necessary in order to Christian Communion. Kennebunk, Pr. by James K. Remich, 1827. 14 p. CSmH; MBAt; MWA; RPB. 28890

Flint, Thomas
The Carolinian spelling book; or, A new and easy guide to the English language... Hillsborough, Pr. and pub. by D. Heartt, 1827. 120 p. NcU. 28891

Florian, Jean Pierre Claris de, 1755-1794
William Tell: or Switzerland delivered. By the Chevalier de Florian. To which is prefixed, the life of the author by Jauffret. Philadelphia, Pr. for the purchasers, 1827. 144 p. IaScW; NjR; PU. 28892

Florida (Territory)
Acts of the Legislative council of the territory of Florida, passed at their fifth session, 1826-7. By authority. Tallahassee, Pr. by A. S. Thruston, 1827. 5, 171 p. F. 28893

The folly of finery; or, The history of Mary Lawson. To which is added, Ripe cherries, and The duty of Sunday scholars to their teachers. Boston, James Loring, 1827. 35 p. MHa; NN. 28894

[Forbes, Charles P.]
The merchant's memorandum and price book: adapted to the principal branches of mercantile business. Particularly designed as a pocket memorandum for the country trader. Boston, J. Marsh, 1827. 182 p. MH-BA; MNBedf. 28895

[----] ---- 3d ed. Boston, Hilliard, Gray, Little & Wilkins, 1827. 192, 16 p. CSmH. 28896

Ford, John
The nature of sin. A sermon ... Newark, N. J., Pr. by W.

Tuttle & co., 1827. 19 p. NjPT; NjR; PSC-Hi; RPB. 28897

Forms of government, containing an abstract of the original charter of Maryland, the bill of rights, and constitution of the state, Declaration of independence, Articles of confederation, and Constitution of the United States, with a brief account of the incidents by which the several forms were connected. Annapolis, From the press of J. Hughes, 1827. 144 p. DLC; MdHi; OCLaw. 28898

Fort Braddock letters. See Brainard, John Gardiner Calkins.

Foster, James

Supreme Court of the U. S. James Foster and Pleasants Elam vs. David Neilson. Appeal from the district court of Louisiana. [New Orleans, Pr. by E. Lyman, 1827] 72 p. PPL. 28899

Foster, John

An essay on the importance of considering the subject of religion addressed particularly to men of education. Boston, Samuel H. Parker, 1827. 172 p. CBPac; CU; CtHT; CtW; CtY; DLC; ICMc; IEG; LNHT; MB; MBAt; MBC; MH; MNtcA; MeBaT; MoSW; NGH; NNG; OO; PLT; PPFr; PPL; PU; RNR; RPB. 28900

400 questions on Murray's abridgment and Murray's English grammar... 2d ed. with imp. Boston, Pub. by John H. A. Frost, 1827. 36 p. MH. 28901

Fowle, William Bentley, 1795-1865

The child's arithmetic or The elements of calculation, in the spirit of Pestalozzi's method, for the use of children between the ages of three and seven years. 2d ed. Boston, Pub. by Thomas Wells, Howe & Norton, prs., 1827. 104 p. DLC; MB; MH; MiU. 28902

---- Practical geography as taught in the Monitorial School, Boston. Part first, comprising modern topography. 2d ed. Boston, Wait, Greene & co., 1827. 162 p. CtHT-W; MB; MBU-E; MH; MNBedf; TxU-T. 28903

---- The true English grammar; being an attempt to form a grammar of the English language... Boston, Munroe & Francis, 1827-29. 2 v. CtHT-W; DLC; ICU; MB; MBAt MH; MiU; NNC; TxU-T; WGr; BrMus. 28904

Fox, George

A declaration of the Christian faith and doctrine, of the Society of Friends, ... Also an epistle from George Fox to Friends in England, written at Dalston, in 1682. Philadelphia, Repr. by Jos. R. A. Skerrett, 1827. 12 p. InRE; MH; OClWHi; PHC; PHi; ScU. 28905

Frances & James; or, Examine yourselves. Revised by the Committee on Publication. (Series iii, No. 115) Philadelphia, American Sunday School Union [1827] 32 p. MH; BrMus. 28906

Franklin, Benjamin, 1706-1790

The Franklin miscellany: consisting of the Way to wealth, Advice to a young tradesman, The whistle, and other essays... Dover, [N. H.] Pub. by Samuel C. Stevens, 1827. 39 p. CSmH. 28907

The Franklin almanac for 1828. By Charles Hoffman. New-York, Caleb Bartlett [1827] 18 l. DLC. 28908

---- Fitted to the meridian and latitude of Belvidere, N. J. By Charles Hoffman. New-York,

Caleb Bartlett [1827] 18 l. DLC. 28909

---- By John Armstrong. Pittsburgh, Johnson & Stockton [1827] 18 l. OClWHi; PPi; WvU. 28910

---- ---- with added "Magazine." Pittsburgh, Johnson & Stockton [1827] 30 l. CSmH; InU; MWA; OClWHi; OMC; PHi; Wv-Ar. 28911

---- Richmond, Pollard & Converse [1827] 24 l. DLC; MWA; NBuHi; PPi; ViHi; ViW. 28912

Franklin Institute, Philadelphia

Address of the committee of premiums and exhibitions of the Institute. And a list of the premiums offered to competition at the exhibition to be held in Oct. 1827. Philadelphia, 1827. 12 p. MH. 28913

The Franklin primer, or, Lessons in spelling and reading... 3d ed. Greenfield, Mass., A. Phelps, 1827. MWA. 28914

Frederick Councy, Va. Citizens.

To the General Assembly of the Commonwealth of Virginia, the memorial of the undersigned, inhabitants of Frederick County, in the said commonwealth, respectfully represents: ...[Winchester? 1827] 2 l. Vi. 28915

Fredonia [N. Y.] Academy

Catalogue of the trustees, instructers [sic] and students of Fredonia Academy, for the year ending Sept. 27, 1827. Fredonia, Hull & Snow, prs. 1827. [8] p. NFred. 28916

Free man's companion; a new and original work, consisting of nunerous moral, political, and philosophical views;... Hartford, A. Brewster, pub., P. Canfield, pr. 1827. 384 p. AMoB; CU; Ct; CtHi; CtW; CtY; MA; MB; MiU; MnSH; Vt. 28917

Free Produce Society of Pennsylvania

Constitution of the Free Produce Society of Pennsylvania. Philadelphia, Pr. on the Vertical Press by D. & S. Neall [1827] 12 p. MH; PPL. 28918

The freeman's almanack for 1828. By Samuel Burr. Cincinnati, N. & G. Guilford; Oliver Farnsworth; W. M. & O. Farnsworth, Jr., prs. [1827] 12 l. ICN; In; InU; MWA; MWHi; OClWHi. 28919

---- ---- Cincinnati, N. & G. Guilford; Oliver Farnsworth; W. M. & O. Farnsworth, Jr., prs. [1827] 24 l. CLU; DLC; MWA; NN; OClWHi; WHi. 28920

Freemasons. Alabama. Grand Chapter

Constitution and regulations of the Royal Arch Grand Chapter of the state of Alabama. Adopted in the city of Mobile, in the state of Alabama, on the 2d day of June, A. D. 1827, A. L. 5827, R. A. M. 2357. Mobile, Commercial Register Office, 1827. 14 p. AMFM; MBFM. 28921

---- ---- Grand Lodge

Proceedings of the Grand Lodge of the state of Alabama, at its annual communication: began[sic] and held in Tuscaloosa, on the fourteenth day of December, eighteen hundred and twenty-six. Tuscaloosa, Pr. by Bro. Dugald M'Farlane, 1827. 24 p. AMFM; DSC; IaCrM; MBFM. 28922

---- Connecticut. Grand Chapter.

General Grand Royal Arch constitution for the United States of America, and by-laws of the Grand Chapter of Connecticut. Hartford, C. Babcock, pr., 1827. 20, 4 p. IaCrM; NNFM. 28923

---- ---- ---- Proceedings of

Grand Chapter of Masonic Lodge in Connecticut; meeting held in 1827. Hartford, C. Babcock, 1827. 16 p. IaCrM. 28924

---- Georgia. Grand Lodge
Constitution of the Grand Lodge of the state of Georgia. Milledgeville, Ga., Pr. by Camak & Ragland, 1827. 16 p. IaCrM. 28925

---- Illinois. Grand Lodge
Proceedings of the Grand Lodge of the state of Illinois, begun and held at the town of Vandalia, on the third day of December, A. L. 5826. Kaskaskia, Ill., Pr. by L. O. Schrader, 1827. 14 p. NN; NNFM; OCM; PPFM. 28926

---- Indiana. Grand Lodge
Proceedings of the Grand Lodge of the most honorable fraternity of Free and Accepted Masons, of the state of Indiana. At its annual communication, held at Salem, on the 1st Monday in October, A. L. 5827. Indianapolis, Pr. by John Douglass, 1827. 56, 1 p. IaCrM; MBFM; NNFM; OCM. 28927

---- Kentucky. Grand Chapter
Proceedings of the Grand Royal Arch Chapter of Kentucky, at a grand annual convocation begun and held at Mason's hall in the town of Lexington, on the third day of September, A. D. 1827. Frankfort, Pr. by Amos Kendall and company, 1827. 27 p. NNFM; NcD. 28928

---- ---- Grand Lodge
Proceedings of the Grand Lodge of Kentucky, at the grand annual communication in August 5827, and at private meetings, called in case of emergency. [Lexington, T. Smith, 1827] 56 p. IaCrM; MBFM; NNFM. 28929

---- Louisiana. Grand Lodge
Extract from the proceedings of the Grand Lodge of Free and accepted Masons of the state of Louisiana. New Orleans, Pr. at No. 20 Conde Street, 1827. 16 p. OCM. 28930

---- Maine. Grand Lodge
Grand Lodge... of Free and accepted Masons of the state of Maine. Portland, Pr. by Arthur Shirley, 1827. 31 p. IaCrM. 28931

---- Maryland. Annapolis Lodge
By-laws of Annapolis Lodge, No. 17. Annapolis, J. Green, pr., 1827. 8 p. MdBJ-G. 28932

---- ---- Grand Lodge
Proceedings [of the Maryland Grand Lodge of Free and Accepted Masons] at its annual grand communication, held in the city of Baltimore, May, A. L. 5827 (A. D. 1827). Baltimore, Pr. by Edes, 1827. 56 p. MdBP. 28933

---- ---- Grand Chapter
Proceedings of the G. R. A. chapter of the state of Maryland, at a communication held at the Masonic hall, in the city of Baltimore, Oct. 25th, A. T. 2826. And at the annual communication held at the same place on the 23d of May, A. T. 2827. Baltimore, Pr. by J. Robinson, 1827. 29 p. MdBP; NNFM. 28934

---- Massachusetts. Grand Chapter
Grand Royal Arch Chapter of Massachusetts. M. E. Daniel L. Gibbon, grand high priest. Boston, Sept. 1827. Boston, Pr. by Comp. E. G. House, 1827. 23 p. MWA. 28935

---- ---- ---- Grand Royal Arch Chapter of Massachusetts. Nov. 1827. Boston, Pr. by E. G. House, 1827. 17 p. IaCrM. 28936

---- ---- Grand Lodge
Grand Lodge... of Free and accepted Masons of Massachusetts, ... Boston, Pr. by E. G. House, 1827. 20 p. NNFM. 28937

---- Michigan. Grand Lodge
[A printed circular letter. Detroit? 1827] 4 p. folder pr. on first page only. DSC. 28938

---- Mississippi. Grand Lodge
Proceedings... at a grand annual communication ... in the city of Natchez, on the 1st Monday in January, A. L. 5827, A. D. 1827, and at two special communications, held on the 30th September, A. D. 1826, and on the 25th June, A. D. 1827, Natchez, Pr. by Wm. C. Grissam & Co., 1827. 63 p. ICS; IaCrM; MBFM; MsMFM; NNFM; PPFM. 28939

---- Missouri. Grand Lodge
Constitution and by-laws of the Grand Lodge of Missouri, as amended; with such regulations as have been adopted for the better government of the Grand and subordinate lodges, subsequent to its formation. St. Louis, Pr. by Edward Charless, 1827. 9 p. MoSHi; NN. 28940

---- ---- ---- Proceedings of the Grand Lodge of the state of Missouri, at their several communications, begun and held in the city of St. Louis, on the second day of April, and the first day of October, eighteen hundred and twenty-seven. St. Louis, Pr. by Edward Charless, 1827. 16 p. DSC; IaCrM; MBFM; NNFM; PPFM. 28941

---- New Hampshire. Grand Chapter
A journal of the proceedings of the Grand Royal Arch Chapter, of the state of New Hampshire, at a special communication, holden at Concord... Concord, Asa McFarland, pr., 1827. 18 p. LNMas; NNFM. 28942

---- ---- ---- Regulations of the Grand Royal Arch Chapter, of the state of New Hampshire... Concord, Statesman & Register office, Asa M'Farland, pr., 1827. 10 p. NNFM. 28943

---- New York. Grand Chapter
Extracts from the proceedings of the Grand Chapter of the state of New York, at its annual meetings, February, 5827. Albany, Pr. by Packard & Van Benthuysen, 1827. [3]-17 p. IaCrM; LNMas; NHi. 28944

---- ---- Grand Lodge
An abstract of the proceedings of the Grand Lodge of the most ancient and honorable fraternity of Free and accepted Masons of the state of New York, at its annual communication in June, A. L. 5827. New York, Pr. by Bro. Wm. A. Mercein, 1827. 46 p. NNFM. 28945

---- ---- ---- The constitution of the ancient and honourable fraternity of Free and accepted Masons, containing all the particular ordinances and regulations of the Grand Lodge of the state of New York... New York, Pr. by Wm. A. Mercein, 1827. 87 p. IaCrM; NNFM. 28946

---- New York City
Order of the ceremony to be observed at the dedication of the Masonic Hall, Broadway, in the city of New York... Oct. 30, A. L. 5827. New York, Wm. A. Mercein, 1827. 10 p. IaCrM; PPFM. 28947

---- North Carolina. Grand Chapter
Fifth annual convocation of the

Grand Royal Arch Chapter of North Carolina. Raleigh, Pr. by Lawrence & Lemay, prs. to the state, 1827. [21] p. NcU. 28948

---- Pennsylvania. Grand Lodge
Annual publication. Grand Lodge of the most ancient and honourable fraternity of Free and accepted Masons of Pennsylvania and Masonic jurisdiction thereunto belonging, according to the old constitutions. Philadelphia, Pr. by Thomas S. Manning, May, 1827. [65]-111 p. IaCrM; NNFM; PPFM. 28949

---- Philadelphia. Columbia Holy Royal Arch Chapter No. 91
By-laws of Columbia Holy Royal Arch Chapter, No. 91. Philadelphia, Pr. by T. S. Manning, 1827. 16 p. PPFM. 28950

---- Rhode Island. Grand Lodge
Proceedings [of the worshipful Grand Lodge of the state of Rhode Island and Providence Plantations at the annual meeting...] Providence, Cranston & Marshall, 1827. 8 p. IaCrM. 28951

---- South Carolina. Grand Lodge
Abstract of the proceedings of the Grand Lodge of ancient Free-Masons of South Carolina, during the year 5826. Charleston, Pr. by Bro. C. C. Sebring, 1827. 32 p. IaCrM; NNFM. 28952

---- Tallahassee. Jackson Lodge No. 23
By-laws... adopted March 1827. [Tallahassee] Pr. at the office of the Florida Advocate [1827] 10 p. CSmH. 28953

---- Tennessee. Grand Lodge
Proceedings of the Grand Lodge of the state of Tennessee, at its annual meeting, held in the town of Nashville, for the year 1826. Nashville, Banner Press, Simpson, pr., 1827. 24 p. IaCrM; MBFM; NNFM. 28954

---- Vermont. Grand Chapter
Extracts from the proceedings of the Grand Chapter of Vermont, at its annual communication, June, A. L., 5827. Castleton, Pr. by Ovid Miner, 1827. 11 p. IaCrM; MBFM; NNFM; VtBFM. 28955

---- ---- Grand Lodge
Journal of the most Worshipful Grand Lodge of Vermont, at their communication holden at Montpelier, Oct. 10, A. L. 5826. Montpelier, Pr. by George W. Hill, 1827. 19 p. DSC; IaCrM; MBFM; MWA; NNFM; VtBFM. 28956

---- Virginia. Grand Lodge
Proceedings of a Grand annual communication of the Grand Lodge of Virginia, begun and held in the Masons' Hall, in the city of Richmond... the second Monday in December, being the tenth day of the month, A. L. 5827, A. D. 1827. Richmond, Pr. by John Warrock, 1827. 47 p. IaCrM; MBFM; NNFM. 28957

---- ---- Knights Templars
Proceedings of Grand commandery of Masonic Lodge, in Virginia: meetings held in 1823 through 1826. Winchester, Samuel H. Davis, 1827. 31 p. IaCrM; ViHi. 28958

The Freewill Baptist register, and Saint's annual visitor... for the year of our Lord, 1828... Limerick, Me., Pr. at the Morning Star Office [1827] 54 p. MHa; MWA; MeLB; NRAB. 28959

The French genders. See Goodluck, W. R.

French spoliations. (Caption title.) [1827?] 22 p. PPL. 28960

Frey, J. S. C. Frederick
The object of the American Society for Meliorating the Condition of the Jews, explained, and objections answered. In a letter, by J. S. C. F. Frey. New-York, Pr. by Daniel Fanshaw, American Tract Society House, sold by W. B. Gilley; G. & C. Carvill; Crocker & Brewster, and J. P. Haven, 1827. 28 p. MiD-B; NNMr; NjPT; PPL. 28961

A friend to the poor, pseud. See Infant education.

A friend of youth, pseud. See Willard, Samuel.

Friendly Fire Society. See Cambridge, Mass. Friendly Fire Society.

Friendly letter to parents and heads of families, particularly those residing in the country towns and villages in America... Boston, True & Greene, prs., 1827. 12 p. CSansS; CtHT-W; MB; MWA. 28962

Friends, Society of. Baltimore Monthly Meeting for the Western District.
A memorial of the Monthly Meeting of Baltimore, for the western district, concerning our friend Evan Thomas... Baltimore, 1827. 12 p. PSC-Hi. 28963

---- Indiana Yearly Meeting.
Extracts, etc. from the minutes of Indiana Yearly Meeting. Held at White-Water, 10th month, 1827. New York, Fanshaw, pr., 1827. 12 p. PSC-Hi. 28964

---- London Yearly Meeting.
The epistle from the Yearly Meeting held in London, by adjournments, from the 23d of the fifth month, to the 31st of the same, inclusive, 1827, to the quarterly and monthly meetings of Friends, in Great Britain, Ireland, & elsewhere. [Mt. Pleasant, O., 1827] 6 p. DLC; OClWHi. 28965

---- Philadelphia Monthly Meeting.
An address from the Monthly Meeting of Friends of Philadelphia, to its members. Pr. by direction of the meeting. [Philadelphia] S. W. Conrad, 1827. 17 p. CSmH; IEG; MH; MWA; PSC-Hi; PPL. 28966

---- ---- An examination of an epistle issued by a meeting of the followers of Elias Hicks, held at Green Street Meeting-house, in Philadelphia, the 4th and 5th of the 6th month, 1827, being a statement of facts relative to their separation from the Society of Friends. Philadelphia, 1827. 54 p. InRE; MA; MH; MNS; NBLiHi; NRAB; OO; PHC; PHi; PPAmP; PPL; PSC-Hi. 28967

---- Philadelphia Yearly Meeting.
An address to friends within the compass of the Yearly Meeting held in Philadelphia. Philadelphia, Pr. on the Vertical Press by D. & S. Neall, 1827. 10 p. CSmH; ICN; InRE; MB; MH; MdToH; NjR; PHC; PHi; PPAmP; PPL; PSC-Hi. 28968

---- ---- An epistle to the members of the religious society of Friends, belonging to the Yearly Meeting of Pennsylvania, New Jersey, Delaware, and the eastern parts of Maryland and Virginia. Philadelphia, Pr. by Solomon W. Conrad, 1827. 20 p. CSmH; DLC; MH; PHC; PPAmP; PPL; PSC-Hi; WHi. 28969

---- ---- Extracts from the minutes of the Yearly Meeting of Friends, held in Philadelphia, by adjournments from the fifteenth of the tenth month, to the nineteenth of the same, inclusive, 1827. Philadelphia, 1827. 10 p. PPFr; PPL; PSC-Hi. 28970

---- Wilmington Monthly Meeting
Address of the Wilmington Monthly Meeting of Friends, to its members, on the subject of the militia law, enacted at the last session of the legislature of Delaware. Wilmington, Delaware, Pr. by R. Porter & son, 1827. 4 p. CSmH; NN; PSC-Hi. 28971

---- (Hicksite) Green Street Monthly Meeting, Philadelphia, Pa.
A statement of facts, exhibiting the causes that have led to the dissolution of the connexion which existed between Philadelphia Quarterly meeting and the Monthly Meeting of Friends, held at Green Street, Philadelphia. Philadelphia, Pr. on the Vertical press by D. & S. Neall [1827] 20 p. CSmH; InRE; MH; MWA; OClWHi; PHC; PHi; PPAmP; PPL; PSC-Hi. 28972

---- ---- The committee appointed at the general meeting held at Green Street, Philadelphia, John Watson, Clerk, Philadelphia, 6th mo. 12th, 1827. Bdsd. MB. 28973

---- (Hicksite) Indiana Yearly Meeting
A testimony and epistle of advice issued by Indiana Yearly Meeting. Cincinnati, Morgan, Fisher & L'Hommedieu, 1827. 12 p. Sabin, 24498, note. 28974

---- ---- A testimony and epistle of advice, issued by Indiana yearly meeting; and approved by the Meeting for sufferings of Ohio. Mountpleasant [O.] E. Bates, 1827. 10 p. CSmH; OClWHi. 28975

---- ---- A testimony and epistle of advice, issued by Indiana Yearly Meeting. [Providence? 1827?] 10 p. CtY. 28976

---- (Hicksite), Philadelphia Yearly Meeting
An epistle from the Yearly Meeting of Friends, held in Philadelphia, by adjournments from the fifteenth day of the tenth month, to the nineteenth of the same, inclusive, 1827, to the Quarterly, Monthly, and particular meetings of Friends, within the compass of the said Yearly Meeting. Philadelphia, 1827. 10, [1] p. CSmH; Ct; InRE; MH; MdToH; NjR; PHC; PHi; PPL; PSC-Hi. 28977

---- ---- An epistle to Friends of the Quarterly & Monthly Meetings within the compass of the Yearly Meeting held in Philadelphia: adopted at a general meeting of Friends at Green Street Meeting House, in that city, by adjournments on the 4th, and 5th of the 6th mo., 1827. Philadelphia, Pr. on the Vertical press, by D. & S. Neall, [1827] 12 p. CSmH; InRE; MB; MH; MiU-C; NjR; PHC; PPAmP; PPL; PSC-Hi. 28978

Frieze, Jacob, d. 1830
Rewards and punishments. A sermon. Preached in Newberry court-house, S. C. Yorkville, S. C., Pr. by Patrick Carey, 1827. 43 p. CSmH. 28979

Frost, John, 1800-1859
Five hundred progressive exercises in parsing... Boston, Hilliard Gray, Little & Wilkins, 1827. 36 p. MHi. 28980

Fruit and flowers. A religious story for children... Boston, Cottons & Barnard, 1827. 76 p. MB; MiD-B. 28981

Fruits of enterprize... See Wilson, Mrs. Lucy Sarah (Atkins).

Fuller, Timothy, 1778-1835
Address delivered at the eleventh anniversary of the Massachusetts Peace Society, Dec. 25, 1826. Boston, Pr. by C. S. Hamilton, 1827. 27 p. CSmH; Ct; DLC; IES; IU; M; MBAt; MBC; MH; MHi; MWA; MeB; NNC; NjPT; NjR; OClWHi; PPL; VtU; WHi; BrMus. 28982

Fuller, Zelotes
Beauties of divine truth; a discourse pronounced before the First Universalist Society in Hartford, Sept. 30, 1827. Hartford, Pr. at the Office of the Religious Inquirer [J. T. Beebe] 1827. 16 p. CSmH; MMeT. 28983

Fullerton, Charles
Dr. Fullerton having returned to Princeton, permanently to remain, offers his professional services to all those who have confidence in his skill. Princeton, [Indiana] 7th Sept. 1827. Bdsd. In. 28984

Fulminea defensio. See Rodriguez, J.

Fulton, pseud. See Carey, Mathew.

Furman, R.
A sketch of the life and character of Matthew Irvine, M. D., late president of the Medical Society of S. Carolina. Read before the said society and published at their request. Charleston, Pr. by A. E. Miller, 1827. 24 p. DLC. 28985

Fyfe, Andrew, 1792-1861
Elements of chemistry, for the use of schools and academies... Boston, Pub. by Richardson & Lord, J. H. A. Frost, pr., 1827. 394 p. CtHT-W; CtY; InI; MB; MH; MdBM; MdBS; NNC; NcU; OCU; OClW. 28986

G

G., E. G.
A star of Virginia by E. G. G. Revised by the Committee of Publication. American Sunday School Union. Philadelphia Depository, 146 Chestnut Street, 1827. 31 p. DLC; KU; BrMus. 28987

Gadsden, James
Oration, delivered by Col. James Gadsden, to the Florida Institute of Agriculture, Antiquities, and Science, at its first public anniversary, on Thursday, the 4th January, 1827. Tallahassee, Pr. at the office of the Florida Intelligencer, 1827. [16] p. DLC; FJ; PPAmP. 28988

The galaxy of wit; or, Laughing philosopher: being a collection of choice anecdotes, many of which originated in or about "the Literary emporium." Embellished with several engravings... Boston, stereotyped by J. Reed, 1827. 2 v. in 1. DLC; MA; MB; MnU; NcD; OU. 28989

Gales's North-Carolina almanac for 1828. By Dr. Hudson M. Cave. Raleigh, J. Gales & Son [1827] 18 l. DLC; MH; NcD; NcHiC. 28990

Gallaher, James
Both sides. A letter to the Rev. Thomas Stringfield, containing remarks on his statements respecting a controversy he had at Rogersville in February, 1826. Preceded by Mr. Manson's and Mr. Springfield's statements. "Knoxville Register" Office. Pr. by Heiskell & Brown, 1827. 67 p. OCHP. 28991

Gallaudet, Thomas Hopkins, 1787-1851
An address on female education; delivered Nov. 21st 1827, at the opening of the edifice erected for the accommodation of the Hartford Female Seminary. Hartford, H. & F. J. Huntington, P. Canfield, pr., 1827. 34 p. MWA. 28992

Gallitzin, Demetrius Augustine. See Golitsyn, Dmitrii Dmitrievich.

[Galt, John,] 1779-1839
The last of the lairds: or, The life and opinions of Malachi Mailings, esq. of Auldbiggings. By the author of "Annals of the parish," "The entail," &c. ... New York, Pr. by J. & J. Harper, 1827. 240 p. CtHT; CtY; DLC; MB; MBC; MWA; NN; NNC; NjR; PU. 28993

Garnett, James Mercer, 1770-1843
Lectures on various topicks of morals, manners, conduct and intellectual improvement. Addressed to Mrs. Garnett's pupils at Elm-wood, Essex County, Virginia, 1825-1826. Richmond [Va.] Pr. and pub. by Thomas W. White, 1827. 159 p. ArU; NcD; NcWsS; ScSch; ViW. 28994

Garrettson, Freeborn
Substance of the semi-centennial sermon, before The New-York Annual Conference. At its session, May, 1826. Preached, and now published, by request of that body. New-York, Pub. by N. Bangs and J. Emory, for the Methodist Episcopal Church... Azor Hoyt, pr., 1827. 46 p. CtW; MBNMHi; MWA; NNMHi; NjR; PHi. 28995

Der gemeinnützige landwirthschafts Calender auf 1828. Lancaster, Wm. Albrecht [1827] 18 l. CLU; DLC; InU; MWA; NN; PHi; PPL; WHi. 28996

Gemeinschaftliches Gesangbuch, zum gotteslienstlichen Gebrauch der Lutherischen und Reformirten Gemeinden in Nord-America ... Reading, G. A. Sage, 1827. 2 p. l., 359, [1] p. DLC; NcWsM; PLT; PNazMHi; PPG; PPL; PPLT; PPeSchw. 28997

General Convention of Agriculturists and Manufacturers, and Others, Friendly to the Encouragement and support of the Domestic Industry in the United States. See Harrisburg Convention.

No entry 28998

The General Protestant Episcopal Sunday School Union.
Circular to the members of the Protestant Episcopal Church in the United States. [New York, 1827] 6 p. NNG. 28999

---- First annual report of the executive committee of the board of managers of the General Protestant Episcopal Sunday School Union; presented to the board of managers at their first annual meeting, held in the city of New-York, June 28th, 1827. New-York, Pr. by Edward J. Swords, 1827. 27 p. CtHT; InID; MBD; MdBD; MnU. 29000

---- System of instruction, for the use of Protestant Episcopal Sunday Schools in the United States. New-York, Pub. by the General Protestant Episcopal Sunday School Union, Edward J. Swords, pr., 1827. 17, [1] p. PPL. 29001

General Synod of the Evangelical Lutheran Church in the United States of America
Minutes of the proceedings of the General Synod of the Evangelical Lutheran Church, in the United States; convened at Gettysburg, Pa. Oct., 1827. Gettysburg, Pr. at the press of the Theological Seminary, H. C. Neinstedt, pr., 1827. 31 p. MBC; PAtM; PHi; PPL; PPLT; PPPrHi. 29002

---- Verhandlungen der General Synode der Evangelisch-Lutherischen Kirche... gehalten zu Gettysburg, im Staate Pennsylvanien, im Oktober, 1827. Gettysburg, Gedruckt in der Druckery des theol. Seminariums, H. C. Neinstedt, Drucker, 1827. 32 p. PPL. 29003

Genet, Edmond Charles, 1763-1834
Air navigation. Mr. Edmond Charles Genet and Mr. Eugene Robertson, well known as an aerostatic experimenter having formed a connection to promote the aerostatic science, and ascertain by actual experiment the practicability of navigating effectually, the air, by means of an aeronaut, constructed on the principles represented above... They respectfully solicit the patronage of the citizens of the United States agreeable to the recommendation of the Philosophical Society of New York hereunto annexed, to carry into effect that important object... They hope, that assisted by liberal subscriptions, they will be able to secure to these republics, the additional scientific honour, after having first improved the navigation of the waters by the power of steam, to be also the first to improve the navigation of the air by aerostatic machine... [New York, 1827] 1 p. DLC. 29004

[----] Vindication of Mr. E. C. Genet's Memorial on the upward forces of fluids, in two letters to Professor Silliman, to which are added Remarks on aerostation. New Haven, Pr. by T. G. Woodward, 1827. 34 p. MB; N; NN; WU. 29005

Geneva College
Catalogue of the trustees, faculty & students of Geneva College, December 28, 1826. Geneva, N. Y., Pr. by James Bogert, 1827. 8 p. MiU; NGH. 29006

A gentleman of Philadelphia county. See The American shooter's manual.

A gentleman of the bar. See Potter, Paraclete.

A geographical view of the United States. See Goodrich, Samuel Griswold.

George Mills, or The little boy who did not love his books. By the author of John Williams. Boston, Pub. by Bowles & Dearborn, Isaac R. Butts, pr., 1827. 25 p. MBMu. 29007

Georgia (State)
Acts of the General Assembly of the state of Georgia, passed in Milledgeville, at an annual session in November and December, 1827. Milledgeville, Pr. by Camack & Ragland, 1827. 296 p. Ar-SC; CSfLaw; G-Ar; GHi; GMBC; GU-De; IN-SC; IaU-L; Ky; L; MdBB; Mi-L; Mo; Ms; NNLI; Nb; Nj; Nv; W; Wa-L. 29008

---- Documents on which the report of the Florida line is founded. [Milledgeville, Ga., 1827] [14], 7 p. MH. 29009

---- Evidence in the case of Ludwell Watts [tried for murder] Pr. by order of Senate. [1827] [Milledgeville, 1827] 13 p. WHi. 29010

---- Journal of the House of Representatives of the state of Georgia, at an annual session of the General Assembly, begun and held at Milledgeville, the seat of government, in November and December, 1826. Milledgeville, Camak and Ragland, 1826 [i. e. 1827] 348 p. GMiW. 29011

---- Journal of the Senate of the state of Georgia, at an annual session of the General Assembly begun and held at Milledgeville, the seat of government, in Nov. and Dec., 1826. Milledgeville, Pr. by Camak & Ragland, 1827. 359 p. G-Ar; GMiW. 29012

---- Report [of the Joint Committee on Agriculture and Internal Improvement] on internal improvement. In Senate 13th Dec. 1827... [Milledgeville, 1827] 8 p. WHi. 29013

---- Report on county academies. In Senate 10th Dec., 1827... [Milledgeville, 1827] 6 p. WHi. 29014

---- Rules of practice at law and in equity established by the judges of the superior courts of the state of Georgia convened in Milledgeville Nov. 1827. Pursuant to the act of the General Assembly of the state of Georgia, passed December 24, 1821. Milledgeville, Pr. at the Statesman & Patriot office, 1827. 31 p. GU-L. 29015

The Georgia and South-Carolina almanac for 1828. By Robert Grier. Augusta, W. J. Bunce [1827] 18 l. GU; MWA; NcD. 29016

Gibbons, William, 1781-1845
Address delivered before the Delaware Academy of Natural Science; together with the constitution. Wilmington, Del., Mendenhall, 1827. 14 p. DeWI; PHi; PPAmP; PPFr; PPWa. 29017

Gibson, William, 1788-1868
The institutes and practice of surgery... 2d ed., with additions. Philadelphia, Carey, Lea & Carey, 1827. 2 v. CSmH; CSt-L; CU; CtY; DLC; GU-M; MB; MBCo; MdBJ; MdBM; MdUM; MnU; NBMS; NNNAM; NbU-M; Nh; PPC; PPHa; ScCMe; TxU; ViNoM; ViRA; ViU. 29018

[Gilbert, Ann (Taylor)] 1782-1866
Hymns for infant minds. By the author of Original poems, Rhymes for the nursery, &c. Hallowell, Pr. and pub. by Glazier & Co., 1827. 69 p. MH; MHi; NN; PPL. 29019

Gildersleeve, Benjamin, 1791-1875
A sermon, preached in the Second Presbyterian Church, Charleston, Oct. 6, 1827, at the funeral of the Rev. T. Carlton Henry, D. D. ... Charleston, Observer office press, 1827. 32 p. PPPrHi; ScU; TxU; WHi. 29020

[Giles, William Branch], comp. 1762-1830
Mr. Clay's speech upon the tariff: or the "American system," so called; or the Anglican system, in fact, introduced here; and perverted in its most material bearing upon society... Richmond, Pr. by T. W. White, 1827. 188 p. CSmH; DLC; ICN; InHi; KyLoF; MBAt; MH; MiD-C; NcD; NjP; PHi; PPL; RPB; ScHi; Tx; Vi; ViU; WHi. 29021

Gilfert, Charles, 1787-1829
Return, O my love sung by Mrs. G. Barrett at the New York

theatre in the melodrama of the Flying Dutchman, the music composed and dedicated to Miss Hosack by Charles Gilfert. New York, Engraved, pr. & sold by E. Riley [c1827] 3 p. CSmH. 29022

Gilles, H. N.
The complete vocal instructor. Baltimore, S. Carusi [1827] 99 p. MH. 29023

---- Improved method of learning the guitar or lyre. Baltimore, Pub. & sold by Geo. Willig [1827] [2], 35 p. MB. 29024

[Gillies, Robert Pearse] 1788-1858
Tales of a voyager to the Arctic Ocean. [1st series]... Philadelphia, H. C. Carey & I. Lea, 1827. 2 v. DLC; MiD; NNA; PFal; PPA. 29025

Gilpin, Henry Dilworth, 1801-1860
An annual discourse before the Pennsylvania Academy of the Fine Arts delivered in the Hall of the Musical Fund Society, on the 29th of November, 1826... Philadelphia, H. C. Carey & I. Lea [Mifflin & Parry, prs.] 1827. 58 p. DLC; MBAt; MH; MHi; MdBJ; NIC; P; PHi; PPAmP; PPL; PU; Vi. 29026

A glance at the times: including an appeal for the Greeks &c. In a poetical epistle... By a Yankee ... Philadelphia, Pub. by R. H. Small, 1827. 52 p. CSmH; MBAt; PPL. 29027

Glenn, James E.
An effort to make all things according to the pattern shewed in the Mount: in ten letters to the Rev. Joseph C. Stiles, in reply to his sermon on predestination. ... Augusta [Ga.] Pr. at the Georgian Courier office, 1827. 46 p. GEU; GMW. 29028

---- ---- Milledgeville [Ga.] Pr. by Camak & Ragland, 1827. 55 p. NcWsM; PHi. 29029

Godfrey Hall: or, Prudence and principle: a tale. By the author of "Rachel," and "The authoress." ... Boston, Munroe and Francis; New-York, C. S. Francis, 1827. 175 p. CSmH; CtY; MB. 29030

Godman, John Davidson, 1794-1830
Lecture introductory to the course of anatomy and physiology in Rutgers Medical College, delivered on Friday, Nov. 2, 1827. Published by the class. New York, W. A. Mercein, 1827. 24 p. CSt-L; MH; NBMS; NNNAM; NNU-M; NjR; PHi. 29031

---- Introductory lecture to the course of anatomy and physiology, Rutgers Medical College, New York, delivered, Nov. 11, 1826. 2d ed. New York, Pub. by H. Stevenson [J. Seymour, pr.] 1827. 44 p. ICMcC; NNNAM. 29032

Goffstown, N. H. Congregational Church
Confession of faith and church covenant. Concord, George Hough, 1827. 24 p. Nh-Hi. 29033

The golden violet. See Landon, Letitia Elizabeth.

Golder, John
The American teacher's lessons of instruction, being a compilation of select speeches and headings from the most eminent American authors... Philadelphia, The author, T. T. Ash, pr., 1827. 250 p. MdBL; P; PP; PPL; PU; RPB. 29034

Goldsmith, J., pseud. See Phillips, Sir Richard.

Goldsmith, Oliver, 1728-1774
The Grecian history, from the earliest state to the death of Alexander the Great. Hartford, S. Andrus, Publisher, stereotyped by H. Wallis, 1827. 2 v. in 1. [316] p. CtY; GEU; PV. 29035

---- Miscellaneous works, with some account of his life and writings and a critical dissertation on his poetry by J. Aiken. New ed. Philadelphia, H. Cowperthwait, 1827. 5 v. GAuY; IEG; MA; NcWfC; OClW; OMC; RP; TNJ; VtU; WaPS. 29036

---- The Vicar of Wakefield, a tale. To which is annexed, The deserted village. Exeter, Stereotyped and pub. by J. & B. Williams, 1827. 288 p. MDeeP; MDovC; MNBedf. 29037

Golitsyn, Dmitrii Dmitrievich, kniaz', 1770-1840
A defence of Catholic principles, in a letter to a Protestant minister, to which is added, An appeal to the Protestant public. 2d Amer. ed. Baltimore, J. Myres, Matchett, pr., 1827. 160 p. CSmH; DLC; ICMcC; MdBS; MdW. 29038

Gonzalez del Valle, Manuel
Diccionario de las musas, donde se esplica lo mas importante de la poetica teorica, y practica con aplicacion de la retorica y mitologia en lo que se juzga necesario... Nueva York, Lanuza, Mendia y c., 1827. [450? p.] CU (lacking all after p. 310); MB (lacking all after p. 46). 29039

Good, John Mason, 1764-1827
The book of nature. Complete in one volume. New-York, Pr. by J. & J. Harper, for E. Duyckinck [etc.] 1827. vii, 530 p. CSmH; CU; CtHT; CtY; GHi; IaGG; MB; MdBM; MdCatS; MdUM; MdW; MoS; NBMS; NNNAM; NbU-M; NjP; O; OMC; PU. 29040

---- The study of medicine. 5th Amer. ed., repr. from the last London ed., greatly imp. and enl. New York, Collins and Hannay, J. & J. Harper, pr., 1827. 5 v. CtY; ICJ; KyLxT; MBC; MBCo; MoSp; NBMS; NBuU-M; NNNAM; NRAM; OO; PPC; RPM; ScCMeS; TU. 29041

No entry 29042

Goodrich, Charles Augustus, 1790-1862
A history of the United States of America, on a plan adapted to the capacity of youths... 12th ed. Bellows Falls, James I. Cutler & Co., 1827. 296, 20 p. CLSU; CSmH; CtHT-W; DLC; LU; MBU-E; MH; MiU; NPV; OClWHi; PU; VtMiS. 29043

---- ---- 22d ed. Boston, Pub. by S. G. Goodrich, 1827. 296, 20 p. ICU; MH; MHad; MoSU; NbOM. 29044

---- ... --- 5th ed. Lexington, Ky., Pr. for and sold by Stephen P. Norton, 1827. 296, 20 p. KyRE; MB. 29045

---- Outlines of modern geography, accompanied by an atlas. Stereotyped by James Conner, New York. Boston, Pub. by S. G. Goodrich, 1827. 252 p. NNC. 29046

---- ---- 5th ed. Boston, Pub. by S. G. Goodrich, 1827. 252 p. CtW; MH; MiU-C; NcWsM. 29047

---- ---- Brattleboro, Holbrook & Fessenden, 1827. 252 p. MB; MH. 29048

Goodrich, Chauncy Allen, 1790-1860
Elements of Greek grammar. 4th ed. Hartford, Pub. by O. D. Cooke & Co., [Treadway and Adams, prs., New Haven] 1827. 247 p. CSmH; CtHT-W; CtY; MB; MH; MeHi; MoS; NjP. 29049

[Goodrich, Samuel Griswold], 1793-1860
A geographical view of the United States. Boston, Pr. for A. K. White [Dutton & Wentworth, prs.] 1827. 130 p. DLC; NNA; PPiHi. 29050

[----] The tales of Peter Parley about America. Boston, S. G. Goodrich [Ingraham & Hewes, prs.] 1827. 142 p. MBAt; MH. 29051

Goodwillie, Thomas, 1800-1867
A sermon, preached at Montpelier, before the Legislature of the state of Vermont, on the day of the anniversary election, Oct. 11, 1827. Montpelier, Pr. by George W. Hill & Co., Patriot Office, 1827. 35 p. CSmH; CtHT; CtY; DLC; MNtcA; N; NN; Vt; VtMiM; VtMiS; VtU; BrMus. 29052

Gordon, Thomas Francis
A digest of the laws of the United States, including an abstract of the judicial decisions relating to the constitutional and statutory law. Philadelphia, Pr. for the author, 1827. xxiv, 884 p. CLSU; IaUL; In-SC; MdBB; MdBP; MiU; MnU; NCH; NIC; NWM; NcD; OClW; PPL; PU-L; RPB; Tx-SC; WM. 29053

---- An inquiry into the propriety and means of consolidating and digesting the laws of Pennsylvania. Philadelphia, Philip H. Nicklin, 1827. 63 p. MH-L; MWA; NjR; OCLaw; P; PHi; PPAmP; BrMus. 29054

Gospel truth accurately stated. See Brown, John.

Gossip, Richard, pseud. ?
The posthumous works of Capt. William Morgan, who was most miraculously kidnapped by a score of freemasons, and afterwards most curiously murdered in no less than twenty different places. Arranged and comp. by Richard Gossip... Ithaca, Pr. by James M. Miller, for the publisher, 1827. 30 p. DLC; NHi. 29055

Gould, Marcus Tullius Cicero, 1793-1860
Trial of twenty-four journeymen tailors charged with a conspiracy: before the Mayor's Court of the city of Philadelphia, Sept. sessions, 1827. Reported by Marcus T. C. Gould, stenographer. Philadelphia, 1827. 167 p. DLC; ICU; MB; MH-BA; MH-L; MHi; MdBB; MoU; N-L; NNC-L; NjR; PHi; PP; PPB; PPL; WHi. 29056

Graham, John
The bishop's office: A sermon, preached in Pittsburg, Pennsylvania: before the students and others, at the close of the late session in the Theological Seminary recently organized by the Associate Reformed Synod of the West, and under its care. Washington, [Pa.] Pr. by John Grayson, Oct., 1827. 24 p. CSmH; OOxM; PPPrHi. 29057

De grandest bobalition dat ever vus be!! 4rt ob July, 1827, cum on de 5ft. [New York? 1827] Bdsd. NN. 29058

[Grattan, Thomas Colley]
High-ways and by-ways, or, Tales of the roadside, picked up

in the French provinces. By a walking gentleman. 3d series. Philadelphia, Carey, Lea & Carey, 1827. 2 v. CtY; LU; NIC. 29059

The graves of the Indians, and other poems. Boston, Hilliard, Gray, Little, and Wilkins, 1827. 72 p. MB; MH; PHi; PU. 29060

Gray, Thomas

Gray's letters and poems: with a life of the author. New-York, Pub. by W. A. Bartow, John Gray & co., pr., 1827. 212 p. GHi; MB; MBC; MWHi; MoSW; NBuU; RWe. 29061

Great Britain

Term reports in the court of King's bench. By Charles Durnford and Edward Hyde East... 2d Amer. ed. Brookfield, E. & G. Merriam; New York, Collins & Hannay, 1827. 8 v. in 4. CoSC; InU; MBeHi; WOshL; WaU. 29062

Green, Beriah, 1795-1874

A sermon preached at Brandon, Vt., Oct. 1827, at the ordination of the Rev. Messrs. Jonathan S. Green and Ephraim W. Clark as missionaries to the Sandwich Islands. Middlebury, Pr. by J. W. Copeland, 1827. 28 p. CtY; MHi; MiD-B; NjPT; NN; RPB; VtMiM. 29063

Green, Jacob

Electro-magnatism being an arrangement of the principal facts hitherto discovered in that science... Philadelphia, Judah Dobson, Jesper Harding, pr., 1827. 216 p. GU; KyLxT; MdAN; MdBS; MiD; MoU; NNE; NSchU; NjP; P; PHi; PPAmP; PPL; PU; WNaE. 29064

Green, Samuel, 1792-1834

Christian faithfulness and zeal essential to the preservation of the church, and the salvation of the world. A sermon preached before the Massachusetts Society for Promoting Christian Knowledge, at its late anniversary, May 30, 1827... with the constitution of the Society, and the annual reports of the directors and treasurer. Boston, Crocker & Brewster 1827. 50, [1] p. CtHT-W; CtY; MB; MBAt; MBC; MWA; OClWHi; WHi; BrMus. 29065

---- The grand theme of the Gospel ministry. A sermon preached at the dedication of the Trinitarian Church in Concord, Mass., Dec. 6, 1826. Concord, Pr. and pub. by Allen & Atwill, 1827. 34, [1] p. CBPac; CSmH; MB; MH-AH; MNtcA; MeBat; MiU; NjPT; BrMus. 29066

Greene, Albert Gorton, 1802-1868

Oration pronounced on the fifty-first anniversary of American independence, before the young men of the town of Providence, July 4, 1827. Providence, Smith & Parmenter, prs., 1827. 28 p. IaU; MBAt; MH; MWA; MiD-B; NN; RP; RPB. 29067

Greene, J. C.

O swiftly glides the bonnie boat: Scotch air. New York, Pub. by E. Riley, 1827. 3 p. CtY. 29068

[Greene, James I.]

Circular. To the voters of the senatorial district composed of the counties of Roane, Morgan, Rhea, Bledsoe, Marion and Hamilton [1827] [2] p. TKL. 29069

Greene, Roscoe Goddard

Murray's theory of the moods and tenses of English verbs, illustrated by an emblematical chart. [Portland] Hill & Edwards, prs., 1827. 16 p. DLC. 29070

---- Questions on the science of book-keeping by double and single entry; adapted to Bennett's system, with explanations of technical words and phrases, accompanied with short methods of calculation, notes, observations, etc. Portland, A. Shirley, 1827. Williamson: 3899. 29071

Greene County almanack for 1828. By Edwin E. Prentiss. Catskill, Samuel Wardwell, Hudson, A. Stoddard, pr. [1827] 18 l. NjR. 29072

Greenleaf, Jeremiah, 1791-1864
Grammar simplified; or, An ocular analysis of the English language. 10th ed., corr., enl. and imp. by the author. New-York, Pub. and sold by Charles Starr [Stereotyped by E. White, New-York] 1827. 50 p. CoGrS; InG; MBevHi; MH; MiHi; OMC; PPeSchw. 29073

Greenleaf, Jonathan
A sermon, delivered at Epping, New Hampshire, Oct. 25, 1826, at the ordination of Rev. Forest Jefferds, Concord, Pr. by Jacob B. Moore, 1827. 15 p. CSmH; MWA; MeBat; MeHi; MeLB; Nh-Hi; NjPT; RPB. 29074

Greenwood, Francis William Pitt, 1797-1843
An essay on the Lord's Supper ... 2d ed. Boston, Bowles & Dearborn, Isaac R. Butts & Co., prs., 1827. 60 p. CtHT-W; MB; MBAt; MH; MHi; MWA; NNG; BrMus. 29075

---- Funeral sermon on the late Hon. Christopher Gore, formerly governor of Massachusetts. Preached at King's Chapel, Bosbon, March 11, 1827. Boston, Wells and Lilly, 1827. 19 p. CSmH; CtY; DLC; ICU; IU; MB; MBC; MH; MHi; MWA; MiD-B; NBLiHi; NjPT; OO; PHi; PPAmP; PPL; RPB; BrMus. 29076

---- The peculiar features of Christianity. A sermon preached at the dedication of the meeting house of the Second Parish in Saco, and the installation of the Rev. Thomas Tracy as their pastor, Nov. 21, 1827. Kennebunk, Pr. by James K. Remich, 1827. 22 p. CSmH; ICMe; MB; MBAt; MH; MHi; MeHi; NN; RPB. 29077

---- Remarks on a popular error respecting the Lord's supper. 2d ed., pr. for the American Unitarian Association. Boston, Bowles & Dearborn [Isaac R. Butts & co., prs.] 1827. 12 p. ICMe; MBAU; MBAt; MH; MMeT; MWA; MeB; MeBat; RPB. 29078

Gregory, John, 1724-1773
A father's legacy to his daughters. New York, Samuel Marks, 1827. 288 p. MMilt; OCY. 29079

[Grierson, Miss.]
Labourers in the East: or Memoirs of eminent men who were devoted to the service of Christ in India. By the author of Pierre and his family. Philadelphia, American Sunday School Union, 1827. [Contains Memoirs of Rev. Claudius Buchanan and Henry Martyn, each with separate titles.] 126, 136 p. MBC; BrMus. 29080

[----] Lily Douglas; a simple story, humbly intended as a premium and pattern, for Sabbath schools. 2d ed. Boston, Crocker & Brewster, 1827. 108 p. KU. 29081

[----] ---- New York, Pub. by William Burgess, Jr., 1827. 107, [1] p. MBC. 29082

[----] Memoirs of the Rev. Claudius Buchanan. By the author of Pierre and his family. Revised

by the Committee of Publication. American Sunday School Union. Philadelphia, 1827. 126 p. LNHT; MBC; ViRUT; BrMus. 29083

[----] Memoirs of the Rev. Henry Martyn. Philadelphia, American Sunday School Union, 1827. 136 p. MBC. 29084

[----] Pierre and his family; or, A story of the Waldenses. By the author of "Lily Douglas." New York, Wm. Burgess [Vanderpool & Cole, pr.] 1827. 162 p. CtHC; DLC; MiKT; NjR. 29085

[----] ---- Philadelphia, American Sunday School Union [Stereotyped by L. Johnson] 1827. MHaHi; MHad; BrMus. 29086

Griffin, Edward Dorr, 1770-1837
A sermon preached September 2, 1827, before the candidates for the bachelor's degree in Williams College. Williamstown, Ridley Bannister, 1827. 23 p. CtY; MH; MNtcA; MPiB; MWiW; MiD-B; NN; NNC; NjPT; PPPrHi. 29087

Griffin, John, 1769-1834
Memoirs of Capt. James Wilson, containing an account of his enterprises and sufferings in India, his conversion to Christianity, his missionary voyages to the South Seas, and his peaceful and triumphant death. 2d. Amer. ed. Portland, James Adams, Jr., 1827. 220 p. CSt; CtHC; CtHT; DLC; MB; MW; MeHi; NhD; NjR; PPi; PU; RPB; TNJ; TxDaM. 29088

[Grigsby, Hugh Blair] 1806-1881
Letters by a South Carolinian. Norfolk, C. Bonsal, Shields & Ashburn, prs., 1827. 89 p. CSmH; DLC; ICN; MdHi; MoSM; NHi; PHi; VtU; WHi; BrMus. 29089

Grimké, Thomas Smith, 1786-1834
An address on the character and objects of science and, especially, the influence of the Reformation on the science and literature, past, present, and future, of Protestant nations, delivered in the First Presbyterian Church, on Wednesday the 9th of May, being the anniversary of the Literary and Philosophical Society of South-Carolina. Charleston, Pr. by A. E. Miller, 1827. 80 p. CSmH; CtHT-W; CtY; DLC; ICN; MB; MBAt; MBC; MH; MeB; NN; NNC; NNG; NNU; NcA-S; NcD; PBL; PHi; PPAmP; RPB; ScCC; ScU. 29090

---- An oration on the practicability and expediency of reducing the whole body of the law to the simplicity and order of a code: delivered in the City-Hall, before the South-Carolina Bar Association, on Saturday, the 17th of March, 1827. Charleston, Pr. by A. E. Miller, 1827. 31 p. DLC; InHi; MBAt; MHi; MH-L; MiU-L; NHi; NN; NcA-S; NcD; OCHP; PPAmP; PU-L; Sc; ScC. 29091

Griswold, Alexander Viets, bp. 1766-1843
An address to the twelfth convention of the Protestant Episcopal Church in the Eastern Diocese, held at Claremont, N.H., Sept. 26, 1827. Middlebury, Pr. by J. W. Copeland, 1827. 16 p. CSmH; CtHT; MBAt; MBD; MHi; MiD-B; RPB; Vt. 29092

Griswold, George
A sermon on preaching the cross, delivered at Northampton, Nov. 25, 1827. Northampton, Pr. by H. Ferry and Company, 1827. 23 p. CtSoP; MB; MHi; MNF. 29093

Grosch, David
Der Lebenslauf von T. Jefferson und J. Adams. Dated: Earl Township [probably pr. in Lan-

caster, Pa.] 1827. Seidensticker p. 234. 29094

The guards. A novel... New York, Collins & Hannay [etc.] 1827. 2 v. DLC; LU; MBAt. 29095

Guldin, J. C.
Betrachtungen u. Gebete, oder Gedanken und Unterhaltungen des Frommen mit Gott... Erster Theil... Reading, Penn., Gedruckt bey Johann Ritter, 1827. 322, [1] p. (Preface dated "2 December, 1826.") 2d & 3d parts have separate titles dated 1826. PPL. 29096

---- ---- Reading, Penn., Gedruckt bey Johann Ritter, 1827. 322, [1] p. (Preface dated "2 Januar. 1827.") PPL. 29097

Gummere, Samuel R., 1789-1866
Elementary exercises in geography, for the use of schools. 6th ed., corr. & imp. Philadelphia, Kimber & Sharpless; Adam Waldie & co., pr. 1827. 180 p. NjR; PPeSchw. 29098

[Gunn, Alexander] 1784-1829
The argument of Domesticus on the question whether a man may marry his deceased wife's sister, considered in a letter to a clergyman of the Reformed Dutch church. By Clericus (pseud.) New-York, W. E. Dean, pr., 1827. 25 p. DLC; MB; MWA; MdHi; NNC; NNG; OClWHi; PPAmP; PPPrHi; BrMus. 29099

[----] Reasons in favour of the erasure of the law which forbids a man to marry his deceased wife's sister: in a second letter to a clergyman of the Reformed Dutch church. By Clericus (pseud.) New-York, G. & C. Carvill, 1827. 38 p. DLC; MB; MdHi; NN;NNC; PPPrHi. 29100

H

H., B. D., comp.
The way to divine knowledge; or, Universal salvation to all men. Compiled by B. D. H. of Rowan County, North Carolina, Salisbury, N. C., 1827. 70 p. NcSal. 29101

Habermann, Johann
Doct. Johann Habermann's Christliches Gebetbüchlein, enthaltend Morgen- und Abendsegen... wie auch Doct. Neuman's Kern aller Gebeter... Reading, Gedruckt bey Schneider und Meyers... 1827. 157 p. MWA; PHi; PReaHi; PPL; PPeSchw. 29102

Hacker, George
The lamp lighter's address... January 1, 1827. G. Hacker. Howe & Norton, prs., Boston [1827] Bdsd. MB. 29103

The Hagerstown town and country almanack for 1828. By Charles F. Egelmann. Hagerstown, J. Gruber and D. May [1827] Drake 2547. 29104

Haines, Lemuel
Universal salvation. A very ancient doctrine!... A sermon delivered at Rutland, (Vt.) in the West Parish, A. D. 1805. Philadelphia, Pr. by J. W. Allen, 1827. 8 p. DLC; PHi. 29105

Hale, Benjamin, 1797-1863
Introduction to the mechanical principles of carpentry. Boston, Pub. by Richardson & Lord, and P. Sheldon, Gardiner, Me., P. Sheldon, pr., 1827. 182 p. CtY; MB; MH; MNan; MWA; MiU; NNC; NNE; NR. 29106

[Hale, David] 1791-1849
Letters on the new theatre. (Addressed to the committee for erecting the Tremont Theatre in

Boston. [Boston, 1827] 15, [1] p. CSmH; CtY; DLC; M; MB; MBAt; MBBC; MBC; MH; MHi; PU; WHi. 29107

Hale, Nathan, 1784-1863
Remarks on the practicability and expediency of establishing a railroad on one or more routes from Boston to the Connecticut River. Boston, Wm. L. Lewis, pr., 1827. 71 p. CSmH; CSt; CtY; DBRE; DLC; ICJ; ICU; M; MB; MBAt; MH; MH-BA; MHi; MNF; MWA; Mi; MiU-T; NN; NNC; NNE; NRU; NbO; PPL; RPB; WU. 29108

[Hale, Salma] 1787-1866
History of the United States from their first settlement as colonies, to the close of the war with Great Britain, in 1815. To which is added, questions adapted to the use of schools. New York, Collins and Hannay, 1827. 281, 24 p. CSt; CU; Ct; CtHT; CtY; DLC; GAU; IGK; IU; KyLxT; M; MH; NCH; NN; NSyHi; NbHi; Nh; OClWHi; OHi; ViU; WM. 29109

Hale, Mrs. Sarah Josepha (Buell), 1788-1879
Northwood; a tale of New England. Boston, Bowles & Dearborn, 1827. 2 v. CSmH; CtW; CtY; DLC; LU; MB; MBAt; MWA; MdBP; MdHi; PPL; RPB; BrMus. 29110

Hall, Basil, 1788-1844
Voyage to the Eastern seas, in the year 1816. Including an account of Captain Maxwell's attack on the batteries at Canton; and notes of an interview with Bonaparte at St. Helena, in August, 1817. New York, G. & C. Carvill, 1827. 331 p. CSmH; CtHT-W; DLC; KyLx; MWA; MiD; NNS; OClW; PPG; PPL; ScC; ViAl; VtU. 29111

Hall, Baynard Rush
Righteousness the safe-guard and glory of a nation. A sermon preached in the representative hall at Indianapolis, Indiana; December 31st, 1826... [Indianapolis] Smith & Bolton, prs. [1827?] 23 p. In; InU; NjPT; PPPrHi. 29112

[Hall, John Elihu]
Memoirs of eminent persons ... written, and in part, selected by the editor of the Portfolio... Philadelphia, Pub. at the Portfolio office, 1827. 457 p. DLC; NcU; TxU; ViRU. 29113

Hall, Robert, 1764-1831
Polemical and other miscellanies, consisting of articles originally inserted in the London Eclectic Review. And an apology for the freedom of the press. From the 7th London ed. Boston, Pub. by James Loring, 1827. 264 p. CU; Ct; CtHC; CtY; GDC; ICMcC; KU; LNHT; MB; MBAt; MBC; MH-AH; MNtcA; MWiW; MeBaT; MoSpD; NNC; NNS; NNUT; NPV; NRU; NcD; NhD; NjP; OHi; OMC; TxU; WBB; WHi. 29114

Hall, Samuel Read, 1795-1877
The child's assistant to a knowledge of the geography and history of Vermont. Montpelier, E. P. Walton, 1827. 90 p. MH; OO; VtStjF. 29115

[Hall, Mrs. Sarah (Ewing)] 1761-1830
Conversations on the Bible. By a lady of Philadelphia. 4th ed., enl. & imp. Philadelphia, Pub. by Harrison Hall, for the author, 1827. 363 p. DLC; NNG; NNUT; NjR; OCHP; PPDrop; TBriK; WHi. 29116

[Halleck, Fitz-Greene] 1790-1867
Alnwick castle, with other poems. New York, G. & C. Carvill, Elliot & Palmer, prs., 1827.

64 p. CSmH; CtW; CtY; DLC; ICU; IU; Ia; InID; MB; MBAt; MH; MHi; MWA; MoKU; NN; NNC; NNS; NcU; NjPT; ODa; PPL; PU; RPB; TxU; BrMus. 29117

Hamersley, Andrew
A dissertation on the remote and proximate causes of phthisis pulmonalis; to which the prize was adjudged for the year 1825, by the New York State Medical Society. 2d ed., rev. and corr. New York, E. Bliss & E. White, 1827. xi, 99 p. CSt-L; DNLM; ICJ; KyLxT; LNT-M; MB; MdBM; NBMS; NN; NNNAM; PPC; BrMus. 29118

Hamilton, pseud. See Carey, Mathew.

Hamilton, James, 1786-1857
Speech of Hames Hamilton, Jr. of South Carolina, in the House of Representatives - Feb. 5, 1827 on the abuses of a government press. 12 p. DLC. 29119

[Hamilton, Thomas] 1789-1842
The youth and manhood of Cyril Thornton. Boston, Wells & Lilly, 1827. 3 v. LNHT; MB; MB-FA; MBAt; MBNEH; PPL. 29120

[----] ---- New-York, Pr. by J. & J. Harper, for Collins and Hannay, Collins and co. [etc.] 1827. 2 v. in 1. DLC; MH; TNJ; ViU. 29121

Hamilton, William
An oration delivered in the African Zion Church, on the fourth of July, 1827, in commemoration of the abolition of domestic slavery in this state. New-York, Pr. by Gray & Bunce, 1827. 16 p. DLC; DHN; NN; BrMus. 29122

Hamilton, William T.
Church manual for the members of the First Presbyterian Church, Newark, N. J. Preceded by a brief history of the church. Newark, N. J., Pr. by W. Tuttle and co., 1827. 43 p. MPiB; Nj; NjN; OHi; PHi; PPPrHi. 29123

Hammond, Antony
A practical treatise on parties to actions and proceedings of civil and criminal; and of right and liabilities with reference to that subject. Exeter, N. H., J. Lamson, pub., J. J. Williams, pr., 1827. ix, 352 p. DLC; NcD. 29124

Hampshire and Hampden Canal Company
To the honourable General Court of the Commonwealth of Massachusetts, now in session. The petition of the Hampshire and Hampden Canal Company, by their agents... respectfully sheweth... Dated at Boston, Jan. 13th, 1827. 1 p. DLC. 29125

Hampshire Bible Society
Tenth annual report of the directors of the Hampshire Bible Society. Northampton, Pr. by Hiram Ferry, 1827. 10 p. N. 29126

Hampshire Education Society
Report of the directors of the Hampshire Education Society, at their thirteenth annual meeting, Oct. 10, 1827. Northampton, Pr. by H. Ferry & Co., 1827. 16 p. MBC; MWA. 29127

Hampshire Sabbath School Union
Address from the standing committee of the Hampshire Sabbath School Union, at an adjourned meeting April 24, 1827. Northampton, Pr. by Hiram Ferry, 1827. 12 p. MBNMHi; MWA; NN. 29128

Hance, James F.
The Cossack, Rondo for the pianoforte... New York, E. Riley, [1827?] NN. 29129

---- Fin ch'han dal vino! Aria from Don Giovanni... New York, Dubois & Stodart [1827?] NN. 29130

---- Polish military waltz. Composed & arranged for the piano forte and dedicated to Miss Lydia Warren by J. F. Hance. New York, Dubois & Stodart [c1827] 3 p. CtY; MB; ViU. 29131

Hanckell, Christian
An address delivered in St. Philip's Church, before the Charleston Protestant Episcopal Sunday School Society, at their eighth anniversary, June 5th, being the Tuesday in Witsun week... Charleston, Pr. by A. E. Miller, 1827. 10 p. NNG. 29132

Handel and Haydn Society, Boston
Collection of church music, psalm and hymn tunes. 5th ed. with additions and imp. Boston, Richardson & Lord, 1827. 360 p. CLU; CtHT-W; ICN; MB; MBC; MH-AH; NjP; PPPrHi. 29133

The happy children. (Series ii, No. 436) Philadelphia, American Sunday School Union, 1827. 16 p. MH; BrMus. 29134

Hardie, James, 1760 (ca)-1826.
The description of the city of New-York... to which is prefixed a brief account of its first settlement by the Dutch, in the year 1629; and of the most remarkable events which have occurred in its history, from that to the present period. New-York, S. Marks, 1827. 360 p. C-S; CSmH; CtHT; CtW; CtY; DLC; ICN; ICU; IU; KHi; MB; MH; MWA; MdBJ; MiD-B; MnHi; NBLiHi; NIC; NNC; NNG; NNLI; NNS; NRU; NSmB; NUtHi; NWM; NbU; Nh-Hi; OC; OClWHi; OO; PPL; RPB; WHi; BrMus. 29135

Hare, Robert, 1781-1858
A compendium of the course of chemical instruction in the medical department of the University of Pennsylvania... Philadelphia, J. G. Auner, Carey, Lea & Carey. Clark & Raser, prs., 1827. xix, 310, 46 p. DNLM; LNT-M; MoSMed; NNC-P; OCo; PPL; PPWI. 29136

Harlan, Richard
American herpetology; or, Genera of North American reptilia, with a synopsis of the species ... Philadelphia, 1827. 87, [1] p. MH-Z; NNM; PPA; PPL; WMMus. 29137

[----] Documents relating to the late election of the professor of surgery in the University of Maryland... [Philadelphia, 1827] [8] p. MdHi; NNC; NHi. 29138

Harmonisches Gesangbuch. Theils von andern Authoren, Theils neu verfasst. Zum Gebrauch für Singen und Musik für Alte und Junge. Nach Geschmack und umständen zu mählen gewidmet. Oekonomie, Beaver county, im staat Pennsylvanien, Gedruckt, im jahr, 1827. 10 p. l., 405, [14] p. CSmH; DLC; PPG; WHi. 29139

The harp of Zion; to which is added, a brief restrospective view of the Baptist Society, by a regular Baptist. Pittsburgh, Johnston and Stockton, prs., 1827. 124 p. CSfU; DLC; NjP; RPB; ViRU. 29140

Harper, Kenton
Proposals, by Kenton Harper, for publishing in Staunton, Virginia, a weekly miscellaneous paper, to be entitled The wreath... Staunton, July 9, 1827. 1 p. DLC. 29141

Harriet and her cousin; or, Prejudice overcome... 1st American from the 4th Edinburgh ed. Salem,

Whipple and Lawrence, 1827. 160 p. KU; MiGr; OClWHi. 29142

---- 2d Amer. from the 4th Edinburgh ed. Salem, Pub. by Whipple and Lawrence, 1827. 160, [1] p. PPPM; RPB; WHi. 29143

Harris, Moses Titcomb, 1797-1879

Extracts, literary, moral, and religious, for the instruction and amusement of youth. Portland, Pub. by W. Hyde, A. Shirley, pr., 1827. 2 v. CtSoP;DLC; ICU; KU; NNG. 29144

Harris, Samuel

Farewell sermon to the people of Windham, N.H., at the close of the author's ministry. January 7, 1827. Amherst, Pr. by R. Boylston, 1827. 24 p. MiD-B; Nh; Nh-Hi. 29145

---- Questions on christian experience & character. Newburyport, Pr. by W. & J. Gilman, 1827. 24 p. MWA; Nh-Hi. 29146

Harrisburg Convention, 1827

General convention of agriculturists and manufacturers, and others friendly to the encouragement and support of the domestic industry of the United States. [Proceedings] Monday, July 30, 1827. [Baltimore, 1827] 76 p. CSmH; CtY; DLC; ICJ; MBAt; MH; MH-AH; NNU; NjR; P; PHi; PPL; TxU; WHi. 29147

Harrison, John P.

Remarks on the influence of the mind upon the body... Louisville, Ky., Pr. by W. W. Worsley, 1827. 16 p. OC "Mussey." 29148

Harrison, Randolph, 1769-1839

Speech of Mr. Randolph Harrison, on the bill authorising [sic] a loan for internal improvement, and for other purposes. Richmond, Pr. by Shepherd & Pollard, 1827. 16 p. Vi; ViV. 29149

Harrod, John J.

Substance of a protest and arguments against the competency of the court and jury to try the members of the Union Society, charged with violating the discipline of the Methodist Episcopal Church; with some remarks on the constitutional law of said church. Baltimore, Pr. by John D. Toy, 1827. 14 p. MdHi; PPL. 29150

[Hart, Miss]

Letters from the Bahama Islands. Written in 1823-4. Philadelphia, H. C. Carey & I. Lea [Mifflin & Parry, prs.] 1827. 207 p. CSmH; LNHT; MB; MBAt; MWA; MdBE; NNS; NjP; PPL; RNR; BrMus. 29151

[Hart, Jeanette M.]

Nahant, or "The Floure of Souvenance"... Philadelphia, H. C. Carey & I. Lea, 1827. Mifflin & Parry, prs. 31 p. CSmH; DLC; ICU; IU; IUC; MB; MH; MWA; MdBP; NjP; P; PHi; RPB. 29152

Hart, Joseph C.

An abridgment of geographical exercises, for practical examinations on maps... Accompanied by an atlas of fourteen maps. 2d ed. imp. New-York, R. Lockwood, 1827. 108 p. CtY; DLC; MH; OCl. 29153

---- Modern atlas. 4th ed. New York, R. Lockwood, 1827. MH. 29154

Hartford Female Seminary

Prospectus, by Catharine E. Beecher. [Hartford?] 1827. 9 p. CtY. 29155

Hartford, Conn. North Church (Congregational)

A brief history of the formation of the North Church in Hartford, Connecticut, together with a summary of Christian doctrine and a form of covenant adopted by the church and read on the admission of members. Hartford, Goodwin, pr., 1827. 16 p. Ct; ICN; MWA. 29156

Hartford, Conn. Retreat for the Insane
Third report of the directors of the Connecticut Retreat for the Insane; presented to the Society, May 11, 1827. Hartford, 1827. 11 p. Ct; MBCo; MWA; N; NNNAM; NjR; OC; OCHP; OClW; WHi. 29157

Hartwick Seminary, Otsego Co., N. Y.
Annual catalogue of the officers and students of Hartwick Theological and Classical Seminary. Albany, 1827. Sabin 30717 (not. loc.) 29158

Harvard University
The annual report of the president of Harvard University to the overseers on the state of the university, for the academical year 1825-6. Cambridge, University press - Hilliard, Metcalf & Co., 1827. 52 p. MH; MiU. 29159

---- A catalogue of the officers and students of Harvard University, for the academical year 1827-8. Cambridge, Mass., University Press, Hilliard, Metcalf & Co., 1827. 24 p. KHi; MH; MS. 29160

---- Catalogus senatus academici, eorum qui munera et officia gesserunt... in universitate Harvardiana... Cantabrigiae, ex universitatis typographeo, Hilliard et Metcalf, et soc., 1827. 79 p. MH; MeHi; MiD-B; TxU. 29161

---- Circular. A meeting of a few individuals, who have received their education at Harvard College, was held in Boston, on the 6th inst. [Regards the erection of a monument to John Harvard.] Boston, 14th Sept., 1827. 3 p. DLC. 29162

---- Harvard University. Catalogue of students attending medical lectures at Boston. Boston, Pr. by J. Shaw, Dec. 1827. 4 p. MBCo; MBilHi. 29163

---- Order of exercises for commencement, Harvard. Cambridge, 1827. 3 p. MWHi. 29164

---- University in Cambridge. Order of performances for exhibition, Tuesday, May 1, 1827. Cambridge, University Press--Hilliard, Metcalf, and Co., 1827. 4 [i.e., 3] p. M; MB. 29165

Harvard University, Divinity School
Theological school at Cambridge. [Cambridge, 1827] 4, 4 p. MH. 29166

Harvard University. Procellian Club
Catalogue of books in the library of the Porcellian Club. Cambridge, Pr. by Hilliard, Metcalf and Co., 1827. 19 p. MHi. 29167

Hastings, Seth, 1762-1831
Remarks made in the Senate upon the manufacturing bill, by the Hon. Messrs. Hastings & Pickering [1827?] 20 p. MWA. 29168

Hastings, Thomas
Juvenile psalmody: prepared for the use of Sunday Schools at the request of the directors of the Western Sunday School Union. Utica, Western Sunday School Union, W. Williams, pr., 1827. 36 p. CtHT-W; MB; MBC; PPAmS. 29169

---- Musica sacra; or Utica and Springfield collections united. Consisting of psalm and hymn tunes, anthems, and chants; arranged for two, three or four voices, with a figured base for the organ or piano-forte. 6th rev. ed. Utica, Pr. and pub. by Wm. Williams, 1827. 262, [2] p. CtHT-W; CtY; ICN; MPiB; OO. 29170

Haven, Kittredge
An address delivered before the fraternity of Free and accepted Masons, convened at Corinth, Vt., for the consecration of Minerva Lodge, and the installation of its officers, Sept. 20, 1827. Royalton, Pr. by W. Spooner [1827] 16 p. IaCrM; MMeT-Hi; NNFM; RPB. 29171

Haven, Nathaniel Appleton, 1790-1826
The remains of Nathaniel Appleton Haven. With a memoir of his life, by George Ticknor. [Cambridge, Hilliard, Metcalf, & Co., prs. to the University] 1827. xl, 351 p. CBPac; CSmH; CtW; ICN; MB; MBAt; MH; MWA; Nh; PPL; PU; RPB. 29172

Hawaiian Islands. Sovereigns, etc. 1824-1854 (Kamehameha III)
He olelo no ke kanawai... King Kauikeaouli. Oahu, Honolulu, Dekemaba 8 1827. 1 p. DLC. 29173

Hawker, Robert
Zion's pilgrim: by Robert Hawker, D. D. Vicar of Charles, Plymouth... 1st Rochester ed. Rochester, Pr. and pub. by E. Peck & Co., 1827. 180 p. NRU; VtMiS. 29174

Hawkes, Pitty
The American companion; or, A brief sketch of geography... Philadelphia, R. Desilver and R. H. Small, 1827. viii, 237 p. 1 l. DLC; MH; NNA; OMC; PPAN; PPAmP; PU. 29175

Hawley, Amos
Wall-Street public sale room. Catalogue of a valuable collection of medical, classical, and miscellaneous books, to be sold... Nov. 2, 1827, at Amos Hawley's auction and commission store. No. 22 Wall-Street [New York, 1827] 1 l. NN. 29176

Hay, George, bp.
An abridgement of the Catholic doctrine, by the Rt. Rev. Bishop Hay. Published with the approbation of the Most Rev. Ambrose Maréchal. Baltimore, Fielding Lucas, Jun., 1827. 108 p. MdBE; MdBS; MdW. 29177

Haydn, Franz Joseph
The creation, an oratorio... Arranged for the organ or piano-forte, by Muzio Clementi. Improved from the 1st Amer. ed. with verbal amendations, from the latest London ed. Boston, Pub. by the Handel and Haydn Society, Pr. by James Loring, 1827. 146 p. CtY; LU; MB; MH; MNF; MeLB; MiGr; NN. 29178

Hayne, Robert Young, 1791-1839
Speech of Mr. Hayne, of S. C., on the bill for the improvement of the navy. In the Senate of the U. S., Feb. 15, 1827. Washington, Pr. by Gales & Seaton, 1827. 21 p. PPL. 29179

Hayward, Caleb
An address, delivered before the school committees, school masters and citizens of Mendon, at the commencement of the free schools in that town, Nov. 19, 1827. Worcester, Griffin and Morrill, prs., 1827. 26 p. CLU; ICN; MTaHi; MWA. 29180

Hazelius, Ernest Lewis, 1777-1853
Exercises at the installation of

the Rev. J. P. Geortner, in St. Paul's Church, Johnstown, January 3, 1827. Sermon by the Rev. E. L. Hazelius, D. D. principal of Hartwick Theological Seminary. Johnstown [N. Y.] Pr. at the office of the Montgomery Republican, 1827. 24 p. IaDuW; N; NCH; NcD. 29181

Hazen, Nathan W.
An oration delivered in Haverhill, Mass. on the fifty-first anniversary of American independence, July 4, 1827. Haverhill, Pr. by A. W. Thayer, 1827. 28 p. CSmH; CtSoP; DLC; MHa; MHi; MeB; MiD-B; Nh-Hi; PHi; PPL; RPB. 29182

Head, Sir Francis Bond, bart., 1793-1875
Rough notes taken during some rapid journeys across the pampas and among the Andes. Boston, Wells and Lilly, 1827. 264 p. CSmH; CU; CtW; CtY; GHi; MB; MH; NBu; NCH; NIC; NNS; NRU; NjP; NjR; OC; OCY; P; PPF; PPL; RNR; ScC; ScU; VtU; WHi. 29183

Head of Medusa. See Potter, Robert.

Headlands in the life of Henry Clay. No. I. from 1797 to 1827. Boston, Leavitt & Alden, [1827] 8 p. CtY. 29184

No entry 29185

Heber, Reginald, bp.
Hymns, written and adapted to the weekly church service of the year. New-York, G. and C. Carvill, Sleight & George, prs., 1827. 132 p. CtY; DLC; GDC; ICU; MBC; MH-AH; MMeT-Hi; MWA; NGH; NJQ; NNUT; NjPT; PP; PPLT; RPB; WNaE. 29186

Hedding, Elijah
The substance of a sermon on the supreme Deity of Christ, delivered in Bath, Me., July 4, 1822, before the New England Conference of Ministers of the Methodist Episcopal Church. Pub. by request of the Conference. New-York, Pub. by N. Bangs and J. Emory, for the Methodist Episcopal Church, Azor Hoyt, pr., 1827. 28 p. MB; MBNMHi. 29187

Hedge, Levi, 1766-1844
Elements of logick; A summary of the general principles and different modes of reasoning. Boston, Hilliard, Gray, Little, and Wilkins, 1827. 178 p. CtHT-W; DLC; MiBatW; MiMus; NNC; PAtM; WHi. 29188

[Heighton, William] 1800-1873
Address delivered before the mechanics and working classes generally of Philadelphia, at the Universalist Church in Callowhill Street, on Wednesday evening Nov. 21, 1827. By the "Unlettered Mechanic."... [Philadelphia] Pr. at the office of the Mechanics' Gazette [1827] 14 p. PHi; PPPrHi. 29189

[----] Address to the members of trade societies, and to the working classes generally... with a suggestion and outlines of a plan, by which they may gradually & indefinitely improve their condition. By a fellow-labourer. Philadelphia, Pub. by the Author, Young, pr., 1827. 45, [2] p. OO; PHi. 29190

Helen of the glen. See Pollock, Robert.

Hemans, Mrs. Felicia Dorothea (Browne)
The forest sanctuary; and oth-

er poems. By Mrs. Felicia Hemans. Boston, Hilliard, Gray, Little, and Wilkins, [Cambridge, University Press, Hilliard & Metcalf] 1827. 4, ii, 231 [1] p. DLC; KyLoN; MB; MBAt; MH; MdBL; MeB; MoSW; NCH; NN; NcAs; OClW; P; RNR; RPB; TNJ; ViU; WvW. 29191

---- Hymns on the works of nature for the use of children. Now first published. Boston, Hilliard, Gray, Little and Wilkins, 1827. 35 p. CtHT-W; DLC; M; MB; MBAt; MH; MWA; NN; NcWsS. 29192

---- Poems by Mrs. Felicia Heman, reprinted from the American octavo ed. Vol. I. Boston, Hilliard, Gray, Little, and Wilkins [Cambridge, University Press; Hilliard, Metcalf & Co.] 296 p. GU; KyLx; LNHT; MB; MoK; MsN; NN; NjP; OClW; RKi; RPB. 29193

---- Poems. 3d Amer. ed. Hartford, E. Hopkins, J. & J. Harper, prs., New York, 1827. 348 p. CtHC; MB; MH; ScOrC; VtU; WBB; WaPS. 29194

Henderson, Thomas, and others, executors.

Executors' sale. The subscribers will offer for sale at public auction, at the court-house of Hamilton county, Ohio, in Cincinnati, on the 21st day of July next, between ten and twelve o'-clock, A. M. the following tracts of land... Also, on the premises near the Great Miami, in Butler County, Ohio, on the 31st day of July next, between 10 and 12 o'-clock, A. M. the following tracts of land, viz.... Cincinnati, Browne, pr. [1827] Bdsd. CSmH. 29195

[Henkel, Ambrose] 1786-1870

Eine Sammlung Auserlesenen Geschichten, zum Gebrauch der Jugend. Neu-Market: Gedruckt in S. Henkel's Druckerey, 1827. Bdsd. ViU. 29196

Henry, John F.

Circular. To the electors of the twelfth congressional district of Kentucky. 8 p. MiD-B. 29197

Henry, Mathew, 1662-1714

An exposition of the Old and New Testament... New ed. John P. Haven, New-York; Robert Patterson, Pittsburgh, Towar & Hogan, Philadelphia, 1827-1828. 6 v. CoD vol. 5 missing; Ia-Ha vol. 5-6; NNAB vol. 1; NN vol. 2, 4, 5. 29198

Henry, Patrick, pseud. See Fendall, Philip Ricard.

Henry, Robert, 1792-1856

A discourse on the beneficial results consequent on the progress of liberal opinions in politics; preached in the chapel of S. Carolina College on the fourth of July, 1824. Columbia, S. C., Pr. by Sweeny and Sims, 1827. 20 p. PPAmP; RPB; ScU. 29199

Henry, Thomas Charlton, 1790-1827

The female labourer in the vineyard, a funeral discourse, occasioned by the death of Miss Elizabeth Robertson. Preached in the Second Presbyterian Church, Charleston, Aug. 26, 1827. Charleston, Observer Office Press, 1827. 29 p. NcD; LNHT; PPPrHi. 29200

---- Hope for the dying infant. A sermon, preached Feb. eighteenth, 1827, in the Second Presbyterian Church, (S. C.). Charleston, Pr. at the Office of the Charleston Observer, 1827. 47 p. MBC; MiD-B; NcD; NjR; OMC; PPPrHi; RPB; BrMus. 29201

---- Letters to an anxious inquirer, designed to relieve the difficulties of a friend, under serious impressions. Charleston, Observer Office Press, 1827. 323 p. CtHC; DLC GDC; ICMcC; IaDuU-S; MB; MBC; NcD; NjR; OO; PPPrHi; ScHi; ScU; TxAuPT; VtU. 29202

Henshaw, John Prentiss Kewley, 1792-1852
An oration delivered before the Associated Alumni of Middlebury College, at the public commencement, on the 15th August, 1827. Middlebury, Pr. by J. W. Copeland, 1827. 48 p. CSmH; CtHT-W; CtY; DLC; MH; MiD-B; NN; NNUT; RPB; Vt; VtHi; VtMiM; VtMiS; VtU; BrMus. 29203

[Hepburn, John M.]
To the honorable the legislature of Maryland. [Washington? 1827] 13 p. MdBP. 29204

Herr, Johannes
Erläuterungs-Spiegel, oder Eine gründ liche Erklärung von der Bergpredigt unsers Herrn Jesu Christi... Lancaster, Gedruckt bey Johann Bär, 1827. 394, [1] p. InGo; MH; MWA; MiU-C; NN; P; PHi; PLFM; PPG; PPL. 29205

Das Herz des Menschen, ein Tempel Gottes oder ein Werkstätte des Satans... Nach der vierten verbesserten Augsburger Auflage. Harrisburg, Gedruckt und zu haben den Moser u. Peters, 1827. 58 p. KMK; MiU-C. 29206

Heselrigge. See Dodge, Mrs. H. M.

High life; a novel. New York, Pr. by J. & J. Harper for Collins & Hannay [etc., etc.] 1827. 2 v. LU; MH; NjR. 29207

High School Society of New York
Third annual report of the trustees of the High School Society of New York, made on Monday, Nov. 12, 1827. pursuant to the act of incorporation. New York, Pr. by Wm. A. Mercein, 1827. 16 p. CtY; DLC; MB; MiKC. 29208

High-ways and by-ways. See Grattan, Thomas Colley.

Hildreth, Hosea, 1782-1835
A discourse on ministerial fidelity. Gloucester, [Mass.] Pr. at the Telegraph Office, 1827. 12 p. CSmH; MBAt; MBC; MH-AH; MiD-B; WHi. 29209

---- ---- 2d ed. Gloucester [Mass.] Pr. at the Telegraph Office, 1827. 12 p. MWA. 29210

Hill, Ebenezer, 1766-1854
A funeral sermon, delivered at Mason, N. H. on Lord's day, December 10, 1826, occasioned by the death of Capt. Hiram Smith... Amherst, Pr. at the Cabinet press [1827] 15 p. CSmH. 29211

---- A sermon delivered at Mason, N. H., Aug. 28, 1826, at the funeral of Joseph Addison Robbins, son of Mr. Joseph B. Robbins, and Hannah his wife. Who departed this life Aug. 26, 1826, aged 4 years, 2 months, and 16 days. New Ipswich [N. H.] S. Wilder, 1827. 16 p. CSmH; MBC. 29212

Hill, Frederic S., 1805-1852
The memorial; a Christmas and New Year's offering for 1828. Edited by F. S. Hill, Boston, Pub. by True & Greene, and Richardson & Lord [1827] 406, [1] p. MH; MWHi. 29213

---- Song. By Frederick S. Hill ... Song. by Rufus Dawes... The angel of art. By W. G. Grosby...

[Boston, 1827] Bdsd. MB. 29214

Hill, Jacob
A discourse on divinity: treating of the old path to Heaven... Cincinnati, Pr. at the Advertiser office, 1827. 20 p. OClWHi. 29215

Hillhouse, James
Remarks of the Hon. James Hillhouse before the joint committee, on the petition of Samuel Hinkley and others, for the extension of the Hampshire and Hampden canal. Boston, True & Greene, Prs., 1827. 11, [1] p. CtHi; M; MA; MB; MBAt; MH-BA; MWA. 29216

Hilliard, William, 1778-1836
An address delivered before the Massachusetts Charitable Mechanic Association Oct. 4, 1827, being the anniversary for the choice of officers, and the seventh triennial celebration of their public festival. Cambridge, Pr. by Hilliard, Metcalf, & Co., 1827. 48 p. CSmH; DLC; MB; MBAt; MH; MHi; MWA; MiD-B; NNC; Nh; PHi; PPL; WHi; BrMus. 29217

Hillsboro County, N.H. Conference of Churches
Constitution and by-laws of the Hillsborough County Conference of Churches. With the proceedings at their annual meeting in Goffstown, Oct. 16 & 17, 1827. Amherst, Pr. by Richard Boylston, 1827. 16 p. CSmH. 29218

Hints for the improvement of early education. See Hoare, Mrs. Louisa (Gurney).

Hints on banking. See McVickar, John.

Hints on public worship; or, The churchman instructed in the use of the Book of Common Prayer. Portland, Pub. by the Prayer Book and Homily Society, James Adams, Jun., pr., 1827. 22 p. NNG. 29219

Historical scenes in the United States. See Barber, John Warner.

The history of Andrew Dunn. Philadelphia, 1827. 48 p. P; PPL. 29220

The history of Betsey Brown. Philadelphia, American Sunday School Union, 1827. 32 p. PPAmS; BrMus. 29221

The history of Emily and her brothers. See Sherwood, Mary Martha (Butt).

The history of John Robins, the sailor. Revised by the Committee of Publication. American Sunday School Union. Philadelphia, 1827. 32 p. DLC; PPL. 29222

The history of Joseph Green, a Sunday scholar. Philadelphia, American Sunday School Union [1827] 48 p. DLC; BrMus. 29223

The history of modern Greece, with a view of the geography, antiquities, and present condition of that country. From the London ed Boston, Pub. by Nathan Hale, Wm L. Lewis, pr., 1827. iv, 503, [5] p. CtHT-W; CtY; DLC; GHi; MB; MWA; MoSW; NNS; Nh; OCY; OClWHi; OO; PPL; TNJ; ViAl. 29224

History of Philip's war. See Church, Benjamin.

History of Sally Preston: with other moral and interesting stories. New-Haven, A.H. Maltby & Co., publishers, 1827. 23 p. CtHi. 29225

The history of Susan Green, a Sunday scholar. Philadelphia, American Sunday School Union. 1827. 48 p. CtY; MB. 29226

History of the Bible. Hartford, J. Gilman, publisher, 1827. 178 p. CSmH; DLC; MNHi; NN; PP. 29227

The history of the pirates... New-York, Stereotyped by James Conner, pub. by Henry Benton, 1827. 283 p. CSmH; DLC. 29228

History of the United States. See Hale, Salma.

The history of Thomas Brown. Philadelphia, American Sunday School Union Depository. 1827. 16 p. CSmH; DLC. 29229

Hitchcock, Edward, 1793-1864
Scientific agriculture. An address delivered before the Hampshire, Franklin, & Hampden Agricultural Society; at Northampton, Oct. 24, 1827. Published by the Society. Amherst, Mass., J. S. & G. Adams, prs. [1827?] 24 p. CSmH; CtY; MB; MH; MWA; RPB. 29230

[Hoare, Mrs. Louisa (Gurney)]
Hints for the improvement of early education. 2d Salem, from the 5th London ed. Salem, Pub. by James R. Buffum, pr. by Bowen & Cushing, Boston, 1827. 168 p. DLC; MBC; MH; MNS; MS; MWA; TxH; TxU. 29231

Hoare, Prince
The prize; or 2, 5, 3, 8. A musical farce, in two acts. Philadelphia, Pub. by C. Neal, Mifflin & Parry, prs., 1827. 32 p. CtY; MH; MWA; PU. 29232

Hobart, John Henry, bp., 1775-1830
An address delivered before the convention of the Protestant Episcopal Church in the state of New York in Trinity Church in the city of New York, on Wednesday Oct. 17, 1827... New York, Pub. by T. & J. Swords, 1827. 19 p. MiD-B; NIC; NNG; PPL; WHi; BrMus. 29233

---- The Christian bishop approving himself unto God, in reference to the present state of the Protestant Episcopal Church in the United States of America. A sermon preached in Christ Church in the city of Philadelphia, on... the 25th day of Oct., A. D. 1827, at the consecration of... Henry U. Onderdonk... as assistant bishop of the Protestant Episcopal Church in the state of Pennsylvania... Philadelphia, Jesper Harding, pr., 1827. 36 p. CtHC; CtHT; DLC; MB; MH; MHi; MWA; MdHi; MiD-B; NCH; NGH; NNG; NNUT; NUT; NjR; PHi; PPAmP; PPL; PPPrHi; RPB; WHi; BrMus. 29234

---- Church catechism enlarged, explained and proved from Scripture in a catechism drawn up, with alterations and additions from various approved catechisms. New York, General Protestant Episcopal Sunday School Union, 1827. 105 p. PPAmS; PPLT. 29235

---- A companion for the Book of common prayer containing an explanation of the service. 4th ed., with additions. Published by the Protestant Episcopal Tract Society. New-York, Pr. by T. & J. Swords, 1827. 108 p. InID; KyDC; MB; MWA; NNG; WHi. 29236

---- ---- 4th ed., with additions. Stereotyped by James Conner, N. Y. New-York, Pub. by the Protestant Episcopal Tract Society [1827] 84 p. CtHC; CtHT; NNG; PHi; PPP; PPPrHi; VtMiM. 29237

Der Hoch-Deutsche Americanische Calender auf 1828. Von Carl Friederich Egelmann. Germantaun, M. Billmeyer [1827] 18 l. CLU; CtY; DLC; MH; NN;

PPL; WHi. 29238

Hochdeutsches reformirtes A B C und Namen-Büchlein, für Kinder welche anfangen zu Lernen. Fünfte Ausgabe. Reading, Gedruckt und zu haben bei Johann Ritter und Co.... 1827. 32 p. PPL; PRHi. 29239

Hodge, Charles
Biblical Repertory. A collection of tracts in Biblical literature... New York, Pub. by G. & C. Carvill, 1827. 604, [8] p. ICMcC; KyDC. 29240

Hogg, Thomas Jefferson
Two hundred and nine days. The journal of a traveller on the continent. New York, Elam Bliss [Jamaica, L. I.: Sleight & George, prs.] 1827. 2 v. CLU; InU; LNHT; MA; MB; MWA; NNS; NT; NjR; OMC; PMA; PPA; ScU; ViRVal. 29241

Hohenlohe, Alexander, prince.
Prince Hohenlohe's prayer book; or, The Christian praying in the spirit of the Catholic Church. Trans. from the German. 1st Amer. ed. Baltimore, Pub. by James Myres. Wm. Wooddy, pr., 1827. 355 p. DLC. 29242

---- ---- Philadelphia, Pub. by Cummiskey, 1827. 335 p. PPCHi. 29243

[Holbach, Paul Henry Thyri, Baron d'] 1723-1789
Ecce Homo! A critical inquiry into the history of Jesus of Nazareth, being a rational analysis of the Gospels... 1st Amer. ed., rev. and corr. New York, Pr. for the proprietors of the Philosophical library, 1827. 212 p. CtY; DLC; ICU; MH; NCH. 29244

Holdich, Benjamin, 1770-1824
Politico-clerico-lay sermon, on the use and abuse of riches. Philadelphia, Pr. by J. Clarke, 1827. 16 p. CSmH; TxU. 29245

Holland Purchase
Proceedings of the meeting held at Lockport, on the 2d and 3d of January, 1827, and of the convention of delegates from the several counties on the Holland Purchase, held at Buffalo, on the 7th and 8th of February, 1827. To consider the relations subsisting between the Holland Company and the settlers on said purchase, and to propose some remedy by which the condition of the settlers may be alleviated. Buffalo, Pr. by Day & Follett, 1827. 23 p. NBu; NN. 29246

[Hollins, William]
Rail roads in the United States of America: or, Protest and argument against a subscription on the part of the state of Maryland to the Baltimore and Ohio Railroad Company. Addressed to the officers and representatives of the people in the several states of the Union, and the general government, By a citizen of Baltimore. Baltimore, Matchett, pr., 1827. 35 p. DBRE; DLC; M; MBAt; MH-BA; MWA; Md; MdHi; MiU-T; N; PPL; PU. 29247

Holmes, Sylvester, d. 1866
A sermon delivered at the ordination of Rev. Freeman P. Howland, at Hanson, Oct. 25, 1826. Plymouth, Pr. by Allen Danforth, 1827. 24 p. CSmH; DLC; MBC; MH; MWA; NjPT; PPPrHi; RPB; BrMus. 29248

Home. (In verse). Philadelphia, American Sunday School Union, 1827. BrMus. 29249

Honestus, pseud.
Revivals of religion, considered as means of grace; a series of plain letters to Candidus, from

his friend Honestus. Ithaca, Pr. by Mack & Andrus, 1827. 39 p. NIC. 29250

Hood, Thomas
The plea of the midsummer fairies, Hero and Leander, Lyons the centaur, and other poems. Philadelphia, E. Littell J. Grigg, 1827. 164 p. DLC; KyLx; MB; MWA; MdBL; MdBP; NN; PHi; PU. 29251

Hooper, William, 1792-1876
A discourse delivered before the Masonic Society, at Chapel-Hill, June 23d, 1827, on the occasion of celebrating the anniversary of St. John the Baptist. Hillsborough, D. Heartt, 1827. 16 p. NcU. 29252

Hope Leslie. See Sedgwick, Catharine Maria.

Hopkinton Academy
A catalogue of the officers, instructers and students of Hopkinton Academy. Fall Term Oct. 1827. Concord, George Hough, pr., 1827, 8 p. Nh. 29253

Horatius Flaccus, Quintus
Quinti Horatii Flacci Opera. Interpretatione et notis illustravit Ludovicus Desprez... Editio Quinta in America, stereotypis impressa cum novissima Parisiensi diligenter collata, E. stereotypis A. D. & G. Bruce fabricatis. Philadelphia, Impensis H. C. Carey & I. Lea, 1827. 559, 61 p. CtY; DLC; MB; MsY; NN. 29254

Horne, Thomas Hartwell, 1780-1862
A compendious introduction to the study of the Bible. Boston, Wells & Lilly, 1827. 528 p. LNB; MNtcA; PPP; ViRUT; WS. 29255

---- An introduction to the critical study and knowledge of the Holy Scripture. 3d Amer. ed. Philadelphia, E. Littell; New York, G. & C. Carvill, 1827. 4 v. CSaT; CoU; CtHC; DLC; IEG; IaScM; KyLoS; KyLx; LNB; MB; MBC; MMeT-Hi; MWiW; MdW; MoSpD; NCaS; OClW; PLT; ScCoB; TBriK; TNJ; ViRU; BrMus. 29256

Horner, William Edmonds, 1793-1853
Lessons in practical anatomy, for the use of dissectors. 2d ed. Philadelphia, H. C. Carey & I. Lea, 1827. xxxiii, 500, 16, 8 p. CtY; DNLM; GEU-M; GU-M; IEN-M KyLxT; MBCo; MdBJ-W; MeB; NBMS; NjR; PPC. 29257

Hornihold, John Joseph. See Hornyold, John Joseph, bp., 1706-1778.

Hornyold, John Joseph, bp., 1706-1778
The real principles of Catholics; or, A catechism of general instruction for grown persons: explaining the principal points of the doctrine and ceremonies of the Catholic Church... Lancaster, Pub. by Peter Fox, Republisher of Catholic standard works, under the patronage of the Archbishop, Bishops, and Clergy, of the Roman Catholic Church of the United States of America, 1827. 329 p. P. 29258

Horrid, brutish and bloody murder. Trial and sentence of Wm. Miller for the murder of David Ackerman, on board the Sloop Phoebe. New York, Pr. and sold wholesale and retail, by C. Brown, 1827. 16 p. N-L. 29259

Hosford's calendar; or The New York and Vermont almanack for 1828. Albany, E. & E. Hosford [1827] 16 l. DLC; MWA; MiGr; N; NHi; NIC. 29260

Howard, pseud. See Carey, Mathew.

Howard Benevolent Society. Boston.
Report of the Standing committee... presented at their annual meeting, Oct. 30, 1827... Boston, T. R. Marvin, pr., 1827. 12 p. MBAt; MWA; PPL. 29261

Howe, John
A journal kept by Mr. John Howe, while he was employed as a British spy... Concord, N. H., L. Roby, pr., 1827. 44 p. DLC; MDeeP; MH; MHi; MLexHi; MWA; Nh; Nh-Hi; PHi; RPJCB. 29262

Hoyt, O. P.
The influence of public opinion. An address: delivered... July 4, 1827. Potsdam, Pr. by Powell & Redington, 1827. 16 p. GDC; NN; PPPrHi. 29263

Hubbard, Austin Osgood
Elements of English grammar; with an appendix, containing exercises in parsing... Baltimore, Cushing, 1827. 220 p. CtHT-W; ICN; NjP; WU. 29264

Hubbard, William
A discourse occasioned by the death of Miss Harriet Bennet... delivered at her funeral Dec. 15, 1826. Including a memoir... Boston, James Loring, 1827. 68 p. CSmH; ICN; MBNEH; MWA; BrMus. 29265

[Hubbell, Seth] 1759-1832
A narrative of the sufferings of Seth Hubbell & family, in his beginning a settlement in the town of Wolcott, in the state of Vermont. Danville, Vt., E. & W. Eaton, prs., 1827. 24 p. CtHi; DLC; MBAt; MH-AH. 29266

Hudson, Charles, 1795-1881
A series of letters, addressed to Rev. Hosea Ballou, of Boston; being a vindication of the doctrine of a future retribution... Woodstock, Pr. by David Watson, 1827. 307 p. CSmH; DLC; ICMe; M; MB; MBC; MBNMHi; MH; MHi; MMeT-Hi; MNtcA; MWA; NcD; NN; NNUT; OO; THi; VtU; VtWood; WHi. 29267

[Hudson, Marianne Spencer (Stanhope)]
Almack's, a novel... New York, Pr. by J. & J. Harper for E. Duyckinck, Collins and Hannay [etc.] 1827. 2 v. CtY; CSmH; MB; MH; NN; PPL; RBr; RPB; ViU. 29268

Huffington, William
An oration delivered at the State-House in Dover, the 4th of July, 1827 on the order of the Delaware Blues, to that corps, and to respectable delegations from other volunteer troops and corps of the second brigade of Delaware militia... Dover, Del., Augustus M. Schee, pr., 1827. 18 p. DLC; MdBP. 29269

Hughes, Mrs. Mary (Robson)
Aunt Mary's tales, for the entertainment and improvement of little boys, addressed to her nephews... A new ed., corr. and imp. by the author. Philadelphia, R. H. Small, 1827. 238 p. CtY. 29270

[----] Aunt Mary's tales for the entertainment... of little girls... 2d Amer. from the 3d London ed. New York, O. A. Roorbach, 1827. vi, 167 p. CtY; MBAt; MHingHi; NN. 29271

---- The new expositor: containing tables of words, from one to seven syllables inclusive;... Philadelphia, R. H. Small, 1827. 192 p. DLC; P. 29272

Hughes, Benjamin F.
An oration... before the Boyer Lodge, 25th of June, 1827... New York, Pr. by Mahlon Day, 1827. 15 p. MB. 29273

Hull, Joseph Hervey
English grammar, by lectures ... 3d ed., rev. and cor. by the author. New-Brunswick [N. J.] Pr. by Terhune & Letson, 1827. 48 p. DLC; NjP. 29274

An humble and affectionate address. See Cresson, Warder.

Hume, David, 1711-1776
Hume and Smollet's celebrated history of England, from its first settlement to the year 1760; accurately and impartially abridged; and a continuation from that period to the coronation of George IV, July 19, 1821. Hartford, D. F. Robinson, Stereotyped by A. Chandler, 1827. 496 p. CU; Ct; CtW; DLC; GM; IU; KyBB; KyDC; KyLo; LNB; MB; MH; MWA; MdU; MnHi; NGH; NIC; OAU; OClW; OOxM; OW; PHi; PU; ScCliTO; TNJ. 29275

Humphrey, Aaron
Sufferings and death of Christ. A sermon delivered in St. Luke's Church, Lanesborough on Good Friday, April 13, 1827. Pittsfield, Pr. by Phinehas Allen, May, 1827. 23 p. MDeeP; MPiB. 29276

Humphrey, Heman, 1779-1861
A sermon delivered at the dedication of the college chapel in Amherst, Mass. Feb. 28, 1827. Amherst, Carter & Adams, 1827. 32 p. CSmH; M; MA; MAJ; MB; MBC; MH; MH-AH; MHi; MNtcA; MWA; MiD-B; NCH; NN; NjP; NjR; RPB; WHi. 29277

Hunt, Ebenezer
Address, delivered before the Danvers Auxiliary Society for the Suppression of Intemperance... April 5, 1827. Salem, Pr. at the office of the Essex Register, 1827. 19 p. MHi; MPeal; MWA; NjR; VtU; WHi; BrMus. 29278

Hurd, Jarvis
Report of Jarvis Hurd, Esq., civil engineer, employed by the Hampshire and Hampden Canal Company, to make a survey, and estimate the expense of a canal from the termination of the Hampshire and Hampden Canal, in Northampton, to the north line of Massachusetts, and thence to Brattleborough, in the state of Vermont. Boston, True & Greene, prs., 1827. 40 p. MB; MBAt; MW. 29279

Hutchings' almanac for 1828. By David Young. New-York, James A. Burtus [1827] 18 l. NHi. 29280

---- ---- New York, N. B. Holmes [1827] 18 l. NBLiHi. 29281

---- ---- New-York, Samuel Marks [1827] 18 l. MWA; NN. 29282

---- ---- New York, Daniel D. Smith [1827] 18 l. CSmH; DLC. 29283

Hutchings' improved almanac for 1828. By David Young. New-York, John C. Totten [1827] 16 l. MWA; NBLiHi. 29284

Hutchings' revived almanac for 1828. By David Young. New-York, John C. Totten [1827] 18 l. Drake 6927. 29285

---- ---- New-York, John Montgomery [1827] 18 l. CtB; NHi. 29286

Hutchins' improved almanac for 1828. New York, C. Brown [1827] 16 l. MB. 29287

Hutchins' improved. Almanac and empheeris [sic] for 1828. New-

York, Caleb Bartlett [1827] 18 l. NBLiHi; NjR (16 l.) 29288

---- ---- New-York, Caleb Bartlett [1827] 18 l. MWA; MnU; NHi; NN. 29289

Hutchins' revived almanac and ephemeris for 1828. New-York, Caleb Bartlett [1827] 18 l. MWA; NBLiHi; NNMus. 29290

Hutchinson, Samuel
An apology for believing in universal reconciliation; or, An appeal from the inferior court of bigotry, superstition, ignorance and unbelief, to the supreme court of proper candor... Norway, Me., Pr. for the author by Asa Barton, 1827. 201, [3] p. CSmH; CtHT-W; KyBC; MeHi; MeLB; MMeT-Hi; NB; PPL. 29291

Hutson, John P.
The Pennsylvania harmonist, containing a choice collection of tunes, grave and sprightly, for divine service and musical refinement... Prepared for the use of schools. In two parts. Part I. Pittsburgh, Cramer & Spear, 1827. xviii, 69 p. ICN; PPi. 29292

Hutton, Isaac G.
The signeron; an essay on the culture of the grape and the makings of wine. Washington, Pub. by the author. 1827. 60 p. DLC; NBuG. 29293

Hutton, Joseph
Omniscience, the attribute of the Father only. 3d ed., No. 4. Pr. for The American Unitarian Association. Boston, Bowles & Dearborn, 1827. [Isaac R. Butts, pr.] 36 p. CBPac; CtY; DLC; ICMe; MH; MHi; MMeT-Hi; MeB; MeBat. 29294

Huzza for Gen. Jackson! Down with the Yankees! [1827] 1 p. DLC. 29295

[Hyde, Jabez Backus]
Analysis of the Seneca language. Na na none do wau gau ne u wen noo da. Buffalo, H. A. Salisbury, pr., 1827. 36 p. 29296

[----] Kau a nau so na na none do wau gau ne u wen noo da. Hymns, in the Seneca language. Buffalo, H. A. Salisbury, pr., 1827. [4], 40 p. CSmH; NBuHi; NRMA. 29297

Hymns for children. New York, Pub. by David Felt, 1827. 52 p. MHi. 29298

Hymns for infant minds. See Gilbert, Ann (Taylor).

Hymns for social and private worship, altered to a devotional form. Boston, Pub. by Wait, Greene and Co., T. B. Wait & son, prs., 1827. 150 p. CBPac; CtHT-W; MBC; MH; MHi. 29299

Hymns for Sunday schools, Pr. for the trustees of the Publishing Fund. Boston, Wait, Greene & co., and Bowles and Dearborn, 1827. 60 p. MB. 29300

Hymns in the Seneca language. See Hyde, Jabez Backus.

Hymns sung at a union meeting of the Sunday schools in Wheeling, January 1, 1827. Bdsd. WvWO. 29301

I

Idle hours employed; or, The new publication. A selection of moral tales. New York, Pub. by W. B. Gilley, Gray & Bunce, prs. 1827. 236 p. CSmH; DLC; KU; PP; ScCliTO. 29302

The ignis fatuus. See Price, James Cave.

Illinois (State)
A bill for an act concerning public roads. [Vandalia, 1827?] 4 p. I-Ar. 29303

---- A bill for an act regulating the salaries, fees, and compensation of the several officers and persons therein mentioned. [Vandalia, 1827?] 16 p. I-Ar. 29304

---- A bill for an act to lease the seminary lands. [Vandalia, 1827?] 2 p. I-Ar. 29305

---- Journal of the House of Representatives of the fifth General Assembly of the state of Illinois, at their first session, begun and held at the town of Vandalia, December 6, 1826. Vandalia, Pr. by Robert Blackwell, public pr., 1826 [i.e., 1827] 595 p. DLC; I-Ar; ICN; IGK; IHi; InU; WHi. 29306

---- Journal of the Senate of the fifth General Assembly of the state of Illinois, at their first session, begun and held at the town of Vandalia, Dec. 6, 1826. Vandalia, Pr. by Robert Blackwell, public pr., 1826 [i.e. 1827] 328 p. CSmH; DLC; I-Ar; ICN; ICU; IGK; IHi; IU; WHi. 29307

---- Laws of a private nature, passed by the fifth General Assembly of the state of Illinois, at their session held at Vandalia, commencing on the fourth day of December, 1826, and ending the 19th of February, 1827. Pub. by authority. Vandalia, Pr. by Robert Blackwell, pr. to the state, 1827. 43 p. DLC; I-Ar; ICLaw; ICN; IHi; IU; NN; NNB. 29308

---- The memorial of the circuit judges of the state of Illinois. Jan. 1, 1827. Vandalia, Ill., Pr. by Robert Blackwell, 1827. 17 p. IHi. 29309

---- The revised code of laws, of Illinois, enacted by the fifth General Assembly, at their session held at Vandalia, commencing on the fourth day of December, 1826, and ending the nineteenth of February, 1827. Vandalia, Pr. by R. Blackwell, pr. to the state, 1827. iv, 406 p. CSmH; DLC; MWCL. 29310

The Illinois Intelligencer--Extra. List of lands entered on the books of the auditor of public accounts for the state of Illinois, subject to taxation for the several years set forth, (With the interest and costs,) and upon which the taxes have not been paid, in conformity to the provisions of the several laws levying and collecting a tax on land. In all cases the lands in the Military Tract are described and advertised in the name of the original patentees, and taxed according to the class to which they belong. [Vandalia, 1827] 33 p. IHi. 29311

Illustrations of Masonry. See Morgan, William.

Illustrations of the four first degrees of female masonry, as practiced in Europe by a Lady. Boston, 1827. 32 p. MB. 29312

The image boys. See Malan, César Henri Abraham.

The importance of revivals. See Philalethes, pseud.

In school and out of school, or, The history of William and John. An interesting tale. By one who knows both. 1st Amer. ed. New York, Wm. Burgess, Jr., 1827. 111 p. CtHT-W; CtSoP; DLC; MH; NN; NNC; NcAS; OClWHi;

PU. 29313

Inchbald, Mrs. Elizabeth (Simpson)
Every one has his fault; a comedy in five acts. Philadelphia, F. C. Wemyss, etc., etc. [1827] 82 p. MH. 29314

---- A Mogul tale; a farce in two acts. New-York, E. M. Murden, 1827. 27 p. MH; MMal; NN. 29315

Indiana (State)
Journal of the House of Representatives, of the state of Indiana, being the eleventh session of the General Assembly, begun and held at Indianapolis, in said state, on Monday the fourth day of December, 1826. Indianapolis, Ia., Pr. by John Douglass [1827] 527 p. In; InU. 29316

---- Journal of the Senate of the state of Indiana, being the eleventh session of the General Assembly, of the state of Indiana, begun and held at Indianapolis, in said state, on Monday the fourth day of December, A. D. 1826. Indianapolis, Ia., Pr. by John Douglass [1827] 287 p. In. 29317

---- Laws of the state of Indiana, passed and published at the eleventh session of the General Assembly, held at Indianapolis, on the first Monday in December, one thousand eight hundred and twenty-six. Indianapolis, John Douglass, pr., 1827. 119 p. In; InHi; InU; In-SC; N. 29318

Indiana Sabbath School Union
First annual report of the Indiana Sabbath School Union, containing its constitution; together with a general plan of forming and conducting Sabbath schools. Indianapolis, Pr. by John Douglass, 1827. 26 p. CSmH; In. 29319

Indigent Widows' and Single Women's Society
The tenth annual report for the year 1826 of the managers of the Indigent Widows' and Single Women's Society; with a list of the officers and manager... Philadelphia, Pr. by order of the Society, Lydia R. Bailey, pr., 1827. 8 p. PPL. 29320

Infant education; or Remarks on the importance of educating the infant poor. From the age of eighteen months to seven years; with an account of some of the infant schools in England, and the system of education there adopted. By A Friend to the Poor. New-York, Pr. by J. Seymour, 1827. 108 p. CtHC; KyBC; MB; MBC; MH; OMC; PPAmS; PPL. 29321

The infant school. See Carey, Mathew.

Infant School Society of Philadelphia. Philadelphia, June 12, 1827. 36 p. MB. 29322

---- Address of the board of managers of the Infant School Society to the benevolent citizens of Philadelphia. [Philadelphia, June 14, 1827] Bdsd. PHi. 29323

Infernal conference, or dialogues of devils. By the Listener. Philadelphia, Pr. and pub. G. G. M. & W. Snider, 1827. vi, 291 p. PLT. 29324

Infidelity, punished; report of a remarkable trial. The King vs. the Rev. Robert Taylor, a minister of the Established Church of England. For a blasphemous discourse against our Lord Jesus Christ. Lord Tenterden on the bench. Wednesday, Oct. 24, 1827. In which the rev. clergyman was found guilty... New York, Pr. and pub. by Robert Wauchope,

1827. 39 p. CU; Ct; Nh. 29325

Ingersoll, Charles
At a... meeting of farmers & manufacturers & friends of farming & manufacturers, of the city & county of Philadelphia, held at the house of John Neville, in Germantown... May 31, 1827... The address... for the promotion of manufactures & the mechanic arts... [1827] 4 p. MWA. 29326

Ingersoll, Joseph R.
Annual discourse before the Philomathean Society of the University of Pennsylvania, pronounced on the 25th July, 1827. Philadelphia, Carey, Lee & Carey; [Mifflin & Parry, prs.] 1827. 32 p. DHEW; DLC; MB; MH; MHi; MWA; MdHi; MiD-B; NN; NjPT; NjR; PHi; PPAmP; PPL; PPPrHi; PU. 29327

[Ingham, Samuel Delucenna] 1779-1860
An exposition of the political character and principles of John Quincy Adams. Showing by historical documents, and incontestible facts, that he was educated a monarchist... Washington, Pr. by Duff Green, 1827. 21 p. CSmH; DLC; MBAt; MH; Nh-Hi; PHi; ScU. 29328

[----] ---- An exposition of the political conduct and principles of J.Q. Adams, showing... that he... has always been hostile to popular government. Burlington, Northern Sentinel, 1827. 15 p. BrMus. 29329

[----] ---- Philadelphia, Pr. at the Office of the American Sentinel, 1827. 15 p. IaU; MWA. 29330

Ingraham, Edward D., 1793-1854
A view of the insolvent laws of Pennsylvania. 2d ed., with considerable additions. Philadelphia, Philip H. Nicklin, Law bookseller. 1827. xxxix, 415 p. C; CSt; DLC; ICLaw; In-SC; MBS; MH-L; NNC-L; NNLI; OCLaw; PP; PPB; PPiAL; PU-L; W; BrMus. 29331

Interesting report of the rise and progress of the Protestant Episcopal Church, Kenyon College, and the new town of Gambier in the diocese of Ohio. [1827] 64 p. Thomson. 29332

Internal improvement. See Luzerne county.

The intolerants. See Comstock, W.

Irving, Christopher
A catechism of Grecian antiquities... 3d Amer. ed. New York, Collins & Hannay, J. & J. Harper, prs., 1827. 108 p. MH. 29333

---- A catechism of Roman antiquities... with a description of the public buildings of Rome. 3d Amer. ed. New York, Collins & Hannay, 1827. 106 p. CtHT-W; MB. 29334

Is this religion? See Tayler, Charles Benjamin.

J

Jackson, Andrew, pres. U.S., 1767-1845
[Enquirer extra. Richmond, Va., Aug. 7, 1827]... To the public. [Speech against Henry Clay, 18 July, 1827] Richmond, Va. [Pr. by the] Enquirer, 1827. Bdsd. ViU. 29335

---- Letter from Gen. Jackson to Mr. Southard [Together with Mr. Southard's answer. 1827] 7 p. DLC. 29336

Jackson, L.
L. Jackson's ornamental writing book;... New York, Engraved by S. Stiles, 1827. 12 l. NhD. 29337

Jackson, Samuel
An introductory lecture to the institutes of medicine... Published by request of the medical class. Philadelphia, Carey, Lea & Carey, Mifflin & Parry, prs., 1827. 41 p. CSmH; DLC; MBAt; MBCo; MWA; NNC-M; NNNAM; PHi; PPAmP; PPL; PU; RPB. 29338

---- Nature improved; or, A new method of teaching languages, exemplified by its application to Latin, Greek and French... Philadelphia, Pub. by Robert H. Small. James Kay, Jun., pr., 1827. 166 p. NNC; PPF; PPL; PU. 29339

Jackson almanac for 1828. Philadelphia [1827] 13 l. DLC. 29340

Jackson Corresponding Committee, Nashville, Tenn.
Circular, Nashville. April 25, 1827. Sir--It is probably not unknown to you, that a Jackson corresponding Committee has been organized in this place, having for its primary object the dissemination of truth, and the rescue of the character of Andrew Jackson... Nashville, 1827. 1 p. DLC. 29341

---- Charlottesville, Virginia
The following resolution was adopted at a meeting of the friends of Gen. Jackson in this county, on the 3d of December, 1827. [Charlottesville? 1827] Bdsd. ViU. 29342

---- Jefferson County, Ohio
Address of the Jackson committee of Jefferson County, Ohio. Under a deep conviction, that the pending presidential contest... Steubenville, Ohio, Sept. 22, 1827. 8 p. OClWHi. 29343

Jackson committee of Nashville
A letter from the Jackson committee of Nashville, in answer to one from a similar committee at Cincinnati, upon the subject of Gen. Jackson's marriage: accompanied by documents in an appendix, thereto annexed. Nashville, Pr. by Hall & Fitzgerald, 1827. 30 p. CSmH; DLC; NcD; NjR; T; WHi. 29344

Jacobs, Friedrich, 1764-1847
The Greek reader. From the 7th German ed., adapted to the translation of Buttman's Greek Grammar. 2d ed. Boston, Hilliard, Gray, Little & Wilkins, 1827. [Cambridge, From the University Press, by Hilliard, Metcalf & Co.] vi, 256 p. IEG; IaU; MB; MBAt; MBC; MH; MeB; MeBat; MeHi; NAlf; NCH; OCl; OO; RNHi; RP; TxHR; TxU-T. 29345

---- ---- 3d Amer. from the 9th German ed. with improvements, additional notes, and corrections, by David Patterson. New York, Collins & Hannay [etc., etc.] 1827. iv, 262, 1 l., 84 p. DLC; IU; KyHi; MH; MNF; MiD-B; MiU; NN; NSyU; OO; BrMus. 29346

---- The Latin reader. First part. From the 5th German ed. Boston, Hilliard, Gray, Little and Wilkins. 1827. [Stereotyped at the Boston Type and Stereotype Foundry.] 240 p. CtHT-W; MB; MH; MeHi; NCH; NNC; PHi; TxU-T. 29347

---- ---- Part II. Chiefly from the 4th German ed. of F. Jacobs and F. W. Doring. 2d ed. Boston, Hilliard, Gray, Little and Wilkins, 1827. 148 p. MH. 29348

Jahn, Johann, 1750-1816
Introduction to the Old Testament... Notes by Samuel H. Terner and Wm. R. Whittingham. New York, G. & C. Carvill, 1827. xxiii, [1], 546, [28] p. ICU; MeB; NIC; NNUT; Nj; OO; OU; PPLT; PPPD; ViU. 29349

James, John Angell, 1785-1859
The Christian father's present, to his children. 2d Northampton ed. Northampton [Mass.] Hiram Ferry, 1827. 237 p. DLC; NPV; BrMus. 29350

---- ---- 4th Amer. ed. Pub. by Jonathan Leavitt, New York: Crocker & Brewster, Boston: Gray & Bunce, prs., 1827. 2 v. MH-AH; MNotn; MNowdHi; MWA; MWiW; NN. 29351

James Somers, the pilgrim's son. Designed for youth. By a Lady of New-Haven. ...New-Haven, Pub. by A. H. Maltby. Treadway and Adams, pr., 1827. 77 p. CtHi; CtY; DLC; MH. 29352

Janeway, Jacob Jones, 1774-1858
Letters on the atonement: in which a contrast is instituted between the doctrine of the old and of the new school... Philadelphia, Pub. by A. Jenley, Clark & Raser, prs., 1827. 242 p. CtHC; CtW; GDC; ICU; KyLoP; NN; NNUT; NjP; NjR; PPPrHi; PPiW; ViRUT. 29353

[Janeway, James]
A token for children. Wendell, J. Metcalf, 1827. 16 p. MNF. 29354

Jay, William, 1769-1853
Prayers for the use of families; or, The domestic minister's assistant. Hartford, S. Andrus, 1827. 266 p. CtHi; MWiW; OrU. 29355

Jay, William, 1789-1858
Prize essays, on the institution of the Sabbath, the former by William Jay, Esq., to whom was awarded the premium of one hundred dollars, by a committee of the Synod of Albany, the latter by Rev. Samuel Nott, Jun. Pastor of the Church in Galway, N. Y. Albany, Pr. by Websters and Skinners, 1827. 56 p. CtHT-W; DLC; ICU; KU; MA; MB; MBAt; MDeeP; MWA; MiD-B; N; NCH; NjPT; NjR; NN; NT; OClWHi; OO; PHi; PPPrHi; TSewU. 29356

---- ---- Sandy-Hill, Wash. Co., N. Y., Pr. at the Sun office, May, 1827. 34 p. CSmH; MA; MNtcA; NN; NNG; VtMiS; BrMus. 29357

Jefferson County Republican Meeting. See National Republican Party. Ohio, Jefferson County.

Jefferson - No. III. See Carey, Mathew.

Jenkins, John
A candid inquiry into the nature and design of Christian baptism... Milton, Pr. by J. Campbell, Jr., 1827. 72 p. NcU. 29358

Jenks, Benjamin
Prayers and offices of devotion. For families, and for particular persons upon most occasions. Philadelphia, Judah Dobson, 1827. 336 p. InGrD; MiD; NNG; NOss; NjP; OCX. 29359

Jennings, Obadiah, 1778-1832
The history of Margaretta C. Hoge, who died May sixth, 1827. Written for the American Sunday School Union. Philadelphia, American Sunday School Union, 1827. 54 p. DLC; OClWHi; WHi. 29360

Jennings, Samuel K.
Dr. Samuel K. Jenning's protests and argument against the proceedings of his prosecutors,

in the Baltimore City Station, who have combined to prefer charges, against him and others ... Baltimore, Pr. by R. J. Matchett, 1827. 24 p. MsJMC; NBLiHi. 29361

Jess, Zachariah
The American tutor's assistant, improved, or, A compendius system of decimal, practical arithmetic... Baltimore, Cushing & Jewett, 1827. 188, ii, 10, [1], 10, [2], 3 p. MdHi; NN; PAtM; PU. 29362

Jews
Compendium of the order of the burial service and rules for the mourners, &c. compiled by desire, and published on account of the Hevrah Hesed v'emet of the Keneset Kodesh sfradiim Shearit Yisrael. New York, Pr. by S. H. Jackson, 5587 [1827] 36 p. NN; NNJ; PPDrop. 29363

John of the score; or, The penitent robber... Philadelphia, Pub. by American Sunday School Union, 1827. 15 p. MWey. 29364

John Williams, or The sailor boy. Boston, Bowles and Dearborn, pub., Isaac R. Butts & co., prs. 1827. 34 p. MB; MBMu. 29365

Johnson, Francis
Speech of Mr. F. Johnson, of Kentucky [1827?] 32 p. MWA; PPL. 29366

Johnson, James, 1777-1845
An essay on morbid sensibility of the stomach and bowels, as the proximate cause, or characteristic condition of indigestion... Philadelphia, B. & T. Kite, 1827. 154 p. CtY; DLC; DNLM; ICU-R; MNF; MdBM; MoSW-M; NBMS; NBuU-M; NNNAM; NjP; OC; OClM; PPC; PPL; TU. 29367

Johnson, Joseph, 1776-1862
Letters addressed to the Agricultural Society of South-Carolina, on the means of improving the health of the lower country. With corr. and additions. Charleston, Pr. and for sale by A. E. Miller, 1827. 12 p. CSmH. 29368

Johnson, Samuel
The rambler. A new ed., corr. from the originals with an historical and biographical preface, by Alex. Chalmers... Philadelphia, Pub. by J. J. Woodward, 1827. 4 v. GAuY; GDC; GMM; IaMp; MA; MB; MdHi; MsJS; NKings; Nh; NhPet; ScDuE; TCU; WMHi. 29369

Johnson, Samuel, 1709-1784
Rasselas, a tale. Hartford, S. Andrus, pub., 1827. 144 p. CtY; ICU; MWHi; MeU; MoSW; NjP; OUrC; TNJ; ViU. 29370

Johnson, Thomas
The last will and testament of Thomas Johnson of Greenfield, County of Franklin, in favour of the trustees of Amherst College. Brattleboro, Pr. for the pub., 1827. 24 p. MB; MBAt; MBC; MHi; MiU; MS; MWiW; NIC; PHi. 29371

Johnston, Charles, b. 1768
A narrative of the incidents attending the capture, detention, and ransom of Charles Johnston, of Botetourt county, Virginia, who was made prisoner by the Indians, on the river Ohio, in the year 1790... New-York, Pr. by J. & J. Harper, 1827. 264 p. CtSoP; CtY; DLC; IC; ICHi; ICN; ICU; IU; In; InHi; KHi; KU; LU; MA; MB; MH; MWA; MdBE; MdBL; MdHi; MiD-B; MiU; MnHi; MoSU; NBLiHi; NIC; NNS; NSmB; NT; NbU; NcD; OFH; OHi; PHi; PPi; PPL; RPA; RPJCB; T; TKL; Vi; ViL; ViRVal; ViU; WHi. 29372

Johnston, Josiah Stoddard, 1784-1833

Speech of Mr. J. S. Johnston, of Lou., on the bill to regulate the commercial intercourse between the United States and the British colonies: delivered in the Senate of the United States, Feb. 23, 1827. Washington, Pr. by Gales & Seaton, 1827. 32 p. DLC; MWA; PPL. 29373

[Johnstone Mrs. Christian I. M.]
Elizabeth de Bruce. By the author of Clan Albin... New York, J. & J. Harper, 1827. 2 v. CtY; LU; MBL; MWalp. 29374

Jones, Mrs.
An account of the loss of the Wesleyan Missionaries, Messrs. White, Hillier... in the Maria Mail boat... Feb. 28, 1826. New York, N. Bangs & J. Emory, 1827. 24 p. MBAt; MBC; MBNMHi. 29375

Jones, Isaac
Questions adapted to the constitution of the United States; designed to be used in academies and common schools. Boston, Richardson & Lord, 1827. 12 p. CtW; M; MH; MHi; Nh-Hi; WHi. 29376

Jones, Peter, Chippewa chief, 1802-1856, tr.
Collection of hymns for the use of native Christians of the Iroquois, to which are added a few hymns in the Chipeway tongue. New York, Pr. at the Conference office by Hoyt, 1827. 54 [i. e. 99) p. CtW. 29377

Jones, Samuel, 1769-1853
...Opinion in the case of Lansing, appellant against Goelet respondent on appeal. Albany, Pr. by Packard & Van Benthuysen, 1827. 55 p. N. 29378

Jones, Thomas
A sermon, delivered on Sabbath evening, Sept. 30th, 1827, in the Independent Church in Gloucester, Mass. Gloucester, Pr. at the Telegraph Office, 1827. 15 p. MiD-B; BrMus. 29379

---- Immortal life, revealed in favor of all mankind... A sermon delivered... July 29, 1827 ...Gloucester [Mass.] Pr. by Wm. E. P. Rogers, 1827. 12 p. CSmH; BrMus. 29380

Jones, Thomas P., 1774-1848
An address on the progress of manufactures and internal improvement, in the United States; and particularly, on the advantages to be derived from the employment of slaves in the manufacturing of cotton and other goods. Delivered in the hall of the Franklin Institute, Nov. 6, 1827. Philadelphia, J. Dobson, 1827. 18 p. CLU; DLC; LU; MBAt; NNNAM; NcU; PHi; PPAmP. 29381

[----] Observations upon the automaton chess player of von Kempelen, and upon other automata and androides, now exhibiting in the United States, by Mr. Maelzel. Philadelphia, J. Dobson, 1827. 12 p. DLC. 29382

Jones, William, 1726-1800
An essay on the church... Philadelphia, Pr. by Jesper Harding, 1827. 52, [1] p. CSmH; IObB; MBAt; MWA; NjR; PPL; PPPrHi; RPB. 29383

Joseph; or, Sketches of scripture history: illustrating the life and character of Joseph, the son of Jacob, and the first ruler of Egypt. 3rd ed., rev. by the Committee of Publication. Philadelphia, American Sunday School Union, 1827. 216 p. C-S; MBL; BrMus. 29384

Josse, Augustin Louis, 1763-1841
A grammar of the Spanish language, with practical exercises ... Rev., amended, imp. and enl. by F. Sales. 3d Amer. ed. Boston, Munroe & Francis, 1827. 468 p. CLSU; CtY; KyDC; KyLo; MA; MB; MH; MdBL; MeBat; MoSW; Ms; NIC; NNC; OCX; RPB; VtU; WM. 29385

Journal of a tour of a detachment of cadets, from the A. L. S. & M. academy, Middletown, to the city of Washington, in December, 1826. Middletown, Conn., W. D. Starr, 1827. 100 p. CSmH; DLC. 29386

Jouy, Étienne, 1764-1846
Sylla, a tragedy, in five acts. Tr. from the French, and adapted for representation at the Chatham theatre, by a citizen of New York. New York, E. M. Murden, 1827. 78 p. 1 l. DLC; ICU; MH; MWA; PU; RPB; BrMus. 29387

[Judah, Samuel Benjamin Herbert]
The buccaneers: a romance of our own count[r]y in its ancient day...[by] Yclept Terentius Phlogobombos [pseud.] ... In five books. Boston, Munroe & Francis, 1827. 2 v. CtY; DLC; ICN; LNHT; MBAt; MH; NN; PU; ViU. 29388

[----] ---- 2d ed. Boston, Munroe & Francis; New York, C. S. Francis, 1827. 2 v. CtHT; CtY; DLC; ICU; LNHT; MB; MBAt; MH; NN; NNS; WHi. 29389

[----] ---- The imprint whereof is at New-York, A. D. 1827. 384 p. (The complete work is in 5 books. This is evidently only books 3 to 5 complete.) CSmH. 29390

Judson, Albert
A series of questions on the selected Scripture lessons for Sabbath schools...In two volumes ... Philadelphia, American Sunday School Union, 1827. 168 p. IaCh; MH; NjR. 29391

---- ---- 3d ed. Philadelphia, American Sunday School Union, 1827. 2 v. NNUT. 29392

Junius, pseud.
The letters of Junius... Boston, Stereotyped by J. Reed, 1827. 2 v. C; CoCsC; Ct; CtHC; DLC; KU; KyHi; MB; MdBL; MiU-C; MoK; OClW; OHi; PP; PPDrop; PReaA; PV; RPB; ViU; WvC; WyU. 29393

The juvenile Plutarch; containing accounts of the lives of celebrated children, and of the infancy of persons who have been illustrious for their virtues or talents. Boston, Munroe and Francis, New-York, C. S. Francis, 1827. 252 p. DLC; KU; MB; MH; NNC; NUtHi; PPL; ScCliTO. 29394

The juvenile souvenir. By the editor of "The juvenile miscellany 1828. Boston, Marsh & Capen [1827] 184 p. MB; MWA; TxU. 29395

K

Keagy, John M.
The Pestallozzian primer; or, First step in teaching children the art of reading and thinking. Harrisburg, Pa., Pr. by John S. Wiestling, 1827. 126, [1] p. CtHT-W; M; MH; MHi; NN; NNC; OO; PPAmP. 29396

Keene, Arthur F.
When rays of summer. New York, Engraved, pr. and sold by E. Riley, 1827. 3 p. MB. 29397

Kelley, Hall Jackson, 1790-1874
First spelling book, or Child's instructor. 8th ed. Boston, Lincoln & Edmands, 1827. 84 p.

MH. 29398

---- Kelley's second spelling book, designed for common schools; containing the elements of the English language... 5th ed. Boston, Lincoln & Edmands, 1827. 168 p. MA. 29399

[Kennedy, Grace] 1782-1825
Anna Ross; a story for children. By the author of "The decision" - "Profession is not principle." "Father Clement," &c. New-York, Pub. by Wm. Burgess, Jr., 1827. 156 p. DLC; MiGr; PPL. 29400

[----] ---- American Sunday School Union. Philadelphia, 1827. 160 p. NN; NSmB; BrMus. 29401

---- The decision; or, Religion must be all, or is nothing. 5th Amer. ed. New York, Wm. Burgess, Jr., 1827. 108 p. IObB; PHi. 29402

[----] ---- 6th Amer. ed. Princeton, D. A. Borrenstein, Princeton Press, 1827. 96 p. MH; NjP. 29403

[----] Dunallan; or, Know what you judge. By the author of "The Decision," "Father Clement," &c. &c. Boston, Pub. by Charles Ewer, and Crocker & Brewster; New York, Jonathan Leavitt, 1827. 2 v. CtY; KU; LNHT; MBL; MH. 29404

[----] Father Clement, a Roman-Catholic story... Boston, Pub. by Crocker & Brewster, New York, Jonathan Leavitt, 1827. 252 p. PPL. 29405

[----] ---- From the 6th Edinburgh ed. New-York, E. Duyckinck, 1827. 246 p. DLC; ICU; MB; NNC; PV; RPB. 29406

[----] Profession is not principle; or, The name of Christian is not Christianity... 3d Amer. ed. New-York, Pub. by John P. Haven, American Tract Society House, Sleight & George, prs., Jamaica L. I., 1827. 162 p. PPL. 29407

[----] ---- 3d Amer. ed. Philadelphia, Pub. by J. J. Woodward, Russell & Martien, prs., 1827. 162 p. CtHC. 29408

Kennedy, Thomas, 1776-1832
Speech of Thomas Kennedy, esq. at the Jackson meeting, held at the court-house in Hagerstown, August 4th, 1827. Hagerstown, Pr. by Wm. D. Bell [1827] 14 p. CSmH; MdBP. 29409

[Kenney, James] 1780-1849
... Sweethearts and wives. In three acts. Philadelphia, A. R. Poole [etc.] Washington, P. Thompson; [etc., etc., 1827] 66 p. DLC; MB; MH; NN; TxU. 29410

Kentish, Mrs.
How to be happy; or, The cottage of content: and the watercress boy. New-Haven, A. H. Maltby and co., 1827. 23 p. CtY; MnS. 29411

Kentucky
An act to remove the unconstitutional obstructions which have been thrown in the way of the Court of Appeals. [Frankfort, 1827] 28 p. NN has photostat of first page of C. P. Everitt copy. 29412

---- Acts passed at the first session of the thirty fifth General Assembly, for the commonwealth of Kentucky. Begun and held in the town of Frankfort, on Monday, the fourth day of December, in the year eighteen hundred and twenty six. Frankfort, Jacob H. Holeman, state pr., 1827. 205 p. A-SC; Ar-SC; CSfLaw; IaU-L; In-SC; Ky; KyLoF;

KyLoU-L; KyLxT; KyU; L; MdBB; Mi-L; Mo; NNLI; Nb; Nj; Nv; OrPML; OrSC; R; RPL; T; W; Wa-L. 29413

---- Journal of the House of Representatives of the commonwealth of Kentucky, begun and held in the town of Frankfort, on Monday, the fourth day of December, in the year of Our Lord 1826. Frankfort, Pr. by Jacob H. Holeman, pr. to the state, 1826 [i. e. 1827] 367 p. Ky; KyBgW; KyHi; KyLxT; KyU; KyU-L. 29414

---- Journal of the Senate of the commonwealth of Kentucky, begun and held in the town of Frankfort on Monday the fourth day of December, in the year of Our Lord 1826. Frankfort, Pr. by Jacob H. Holeman, pr. for the state, 1826 [i. e. 1827] 332 p. Ky; KyLo; KyLoF; KyLxT; KyU; KyU-L; MHi. 29415

---- Reports of cases at common law and in equity argued and decided in the Court of appeals, of the commonwealth of Kentucky. By Thomas B. Monroe, reporter. Containing the cases decided in the year 1825 and 1826. Frankfort, Pr. by Albert C. Hodges-Commentator office, 1827. 622 p. Az; CoSC; DLC; IDaGL; Ky; KyBgW; KyDC; KyLxT; MH-L; MdBB; MnDuB; N-L; NNB; PPB; RPL; W; WvW-L. 29416

Keppel, George. See Albemarle, George Thomas Keppel, 6th earl of.

Kératry, Auguste Hilarion de, 1769-1859
Tower of Helvin; or The last of the Beaumanoir... Philadelphia, Desilver, 1827. 2 v. CtHT; PWW. 29417

Kerr, Robert B.
A review of some parts of the Rev. S. W. Crawford's sermon on creeds and confessions. Chambersburg, Pa., Pr. by J. Pritts, 1827. 58 p. DLC; PPPrHi. 29418

[Kesley, William]
A few plain and candid objections, to the committee appointed by the Rev. J. M. Hanson, to try the charges exhibited against the reforming local ministers in the Baltimore City Station. By one of the accused. Baltimore, Pr. by Wm. Wooddy, 1827. 16 p. MdBS; MdHi. 29419

Key, Francis Scott
A discourse on education, delivered in St. Anne's Church, Annapolis, after the commencement of St. John's College... Office of the Maryland Gazette, Annapolis, J. Green, pr., 1827. 26, xviii p. DLC; KyLx; MMeT; MdAS; MdBP; MdHi; NNG; PLERC-Hi; WStfSF. 29420

Key to Vivian Grey... 1st Amer. from the 10th London ed. Philadelphia, Carey, Lea & Carey, 1827. 25 p. NN. 29421

Kimball, Charles Otis
The claims of Free-Masonry. An address delivered at the consecration and installation of Mt. Horeb Royal Arch Chapter, in Lowell, Mass., Aug. 31, 1826. Boston, Pr. by Beals and Homer, 1827. 19, [1] p. MH; MWA; NNFM; NNUT. 29422

The kind little boy. See Cameron Mrs. Lucy Lyttleton (Butt).

Kinne, William, 1781-1848
A short system of practical arithmetic, compiled from the best authorities, to which is annexed a short plan of bookkeeping. 6th ed., rev., corr. & greatly enl. by Daniel Robinson. Hallowell, Pr. and pub. by Glaz-

ier & Co., 1827. 240 p. DAU. 29423

Kirkham, Samuel

English grammar in familiar lectures, accompanied by a compendium... 5th ed., enl. and much imp. Cincinnati, Pub. by N. & G. Guilford, and by the author. W. M. & O. Farnsworth, jr., prs. 1827. 192 p. InGrD. 29424

Kite's town and country almanac for 1828. By William Collom. Philadelphia, Benj. & Thomas Kite, [1827] 18 l. CLU; DLC; InU; MWA; N; PHC; PHi. 29425

Kittredge, Jonathan, 1793-1864

An address, upon the effects of ardent spirits, delivered in the town hall of Lyme, N. H., Jan. 8, 1827. Canandaigua, Pr. by Bemis, Morse & Ward, 1827. 24 p. CSmH; MWA; NCanHi; WHi. 29426

---- ---- Pub. by the Lyme Association for the Promotion of Temperance. Concord, Pr. by Jacob B. Moore, 1827. 32 p. CSmH; DLC; MBAt; MBC; MHi; MWA; MeHi; NNC; PPL; PPPrHi. 29427

---- Intemperance. Extracts from an address upon the effects of ardent spirits, delivered in the town hall of Lyme, N. H. [Lyme, 1827] 12 p. DNLM; MB. 29427a

Die kleine Lieder Sammlung, oder Auszug aus dem Psalterspiel der Kinder Zions... 2. Auflage. Ephrata, Gedruckt bey Joseph Baumann, 1827. 216 p. PPL. 29428

Kneeland, Abner

Kneeland's key to the new orthography. New York, Pub. and sold by the author, no. 80 Prince street... 1827. 96 p. MB; NNC. 29429

Knickerbocker's almanac for 1828. By David Young. New-York, Caleb Bartlett [1827] 18 l. DLC; MWA; NHi. 29430

Knight, Richard, 1771-1863

History of the General or Six Principle Baptists in Europe and America: in two parts. Pub. under the patronage of the Rhode Island Yearly Meeting. Providence, Smith and Parmenter, 1827. 367 p. DLC; ICU; KyLoS; LNB; MB; MBAt; MBC; MH-AH; MWA; MeLB; NBuG; NNUT; NRAB; PPL; RNHi; RNR; RP; TxHuT. 29431

Knox, Samuel

A letter to the trustees of Frederick Academy, from the late principal. Baltimore, Pr. by Richard J. Matchett, 1827. 36 p. MdHi. 29432

Knowledge. New York, 1827. 8 p. (Friedman (N. Y.) catal. 173 (1931), item 77. From NN imp. catal., but not in NN. (1932)) 29433

Kotzebue, August Friedrich Ferdinand von, 1761-1819

Pizarro; a tragedy; taken from the German drama of Kotzebue. Boston, J. H. A. Frost, 1827. 70 p. MH; RPB. 29434

---- ---- .... carefully corr. from the prompt books of the Philadelphia theatre, by M. Lopez, prompter. Philadelphia, A. R. Poole, and Ash & Mason; New York, E. M. Murden; [etc., etc.] 1827] 59 p. CtY; DLC; NjR. 29435

Kurtz, Benjamin, 1795-1865

Pastoral address... transmitted as testimonial of affection to his congregation in Hagerstown, Md., and vicinity. Gettysburg, Pa., Pr. by the Theological Seminary, 1827. 15 p. PPLT. 29436

---- Sendschreiben, des Ehrwürden Herrn Benjamin Kurtz, der jetzt Europa durchreist, als

Agent sum Bosten des Theologischen Seminars, errichtete durch die General Synode der Evangelisch Lutherischen Kirche in den Vereinigten Staaten von Nordamerika als ein Beweis der Liebe seiner Gemeinden, in und um Heogerstadt zugesandt, und durch genannte Gemeinden zum Druck befördert. Gettysburg, Pa., H. C. Neinstedt, Drucker, 1827. 16 p. C; P; PPL; PPLT. 29437

Kurtz, Heinrich
Gott ist die Liebe; eine Predigt Über 1. Brief Johannis, Cap. 4, Vers 16. Seinen lieben Gemeinen in Northampton Caunty und allen seinen Freunden dortiger Gegend zum Andenken hinterlassen von Heinrich Kurtz. [Easton, Pa.] Gedruckt auf Kosten des Verfassers; H. Held, Drucker [1827] 14 p. PHi. 29438

Kurzgefasster Bericht des Mords, Verhörs und Betragen des James Quinn, welcher auf den 9ten Februar, 1827... für die Ermordung seiner Gattin, Bäddy Quinn, hingerichtet worden ist. Libanon, Gedruckt für den Liebhaber, 1827. 8 p. PHi; PPL. 29439

L

Labourers in the East... See Grierson, Miss.

Laconics; or Instructive miscellanies, selected from the best authors, ancient and modern. By a general reader. Philadelphia, Pr. by Wm. Brown, 1827. 188 p. MH; OFH; PPL. 29440

Ladd, William, 1778-1841
Address to seamen, delivered at Portland, before the Portland Marine Bible Society, Dec. 17, 1826. Portland, Pr. by Arthur Shirley, 1827. 16 p. MBC; MeBat; MeHi; MiD-B; NjPT; RPB. 29441

[----] The essays of Philanthropos [pseud.] on peace & war, which first appeared in the Christian mirror, pr. at Portland, Maine. Rev. and cor. by the author. 2d ed. Exeter, N. H., J. T. Burnham in behalf of the Exeter, and other peace societies, 1827. 173 p. 1 l. DLC; KU; MB; MBC; MH; MMeT-L; MNe; NB; Nh-Hi; NhPet; PCC; TNF; VtMiM; WHi; BrMus. 29442

[----] Essays on peace & war, which first appeared in the Christian Mirror, printed at Portland, Me. New series. By Philanthropos [pseud.] Rev. and corr. by the author. Portland, Pr. by A. Shirley, 1827. 279, [3] p. CtHC; DLC; GDC; MB; MNe; MeHi; MeLB; NN; NhD; PPL; PU; RPB. 29443

Lady, A., pseud. See Illustrations of the four first degrees of female masonry.

A lady of Boston, pseud. See Tales of the fireside.

A lady of Charleston, S. C., pseud. See Murden, Mrs. Eliza (Crawley).

A lady of Maine. See Wood, Sally Sayward.

A lady of New-Haven, pseud. See Sowers, James.

A lady of Philadelphia. See Hall, Mrs. Sarah (Ewing).

Lafayette almanac for 1828. Baltime, James Lovegrove; Wm. Wooddy, pr. [1827] 18 l. MWA; NjR. 29444

Lafitte; or, The Baratarian chief. A tale. Fall River, Pr. by Nathan Hall, 1827. 70 p. RPB. 29445

Lambert
Little Henri, a German tale; translated from the French of M. Lambert. New York, O. A. Roorbach, W. E. Dean, pr., 1827. 106 p. DLC; MH; NNU. 29446

Lamson, Alvan, 1792-1864
A discourse, preached at the dedication of the Bethlehem Church, in Augusta, Maine. Oct. 18, 1827. Augusta, Pr. by Eaton & Severance, 1827. 32 p. CSansS; CtSoP;DLC; ICMe; MBAt; MB-FA; MBC; MH; MHi; MeBat; MeHi; NjR; RPB. 29447

---- The foundation of our confidence in the Saviour, a sermon, preached at the ordination of the Rev. Charles C. Sewall, as minister of the First Unitarian Church, in Danvers... Apr. 11, 1827. Pub. for the First Unitarian Church in Danvers. Dedham, Pr. by H. & W. H. Mann, 1827. 46 p. ICMe; MBAt; MBC; MH; MHi; MWA; MeB; MiD-B; RPB; BrMus. 29448

---- ---- 2d ed. Boston, Bowles & Dearborn, Isaac R. Butts & Co., prs. 1827. 36 p. CBPac; CtSoP; ICMe; ICU; MA; MB; MBAt; MH; MHi; MWA; NjR; OClWHi; WHi. 29449

Lancaster agricultural almanac for 1828. By Charles F. Egelman. Lancaster, John Bear [1827] 18 l. DLC; MWA; PHi; PYHi. 29450

[Landon, Letitia Elizabeth, afterwards Mrs. George McLean] 1802-1838
The golden violet, with its tales of romance and chivalry: and other poems. By L. E. L. ... Philadelphia, H. C. Carey & I. Lea, 1827. 244 p. DLC; MB; MBr; MH; MNBedf; NNS. 29451

La Roche, René, 1795-1872
An oration delivered before the Philadelphia Medical Society, pursuant to appointment. February 3, 1827. Pub. by the society. Philadelphia, Mifflin & Parry, prs., 1827. 31 p. DLC; DNLM; MB; MdBJ-W; MiD-B; NBuU-M; NNNAM; OC; PHi; PPAmP; PPHa; PPL. 29452

A lash for petty tyrants, or Government of laws, not despotism. Being an account of outrages committed by some of the police officers of New York. In English and Spanish. ... New-York, Pr. for the Translator, 1827. 13 p. Sabin 39130 (not loc.) 29453

The last day of the week... Philadelphia, American Sunday School Union [1827] 107 p. MiD-B; MiHi. 29454

The last of the lairds. See Galt, John.

Last of the Mohicans. See Cooper, James Fenimore.

A late member of the craft, pseud. See Revelations in masonry.

Law, John
To the citizens of Knox, Daviess & Martin counties. Fellow citizens--On my return to this place last Wednesday, after an absence of nearly two months, I found a pamphlet of twenty-two pages in circulation... by the writer, Mr. John Ewing... John Law. Vincennes, May 29, 1827. In. 29455

Law Academy of Philadelphia
Constitution and by-laws of the Law Academy of Philadelphia. Philadelphia, Pub. by the Law Academy, Mifflin & Parry, prs.,

1827. 14 [2] p. PHi; PU. 29456

The law and the facts, submmitted [sic] to the consideration of the militia of the United States. [n. p., 1827?] 24 p. MiU-C. 29457

Lawrence, Myron, 1799-1852
An oration, delivered at Barre, Massachusetts, before Mount Zion lodge of Free and accepted Masons, at the festival of St. John the Baptist, June 23, A. L. 5827. Belchertown [Mass.] Pr. at the Sentinel and Journal office, 1827. 20 p. CSmH. 29458

Lawrence & Lemay's North Carolina almanac for 1828. By Wm. Collom. Raleigh, Lawrence & Lemay [1827] 18 l. NcD; NcHiC; NcU. 29459

A Layman, pseud. See A review of the Rev. Dr. Channing's discourse.

Lea, Isaac, 1792-1886
Description of six new species of the genus Unio... anatomical observations... Read before American Philosophical Society, Nov. 2, 1827. [Philadelphia] 1827. 38 p. IaDaM; PPF. 29460

[Lea, Pryor]
Circular. To the voters of the Second Congressional District of Tennessee. Fellow-citizens, will you do yourselves the justice and me the favor to read this circular, and weigh well its import? ...[1827] 12 p. MBAt. 29461

Leavitt
Lines in memory of Porter Leavitt, aged 25 years, 4 months, and 16 days; late master of Schooner Leander, of Portland who was washed overboard, from the wreck of said vessel, and lost, on his passage from Portland for St. Michael's at the dawning of day, (5 o'clock) Monday, Feb. 19th, 1827... Written by his father. 1 p. DLC. 29462

Leavitt, Joshua, 1794-1873
Easy lessons in reading: for the use of the younger classes in common schools. 7th ed. New Haven, A. H. Maltby, 1827. 179 p. CtY; MWA. 29463

---- ---- 8th ed. Stereotyped by T. H. Carter & Co., Boston. Keene, N. H., Pub. by John Prentiss, 1827. 156 p. MFiHi; NbL; NhD. 29464

---- ---- (7th New-England and) 3d Watertown ed. Watertown, N. Y., Pub. by Knowlton & Rice, 1827. MWA. 29465

Leavitt's improved New-England farmer's almanack for 1828. By Dudley Leavitt. Concord, Jacob B. Moore [1827] 12 l. CLU; CtHi; DLC; MBAt; MWA; MiD-B; NBLiHi; Nh-Hi; NjR; OClWHi; WHi. 29466

Lee, Anna Maria
Memoirs of eminent female writers, of all ages and countries. Philadelphia, J. Grigg, 1827. 183 p. CtHT; DLC; KU; LNHT; MBAt; MWA; OO; PPA; ViU. 29467

---- ---- Philadelphia, T. Desilver and Towar & Hogan. J. Harding, pr., 1827. 183 p. DLC; IC; IObB; LN; MWA; NN; PPi; TNJ. 29468

Lee, Henry, 1756-1818
Memoirs of the war in the southern department of the United States... New ed., with corr. left by the author, and with notes and additions by H. Lee, the author of the campaign of '81. Washington, Pr. by P. Force, 1827. 466 p. CSmH; CtW; DLC; GA; IU; KHi; KyBg-W; LN; MA; MB; MH;

MdBE; MiD-B; NBLiHi; NN; NWM; NcU; Nh-Hi; NjP; NjR; OClWHi; PHC; PHi; PPAmP; PU; RPB; ScU; TNJ; TxU; ViU; WHi; BrMus. 29469

Lee, Jonathan
The truths of the Bible harmonious, and inseparably united. A sermon, preached at Otis, Mass. Sept. 16, 1827. Pittsfield, Pr. by Phinehas Allen, 1827. 20 p. OO; RPB. 29470

Lehigh Coal and Navigation Company
Facts illustrative of the character of the anthracite, or Lehigh coal, found in the great mines at Mauch Chunk, in possession of the Lehigh Coal and Navigation Company... Philadelphia, Pr. by S. W. Conrad, 1827. 20 p. DLC; MHi; PPAmP. 29471

Leigh, Hezekiah G.
Funeral sermon of the Rev. Benjamin Ogburn preached by Rev. Hezekiah G. Leigh minister of the Methodist Episcopal Church. New York, Pr. for the author at the Conference Office, Azor Hoyt, pr., 1827. 22 p. TxDaM. 29472

Leland, Aaron Whitney, 1787-1871
Christian mourning: a funeral discourse, occasioned by the death of Mrs. Sarah Hibben... on the 26th of July, 1827. Charleston, Pr. by C. C. Sebring, 1827. 31 p. MBC. 29473

Lemprier, John, 1765?-1824
Lempriere's Biographical dictionary... Hartford, D. F. Robinson & Co., 1827. 444 p. PPL. 29474

---- A classical dictionary containing a copious account of all the proper names mentioned in ancient authors. 6th Amer. ed. New York, Pub. by Evert Duyckinck, Collins & Co. [etc., etc.] W. E. Dean, pr., 1827. xvi, 890 [12] p. AMob; FDef; Ky; LNMus; MB; MBC; MH; MWA; MoSMa; NBuCC; NbCrD; NcEc; OBerB; Vi. 29475

Leonard, Ezra
A sermon, the substance of which was delivered at the Third Parish, in Gloucester, May 20, 1827... Gloucester [Mass.] Pr. at the Telegraph office, 1827. 20 p. CSmH; NjR. 29476

Leonard, Levi Washburn, 1790?-1864
The literary and scientific class book, embracing the leading facts and principles of science... Keene, N. H., John Prentiss, 1827. xii, 318 p. CtHT-W; DLC; IU; MB; MH; MWHi; NCH; NNC; OU. 29477

Le Sage, Alain Rene, 1668-1747
The adventures of Gil Blas of Santillane, trans. from the French of Le Sage by T. Smollet, M. D., to which are prefixed Memoirs of the author. New York, S. Marks, 1827. 3 v. MdBS; NcC; NcHil; RPB; ScNC; WyU. 29478

---- The Devil upon two sticks. Trans. from the Diable boiteaux of M. Le Sage. To which are prefixed Asmodens's crutches. A critical letter upon the work; and Dialogues between two chimneys of Madrid. Boston, Pub. by J. P. Peaslee, 1827. 340 p. ICMe; NP; NRAB; NWatt. 29479

Leslie, Eliza, 1787-1858
Miss Leslie's seventy-five receipts for pastry, cakes and sweetmeats. 20th ed. enl. New York and Boston, C. S. Francis and co., [1827] 120 p. DLC; OCl; TNJ. 29480

Lesueur, Charles Alexandre
American ichthyology, or, Natural history of the fishes of North America with coloured figures from drawings executed from nature. New Harmony, Ia., 1827. 8 unnumbered pages of text and 4 unnumbered plates. Muséum d'Histoire Naturelle, Le Havre, France. 29481

A letter on devotion at Church, from the Christian Examiner Vol. IV. no. IV. Boston, The Christian Examiner. Stephen Foster, pr., 1827. 12 p. DLC; ICMe; MBAU; MBAt; MH; MWA; MiD-B; PPL. 29482

Letter on the use and abuse of incorporations, addressed to the delegation from the city of New-York, in the state Legislature. By one of their constituents. New-York, G. & C. Carvill, H. C. Sleight, pr., Jamaica, 1827. 59 p. CtHC; CtY; MB; MH; MH-BA; MdHi; NIC; P; PPAmP; PPL; PPiW; PU. 29483

Letter to the citizens of Lancaster county... See Miner, Charles.

A letter to the editor of the Charleston Observer. See Upham, Charles Wentworth.

Letter to the Secretary of War. See Scott, Winfield.

A letter to the Trinitarian Congregational Church in Waltham, Massachusetts. By a layman. Boston, Christian Examiner, 1827. 18 p. CBPac; ICMe; M; MH; MWA; NNUT. 29484

The letter writer: containing a great variety of letters on the following subjects: relationship-business- love, courtship, and marriage-friendship, and miscellaneous letters... Charlestown, G. Davidson, 1827. 276 p. MB; NIl; NN; NNe. 29485

Letters by a South Carolinian. See Grigsby, Hugh Blair.

Letters explanatory of the difficulties existing in the Baptist Church at Salisbury, N. H. Concord, 1827. 24 p. DLC; Nh-Hi. 29486

Letters from the Bahama Islands. See Hart, Miss.

Letters of Christian sympathy to mourners. New York, Pub. by John Midwinter, 1827. 146 p. CtW; CtY; MB; RPB. 29487

Letters on religious persecution. See Carey, Mathew.

Letters on the new theatre... See Hale, David.

Letters to the Rev. John Potts; being a reply to his Sermon on Predestination delivered in the Methodist Episcopal Church in Bridgeton, W. N. J. Feb. 18th, 1827. By a Calvinist. Pr. by Robert Johnston. Bridgeton, W. N. J. 1827. 48 p. TxDaM; WHi. 29488

Levings, Noah, 1796-1849
The Christian's instructor instructed, containing remarks upon a late publication of the Rev. Josiah Hopkins, A. M., pastor of the Congregational Church in New Haven, Vt., with a short appendix containing extracts from the articles of Addison Consociation, ... Middlebury, Pr. by J. W. Copeland, 1827. 237 p. CtW; CtY; IaFayU; MoS; NNMHi; NSyU; VtHi; VtMiS; VtU. 29489

Levizac, Jean Pons Victor Lecountz de, d. 1813
A theoretical and practical grammar of the French tongue: in which the present usage is dis-

played agreeably to the decision of the French Academy. 5th Amer. from the last London ed., rev. and corr. by Mr. Stephen Pasquier... New York, Evert Duyckinck, G. Long, Collins & Co., Collins & Hannay, G. & C. Carvill, O. A. Roorbach. W. E. Dean, pr., 1827. x, 444 p. CtHT-W; MB; MBC; MH; NHem; NNC; NjP. 29490

Lewis, Enoch, 1776-1856
Solutions of the most difficult questions in Lewis' Algebra. Philadelphia, Pub. by Kimber & Sharpless, I. Ashmead, pr., 1827. 40 p. CtHT-W. 29491

Lewis, Isaac, 1773-1854
A sermon addressed to the Legislature of the state of Connecticut at the annual election in Hartford, May 2, 1827. Hartford, C. Babcock, pr., 1827. 21 p. CSmH; Ct; CtHi; CtHT; CtSoP; DLC; M; MB; MBC; MHi; NCH; NIC; NN; NhHi; OClWHi; VtMiM. 29492

Lewis, John, 1784-1858
Observations on the objects and progress of Philological enquiries; with remarks on some of the principles of technical grammar now used as instruments in the acquisition of languages. Fredericksburg, Pr. by John Minor, 1827. 36 p. CSmH; NIC; NN; PPAmP. 29493

Lewis, William
Elements of the game of chess; or, A new method of instruction in that celebrated game, founded on scientific principles... Rev. and corr. by an American amateur. New-York, G. & C. Carvill, 1827. 275 p. MWA; MdBE; NN; NNC; NNS; NR; OCl; PP; PU; RPB; WU; BrMus. 29494

Lexington, Ky. Church of Christ on Mill Street
Address of the Church of Christ on Mill-Street, in Lexington, Kentucky, to the moderator of the Elkhorn Association. Lexington, Ky., Pr. for the Church, by Thomas T. Skillman, 1827. 64 p. KyLoS; MNtcA; NNUT; OCHP. 29495

---- First Baptist Church
A response, by a committee of the First Baptist Church, in Lexington, Ky. (To an address, pub. by those of her body who have separated from her under the name of The Church of Christ, on Mill Street, in Lexington.) To the moderator of the Elkhorn Association. Lexington, Ky., Pr. by A. G. Meriwether, 1827. 24 p. KU; KyLoS; KyU. 29496

Library Society of Richmond
A catalogue of the books, belonging to the Richmond Library Society, with the rules and regulations and act of incorporation. Richmond, Pr. by John Warrock, 1827. 56 p. CSmH--The Brock collection. 29497

The life and death of Lady Jane Grey. Philadelphia, American Sunday School Union. Stereotyped by L. Johnson, 1827. 32 p. MLex. 29498

The life of Christian F. Swartz. An early missionary in India. Revised by the Committee of Publication. American Sunday School Union. Philadelphia, 1827. 86, 2 p. IObB; NcWsS; ViRUT. 29499

The life of Martin Luther. Revised by the Committee of Publication... American Sunday School Union. Philadelphia, John Clarke, pr., 1827. 159 p. IObB; MiToC; PPLT. 29500

The life of Napoleon Buonaparte. See Scott, Sir Walter.

Life of Philip, the Indian chief. See Savage, Sarah.

Life of the late Reverend and learned Dr. Cotton Mather. See Mather, Samuel.

Lily Douglas... See Grierson, Miss.

Lincoln, Solomon, 1804-1881
History of the town of Hingham, Plymouth county, Mass. Hingham, C. Gill, jr. and Farmer and Brown, 1827. 183 p. DLC; MH. 29501

Lindsley, Philip, 1786-1855
Baccalaureate address, pronounced on the evening of the anniversary commencement of the University of Nashville, Oct. 3, 1827. Nashville, Pr. by J. S. Simpson, 1827. 30 p. DLC; MH; NjP; PPAmP; T; TKL; TNJ. 29502

Lingard, John, 1771-1851
A history of England. Philadelphia, Eugene Cummiskey, publisher, J. Harding, pr., 1827-31. 14 v. CtHT; DGU; GHi; GU; ICLoy; IaDuC; In; InCW; KMK; KyDC; M; MA; MB; MBL; MH-AH; MMidb; MWA; Md; MdBS; MdCatS; MdW; Me; MeLB; MiDSH; MiDu; MoS; MsU; NCH; NCaS; NcW; Nh; Nj; NjP; OCY; OClWHi; PHC; PPL; PPP; PRosC; PV; RBr; ScNC; ScU; TN; Vi; ViAl; VtU; WHi. 29503

Linsley, Joel Harvey, 1790-1868
A sermon delivered at the dedication of the Second or South Congregational Church in Hartford, Conn., April 11, 1827. Hartford, D. F. Robinson, publisher, P. Canfield, pr., 1827. 32 p. CSmH; Ct; CtHC; CtHi; CtY; ICN; MA; MBC; MeHi; MiU-C; NjPT; NjR; RPB; Vt; VtMiM. 29504

Lionel Lincoln. See Cooper, James Fenimore.

List, Friedrich, 1789-1846
Outlines of American political economy, in a series of letters addressed by Frederick List... Philadelphia, Pr. by S. Parker, 1827. 40 p. DLC; DeWI; ICU; KU; KyLx; MBAt; MH; MWA; MdBP; O; P; PHi; PPB; PPL; PU; RPB; BrMus. 29505

---- Appendix to The outlines of American political economy, in three additional letters, Nos. IX. X. XI. Addressed by Professor Frederick List, of the University of Tubingen in Germany, to Charles J. Ingersoll, Esq. Vice-President of the Pennsylvania Society for the Promotion of Manufactures and the Mechanic Arts. Philadelphia, Pr. by Samuel Parker, 1827. 13 p. DLC; MWA; PPL; PU; BrMus. 29506

---- Proposals, for publishing a work, to be entitled The American Economist; in two volumes by Frederick List, of Pennsylvania ... Reading, Dec. 22, 1827. 1 p. DLC. 29507

List of jurors in the city of New York, taken 1825. New York, Pr. by P. & H. Van Pelt, 1827. 139 p. WHi. 29508

The listener, pseud. See Infernal conference.

Literary Cadet - Extra. January 11, 1827. See Burges, Tristam.

The literary gem; or, Legends and lyrics, etc.... For the amusement of winter nights and summer mornings... Boston, Pr. by J. H. Eastburn for Benjamin Davenport, 1827. 238 p. CtY; MBAt. 29509

The little girl who was taught by experience. Boston. Bowles and Dearborn, I. R. Butts & Co., prs. 1827. 50 p. DLC. 29510

Little Patrick, the weaver's son. American Sunday School Union. Philadelphia, 1827. 8 p. WHi. 29511

Little Sally or the good girl. Philadelphia, American Sunday School Union, 1827. 7 p. ICU; BrMus. 29512

Little Susan and her lamb. Philadelphia, American Sunday School Union. 1827. 15 p. MWey; NNC. 29513

Little Tom, the huntsman's boy. Philadelphia, American Sunday School Union, 1827. 16 p. DLC; BrMus. 29514

Livermore, Harriet
An epistle of love, addressed to the youth & children of Germantown, Pennsylvania, county of Philadelphia. By Harriet Livermore, a mourning pilgrim, bound to the promised land... 2d ed. Philadelphia, Joseph Rakestraw, 1827. 84 p. MB; MHa; NN; P. 29515

Livermore, Samuel, 1786-1833
An argument, in a cause depending before the Supreme Court of Louisiana, between the Bank of the United States, the Bank of Louisiana, the Bank of Orleans and others, creditors of Joseph Saul, appellants; and Thomas H. Saul and others... appellees: in which is discussed the question, whether in the case of a marriage contracted in a state, governed by the common law of England, between parties there residing, but who afterwards remove to Louisiana and there acquire property, such property will be held in community between such husband and wife? By Samuel Livermore. New-Orleans, Pr. by Benj. Levy, 1827. 1 p. l., 80 p. MHi; BrMus. 29516

The living and the dead. See Neale, Erskine.

Livingston, Edward, 1764-1836
Introductory report to the code of prison discipline: explanatory to the principles on which the code is founded. Being a part of the system of penal law, prepared for the state of Louisiana. Philadelphia, Carey, Lea & Carey, sold in New York, by G. & C. Carvill, 1827. 78, [4] p. CU; CtHC; DNLM; IGK; MB; MBAt; MH-L; Me; MnU; NN; NNC-L; NcD; O; PHC; PHi; PPA; PU; RP; BrMus. 29517

Livingston, Edward
Introductory report to the code of prison discipline... Philadelphia, Pr. for gratuitous distribution, at the expense of Roberts Vaux, Robert Ralston, Richard Price, Robert Earp, and Mathew Carey, 1827. 78 p. PPL. 29518

Livius, Titus
Titi Livi Patavini Historiarum libri quinque priores; ad optimas editiones castigati... Hallowell, C. Spaulding, 1827. 300 p. CtW; DLC; IaHi; InCW; KyLxT; MA; TxU. 29519

Lloyd, W. F.
A catechism on the principal parables of the New Testament. Philadelphia, American Sunday School Union, 1827. 90 p. MH-AH; PAtM; PPAmS. 29520

Locke, John, 1792-1856
An English grammar for children; according to the elementary method of Pestalozzi... Cincinnati, W. M. & O. Farnsworth, jr., prs., 1827. 228 p. DLC; InIB; NNC. 29521

Lohra, Peter
Peter Lohra vs. A. Morhouse. In the state of Louisiana. Case stated. [Philadelphia, Pr. by Lydia R. Bailey, 1827?] 8 p. PPL. 29522

Long, John
Circular to the freemen of the tenth Congressional district in North Carolina. Washington, 1827. 8 p. NcU. 29523

Long, Stephen H.
Letter from Lt. Col. S. H. Long, U. S. topographical engineer to Philip E. Thomas, Esq. on the subject of railroads. Baltimore, Pr. by Samuel Sands, 1827. 15 p. DBRE; DLC; MdHi; PPAN; PPL. 29524

The Long-Island almanack for 1828. By Thomas Spofford. New-York, David Felt [1827] 18 l. NHi. 29525

Long Island Sound.
Chart of Long Island Sound, 1827. (Edmund & Geo. C. Blunt, Engraved by Hooker. 8-1/2 x 17-1/4". Rare. New York, 1827. Argosy Book Stores. Cat. 131, Sep. 1938. no. 425. 29526

Longworth's American almanac, New-York register, and city directory, for the fifty-second year of American independence... New-York, Pub. by Thomas Longworth, [J. Seymour, pr.] 1827. 557 p. MBAt; NNMus; NNS; NjR. 29527

Lopez, Mathias
Lopez and Wemyss' edition. Acting American theater, containing the most popular plays, as they are performed at the Philadelphia Theatre. Philadelphia, A. R. Poole, and Ash and Mason, P. Thompson, Washington, H. W. Boal, Baltimore, E. M. Murden, New York, [etc.] 1827. v. p. NjR. 29528

Lost child. Revised by the Committee of Publication. Philadelphia, American Sunday School Union, 1827. 31 p. MNBedfHi. 29529

Lothrop, Jason
The pilgrim's companion; being a collection of hymns in general use in private circles and conference meetings: with a few never before published. Newport, J. Lothrop, 1827. 140 p. RPB. 29530

Lotteries exposed. Or, an inquiry into the consequences attending them... by a foe to deception. Philadelphia, B. & T. Kite and Shadrach Taylor, John Richards, pr., 1827. 24 p. MBC; PPL. 29531

The lottery ticket: an American tale. To which is added, The destructive consequences of dissipation and luxury. Hartford, D. F. Robinson & co., 1827. 105 p. CtHi; DLC; IaU; MH; NcD; OU; PU. 29532

Loubat, Alphonse
The American vine dresser's guide... New-York, Pub. by G. & C. Carvill, Joseph Desnoues, pr., 1827. 123 p. GHi; IU; KyBgW; MB; MBHo; MW; MiD; MoU; NBuB; NBuG; NIC-A; NNC; NNBG; NjP; NjR; P; RNR; Vi. 29533

Louaillier, Louis, sr.
The appeal of L. Louaillier, sen., against the charge of high treason, and explaining the transactions at New-Orleans... [New Orleans] 1827. 28 p. CSmH; DLC; ICN; MH; NN; Nh; PHi; WHi; BrMus. 29534

---- Speech delivered by Mr. Lewis Louaillier at a meeting of the inhabitants of the County of Opelousas, state of Louisiana, friendly to the administration of the general government, held pursuant to public notice, at the court-house, in the town of Opelousas, on Monday, the twentieth of August, 1827. New Orleans, Pr. by John Gibson, 1827. 30 p. DLC; MH; MHi; PHi. 29535

Loughborough, Preston S.
Speech of Preston S. Loughborough, delivered, by request, near Frankfort on the 10th of September, 1827, at the celebration of Perry's victory on Lake Erie; and of the success of the cause of Andrew Jackson, in the late election of Representatives in Congress from Kentucky. Frankfort, Pr. for the author, by A. G. Hodges, 1827. 24 p. NN; T. 29536

Louisiana
Acts passed at the first session of the eighth Legislature of the state of Louisiana, begun and held in the city of New Orleans, on Monday [Jan. 1, 1827]... By authority. New Orleans, John Gibson, state pr., 1827. 211 p. IU; LNHT; LU. 29537

---- Journal de la chambre des representants [sic] durant la premiere session de la huitieme législature, de l'état de la Louisiane. Par autorité. Nouvelle Orleans, imprimé par John Gibson, imprimeur de l'état, 1827. 97 p. DLC; LU. 29538

---- Journal du senat durant la première session de la huitième législature de l'état de la Louisiane. Nouvelle Orleans, imprime par John Gibson, imprimeur de l'état, 1827. 75 p. LU. 29539

---- The journal of the House of Representatives during the first session of the eighth Legislature of the state of Louisiana. New Orleans, Pr. by John Gibson, state pr., 1827. 99 p. DLC; LNHT. 29540

---- The journal of the Senate during the first session of the eighth Legislature of the state of Louisiana. By authority. New Orleans, Pr. by John Gibson, state pr., 1827 [72] p. LNHT; LU. 29541

---- The opinion of the supreme court of the state of Louisiana, on a question arising in the cause of Saul vs. his creditors... New-Orleans, Pr. by Benjamin Levy, 1827. 24 p. PPL. 29542

The Louisiana almanack for 1828. By William Collom. New Orleans, William M'Kean [1827] 24 l. Ms-Ar. 29543

Lounsbury, Thomas
Universalism: or The rich man and Lazarus. A sermon. 3d ed. Rochester, Pr. for D. Clark, Jr., 1827. 16 p. NjR; PPPrHi. 29544

Lovell, John E.
Introductory arithmetic; prepared for the pupils of the Lancasterian School, New Haven. Accompanied by a key for the use of the monitor. Part First. New-Haven, Pub. by S. Wadsworth, N. Whiting, pr., 1827. 228 p. DAU; DLC; CtW; CtHT-W; CtHi; CtY. 29545

A lover of the souls of men. See Coleman, H.

Lowe, Abraham T.
Columbian class book; consisting of geographical, historical, and biographical extracts... 3d ed. Pub. by Dorr & Howland. Sold by Richardson & Lord, and Hillard, Gray & Co., Boston: John Hutchens, Providence, 1827. 354 p. CtHT-W; MH; MWHi; NNNAM; PU. 29546

Lowell, Charles, 1782-1861
...A sermon preached at the ordination of Mr. George Wadsworth Wells, as one of the ministers of the First Parish in Kennebunk. Cambridge, Hilliard, Metcalf, and Co., prs. for the University, 1827. 15 p. CtHC;

ICU; M; MBAt; MDeeP; MBNEH; MH; MHi; MWA; MeBa; MeHi; MiD-B; NjPT; RPB; BrMus. 29547

[Lowell, John] 1769-1840
The rights of the Congregational parishes of Massachusetts. Review of a pamphlet entitled "The rights of the Congregational churches of Massachusetts." Boston, Bowles & Dearborn; Isaac R. Butts & Co., prs., 1827. 32 p. CBPac; CSmH; M; MB-FA; MH; MWA; MeBat; MiD-B. 29548

[----] ---- 2d ed. Boston, Bowles & Dearborn; pr. by Dutton & Wentworth, 1827. 36 p. ICMe; ICN; ICU; KHi; M; MBAU; MBAt; MBC; MH; MWA; MiD-B; MnHi; NjPT; NjR; OO; PPAmP; PPL; WHi. 29549

Lowry, William
A sermon delivered at the funeral of Mrs. Anna B. Bush, late consort of the Rev. George Bush, pastor of the Presbyterian Church at Indianapolis, Nov. 11, 1827. [Indianapolis] John Douglass [1827?] 16 p. InHi. 29550

Lucas, Fielding
Lucas' progressive drawing book... Baltimore, F. Lucas, jun'r [c1827] John D. Doy, pr. 3 v. in 1. CSmH; DLC; MH; MdHi. 29551

Lucy and her Dhaye. Revised by the Committee of Publication. Philadelphia, American Sunday School Union, 1827. 72 p. DLC; ICU; ScCliTo; BrMus. 29552

Lunn, Joseph
Fish out of water. A farce in two acts... New York, Pub. by E. M. Murden, Circulating Library & Dramatic Repository, 1827. 38 p. MH; MWA. 29553

Luther, Martin
Three sermons of Dr. Martin Luther as they were written by himself, in the German language and now translated into the English tongue... New-Market, Pr. in Dr. S. Henkel's Office by Ireneus N. and Samuel B. Henkel, 1827. 64 p. DLC; NcD; PPLT; ViU. 29554

Luzerne County, Penna.
Internal improvement. (cap. title) [Wilkesbarre? 1827?] Bdsd. PPL. 29555

Lyon, Lucius
Ypsilanti village lots at auction. On Friday, the 8th day of June next, the subscriber, one of the proprietors of the village of Ypsilanti, in the County of Washtenaw, will offer for sale at the time and place of the sale of the contracts on the Chicago road. Detroit, May 24, 1827. Pr. by Chipman & Seymour, Detroit [1827] Bdsd. MiU-C. 29556

M

M. B. Roberts's almanac for 1828. Baltimore, M. B. Roberts; R. J. Matchett, pr. [1827] 18 l. MWA. 29557

M. Robinson's Circulating Library
Catalogue of additions, for 1827. [Providence, 1827] 7 p. RPB. 29558

M'Caine, Alexander, 1775-1856
The history and mystery of Methodist episcopacy; or, A glance at "the institutions of the church"... Baltimore, Pr. by Richard J. Matchett, 1827. 76 p. CBDP; CSmH; GDC; IEG; MB; MBAt; MBNMHi; MH; MWA; MdBBC; MdBP; MdHi; NNG; NcD; NcWfC; PPL; TxU. 29559

McCarrell, Joseph
Answer to a discourse preached by Dr. Wm. E. Channing, at the dedication of the Second Congregational Unitarian Church, New York, Dec. 7th, 1826. New York, J. Seymour, 1827. 47, 32 p. CtHC; DLC; ICMcC; MBAU; NNUT; NjPT; NjR; PPL; PPPrHi; RHi; WHi. 29560

[McClelland, Alexander]
The doctrine of incest stated, with an examination of the question, whether a man may marry his deceased wife's sister, in a letter to a clergyman of the Presbyterian Church, by Domesticus, 2d ed. New-York, G. & C. Carvill, 1827. 48 p. DLC; MB; MH-AH; MdHi; NjR; NNG; OClWHi; OO; PPL; PPPrHi; BrMus. 29561

McClung, James W.
Defense against accusations of Huntsville Democrat. [Huntsville, 1827] Bdsd, described in Huntsville Democrat, June 29, 1827, p 2. 29562

---- To the public. Second defense against accusations of Huntsville Democrat, [Huntsville, 1827]. Bdsd. copied in Huntsville Democrat, July 6, 1827, p. 2. 29563

M'Conaughy, David, 1775-1852
Drunkenness excludes from heaven: a discourse on 1 Corinthians 6:10. Gettysburg, Pa., Pr. by R. G. Harper, 1827. 15 p. NbOD; O; P; PPPrHi. 29564

M'Cord, David James, 1797-1855
Speech of Mr. M'Cord, at a meeting of inhabitants, in the town hall of Columbia, S. C. opposed to the proposed woollens bill, on the second July, 1827. Columbia, So. Carolina, Pr. by Sweeny & Sims, 1827. 50 p. ICN; ICU; MBAt; MHi; MWA; N; NNS; NcD; PPAmP. 29565

McCoy, Isaac, 1784-1846
Remarks on the practicability of Indian reform embracing their colonization... Boston, Pr. by Lincoln & Edmands, 1827. 47 p. CSmH; CtHT-W; DLC; ICHi; ICN; In; InHi; KHi; MBAt; MBC; MH; MWA; MnU; MoK; Nh-Hi; OClWHi; RPB; WHi; BrMus. 29566

Macdonald, Norman
Maxims and moral reflections. New York, Collins & Hannay [etc., etc.] Pr. by J. & J. Harper, 1827. 214 p. DLC; MH; MLow; NIC. 29567

M'Dowell, John, 1780-1863
Questions on the Bible, for the use of schools... With the author's last corr. 15th ed. Elizabethtown, N. J., Pub. by J. J. Bryant, 1827. 152 p. MH. 29568

---- ---- Stereotype ed. Utica, Pr. and pub. by Hastings & Tracy, 1827. 152 p. NUt; NjP. 29569

McFarland, James C.
Memorial to the Baltimore and Ohio Railroad Company. [Baltimore, R. Edes, prs., 1827.] 16 p. DBRE; MdBJ; MdHi; NN. 29570

McFarlane, Alexander
The scriptural doctrine of predestination, in reference to the present and eternal condition of men, stated and vindicated. Bridgeton (W. N. J.) Pr. by Franklin Ferguson, 1827. 32 p. CSmH; NN; OO; PPPrHi. 29571

MacGowan, John
The dialogues of devils on the many vices which abound the civil and religious world. Philadelphia, Pub. by G. M. & W. Snider, 1827. vi, 291 p. CtHC; KyLo; PAtM. 29572

McIlvaine, Charles Pettit, bp., 1799-1873
Rev. Mr. M'Ilvaine in answer

to the Rev. Henry U. Onderdonk, D. D. Philadelphia, W. Stavely, 1827. 43 p. CtHT; DLC; MB; MH; MnHi; NBLiHi; NNG; NjPT; NjR; OCHP; PHi; PLT; PMA; PPFM; PPL; PPPrHi; TxDaM; ViRUT. 29573

McIver, Colin
Ecclesiastical proceedings in the case of Mr. Donald McCrimmon, a ruling elder... to which is added a speech... in opposition to Mr. McCrimmon's appeal. Fayetteville [N. C.] Pr. for the author and publisher, 1827. 42 p. CSmH; NcU; OCHP; PPPrHi. 29574

McKenney, Thomas Lorraine, 1785-1859
Sketches of a tour to the Lakes, of the character and customs of the Chippeway Indians, and of incidents connected with the treaty of Fond du Lac... Baltimore, F. Lucas, jun'r., J. D. Toy, pr., 1827. 493, [1] p. C; CSmH; CtHT-W; DLC; FOA; GU; ICHi; ICN; IP; IaGG; In; InLW; KSalW; KyLx; M; MB; MBAt; MH; MWA; MdBE; MdBL; MdHi; MiD-B; MiGr; MiU; MnU; MoSW; MoSU; MsWJ; NN; NNG; NWM; NbO; NcU; Nh; NjP; NjR; OClWHi; OO; P; PPL; PU; RP; RPJCB; Vi; ViU; VtU; WHi; BrMus. 29575

Mackentosh, John
Receipts for the cure of most diseases incident to the human family. By the celebrated Indian doctor John Mackentosh, of the Cherokee Nation; none of which have ever before been communicated to the world. New-York, Pr. for the pub. [i. e., Seth Holderwell] 1827. 12 p. Ct; CtY; GU-M; InLP; MWA; NN; NNNAM; OClWHi; OkU; PPL; T; WHi. 29576

Mackenzie, Colin
Five thousand receipts in all the useful & domestic arts... Philadelphia, Pr. by James Kay, jun. for John Grigg, Uriah Hunt, Towar & Hogan, R. H. Small, M'Carty & Davis, Thomas De Silver, O. A. Roorback, New York, 1827. 661 p. MBP; NN; NcRA; OMC; P; PPL; TN; ViU. 29577

Mackenzie, John, 1806-1848
Memoir of the life and writings of John Calvin, to which is prefixed a brief sketch of the history of the Reformation. Pr. from the last London ed., with additions. Philadelphia, Pub. & sold by Towar & Hogan, 1827. [J. Robertson, pr., Dover, Del.] 320 p. CtY; MNBedf; MsJMC; NcMHi; PAtM; ScU. 29578

---- ---- Pr. from the last London ed., with additions. 2d Amer. ed. Philadelphia, Pub. by Towar & Hogan [J. Robertson, pr., Dover, Del.] 1827. 320 p. CtHC; GMM; MBC; MH; MW; MoSpD; NcDaD; NcG; NjR; OO; OSW; PHi; PPPrHi; ScU; ViRUT; WHi. 29579

McLeod, Alexander
Address to the Synod of the Reformed Presbyterian Church in America, on submitting to their consideration the plan of correspondence with the General Assembly, by the chairman of their committee, in May 1827. 48 p. New York, G. & C. Carvill, 1827. 48 p. MBC; MH-AH; PPPrHi. 29580

McNamee, Elias
Vincennes, (Ia) Aug. 27th, 1827. Dear Sir--Having opened a medicine store, in this place, I propose to furnish you medicines at the prices affixed... J. D. Woolverton, for Elias McNamee. Bdsd. In. 29581

MacNish, William
The confessions of an unexecuted femicide. "no fiction." Published by R. Matthews. Brooklyn,

Pr. by Geo. L. Birch, 1827. 16 p. NJQ. 29582

Macomb, David B.
Answer to inquiries relative to middle Florida, propounded by a gentleman in Switzerland... Tallahassee, Pr. at the office of the Advocate, 1827. 5 l. NN imprint cat. 29583

McPherson, James, 1736-1796
The poems of Ossiam, translated by James McPherson... New York, Dixon & Sickels, 1827. 2 v. KHi; MB; MB-FA; MFi; MH; MdBP; MoSpD; NbL; OBerB; RJPHL; RRu; WKen. 29584

[McVickar, John] 1787-1868
Hints on banking, in a letter to a gentleman in Albany; by a New Yorker. New-York, Pr. by Vanderpool & Cole, 1827. 43 p. DLC; ICU; KU; MB; MH-BA; NIC; NN; NNC; NNS; PHi; PPAmP; PPL; PU; RNR. 29585

Madam, without being able to ascertain. See Carey, Mathew.

Maddock, Henry, d. 1824
A treatise on the principles and practices of the High Court of Chancery... 3d Amer. from the last London ed. With the addition of the principal American decisions in chancery, upon the plan of the original work, by Thomas Huntington. Hartford, O. D. Cooke, 1827. 2 v. C; CL; CSfL; FTU; GU-L; IaU-L; InSC; KyU; MB; MH-L; NNLI; NNU; NcD; NhD; OCLaw; OU; PU-L; RPL; TMB; ViU-L; WaU-L. 29586

Madison College, Uniontown, Pa.
An act for the establishment of a college at Uniontown, in the county of Fayette. Pittsburgh, Pr. by J. C. Andrews [1827] 7 p. DLC 29587

---- Catalogue of officers, system of education, and laws of Madison College, Uniontown, Fayette County, Pennsylvania. Pittsburgh, Pr. by John C. Andrews, 1827. 19, [1] p. DLC. 29588

Magdalen Society of Philadelphia
Report of the managers of the Magdalen Society, for 1826. [Philadelphia, 1827] 14 p. DNLM; PPL. 29589

Magendie, François, 1783-1855
Formulary for the preparation and employment of many new medicines... Trans. from the 5th ed., rev., and additions. New York, G. H. Evans and co., 1827. xii, 138, [2] p. CSt-L; MB; MBP; NBMS; NNNAM; NRU-M; WU. 29590

[Maginn, William] 1793-1842
The military sketch-book. Reminiscences of seventeen years in the service abroad and at home. By an officer of the line... New York, Pr. by J. & J. Harper for Collins and Hannay [etc.]; Philadelphia, Carey, Lea and Carey; [etc., etc.] 1827. 2 v. CtW; DLC; IaDm; LNHT; MA; NWM; NjR. 29591

Maine
Land agent's report. Report of the land agent of Maine, together with the report of the auditor. Jan. 5, 1827. 28 p. MeHi. 29592

---- Laws of the state of Maine passed by the Legislature. Portland, Pr. by Todd & Smith, 1827. [5], 2552 p. Me. 29593

---- Letter from the treasurer of the state, of the president of the Senate, and the speaker of the House of Representatives, transmitting his annual report on the state of finances. Dec. 31, 1826. Portland, Pr. by Thomas Todd, pr. to the state, 1827. 27 p. MeHi. 29594

---- ---- Portland, Pr. by Thomas Todd, pr. to the state, 1827. 128 p. MeHi. 29595

---- Private acts of the state of Maine passed by the Seventh Legislature, at its session held in January, 1827. Portland, Pr. by Thomas Todd, pr. to the state, 1827. [3], 727-809, [4] p. CSfLaw: Me-LR; MeU; MeWebr; Mo; TxU-L. 29596

---- A proclamation for a day of public humiliation, fasting and prayer. By advice of the council and in compliance with a venerated usage, I appoint Thursday, the fifth day of April next, for humiliation, fasting and prayer... Council Chamber, Portland, Mar. 3rd, 1827. Augusta, Pr. at the Journal Office [1827] Bdsd. DLC; MeHi. 29597

---- Public Acts of the state of Maine, passed by the Seventh Legislature, at its session held in January, 1827. Pub. agreeably to the resolve of the 29th of June, 1820. Portland, Pr. by Thomas Todd, pr. to the state, 1827. [3], 1105-1136, [4] p. Me-LR; MeBa; MeU; Nb; TxU-L. 29598

---- Report of the Commissioners appointed... to examine into the doings and transactions of the banks in this state. Portland, Pr. by Thomas Todd, 1827. 47 p. MH. 29599

---- Resolves establishing the seat of government. 2 p. (Caption title. At head of title: State of Maine. In the year of Our Lord one thousand eight hundred and twenty seven.) MeHi. 29600

---- Resolves of the Seventh Legislature of the state of Maine, passed at the session which commenced on the third day of January, and which ended on the twenty-sixth day of February, one thousand eight hundred and twenty-seven. Portland, Pr. by Thomas Todd, pr. to the state, 1827. [5], 534-607, [6] p. CSfLaw; IaU-L; InSC; MeU; MeWebr; Mo; Nb; Nj; TxU-L. 29601

---- Rules and orders to be observed in the House of Representatives of the state of Maine, during the continuance of the Seventh Legislature, 1827. Portland, Pr. by Thomas Todd, 1827. 44 p. MeHi. 29602

---- Speech of the Governor of the state of Maine, delivered to both branches of the Legislature, January 4, 1827. 8 p. MHi; MeHi. 29603

---- ... With the advice of the Council I appoint Thursday... a day of thanksgiving and praise... By the Governor, Amos Nichols, Secretary of State. Council Chamber, Portland, Oct. 18, 1827. Bdsd. MeHi. 29604

The Maine farmers' almanac for 1828. By Daniel Robinson. Hallowell, Glazier & Co. [1827] 24 l. DLC; MB; MBAt; MH; MWA; MeB; MeHi; WHi. 29605

Maine Missionary Society

Report of the trustees of the Maine Missionary Society at their twentieth annual meeting, in Hallowell, June 27, 1827. Portland, Pr. at the Mirror Office, 1827. 35 p. DLC; MH; MeBa; MeBat; MeHi. 29606

The Maine register, and United States calendar for 1828. Hallowell, Glazier & Co. [1827] 18 l. DLC; MWA; MeBa; MeHi; MeU; Nh. 29607

Maine Sabbath School Union
First annual report of the Maine Sabbath School Union, auxiliary to the American Sunday School Union. Portland, Pr. at the Mirror Office, 1827. 24 p. CSmH; MBC; MeBat. 29608

Maine Wesleyan Seminary, Kent's Hill, Me.
Catalogue of the officers and students of Maine Wesleyan Seminary, Spring term, 1827. [8] p. MBC. 29609

Malan, César, 1787-1864
Idle Dick: or, The history of Richard Watson. Trans. from the French (Children should come to the Lord Jesus). Philadelphia, American Sunday School Union, 1827. BrMus. 29610

[----] The image boys. Trans. from the French. New York, Pub. by The New-York Religious Tract Soc., D. Fanshaw, pr. [ca. 1827] 16 p. NNC-T. 29611

Malles de Beaulieu, Mme. d. 1825
The modern Crusoe. A narrative of the life and adventures of a French cabin boy, who was shipwrecked on an uninhabited island. Trans. from the French of Mad. Malle de Beaulieu. 1st Amer. ed. Boston, James Loring, 1827. 217 p. DLC; PP. 29612

Malte-Brun, Conrad, 1775-1826
Universal geography, or description of all parts of the world on a new plan... Philadelphia, Anthony Finley, Wm. Brown, pr., 1827 -1832. 6 v. CLCM; CSansS; CSt; CtHT; CtW; DLC; GEU; GHi; GU; ICU; IU; IaCr; IaDL; InU; KU; KyLx; KyLxT; LNT; LU; MA; MB; MH; MHi; MWA; NN; NP; NT; NcAS; NcU; NjP; MdBJ; MdW; MeBaT; Mi; MiD-B; MnU; MoS; OClW; OO; OkU; PLFM; PP; PU; ScC; ScCC; TC; TJaU; TN; TxD-T; TxSaU; ViRU; ViU; WM; Wv. 29613

[Mampel, Johan Christian]
The young rifleman's comrade: a narrative of his military adventures, captivity and shipwreck. Philadelphia, H. C. Carey & I. Lea, 1827. 308 p. GHi; KyLx; LU; PPL; TxU. 29614

Mansfield, Edward Deering
Sketch of a journey through the western states of North America and the city of Cincinnati. Cincinnati, 1827. Sabin 44375. 29615

[Mant, Alicia Catherine]
Tales for Ellen, by the author of "Ellen, the young Godmother;" The "Young Naturalist," &c. Boston, Monroe & Francis, etc., etc. [1827] 47 p. MBMu; MH. 29616

---- The young naturalist; a tale. Boston, Munroe & Francis; New York, C. S. Francis, 1827. 226 p. MH; KU; PP; ScCliTO. 29617

[----] A boat to Richmond; or, The excursion. By the author of "Ellen, the Young Godmother." "The Young Naturalist;" etc. Boston, Munroe & Francis [c1827] 26 l. PP. 29618

The manufacturers. [Wilmington, Del. ? 1827] 7 p. PPL. 29619

Manufacturers & Growers of Wool in the State of Vermont
Proceedings of the meeting... held at Woodstock, Dec. 13, 1826. [1827?] 12 p. MH-BA. 29620

[Marcet, Mrs. Jane (Haldimand)] 1769-1858
Conversations on natural philosophy... 8th Amer. ed. Boston, Lincoln & Edmands, 1827. CtY; MH; RPB. 29621

Marcia's reward; or, The voice of the dead. By the author of

Jane and her teacher [etc.] 1st Amer. ed. Hartford, D. F. Robinson, publ., 1827. 167 p. CSmH; CtHi; MA; NNG. 29622

Markham, Mrs., pseud. See Penrose, Elizabeth (Cartwright).

[Marks, Richard]
The thatcher's wife. Philadelphia, American Sunday School Union [1827] 52 p. NN. 29623

Marine Bible Society of New York
Eleventh annual report of the managers of the Marine Bible Society of New-York auxiliary to the American Bible Society, presented April 25, 1827. New York, Pr. by Gray & Bunce, 1827. 12 p. MNtcA. 29624

Marot & Walter's almanack for 1828. By Joshua Sharp. Philadelphia, Marot & Walter [1827] 16 l. MiU-C. 29625

Marrion Wilder; or, The passionate little girl. Boston, Bowles & Dearborn, 1827. 30 p. MiD-B. 29626

Marsh, John, 1788-1868
An epitome of general ecclesiastical history, from the earliest period to the present time. With an appendix, giving a condensed history of the Jews from the destruction of Jerusalem to the present day. New York, Pr. by Vanderpool & Cole, 1827. 420, 32 p. Ct; CtHT-W; DLC; LNB; MnHi; NIC; NN; NRU; NjP; OO; PPPrHi; PSC-Hi; TxH. 29627

Marshall, Elihu F.
Marshall's Spelling book of the English language... Concord, N.H., Pub. by Jacob B. Moore, 1827. 156 p. MH; Nh. 29628

---- A spelling book of the English language; or, The American tutor's assistant... Stereotype ed. Plymouth, Mass., Ezra Collier, 1827. 156 p. KU. 29629

Marshall, Mrs. L. A.
A sketch of my friend's family, intended to suggest some practical hints on religion and domestic manners. 6th ed. Exeter, Pub. by J. & B. Williams, 1827. 128 p. ICN; MAm; Nh; Nh-Hi. 29630

---- ---- American Sunday School Union. Philadelphia, 1827. 108 p. IObB; ViU; BrMus. 29631

Martin, François Xavier, 1762-1846
The history of Louisiana from the earliest period. New Orleans, Pr. by Lyman and Beardslee, 1827-29. 2 v. CLU; CSmH; CU-B; FSa; I; ICU; IGK; IHi; Ia; KU; KyBgW; LNHT; LU; MB; MBAt; MBNEH; MH; MdBJ; MnHi; MoK; MoSM; MsJS; NBLiHi; NIC; NN; NNC; NNS; NUtHi; O; OC; OCl; P; PPA; PPAmP; PPL; RHi; RPJCB; ScC; TU; Vi; ViU; WHi; BrMus. 29632

Martin and his two little scholars. See Cameron, Mrs. Lucy Lyttleton (Butt).

Martinet, Louis
Manual of pathology containing the symptoms, diagnosis and morbid characteristics of diseases... Trans. with notes and additions, by Jones Quain. Philadelphia, Carey, Lea & Carey, 1827. 310, xii p. LNT-M; MB; MBCo; MsU; NBMS; Nh; PMA; PPC. 29633

Martinsburg Gazette
The address of the carriers of the Martinsburg Gazette to its patrons on the commencement of the year 1827. [Martinsburg] Bdsd. WvU. 29634

Mary and Betsey. Wendell, J. Metcalf, 1827. 8 p. MNF. 29635

Maryland (State)
An act to incorporate the Baltimore and Ohio Railroad Company, passed at December session, 1826. Baltimore, Pr. by Wm. Wooddy, 1827. 24 p. CtY; DLC; MBAt; MCM; MH-BA; MdBJ; MdHi; NN; NNP; PHi; BrMus. 29636

---- A catalogue of books in the Maryland State Library. Annapolis, Pr. by J. Green [1827] 8 p. MdBP. 29637

---- Correspondence between the treasurer of the W. shore of Maryland, and the third auditor of the United States treasury, on the subject of the claim of the state of Maryland upon the United States, for interest due upon sums advanced by the state during the late war. Annapolis, Pr. by Jeremiah Hughes, 1827. 35 p. DLC; MBAt; MdHi. 29638

---- The general report for 1827, of the Treasurer for the Western Shore to the General Assembly. Annapolis, Pr. by Jeremiah Hughes, 1827. 4 p. MdBP. 29639

---- Message of the governor to the General Assembly of Maryland. December 27th, 1826. [Annapolis? 1827?] 36 p. MdHi. 29640

---- The hoop-pole law: entitled "An act to declare certain trespasses felony, and for other purposes," passed December session, 1826. [Baltimore, 1827] 8 p. Sabin 45162. 29641

---- Index to the laws of Maryland, from the year 1818 to 1825, inclusive. Prepared and published by authority. By William Kilty, attorney at law. Annapolis, Jeremiah Hughes, pr., 1827. [237] p. C; CSfLaw; Ct; DLC; LU-L; M; MCM; MH-L; Md; MdBB; MdBJ; MdLR; MdUL; Mi-L; Nb; Nj; OCLaw; OClW; WaU. 29642

----Journal of the proceedings of the House of Delegates of the state of Maryland. December session, 1826. Annapolis, J. Green, 1827. 600 p. MdBB; MdHi; MdLR. 29643

---- Journal of the proceedings of the Senate of the state of Maryland; December session, 1826. Annapolis, Wm. M'Neir, 1827. 232 p. MdBB; MdHi; MdLR. 29644

---- Laws made and passed by the General Assembly of the state of Maryland, at a session begun and held at the city of Annapolis, on the last Monday of Dec. 1826. Annapolis, Pr. by Jonas Green, 1827. 304 p. A-SC; C; CU; Ia; IaU-L; L; MWCL; MdBB; MdHi; MdUL; Mi-L; Mo; Ms; NNLI; Nb; Nc-SC; Nj; Nv; R. 29645

---- Message from his excellency the governor transmitting memorials respecting the Chesapeake and Ohio canal, and the Chesapeake and Delaware canal: Annapolis, Pr. by Jeremiah Hughes, 1827. 8 p. MdHi. 29646

---- The petition of Daniel Bussard, to the General Assembly of Maryland. Annapolis, Pr. by Wm. M'Neir, 1827. 5, 18 p. Md. 29647

---- Proposals for tobacco warehouses and accompanying documents. Annapolis, Pr. by Jeremiah Hughes, 1827. 16 p. MdBP. 29648

---- Report of the board of public works to the General Assembly of Maryland. Annapolis, Pr. by Jeremiah Hughes, 1827. 10, [2] p. MdBJ-G. 29649

---- Report of the committee to investigate the state and condition of the Maryland Penitentiary. Annapolis, Pr. by Jeremiah Hughes, 1827. [73]-96 p. Doc. 8 of a series not separately paginated. MdBJ-G. 29650

---- Report of the state's agent of the Western Shore of Maryland. January 26, 1827. Referred to the Committee on Ways and Means. [Annapolis, 1827] 4 p. MdHi. 29651

---- Rules and regulations to be observed in the library of the Legislature of Maryland. Annapolis, Jeremiah Hughes, pr., 1827. 6 p. MdBP. 29652

Maryland Colonization Society
African colonization. Proceedings of a meeting of the Friends of African Colonization, held in the city of Baltimore... [Baltimore, 1827] 19 p. DLC; KyLxT; MH; MdHi; PPL; RP. 29653

Maryland Institute for the Promotion of the Mechanic Arts
Proposals of the Maryland Institute for the Promotion of the Mechanic Arts, for the exhibition of November, 1827, addressed to the mechanics and manufacturers of the United States. Baltimore, Pr. by John D. Toy, 1827. 11 p. MdHi. 29654

Maryland. University.
Report of the trustees of the University of Maryland, to the General Assembly of Maryland. Annapolis, Pr. by Jeremiah Hughes, 1827. 6, [1] p. MdBJ-G. 29655

Mason, A. See Burt, Daniel.

Mason, Henry
A poem... at the fifth anniversary of the Franklin Debating Society, on the birthday of Benjamin Franklin, January 17, 1827. Boston, [Isaac R. Butts & Co., prs., 1827] 8 p. RPB. 29656

Mason, Lowell
Address on church music... Revised ed. Boston, Hilliard, Gray, Little and Wilkins, T. R. Marvin, pr., 1827. 44 p. CBPac; ICN; MAnP; MB; MBC; MHi; MeLewB; MiD-B; NNC; NjR; OClW; PPL; RPB; TxU. 29657

Mason, William Powell, 1791-1867
An oration delivered Wednesday, July 4, 1827, in commemoration of American Independence, before the Supreme Executive of the Commonwealth and the City Council and inhabitants of the city of Boston. Boston, Nathan Hale, city pr., 1827. 31 p. CSmH; CtSoP; DLC; ICMe; KHi; MB; MBAt; MBB; MBC; MH; MHing; MNtcA; MiD-B; NCH; NjPT; NjR; PPL; RPB; WHi; BrMus. 29658

Massachusetts
An act, to confirm an act of the General Assembly of the state of Vermont, entitled "An act to provide for improving the navigation in the valley of Connecticut River." Boston, 1827. 36 p. Thomson, 158. 29659

---- An act to establish the Warren bridge corporation. [Boston, 1827] 4 p. MH. 29660

---- An act to provide for the instruction of youth, passed March 10, 1827. [1827] 21 p. MH. 29661

---- Acts and resolves passed by the General Court of Massachusetts in the year 1827. Boston, Dutton & Wentworth, prs. to the state [1827] [1], 589-623, l. ii p. MHam-BA. 29662

---- Commonwealth of Massachusetts. By His Excellency Levi Lincoln, Governor of the Commonwealth of Massachusetts, A proclamation for a day of public thanksgiving and praise... I have thought fit with the advice and consent of the Council, to set apart Thursday, 29th of November to be observed... Council Chamber... Boston... 17th of Oct., 1827. Bdsd. MBB; MHi. 29663

---- By His Excellency Levi Lincoln, a proclamation: The period in the season of the year having arrived, when it has been usual for the supreme executive of this Commonwealth to set apart a day... Thursday the fifth day of April next... [Boston, 23 Feb. 1827] Bdsd. MHi. 29664

---- An extract from the report of the directors of Massachusetts State Prison, made to his excellency the governor and the honourable council, October 18, 1827. Boston, Dutton and Wentworth, prs., 1827. 28 p. DNLM; IU; M; MBAt; MBC; MH; MHi; MWA; MiD-B; NNC; NcD; PPL. 29665

---- The general laws of Massachusetts, from June 1822, to June 1827. Ed. by Theron Metcalf. Boston, Wells & Lilly, 1827. 3 v. C; CSfLaw; ICLaw; M; MBr; MH-L; MHam-BA; MNS; MSH; MSbri; MdBB; OCLaw; R; W. 29666

---- In the House of Representatives, Feb. 16, 1827. The committee... to examine into and ascertain the state of the several goals... Report. [Boston, 1827] 41, lxx p. (H. R.-No. 50) PPL. 29667

---- Governor's message relative to the Salem Mozart Association. [Boston, Feb. 16, 1827] 8 p. MHi. 29668

---- The Joint Committee on Roads and Canals, who were directed "to consider the expediency of providing for a Board of Commissioners for Internal Improvements," ... report the following resolutions. For the committee. L. M. Parker. [Boston, 1827] [1] p. M; MB; MH. 29669

---- Laws of the commonwealth of Massachusetts, passed by the General court, at their session, which began on Wednesday, the third of January, and ended on Saturday, the tenth of March, one thousand eight hundred and twenty seven. Boston, Pr. by True & Greene, state prs., 1827. 387-588 [10] p. L; MH-L; MdBB; Ms; Nj. 29670

---- Laws of the commonwealth of Massachusetts, passed by the General court, at their session, which commenced on Wednesday, the thirteenth day of May, and ended on Saturday the sixteenth of June, one thousand eight hundred and twenty-seven. Boston, Dutton & Wentworth, prs. to the state, 1827. [3], 590-623, ii p. CSfLaw; IaU-L; MH-L; MHa; MKiTH; MMat; Mo. 29671

---- Message of his excellency Levi Lincoln, transmitted to both branches of the Legislature, January 3, 1827. Boston, True & Greene, state prs., 1827. 24 p. DLC; M; MBAt; MH; MHi; MWA; MiD-B; NjPT. 29672

---- H. R.-No. 5... Report of the commissioners, by virtue of a resolution of the House of Representatives, of the 22d February, 1826. The subject of the establishment of a seminary of practical arts and sciences... [Boston, 1827] 23 p. MB. 29673

---- Senate. No. 15. ...The Committee of both Houses to whom were referred the petitions of the trustees of Amherst College and of Williams College, have had the same under consideration, and ask leave to report... [Boston, 1827] 12 p. MB; MH. 29674

---- [Report of the joint committee on petition for survey for railway on one or more routes from Boston to Hudson river. Boston? 1827] 2 p. M; MWA. 29675

---- ... Report [of the Joint Committee on roads and canals, to whom was referred the petition of Samuel Hinkley and others, praying that they may be authorized to extend the Hampshire and Hampden Canal to the north line of the State]. [Boston, 1827] 20 p. M. 29676

---- Report of the select committee of the House of Representatives of Massachusetts, on the practicability and expediency of constructing a railway from Boston to the Hudson river, at or near Albany... January 19, 1827. Boston, True & Greene, 1827. 37, [1] p. DBRE; KU; M; MB; MBAt; MCM; MH; MH-BA; MWA; MiU-T; NN; NNC. 29677

---- Report of the select committee to whom was referred the bill from the House, respecting the Indians in Dukes county. [Boston, 1827] 28 p. MH. 29678

---- [Resolve that the commissioners of internal improvements be directed to survey the railway from Boston, state line of Rhode Island. 1827] 2 p. M; MB; MBAt; MWA. 29679

---- Resolves of the General court of the commonwealth of Massachusetts, passed at their session, which commenced on Wednesday, the third of January, and ended on Saturday, the tenth of March, one thousand eight hundred and twenty-seven. Boston, Pr. by True & Greene, prs. to the state. 1827. 435-553, 1, vi p. Ia; MKiTH; MNBedf. 29680

---- Resolves of the General court of the commonwealth of Massachusetts, passed at their session which commenced on Wednesday, the thirtieth of May, and ended on Saturday, the sixteenth of June, one thousand eight hundred and twenty-seven. Boston, Dutton & Wentworth, prs. to the state, 1827. 555-620, 1, iii p. Ia; IaU-L; MKiTH; MNBedf. 29681

---- Rules and orders to be observed in the House of Representatives of the commonwealth of Massachusetts, for the year 1827-8. Boston, Pr. by True & Greene, 1827. 36 p. MRev; Mi. 29682

No entry 29683

---- Speech of His Excellency Levi Lincoln, before the two branches of the Legislature, in convention. June 6, 1827. Boston, True & Greene, state prs., 1827. 16 p. M; MBC; MH; MH-BA; MHi; MWA; NcD; PHi. 29684

---- To the Honorable the Senate and House of Representatives. The commissioners appointed by a resolve of the Legislature, March 3d, 1826, on the subject of the discipline of the prisoners ... Report... [Boston, 1827] 30 p. (Senate, No. 6) PPL. 29685

---- A true abstract from the statements of the presidents and directors of the different banks. Rendered May, 1827... [Boston, 1827] Bdsd. IU. 29686

Massachusetts Charitable Eye and Ear Infirmary, Boston.

Second annual report of the Massachusetts Charitable Eye & Ear Infirmary. Boston, Pr. by Beals and Homer, 1827. 7 p. DLC; DNLM; MB; MBC. 29687

---- Third annual report of the Massachusetts Charitable Eye & Ear Infirmary. Boston, Pr. by John G. Scobie, 1827. 12 p. DLC; DNLM; MB; MBC; MHi. 29688

Massachusetts Charitable Mechanic Association.

Constitution of the Massachusetts Charitable Mechanic Association... Boston, Pr. by Monroe & Francis, 1827. 36 p. MB. 29689

Massachusetts Episcopal Missionary Society

Proceedings of the Massachusetts Episcopal Missionary Society, and trustees of the Massachusetts Episcopal Prayer Book and Tract Society, at the annual meeting held in St. Paul's Church, Boston, June 20, 1827. Boston, J. Putnam, pr., 1827. 24 p. MBD; MWA; NcD; PPL. 29690

Massachusetts Missionary Society

Twenty-eighth annual report of the trustees of the Massachusetts Missionary Society. Salem, Pr. at the office of the Essex Register, 1827. 19, [1] p. NjR; WHi. 29691

The Massachusetts register and United States calendar for 1828. Boston, Richardson & Lord; James Loring [1827] 126 l. CSt; CtHT-W; ICN; MB; MH; MWA; MdBJ; MiD-B; MeB; NN; RPB. 29692

Massachusetts Sabbath School Union

Second annual report, May 31, 1827... Boston, J. Putnam, 1827. 64 p. CtHC; MBC; MHi; MWA; RPB; WHi; BrMus. 29693

Massachusetts Society for the Suppression of Intemperance

Fourteenth annual report of the Massachusetts Society for the Suppression of Intemperance, with resolutions. Passed at a public meeting held November 5, 1827. Boston, N. S. Simpkins and Co., Stephen Foster, pr., 1827. 21 p. ICMe; MWA; PHi; PPPrHi. 29694

Massey, A.

Auction. Will be sold without reserve, for cash on Thursday, the fifth day of April, 100 barrels of salt, a few barrels of dryed apples, and a few barrels of dryed peaches. A. Massey, auctioneer. Vincennes, Mar. 27, 1827. Bdsd. In. 29695

Massinger, Philip, 1583-1640

...A new way to pay old debts. Philadelphia, F. C. Wemyss [etc.] New York, G. M. Bourne [etc., etc.] [1827] 80 p. AzU; DLC; MB; MH; NN. 29696

Matchett's Baltimore directory for 1827... Baltimore, Pr. and pub. by R. J. Matchett, 1827. 285, 30 p. DLC; MBNEH; MWA; MdBB. 29697

[Mather, Samuel] 1706-1785

The life of the late Rev. and learned Dr. Cotton Mather, of Boston, New England... Revised by the Committee of publication. Philadelphia, American Sunday-School Union, I. Ashmead, pr., 1827. 115 p. CSmH; GAU; ICN; KyLoS; MBC; MH; MWA; OMC. 29698

Matters of fact relative to late occurrences among professional Quakers. Philadelphia, 1827. 23 p. CSmH; DLC; MiU-C; PPL; PSC-Hi. 29699

[Matthews, John]

The Divine purpose; displayed in the works of providence and grace; in a series of twenty letters, addressed to an inquiring friend. 2d ed. Richmond, Va., Pub. by Pollard and Converse, 1827. 138 p. DLC; MH-AH; NcD; NcU; NjR; OMC; PPWa; ViRUT. 29700

Maturin, Charles Robert
Bertram, or The castle of St. Aldobrand; a tragedy, in five acts. New York, O. Phelan [1827?] 63 p. CSmH; MH. 29701

Maurice, Mark
The manuscript, comprising the Fratricide, and miscellaneous poems. Boston, J. H. Eastburn, 1827. 69+ p. ICU; MB; MH; NBuG. 29702

May, R.
The advantages of early religion. Boston, Samuel Armstrong, 1827. 36 p. KU. 29703

Mayer, Charles F.
The second annual oration, delivered before the Belles Lettres and Union Philosophical Societies of Dickinson College, at their request, in the Lutheran Church, in Carlisle, on Tuesday evening the 28th day of Sept., 1827. Carlisle, Pr. at the office of the "Herald." 1827. 28 p. DLC; IU; MH; MdHi; N; NN; NjR; PCarlD; PHi; PPAmP; PPPrHi. 29704

Maynard, Lyman
God the Saviour of all men. A sermon, delivered before the First Society of United Christian Friends in Medway, Mass. on the second Sabbath in June, 1827. Dedham, Pr. by H. & W. H. Mann, 1827. 15 p. MB; MMeT; MWA. 29705

---- Reconciliation of all things. A sermon delivered at the Meeting-House in Sherburne, Mass., on the fourth Sabbath evening in August, 1827. Providence, John S. Greene, pr., 1827. 14 p. CSmH; MMeT-Hi; RHi. 29706

Maysville and Lexington Turnpike Road Company
An act to incorporate the Maysville and Lexington Turnpike Road Company. [Frankfort? 1827] 16 p. DNA. 29707

Mead, Asa, 1792-1831
A sermon addressed to the temperate. Portland, Shirley & Hyde, 1827. 20 p. CSmH; MB; MHi; MNtcA; MWA; MeHi; MeLB; RPB. 29708

Mead, Mathew
The almost Christian discovered... Philadelphia, Pr. and pub. by Wm. Stavely. Stereotyper, E. L. Johnson, 1827. viii, 204 p. PLT. 29709

Mechanics and Manufacturers Bank, Providence, R. I.
The charter of the Mechanics and Manufacturers Bank, in Providence. Granted in June, A. D. 1827. [Providence] Jones & Simons, prs., 1827. 8 p. CSmH; RHi; RPB. 29710

The Mechanics' assistant; or, Universal measurer, containing a collection of tables of measures, weights and powers... Providence, John Hutchins; Miller and Grattan, prs., 1827. 58, [1] p. InLP; NjR; PPF; RPB. 29711

Medford, Mass. First Church
Order of exercises at the ordination of Mr. Caleb Stetson to the pastoral care of the First Congregational Church and Society in Medford; on Wednesday, February 28, 1827. [Boston? 1827] Bdsd. MB. 29712

Medical and Philosophical Society of New York
Constitution and by-laws of the Medical & Philosophical Society

of New York. Revised & adopted February 19, 1827. New York, Pr. for the Society by Dixon & Sickels, 1827. 12 p. NNNAM. 29713

Medical College of Ohio, Cincinnati.
Catalogue of the officers and students, in the Medical College of Ohio, during the session of 1826-7. Cincinnati, Morgan, Lodge, and Fisher, prs., [1827?] 8 p. OCHP. 29714

Medical College of South Carolina
Announcement of the Medical College of the state of South Carolina. Charleston, W. Riley, pr. to the Medical College, 1827. 7 p. CSmH; NHi; NNNAM. 29715

The medical companion. See Ewell, James.

Medical Society of the County of New York
Reports of the Medical Society of the City of New York, on nostrums, or secret medicines. Part I. Published by order of the Society, under the direction of the Committee on Quack remedies. New-York, Pr. by E. Conrad, 1827. 52 p. DLC; DNLM; MH; MBCo; NNNAM; PU. 29716

Medicus, pseud. See An address to the guardians of the Washington Asylum.

Meeker, Eli
Sermons; on philosophical, evangelical, and practical subjects ... Ithaca, Pr. by Mack & Andrus, 1827. 400 p. CSmH; ICU; N; NIC; NNR; NRU; NjR; PWW. 29717

Meineke, C.
Brignal banks. A favorite Scotch air with variations for the piano forte. Baltimore, Geo. Willig, Jr., [c1827] 9 p. ViU. 29718

Melford, Charlotte
The twin sisters: or, Two girls of nineteen: being the interesting adventures of Sophia and Charlotte Melford, An affecting narrative written by Charlotte, one of the sisters. To which is added, The orphan of the castle: a Gothic tale, or, The surprising history and vicissitudes of Allan Fitz-Robert, the orphan heir of the Castle of Lindisfarne. Philadelphia, Pub. and for sale, wholesale only by Freeman Scott, 1827. 72 p. CSmH; DLC; PHC; PHi. 29719

[Mellen, Grenville] 1799-1841
Our chronicle of '26; a satirical poem... Boston, Wells & Lilly, 1827. 40 p. CSmH; CtW; DLC; ICN; ICU; IaU; MB; MBAt; MH; MeHi; MeU; NIC; NNC; NjP; PU; RPB; BrMus. 29720

Melmoth, Sydney
The confessions of Cuthburt, a ballad. Bunker Hill, a poem. Migration, a poem. Boston, Hilliard, Gray, Little, and Wilkins, 1827. 124 p. DLC; M; MB; NPV; RPB; BrMus. 29721

A member of the bar. See A brief sketch of the occurrences on board the Brig Crawford.

A member of the Staunton Convention. See The Constitution of '76.

Memoir of Ann Eliza Starr, of Connecticut. Philadelphia, American Sunday School Union, 1827. 31 p. MB. 29722

Memoir of Barron Clarke. Boston, Crocker & Brewster, 1827. 16, [2] p. KU. 29723

Memoir of the Rev. William Ward, one of the Serampore missionaries... Revised by the Committee of Publication... Philadelphia, American Sunday School Union, 1827. 36 p. Ct; KU; MBAt. 29724

Memoirs of David Brainard. By a Sunday School teacher. Prepared for the American Sunday School Union. American Sunday School Union. Philadelphia, Depository, 1827. 141 p. IObB; NCanHi. 29725

Memoirs of eminent persons. See Hall, John Elihu.

Memoirs of the life of the Rev. William Tennent. See Boudinot, Elias.

Memoirs of the Rev. Claudius Buchanan. See Grierson, Miss.

Memoirs of the Rev. Henry Martyn... See Grierson, Miss.

Memorial to the Baltimore and Ohio Rail Road Company. [Baltimore, B. Edes, pr., 1827] 16 p. MdBJ-G. 29726

Memorial to the Hon. Senate and House of Representatives, of the merchants and traders of New-York, having claims upon France and other European states, for spoliations committed on their commerce. New-York, Pr. by J. Seymour, 1827. 18 p. MB; MHi; MiD-B; MiU-C; PPL. 29727

Memory. By the author of "Margaret Whyte" Philadelphia, American Sunday School Union [1827] 35 p. MH. 29728

Men and manners, in verse. Concord, Pr. and sold by J. B. Moore, 1827. 10 l. PPL. 29729

The merchant's memorandum. See Forbes, Charles P.

Merrill, Joseph A.
A discourse on the doctrine of the Trinity, delivered in the chapel, Bromfield Lane, December 31, 1826... Boston, Pr. by T. R. Marvin, 1827. 31 p. ICN; IEG; MBNMHi; MiD-B; MnHi; NNMHi; Nh; OO; BrMus. 29730

Merrill, Samuel
To the public. [Indianapolis, 1827] 24 p. In. 29731

Merritt, Timothy, 1775-1845, comp.
The Christian's manual, a treatise on Christian perfection; with directions for obtaining that state. Compiled principally from the works of the Rev. John Wesley. By the Rev. T. Merritt. 4th ed. New York, Pub. by N. Bangs & J. Emory for the Methodist Episcopal Church, 1827. 160 p. DLC. 29732

Metamorphosis; or, A transformation of pictures, with poetical explanations, for the amusement of young persons. New-York, Sold by Samuel Wood & Sons, Pr. by J. Rakestraw, Philadelphia, 1827. 14 x 9 cm. NNFL. 29733

Methodist Episcopal Church
A collection of hymns for the Methodist Society. Abridged and rev. from the London ed. of the Rev. John Wesley's hymn book... 1st ed. New York, Pub. by Aaron G. Brewer, Stereotyped by A. Chandler, 1827. 522 p. GAGTh; NBliHi. 29734

---- Minutes taken at the several annual conferences of the Methodist Episcopal Church for the year 1827. Cincinnati, Pub. by Martin Ruter for the Methodist Episcopal Church. W. M. and O. Farnsworth, jr., prs., [1827] 64 p. Private library of C. E. Andrews, Steubenville, Ohio, 1938. 29735

---- Minutes taken at the several annual conferences of the Methodist Episcopal Church. For the year 1827. New-York, Pub. by N. Bangs & J. Emory, for the Methodist Episcopal Church, Azor Hoyt, pr., 1827. 72 p. CLU; CoDI; NNMHi; NbHi; PPL; TNS; TxGeoS. 29736

---- Baltimore

Address of the male members of the Methodist Episcopal Church in Baltimore to their brethren throughout the United States. [Baltimore, 1827] 8 p. MdBBC; PPL. 29737

---- Proceedings of the general convention of delegates from the members and local preachers of the Methodist Episcopal Church, friendly to reform, assembled in the First English Evangelical Lutheran Church, in Baltimore... 1827. Baltimore, John D. Toy, 1827. 36 p. MdBBC; OClWHi; OSW; PHi. 29738

The Methodist harmonist. Great variety of tunes collected from the best authors. Also, anthems and pieces for particular occasions. New York, Azor Hoyt, 1827. 247 p. MBNMHi. 29739

Methodist Preachers' Aid Society, Baltimore

Constitution and by-laws of the Methodist Preachers' Aid Society. Baltimore, J. D. Toy, pr., 1827. 11 p. MdBE. 29740

Methodist Society, New York

Extracts from the minutes, &c. of the sixth yearly conference, and the first annual state conference, of the Methodist Society. Held in the city of New-York, in November, 1826, and June, 1827. New-York, Pub. for the Society by Aaron G. Brewer, 1827. 24 p. DWT; MiD-B. 29741

Miami University. Oxford, Ohio

Catalogue of the officers and students of the Miami University, Oxford, Ohio. July, 1827. Hamilton, O., Pr. by James B. Camron [1827] 10 p. ICU; OCHP; OMC; OOxM; PPL; PPPrHi. 29742

---- Report of the trustees of the Miami University, 1827. 4 p. OClWHi. 29743

Michigan (territory)

Actes, relatifs aux townships, aux grands chemins, aux elections, &c. Publies conformement à certaines résolutions, passés pendant la seconde session du second conseil législatif du Michigan. Detroit, Imprimé par Sheldon & Wells, 1827. 69 p. MiD-B; WHi. 29744

---- Acts, relative to townships, highways, & elections. Published agreeably to certain resolutions, passed during the second session of the second legislative council of the territory of Michigan. Detroit, Pr. by Sheldon & Wells, 1827. 55 p. MiD-B. 29745

---- A communication from the secretary of the territory, and a report thereon, from the select committee, to whom the communication and the documents accompanying it were referred; made the 27th February, 1827. Detroit, Pr. by Sheldon & Wells, 1827. 14 p. Mi. 29746

---- Journal of the Legislative council of the territory of Michigan, being the second session of the second council begun and held at the city of Detroit. Jan. 1, 1827. Monroe, Pr. by Edward D. Ellis, 1827. 138 p. DLC; M; Mi; Mi-Hi; Mi-L; MiD-B; MiGr; MiU; NHi; NN; WHi. 29747

---- Laws of the territory of Michigan, comprising the acts of a public nature, revised by commissioners appointed by the first legislative council and passed by the second council; the acts and resolutions of the first and second councils; and the acts, now in force, adopted by the governor and judges of the territory; together with the Declaration of Independence, the Constitution of the United States, and certain acts of Congress relative to said Territory. Detroit, Pr. by Sheldon & Wells, 1827. 709 p. C-L; Ct; DLC; ICLaw; Ia; MH; Mi; Mi-L; MiD-B; MiDSH; MiDU-L; MiU-L; MnU; Mo; Ms; NN; NNLI; Nb; Nj; Nv; OCLaw; OrPML; PU-L; RPL; T; W; WHi; WMMU-L; WaU-L. 29748

Middlebrook's almanack for 1828. By Elijah Middlebrook. Bridgeport, J. B. & L. Baldwin [1827] 12 l. Ct; CtHi; DLC; InU; MWA; NjR. 29749

---- ---- New-Haven, S. Babcock [1827] 12 l. Ct; CtHi; CtY; InU; MWA. 29750

Middlebury College. Middlebury, Vermont

Catalogue of the officers and students of Middlebury College, and the Vermont Academy of Medicine, in connexion. November, 1827. Castleton, Press of the Vermont Statesman [1827] 16 p. OCHP. 29751

---- Middlebury College. Celebration of the Philomathesian & Beneficient Societies. Tuesday, Aug. 14, 1827. Bdsd. VtU. 29752

---- Speakers for the Parkerian Premiums. Middlebury College, Tues. eve, Aug. 14th, 1827. Bdsd. VtU. 29753

Midnight horrors, or, The bandit's daughter. An original romance... Philadelphia, Pub. and sold wholesale only, by Freeman Scott... 1827. 72 p. Collection of Wilbur Macy Stone, East Orange, N. J. 29754

Mignet, François Auguste Alexis, 1796-1884

History of the French revolution from 1789 to 1814. Rev. & corr. from the London ed. New York, Pub. by G. & C. Carvill. John M. Danforth, pr., 1827. 447 p. C-S; CSmH; CtHT-W; CtW; KyBC; KyLx; LNHT; MA; MB; MH; Me; MoU; NBLiHi; NNS; NNUT; NR; NSyU; NWM; NbCrD; NcU; O; PLFM; RNR; TMeC; WBB; WHi. 29755

Miles, Barzillai H.

The new Christian hymn-book. Being a selection from the most approved authors, carefully compiled and corrected; for the use of the Church of Christ. 1st ed. Athens, O., Pub. by A. G. Brown, for the author, 1827. I. Maxon, pr. 368 p. MWA. 29756

Military! He took the field, not as a victor crowned with glorious deeds, in battle won, nor solely bent, his troops in martial prowess to display... Gorham, Oct. 8, 1827. Bdsd. MeHi. 29757

The military sketch-book. See Maginn, William.

Milk for babes, or A catechism in verse: For the use of Sunday schools. Philadelphia, American Sunday School Union [1827?] 32 p. MHi; RPB; BrMus. 29758

Miller, H.

A new selection of hymns and spiritual songs. From the best authors, designed for the use of conference meetings, private circles and congregations. Cincinnati, 1827. 660 p. KyWinK. 29759

Miller, Nathaniel
A dissertation, read before the Massachusetts Medical Society, on the importance and manner of detecting deep seated matter... Boston, Pr. by John G. Scobie, 1827. 16 p. MBC; MBCo; MiDW-M; NNNAM; RPB. 29760

Miller, Samuel, 1769-1850
The importance of the Gospel ministry: an introductory lecture delivered at the opening of the winter session of the Theological Seminary at Princeton, New Jersey Nov. 9, 1827. Princeton, N. J., Pr. by D. A. Borrenstein, 1827. 56 p. CSmH; DLC; GDC; MH; MoSpD; NCH; NNG; NNUT; NjP; NjR; OC; OCHP; OO; PHi; PPL; PPLT; PPPrHi; ScCoT. 29761

---- Letters on clerical manners and habits, addressed to a student at Princeton, N. J. in the Theological Seminary. New York, Pub. by G. & C. Carvill [D. A. Borrenstein, pr., Princeton, N. J.] 1827. 476 p. CSmH; CU; CtW; CtY; DLC; GDC; ICN; ICU; InCW; MB; MBAt; MBC; MH; MdBS; MeB; MiU; MdBP; NBLiHi; NIC; NN; NRU; Nh; NjP; OO; PPPrHi; PU; PV; TCU; TNJ; TxAuPT; ViU; WBB; BrMus. 29762

---- ---- 2d ed. New York, Pub. by G. & C. Carvill [Princeton, N. J., D. A. Borrenstein, pr., 1827] 423 p. Ct; KyLoS; MH; MiToC; NNC; NNUT; NRAB; NjR; OCl; OMC; OO; PAtM; PPPrHi; PU; BrMus. 29763

Miller's agricultural almanac for 1828. By Joshua Sharp. Charleston, A. E. Miller [1827] 24 l. DLC; MWA; ScC; ScU. 29764

Miller's planters' & merchants' almanac for 1828. 2d ed. Charleston, A. E. Miller [1827] 24 l. MWA. 29765

Mills, John B.
A survey for a proposed canal along the Delaware river, from the mouth of the Lackawaxen river to the village of Deposite. Done in Oct. and Nov., 1826... Albany, Pr. by Croswell & Van Benthuysen, 1827. 16 p. CSmH. 29766

---- ---- New-York, Pr. by Elliott & Palmer, 1827. 17 p. MWo; NN; NNE; NRom. 29767

[Miner, Charles] 1780-1865
Letter, to the citizens of Lancaster county, on the woollens-bill. [Philadelphia? 1827?] 15 p. LNHT; MB. 29768

Ming's Hutchins' improved; almanac and ephemeris for 1828. New-York, Alexander Ming [1827] 18 l. NB; NBLiHi; NHi. 29769

Miniature almanack, for the year of our Lord, 1828. Boston, Pub. and sold wholesale and retail by Richardson & Lord, J. H. A. Frost, pr., [1827] [20] p. DLC; MWA; MnU; WHi; BrMus. 29770

The minstrel, or, Pocket songster. New-York, Pr. for the booksellers, 1827. 144 p. RPB. 29771

Minstrel boy. A collection of the most fashionable and delightful songs. Philadelphia, F. Scott, 1827. PPins. 29772

The minstrel lyre. See Ellen, pseud.

Minutoli, Wolfardine Auguste Louis Menu
Recollections of Egypt. By Baroness von Wolfardine Auguste Louis Menu Minutoli. Philadelphia, Carey, Lea & Carey, 1827. xii, 252 p. DLC; DeWI; LU; MA; MMedHi; MdW; NNS; NP; NT; NjR; PPA; PPL; PU; UU; ViAl; WM. 29773

Miscellaneous poems. See Murden, Mrs. Eliza (Crawley)

The Miss Gillinghams' second concert... Thursday ev'g. Jan. 25, 1827. Washington city, Wm. Cooper, jun., pr., [1827] 1 p. DLC. 29774

Missionary Society of Connecticut

Twenty-eighth annual narrative of missions... with an account of books sent to the new settlements, and a statement of the funds for the year 1826. Hartford, P. B. Gleason, pr., 1827. 24 p. CtHC; CtHT-W. 29775

Mississippi

Journal of the House of Representatives, of the state of Mississippi: at their tenth session, held in the town of Jackson. Jackson [Miss.] Pr. by Peter Isler, 1827. 308 p. Ms; MsU; MsWJ; NN. 29776

---- Journal of the Senate of the state of Mississippi, at their tenth session, held in the town of Jackson. Jackson [Miss.] Pr. by Peter Isler, 1827. 235 p. DLC; Ms; MsU; MsWJ; NN; WHi. 29777

----Laws of the state of Mississippi, passed at the tenth session of the General Assembly, held in the town of Jackson. Jackson, Peter Isler, state pr., 1827. 155, viii, [11] p. C-L; DLC; I; ICLaw; Ia; In-SC; LU-L; M; MH-L; MdBB; MiU-L; Ms; Ms-Ar; MsU; MsWJ; NN; NNB; NNC-L; NNLI; Nb; Nj; Nv; OCLaw; O-SC; Or-SC; RPL. 29778

Missouri

Journal of the House of Representatives of the 4th General Assembly, of the state of Missouri, begun and held at the city of Jefferson, on Monday, the twentieth day of November, in the year of our Lord one thousand eight hundred and twenty-six. City of Jefferson, C. Gunn, pr., 1827. 151 p. DLC; Mo; MoSL. 29779

---- Journal of the Senate of the fourth General Assembly of the state of Missouri, begun and held at the city of Jefferson, on Monday, the 20th day of November, 1826. City of Jefferson, C. Gunn, pr., 1826! [1827] 135 p. Mo; MoHi; MoSL. 29780

---- Laws, of the state of Missouri; passed at the second session of the third General Assembly, begun and held at the town of St. Charles, January 19, 1826; and, at the first session of the fourth General Assembly, begun and held at the city of Jefferson, Nov. 20, 1826. St. Louis, C. Keemle, pr., 1827. 83, [1], [3] p. DLC; I; ICLaw; MH-L; MoHi NNB; P. 29781

.... Mr. Clay and General Jackson... a complete history of the case between General Jackson and Mr. Clay... [Baltimore, Patriot Office, August, 1827] 16 p. CtY; MBAt; NIC; NcU; OCHP; PHi; PPAmP. 29782

Mr. Clay's speech upon the tariff. See Giles, William Branch.

Mitchell, Joseph

The missionary pioneer; or, A brief memoir of the life, labours, and death of John Stewart... New-York, Pr. by J. C. Totten, 1827. 96 p. DGU; DLC; ICN; IEG; IaU; InHi; InU; KU; MiD-B; MiDSH; MiGr; MnHi; MnU; MoSM; NN; NcD; NhD; NjMD; OC; OClWHi; OHi; OMC; OkU; TNF; WHi. 29783

Mitchell, Stephen T.

The spirit of the Old Dominion. By Stephen T. Mitchell... [no. 1]

Richmond, Pr. by Shepherd & Pollard, 1827. 298 p. DLC; MWo; NN; Vi; ViU. 29784

Mohawk and Hudson Rail Road Co. See Albany and Schenectady Railroad Co.

The monkey's frolic. A humorous tale. Baltimore, Pub. by Fielding Lucas, Jun. [Philadelphia, Ash & Mason, 1827?] 16 l. MdHi. 29785

Monroe Academy, Henrietta, N. Y.
The charter of the Monroe Academy, located at Henrietta, near Rochester, N. Y. To which is added, the general act of the legislature, passed Feb. 23, 1821. Also the by-laws, rules, and regulations, of the Academy. Rochester, Pr. for the trustees, by E. Peck & Co., 1827. 12 p. MH. 29786

Montgomery, James
The Pelican Island. Philadelphia, E. Littell, 1827. 156 p. MBC; MBL; MWHi; PHi. 29787

Moore, Theophilus
Marriage customs & ceremonies, & modes of courtship, of the various nations of the universe... New York, W. Borradaile, 1827. 269 p. Ct; FOA; MH; MdBL; NHuntHi; TJoT. 29788

Moore, Thomas, 1779-1852
The Epicurean, a tale. Boston, Wells & Lilly, 1827. 275 p. MAnP; MB; MBAt; NNS; PPL. 29789

---- ---- Philadelphia, The Olive-Branch book store, 1827. 192 p. CtHT; LNHT; MNS; MeLB; MiD; NcAS; NjP; OHi; PPL. 29790

---- ---- Philadelphia, Carey, Lea, & Carey and R. H. Small, 1827. 260 p. CtHT-W; LU; MB; MH; NNC; OCL; P; PHi; PPL; RPB. 29791

---- The works of Thomas Moore, complete in two volumes. 4th ed. Philadelphia, 1827-1828. 2 v. IU. 29792

Moore, Thomas Patrick, 1797-1853
Speech of Thomas P. Moore, esq. delivered in the court house in Harrodsburg, June 3d, 1827. Harrodsburg, K. [Ky.] Pr. at the Watchtower office, 1827. 36 p. CSmH; NN; NjR; TxU. 29793

Moore, Zephaniah S.
Articles of faith and form of covenant... Worcester, Griffin and Morrill, prs., 1827. 12 p. MWA. 29794

Moral stories for boys and girls. [Story I: Maria; or, The good girl] Providence, 1827. 8 p. RPB. 29795

Moran, P. K.
A collection of favorite songs arranged for the Spanish guitar. New York, Engraved, pr. and sold by E. Riley [c. 1827] v p. MdBP. 29796

Moravians
Die taglichen Loosungen und Lehrterte der Brudergemeine fur das Jahr 1828. Allentaun, Penn., Gedruckt bey Heinrich Ebner und Comp., 1827. 132, [1] p. DLC; MA; P; PNazMHi. 29797

More, Hannah, 1745-1833
The works of Hannah More, with a sketch of her life... Boston, S. G. Goodrich, 1827. 2 v. ArCa; IaU; InID; MnS; NRSB; OO; PAtM; PSC-Hi; RNR; TxDaM; Vi. 29798

More light on masonry; or, Morgan revived. With an appendix. By one of the fraternity, who has devoted thirty years to the subject... Rochester, Pr. for the author, 1827. 88 p. DLC; NRU; PPFM. 29799

Morgan, Thomas
Proposals by Thomas Morgan for publishing a weekly newspaper in the borough of Washington, Washington County, Penna. to be entitled The Herald of the Cross, and Democratic Eagle. Washington [Pa.] Mar. 15, 1827. 1 p. DLC. 29800

[Morgan, William] 1774-ca. 1826
Illustrations of Masonry, by one of the fraternity, who has devoted 30 years to the subject. [Batavia?] Pr. for the proprieter [sic] 1827. ix, [10]-82 p. (Probably pr. at Batavia or Rochester.) NCanHi. 29801

[----] ---- 2nd ed. With an account of the kidnapping of the author. [Batavia?] Pr. for the author, 1827. 92 p. NRU; WMFM. 29802

---- ---- 3d ed. New York, Pr. for the author, 1827. 99 p. CtHC; DLC; MB; MH; MdHi; NN; PPFM; WHi. 29803

[----] ---- Rochester, Pr. for the author, 1827. 96 p. DLC; IaCrM; MH; MiD-B; NN; NNFM; NRM. 29804

[----] ---- 3d ed. Rochester, Pr. for the author, 1827. 95, [1] p. CSmH; DLC; MB; MH; NN; NRHi; PHi; PPFM; WHi. 29805

---- ---- [Rochester] Pr. for the author, Wm. Morgan, 1827. 94 p. ICAC; NN; NNFM; NRHi. 29806

[----] ---- 4th ed. Rochester, Pr. for the Proprietors, 1827. ix, [11]-96 p. MDeeP;NBuHi; NN. 29807

[----] ---- 12th ed. Rochester, For the proprietors, 1827. x, 98 p. CSmH; NRHi; PPFM; WHi. 29808

---- Ilustraciones de masoneria, por Guillermo Morgan, uno de la fraternidad, que ha dedicado treinta años á este objeto... Traduccion literal del original. Boston, 1827. 95 p. DLC. 29809

Morgan confirmed: or, The secrets of freemasonry made known to all the world... New York, Pr. for the author, 1827. 86 p. 1 l. DLC; PPFM. 29810

Morgan's pamphlet. An authentic key to the door of Free Masonry, calculated not only for the instruction of every new made Mason, but also for the information of all who intend to become brethren; containing a circumstantial account of all the proceedings in making a Mason... New-York, Pr. for the pub., 1827. 62 p. Nj; PPFM. 29811

Morris Academy, Morris, Conn.
Prospectus of Morris Academy in Litchfield, (South-Farms), Conn. Litchfield, Conn., S. S. Smith [1827] 25 p. Ct; CtHC; MH. 29812

Morris Canal and Banking Company
A report to the directors of the Morris Canal and Banking Company; made by May 1st, 1827 with a statement of the work ther done upon the canal. A report from the Chief Engineer, and a communication from Governor Clinton. Pr. by order of the Board of Directors. New-York, Wm. Davis, jr., pr., 1827. 22 p. DLC; NBuG; NN; NNC; NRU; NjR. 29813

Morse, Intrepid
Christian piety and knowledge, or literature & religion; a sermon. Preached at the laying of the corner-stone of the Theological Seminary & Kenyon College, at Gambier, Knox County, Ohio, June 9th, 1827. Steubenville, Pr. by James Wilson, 1827. 24 p. DLC; MiD-B; NjR; OCHP;

OClWHi; OHi. 29814

Morse, Pitt
An oration, delivered in the village of Adams, Jefferson County, N. Y. on the fifty-first anniversary of the national independence of the United States of America. Watertown, Pr. by W. Woodward, 1827. 11 p. NCaS. 29815

Morse, Samuel Finley Breeze, 1791-1872
Academies of arts. A discourse delivered on Thursday, May 3, 1827, in the chapel of Columbia College before the National Academy of Design on its first anniversary. G. and C. Carvill, New-York. Elliot and Palmer pr., 1827. 60 p. DLC; LU; MB; MBAt; MH; MiD-B; NIC; NNC; NNUT; PHi; PPL; ScC; ScU; WHi. 29816

Morse, William
A sermon wherein is shown that sin is finite, or limited, in its nature and consequences: delivered in the First Universalist Church, Nantucket, Sunday afternoon, Jan. 28, 1827. Nantucket [Mass.] Pr. at the Inquirer office, 1827. 23 p. CSmH; MB. 29817

Morton, Daniel Oliver, 1788-1852
A sermon, delivered in Shoreham, January 31, 1827, at the funeral of Deacon Stephen Cooper. Castleton, Pr. by Ovid Miner, 1827. 22 p. MBC; MDeeP; VtMiM. 29818

Morton, Thomas, 1764?-1838
A school for grown children: a comedy, in five acts... New-York, E. M. Murden, 1827. 86 p. CSmH; DLC. 29819

---- Town and country; a comedy, in five acts. Baltimore, Pr. and pub. by J. Robinson, Circulating Library, and Dramatic Repository, 1827. 80 p. MWA. 29820

---- ---- Philadelphia, Pub. by C. Neal, Mifflin & Parry, prs., 1827. 72 p. MB; MH. 29821

A mother, pseud. See Always happy.

[Mott, Mrs. Abigail (Field)] 1766-1851
Observations on the importance of female education & maternal instruction, with their beneficial influence on society, by a mother ... 2d ed. New York, Mahlon Day, 1827. 84 p. InRE; MH; OO; PSC-Hi; PU. 29822

Mott, Samuel, N.
An exhortation to all professing the Christian name... New York, Dixon and Sickels, 1827. 18 p. PHC. 29823

Mott, Valentine
Successful ligature of the common iliac artery. [Philadelphia, 1827] 8 p. NNNAM. 29824

Motte, Mellish Irving
Simplicity in the Christian faith alike scriptural and powerful. A sermon, delivered on the morning of Lord's Day, July 1, 1827. At the second Independent Church in Charleston, S. C. Charleston, Pr. by C. C. Sebring, 1827. 23 p. ICMe; MB; MBAU; MH; NNC; PPL; RPB; WHi. 29825

Moultrie, James, 1783-1869
An eulogium on Dr. Samuel Wilson read before the Medical Society of South Carolina, and published at their request... Charleston, A. E. Miller, 1827. 14 p. DLC. 29826

Much instruction from little reading; or, Extracts from some of the most approved authors, ancient and modern... New York, Pr. by Mahlon Day, 1827. 5 v. C-S; CtHT; CtW; ICMcC; MB; MH;

NBF; NbOU; NcGu; NjR; PHC; RNHi; UPB. 29827

Muckarsie, John
The children's catechism. West Union, O., R. M. Voorheese, pr., 1827. 24 p. PPPrHi. 29828

Mulford, James H.
James H. Mulford and al appellants, vs. Abraham Bradley and al appellees. Motion in error by appellees. At a Court of probate, 2d May, 1825, on the estate of Abraham Bradley, deceased. [New Haven? 1827?] 27 p. CtY. 29829

[Mumford, Paul M.]
A defence. Providence, Jones & Simons, 1827. 17 p. RNHi. 29830

Munchausen
The surprising adventures of Baron Munchausen; containing his singular travels, miraculous escapes, &c. To which is added The life of Bamfylde Moore Carew, king of the beggars. Philadelphia, F. Scott, 1827. 72 p. DLC; TSewU. 29831

Mundy, William
A treasure for the honest inquirer. after truth. Baltimore, Pr. for the author, 1827. 40 p. ICMe. 29832

[Murden, Mrs. Eliza (Crawley)]
Miscellaneous poems, by a lady of Charleston, S. C. 2d ed. New York, the author, Samuel Wood & Sons, prs., 1827. 179 p. DLC; IU; MH; NBLiHi; NIC; NcAS; NcD; ScCleA. 29833

Murdock, James, 1776-1856
On coming unworthily to the Lord's supper. A sermon, delivered in the South Parish of Andover, Oct. 28, 1827... Andover, Flagg & Gould, prs., 1827. 22 p. CBPac; CSmH; ICT; MAnP; MBC; MH-AH; MHi; MWA; MeBat; MiD-B; MoSpD; NNG; OClW; PPL; RPB; VtU; BrMus. 29834

Murphey, Archibald DeBow, 1777-1832
An oration delivered in Person Hall, Chapel Hill, on the 27th of June, 1827, the day previous to the commencement, under the appointment of the Dialectic Society. Raleigh, Pr. by J. Gales & Son, 1827. 18 p. CSmH; MWeA; NCH; NcU. 29835

[----] To the honourable the General Assembly of North-Carolina, the memorial of the subscriber. [Hillsborough, D. Heartt, pr., Jan. 1, 1827] 3 p. NcU. 29836

Murray, Benjamin Bixby, b. 1801.
A sermon delivered in the Universalist Meeting House, Norway Village, on the annual Thanksgiving, November 29, 1827. Norway, [Me.] Pr. at the Observer office, 1827. 12 p. MH. 29837

[Murray, Hannah Lindley] 1771-1836
... The American toilet. 2d ed. New-York, Pr. and pub. at Imbert's Lithographic Office [1827?] 20 pl. MBAt; NN. 29838

Murray, John, 1742-1793
Records of the life of the Rev. John Murray... written by himself. 2d ed. Boston, Pub. by Bowen & Cushing, 1827. 348 p. CSmH; MB; MH; MLow; MWA; TJoT. 29839

Murray, Lindley, 1745-1826
An abridgment of Murray's English grammar. Containing also lessons in parsing... From the 2d Portsmouth ed., enl. and imp. Boston, Hilliard, Gray, Little & Wilkins, 1827. 99 p. DLC; MB. 29840

---- ---- Concord, J. B. Moore, Stereotyped by T. Woolson, Claremont, N. H., 1827. 100 p. CtSoP;

MH; MLex; NNC; Nh-Hi. 29841

---- ---- Ithaca, N.Y., Pr. and sold by Mack & Andrus, Pub. by Collins & Hannay, New York, 1827. 107 p. CtHT-W; DLC; MH; MNBedf; WU. 29842

---- ---- Philadelphia, Pub. by John Grigg, 1827. 105 p. PWCHi. 29843

---- The duty and benefit of a daily perusal of the Holy Scriptures in families... Philadelphia, Pr. by Adam Waldie & Co., 1827. 30 p. MH; PPF; PU. 29844

---- English exercises, adapted to Murray's English grammar... Designed for the benefit of private learners, as well as for the use of schools. Loring's 13th Boston ed. Boston, Pub. & sold by James Loring, 1827. 213, [3] p. CtMMHi; MH; NNC; RNHi; RPB. 29845

----- ----- Stereotyped from the last English ed. By B. & J. Collins, New York. Philadelphia, Pub. and for sale by John Grigg, 1827. 192 p. CoGrS; MH; TNT. 29846

---- English grammar, adapted to the different classes of learners, with an appendix... Baltimore, Fielding Lucas, Jun. and Armstrong and Plaskitt, 1827. CtHT-W; MChiA. 29847

---- ---- Stereotyped by B. & J. Collins, from the last English ed. Bridgeport, J. B. & L. Baldwin, 1827. 312 p. CtHT-W; MH; WGr. 29848

---- ---- Stereotyped by H. & H. Wallis... New York, Pr. and pub. by J. & J. Harper, 1827. 232 p. NBP. 29849

---- ---- Philadelphia, Freeman Scott, 1827. Stereotyped by L. Johnson. 108 p. NcWsM;P. 29850

---- ---- Philadelphia, Pub. and for sale, (wholesale only) by Freeman Scott, Stereotyped by L. Johnson, 1827. 210 p. ViRVal. 29851

---- The English reader; or, pieces in prose and poetry... Bellows Falls, James I. Cutler & Co., 1827. 249 p. CtY; MH; OO; RPB; VtHi. 29852

---- ---- Brattleboro, Holbrook & Fessenden, 1827. 204 p. DLC; IaScM; N; NN; PSC-Hi. 29853

---- ---- Bridgeport, J. B. & L. Baldwin, 1827. 263 p. MH. 29854

---- ---- Cincinnati, Pub. & sold by N. & G. Guilford, 1827. W. M. & O. Farnsworth, Jr., prs. 204 p. In. 29855

---- ---- Stereotyped by H. & H. Wallis, New York. Concord, N.H., Pr. and pub. by Manahan, Hoag & Co., 1827. 252 p. MBeHi; MH; MeHi. 29856

---- ---- Cooperstown, Stereotyped, pr. and pub. by H. & E. Phinney, 1827. 252 p. CSmH; DLC; IaHA; MiU-C; NCH; NSyU. 29857

---- ---- Stereotyped by A. Chandler, New-York. Hallowell, Pub. by Calvin Spaulding, 1827. 258 p. MTaHi. 29858

---- ---- New York, Pub. by Wm. Burgess, Jun., 1827. 204 p. MeBat. 29859

---- ---- New York, Stereotyped by H. & H. Wallis. Pub. by Collins & Co., 1827. Ct; CtY; MBU-E; MWA; WHi. 29860

---- ---- New York, Pub. by John Montgomery. Stereotyped by James Conner, 1827. 204, 60 p. CSfCW; MH; MPiB. 29861

---- ---- Philadelphia, Pub. by L. B. Clarke, 1827. [20], 189 p. CtHi; PReaHi. 29862

---- ---- Stereotyped by H. & H. Wallis, New York. Rochester, Pr. and pub. by E. Peck & Co., 1827. 252 p. MiGr; NRHi; NRU. 29863

---- ---- Stereotyped by J. Reed, Boston. Saco, Pub. by Putnam & Blake, 1827. 304 p. CSmH; CoFcS; ICU; LT; MB; MH; MeHi; NNC-T. 29864

---- ... Introduction to the English reader; or, Pieces in prose and poetry... Boston, Lincoln & Edmands; Baltimore, Cushing & Jewett [Stereotyped by T. H. & C. Carter] 1827. 264 p. CSt; MH. 29865

---- ---- Boston, N. S. Simpkins & Co., Hilliard Gray, Little & Wilkins, 1827. viii, 220 p. NNC-T. 29866

---- ---- Rochester, N. Y., Pub. and sold by E. Peck & Co., 1827. 156 p. CtHT-W; CtHi; Vt. 29867

---- Key to the exercises adapted to Murray's English grammar. Calculated to enable private learners to become their own instructors in grammar and composition... Stereotyped from the last English ed. by B. & J. Collins, New York. New York, Pub. by Collins & co., 1827. viii, [1], 168 p. MH. 29868

---- Memoirs of the life and writings of Lindley Murray, in a series of letters, written by himself. With a preface and a continuation of the memoirs, by Elizabeth Frank. New York, Pub. by Samuel Wood & Sons, Richard Wood, Collins & Hannay, Collins & Co. [Samuel Wood & Sons, prs.] 1827. viii, 280 p. ArU; CSmH; CSt; CtHT; ICU; IaU; InRE; KU; MA; MB; MH; MW; MiU; MoSU; NIC; NNS; NNUT; NcGuG; Nh-Hi; OC; OClWHi; PHi; PLFM; PP; PPF; PSC-Hi; PU; RP; RPB; UU; WHi; BrMus. 29869

---- A new abridgement of Murray's English grammar, with questions, containing all that is generally used in the duodecimo and octavo editions, condensed and arranged to facilitate the learner... By Stephen W. Taylor ... Watertown [N. Y.] R. Clapp, Pr. by T. Parsons & Co., 1827. 137 p. CSmH; DLC; NN; NNC. 29870

---- The pronouncing introduction. Introduction to the English reader: or, A selection of pieces, in prose and poetry... Boston, Pub. by Lincoln & Edmands, 1827. 168 p. CtSoP. 29871

---- Sequel to the English reader, or Elegant selections in prose and poetry... New York, Stereotyped by H. & H. Wallis. Pub. by Collins & Co., 1827. 4, 299 p. CtSoP. 29872

---- ---- Philadelphia, Pr. and pub. by S. Probasco, 1827. 244 p. MoFloSS; NjR; OO; PHi; PPeSchw; PU-Penn. 29873

---- Murray's system of English grammar, improved, and adapted to the present mode of instruction in this branch of science. 2d ed. Worcester, Pub. by Dorr & Howland, 1827. 55 p. MHi. 29874

Musical Fund Society of Philadelphia

14th concert... 28 November, 1827. [Philadelphia, 1827] Bdsd. PPL. 29875

Mututal Assurance Company of the City of Norwich, Conn.

An act of assembly, incorporating the Mutual Assurance Company of the City of Norwich; also, the deed of settlement to be subscribed by the members of said company. Norwich [Conn.] L. H. Young, pr., 1827. 15 p. CSmH; CtHi. 29876

N

Nack, James, 1809-1879
The legend of the rocks, and other poems... New York, Pr. by E. Conrad, 1827. 204 p. CSmH; CtHT-W; CtW; DLC; IU; MB; MH; NCaS; NGH; NNC; NjP; OCHP; PU; TxU; VtMiM; WHi. 29877

Nahant. See Hart, Jeanette M.

[Nares, Edward]
Thinks-I-to-myself; a serio-ludicro, tragico-comico tale. Written by Thinks-I-to-myself, Who? (pseud.) Boston, J. P. Peaslee, 1827. 2 v. AMob; MBBC; MH; MHi; MnU; NRMA; NjR. 29878

A narrative of the facts and circumstances relating to the kidnapping and presumed murder of William Morgan, and of the attempt to carry off David C. Miller, and to burn or destroy the printing office of the latter, for the purpose of preventing the printing and publishing of a book, entitled "Illustrations of Masonry." Prepared under the direction of the several committees, appointed at meetings of the citizens, of the counties of Genesee, Livingston, Ontario, Monroe, and Niagara, in the state of New York... Batavia, Pr. by D. C. Miller, under the direction of the Committees. 1827. 37, [1], xxxv p. CSmH; KU; MBFM; N; NHi; WHi. 29879

---- Rochester, N. Y., Pr. by Edwin Scrantom, under the direction of the Committees, 1827. 88 p. IaCrM; MBFM; NIC; NN; PPFM; RPJCB. 29880

Narrative of the sufferings of Seth Hubbell. See Hubbell, Seth.

Nash, W.
Canton March. For the piano forte. Composed for, and dedicated to Miss E. A. Gedney by W. Nash. New York, Engraved, pr. & sold by E. Riley [c1827] 1 p. ViU. 29881

---- Lassie wi' the lint white locks. New York, Engraved, pr. & sold by E. Riley, 1827. 2 p. MB. 29882

Nashua Manufacturing Company
The acts of incorporation, and by-laws of the Nashua Manufacturing Company. Together with extracts from the statute laws of New Hampshire, relative to manufacturing corporations. Boston, Pr. by Beals and Homer, 1827. 24 p. MCM; MHi. 29883

Nashville Republican & State Gazette
[Reprint of the Nashville Republican & State Gazette containing "An important letter from the Jackson Committee on the Six Militia Men."] [Nashville, Oct. 5, 1827] 2 p. DLC. 29884

Natchez Fencibles
Constitution of the Natchez Fencibles, as adopted on the 21st day of April, 1824, and revised on the 22nd of January, 1827. Natchez, Pr. at the office of the Ariel. 1827. 10 p. Ms-Ar; MsJS. 29885

Natchez, Miss. Trinity Church
The charter of Trinity Church, in the city of Natchez, granted January 30, 1827. Also the bye-laws of the corporation of said church adopted July 6, 1827. Natchez, Pr. at the Ariel Office,

1827. 8 p. DLC. 29886

National Anthracite Coal Company of Pennsylvania
Maps of the lands of the National Anthracite Coal Co. & of the anthracite coal region of Pa. New York, 1827. PPL not located, 1969. 29887

The national calendar and people's almanac for 1828. Baltimore, Wooddy [1827] 18 l. MdBE. 29888

The national calendar for 1828. By Peter Force. Washington City, Peter Force [1827] 144 l. CtY; DLC; DWP; In; InU; MBAt; MWA; NBLiHi; NjP; NjR; PHi. 29889

[National Republican Party. Kentucky]
Address to the freemen of Kentucky, from a convention of delegates friendly to the re-election of John Quincy Adams, as president of the United States, held in the town of Frankfort, on the 17th, 18th and 19th days of December, 1827. Maysville, Ky., Pr. at the office of the Eagle [1827?] 15, [1] p. DLC. 29890

[----] Proceedings of the administration convention held at Frankfort, Kentucky, on Monday, December 17, 1827. [Frankfort? Pr. by J.H. Holeman, 1827?] 23 p. DLC; OCHP; WHi. 29891

---- Jefferson County.
Administration convention. Proceedings had at a meeting of the friends of the administration at Louisville, Ky. [Louisville, Ky., W.W. Worsley, pr., 1827] 8 p. CSmH. 29892

[National Republican Party. Louisiana]
Proceedings of the delegates of the friends of the administration of John Quincy Adams, assembled in convention at Baton Rouge. New-Orleans, Pr. by B. Levy, 1827. 28 p. DLC; MBAt; MdBP; MiD-B; NN; PHi; PPL; RP. 29893

[---- Maryland]
Proceedings of the administration meeting in Baltimore County, June, 1827. Baltimore, Pr. at the Baltimore Patriot Office, 1827. 12 p. MBAt. 29894

[---- ----] Proceedings of the Maryland administration convention, delegated by the people, and held in Baltimore, on Monday and Tuesday, July 23d. and 24th, 1827. [Baltimore,] Pr. at the office of the Baltimore patriot, 1827. 24 p. CSmH; DLC; MB; MBAt; MdBE. 29895

[---- North Carolina]
Address of the administration convention, held in the capital at Raleigh, Dec. 20th, 1827. To the freeman of North-Carolina. Raleigh, Pr. by J. Gales & Son, 1827. 15 p. ICJ; MBAt; MWA; MiD-B; NN; NcU; NjR; OClWHi; WHi. 29896

[---- Ohio]
Proceedings and address of the convention of delegates, that met at Columbus, Ohio, Dec. 28, 1827, to nominate a ticket of electors favorable to the reelection of John Quincy Adams, president of the United States, to be supported at the electoral election of 1828. [Columbus?] Pr. by P.H. Olmsted, 1827. 17 p. CSmH; DLC; PPL. 29897

[---- Ohio. Hamilton County]
An address from the administration committee of Hamilton County, to their fellow citizens. [Cincinnati? 1827] 8 p. O. 29898

[---- Ohio. Jefferson County]
Jefferson County Republican meeting. A meeting of the citizens of the county of Jefferson, friendly to the present administration of the general government, was held at the court house, in the town of Steubenville, pursuant to public notice, on Tuesday evening, June 5, 1827. The meeting was organized, by appointing the Hon. J. H. Hallock, president, and David Sloan, Esq. vice president, Dr. Anderson Judkins and David Moodey, secretaries. The following preamble and resolutions were offered, and, after some discussion, adopted. [Steubenville? 1827] 12 p. OClWHi. 29899

[---- Ohio. Warren County]
Warren County administration meeting. [Lebanon, office of the Western Star, Nov. 19, 1827] 8 p. CSmH; O; OClWHi. 29900

[---- Pennsylvania. Washington County]
To the citizens of Washington County. [Washington, Pa. ? 1827] 32 p. CSmH; PPL. 29901

[---- Pennsylvania. Westmoreland County]
Proceedings of a meeting of the friends of the general administration, held in the borough of Greensburgh, Westmoreland county, Pennsylvania, on the 20th November, 1827. F. A. Wise, pr., 1827. 16 p. DLC. 29902

[---- Philadelphia]
Address from a meeting of Democratic citizens of Philadelphia opposed to the election of Gen'l Jackson. Oct. 5, 1827. [Philadelphia, Pr. by John Binns, 1827.] 15 p. ICN; MnHi; PHi. 29903

[---- Virginia]
Preamble and resolutions of a meeting... in Richmond, October 24, 1827, disapproving the election of Gen. Andrew Jackson to the Presidency of the United States. [Richmond? T. W. White, pr., 1827] 8 p. Vi. 29904

[---- Virginia]
To the people of the state of New York. [Virginia anti-Jackson convention, Saturday Dec. 12, 1827. Richmond? 1827] 16 p. MBAt; NNC. 29905

Natural history. Selected from the Youth's Friend. American Sunday School Union, Philadelphia, [1827] vi, 144 p. DLC; PU; ViRVal; BrMus. 29906

[Neale, Erskine]
The living and the dead, by a country curate. New York, Pr. by J. & J. Harper, 1827. 232 p. GDC; KyLx; MB; NCH; NNG; NRU; ViAl. 29907

Neals' almanac for 1828. Baltimore, Wm. & Joseph Neal; R. J. Matchett, pr. [1827] 18 l. DLC; MWA. 29908

Nelson, John
Address, delivered in Leicester, Jan. 26, 1827, before a meeting of delegates from several "Lyceums for Mutual Instruction" in the county of Worcester. Worcester, William Manning, pr. [1827?] 23 p. MBAU; MBAt; N. 29909

Nettleton, Asahel, 1783-1844
Remarks of the Rev. Mr. Nettleton on a recent sermon by Rev. Mr. Finney, in a letter addressed to Rev. Dr. Spring... Durham, N. Y., 1827. 8 p. CtHC; MBC. 29910

---- Village hymns for social worship... 7th ed. New York, E. Sands [Sleight & George, prs., Jamaica, L. I.] 1827. 416 p. CtHT-W; GDC; MBC; NBuG; NN;

NNUT; OO; PPL; PPPrHi; TxShA; ViRU. 29911

Der Neue Allentauner Calender auf 1828. Von Carl Friedrich Egelmann. Allentaun, Carl Ludwig Hutter [1827] 18 l. PPeSchw. 29912

Der Neue, Americanische Landwirthschafts-Calender auf 1828. Von Carl Friedrich Egelmann. Reading, Johann Ritter u. Comp. [1827] 18 l. DLC; InU; MWA; PHi; PPL; PR; WHi. 29913

Der Neue Pennsylvanische Stadt- und Land-Calender auf 1828. Allentaun, Heinrich Ebner und Comp. [1827] 18 l. CLU; CtY; DLC; InU; MWA; NN; NjR; OC; PHi; PAtM; PPL. 29914

Neuman, Henry

Neuman and Baretti's dictionary of the Spanish and English languages ... 2d Amer. from the 4th London ed. Boston, Hilliard, Gray, Little and Wilkins, 1827. 2 v. IEG; MB; MdBJ; NN; PPL; PU; RPA; ScU. 29915

Nevin, John Williamson, 1803-1886

Address on sacred music; delivered at the anniversary of the Handel and Hastings Society, in the Theological Seminary, Princeton, N. J., Dec. 5, 1827. Princeton, N. J., Pr. by D. A. Borrenstein, 1827. 24 p. DLC; MH; MoSpD; NNUT; OO; PPPrHi. 29916

New & complete preceptor for the Spanish guitar with progressive exercises selected from the works of the best authors. Philadelphia, John G. Klemm [c 1827] 15 p. Plate No. 321. PPi; ViU. 29917

A new and universal history of the United States: embracing the whole period from the earliest discovery down to the present time. By a citizen of the United States. New Haven, Pub. by subscription only. 1827. 452, [1] p. CoHi; OClW; OWoC; N. 29918

New Arabian nights. See Arabian nights.

New-Bedford, Mass. Social Library

Catalogue of books, belonging to New-Bedford Social Library. New Bedford, Benjamin Lindsey & Co., prs., 1827. 24 p. MNBedf. 29919

New Brunswick, (N. J.) almanack for 1828. By Joseph Cramer. Philadelphia, Griggs & Dickinson, for Joseph C. Griggs, New Brunswick, (New Jersey) [1827] NjR. 29920

New Brunswick, N. J. almanack for the year 1828... calculated by Joseph Cramer. Philadelphia, Pr. and pub. by Griggs & Dickinson [1827] [30] p. MB; MWA; NjR. 29921

---- By Joshua Sharp. Philadelphia, Griggs & Dickinson, for Joseph C. Griggs, New Brunswick, (N. J.) [1827] 18 l. MWA; NjHi. 29922

The New-England almanack, and farmer's friend for 1828. By Nathan Daboll. New-London, Samuel Green [1827] 16 l. CLU; CU; CtY; DLC; InU; MB; MWA; MiD-B; NHi; NN; NNC; OClWHi; WHi. 29923

The New England almanack, and Masonic calendar for 1828. Boston, Marsh and Capen; J. Putnam, pr. [1827] 30 l. CLU; CtHi; InU; MB; MBAt; MH; MWA; NHi; NNFM. 29924

The New-England farmer's almanack for 1828. By Truman

Abell. Alstead, N.H., Newton & Tufts; Windsor, Simeon Ide, pr. [1827] 24 l. CLU; CtY; DLC; InU; MWA; N; NCooHi; Nh-Hi; VtU; WHi. 29925

---- By Thomas Green Fessenden. Boston, John B. Russell [1827] 20 l. CLU; CtY; DLC; InU; MH; MHi; MWA; NN; Nh-Hi; OClWHi; VtHi; WHi. 29926

New England Palladium
Address of the carriers to the patrons of the New England Palladium... Boston, January 1, 1827. [Boston, 1827] Bdsd. MB. 29927

The New England Primer, improved; ... Boston, Pub. by Amos B. Parker, J.K. Remich, pr., Kennebunk, 1827. 32 l. NN. 29928

---- Kennebunk, Pr. by J.K. Remich, 1827. 63 p. CtHT-W; CtSoP; DLC; NN; NNC; BrMus. 29929

---- Middletown (Conn.), Pr. and pub. by E. & H. Clark, 1827. 72 p. CtHi; DLC. 29930

---- Stereotyped by J. Howe, Philadelphia. Philadelphia, Pub. by M'Carty and Davis [1827?] 36 p. MB. 29931

---- Pr. by E. Peck & Co. Rochester, N.Y., 1827. [64] p. CtHT-W; MWA; NN. 29932

A new family receipt book, containing all the truly valuable receipts for various branches of cookery ... Hartford [E. Strong] 1827. 24 p. CtSoP; NjR. 29933

New Hampshire
Journal of the House of Representatives of the state of New-Hampshire, at their session, holden at the capitol in Concord, commencing Wednesday, June 6, 1827. Concord, Pr. by Isaac Hill, for the state, 1827. 435 p. IaHi; Mi. 29934

---- Journal of the Senate of the state of New Hampshire, at their session, holden at the capitol in Concord, commencing Wednesday, June 6, 1827. Concord, Pr. by Isaac Hill, 1827. 270 p. IaHi; Mi. 29935

---- Laws of the state of New Hampshire, passed June session ... 1827. Concord, Pr. by Isaac Hill for the state, 1827. 154-271 p. Ar-SC; IaU-L; In-SC; MdBB; MiD-B; Mo; Nb; Nv; OrSC. 29936

---- Opinion of the justices of the Superior Court, on certain questions, proposed to them by order of the House of Representatives, passed June 25, 1827. [1827?] 8 p. DLC; MBC. 29937

---- Report of a committee, appointed by a resolve of the Legislature, June 30, 1826, to revise the laws of this state relating to towns and town officers. [Concord? 1827] 8 p. MH. 29938

---- Rifle drill, extracted from the system of tactics for the infantry, light infantry and riflemen of the United States, lately revised by order of the War Department. Baltimore, Pub. by F. Lucas Jun'r, 1825 [i.e. 1827] Reissue of 23124, with 6 p. special instructions added between the engraved and printed titles by the N.H. "Adjutant General's Office, Concord, Aug. 20, 1827," as the official handbook for the state militia. MdBE. 29939

---- Rules and orders of the House of Representatives of the state of New Hampshire. A.D. 1827 ... Concord [N.H.] Pr. by J. B. Moore, 1827. 28, 44 p. NBuG. 29940

---- State of New-Hampshire. A proclamation, for a day of humiliation and prayer ... I have thought fit ... and do, hereby appoint Thursday the twelfth day of April next, to be observed, ... for the purpose of public humiliation and prayer ... Dated at Goffstown, the tenth day of March, in the year of our Lord, one thousand eight hundred and twenty-seven ... David Lawrence Morril. [1827] 1 p. DLC. 29941

---- State of New-Hampshire. A proclamation for a day of public thanksgiving and prayer ... appoint Thursday, the twenty-ninth day of November next, to be observed as a day of public thanksgiving and prayer throughout this State ... Given at Hillsborough, this eighteenth day of October, in the year of our Lord one thousand eight hundred and twenty-seven ... Benjamin Pierce. [1827] 1 p. DLC. 29942

The New-Hampshire annual register, and United States calendar for 1828. By John Farmer. Concord, Jacob B. Moore [1827] 72 l. CtY; ICN; MB; MWA; MdBP; MiD-B; NHi; Nh; Nh-Hi. 29943

New Hampshire Auxiliary Colonization Society

The third annual report of the New Hampshire Auxiliary Colonisation[!] Society, presented and read at the meeting of the Society, held in Concord, June 7, 1827. Concord, Pr. at the Repository and Observer Office, 1827. 15 p. MsJS; Nh; WHi. 29944

New Hampshire Bible Society

The sixteenth report of the New-Hampshire Bible Society, communicated at the annual meeting, holden at Rindge, September 5, 1827 ... Concord, Pr. by George Hough, for the Society, 1827. 32 p. CtHC. 29945

New Hampshire Branch of the American Education Society

Constitution of the New-Hampshire Branch of the American Education Association, with an address of the directors. [Concord, N. H., Pr. at the Repository and Observer office, 1827] 11, [1] p. MBC. 29946

---- First annual report of the ... for the year ending September, 1827. Hanover, Pr. by Thomas Mann, 1827. 23, [1] p. MBC. 29947

New Hampshire. Citizens

Memorial. To the Honourable the Senate and House of Representatives of the United States of America, in Congress assembled ... We, therefore, the undersigned inhabitants of New Hampshire, would, respectfully present, for the wise consideration of Congress, our views and most earnest wishes upon a subject which we deen to be of pressing and vital interest to a very large portion of this great country [regarding tariff] New Hampshire, December 21, 1827. 1 p. DLC. 29948

New Hampshire Missonary Society

Twenty-sixth annual report ... Missionary Society ... Holden at Rindge ... Concord, Pr. by George Hough, 1827. 30 p. MB; MiD-B. 29949

New Jersey (State)

Acts of the fifty-second General Assembly of the state of New Jersey. At a session begun at Trenton, on the twenty-third day of October, one thousand eight hundred and twenty-seven, and continued by adjournments: being the first sitting ... Trenton, William L. Prall, pr., 1827. 233 p.

IaU-L; In-SC; Ky; MWCL; MdBB; Mi-L; NNLI; Nb; Nj; NjR; Nv; R; T; W. 29950

---- Journal of the proceedings of the Legislative Council of the state of New Jersey ... 24th day of October ... 1826. Being the 51st session. Woodbury, N. J., Pr. by P. J. Gray, 1827. 95, 40 p. NN; NjR. 29951

---- Memorial of the convention of delegates assembled on the 22nd of August 1827, on the subject of revising and amending the constitution of New Jersey. [Trenton? 1827?] 7 p. NjP; NjR; PPL. 29952

New-Jersey almanac for 1828. By David Young. Newark, Benj. Olds [1827] 18 l. CtY; DLC; MH; MWA; NjR. 29953

---- ---- Newark, Benjamin Olds [1827] 18 l. CtB; NjR; ViHi. 29954

---- Trenton, George Sherman [1827] 18 l. DLC; MWA; NjR; NjT. 29955

New Jersey Colonization Society

Proceedings of the third annual meeting of the New Jersey Colonization Society, Held at Princeton, N. J. August 15, 1827 ... Princeton Press, Pr. for the Society by D. A. Borrenstein, 1827. 32 p. NjP; NjR. 29956

New Jersey Society for the Promotion of Manufactures and the Mechanic Arts

[Circular on tariff duties.] Paterson Dec. 10th, 1827. 1 p. DLC. 29957

New Jerusalem Church

Journal of the proceedings of the ninth general convention of receivers of the doctrines of the New Jerusalem in the U. S., held at the temple, in Baltimore, June 7th, 8th and 9th, 1827-71. Boston, Office of the New Jerusalem Magazine [1827] 32 p. MH. 29958

New Robinson Crusoe. See Campe, Joachim Heinrich von.

New-Salem Academy

Catalogue of the trustees, instructers and students of New-Salem Academy, October 1827 ... J. Metcalf, pr., Wendell, Mass. Bdsd. MH; MNSaS. 29959

A new selection of revival hymns. Washington, Pr. at the Columbian Office, 1827. 74 p. IEG. 29960

The New Year's Sabbath. The holidays, and dutiful George with many other interesting stories for Sunday scholars. Boston, Pub. by James Loring, 1827. 35 p. MH. 29961

New York (City)

Annual report of deaths, in the city & county of N. York, for the year 1826. ... New-York, Pr. by P. & H. Van Pelt, 1827. 12, [2] p. NNNAM. 29962

---- Laws and ordinances, made and established by the mayor, aldermen, & commonalty of the city of New York; in Common council convened, A. D. 1827. New York, Pr. by E. Conrad, 1827. 208 p. MH; NIC; NNLI. 29963

---- Report of the select committee, on erecting a monument, to the memory of John Paulding, with an address by the mayor of the city of New York. New York, W. A. Davis, pr., 1827. 47 p. CtHT-W; DLC; NIC; NN; NTaHi; WHi. 29964

New York (State)

Analysis and contents of Chapters I and II, of the first part, of the proposed revision of the statute laws of this state. Albany (N. Y.), Pr. by Croswell and Van Benthuysen, 1827. xxx p. IaU-L; NLitf; NNLI; RPL. 29965

---- Analysis and contents of Chapter V, of the first part of the proposed revision of the laws of this state. Albany (N. Y.), Pr. by Croswell and Van Benthuysen, 1827. xviii p. IaU-L. 29966

---- Analysis and contents of Chapter VIII, of the first part of the proposed revision of the statute laws of this state. Albany (N. Y.): Pr. by Croswell and Van Benthuysen, 1827. xiii p. IaU-L; RPL. 29967

---- Annual report of the acting superintendent of common schools, made to the Legislature Jan. 23, 1827. [Albany, 1827] 61 p. MHi. 29968

---- Annual report of the Canal commissioners of the state of New-York. Made to the Assembly, Feb. 10, 1827. Albany, Pr. by Croswell and Van Benthuysen, 1827. 35 p. MCM; N; NRom. 29969

---- Canal laws. The several laws relative to the canals of the state of New-York. Taken from the laws. Published by order of the Canal board, April, 1827. Albany, Pr. by Croswell & Van Benthuysen, 1827. 43 p. N. 29970

---- Chapter II, of the second part of the proposed revision of the statute laws of the state of New York. Albany, Pr. by Croswell & Van Benthuysen, 1827. 10 p. MMeT; NNLI. 29971

---- Chapter III of the second part of the proposed revision of the statute laws of the state of New York. Albany, Pr. by Croswell & Van Benthuysen, 1827. 16 p. MMeT; NNLI. 29972

---- Chapter IV of the second part of the proposed revision of the statute laws of the state of New-York. Albany, Pr. by Croswell and Van Benthuysen, 1827. 17 p. NNLI. 29973

---- Chapter V of the first part of the proposed revision of the statute laws of the state of New-York. As reprinted by the revisers. Albany, Pr. by Croswell and Van Benthuysen, 1827. 47 p. IaU-L; NNLI; NjR; RPL. 29974

---- Chapter VI, of the second part of the proposed revision of the statute laws of the state of New-York. Albany, Croswell and Van Benthuysen, 1827. 7, 115 p. MMeT; N; NNLI; RPL. 29975

---- Chapter VII of the second part of the proposed revision of the statute laws of the state of New York. Albany, Pr. by Croswell and Van Benthuysen, 1827. 4, 17 p. NNLI. 29976

---- Chapter VIII of the second part of the proposed revision of the statute laws of the state of New York. Albany, Pr. by Croswell and Van Benthuysen, 1827. 35 p. NNLI. 29977

---- Chapter XI. Of the first part of the proposed revision of the statute laws of the state of New-York. Croswell and Van Benthuysen. Albany, N. Y. , 1827. viii, 42 p. NjR; RPL. 29978

---- Chapter XII. Of the first part of the proposed revision of the statute laws of the state of New-York. Albany, Pr. by Croswell and Van Benthuysen, 1827. [2], 35 p. NNLI; NjR; RPL. 29979

---- Chapter XIII of the first part of the proposed revision of the statute laws of the state of New-

York. Albany, Pr. by Croswell and Van Benthuysen, 1827. x, 55 p. NNLI; NjR; RPL. 29980

---- Chapter XIV of the first part of the proposed revision of the statute laws of the state of New-York. Albany, Pr. by Croswell and Van Benthuysen, 1827. viii, 48 p. NNLI; NjR. 29981

---- Chapter 14th of the revised statutes; Of the public health. Relating to the port, harbour and state of New York. [New York] N. B. Penfield [1827?] 48 p. IEN-M; MH. 29982

---- Chapter XV, of the first part of the proposed revision of the statute laws of the state of New York. Albany (N. Y.), Pr. by Croswell and Van Benthuysen, 1827. x, 71 p. IaU-L; MB; NNLI; RPL. 29983

---- Chapter XVI of the first part of the proposed revision of the statute laws of the state of New York. Albany, Pr. by Croswell and Van Benthuysen, 1827. viii, 38 p. NNLI; RPL. 29984

---- Chapter XVII of the first part of the proposed revision of the statute laws of the state of New York. Albany, Pr. by Croswell and Van Benthuysen, 1827. 65 p. NNLI; RPL. 29985

---- Chapter XVIII. Of the first part of the proposed revision of the statute laws of the state of New York. Albany, Pr. by Croswell and Van Benthuysen, 1827. 74 p. MB; NNLI; RPL. 29986

---- Chapter XX of the first part of the proposed revision of the statute laws of the state of New York. Albany, Pr. by Croswell and Van Benthuysen, 1827. 171 p. NNLI; RPL. 29987

---- A communication from the Comptroller, transmitting a report of Philip Church and Sylvanus Russell, Esqrs. relative to a road from Angelica to Hamilton: together with a petition of sundry persons. Made to the Senate Feb. 9, 1827. Albany, Pr. by Croswell & Van Benthuysen, 1827. 21 p. N; PPL. 29988

---- The constitution of the state of New-York together with the rules and orders, standing committees, and list of members of the state assembly, for 1827. Albany, Pr. by Croswell and Van Benthuysen, 1827. 117, [2] p. NHi; NWatt; BrMus. 29989

---- No. 91. In Assembly, February 16, 1827. Report of the committee on canals and internal improvements, in relation to the Chenango Canal. [Albany, 1827] 7 p. DLC. 29990

---- In the court for the trial of impeachments and the correction of errors. Samuel F. Lambert, plaintiff in error, vs. The People of the state of New York, defendants in error. Error book. New York, Geo. F. Hopkins, 1827. ICLAW, Now missing 1969. 29991

---- Joint rules of the Senate and Assembly during the present meeting of the Legislature. [Albany, 1827] 3 p. N. 29992

---- Journal of the Assembly of the state of New-York; at their fiftieth session, begun and held at the capitol in the city of Albany, the 2nd day of January 1827. Albany, Pr. by E. Croswell, pr. to the state, 1827. 1153 p. NNLI. 29993

---- Journal of the Assembly of the state of New York; at their fiftieth session, second meeting;

begun and held at the capitol, in the city of Albany, Tuesday, 11th September, 1827. Albany, Pr. by E. Croswell, pr. to the state, 1827. 113 p. NNLI. 29994

---- Journal of the Senate of the state of New-York; at their fiftieth session begun and held at the capitol in the city of Albany, the 2nd day of January, 1827. Albany, Pr. by E. Croswell, pr. to the state, 1827. 626, 170, 32, xxi p. NNLI. 29995

---- Journal of the Senate of the state of New York; at their fiftieth session, second meeting. Begun and held at the capitol, in the city of Albany, Wednesday, 27th June, 1827. Albany, Pr. by E. Croswell, 1827. Variously paged. NNLI; WGr; WHi. 29996

---- Laws of the state of New-York, passed at the fiftieth session of the Legislature, begun and held at the city of Albany, the second day of January, 1827. Albany, Pr. by E. Croswell, for Wm. Gould and Co. Albany, and Gould and Banks, Law Booksellers, New-York, 1827. 425 p. Ar-SC; CtHT-W; In-SC; MdBB; Mi-L; Nb; Nj; N; NMinNCL; NN; NNebgL; NNIA; NNLI; NNowiSC; NNU; NPot; NSyHi; NTSC; NTiHi; NUtSC; R; RPL; T; TxU-L; ViU; W; Wa-L. 29997

---- Laws of the state of New-York. Passed at the second meeting of the fiftieth session of the Legislature, begun and held at the city of Albany, the eleventh day of September, 1827. Albany, Pr. by E. Croswell, 1827. 22, 2, 479 p. MH-L; NBuU; OCLaw; TxU-L. 29998

---- Laws of the state of New-York, relating particularly to the city of New-York, published by the authority of the corporation of the said city. New-York, W. A. Davis, 1827. 602 p. MH; MH-L; NIC; NNC; NNLI. 29999

---- The message from the governor to the Legislature of the state of New-York, on the opening of the session, January 2, 1827. Albany, Pr. by John B. Van Steenbergh, 1827. 18 p. CSmH; NbU. 30000

---- No. 1. Report of the commissioners appointed by the act of April 21, 1825 to revise the statute laws of this state, made to the Senate, January 5, 1827. Albany, Pr. by Croswell and Van Benthuysen, 1827. 39 p. IaU-L; NNLI; NjR; PPL; RPL. 30001

---- No. 2. Report of the commissioners appointed by the act of April 21, 1825, to revise the statute laws of this state, made to the Assembly, Jan. 9, 1827. Albany, Pr. by Croswell and Van Benthuysen, 1827. 295, [1] p. NNLI; NjR; RPL. 30002

---- No. 3. Report of the commissioners appointed by the act of April 21, 1825, to revise the statute laws of this state, made to the Senate, Jan. 13, 1827. Albany, Pr. by Croswell and Van Benthuysen, 1827. 13 p. NNLI; NjR; PPL; RPL. 30003

---- No. 4. Report of the commissioners appointed by the act of April 21, 1825, to revise the statute laws of this state, made to the Senate, Jan. 29, 1827. Albany, Pr. by Croswell and Van Benthuysen, 1827. 9 p. IaU-L; NNLI; NjR; RPL. 30004

---- No. 5. Report of the commissioners appointed by the act of April 21, 1825 to revise the statute laws of this state, made to the Senate Feb. 1, 1827. Albany, Pr. by Croswell and Van Benthuysen, 1827. 28 p. IaU-L; NNLI; RPL. 30005

---- No. 6. Report of the commissioners appointed by the act of April 21, 1825, to revise the statute laws of this state, made to the Assembly, Feb. 5, 1827. Albany, Pr. by Croswell and Van Benthuysen, 1827. 44 p. IaU-L; MH; NNLI; NjR; RPL. 30006

---- No. 7. Report of the commissioners appointed by the act of April 21, 1825, to revise the statute laws of this state. Made to the Senate, Feb. 10, 1827. Albany, Pr. by Croswell and Van Benthuysen, 1827. 28 p. NNLI; NjR; RPL. 30007

---- No. 8. Report of the commissioners appointed by the act of April 21, 1825, to revise the statute laws of this state. Made to the Senate, Feb. 24, 1827. Albany, Pr. by Croswell and Van Benthuysen, 1827. 53 p. CSmH; MH; N; NNLI; NjR; RPL. 30008

---- No. 9. Report of the commissioners appointed by the act of April 21, 1825, to revise the statute laws of this state. Made to the Assembly, March 13, 1827. Albany, Pr. by Croswell and Van Benthuysen, 1827. xxii, 132 p. NNLI; NjR; RPL; WHi. 30009

---- No. 10. Report of the commissioners appointed by the act of April 21, 1825, to revise the statute laws of this state. Made to the Assembly, March 14, 1827. Albany, Pr. by Croswell and Van Benthuysen, 1827. 80 p. IaU-L; NLitf; NNLI; NjR; RPL. 30010

---- No. 19. Report of the commissioners appointed by the act of April 21, 1825, to revise the statute laws of this state. Made to the Senate April 4, 1827. Albany, Pr. by Croswell and Van Benthuysen, 1827. 46 p. MB; NNLI; RPL. 30011

---- Part of the revised statutes, passed at the second meeting of the fiftieth session of the Legislature of the state of New York; begun and held at the city of Albany, the 11th day of September, 1827. Consisting of Chapters VI, VIII, IX, X, XIII, XIV, XV, XVI, XVII, and XVIII, of the first part. Albany, Pr. by E. Croswell, pr. to the state, 1827. 479 p. In-SC; MB; NNLI; NNU; Wa-L. 30012

---- Proclamation of the Governor convening the Senate, dated 15 June 1827. 1 p. sq. MHi. 30013

---- Report of the commissioners appointed to revise the statute laws of this state. Made to the Legislature, September 11, 1827. Albany, Croswell and Van Benthuysen, 1827. 28 p. NN; NNLI. 30014

---- Report of the commissioners appointed to revise the statute laws of this state. Made to the Senate, November 2, 1827. Albany, Pr. by Croswell and Van Benthuysen, 1827. 14 p. NNLI; W. 30015

---- Report of the commissioners, directed by the act of 17th April, 1826, to visit the state-prison at Auburn. Made to the Senate, Jan. 13, 1827. Albany, Pr. by Croswell & Van Benthuysen, 1827. 88 p. N; PPL. 30016

---- Report of the committee on canals on the engrossed bill from the Assembly, authorizing the construction of the canal. From Seneca Lake to Newtown. Albany,

N. Y., Pr. by Croswell and Van Benthuysen, 1827. 55 p. MPlyP; N. 30017

---- Report of the committee on canals on the petition of David E. Evans, and others. Made to the Senate, Feb. 12, 1827. Albany, Pr. by Croswell and Van Benthuysen, 1827. 36 p. DLC; N; NBu; NN; NRom; PPL. 30018

---- Report of the committee on literature, relative to common schools and academies, made to the Senate, Feb. 21, 1827. Albany, Pr. by Croswell and Van Benthuysen, 1827. 18 p. DLC; M; MB; MHi; N. 30019

---- Report of the Joint committee of the Senate and Assembly, on the application for the relief of the Greeks. Made March 1, 1827. Albany, Pr. by Croswell and Van Benthuysen, 1827. 9 p. DLC; N. 30020

---- Reports of cases argued and determined in the court of chancery of the state of New York. By Samuel M. Hopkins ... New York, Pub. by Oliver Halstead, law bookseller; Hosfords Print, Albany, 1827. xv, [1] 616 p. DLC; FTU; MBS; MWCL; MWiW; Md; MoKB; NCH; Nj; PU-L; RPL. 30021

---- Reports of committees in relation to the Long Island Canal Company. Albany, 1827. 14 p. N. 30022

---- Revised statute. Chapter IX., Title IX., relating to canals; passed at the extra session of the legislature ... Dec. 3, 1827. Albany, Pr. by E. Croswell, 1827. 40 p. MH-L; PPL. 30023

---- Revised statute, chapter X. Part I. Relating to the militia, and public defence, passed at the extra session of the Legislature of the state of New-York, December 3, 1827. Albany, E. Croswell, pr. to the state, 1827. 7, 60, 23 p. CSmH; DLC; MB; MH; NNC. 30024

---- Revised statute, chapter XIII, relating to the assessment and collection of taxes, passed at the extra session of the Legislature of the state of New York. Dec. 3, 1827. Albany, E. Croswell, 1827. 43 p. MH-L; N. 30025

---- Revised statute, chapter XVI relating to highways, bridges and ferries, passed at the extra session of the Legislature, Dec. 3, 1827. Albany, 1827. E. Croswell, 31 p. NIC. 30026

---- Revised statute, relating to common schools, being title II. of Chapter XV. Passed at the extra session of the Legislature of the state of New-York, December 3, 1827, with forms and regulations prepared by the Superintendent of common schools, in obedience to sections 9 and 10 of this Title. Albany, Pr. by E. Croswell, pr. to the state, 1827 50 p. MH-L; MiD-B. 30027

---- Rules and orders of the Senate of the state of New York. Albany, Croswell, 1827. 10 p. NCH. 30028

---- State of New York. In the Court for the trial of impeachments and the correction of errors, between Peter McCartee, one of the executors of the last will and testament of Philip Jacobs ... New York, William A. Mercein, 1827. 39 p. NNC-L. 30029

---- State of New York. In the Court for the trial of impeachments and the correction of errors. Between the Orphan Asylum

Society, in the City of New York, respondents, and Peter M'Cartee, one of the executors of the last will and testament of Philip Jacobs, deceased ... New York, Clayton & Van Norden, 1827. 63 p. NNC-L. 30030

---- Statement of lands sold in March 1826, for quit-rents... Albany, Pr. by Croswell & Van Benthuysen, 1827. 132 p. NN; PPL. 30031

The New York almanac for 1828. By David Young. Newark, Benjamin Olds [1827] 18 l. CtY. 30032

The New-York almanack for 1828. By Thomas Spofford. New-York, David Felt [1827] 18 l. MB; MWA; NSyOHi. 30033

New York. American Academy of the Fine Arts

Catalogue of paintings and engravings exhibited ... May, 1827. The thirteenth exhibition. New-York, William A. Mercein, pr., 1827. 13 p. CSmH; CtY; MH; PPAmP; PPL. 30034

New York & New Jersey almanac for 1828. By David Young. New York, John C. Totten [1827] 18 l. MWA. 30035

New York Asylum for Lying-in Women

Fourth annual report of the managers... March 8, 1827. New York, Pr. by D. Fanshaw, 1827. 20 p. DLC. 30036

New York. Chatham Theatre

Brian Boroihime, or, the maid of Erin with a description of the splendid drama of that name as performed at the Chatham Theatre, on Monday evening, January 22, 1827. New York, Pub. by E. M. Murden, 1827. 12 p. DLC. 30037

New York. College of Physicians and Surgeons

Catalogue of the faculty and students of the College of Physicians and Surgeons of the state of New-York, in the city of New-York. New-York, Pr. by Vanderpool & Cole, 1826-1827. 8 p. NNC; NNNAM. 30038

---- Catalogue of the regents of the University; and faculty, fellows and students of the College of Physicians and Surgeons of the state of New York, in the city of New York. New-York, Pr. by Alexander Ming, Jr., 1827-8. 12 p. DLC; NNC. 30039

---- Circular and catalogue of the faculty and students of the College of Physicians and Surgeons of the Western District of the state of New York, in Fairfield, (Herkimer county). Albany, Pr. by Webster and Skinners, 1827. 8 p. CSmH; KU. 30040

---- New York, August 12th, 1827. The twenty-first session of the College will commence on the first Monday of November next ... Bdsd. NjR. 30041

New York Female Auxiliary Bible Society

Eleventh annual report of the New York Female Auxiliary Bible Society. Together with the first report of the Young Ladies' Bible Society. New-York, Pr. by J. Seymour, John-Street, 1827. 21 p. DLC; OClWHi; PPL. 30042

New York Female Union Society

The eleventh report of the New York Female Union Society ... New York, Gray & Bunce, pr., 1827. 36 p. NjR. 30043

The New-York gardener. See Agricola, P., pseud.

The New York guide in miniature, containing hints and cautions to all little strangers in New York ... New York, Mahlon Day, 1827. 23 p. Goodspeed (Bost.), catal. 252 (1936), item 218. From NN imp. catal., but not in NN. (1936). 30044

New York Historical Society
[Memorial to the Legislature of the state asking an appropriation for the relief of the society. With a list of members, 1827.] [New York, 1827] 32 p. DLC; MHi; NN; NNC; PHi; PPAmP. 30045

New York Institution for the Instruction of the Deaf and Dumb
Eighth annual report of the directors of the New York Institution for the Instruction of the Deaf and Dumb, to the Legislature of the state of New York, for the year ending 31 Dec. 1826; accompanied by documents illustrating the ... state and condition of the institution. New York, 1827. 39 p. MWA. 30046

New York Medical Academy
Circular. To editors and printers of public journals throughout the United States. Should the following circular meet your approbation, and should you feel disposed to promote the interests of this Institution, by giving it publicity in your respective journals; to such the proprietor makes the following proposition [1827] 1 p. DLC. 30047

The New-York medical almanac, and repository of useful science and amusement for 1828. By David Young. New-York, Caleb Bartlett [1827] 18 l. DLC; InU; MWA; NBLiHi; NN. 30048

New York. Northern Dispensary
Constitution and by-laws of the Northern Dispensary, of the city of New-York. New-York, Pr. by John Post, 1827. 12 p. NNNAM; PPL. 30049

New York Protestant Episcopal Missionary Society
The tenth annual report of the board of managers ... adopted by the Society at the anniversary meeting held in December, 1826 ... New-York, Pr. by T. and J. Swords, 1827. 23 p. NjR. 30050

---- The eleventh annual report of the board of managers of the New-York Protestant Episcopal Missionary Society ... New-York, Pr. by T. and J. Swords, 1827. 8, 35 p. NNG; PHi. 30051

The New York reader, No. 2: Being selections in prose and poetry, for the use of schools. New York, Pub. by Samuel Wood & Sons, R. & G. S. Wood, prs. [1827] 215 p. CSmH; MH; OOxM; BrMus. 30052

New-York scenes. Designed for the entertainment and instruction of children of city and country. New-York, Pr. and sold by Mahlon Day, 1827. 23 p. PPL. 30053

New-York South American Steam-Boat Company
That part of South America which the New York South American Steam Boat Association contemplates making the field of thei operations, is at present little known. It is their intention to explore one of the most important rivers in the world- the River Amazon and branches... Albany, April 10, 1827. 2 p. DLC. 30054

New York (state) University
Annual report of the regents of the university, to the legislature of the state of New-York. Made to the Senate April 13, 1827. Albany, Croswell and Van Benthuy-

sen, 1827. 5 p. CSmH; CtHT; N; NNNAM; P; PU. 30055

New York Sunday School Union Society
The eleventh annual report ... New York, Gray, 1827. 32 p. DLC; NUt. 30056

New York. Trinity Church
This indenture, made this twenty-second day of May, in the year of our Lord one thousand eight hundred and twenty-seven, between the rector, church wardens, and vestrymen of Trinity Church, in the city of New-York, of the first part, and the several persons whose names and seals are hereunto affixed, parties of the second part ... [Geo. F. Hopkins, pr., 19 Nassau-street, New York, 1827] 16 p. DLC; NN; NNB. 30057

A New-Yorker, pseud. See Mc Vickar, John.

Newman, Samuel P.
A practical system of rhetoric; ... Portland, Pub. by Wm. Hyde, A. Shirley, pr., 1827. 215 p. CtHT-W; CtSoP; KU; MH; MNBedf; MeB; MeHi; MnU; NN; NNC; TxU-T. 30058

The Newtonian reflector, or New-England almanac for the year 1828. By Anson Allen. Hartford, Roberts and Burr, prs. [1827?] 12 l. Ct; CtHi; CtY; DLC; InU; MB; MWA; MiD-B; N; NN; WHi. 30059

Nicholson, Peter, 1765-1844
The carpenter's new guide... Being a complete book, of lines for carpentry and joinery. 9th ed. Philadelphia, Pub. by John Grigg. Clark & Raser, prs., 1827. 127 p. MNBedf; PP; PU. 30060

Nicolai, V.
... Nicolai's celebrated sonata. A corrected ed., 1827. Boston, Pub. at Browne's Musical Seminary, 1827. 8 p. MB. 30061

Niles, Hezekiah, 1777-1839
Agriculture of the United States, or An essay concerning internal improvement & domestic manufactures, shewing their inseparable connection with the business and interests of agriculture... First pub. in Niles's Register of March 24, 1827 ... [1827?] 16 p. DLC; MBAt; MdBP. 30062

---- ---- Wheeling [Curtis, pr.] 1827. 16 p. Norona 601. 30063

[Niles, John Milton]
A view of South America and Mexico, comprising their history, the political condition, geography, agriculture, commerce, &c. of the republics of Mexico, Guatamala [!], Columbia, Peru, the United Provinces of South America and Chile ... By a citizen of the United States ... New York, Pub. for subscribers, 1827. 2 v. in 1. CU-B; DLC; GHi; IHi; KyBgW; KyU; MWeA; NNU; NRU; NcAS; NcWfC; PPL; PU; RPB; ScDuE; TxGR; Vi; ViU; VtU; BrMus. 30064

Niles, Nathaniel
Medical statistics; or A comparative view of the mortality in New-York, Philadelphia, Baltimore, and Boston, for a series of years, including comparisons of the mortality of whites and blacks in the two former cities; and of whites, free blacks, and slaves, in Baltimore. New-York, Pub. by Elam Elias, J. Seymour, pr., 1827. 10 p. DLC; NNNAM; PHi; PPL; PU; BrMus. 30065

Nina, an Icelandic tale. By a mother, author of "Always Happy," &c. New-York, O. A. Roorbach,

1827. 105 p. MH; NjN. 30066

Nisbet, Alexander
A view of the claim of Alexander Nisbet, A. D. B. N. of Thomas Cockey Deye, containing an examination of the report of the treasurer of the state, made to the last General Assembly, together with all the proceedings of the legislature on the subject. Baltimore, Pr. by John D. Toy, 1827. 41 p. MdBJ-G. 30067

Nobody, pseud. See Richmond, James Cook.

The North American calendar, or the Columbian almanac for 1828. By W. Collom. Wilmington, R. Porter & Son [1827] 18 l. DeU; InU; MWA; NHi; NjR. 30068

North American Coal Company
A brief sketch of the property belonging to the North American Coal Company, with some general remarks on the subject of coal and coal mines. New-York, Pr. by William Davis, Jun, 1827. 14 p. DLC; MH-BA; OC; OCHP; P; PHi; PPAmP; PPL. 30069

North Carolina (State)
Acts passed by the General Assembly of the state of North Carolina, at its session, commencing on the 25th of December, 1826. Raleigh, Pr. by Lawrence & Lemay, prs. of the state, 1827. 92 p. Ar-SC; C; IaU-L; MdBB; Mi-L; NNLI; Nb; NcU; Nj; T. 30070

---- Comptroller's statement, 1827. [Raleigh] Lawrence & Lemay, prs. to the state [1827] [16] p. NcU. 30071

---- Journals of the Senate & House of Commons of the General Assembly of the state of North Carolina, at the session of 1826-27. Raleigh, Pr. by Lawrence & Lemay, prs. to the state, 1827. 235 p. NcU; NcWfC. 30072

---- Message of His Excellency Governor H. G. Burton, To the General Assembly of North-Carolina, 1827. Raleigh, Pr. by Lawrence & Lemay, prs. to the state, 1827. 7 p. NcU. 30073

---- ... Report of the Adjutant General of North Carolina. 1827. Raleigh, Pr. by Lawrence & Lemay, prs. to the state, 1827. 4 p. [Dated January 17, 1827] NcU. 30074

---- ... Report of the Adjutant General of North Carolina, 1827. Raleigh, Pr. by Lawrence & Lemay, prs. to the state, 1827. 11 p. [Dated December 1, 1827] NcU. 30075

---- ... Report of the Board for Internal Improvements. Raleigh, Pr. by Lawrence & Lemay, prs. to the state, 1827. 28 p. NcU. 30076

---- [No. 4] Report of the board for internal improvements, November 1827. Raleigh, Pr. by Lawrence & Lemay, prs. to the state, 1827. 35 p. DLC; NcU. 30077

---- Report of the Committee on the resolutions of Georgia relative to the election of president and vice president. Raleigh, Lawrence & Lemay, 1827. 7 p. NcU. 30078

---- Report of the Joint select committee appointed to investigate the accounts of the Treasury Department. Raleigh, Lawrence & Lemay, 1827. 88 p. NcU. 30079

---- Report of the Joint select committee appointed to make suitable arrangements to secure the debt due the state from the late treasurer. Raleigh [1827] 4 p. NcU. 30080

---- Report of the speaker of the Senate relative to the state bank, 1827. Raleigh, Lawrence & Lemay, 1827. 7 p. NcU. 30081

---- Report relative to Ocracoke Inlet. 1827. Raleigh, Lawrence & Lemay, prs., 1827. 6 p. NcU. 30082

---- Report relative to the Cherokee lands, December, 1827. [Raleigh, 1827?] 3 p. NcU. 30083

---- ... Reports relative to the swamp lands in North-Carolina, 1827. Raleigh, Pr. by Lawrence & Lemay, prs. to the state, 1827. 28 p. NcU. 30084

---- A revisal of the laws of the state of North-Carolina, passed from 1821 to 1825 (both years inclusive.) With marginal notes and references. Revised by John L. Taylor ... Raleigh, J. Gales & son, 1827. 203 (i.e. 205) p. C; Ct; FU-L; InSC; M; MB; MH; MdBB; Mi-L; NN; NNLI; NcAS; NcD; NcU; OrSC; W. 30085

---- Statement of expenditures on internal improvements. Raleigh, Lawrence & Lemay, 1827. 5 p. NcU. 30086

---- A statement of the revenue of North Carolina [based on returns filed in Comptroller's office] [Raleigh] Pub. by the Comptroller, Jno. L. Henderson, 1 Nov., 1827. Bdsd. NcU. 30087

North Carolina Literary Fund
... Report of the President and directors of the Literary Fund, 1827. Raleigh, Pr. by Lawrence & Lemay, prs. to the state, 1827. 7 p. NcU. 30088

North Carolina University. Dialectic Society
Catalogue of books belonging to the library of the Dialectic Society at Chapel-Hill, 1827. Raleigh, Pr. by J. Gales & son, [1827?] 32 p. NcU. 30089

North River Steam Boat Line
For Albany at 6 o'clock A. M. The low pressure steam boat Albany ... regular days of starting, are for Albany ... New York ... 1827. Bdsd. MHi. 30090

Northern regions; or Uncle Richard's relation of Captain Parry's voyages for the discovery of a north-west passage and Franklin's and Cochrane's overland journeys to other parts of the world. New York, O. A. Roorbach, W. E. Dean, pr., 1827. 256 p. DLC; LN; MB; MHi; MPiB; MWA; NN; NNMr; NRom; NjR; RPA; ViU. 30091

Der Northampton Bauern Calender auf 1828. Easton, Heinrich und Wilhelm Hutter [1827] 18 l. DLC. 30092

The Northampton farmer's almanac for 1828. Easton, Henry & William Hatter [1827] 18 l. MBAt; MWA. 30093

Northwest Territory, U. S.
Journal of the convention, of the territory of the United States North West of the Ohio, begun and held at Chillicothe, on Monday the first day of November, A. D. 1802, and of the Independence of the United States the twenty-seventh. ... Columbus, George Nashee, state pr., 1827. 42 p. OU. 30094

Norwich University, Northfield, Vt.
Catalogue of the officers and cadets, together with the prospectus and internal regulations of the American literary, scientific and military academy, at Middletown, Connecticut. Middletown, Pr. by E. & H. Clark, 1827. 51 p.

CSmH. 30095

Notes and reflections during a ramble in Germany ... See Sherer, Moyle.

Notes on Colombia. See Bache, Richard.

Nothing is secret. See Powell, Thomas Spencer.

Nott, Samuel, 1754-1852
'Hitherto hath the Lord helped us." An address, delivered by request, to the citizens of Norwich, July 4, 1827 ... Norwich [Conn.] Pr. by J. Dunham [1827?] 16 p. CSmH. 30096

Nott, Samuel, Jr.
The Sabbath as a rest to be occupied in personal, domestic and social religion. Albany, Websters & Skinners, 1827. 21 p. Ct; MBC. 30097

Nugent, Thomas
A new pocket dictionary of the French and English languages, In two parts. 4th Amer. ed. from the last London ed. ; with additions of the new words by J. Ouiseau, A. M. New York, Pr. and pub. by George Long. Stereotyped by A. Chandler, 1827. liv, 452 p. MBC; MDux. 30098

Nuttall, Thomas, 1786-1859
An introduction to systematic and physiological botany... Cambridge, [Mass.] Hilliard and Brown; Boston, Hilliard, Gray, Little & Wilkins, [etc.] [Cambridge: University press - Hilliard Metcalf & Co.] 1827. xi, 360 p. CSmH; CU; CtHT-W; IU; KU; KyLxT; MB; MH; MHi; MdUM; MeU; MoSB; NIC; NNNAM; NcAS; OU; PHi; PPL; PU; RPB; TNJ; WU. 30099

O

Oakwood, Oliver, pseud. See Potts, Stacy Gardner.

Observations on penitentiary discipline. See Allen, Stephen.

Observations on some extracts from a volume of sermons said to be preached by Elias Hicks, & published in Philadelphia by J. & E. Parker, 1825. Pr. by Daniel Fanshaw, American Tract Society House, 1827. 19 p. MWA; NNMHi; PHC; PSC-Hi. 30100

Observations on the floating dock. See Shipwright, pseud.

Observations upon the automaton chess player. See Jones, Thomas P.

Odd Fellows, Independent Order of.
Allgemeine Gesetze der Wilhelm Tell's Loge No. 4 von dem Orden der Independent Odd Fellows oder unabhängigen Sonderbaren Brüder ... Baltimore, Johann T. Hanzsche, 1827. 24 p. MdBE. 30101

---- Proceedings of the ... Grand Lodge of the United States ... held at Baltimore. Baltimore, 1827. Sabin 56696 (not loc.) 30102

The odd volume ... See Corbett, Misses.

An officer of the line, pseud. See Maginn, William.

An officer of the United States army, pseud. See Bache, Richard.

Oft in a stilly night. With variations for the piano forte, by a lady. Philadelphia, Geo. Willig [c 1827] 5 p. ViU. 30103

Ogden, David Longworth
Public worship: A sermon delivered at the dedication of the New Congregational Church in Cheshire, August 1, 1827. New Haven, Pr. by Hezekiah Howe, 1827. 24 p. CtHC; CtHi; CtY; MBC; MH-AH; MWA; MiD-B; OClW; PPPrHi. 30104

O'Hara family, pseud. See Banim, John.

Ohio (State)
Journal of the House of Representatives. Columbus, George Nashee, state pr., 1827. 341 p. O. 30105

---- Journal of the Senate of the state of Ohio: being the first session of the twenty-fifth General Assembly, begun, and held in the town of Columbus, in the County of Franklin, Monday, December 4, 1826 ... Columbus, George Nashee, state prs., 1827. 322, 42 p. DLC. 30106

---- Message of the governor of the state of Ohio, to both houses of the General Assembly, at the commencement of the 26th session of the Legislature. Tuesday, December 4, 1827. Read and ordered to be printed. Columbus [O.], P.H. Olmsted, state pr., 1827. 14 p. CSmH; NN. 30107

---- Pennsylvania and Ohio canal law. [Columbus, 1827] 12 p. DLC. 30108

---- Report. The standing committee on canals to whom was referred the memorial of sundry citizens, residents of the Miami county, praying for an alteration of the law prescribing the mode for the assessment of damages for materials, &c. taken for the construction of canals, have had the same under consideration, and ask leave to report: [January 18, 1827] 3 p. OClWHi. 30109

O'Keefe, John, 1747-1833
Recollections of the life of John O'Keefe, written by himself. Philadelphia, H. C. Carey & I. Lea, 1827. 2 v. in 1. CSf; KU; KyBgW; KyLx; LNX; MA; MB; MBAt; MNe; NNG; NR; OU; P; PLFM; PPL; PRea; ScC; WHi. 30110

---- Sprigs of laurel: a comic opera, in two acts ... Baltimore, Pr. and pub. by J. Robinson, Circulating Library and Dramatic Repository, 1827. 36 p. MH; MWA. 30111

Old Colony Auxiliary Foreign Mission Society
Proceedings at the second annual meeting of Old Colony Auxiliary Foreign Mission Society, holden at Plymouth, April 25, 1827. Plymouth, Pr. by Allen Danforth, 1827. 16 p. MNBedf. 30112

Old Dominion. Charlottesville, Va.
The carrier's Christmas present, to the patrons and friends of the Old Dominion. Christmas, Dec. 25, 1827. [Charlottesville, Va. 1827] 1 p. DLC. 30113

Oliver, Benjamin Lynde, 1788-1843
Practical conveyancing, a selection of forms of general utility, with notes interspersed ... 2d ed., corr. and enl. Pub. by Glazier & Co., Hallowell, Me.; Boston, Hilliard, Gray, Little & Wilkins, Richardson & Lord, and Wells & Lilly. Glazier & Co., prs., 1827. 581 p. CU; DLC; LU; MAnP; MBU-L; MH-L; MiD-B; N-L; PU-L. 30114

Olmstead, Denison
An oration on the progressive state of the present age; delivered

at New Haven, before the Connecticut Alpha of the Phi Beta Kappa, September 11, 1827. New Haven, Pr. by Hezekiah Howe, 1827. 24 p. CtHi; CtHT-W; CtY; MB; MH; MHi; MiD-B; NNC; NNG; PHi; RPB. 30115

Olney, Jesse, 1798-1872
Practical geography, for the use of schools, accompanied with problems for the use of the globes. Hartford, D. F. Robinson, 1827. 116 p. CtHT-W; IHi; MH. 30116

---- A system of geographical questions, for the use of schools, accompanied with problems for the use of the globes... Hartford, D. F. Robinson, 1827. 57 p. Ct; CtHi. 30117

On experimental religion. See American Unitarian Association.

On religious phraseology. See Dewey, Orville.

Onderdonk, Benjamin Tredwell, bp., 1791-1861
A sermon preached in St. Thomas's Church, New York, at the funeral of the Rev. Cornelius R. Duffie ... on Tuesday August 21, 1827 ... New York, T. & J. Swords, pr., 1827. 21 p. CtHT; MBC; MH; MHi; MiD-B; NGH; NNC; NNG; PHi; RPB; WHi. 30118

Onderdonk, Henry Ustick, bp.
The Rochester correspondence. [New York, 1827] 11 p. MB. 30119

One hundred scriptural arguments. See American Unitarian Association.

O'Neall, John Belton, 1793-1863
Oration delivered at Newberry court house, on the fourth of July, 1827. Columbia, So. Carolina, Pr. by Sweeny & Sims, 1827. 27 p. LU; NcD. 30120

---- An oration delivered before the Clarisophic Society incorporate, and the inhabitants of Columbia, on the anniversary of the Society, Dec. 5th, 1826. Charleston, A. E. Miller, 1827. 18 p. NcD; ScC; ScU. 30121

Ontario Agricultural Society
Premiums for 1827 ... Pr. by Bemis, Morse & Ward, Canandaigua. Bdsd. NCanHi. 30122

Ontario Female Seminary
Catalogue of the trustees, teachers and pupils, of the Ontario Female Seminary, opened in Canandaigua, N. Y., June 1, 1826; together with the terms of admission, and the course of studies to be pursued in the seminary. Canandaigua, Pr. by Bemis, Morse and Ward, 1827. 8 p. NCanHi; NN. 30123

Opie, Mrs. Amelia (Alderson), 1764-1853
Illustrations of lying, in all its branches. 2d Amer. ed. Boston, Monroe and Francis; New York, C. S. Francis, 1827. 276 p. CBPac; DLC; KyDC; MBr; MH; MnU; MoSW; OO; PPL; PU; RPB; VtMiM. 30124

---- ---- From the 2d London ed. Hartford, S. Andrus, publisher, 1827. 283 p. CSmH; CtHi; CtSoP; ICN; ICU; MNBedf; MWA; NbOU; NjN; NjR; OMC; OrU; PPL; PSC-Hi; VtU. 30125

---- Works. Boston, Pub. by S. G. Goodrich. Sold by Bowles & Dearborn, Boston; G. & C. Carvill, New York, and H. C. Carey and I. Lea, Philadelphia, 1827. [Boston, Isaac R. Butts, prs.] 12 v. in 11. GU; MB; MBAt; MH; MdHi; MoSW; NNUT; PHC; PPL; PWW; TJoT; TNJ; ViRU; VtMiM. 30126

The opinions of a layman, on the

method of treating the marriage of a deceased wife's sister, by some modern divines ... New-York, Pr. by Elliott and Palmer, 1827. 46 p. MB; MBC; MdHi; NNC; NNG; NjR; PPPrHi. 30127

An oration, delivered at Potter's field. See Whitehead, David.

Origin of the terms high and low Churchman. Philadelphia, 1827. 8 p. NNG; PPPrHi; WHi. 30128

Original and select poems. See Story, Isaac.

Original moral tales intended for children and young persons. Containing The advantages of a good resolution. ... Boston, Bowles and Dearborn. Isaac R. Butts & Co., prs., 1827. Vol. I. 215 p. DLC. 30129

Osbourn, James
Spiritual lessons from a military school, in three letters to a female soldier, (Mrs. Ann Fradgley,) in the royal army of reserve, quartered at Salem on the borders of Zion. Baltimore, Pr. by John D. Toy, 1827. 35 p. MdHi. 30130

Osgood, Samuel
A sermon delivered at Springfield, Mass., before the Colonization Society of Hampden County, July 4, 1827... Springfield, Tannatt & Co., prs., 1827. 18 p. CSmH; CtHC; MHaHi; MSHi; MsJS; OClWHi; PPPrHi; VtU. 30131

Otter, William, 1768-1840
The life and remains of Edward Daniel Clarke: professor of mineralogy in the University of Cambridge. 2d ed. New York, Collins & Hannay [etc.] 1827. 528 p. CSt; CtHC; CtHT; CtW; GU; ICU; InCW; KyDC; KyLx; LN; MB; MBC; MBNEH; MH-AH; MWA; MWiW; MdBJ; MoSW; NCH; NNC; NNG; NNUT; NRU; NcDaD; NjR; NmU; OClW; PU; ScCC; VtU; WM. 30132

Otway, Thomas
Venice preserved, a tragedy ... 2d Amer. ed. Baltimore, Pr. and pub. by J. Robinson, Circulating Library and Dramatic Repository, 1827. 67, [4] p. MWA. 30133

Our chronicle of '26. See Mellen, Grenville.

Ovidius Naso, Publius
Ovid's art of love; together with his remedy of love. Translated into English verse; to which are added, "The court of love," and "The history of love." A new edition. New York, 1827. 134 p. LNHT. 30134

---- Excerpta ex scriptis Publii Ovidii Nasonis. Accedunt notulae anglicae et questiones. Bostoniae, Sumptibus Hilliard, Gray, Little et Wilkins, 1827. [Cambridge. From the University Press- By Hilliard, Metcalf, & Co.] 312 p. GAGTh; IEG; KyBC; KyLxT; MB; MBAt; MH; MHi; MPiB; TxU-T. 30135

---- Publi Ovidii Nasonis Metamorphoseon, libri XV, interpretatione et notis, illustravit D. C. Helsetius ... recensuit et emendavit Thomas S. Joy. New York, J. & J. Harper, 1827. 475 p. In; NbOC; ODaB; PPFM; ScNC. 30136

Owen, John, 1616-1683
The death of death in the death of Christ. A treatise of the redemption and reconciliation that is in the blood of Christ ... Philadelphia, Green, and M'Laughlin, Russell & Martien, prs., 1827. 392, [3] p. ICMcC; IObB; InCW; MiU; OT; PPL; PPiRPr; PU. 30137

---- Pneumatologia: or, A discourse concerning the Holy Spirit ... Abridged by the Rev. G. Burder, from the 3d London ed. ... Philadelphia, Pub. and sold by Towar & Hogan, J. H. Cunningham, pr., 1827. 391 p. CtW; GDC; MBC; MH; MiOC; MoFuWC; OO; PU. 30138

Owen, Robert
Address delivered at a public meeting.. Franklin Institute, Philadelphia, June 25, 1827, to which is added an exposition of the pecuniary transactions between that gentlemen and William M'Clure. Philadelphia, Gould, 1827. 39 p. PPAmP; PPL; PHi; BrMus 30139

P

Page, Charles Henry
A sermon delivered on the 27th December, 1826, being the anniversary of St. John the Evangelist ... New York, Dixon and Sickels, 1827. 24 p. NNG. 30140

Paine, Thomas
The age of reason ... New York, Pr. by G. N. Devries, 1827. 179 p MAnHi; PPL. 30141

Paley, William, 1743-1805
... The principles of moral and political philosophy. Boston, N. H. Whitaker, 1827. 2 v. MB; MH; MQ; MiD; MiDM; OFH; PHi; RJa; TNJ. 30142

---- ---- Bridgeport, Pub. by M. Sherman, 1827. 374 p. CtMMH; ICMcC; InU; MH-AH; MdBE; MnSM; NcAS; OO; RPA; Wv. 30143

---- Sermons on various subjects. 1st Amer. ed. Boston, Hilliard, Gray, Little & Wilkins, 1827. xv, 438 p. CBPac; CtHC; MB; MBC; MH; MMeT-Hi; MiU; MoSpD; NNUT; NSyU. 30144

[Palfrey, John Gorham] 1796-1881
The child's prayer book. Boston, Nathan Hale, 1827. 32 p. MBC; MH; PP. 30145

---- Discourses on intemperance, preached in the church in Brattle Square, Boston, April 5, 1827, the day of annual fast, and April 8, the Lord's day following. By John G. Palfrey ... [Boston] N. Hale, 1827. 111 p. DLC; M; MBAt; MBAU; MBC; NCH; NIC; Nh; RPB; W; BrMus. 30146

---- ---- 2d ed. Boston, Bowles and Dearborn, I. R. Butts & Co., prs., 1827. 108 p. CU; CtHT; MH; MH-AH; MW. 30147

[----] The youth's prayer book. Boston, Nathan Hale, 1827. 55p. MH. 30148

Park, Avery
A chronological compendium of the history of the United States, extending from the discovery of America, A. D. 1492, to the present day, A. D. 1827: according to the best authorities. Albany, Webster and Wood [1827] 2 folded sheets. MiMu. 30149

Parker, Edward Lutwyche
The supreme divinity of Jesus Christ. A sermon delivered October, 1827. Concord, N. H., Pr. by Isaac Hill, 1827. 63 p. ICN; MB; MBC; MH; MHi; MeBat; MiD-B; Nh; Nh-Hi. 30150

Parker, Jeroboam
A sermon delivered at Southborough, Mass., July 17, 1827 ... A century from the incorporation of the town. Boston, John Marsh, 1827. 39 p. CSansS; ICMe; ICN; M; MB; MBAt; MH; MHi; MW; MWHi; MiD-B; MnHi; NBLiHi; Nh; WHi; BrMus. 30151

Parker River Bridge Corporation
Act and by-laws and rules ... Newburyport, Pr. by W. & J. Gilman, 1827. 8 p. MH-BA. 30152

Parley, Peter, pseud. See Goodrich, Samuel Griswold.

Passages cited from the Old Testament by the writers of the New Testament compared with the original Hebrew and the Septuagint version. Arranged by the junior class in the Theological Seminary, Andover, and published at their request ... Andover, Flagg & Gould, publishers. Codman Press, 1827. 37 p. ICT; KyBC; MA; MB; MBC; MH; NNUT; PAtM; PPiW; PPL; WHi; BrMus. 30153

Paul, Nathaniel
An address, delivered on the celebration of the abolition of slavery, in the state of New-York, July 5, 1827 ... Albany, Pr. by John B. Van Steenbergh, 1827. 24 p. N; NN. 30154

Paul and Virginia. See Saint-Pierre, Jacques Henri Bernardin de.

[Paulding, James Kirke]
The diverting history of John Bull and Brother Jonathan. By Hector Bull-us [pseud.] 3d ed., imp. Philadelphia, Robert Desilver; R. Wright, pr., 1827. 114 p. MH; MWA; MdCatS; MdHi. 30155

Pauperism. See Carey, Mathew.

Paxton, James, 1786-1860
Illustrations of Paley's Natural Theology, with descriptive letter press. Boston, Hilliard, Gray and Wilkins, etc., 1827. 40 l. CtHC; CtHT; GaGTh; ICMcC; ICMe; ICJ; MB; MH; MWiW; MdBM; MiOC; MoSpD; NBMS; NIC-A; NNS; NWM; OC; P; RNR. 30156

Payne, John Howard, 1791-1852
Brutus; or, The fall of Tarquin. An historical tragedy, in five acts. Baltimore, J. Robinson, 1827. 57, [2] p. DLC; ICU; MB; MdHi. 30157

---- 'Twas I, or, The truth a lie. A farce, in two acts. New York, E. M. Murden, 1827. 31 p. CSmH; ICU; MB; MH; MnU; NSmB; PU; RPB. 30158

The peace catechism. See Worcester, Noah.

Peace Society of Windham County, Conn.
Peace Society of Windham County, its institution, sentiments and purposes. By order of the Society. Brooklyn, Con. Advertiser Press. John Gray Jr. 1827. 24 p. ICMe; MHi; MeB; MiD-B; WHi. 30159

The peaceful valley; or, The influence of religion, a narrative of facts. By a clergyman of the Church of England. 1st Amer. ed. Hartford, D. F. Robinson, pub., 1827. 108 p. CtHi; GDC; MH; MWA; NRAB; PCC; PPAmS. 30160

[Peacock, Lucy]
Visit for a week, or Hints, on the improvement of time. Containing, original tales, entertaining stories, interesting anecdotes, &c. New York, Pub. by N. B. Holmes [Pr. by Vanderpool & Cole] 1827. 216 p. CSmH; NHem. 30161

Peck, George
Universal salvation considered, and the eternal punishment ... Wilkesbarie, Pa., Pr. by S. D. Lewis, 1827. 148, [4] p. CtW; MMeT-Hi; PPL. 30162

Peck, John
A short poem, containing a descant on the universal plan ... 5th ed. Philadelphia, Pr. for the purchaser, 1827. 95 p. KyDC; RPB. 30163

Pengilly, Richard, 1782-1865
The Scripture guide to baptism; or, A faithful citation of all the passages of the New Testament which relate to this ordinance; ... 2d Amer. ed. Boston, Lincoln & Edmands, 1827. 48 p. MCET; MeLB; NNUT; PPPrHi; RPB. 30164

---- ---- 2d Amer. ed. Troy [N. Y.] Pr. by Tuttle and Richards, 1827. 44 p. CSmH. 30165

Penn, James, 1727-1800
Life of Miss Davis, the farmer's daughter of Essex. Also, Lisette & Login: a Russian tale. Philadelphia, Freeman Scott, 1827. 71 p. PHi not loc., 1969. 30166

Penn, William
The sandy foundation shaken, to which is added, Innocency with her open face, by way of apology. Trenton, F. S. Wiggins, 1827. 61 p. MH; PSC-Hi. 30167

Pennsylvania (State)
An act for establishing a health office, and to secure the city and port of Philadelphia from the introduction of pestilential and contagious diseases ... [Philadelphia?] Jacob Frick & Co., prs., 1827. 48 p. PPL. 30168

---- Communication from the Governor, accompanied with a report of the Board of Canal commissioners of Pennsylvania, and documents accompanying the said report. Read in the House of Representatives, January 1, 1827. Harrisburg, Pr. by John S. Wiestling, 1827. 96 p. DLC; ICJ; MB; N; P; PPL; PPAmP; PU. 30169

---- ---- No. 2. Read in the House of Representatives, February 7, 1827. Harrisburg, Pr. by John S. Wiestling, 1827. [135] p. DLC; M; MB; MH-BA; P; PPAmP; PPL. 30170

---- First report of the Pennsylvania Canal Commissioners, accompanied with official documents. Harrisburg, Pr. by Cameron & Krause, 1827. 96 p., 3 folded tables. CtY; DBRE; DLC; MH-BA; N; NN; PHi; P; PPAmP; PPF. 30171

---- Laws of the General Assembly of the state of Pennsylvania, passed at the session of 1826-27 in the fifty-first year of independence. Also acts relating to the circuit courts of Pennsylvania, published by way of appendix to the pamphlet laws ... Harrisburg, Cameron & Krause, 1827. [3]-512, [3]-14, 37 p. C; IaU-L; In-SC; MdBB; Mi-L; Mo; Ms; NNLI; Nb; Nc-S; Nj; PAtM; PLL; PPL; RPL; T; TxU-L; W. 30172

---- Minutes of the testimony taken by the Committee appointed by the House of Representatives to investigate the official conduct of Samuel D. Franks, Esq. President Judge of the Twelfth Judicial District of Pennsylvania. Harrisburg, Pr. by J. S. Wiestling, 1827. 151 p. NN; OCl; PPAmP. 30173

---- Ninth annual report of the Controllers of the public schools of the First school district of the state of Pennsylvania ... Philadelphia, Pr. by order of the boar of control, William Fry, pr., 1827. 14 p. PPL. 30174

---- Report of the Auditor General, giving a statement of the accounts of the commissioners and engineers, of the Pennsylvania Canal. Harrisburg, Pr. by Cameron & Krause, 1827. 23 p. PPAmP. 30175

---- Report of the canal commissioners of Pennsylvania to the Legislature. [Harrisburg, 1827] 320 p. CtY; ICJ; OCHP; PPF; PPL. 30176

---- Report of the Committee of Ways and Means, relative to the finances of the Commonwealth. Mr. Harrison, chairman ... Read in the Pennsylvania House of Representatives, March 7, 1827. Harrisburg, Pr. by J. S. Wiestling, 1827. 7 p. PHi; PPi. 30177

---- Report of the Committee on inland navigation and internal improvement, relative to the further extension of the Pennsylvania Canal accompanied with a bill, Mr. Lehman, Chairman. Harrisburg, J. S. Wiestling, 1827. 18 p. DLC; IU; MH-BA; N; P; PPAmP. 30178

---- Report of the engineer appointed by the commissioners for the improvement of the navigation of the river Susquehanna ... read ... Mar. 8, 1827. Harrisburg, J. S. Wiestling, 1827. 19 p. PPAmP; PPi. 30179

---- Report of the State Treasurer, shewing the receipts and expenditures at the Treasury of Pennsylvania, from the first day of December, 1826, to the thirtieth of November, 1827, inclusive. Harrisburg, Pr. by Simon Cameron, 1827. 412 p. PPi. 30180

---- Second report of the canal commissioners, together with reports and estimates of the engineers. Harrisburg, Pr. by Cameron & Krause, 1827. 139 p. Dated Feb. 6, 1827. CtY; MWA; MiU-T; N; NN-P; P; PPF; PPL. 30181

---- The several acts of Assembly providing for the education of children at public expense, within the city and county of Philadelphia. Philadelphia, Pr. by W. Stavely, 1827. 40 p. CU; DLC; PHi; PPL. 30182

---- Tagebuch des Senats der Republik Pennsylvanien 1826-1827. Reading, Pr. by Schneider u. Meyers, 1827. Seidensticker p. 235. 30183

Pennsylvania Academy of the Fine Arts

Sixteenth annual exhibition ... 1827. Philadelphia, 1827. 24 p. MHi. 30184

Pennsylvania Agricultural Society

Hints for American husbandmen; with communications to the Pennsylvania Agricultural Society. By order of the directors. Philadelphia, Pr. by Clark & Raser, 1827. [178] p. DLC; ICU; IU; M; MH; NNC; NcRA; P; PHi; PPL; PPi; PU; RPA. 30185

Pennsylvania almanac for 1828. By John Ward. Philadelphia, M'Carty & Davis [1827] 18 l. PDoBHi; PP; PPiHi. 30186

---- ---- Philadelphia, G. W. Mentz, and M'Carty & Davis [1827] 18 l. CtY; DLC; InU; MWA; NN; NjR; PHi; PLF. 30187

Pennsylvania and New Jersey almanack for 1828. Philadelphia, Griggs & Co. [1827] CtY. 30188

---- By Joseph Cramer. Philadelphia, Isaac Pugh [1827] 18 l. FSaHi; InU; MWA; NjR; PHi; PP. 30189

Pennsylvania Colonization Society

The first report of the board

of managers of the Pennsylvania Colonization Society, read at the annual meeting held April 9th, 1827. With an appendix. Philadelphia, Pub. by order of the Society. T. Town, pr., 1827. 16 p. PPPrHi. 30190

Pennsylvania Domestic Missionary Society
Statement of the origin, nature and operations of the Pennsylvania Domestic Missionary Society. Philadelphia, John W. Allen, 1827. 15 p. PHi; PPPrHi. 30191

Pennsylvania Historical Society
Memoirs of the Historical Society of Pennsylvania. Vol. II ... Philadelphia, Carey, Lea & Carey, 1827. 247 p. CtSoP; ICU; MNBedf; PPFM; PSC-Hi. 30192

Pennsylvania Horticultural Society, Philadelphia.
Constitution of the Pennsylvania Horticultural Society at Philadelphia. Philadelphia, Clark & Raser, prs., 1827. 7 p. PPL. 30193

Pennsylvania Society for Discouraging the Use of Ardent Spirits.
Constitution of the Pennsylvania Society for Discouraging the Use of Ardent Spirits. Adopted July 24, 1827. [Philadelphia? 1827?] 4 p. PPL. 30194

Pennsylvania Society for the Promotion of Manufactures and the Mechanic Arts.
Farmers' and Manufacturers' Meeting. At a meeting of the Pennsylvania Society for the Promotion of Manufactures and the Mechanic Arts, held at Philadelphia, on the 14th day of May, 1827. Charles Jared Ingersoll, Esq., Vice President, in the chair, and Redwood Fisher, Esq., Secretary. Boston, June 1, 1827. Bdsd. NjR. 30195

---- ... At a meeting of "The Pennsylvania Society for the Promotion of Manufactures and the Mechanic Arts," held on Tuesday evening, the 16th inst. the following officers were elected. [Philadelphia, Jan. 19, 1827] Bdsd. PU. 30196

---- At a meeting of the ... held in Philadelphia, on the 14th day of May, 1827 ... [Philadelphia, 1827] 12 p. MB; PPL. 30197

---- To the citizens of the United States ... [Philadelphia, 1827] 12 p. MB; MH-BA. 30198

Pennsylvania. University.
Annual statement of the funds of the University of Pennsylvania, as reported by the Committee of finance. Philadelphia, 1827. 8, [1] p. PPL. 30199

[----] Report on the application of the Widow of C. Carpenter. [Philadelphia, 1827] 8 p. PPL. 30200

[Penrose, Elizabeth (Cartwright)] 1780-1837
Amusements of Westernheath: or, Moral stories for children ... By Mrs. Markham [pseud.] New York, Orville A. Roorbach, 1827. 300 p. CtHT-W. 30201

Percival, James Gates, 1795-1856
Clio. [No. III] ... New York, G. and C. Carvill, 1827. 203, [1] p. CSmH; CtB; CtSoP; DLC; GMWa; ICU; IU; MeBat; NNC; NcU; PHi; PU; RNR; RPB; ScC; TxU; WHi. 30202

Perkins, Ephraim
Letter to the Presbytery of Oneida County, New-York, and their "Committee, the Rev. John Frost, Rev. Moses Gillet, and Rev. Noah Coe," appointed to receive communications from minis-

ters and others respecting the late revival, in this county, Utica, Pr. for the author by Dauby & Maynard, 1827. 23 p. ICMe; MH; MWA; NN; NUtHi. 30203

Perkins, Joseph, 1788-1842
The American penman, by Perkins and Rand. Philadelphia, 1827. 12 p. 33 plates. WHi. 30204

Perkins, Samuel
Address delivered before the Peace Society of Windham County, at their semi-annual meeting in Pomfret. Feb. 14, 1827. Brooklyn, Con. Advertiser Press, John Gray, Jr. [1827] 20 p. CSmH; DLC; MeB. 30205

Perrin, Jean Baptiste
A selection of M. Perrin's Fables, accompanied with a key ... By A. Bolmar. Philadelphia, Pr. by P. M. Lafourcade, 1827. 84 p. PHi. 30206

Peter, John
To the public. [Refers to slanderous publications against him by Col. Braxton Davenport] John Peter. Jefferson County. 24th May, 1827. [Martinsburg] Bdsd. WvU. 30207

Phaedrus
Phaedri Augusti Liberti Fabularum Aesopiarum libri quinque. Or a correct Latin edition of the fables of Phaedrus: With English notes, and a copious construing and parsing vocabulary. Baltimore, Pub. by Fielding Lucas, Jun'r. [John D. Toy, pr.] 1827?] xvi, 242 p. LNHT; NIC. 30208

---- Phaedri Fabulae expurgatae accedunt tractatus de versu Iambico, notulae anglicae et quaestiones in usum scholae Bostoniensis. Bostoniae, Sumptibus Hilliard, Gray, Little, et Wilkins. 1827. [Cambridge, Hilliard, Metcalf & Company, prs. to the University] vii, [1], 130 p. CtHT-W; IJI; KyLxT; MB; MBedf; MH; MdCatS; MeB. 30209

Phi Beta Kappa. New York Alpha. Union College
A catalogue of the fraternity of ØBK, Alpha of New-York, Union College, Schenectady, 1827. Schenectady, Pr. by Isaac Riggs, 1827. 18 p. MB; MHi; MWA; NSchU. 30210

Philadelphia
Act to incorporate the district of Spring Garden ... Philadelphia, Pr. by order of the Commissioners, Jacob Frick & Co., 1827. 108, xiii p. PHi. 30211

---- Ordinances of the corporation of the city of Philadelphia; passed since June 8, 1826. Philadelphia, Pr. by Lydia R. Bailey, 1827. 28 p. P. 30212

---- Report of the Committee appointed at a town meeting of the citizens of the city and county of Philadelphia, on the 23rd of July, 1827 to consider the subject of the pauper system. Philadelphia, Pr. by Clarke & Raser, 1827. 28, [6] p. CU; IU; InRE; MB; MH; MdBM; MdHi; PPAmP; PPC; PPL; PPPrHi; PPi; PU; WHi. 30213

---- Report of the committee appointed by the Board of Guardians of the Poor of the city and districts of Philadelphia, to visit the cities of Baltimore, New-York, Providence, Boston, and Salem. Philadelphia, Pr. by S. Parker, 1827. 38 p. CU; DLC; MH; MHi; NNC; NjP; PHC; PHi; PPAmP; PPL; PPi; WHi. 30214

---- Report of the Watering committee, to the Select and Common Councils. Read January 11, 1827. Published by order of the councils. Philadelphia, Pr. by Lydia R. Bailey, 1827. 24 p. PPL; THi. 30215

---- Report of the Watering committee, to the Select and Common Councils of the city of Philadelphia, relative to the Fair Mount water works. Read January 9, 1823. 2d ed., with additions. Philadelphia, Pr. by Lydia R. Bailey, 1827. 27 p. PHi; THi. 30216

---- Statement of the expenditures of the city commissioners for the year 1826. Read March 8, 1827. Philadelphia, Lydia R. Bailey, 1827. 15, [29] p. PHi. 30217

Philadelphia Album
The carrier of the Philadelphia Album respectfully present to its patrons the following New Year address, for 1827. Philadelphia, Album office, J. B. Kenney, pr. [1827] 1 p. DLC. 30218

Philadelphia. Apprentices' Library
Cautions against the use of tobacco, affectionately addressed to the youth using the Apprentices' Library of Philadelphia. [Philadelphia, 1827] 4 p. PPL. 30219

---- ---- Variant issue. 4 p. PPL. 30220

---- Report of the managers of the Apprentices' Library ... Philadelphia, I. Ashmead, pr., 1827. 12 p. PHi. 30221

Philadelphia Bible Society. See Bible Society of Philadelphia.

Philadelphia Cemetery
Copy of deed of trust. April 2, 1827. [Philadelphia, 1827] 13 p. PPL. 30222

---- ---- Variant issue 12 p. PPL. 30223

Philadelphia. Chestnut Street Theatre
[Program for Le Macon and Le Bouffe et Le Tailleur, 30 September] Philadelphia [1827] [Bdsd.] PU. 30224

Philadelphia. Citizens
To the honourable the Senate and House of Representatives of the United States ... The memorial of the subscribers, citizens of the city and county of Philadelphia. [Philadelphia, Sept. 20, 1827] 12 p. MH; MWA; PPL. 30225

---- ---- 2d ed., Nov. 9, 1827. [Philadelphia, 1827] 12 p. PPL. 30226

Philadelphia. Committee for the Relief of the Greeks
Extract of a letter from a young Greek ... The cause of suffering humanity. [Philadelphia, 1827] 4 p. PPL. 30227

---- ---- 2d ed. [Philadelphia, 1827] 4 p. PPAmP. 30228

---- Sir, the annexed resolution, and the appended papers, are respectfully submitted to your consideration by a member of the Greek Committee. [Philadelphia, 1827] 7 p. PPL. 30229

---- Sir. We have the pleasure to inform you, that at length, after much difficulty, we have succeeded in chartering a vessel to convey to the Greeks, the supplies of food and clothing, contributed by the liberality of our citizens, for the relief of the noncombatants of that heroic nation ... Philadelphia, May 19, 1827. 1 p. DLC. 30230

---- To the friends of humanity. The following truly eloquent letter is respectfully submitted to the most serious consideration of the citizens of Pennsylvania ... The suffering Greeks ... [Philadelphia, 1827] 8 p. PU. 30231

---- To the Public. ["The following letter, received by yesterday's mail, is most respectfully and earnestly recommended ..."] [Philadelphia, 1827] 3 p. PPL. 30232

Philadelphia. Friends Asylum for the Insane

Tenth annual report on the state of the Asylum for the Relief of Persons Deprived of the Use of their Reason. Published by direction of the contributors, third month, 1827. Philadelphia, Pr. by Solomon W. Conrad, 1827. 12 p. TNJ. 30233

Philadelphia. Harmony Fire Company

Constitution of the Harmony Fire Company. Philadelphia, John Richards, 1827. 16 p. PHi. 30234

Philadelphia. Mariners' Church

Report on the state of the Mariners' Church, at the port of Philadelphia. With an appendix, containing extracts from sundry letters, and a list of new subscribers and donations. Philadelphia, Pr. by J. W. Allen, 1827. 24 p. InRE; PHi; PP; PPAmP; PPPrHi. 30235

Philadelphia Monthly Magazine

Prospectus of a literary magazine to be published in Philadelphia ... [Philadelphia, R. H. Small, 1827] 2 p. PPL. 30236

Philadelphia. Northern Dispensary for the Medical Relief of the Poor.

Rules and regulations of the Northern Dispensary ... and the annual report for 1826. [Philadelphia, 1827] 11 p. PPL. 30237

Philadelphia. Passyunk Township

Sherriff's sale, July 16, 1827. Tract of land bounded on the North and East by property granted by John Jacob Cubler to the Old Lutheran Church, Southward by Beggarstown Lane ... Philadelphia, 1827. 1 p. PHi. 30238

Philadelphia. St. Mary's Church

A continuation of references relative to St. Mary's Church. 13, 1 p. DGU. 30239

---- Rev. W. V. Harold, D. D.

Rev. Sir. - On the 24th ult. a large and respectable meeting of the pewholders and other Roman Catholics, worshipping in St. Mary's Church, disapproving of your suspension appointed the following citizens ... "to open a correspondence with the proper authorities ..." [Philadelphia, May 2, 1827] 22 p. PU. 30240

---- To the Congregation of St. Mary's Church. [Philadelphia, March 29, 1827] Bdsd. MB. 30241

Philadelphia Society for the Establishment and Support of Charity Schools.

Annual report of the board of managers of the ... Philadelphia, Pub. by order of the Society, Samuel Parker, pr., 1827. 11 p. PPL. 30242

Philadelphia Theatre

[Playbills] July 2, 1827 - July 27, 1827. [Philadelphia, Thomas De Silver, 1827] 12 bdsds. PPL. 30243

Philalethes, pseud.

The importance of revivals as exhibited in the late convention at New-Lebanon, considered in a brief review of the proceedings of that body. By Philalethes. Ithaca, Pr. by Mack & Andrus, 1827. 19 p. CtY; MH; MWA; N. 30244

Philanthropos, pseud. See Ladd, William.

Phillips, counsellor.
The new American dictator, containing a number of useful precedents, agreeable to the individual laws of the United States ... New York, Pub. for the proprietor, [1827?] 12 p. MH-BA. 30245

[Phillips, Jonas B.]
Tales for leisure hours ... Philadelphia, Atkinson & Alexander, prs., 1827. 162 p. PPL. 30246

[Phillips, Sir Richard]
The first catechism for children ... By the Rev. David Blair [pseud.] Loring's 7th Boston ed. Boston, Pr. and sold by James Loring [1827?] 72 p. MB; NNC. 30247

[----] A geographical view of the world embracing the manners, customs and pursuits of every nation founded on the best authorities ... illustrated by engravings. Boston, Reed & Jewett, 1827. 406, [2], 46 p. IEG; ILebM; NhD; ViU. 30248

[----] ---- 3d ed. Boston, Pr. for Reed and Jewett, New York. 1827. 406, [2], 46 p. CSmH; NKings. 30249

[----] ---- By Rev. J. Goldsmith [pseud.] 7th ed. Boston, New York, Pr. for Reed and Jewett, 1827. 406, [2], 46 p. CLSM; KyLxT; MPiB; MiU; Nh-Hi. 30250

[----] ---- By Rev. J. Goldsmith [pseud.] ... rev. and corr. and imp. by James G. Percival ... 8th ed. Boston, New York, Pr. for Reed and Jewett, 1827. 406, [2], 46 p. MiKC; ViU. 30251

[----] ---- 9th ed. Boston, Pr. for Reed and Jewett, New York, 1827. [8], 406, [3], 46 p. TxSani. 30252

[----] ---- 10th ed. Boston, Pr. for Reed and Jewett, New York, 1827. 406, [2] index, 46 p. KyHi; MsCliM; TNJ. 30253

[----] A grammar of chemistry ... Corr. and rev. by Benjamin Tucker ... 5th ed. Philadelphia, Towar and Hogan, 1827. 211 p. DLC; MH; NRU-W; NhPet; NjR; PHi; PPF; PV. 30254

Philo Pacificus, pseud. See Worcester, Noah.

Phinneys' calendar, or Western almanac for 1828. By Edwin E. Prentiss. Cooperstown, H. & E. Phinney [1827] 18 l. CLU; DLC; InU; MWA; NIC; NN; PHi; WHi. 30255

Phinney's calendar, or Western almanac for 1828. By Edwin E. Prentiss. Little Falls, Sprague & McKenster [1827] 18 l. DLC; MWA; WHi. 30256

Phlogobombos. Yclept Terentius, pseud. See Judah, Samuel Benjamin Herbert.

Pickens, Francis Wilkinson, 1805-1869
The anniversary oration of the Clariosophic Society, delivered in the Chapel of the South Carolina College, on the 2nd of February, 1827. Columbia, S. C. Sweeny & Sims, at the Telescope press, 1827. 23 p. A-Ar; ScU. 30257

Pickering, David, 1788-1859
The effects of intemperance, a discourse delivered on January 14, 1827, at the Universalist Chapel. 2d ed. Taunton, Samuel W. Mortimer, pr., 1827. 22 p. CSmH; MH; NN; PPPrHi; RHi; RPB; BrMus. 30258

---- Reflections for the New Year; a discourse delivered on Sabbath morning, Jan. 7, 1827, at the Universalist Chapel ... Providence, Miller and Grattan, prs., 1827. 15 p. NcAS; RHi; RPB. 30259

Picket, Albert, 1771-1850
The juvenile expositor, or American school class book, improved and enlarged ... Stereotyped by A. Chandler & Co. New York; Pr. and pub. at the American School class-book warehouse by C. Bartlett, 1827. 381 p. CtHT-W; IaDmDC; NNC-T; NcGW; OClW; TNJ; BrMus. 30260

---- American school class book, No. 1. Picket's juvenile spelling book ... New-York, Pr. and pub. by Caleb Bartlett, 1827. 214 p. NNC. 30261

---- Picket's juvenile spelling book; or, Analogical pronouncer of the English language ... New York, Caleb Bartlett, 1827. iv, 5-211 p. CSt; ICU. 30262

---- Supplement to Picket's juvenile, or universal primer. The child's first lesson in definitions. Cincinnati, Pr. and pub. by G. T. Williamson, 1827. 48 p. DLC. 30263

Pickett, Aaron
A sermon, occasioned by the death of Mrs. Abigail Lothrop, wife of Capt. Daniel Lothrop, of Cohasset; preached July 1, 1827, the Sabbath succeeding her funeral. Boston, T. R. Marvin, pr. 1827. 20 p. CBPac; Ct; MH; MHi; MWA; NBLiHi; RPB; BrMus. 30264

Pierce, Benjamin
Message from the governor of New Hampshire ... Concord, Jacob B. Moore, pr., 1827. 8 p. Nh-Hi; NjR. 30265

Pierpont, John, 1785-1866
A discourse delivered in Hollis Street Church, Boston, September 2, 1827: occasioned by the death of Horace Holley, LL. D., late President of Transylvania University. Boston, from the press of the Christian Examiner, Stephen Foster, pr., 1827. 31 p. CBPac; CLU; CSmH; CoD; CtHC; CtSoP; DLC; ICMe; ICU; KyBgW-K; MA; MB; MBAt; MBC; MH; MHi; MWA; MiD-B; MeBat; NCH; NIC-L; PHi; PPL; PPPrHi; RPB; BrMus. 30266

---- "Knowledge is Power," ... A sermon, preached in Hollis Street Church, Boston, on Fast Day, April 5, 1827. Boston, Hilliard, Gray, Little and Wilkins [Cambridge, From the University Press by Hilliard, Metcalf & Co.] 1827. 16 p. CSmH; CtHT-W; DLC; ICMe; M; MBAU; MH; MWA; MiD-B; NUt; PPAmP; RPB; BrMus. 30267

---- The national reader; a selection of exercises in reading and speaking ... Boston, Hilliard, Gray, Little, and Wilkins [etc.] 1827. 276 p. CtHT-W; MB; MH; NCH; RPB. 30268

Pierre and his family. See Grierson, Miss.

Pike, Nicholas, 1743-1819
Pike's system of arithmetic abridged ... 2d ed., rev., cor., and improved. By Dudley Leavitt. Concord [N. H.] J. B. Moore, 1827. 201, [7] p. CSt; CtHT-W; MH; NNC. 30269

Pike, Stephen
The teacher's assistant, or, A system of practical arithmetic ... A new ed. ... Philadelphia, M'Carty & Davis, stereotyped by L. Johnson, 1827. 198 p. PPL. 30270

Pilkington, Mary (Hopkins), 1766-1839
Scripture histories; or Interesting narratives, extracted from the Old Testament ... 2d Princeton ed., carefully rev. and cor. Princeton Press, Pr. by D. A. Borrenstein, 1827. 105 p. DGU. 30271

The Pilot. See Cooper, James Fenimore.

Pinkerton Academy. Derry, N. H.
Catalogue of the officers and members of the Pinkerton Academy, in Derry N. H. November--1827. Concord, Pr. by Isaac Hill, 1827. 7, [1] p. CSmH. 30272

The Pioneers. See Cooper, James Fenimore.

The pious gift: consisting of a dialogue between two seamen after a storm; and, The wonderful cure of General Naaman. New York, Mahlon Day, 1827. 23 p. OClWHi. 30273

The pious guide to prayer and devotion. Baltimore, Pub. by Fielding Lucas, Jr. [1827?] (verso:) ["James C. Dunn, printer. Georgetown, D. C."] 387 p. DGU. 30274

A pious inquirer with respect to the Lord's supper, answered by a minister of the Gospel. Philadelphia, William Stavely, 1827. 12 p. WHi. 30275

Pise, Charles Constantine
A history of the church, from its establishment to the present century. Baltimore, Pub. by P. Blenkinsop, 1827-30. 5 v. DGU; DLC; InNd; MB; MdBL; MdW; MiDSH; MoSU; NNF; PPCHi; PV. 30276

Pittsburgh. Canal Committee.
Narrative of facts relative to the location of the western section of the Pennsylvania canal, and the proceedings of the canal commissioners, prepared under a resolution of the canal committee of Pittsburgh. Pittsburgh, Pr. at the office of the Statesman, 1827. 35 p. PPiHi; PPL. 30277

Pittsburgh. Methodist Episcopal Church.
An address to the members of the Methodist Episcopal Church; by a meeting of Methodists, held in Pittsburgh May 23d, 1827. To which are prefixed the resolutions of the meeting. Pittsburgh, Pr. by John C. Andrews, 1827. 15, [1] p. In; OCHP. 30278

Plain Fact, pseud.
"Prove all things; hold fast that which is good." An answer to a pamphlet, recently addressed to the Episcopalians of Pennsylvania, under the signature of Plain Truth, by Plain Fact. Philadelphia, 1827. 27, [1] p. CtHT; IEG; MH-AH; MWA; MiD-B; NNG; P; PHi; PPAmP; PPL; PPPrHi. 30279

Plain Truth
Proposals for publishing at Buffalo, N. Y. A new series of Plain Truth! ... [Buffalo, 1827] Bdsd. McMurtrie 25. 30280

Plain Truth, pseud. See DeLancey, William Heathcote, bp.

Plain Truth, Junior, pseud.
Another candid address to the Episcopalians of Pennsylvania in relation to the present situation of affairs in the diocess. [Philadelphia? 1827?] 22 p. MH; MWA; NNG; PPL; PPiU. 30281

[Plumer, William] 1759-1850
Remarks on the letter of Domesticus, containing the doctrine of incest stated, with an examination of the question, "Whether a man may marry his deceased

wife's sister." New York, G. and C. Carvill, 1827. 40 p. LNHT; MB; MH-AH; MdHi; N; NjR; OClWHi; PPL; PPPrHi; RPB. 30282

Plummer, Frederick
Disquisition on the text, "What think ye of Christ? Whose son is he?" ... Philadelphia, Pr. by the request of those that heard it delivered, 1827. 12 p. CtHT-W. 30283

Plutarch, pseud. See A sketch of the life and public services of John Quincy Adams.

Pocock, Isaac, 1782-1835
John of Paris; a comic opera, in two acts. New-York, Pub. by E. M. Murden, Circulating-Library and Dramatic Repository, 1827. 32 p. MB; MH; MWA; NRU; PPL. 30284

[Poe, Edgar Allan] 1809-1849
Tamerlane and other poems. By a Bostonian ... Boston, Calvin F. S. Thomas ... printer, 1827. 40 p. CL; CLU; MH; MoSW; NN; NjP; RPB; ViU; BrMus. 30285

Poems, by the author of "Moral pieces." See Sigourney, Mrs. Lydia Howard (Huntley).

Poetical illustrations of the Athenaeum gallery of paintings. See Crosby, William George.

The political memorial: containing Washington's Farewell address to the people of the United States, The Federal Constitution, with the amendments to the same, names of the delegates who formed the Constitution and Washington's letter to the president of Congress. To which is prefixed a biographical memoir of Gen. George Washington. Concord, G. Hough, 1827. 105 p. CSmH; DLC; Nh-Hi; NjR. 30286

Polk, Charles
Inaugural address of Governour Polk to the Legislature of the state of Delaware delivered January 16, 1827. Dover, Pr. by J. Robertson, 1827. 8 p. DLC. 30287

[----] The banks of the Irvine ... By the author of "Helen of the Glen." Boston, Pub. and sold by James Loring, 1827. 144 p. IU. 30288

[Pollok, Robert] 1798-1827
Helen of the glen. A tale for youth. New York, W. E. Dean for Orville A. Roorbach, 1827. 72 l. PP. 30289

Polly Hopkins and Tommy Tompkins. Comic duett. Baltimore, Willig, 1827. 3 p. MB. 30290

Poole, John, 1786?-1872
Paul Pry; a comedy in three acts. New York, E. M. Murden, 1827. 72 p. CU; MWA; RP. 30291

---- Simpson & Co., a comedy, in two acts. Philadelphia, F. C. Wemyss, and Ash & Mason; New York, E. M. Murden, and L. Godey; etc., etc., 1827. 46 p. NIC-L; NNC. 30292

Poor Richard revived. Almanac for 1828. By David Young. New-York, John C. Totten [1827] 18 l. MWA; NBLiHi; NN. 30293

Poor Wills almanac for 1828. By William Collom. Philadelphia, J. Rakestraw [1827] 18 l. MWA; NHi. 30294

---- ---- Philadelphia, Kimber & Sharpless [1827] 18 l. CtY; DLC; InU; MB; MWA; N; NjR; PPL; WHi. 30295

Poor Will's pocket almanack for 1828. Philadelphia, Kimber & Sharpless [1827] 24 l. MWA;

NjR; PHi. 30296

Pope, Alexander, 1688-1744
An essay on man ... Hartford, S. Andrus, 1827. 110 p. LND. 30297

---- ---- Norway, Me., A. Barton, 1827. 54 p. CtY. 30298

Popular songs. Vergennes. [Gamaliel Small, pr. ?] 1827. 16 p. VtU. 30299

Porney, Mr., pseud. See Pyron du Martre, Antoine.

Porter, Anna Maria
Honor O'Hara. A novel ... New York, Pr. by J. & J. Harper. New York, Pub. by E. Duyckinck, Collins & Hannay, and Collins & Co. Philadelphia, H. C. Carey & I. Lea. R. H. Small and J. Grigg. Boston, Hilliard, Gray & Co., 1827. 2 v. LU; MB; MBBC; MBC; MH; NcU; PFal; PP; RPB. 30300

---- The Hungarian brothers ... Exeter, N. H., Pub. by J. C. Gerrish, 1827. 2 v. MH; NbOM; RP. 30301

Porter, Ebenezer, 1772-1834
Analysis of the principles of rhetorical delivery as applied in reading and speaking. Andover, Pub. by Mark Newman, Hilliard, Gray & company, Boston, J. Leavitt, New York, Pr. by Flagg & Gould, 1827. 404 p. CSmH; KU; MA; MB; MH; MWiW; NNC; NbCrD; NjP; PPL; PU; RPB; TNJ; TxU-T. 30302

---- The duty of Christians to pray for the missionary cause. A sermon preached in Boston, November 1, 1827, before the Society for Propagating the Gospel among the Indians and Others in North America. Andover, Pr. by Flagg & Gould, 1827. 42 p. CtHT-W; MAnHi; MBAU; MBC; MH-AH; MHi; MWA; MiD-B; MeHi; RPB; VtMiM; WHi; BrMus. 30303

---- Unity of ministerial influence. A sermon, preached in Boston, May 29th, 1827 before the pastoral association of Massachusetts. Andover [Mass.] Pub. by Flagg & Gould, 1827. 36 p. CSmH; CtHT-W; DLC; GDC; ICN; MA; MB; MH-AH; MWA; MeB; MoSpD; NIC-L; NjR; PPPrHi; RPB; BrMus. 30304

Porter, Jane, 1776-1850
The Scottish chiefs; a romance. Exeter, Pr. and pub. by J. & B. Williams, 1827. 3 v. CtHC; IaDmD; MPlyA; MiToC; Nh-Hi; OClW; PU. 30305

---- ---- Hartford, S. Andrus, 1827. 5 v. in 3. MSwan. 30306

---- Thaddeus of Warsaw ... Exeter, N. H., J. C. Gerrish, 1827. 2 v. MWbnHi; NbOM; RAp; RPE. 30307

Portland Athenaeum
By-laws and regulations of the Portland Athenaeum. Portland, Pr. by James Adams, Jr., 1827. 64 p. MeHi. 30308

The Portland directory & register; containing the names, professions and residence, of the heads of families & persons of business ... Accompanied with a new and correct plan of the town. Portland, J. Adams, jr., 1827. vol. 2. DLC; MHi; MeHi; PHi. 30309

Portland. Fire Society.
Rules and orders to be observed by the Fire Society, instituted in Falmouth, now Portland, February 24th, 1783. Revised by the Society in March, 1805, also

in March, 1816, also in March, 1827. Portland, Pr. by James Adams, Jun., 1827. 18 p. MeHi. 30310

Portland. First Parish.
Sunday school regulations, First Parish, Portland. Instituted April, 1824. Portland, Thomas Todd, pr., 1827. 8 p. CBPac; MeHi. 30311

Portsmouth Athenaeum
Annual report of the directors ... January, 1827. [Portsmouth, Miller & Brewster, prs., 1827] 8 p. MBC. 30312

---- Catalogue of books in the Portsmouth Athenaeum. [Portsmouth] Charles Turell, pr., 1827. 24 p. Nh-Hi. 30313

Portsmouth, N. H. North Parish Library
[Catalogue. Portsmouth, Jan. 1, 1827] 12 p. MBC. 30314

The Portsmouth directory, containing names of inhabitants, their occupations, places of business, and dwelling houses; lists of the streets, lanes and wharves; the town officers, the public offices and banks; and other useful information. Portsmouth, Pub. by Wibird Penhallow ... 1827. 83, [1] p. MHi; MWA; NhPoA; NhPo. 30315

Potter,
New-year's address, of a street sweeper. Presented by Potter ... January 1, 1827. [Boston? 1827] Bdsd. MB. 30316

[Potter, Paraclete]
Every man his own lawyer, or The clerk and magistrate's assistant. By a gentleman of the bar. Stereotyped by James Conner, New-York. Poughkeepsie, P. Potter & co., 1827. 126, 62 p. CSmH; DLC; GAuY; IaHi; NNLI; NP. 30317

Potter, Ray, 1795-1858
A vindication of the doctrine of the final perseverance of the saints ... Pawtucket [R. I.] Pr. for the author, 1827. 119, [1] p. CSmH; DLC; MH; MWA. 30318

[Potter, Robert] 1800-1842
Head of Medusa; a mock-heroic poem, founded on fact, in which "the word is suited to the phrase, and the phrase to the action," by Rienzi. Halifax [Office of the Free press] 1827. 86 p. NcU. 30319

Potts, John
Letters to the Rev. A. M'Farlane; being a reply to his essay on predestination. Pr. by Robert Johnston, Bridgeton, W. N. J. 1827. 26 p. PHi; PPPrHi; TxDaM. 30320

---- A sermon on predestination. Delivered in the Methodist Episcopal Church at Bridgeton, W. N. J. on the evening of the 18th of February, 1827. Bridgeton, W. N. J., Pr. by Robert Johnston, 1827. 24 p. NjR; PHi; PPL; PPPrHi. 30321

[Potts, Stacy Gardner] 1799-1865
Village tales; or, Recollections of by-past times. By Oliver Oakwood [pseud.] Trenton, N. J., Joseph Justice, 1827. 252 p. CSmH; DLC; ICU; MH; NjP; NjT; PHi; PU; RPB. 30322

[Powell, Thomas Spencer]
"Nothing is so Secret, but Time and Truth will reveal it." To the Honorable Members of the General Assembly of Georgia. [1827?] 8 p. GU-De. 30323

Powers, Grant, 1784-1841
The government of God universal. A sermon, delivered at the

installation of the Rev. Elderkin J. Boardman to the pastoral care of the Church of Christ in Danville, Vt., January 3, 1827. Danville, Pr. by E. & W. Eaton, 1827. 22 p. MBAt; NN; OClWHi; VtHi. 30324

The prairie. See Cooper, James Fenimore.

Preamble and resolutions. See National Republican Party, Virginia.

Presbyterian Church in the U. S. A.

The constitution of the Presbyterian Church in the United States of America; containing the Confession of faith, the catechisms and the directory for the worship of God; together with the plan of government and discipline as amended and ratified by the General Assembly at their session in May, 1821. Philadelphia, Towar & Hogan, 1827. 466 p. CSansS; CtHC; CtHT; ICLaw; KWiU; LShD; MA; MBC; MH; MiNazC; MoS; MtH; NB; NcMHi; P; PPPrHi; RBr; ScP; ViU. 30325

---- Minutes of the General Assembly of the Presbyterian Church in the United States of America: with an appendix, A. D. 1827. Philadelphia, Pr. by Jesper Harding, 1827. [3], 108-213, [3] p. InU; KyLoP; MsJS; NcMHi. 30326

---- Narrative of the state of religion, within the bounds of the General Assembly of the Presbyterian Church, in the United States of America. May, 1827. Philadelphia, Pr. by William F. Geddes, 1827. 8 p. MWA; PPPrHi. 30327

---- Presbytery of Buffalo.

A review of the minutes and proceedings of The Presbytery of Buffalo, at their special session in that village, October 16, 17 and 18, 1827; for the trial of the Rev. Jabez B. Hyde, on charges preferred against him by Rev. T. S. Harris, missionary among the Seneca Indians. Buffalo, H. A. Salisbury, pr., 1827. 73 p. NBuHi. 30328

---- Presbytery of Lexington, Va.

A pastoral letter, of the Presbytery of Lexington, addressed to the churches: under their care ... Staunton [Va.] Spectator office, 1827. 14 p. CSmH; PPPrHi. 30329

---- Presbytery of Mississippi

Extracts from the minutes of the Mississippi Presbytery. With the narrative of the state of religion: and extracts from the minutes of the Missionary & Education Societies. Pr. by Andrew Marschalk, Natchez, 1827. 35 p. Ms-Ar; MsJS. 30330

---- Presbytery of Oneida.

A narrative of the revival of religion in the county of Oneida; particularly in the bounds of the Presbytery of Oneida, in the year 1826. Utica, Pr. by Hastings & Tracy, 1826. Princeton, N. J., Repr. by D. A. Borrenstein, 1827. 67 p. CBPac; CSmH; CtHC; NN; NUt; PPL; BrMus. 30331

---- ---- Washington, Way & Gideon, 1827. 44 p. KyDC; MH-BA; MNF; PPPrHi. 30332

---- Synod of Indiana

A memorial to the General Assembly of the Presbyterian Church in the United States. On the subject of African slavery, from the Synod of Indiana, adopted at their meeting at Salem, Indiana, Oct. 1827. Madison, Ia., Pr.

by C. P. J. Arion [1827?] 10 p. OC; PPPrHi. 30333

---- Synod of Philadelphia.
Minutes of the Synod of Philadelphia; at their meeting held in Harrisburgh, Pa. from Oct. 31st, to Nov. 2d, 1827. [Harrisburg, Pr. by Wm. F. Geddes, 1827] 8 p. PPPrHi. 30334

Presbyterian Education Society, New York.
Ninth annual report of the ... Presbyterian Education Society ... New York, J. &J. Harper, pr. 1827. 16 p. NjR. 30335

The presidential question. Fairfax, Pr. by J. Caldwell, 1827. 16 p. DLC. 30336

[Supplement to the Democratic Press] The Presidential question. To the friends of equal rights ... Philadelphia, Oct. 13, 1827. 8 p. DLC; MB. 30337

Preston, Lyman
Preston's manual on book keeping: or Arbitrary rules made plain ... Utica, Pr. by Dauby and Maynard, 1827. 94, [2] p. DLC; IU; NBatHL; NNC. 30338

Preston, William Scott
A practical treatise on the law of legacies. New York, Pr. at the Coke law-press, by S. Gould, for the proprietor, 1827. 379 p. C; CU; IU; MH-L; MWCL; NIC-L; NNIA; NNLI; NRAL; NUtSC; NcD; OU; PPB; W; BrMus. 30339

Pretty pictures, with pretty verses. Wendell, J. Metcalf, 1827. 8 p. MWA. 30340

[Price, James Cave]
The ignis fatuus; or, A voice from the clouds. ... Comprising The climax of iniquity, an opera; The quinciad, and other poems. Richmond [Va.] Pr. for the author by Thomas W. White, 1827. 136 p. CSmH; DLC; ICU; MB; RPB; Vi. 30341

Priest, Josiah, 1788-1851
A view of the expected Christian millennium, which is promised in the Holy Scripture... with a chart, of the dispensations from Abraham to the end of time ... 2d ed. Albany, Pub. for the subscribers, Loomis' press, 1827. 372 p. CL; CLCM; CtW; DLC; IC; NBuG; NN; NTiHi; VtMiS. 30342

Princeton Theological Seminary
Catalogue of the officers and students of the Theological Seminary, Princeton, N. J., January 1827. Princeton, Borrenstein [1827] 7 p. MB; MBC; NCH; Nh; NjP. 30343

---- Charter of the Theological Seminary of the Presbyterian Church. Elizabeth-town, N. J., Pr. by Edward Sanderson, 1827. 8 p. CSmH; PPL. 30344

Princeton University
Catalogus collegii Neo-Caesariensis. Rerumpublicarum foederatarum Americae summae potestatis, anno LII. Princetoniae, typis D. A. Borrenstein, 1827. 46 p. DLC; MH; OCHP; PPL; TNJ. 30345

Prindle's almanack for 1828. By Charles Prindle. New-Haven, A. H. Maltby [1827] 12 l. CtHi; CtY; DLC; MB; MWA; NjR. 30346

Prison Discipline Society, Boston.
First annual report of the Board of Managers of the Prison Discipline Society, Boston, June 2, 1826. 4th ed. Boston, Pr. by T. R. Marvin, 1827. 88 p. CLU; CU; ICU; MB; MH; MW; OU; PHC; PHi; PPL; PPPrHi; PU; WaPS. 30347

---- ---- 5th ed. Boston, T. R. Marvin, pr., 1827. 48 p. PPL. 30348

---- Second annual report of the Board of Managers of the Prison Discipline Society, Boston, June 1, 1827. Boston, T. R. Marvin, pr., 1827. 164 p. DLC; ICME; MeHi; PPL; ScU. 30349

The prize, or The three half crowns. By the author of "Self Conquest" ... Boston, Bowles & Dearborn, 1827. 112 p. CtSoP; MH; NIC; NdFM. 30350

Proceedings and address of the convention of delegates. See National Republican Party, Ohio.

Proceedings of a convention of medical delegates, held at Northampton, in the state of Massachusetts on the 20th day of June, 1827. Boston, Wells and Lilly, 1827. 12 p. CtY; ICJ; ICU; M; MB; MBCo; MHi; MWA; MdHi; MiD-B; NBMS; NNNAM; RPB. 30351

Proceedings of a meeting held in [Boston] ... to take into consideration the present state of the wool-growing and wool-manufacturing interests ... and to appoint delegates to attend a general convention, for these purposes, to be held at Harrisburg on the 30th day of July next ... Boston, 1827. 16 p. MH-BA. 30352

Proceedings of a meeting of the friends of the general administration. See National Republican Party. Pennsylvania Westmoreland County.

Proceedings of the administration convention. See National Republican Party, Kentucky.

Proceedings of the delegates of the friends of the administration. See National Republican Party, Louisiana.

Proceedings of the friends of Gen. Jackson, at Louisville & Frankfort, Ky. At a meeting of the friends of Gen. Andrew Jackson, at the court house in Louisville, on the 22d day of Sept. 1827 ... [S. Penn Jr., pr.] 12 p. MWA. 30353

Proceedings of the Maryland administration convention. See National Republican Party, Maryland.

The prodigal daughter ... [Hudson, N. Y., Ashbel Stoddard, circa 1827.] RPB. 30354

The Prodigal Son. Philadelphia, American Sunday School Union, 1827. 32 p. BrMus. 30355

Profession is not principle. See Kennedy, Grace.

Proposals for making a geological and mineralogical survey of Pennsylvania, for publishing a series of geological maps, and forming state and county geological and mineralogical collections. [Philadelphia, 1827.] 20 p. DLC; MH; P. 30356

Protestant Episcopal Church in the U. S. A.

The book of common prayer, and administration of the sacraments and other rites and ceremonies of the church, according to the use of the Protestant Episcopal Church in the U. S. A.; together with the Psalter or Psalms of David. Hartford, S. Andrus, publisher, stereotyped by A. Chandler, 1827. 576 p. CtHi; NNG; TxDaM. 30357

---- ---- New York, W. Burgess, Jr., 1827. 360, 80, 106 p. MB. 30358

---- ---- Stereotyped by E. & J.

White. New-York, Pr. and pub. by C. Bartlett, 1827. 360, 142 p. CSmH. 30359

---- ---- New York, S. Marks, 1827. 226 p. CSansS; CtW; IaDuU; KySo; MB; MBD; MCET; MWA; NNG; NPV; BrMus. 30360

---- ---- Philadelphia, S. F. Bradford, 1827. 371 p. CBPac. 30361

---- Hymns of the Protestant Episcopal Church in the United States of America. Set forth in general conventions of said church, in the years of our Lord, 1789, 1808 & 1826. Standard stereotype ed. Philadelphia, S. F. Bradford, 1827. 132 p. CBDP; CtHC; CtHT; ICN; KyDC; LNB; MBD; MdBE; NGH; NN; NNC; NNG; OClWHi; OSW; PHi; PLT; PPL; PPLT; PU; TxU; ViU; VtMiS; WNaE; BrMus. 30362

---- Domestic & Foreign Missionary Society.

Proceedings of the board of directors of the Domestic and Foreign Missionary Society of the Protestant Episcopal Church in the United States of America, at a special meeting, held in the city of Philadelphia, on the 24th and 25th days of October, 1827. Philadelphia, Jesper Harding, pr., 1827. 24 p. CtHT; InID; MHi; MnHi; RPB. 30363

---- Connecticut (Diocese)

Journal of the proceedings of the annual convention of the Protestant Episcopal Church, in the diocese of Connecticut, held in Christ Church, Hartford, June 6th and 7th, 1827. Middletown, Pr. by William D. Starr, 1827. 32 p. CtHC. 30364

---- Maryland (Diocese)

Journal of a convention of the Protestant Episcopal Church of Maryland, held in Chester Town, Kent County, June 13th, 14th, 15th, 1827. Baltimore, J. Robinson, 1827. 39 p. DLC; NBuDD; NNG. 30365

---- Mississippi (Diocese)

Journal of the proceedings of the second annual convention of the Protestant Episcopal Church, in the diocese of Mississippi, held in Trinity Church, Natchez, on the second and third days of May, 1827. Natchez, Pr. at the office of the Ariel, 1827. 14 p. CtHT; MsJPED; NN. 30366

---- New Jersey (Diocese)

Journal of the proceedings of the forty-fourth annual convention of the Protestant Episcopal Church in New Jersey ... Paterson ... New-Brunswick, Pr. by Terhune & Letson, 1827. 62 p. NjR. 30367

---- New York (Diocese)

Journal of the proceedings of the forty-second convention of the Protestant Episcopal Church in the state of New York; A. D. 1827. To which is prefixed a list of the clergy of the diocese of New York. New York, Pr. by T. & J. Swords, 1827. 75 p. MBD; MiD; NBuDD; NGH; BrMus. 30368

---- North Carolina (Diocese)

Journal of the proceedings of the eleventh annual convention of the Protestant Episcopal Church in the state of North Carolina ... 1827. Newbern, N. C., Pr. by Watson & Machen, 1827. 43, 4 p. MBD; MH; NN; NcU. 30369

---- Ohio (Diocese)

Journal of the proceedings of the tenth annual convention of the Protestant Episcopal Church in the state of Ohio, held in Mount Vernon and Gambier, September 5th & 6th, 1827. Chillicothe,

Ohio, Pr. by John Bailhache, 1827. 31 p. CSmH; MBD; NN; OHi. 30370

---- Pennsylvania (Diocese)
The decision of the bishops who united in the consecration of the Rev. Henry U. Onderdonk, D. D. on the reasons presented to them against the said act. Published by the standing committee of the Diocese of Pennsylvania. Philadelphia, Jesper Harding, pr., 1827. 16 p. CtHT; InID; MB; MiD-B; NNG; NNUT; P; PHi; PPAmP; PPL; RPB; BrMus. 30371

---- ---- Journal of the proceedings of the forty-third convention of the Protestant Episcopal Church, in the state of Pennsylvania. Held in the chamber of the House of Representatives, in the borough of Harrisburgh, on Tuesday May 8th, Wednesday, May 9th and Thursday, May 10th, 1827. Philadelphia, Pub. by order of the convention. Jesper Harding, pr., 1827. 70 p. DLC; MiD-B; NBuDD; PPL. 30372

---- ---- Narrative of the consecration of the Rev. Henry U. Onderdonk, D. D. with the address of the presiding bishop ... Philadelphia, Jesper Harding, pr. 1827. 22 p. CtHT; MBAt; MiD-B; NBLiHi; NNG; NjR; PPAmP; PPL; RPB; WHi. 30373

---- ---- Society for the Advancement of Christianity in Pennsylvania.
Fifteenth annual report of the trustees of the Society of the Protestant Episcopal Church for the Advancement of Christianity in Pennsylvania ... Philadelphia, J. Harding, pr., 1827. 32 p. PPL. 30374

---- South Carolina (Diocese)
Journal of the proceedings of the 39th annual convention of the Protestant Episcopal Church in the Diocese of South Carolina ... 1827. Charleston, Pr. by A. E. Miller, 1827. 37 p. MBD; NBuDD; NN. 30375

---- Vermont (Diocese)
Journal of the proceedings of the convention of the Protestant Episcopal Church in the state of Vermont. Woodstock, Pr. by David Watson, 1827. 19 p. MB; MBD. 30376

---- Virginia (Diocese)
Journal of the proceedings of a convention of the Protestant Episcopal Church of the Diocese of Virginia, which assembled in the town of Fredericksburg, on Thursday the 17th day of May, 1827. Richmond, Pr. by John Warrock, 1827. 39 p. ViAlTh. 30377

Protestant Episcopal Sunday and Adult School Society of Philadelphia.
The annual report of the Protestant Episcopal Sunday and Adult School Society of Philadelphia, read December 28th, 1826. Philadelphia, Pr. by William Stavely, 1827. 25 p. NNG. 30378

Prove all things. See Plain Fact, pseud.

Providence. Town Council.
A list of persons assessed in the town tax of forty thousand dollars, voted by the freemen of Providence, June, 1827. With the amount of the valuation and tax of each. Providence, Miller and Hammond, prs., 1827. 40 p. RHi. 30379

Providence Association of Mechanics and Manufacturers.
The charter, articles of agreement, and by-laws, rules and regulations of the Providence As-

sociation of Mechanics and Manufacturers. Also a catalogue of names and members. Pub. by order of the association. [Providence, Walter R. Danforth, 1827] 28 p. Sabin 66305 (not loc.) 30380

Providence Charitable Fuel Society

Constitution of the Providence Charitable Fuel Society. Adopted 1826. Providence, Miller & Grattan, prs., 1827. 8 p. MH. 30381

Provident Society for Employing the Poor

Third annual report of the Provident Society for Employing the Poor ... Jan. 9, 1827. Philadelphia, Pr. by Samuel Parker, 1827. 7, [1] p. PPL. 30382

Providential care. See Sandham, Mrs. Elizabeth.

Public School Society of New York.

Twenty-second annual report of the trustees of the Public School Society of New-York. New-York, Pr. by Mahlon Day, 1827. 21 p. MiD; PHC; PHi; PP; PPL; PU. 30383

Puffer, Reuben

Two sermons, delivered at Berlin. One, a valedictory discourse, on leaving the old meeting-house, March 19th, 1826. The other a dedication sermon, on entering the new meeting house November 15th, following. Boston, Pr. by Lincoln & Edmands, 1827. 31 p. Ct; CtHC; ICMe; IEG; MBC; MW; MWHi; RPB; BrMus. 30384

Pursuant to public notice ... requesting the freeholders of Hanover, who are opposed to the present administration for the purpose of taking into consideration the necessary measures for ensuring a proper representation of the county in the House of Delegates ... Hanover Courthouse. March 2d 1827. [Hanover, 1827?] Bdsd. NcU. 30385

Putnam, Charles F.

Medicine chests with new and approved directions. Salem, 1827. 36 p. MBCo. 30386

Putnam, John March

English grammar, with an improved syntax. Concord, Pub. by John M. Putnam, 1827. 56 p. Nh-Hi. 30387

Putnam, Rufus Austen

The causes, evils and the remedy of intemperance, a sermon delivered in Fitchburg, Mass., at the annual fast, April 5, 1827 ... Boston, Pr. by T. R. Marvin, 1827. 36 p. Ct; M; MAnP; MBAt; MBC; MFiHi; MWA; BrMus. 30388

Putnam, Samuel

The analytical reader, containing lessons in simultaneous reading & defining, with spelling from the same ... 2d ed. Dover, N.H., S.C. Stevens, 1827. 160 p. DLC; InGrD; NNC. 30389

[Pyron du Martre, Antoine]

Syllabaire François, or French spelling book ... by Mr. Porney ... Baltimore, Pub. by E.J. Cole, Benjamin Edes, pr., 1827. 166, [1] p. MH; MdW; PPL. 30390

Q

The Quaker, being a series of sermons by members of the Society of Friends ... Taken in short hand by Marcus, T. C. Gould ... Philadelphia, 1827-30. 4 v. CLCM; CSmH; DeWI; IEG; InRE; MH; MdBF; MiD; NBF; NBu; NjR; OU; PHC; PPFHi; PPL; PSC-Hi; PU; ScU; WHi;

WMMD. 30391

Quandary, Christopher, pseud.
Some serious considerations on the present state of parties, with regard to the presidential election ... Richmond, Pr. by T. W. White, 1827. 24 p. CSmH; DLC; ICN; MH; RPB; Vi; ViL; ViU; WHi. 30392

The question of the tariff discussed in a few selected communications originally published in the Charleston City Gazette and Charleston Courier, during the last summer. Charleston, Pr. by C. C. Sebring, 1827. 47 p. DLC; ICU; MB; NcD; PHi; WHi. 30393

Questions on the collects, with Scripture proofs and illustrations; for the use of Protestant Episcopal Sunday School ... New York, Edward J. Swords, pr., 1827. 88 p. NcD. 30394

Quincy, Josiah
An address to the board of aldermen, and members of the common council, of Boston, on the organization of the city government. January 1, 1827. By Josiah Quincy, Mayor of the city of Boston, True & Greene, city prs., 1827. 20 p. MB; MBAt; MBB; MHi; MiD-B. 30395

Quinebaugh Canal Association
Survey and charter ... Norwich [Conn.] Pr. at the Courier office, 1827. 15 p. CSmH. 30396

R

Radcliffe, Ann (Ward), 1764-1823
The romance of the forest interspersed with some pieces of poetry. By Mrs. Ratcliffe [sic] New York, Pub. for the booksellers, 1827. 2 v. MH. 30397

Rail-roads. See Carey, Mathew.

Rail roads in the United States. See Hollins, William.

The rainbow after the thunderstorm. Philadelphia, American Sunday School Union, 1827. BrMus. 30398

Ramsay, Mrs. Martha (Laurens), 1759-1811
Memoirs of the life of Martha Laurens Ramsay ... 3d ed. Boston, Crocker and Brewster; New York, J. Leavitt, 1827. 252 p. MDeeP; NHuntHi; NNC; TC; TxU. 30399

---- ---- 4th ed. Boston, Pub. by Crocker & Brewster; New York, Jonathan Leavitt, 1827. [iii]-x, 252 p. AB; CSmH; ICU; NHuntHi; PPL; ViL; BrMus. 30400

Randall, Benjamin, 1749-1808
A sermon delivered at Farmington, New Hampshire, February 27, 1803, at the interment of Murmoth Fortune Herrick. Limerick, Repub. at the Star Office, 1827. 24 p. CSmH; MeLB. 30401

Rankin, Andrew
A discourse, on the intemperate use of spirituous liquor, delivered at Thornton, N. H., on the day of the annual fast, April 12, 1827. Concord [N. H.] Pr. by J. B. Moore, 1827. 32 p. DLC; MBC; MWA; MoSpD; NCH. 30402

Rapp, George
Hymn Book. Economy, Pa., 1827. Sabin 67917 (not loc.) 30403

Ratcliffe, Mrs. See Radcliffe, Ann (Ward).

Raymond, James
Prize essay on the compara-

tive economy of free and slave labour, in agriculture. Frederick, Pr. by John P. Thomson, 1827. 20 p. MdBP. 30404

Rayner, Menzies, 1770-1850
Universal grace, a doctrine worthy of all acceptation. A sermon delivered at Monroe, Conn. ... Nov. 4th, 1827. Hartford, R. Canfield, pr., 1827. 24 p. CSmH; Ct; CtHT; CtHi; CtY; MWA; PLT; RNHi; RPB. 30405

Read, William George
An address delivered before the South-Carolina Society on the occasion of opening their male academy on the 2d of July, 1827. Charleston, A. E. Miller, 1827. 28 p. MH; MHi; NN; NcD; ScC; ScCC; ScCleA; ScU. 30406

Reasons in favour of the erasure of the law which forbids a man to marry his deceased wife's sister. See Gunn, Alexander.

The Red Rover. See Cooper, James Fenimore.

Redford, George
The pastor's sketch book; or, Authentic narratives of real character. New York, Pub. by John P. Haven, American Tract Society House ... 1827. 219 p. CtHT; MBC; NcWsM; VtU. 30407

Reed, Ephraim
Musical monitor, or New-York collection of church musick: to which is prefixed, The elementary class-book, or An introduction to the science of musick ... 5th rev. ed., enl. and improved. Ithaca, Pr. by Mack & Andrus, 1827. 29, ii, [1], [29]-246, [2] p. CtY; ICN; MH; MWA; NBuG; NCH; NIC; NRU. 30408

Reed, Thomas Buck, 1787-1829
An address, by Thomas B. Reed, of Mississippi, to the cadets at West Point, June 20, 1827. New York, Pr. by J. Seymour, 1827. 40 p. CtHT-W; MdHi; NCH; NNC; PPL. 30409

Reel, David
Ali Bey. This celebrated horse will stand at the stable of the subscriber, in Harrison township, the ensuing season ... Ali Bey will be let to mares at 4 dollars the season ... 2 dollars the single leap ... David Reel. Knox county, February 19th, 1827. In. 30410

Reese, Daniel E.
Protests, arguments, and address against the whole of the proceedings of his prosecutors, &c. in the Baltimore City Station ... Baltimore, 1827. Pr. by R. J. Matchett, 16 p. MdBP; MdBS. 30411

Reese, Levi R.
Argument and protest against the whole of the proceedings of his prosecutors &c. in the Baltimore City Station ... Baltimore, Pr. by R. J. Matchett, 1827. 15 p. MdBBC; MdBP. 30412

Reformed Church in North America.
The acts and proceedings of the General Synod of the Reformed Dutch Church, in North America, at Philadelphia, June, 1827. New-York, Pr. by Vanderpool & Cole, 1827. 80 p. IaPeC; NSchHi; NcMHi. 30413

---- The fifth annual report of the Missionary Society of the Reformed Dutch Church in North America ... New York, Pr. by Vanderpool & Cole, 1827. 50 p. NjR. 30414

---- Minutes of the particular synod in Albany, May, 1827. Albany (N. Y.), Webster & Wood, 1827. 15 p. IaPeC. 30415

---- The Psalms & hymns, with the catechism, confession of faith, and liturgy of the Reformed Dutch Church in North America ... By John H. Livingston ... New-York, Daniel D. Smith, and John Montgomery [1827] 493 p. DLC; MiU-C. 30416

Reformed Church in the United States. Synod.

Kirchen-ordnung der Reformirten Kirche in den Vereinigten Staaten von Nord America, durch eine von der Synode dazu bestimmten Committee aufgesucht und zur Annehmung vorzuschlagen. Harrisburg, Gedruckt bey Moser und Peters, 1827. 30 p. DLC; PHi; PLFM. 30417

---- Synodal Verhandlung der Hochdeutschen Reformirten Kirche in den Vereinigten Staaten von Nord Amerika. Gehalten in Friedrich City vom 23 bis zum 29 September, 1826. Philadelphia, Gedruckt bey Conrad Zentler, 1827. 43 p. MoWgT; PPL. 30418

... Register of civil, judicial, military, and other officers in Connecticut and United States Record, for the year 1828 ... Hartford, Norton & Russell, prs. and publishers [1827?] 144 p. Ct; CtHi; CtNwchO; CtY; InU; MB; MBNEH; MWA; N. 30419

Religion and its image. See Cameron, Mrs. Lucy Lyttleton (Butt).

Remarks on a review of Symmes' theory. See Reynolds, Jeremiah N.

Remarks on Christian liberty, designed to promote peace and harmony in the church. By a layman ... Penn-Yan, [New York] E. J. Fowle, 1827. 12 p. ICN. 30420

Remarks on the character of Napoleon Bonaparte. See Channing, William Ellery.

Remarks on the letter of Domesticus. See Plumer, William.

Remarks on the policy and practice of the United States. See Cass, Lewis.

Remarks on the practicability and expediency of establishing a railroad on one or more routes from Boston to the Connecticut River. By the editor of the Boston Daily Advertiser, Boston, Springfield, 1827. 71 p. ICJ. 30421

Remarks upon Christian discipline and church government, extracted principally from the writings of some of the most eminent members of the Society of Friends. Philadelphia, B. & T. Kite; S. W. Conrad, pr., 1827. 16 p. CSmH; DLC; MH; NNFL; OClWHi; PHC; PPL; PSC-Hi. 30422

Remarks upon Mr. Carter's outline of an institution for the education of teachers. From the U. S. Review. Boston, Pub. by Bowles and Dearborn, from the University Press, 1827. 25 p. CtHT-W; ICU; MB; MBAt; MH; MWA; NIC; NNC-T; PPL; BrMus. 30423

Renwick, James, 1790-1863

Report on the water power, at Kingsbridge, near the city of New-York, belonging to the New-York Hydraulic Manufacturing and Bridge Company. New York, Pr. by S. Marks, 1827. 12 p. CSmH; DLC; NN; NNC; NNNAM. 30424

A reply to a letter remonstrating against the consecration of the Rev. Henry U. Onderdonk ... Philadelphia, Jesper Harding, pr. 1827. 16 p. CtHT; DLC; NNG; P; PHi; PPAmP; PPL; RPB; BrMus. 30425

Reply to the address of the male members. See Union Society of Queen Ann's County.

A report of the proposed Saugatuck and New-Milford Canal. See Cruger, Alfred.

Report of the trial and acquittal of the Honourable Robert Porter president judge of the Third Judicial District of Pennsylvania, befor the Senate ... Reported by James Madison Porter. Easton, Pa., Pr. by Weygandt & Innes, 1827. vi,, [1] 288 p. DLC; InSC; MH-L; MWCL; MnU-L; N-L; P; PP; PHi; PPB; PPiAL; PU. 30426

Republican Party. Massachusetts. Suffolk Co.

A meeting of the Suffolk Republican administration will be held ... this evening ... D. L. Child, sec'y. July 11th, 1827. [Boston, 1827] Bdsd. MB. 30427

---- Member of Congress. Fellow citizens! On Monday next, you will be called upon ... Saturday, July 21, 1827. [Boston, 1827] Bdsd. MB. 30428

---- Republicans of Boston! Rally to the polls on Monday, and support ... the Hon. David Henshaw ... [Boston, 1827] Bdsd. MB. 30429

Reuben Apsley. See Smith, Horatio.

Revelations in masonry, made by a late member of the craft. A new ed., carefully rev. and corr. by the author. New York, Pr. for the author, 1827. 4 v. NIC. 30430

Review of Mr. McClintock's History and mystery! &c. &c. Philadelphia, Pr. on the Vertical Press by D. & S. Neall [1827] 19 p. PHi. 30430a

A review of Rev. Mr. Whitman's discourse, preached before the Second Religious Society in Waltham. Boston, T. R. Marvin, pr. 1827. 48 p. CoD; M; MBC; MLow; MNe; MeBat; OO; PPPrHi; BrMus. 30431

Review of the answer to the remonstrance sent to the bishops of the Protestant Episcopal Church. Philadelphia, 1827. 15 p. CtHT; MH-AH; NBLiHi; NNG; PHi; PPL. 30432

Review of the case of the free bridge between Boston and Charlestown ... including public documents. Boston, Dutton & Wentworth, prs., 1827. 106 p. Ct; ICN; IU; M; MB; MH; MH-L; MHi; MWA; MiD-B; NN; NNE; NjR; BrMus. 30433

Review of the Doctrines of the Church vindicated. See Rice, John Holt.

Review of the report of a committee of the Medical Society of the City of New York, on Dr. Chambers' remedy for intemperance. No. 1. New-York, Pr. for the publisher, 1827. 12 p. NNNAM. 30434

A review of the Rev. Dr. Channing's discourse preached at the dedication of the Second Congregational Unitarian Church, New York, December 7, 1826. Boston, Hilliard, Gray, Little & Wilkins, 1827. 91 p. CBPac; CSmH; Ct; CtHC; DLC; GDC; ICMe; KWiU; MAnP; MB; MBC; MH; MHi; MNtcA; MeBat; MiD-B; NGH;

NNUT; NjR; PHi; PPAmP; PPL; PPPrHi; BrMus. 30435

---- By a layman. Providence, Jones & Simons and H. H. Brown, 1827. 36 p. CtSoP; MB; MBC; MH; MHi; MeBat; BrMus. 30436

Revivals of religion. See Honestus, pseud.

[Reynolds, Jeremiah N.] 1799-1858

Remarks on a review of Symmes' theory, which appeared in the American quarterly review, by a "citizen of the United States." Washington, Pr. by Gales & Seaton, 1827. 75 p. DLC; MHi; MdBP; MdHi; NNM; OMC. 30437

Rhees, J. L.

Error refuted; or, A brief exposition of the leading features of the Baptist controversy in Philadelphia and its vicinity for some years past; intended as a biographical notice of Henry Holcombe, D. D. and supplementary to his work intitled "First fruits" and etc. Philadelphia, William Stavely, 1827. 59 p. PHi; PPAmP. 30438

---- A pocket manual of the Lancasterian system of education, in its most improved state ... Philadelphia, 1827. 30, [6] p. PPAmP; PPL. 30439

Rhode Island

Acts of General Assembly, May 1827. 73, [2] p. Ia; Mi. 30440

---- At the General Assembly of the state of Rhode Island and Providence Plantations, begun and holden, (by adjournment) at East Greenwich, within and for said state on the second Monday in January, in the year of our Lord, one thousand eight hundred and twenty-seven ... Providence, 1827. 33, [2] p. Ia; Mi; RNCH. 30441

---- At the General Assembly of the state of Rhode Island and Providence Plantations, begun and holden, [by adjournment] at Newport, within and for said state, on the fourth Monday of June, in the year of our Lord, one thousand eight hundred and twenty-seven ... Providence, 1827. 49, [2] p. Ia; Mi; R. 30442

---- At the General Assembly of the state of Rhode Island, began and holden at S. Kingston on the last Monday of Oct., in the year of our Lord, one thousand eight hundred and twenty-seven... Providence, 1827. 74, [2] p. Ia; Mi; R. 30443

The Rhode-Island almanack for 1828. By Isaac Bickerstaff. Providence, H. H. Brown [1827] 18 l. CLU; DLC; ICN; InU; MB; MH; MWA; NHi; NjR; PHi; RPB; WHi. 30444

Rhode Island Historical Society

Collections of the Rhode-Island Historical Society. Vol. 1. Providence, John Miller, pr., 1827. 163 p. CU; DLC; GU; InU; MB; MH; MiD-B; MoK; NNU; Nh-Hi; OClW; PPL; PU; RHi; RP; TxU; WHi. 30445

The Rhode-Island register and United States calendar for 1828. Providence, H. H. Brown [1827] 48 l. InU; MH; MWA; NHi; NN; RPB. 30446

[Rice, John Holt] 1777-1831

Review of the "Doctrines of the Church vindicated from the misrepresentations of "Dr. John Rice;" and the integrity of the revealed religion defended against the "no comment principle of promiscuous Bible Societies; by the Right Rev. John S. Ravenscroft," Bishop of the Diocese of

North Carolina." Richmond, Va., Pr. at the Franklin Press, 1827. 1 p. 1, 214 p. CSmH; N; NBuG; NNC; NcD; NcMHi; PPL; PPPrHi; Vi; VtU. 30447

Richard, Gaspard
Prospectus of a new plan to make a large fortune by a new system of power as substitute of steam by weight and lever ... New York, The author, 1827. 50 p. DLC; NN. 30448

Richmond, Edward
A sermon, preached at Dorchester, third parish, June 24, 1827. Boston, Thomas B. Wait, and Son, 1827. 16 p. DLC; ICMe; MBAt; MBC; MH; MWA; MeB; MeHi; MiD-B; MiU; OO; PPAmP; RPB; BrMus. 30449

[Richmond, James Cook] 1808-1866
Nothing, by Nobody ... Philadelphia, E. Littell, 1827. 222 p. CSmH; CtY; ICU; MH; NN; PHi; PU. 30450

[Richmond, Legh)
The dairyman's daughter; an authentic narrative. Communicated by a clergyman of the Church of England. Revised by the committee of publication. American Sunday School Union. Philadelphia, Stereotyped by L. Johnson, 1827. [2], 120, 2 p. KN; PHi; BrMus. 30451

[----] ---- Philadelphia, Pub. by the Philadelphia Tract Society, William Bradford, agent [1827?] 12 p. PPL. 30452

Richmond, Va.
An ordinance, for regulating the meetings and defining the conduct of the members of the common hall passed April 5, 1827. [Richmond, 1827] 1 p. DLC. 30453

Richmond and Manchester Colonization Society, Richmond, Va.
Richmond and Manchester Colonization Society. [Richmond, 1827] 7 p. CSmH. 30454

Richmond Constitutional Whig. Richmond, Va.
To the friends and patrons of the Richmond Constitutional Whig, the carrier, with the compliments of the season, according to the good old custom of giving and receiving Christmas presents, respectfully presents the following Christmas ode. Christmas, 1827. [Richmond, Va. 1827] 1 p. DLC. 30455

Richmond, Va. Library Society of Richmond
A catalogue of the books ... Richmond, Pr. by John Warrock, 1827. 56 p. CSmH. 30456

Richmond; or, Scenes in the life of a Bow Street officer. See Surr, Thomas Skinner.

Riedesel, Friederike Charlotte Luise (Von Massow) freifrau von 1746-1808
Letters and memoirs relating to the war of American independence, and the capture of the German troops at Saratoga. By Madame de Riedesel. Tr. from the original German . . . New York, G. & C. Carvill, [Sleight and George, prs., Jamaica, L.I.] 1827. 323 p. CL; CSmH; CtHC; CtHT-W; CtW; DLC; GU; IC; ICN; IaU; InU; MB; MH; MMeT; MWA; Md; MiD-B; MiU-C; MoSW; NIC; NN; NNC; NNS; NcU; Nh; Nh-Hi; NjP; OO; P; PPL; PU; RPB; RPJCB; ScC; Vi; ViU; VtU; WHi; BrMus. 30457

Rienzi. See Potter, Robert.

The rights of the Congregational parishes. See Lowell, John.

Rime of the ancient mariner. See Coleridge, Samuel Taylor.

Ripley, David B.
Zeal employed upon the mere circumstantials of religion, reprehensible and dangerous. A sermon, delivered at Abington, in Pomfret, on the first Sabbath in October, 1827. Brooklyn, Con., Advertiser Press, John Gray, Jr., 1827. 13 p. IaDuU; MiD-B; BrMus. 30458

Ripley, Ezra, 1751-1841
A history of the fight at Concord, on the 19th of April, 1775 ... showing that then and there the first regular and forcible resistance was made ... and the Revolutionary war thus commenced. Concord, Pr. and pub. by Allen & Atwill, 1827. 60 p. CSmH; CtSoP; DLC; ICN; MB; MH; MWA; MeHi; MiU-C; NN; NNUT; NjR; OClWHi; PHi; PPAmP; RPB; BrMus. 30459

Ripley, William, 1739-1784?
Memoirs of William Ripley, Minister of the Gospel, Whitby, England. Philadelphia, J.H. Cunningham, pr., 1827. 87, [1] p. CtW; NRAB; BrMus. 30460

Rippon, John
A selection of hymns from the best authors ... Charleston, S.C., W. Riley, 1827. 588 p. GDC. 30461

Ritchie, William
Christian sincerity; A sermon delivered in the First Parish in Needham, June 18, 1826, the Sabbath after the interment of Deacon Zacheriah Cushman. Dedham, Pr. by H. & W.H. Mann, 1827. 12 p. CtSoP; MBC; MH; MWA; RPB. 30462

The rivals of Acadia. See Cheney, Mrs. Harriet Vaughan (Foster)

Roanoke Navigation Company
... Report of the Roanoke Navigation Company, 1827. Raleigh, Pr. by Lawrence & Lemay, prs. to the state, 1827. 13 p. NcU. 30463

Robbins, Asher
Oration, delivered on the Fourth of July A.D. 1827, at Newport, R.I. Providence, Miller and Hammond, 1827. 27 p. CSmH; DLC; MBC; MiU-C; NCH; RHi; RPB; BrMus. 30464

[Robbins, Eliza] 1786-1853
American popular lessons, chiefly selected from the writings of Mrs. Barbauld, Miss Edgeworth, and other approved authors, designed particularly for the younger classes of children in school. New York, W.B. Gilly, 1827. 34 p. MdToN; NNC. 30465

[----] Sequel to American popular lessons, intended for the use of schools: by the author of American popular lessons "Songs of the muses, Sage historic tale," and "Word of Holy writ." New York, Pub. by Collins and Hannay, 1827. 376 p. MB; MH; OMC. 30466

Roberdeau, Isaac, 1763-1829
Observations on the survey of the sea coast of the United States. [Washington?] 1827. 24 p. DLC; PPL. 30467

Roberts, Robert
The house servant's directory, servants' work, the art of waiting. Boston, Munroe and Francis, and Charles S. Francis, New York, 1827. xiv, 180 p. ICJ; MB; MH; MHi; MPlyA; NPV; Nh-Hi; PPL. 30468

Robin Hood
The extraordinary life and adventures of Robin Hood, captain of the robbers of Sherwood Forest ... Philadelphia, Pub. and for sale, wholesale only, by Freeman Scott, 1827. 71 p. DLC; MLex; PPL. 30469

Robinson, Isaac, 1780-1854
A review of Remarks by Rev. T. R. Sullivan, upon A sermon, illustrating the human and official inferiority and supreme divinity of Christ. Keene, N. H., Pr. by John Prentiss, 1827. 56 p. CBPac; CSmH; CtHC; MB; MBC; MWA; Nh; PPL. 30470

---- A sermon, illustrating the human and official inferiority and supreme divinity of Christ. 2d ed. Keene, N. H., Pr. at the Sentinel office, 1827. 16 p. CSmH. 30471

Robinson, James, Jun.
Elements of arithmetick, by question and answer. Designed for the use of the younger classes in publick and private schools. 3d ed. imp. Boston, Pr. and pub. by Lincoln & Edmands, 1827. 72 p. CtHT-W; MB; MH; NNC; BrMus. 30472

Roche, Regina Maria (Dalton), 1764?-1845
The children of the abbey. A tale. Philadelphia, Pub. by J. & J. Woodward, 1827. 3 v. CN; DLC; GU; InLW; MH; MdBE; NSy; PPL; RJA; TNJ; ViL. 30473

Rochester. Fire Company, No. 1.
By-laws of Fire Company, No. 1, adopted December 3, 1827. Rochester, Pr. by E. Peck & Company, 1827. 8 p. NRHi. 30474

The Rochester selection of hymns for conference meetings, and for private and family worship. Rochester, Pr. and pub. by E. Peck, 1827. 160 p. Copy belonging to Rev. Van Nostrand seen by McMurtrie in 1938. 30475

Rock Spring Theological and High School
Rock Spring Theological and High School, Rock Spring, Ill. The Rock Spring Theological and High School is established on the most liberal principles--encouraged by a numerous list of patrons and shareholders in Illinois, Missouri, and Indiana... J. M. Peck, secretary. Rock Spring, St. Clair Co., Illinois, Sept. 1st, 1827. Bdsd. MHi. 30476

[Rodriguez, J.]
Fulminea defensio violati populi juris. Defense fulminante contre la violation des droits du peuple. Nouvelle-Orleans, 1827. 67, [1], 7, 3 p. MB. 30477

Rogers, John
Statements, calculations and hints, relative to rail-roads, and moving power locomotive engines to be used thereon ... Baltimore, Matchett, pr., 1827. DBRE; DLC; MB; MCM; MH-BA; MWA; MdHi; MdBP; NN; PHi; PPL; WU. 30478

Rollin, Charles, 1661-1741
The ancient history of the Egyptians, Carthaginians, Assyrians, Babylonians, Medes & Persians, Macedonians, and Grecians. New and imp. ed. Boston, S. Walker, 1827. 2 v. AMob; CU; MB; NBu; NBuDC; PPP; TNJ. 30479

Rome, in the nineteenth century. See Eaton, Mrs. Charlotte Anne (Waldie).

[Romer, John]
Christian revolutioner in the similitude of David with his sling and five stones, containing a statement of the new methodizing

reformation which commenced Dec. 11, 1825 in ... Sawpit village, by a branch of the Church of Christ, called Christians ... New York, Pr. for the author, 1827. 95 p. NNC. 30480

Rosabella; or, The queen of May, by the author of the "Star of Virginia." Philadelphia, American Sunday School Union, 1827. 36 p. DLC; BrMus. 30481

Ross, James, 1744-1827
A short plain comprehensive, practical Latin grammar ... 8th ed. rev. and imp. Philadelphia, Desilver, 1827. Lydia Baily, pr. viii, 184 p. CtHT; CtW; NNC; OOxM; OrSaW; P; BrMus. 30482

Rossini, Gioacchino Antonio
(Tancredi.) Di tanti palpiti. Recitativo e cavatina ... Arranged for the voice and piano forte. New York, Dubois & Stodart [1827] 7 p. MB. 30483

Rost, Pierre Adolphe, 1797-1868
A speech, delivered before the Senate of the state of Louisiana, on the subject of a contested election. New-Orleans, Pr. for the publisher, by John Gibson, 1827. 16 p. MB; PPL. 30484

Rowley, William, 1585?-1642?
... A woman never vext; or, The widow of Cornhill. A comedy, in five acts ... Philadelphia, A. R. Poole, and Ash & Mason; New York, E. M. Murden, and L. Godey; [etc., etc.] [1827] 78 p. DLC; ICU; MB; MH; NNC; TxU. 30485

Rowson, Susanna (Haswell), 1762-1824
Charlotte Temple: A tale of truth. Cincinnati, Pub. by William Hill Woodward, 1827. 186, [2] p. CtY; MWA. 30486

---- ---- Hartford, S. Andrus, pub., 1827. 138 p. CSmH; MWA; NcU; OU; OkU; ViRC. 30487

---- ---- New York, R. Hobbs, 1827. CtY; MWA. 30488

Royall, Mrs. Anne (Newport), 1769-1854
The Tennessean; a novel, founded on facts. New-Haven, Pr. for the author, 1827. 372 p. CtHi; CtY; DLC; MA; MB; MH; MWA; NN; PPL; PPiU; PU. 30489

Ruddiman, Thomas, 1674-1757
The rudiments of The Latin tongue; or, A plain and easy introduction to Latin grammar ... Carefully rev. and cor. from the latest Edinburgh ed. New York, Collins and Hannay, 1827. 168 p. InThR; PU; Vi. 30490

Rules of prosody, for the use of schools ... A new edition, corrected and enlarged. New-York, Pr. and sold by T. & J. Swords, 1827. 23 p. MH. 30491

[Rundell, Maria Eliza (Ketelby)] 1745-1828
The experienced American housekeeper; or, Domestic cookery ... Hartford, S. Andrus, publisher, 1827. 213 p. CtHi; MH; NhHi; TxBrdD. 30492

Rural scenes. See Taylor, Jane.

Rush, Benjamin, 1745-1813
Extracts from Dr. Benjamin Rush's Inquiry into the effects of ardent spirits upon the human body and mind. Philadelphia, To be had of Benjamin & Thomas Kite, 1827. 16 p. InRE. 30493

---- Medical inquiries and observations, upon the diseases of the mind. 3d ed. Philadelphia, J. Grigg, 1827. 365 p. CSt-L; CU; DNLM; ICU-R; KBB; MB; MBCo;

MWC; MdBJ; MdUM; MiD; MoSMed; NBMS; NIC; NNC; NNNAM; NcD; NjP; OC; OClW; OrUM; PPC; PPL; PPiAM; Vi; WU-M; WvW. 30494

Rush, James, 1786-1869
Philosophy of the human voice: embracing its physiological history ... Philadelphia, J. Maxwell, pr., 1827. 586 p. CtHT; DLC; DNLM; ICJ; KU; KyLxT; MB; MBAt; MBCo; MH; MdBM; MeB; NCaS; NIC; NNF; NjP; PHC; PPC; PPF; PPL; RPB; ScCMeS; VtB. 30495

Russell, John B.
Catalogue of kitchen garden, herb, tree, field and flower seeds, bulbous flower roots, agricultural books, &c. for sale at the office of the New England Farmer, No. 52 North Market Street Boston, ... With a list of agricultural implements, for sale ... in the same building, by Joseph R. Newell. Boston, Pr. at the New England Farmer office, 1827. 40 p. MB; BrMus. 30496

Ruter, Martin, 1785-1838
The juvenile arithmetick, and scholar's guide ... Cincinnati, N. & G. Guilford, 1827. 216 p. DLC. 30497

Rutgers Medical College, New York
Catalogue of the faculty and students of Rutgers Medical College, Duane-street, city of New-York. Session of 1826-7. New-York, Pr. by John Gray, 1827. 7 p. MBCo; NNNAM; NjR. 30498

---- Circular. New-York, 13th January, 1827. [2] p. NjR. 30499

---- Rutgers Medical College, Duane-Street, New-York. [New-York] Pr. at the Rutgers Press, by William A. Mercein, 1827. 8 p. DNLM; N; NNNAM; NjP; NjR; PPC. 30500

Rutgers Medical Faculty. Geneva College.
This college will commence the course of lectures, for the ensuing Winter session ... New-York, Nov. 3d, 1827. Bdsd. NjR. 30501

Rutledge, Edward, 1797-1832
An address, delivered before the inhabitants of Stratford, July 4, 1827 ... New-Haven, A. H. Maltby, 1827. 15 p. CSmH; CtHT-W; CtY; DLC; MHi; MiD-B; NN; Nh; OO; PPL; RPB. 30502

Ryan, James
An elementary treatise on arithmetic, in theory and practice ... New York, Pub. by Collins & Hannay. J. & J. Harper, prs., 1827. 272 p. CtHT-W; DLC; IObB; MB; NH; NcU; VtMiM. 30503

---- The new American grammar of the elements of astronomy, on an improved plan. New York, Collins & Hannay, 1827. 375 p. CtHT; DLC; GU; IU; MiU; NCanHi. 30504

S

Sabin, Benjamin
A short narrative of the revival of religion in Ithaca, from its commencement till the last week in January. Ithaca, Pr. by Mack & Andrus, 1827. 8 p. NIC. 30505

Saco, Maine. Second Parish.
Dedication of the Second Parish Meeting House in Saco, and installation of the Rev. Thomas Tracy, Nov. 21, 1827. Order of performances ... Bdsd. KHi. 30506

Sacred concert, to be performed at the Rev. Dr. Bancroft's

church in Worcester, on Wednesday evening, March 7, 1827. Boston, Pr. by Isaac R. Butts and Co., 1827. 8 p. MWA. 30507

Sagra, Ramon de la, 1798-1871
Memorias para servir de introduccion a la horticultura cubana. Por d. Ramon de la Sagra ... Nueva York, Lanuza, Mendia y c., 1827. viii, 24 p. CU-B; DNA; BrMus. 30508

The sailor's son. Philadelphia, American Sunday School Union, 1827. 7 p. MWHi; BrMus. 30509

St. George, George Glascott
An oration on the present state of Ireland ... As delivered at Tammany-Hall ... Feb. 13, 1827 ... New York, R. Wauchope, 1827. 10 p. NN. 30510

St. Patrick's Beneficial Society of Pennsylvania
Constitution and bye-laws of the St. Patrick's Beneficial Society of Pennsylvania. Founded March 17, 1827. [Philadelphia] John Young, pr., 1827. 26 p. PPL. 30511

[Saint-Pierre, Jacques Henri Bernardin de] 1737-1814
Paul and Virginia, her compulsive visit to her aunt beyond sea; her return home, and happy union with Paul, &c. to which is added adventures of Don Quixote, and his humorous squire, Sancho Pancha ... Philadelphia, Pub. and sold, wholesale only, by Freeman Scott, 1827. 72 p. MWA. 30512

---- ---- Trans. from the French by Helen Maria Williams. Providence, Pub. by Doyle and Hathaway [Smith & Parmenter, prs.] 1827. 187 p. KyHi; MNBedf. 30513

Salem, Mass. First Church.
First Church in Salem. At a meeting of the brethren of the Church, held ... Nov. 28th, and continued by adjournment to Dec. 1st, 1827 ... Report ... [Salem? 1827] Bdsd. NN. 30514

Salem Mill Dam Corporation
Report of the directors of the Salem Mill Dam Corporation, at a meeting of the stockholders, held May 7th, 1827. Salem, Pr. by W. & S. B. Ives, Observer Office, 1827. 9 p. CtSoP; DLC; MH; MH-BA; MWA; PPL. 30515

Salem, Mass. North Church.
A catalogue of the members of the North Church in Salem, with an historical sketch of the church. Salem, Pr. by W. & S. B. Ives, 1827. 36 p. MBNEH; MH; MWA; NBLiHi; OClWHi. 30516

Salem witchcraft: or The adventures of Parson Handy, from Punkapog Pond. 2d ed. with cor. New York, Elam Bliss, 1827. 70, [1] p. DLC; IEG; MB. 30516a

Salisbury and Amesbury, Mass. Congregational Church.
Order of exercises at the dedication of the new meeting-house of the Congregational Society in Salisbury and Amesbury, Thursday, 17th May, 1827. Newburyport, W. & J. Gilman, prs. [1827] 1 p. DLC. 30517

Salisbury, N. C. Lutheran Church
A misstatement in the "Episcopal journal" of Bishop Ravenscroft corrected. Salisbury, Philo White, 1827. 7 p. NcU. 30518

Eine Sammlung auserlesenen Geschichten. See Henkel, Ambrose.

Sampson, Joseph Adam Hall, 1805-1825
Remains of Joseph A. H.

Sampson, who died at New-Lebanon, 12 mo. 14, 1825, aged 20 years. Rochester, N. Y., Pr. by E. F. Marshall, for Procter Sampson, 1827. 59, [1] p. DGU; DLC; ICU; IU; MWA; NBuG; NN; NNC; NRHi; OClWHi; RPB; BrMus. 30519

No entry 30520

Samuel, pseud.
A chapter of modern chronicles in which certain events which lately took place in the city of Gotham are truly set forth. [New York? 1827?] 4 p. (Photostat reproduction (negative) from a copy owned by Mrs. Edward Ingram, Cambridge, Mass.) MH. 30521

[Sandham, Mrs. Elizabeth]
Providential care: a tale, founded on facts. By the author of "Twin Sisters," "Boys' School" "School-fellows" etc. 1st Amer. ed. New York, Pub. by William Burgess, Jr., 1827. 161 p. MH; MeSaco; NcWsS. 30522

Sangmeister, Ezechiel
Folgendes ist der vierte Theil von meinem armen Lebens-Lauf; nimmt seinen Anfang im Jahr 1766. Erste Auflage. Ephrata, Pr. by Jos. Bauman, 1827. 72 p. PHi. 30523

Satire on modern piety, and gilded prayers. Portraitures, of certain worthy personages residing in a certain city, where they emigrated some years since; and having obtained Dame Fortune's propitious smiles, they now endeavor to "astonish the natives." Published for the author. Cincinnati, 1827. 22 p. KyDC. 30524

Saunders, Ann
Narrative of the shipwreck and sufferings of Miss Ann Saunders, who was a passenger on board the ship Francis Mary, which foundered at sea on the 5th Feb. 1826 on her passage from New Brunswick to Liverpool ... Providence, Pr. for Z. S. Crossmon, 1827. 38 p. CSmH; CtHi; DLC; MB; MBAt; MH; MHi; MLexHi; MeHi; PHi; PPL; PPPrHi; RHi; RP. 30525

---- "There is nothing true but Heaven!" lines composed by Miss Ann Saunders, on the melancholy death of James Frier, to whom she expected to be married in a few weeks, but who with fourteen of his ship companions, perished on board the wreck of the Ship Francis Mary. [Providence, 1827] 1 l. MH. 30526

Saurin, Jacques, 1677-1730
Sermons of the Rev. James Saurin ... A new ed., with additional sermons; rev. and cor. by Sam. Burder ... Pr. from the last London ed. Princeton, N. J., D. A. Borrenstein, 1827. 2 v. CSt; CU; MBC; MH; MiDSH; MoSpD; NNG; NSyU; NbOP; NjP; NjR; OO; RPA; ViU. 30527

[Savage, Sarah] 1785-1837
Life of Philip, the Indian chief. By the author of "The factory girl," "The badge" ... Salem, Pub. by Whipple and Lawrence [Pr. by W. Palfray, jr. and J. Chapman] 1827. 53 p. ICN; KU; MH; NN; Nh; PU. 30528

Savannah. First Presbyterian Church.
Rules and confessions of faith

of the First Presbyterian Church constituted in Savannah, June 6, 1827. Charleston, Pr. at the office of Charleston Observer, 1827. 11 p. TxU; WHi. 30529

Sawyer, John York, et al.
The memorial of the circuit judges of the state of Illinois: Presented January 1, 1827. Vandalia, Pr. by Robert Blackwell, 1827. 17 p. IHi. 30530

Say, Jean Baptiste, 1767-1832
A treatise on political economy; or, The production, distribution and consumption of wealth. Trans. from the 4th ed. of the French, by C. R. Prinsep, M. A. 3d Amer. ed. Philadelphia, J. Grigg, 1827. lvii, 455 p. C; CtHT-W; CtW; DLC; GEU; ICU; InCW; KU; KyLx; MB; MH; MH-BA; MHi; MWA; MdBJ; MeLB; MeU; MiU; MtGr; NGH; NIC; NT; OWoC; PPAmP; PU; RPB; ScU; TCU; TxU; Vi; ViU; WaU. 30531

Schmucker, Samuel Simon
Antrittsrede gehalten in Gegenwart des Direktoriums des Theologischen Seminariumus, errichtet durch die General-Synode der Evangelisch-Lutherischen Kirche in Nord-Amerika, zu Gettysburg ... York-Town, Gedruckt bey Heinrich C. Neinstedt, 1827. 40 p. PPL. 30532

The school; or, Lessons in morals, #2. Boston, Cottons & Barnard, 1827. 36 p. TxDaM (not loc. 1969) 30533

Schuylkill Navigation Co.
Report of the president and managers ... to the stockholders. Jan. 1, 1827. [Philadelphia] Pr. by Lydia R. Bailey, 1827. 12 p. PHi; PPi. 30534

Scott, John, 1777-1834
The life, letters, and papers of the late Rev. Thomas Scott, D. D. ... In two parts. By Rev. John Scott, A. M. To which is added The force of truth. New-Haven, Pub. by N. Whiting, 1827. 592 p. CSansS; CSt; IU; NRU; NSyU; NcMHi; NjNbS; TNJ. 30535

Scott, Robert G.
To the public. The annexed statement of my agency in the fete at the village of York in 1824, is submitted to the citizens of Virginia, as concerning a full and fair development of my concern in that affair; and a defence of my conduct in making the preliminary arrangements for its consummation. [Richmond? 1827?] 28 p. ViW. 30536

Scott, Thomas, 1747-1821
The force of truth: an authentic narrative. From the last London ed. Philadelphia, G. M. & W. Snider, 1827. 141 p. DLC; PPL. 30537

---- ---- New-Haven, Pub. by Nathan Whiting, 1827. 153 p. Ct; CtHi; MB; MW; OMC. 30538

---- ---- Princeton Press, Pub. by D. A. Borrenstein, 1827. 144 p. CtY; MH; OO. 30539

[Scott, Sir Walter] bart
Chronicles of the Cannongate ... New York, Pr. by J. & J. Harper, for Collins and Hannay, Collins and co., and G. and C. Carvill; Philadelphia, Carey, Lea and Carey, R. H. Small, and Towar and Hogan; Boston, Richardson and Lord, and Hilliard, Gray, and co., 1827. 2 v. LNT-N; MB; NjR; PU; PWW; RJa. 30540

[----] ---- Philadelphia, Carey, Lea & Carey, 1827. 2 v. CSfA; DLC; KyLoP; MBAt; MBC; MNF; NCH; NCaS; NN; PPL; RPB; TNJ; ViU; VtMiM; WyU. 30541

[----] ---- Philadelphia, L. B. Clarke, 1827. 2 v. CSmH. 30542

---- The lady of the lake; a poem. By Walter Scott. New York, S. King, 1827. 275 [i. e. 265] p. CtHT-W; MB; MBAt; MChiA; PPL. 30543

[----] The life of Napoleon Buonaparte, emperor of the French. With a preliminary view of the French revolution. By the author of "Waverley," etc. ... Philadelphia, Carey, Lea & Carey, Stereotyped by J. Howe, 1827. 3 v. CBPac; CL; CtHT; CtW; DLC; GU; ICU; InCW; InU; KWiU; KyU; LNB; MB; MH; MWHi; MWiW; MdBJ; MeLB; MiU; MnSS; MoSW; NNC; NWM; NcU; NjP; NjR; PU; PPL; RPB; ScU; TNJ; ViU; VtMiS; WHi. 30544

[----] ---- Abridged. By an American gentleman. New York, Pub. by Collins & Hannay, 1827. 3 v. in 1. DLC; GDC; GEU; ICMcC; InRE; MBC; MBNEH; MH; MdAS; MoS; NNC; OC; OClW; OrBe; PU; ViU; BrMus. 30545

[----] ---- Exeter, J. & B. Williams, 1827. 2 v. IU; MB; MDeeP; MH; NNUT. 30546

---- The lay of the last minstrel, a poem by Walter Scott. Boston, Timothy Bedlington, 1827. 304 p. KyU. 30547

---- Marmion, a poem by Walter Scott. Boston, Timothy Bedlington, 1827. 341 p. KyU. 30548

---- Poetical works. Philadelphia, J. Maxwell, agent, 1827. 5 v. DLC; IRA; KyLoP; MB; NN; PWW; WyU. 30549

[Scott, Winfield] 1786-1866

Letter to the Secretary of War, or, Review of the controversy on a question of rank between Generals Scott and Gaines. [New York, 1827] 88 p. DS; MB; MH; NIC; PHi; PPAmP; PPL; WHi. 30550

Scougal, Henry

The life of God in the soul of man. New York, N. B. Holmes, 1827. 90 p. NNG. 30551

---- ---- Philadelphia, Pr. and pub. by G. M. & W. Snider, 1827. 140 p. ArBaA; KyU. 30552

Scripture illustrations, first series. American Sunday School Union. Philadelphia, 1827. 126 p. MB; NcGu. 30553

Seabrook, Whitemarsh Benjamin, 1795-1855

A report accompanied with sundry letters on the causes which contribute to the production of fine sea-island cotton; read before the Agricultural Society of St. John's Colleton, on the 14th March, 1827. Charleston, A. E. Miller, 1827. 36 p. ICU; OCHP; ScC. 30554

Seall, Stephen P.

A selection of Christian hymns ... Bloomington, Ia., Lowe and Brandon, prs., 1827. 270 p. Byrd, Indiana, item 331. 30555

Seaman, James N.

Importance of early religious instruction; a discourse, delivered at the anniversary of the Providence Sabbath School Union, June 17, 1827. Providence, Pr. by H. H. Brown, 1827. 16 p. RHi; RPB. 30556

Seamen's Union Bethel Society of Baltimore

Fourth annual report ... 1827. Baltimore, Pub. for the Society by Wm. Wooddy, 1827. 8 p. MdBP. 30557

Searle, Moses C.
On slander. A sermon, preached in Grafton, September 9, 1827, and also in Westborough, October 7, 1827. Worcester, William Manning, pr. [1827?] 16 p. MB; MWA. 30558

Sears, James H.
A standard spelling book; or, The scholar's guide to an accurate pronunciation of the English language ... The rev. ed. Greenfield, Mass., A. Phelps, 1827. 144 p. PU; TxU-T. 30559

Sears, Reuben
The farewell sermon, delivered to the Presbyterian Church and Society in Dracut, August 26, 1827 ... Lowell, Pr. at the Journal office, 1827. 12 p. MBC. 30560

Secker, Thomas, abp. of Canterbury, 1693-1768
Five sermons against popery. Windsor, Vt., Pr. by S. Ide, 1827. 118 p. DLC; MB; MBC; MH; MWA; Vt; VtU; VtWinds. 30561

The second book of masonry ... See Burt, Daniel.

The second book of modern chronicles. [Philadelphia? 1827?] 7 p. NN. 30562

The second part; or, A key to the higher degrees of freemasonry ... By a member of the craft. Cincinnati, Pr. for the proprietor [L. Smith] 1827. 71, [1] p. DLC; OCHP. 30563

Secondary lessons. See Willard, Samuel.

[Sedgwick, Catharine Maria] 1789-1867
Hope Leslie; or, Early times in the Massachusetts. By the author of Redwood ... New York, White, Gallaher, and White, 1827. 2 v. CLU; CSmH; CSt; CtHT; DLC; ICU; IU; Ia; MA; MB; MBAt; MH; MWiW; MnM; NCH; NIC; NN; NPV; NjP; NjR; PHi; PPL; PU; RPB; USl. 30564

Sedgwick, Elijah
The plain physician, giving directions for the preservation of health, and the cure of disease. Rochester, Pr. by E. F. Marshall, 1827. 48 p. NRHi; NRU-M. 30565

[Sedgwick, Henry Dwight]
Circular. [Concerning the Rhode Island Coal Company. Boston, W. L. Lewis, pr. 1827] 20 p. MB; MH; MWA; BrMus. 30566

Select hymns for the use of Sunday schools and families. Cambridge, Hilliard and Brown, 1827. 64 p. MH. 30567

A selection of hymns for the use of children ... Providence, 1827. 24 p. RPB. 30568

Selections from Scripture, designed as lessons in reading for the use of adults; with lessons in spelling. Cambridge, Pr. by Hilliard, Metcalf, and Co., 1827. MB; MWA. 30569

Self conquest; or, The sixteenth birthday; a tale of youth. Boston, Isaac R. Butts & Co., prs., 1827. 82 p. RPE; WHi. 30570

[Selfridge, Thomas Oliver]
The tulip, or Selina's favourite ... Philadelphia, American Sunday School Union, 1827. 32 p. DLC; BrMus. 30571

A sentimental journey. See Sterne, Laurence.

Sequel to American popular lessons. See Robbins, Eliza.

A serious address to Unitarians and Trinitarians, to which is added a series of questions which divide these two classes of Christians ... By a friend of truth. Harrisburg, Pr. at the office of the Intelligencer, 1827. 24 p. DLC; ICMe; MB; MBAU. 30572

Sewall, Edmund Q.
On human depravity ... 4th ed. Printed for the American Unitarian Association. Boston, Bowles and Dearborn, Pr. by Isaac R. Butts & Co., 1827. 42 p. CBPac; ICMe; MB; MH; MMeT. 30573

Sewall, Samuel Edmund
Remarks on slavery in the United States. From the Christian Examiner, Vol. IV. No. 111. Boston, Bowles & Dearborn. I. R. Butts and Co., prs., 1827. 28 p. MB; MH; MiD-B. 30574

Seymour's almanac for 1828. By Matthew Seymour. Danbury, O. Osborn [1827] 12 l. Mi. 30575

Sganzin, Joseph Mathiew
An elementary course of civil engineering ... From the 3d French ed. ... Boston, Hilliard, Gray, Little, and Wilkins, 1827. 220 p. IC; ICJ; LNHT; MA; MB; MiD; MnHi; NjP; NjR; P; PPL; PU; VtU. 30576

Shakers
Testimonies concerning the character and ministry of Mother Ann Lee and the first witnesses of the gospel of Christ's second appearing; given by some of the aged brethren and sisters of the United Society ... Albany, Pr. by Packard & Van Benthuysen, 1827. 178 p. ArCH; CSf; CSmH; CtHC; DLC; IaHA; ICN; ICU; IU; KyBgW; MB; MH; MWA; MeHi; MiD-B; MnHi; NIC; NN; OClWHi; OO; PHi; PPL; PU; TxDaM; WHi; BrMus. 30577

Shakespeare, William, 1564-1616
The beauties of Shakespeare regularly selected from each play, with a general index ... by the late Rev. W. Dodd ... Boston, Bedlington, 1827. 345 p. CtHT; GDC; IU; MB; MH; MeBaT; MiDU; RPB; WHi. 30578

Sharp, L. J.
Vindication of the character of the late Col. Solomon P. Sharp, from the calumnies published against him since his murder by Patrick Darby and Jeroboam O. Beauchamp ... Frankfort, Pr. by Amos Kendall and Co., 1827. 140 p. CtSoP; DLC; ICU; KyHi; NN; OCHP. 30579

Shaw, Elijah, jr.
Hymns, original and selected, for the use of Christians: designed as a supplement to the general collection by R. Foster, and containing no hymns found in that book. Lockport [N.Y.] Pr. for the authors, 1827. 191, [1] p. CSmH; RPB. 30580

Shaw, Oliver, 1779-1848
Julia; an original song written by Graham, author of Killdeer. Composed with accompaniment for the pianoforte by Oliver Shaw. Providence, Pub. and sold by the author, 1827. 2 p. Tuttle. 30581

Sheet almanack for 1828. New-London, Samuel Green. Advertised in the "New London Gazette," Dec. 19, 1827 [1827] 30582

Sheffield, William
An address delivered before the Marine Bible Society of New Haven, at their annual meeting October 4, 1827. New Haven, Pr. by Treadway & Adams, 1827. 12 p. CtH. 30583

Sheil, Richard Lalor
The apostate; a tragedy, in

five acts. Baltimore, J. Robinson, 1827. 64 p. MH. 30584

[Shepard, John]
The artist & tradesman's guide. Embracing some leading facts & principles of science ... Utica, Pr. by William Williams, 1827. 216 p. CSmH; IU; LU; MH; MH-BA; MWA; NUt; PHi. 30585

The shepherd boy. Philadelphia, American Sunday School Union, 1827. 15 p. DLC. 30586

[Sherer, Moyle] 1789-1869
Notes & reflections during a ramble in Germany, by the author of Recollections in the Peninsula ... Boston, Wells & Lilly, 1827. 246 p. MB; MNF; NBu; OClW; ViAl; WBB. 30587

Sheridan, Richard Brinsley, 1751-1816
The school for scandal; a comedy, in five acts. Philadelphia, F. C. Wemyss, etc., etc. [1827] 102 p. MH; PU. 30588

Sherman, John
A description of Trenton Falls, Oneida County, New York. Utica, Pr. by William Williams, 1827. 18 p. N; NNM; WHi; BrMus. 30589

Sherwood, Adiel, 1791-1879
A gazetteer of the state of Georgia. Charleston, Pr. by W. Riley, 1827. 143 p. DLC; G; GA; GAU; GU; NNMer; NCRA; OO. 30590

Sherwood, Mrs. Mary Martha (Butt) 1775-1851
Edward Mansfield, a narrative of facts. Salem, Pub. by Whipple and Lawrence. [W. Palfray Jr. and J. Chapman, prs.] 1827. 34 p. DLC; MH. 30591

---- Ermina; or, The second part of Juliana Oakley. Philadelphia, American Sunday School Union, 1827. 108 p. DLC; MnU; PHi; PPL; BrMus. 30592

---- The gipsy babes; a tale of the last century. Revised by the Committee of publication. Philadelphia, American Sunday School Union, 1827. 54 p. MH. 30593

---- The governess, or The young female academy. From the 3d English ed. New York, Pr. for O. D. Cooke & Co., Hartford, J. & J. Harper, pr., 1827. 222 p. CtHi; MH; RLa; VtMiS. 30594

[----] The history of Emily and her brothers. Philadelphia, American Sunday School Union, 1827. BrMus. 30595

---- The history of Henry Milner, a little boy who was not brought up according to the fashions of this world. Princeton, D. A. Borrenstein, 1827. 184 p. NjP; PP. 30596

---- Julian Percival. Salem [Mass.] Pub. by Whipple & Lawrence [W. Palfray, jr. and J. Chapman, prs.] 1827. 35 p. MB; PP. 30597

---- Juliana Oakley. A tale ... 2d ed. Philadelphia, Stereotyped by L. Johnson for the American Sunday School Union, 1827. 88 p. MHi; OO; PP; BrMus. 30598

---- Little Henry and his bearer. New York, Pub. by the American Tract Society [1827?] 32 p. WHi. 30599

---- The little woodman, and his dog Caesar. Philadelphia, American Sunday School Union, 1827. 34 p. DLC. 30600

---- ---- Philadelphia, American Sunday School Union, 1827. 36 p. DLC. 30601

---- New stories, comprising the Shepherd of the Pyrenees, The little woodman, and The errand boy ... Recommended by the American Sunday School Union. New York, Pub. for O. D. Cooke & Co. - Hartford [Vanderpool & Cole, prs., New York] 1827. 46 p. MH; NBuG. 30602

---- The orphans of Normandy; or, Florentin and Lucie. 1st Amer. ed. Hartford, D. F. Robinson, 1827. 106 p. CtHi; CtY; DLC; ICN; MAm; NN; NNC; NRHi; NcD. 30603

---- The re-captured negro. Providence, 1827. 63 p. RHi. 30604

---- Religious fashion, or, The history of Anna ... Philadelphia, American Sunday School Union, 1827. 138 p. OW; BrMus. 30604a

Shinn, Asa

An appeal to the citizens of the United States. Baltimore, Pr. by R. J. Matchett, 1827. 16 p. MdHi. 30605

---- A brief review of Doctor Bond's "Appeal to the Methodists." Baltimore, Pr. by Richard J. Matchett, 1827. 52 p. MHi; MdBBC; MdBS; MdHi; MsJMC. 30606

---- A finishing stroke to the high claims of ecclesiastical sovereignty, in reply to the address of a meeting of male members of the Methodist Episcopal Church in Baltimore ... Baltimore, Pr. by John D. Toy, 1827. 29 p. MdBS; MdHi; MsJMC; OClWHi. 30607

Shipwright, pseud.

Observations on the floating dock, invented by Commodore Barron; as described in the Franklin Journal for Jan. 1827, & recommended by a select committee, to the merchants of Philadelphia. Philadelphia, Harding, 1827. 8 p. PPAmP. 30608

Short, J. C.

An address, delivered before the Hamilton County Agricultural Society ... September, at the Court House in Cincinnati, 1827. Title from Western Monthly Review, v. 1, Sept. 1827, p. 304 (Rusk 11:306, and Kyle 259). 30609

Short stories. Philadelphia, American Sunday School Union, 1827. BrMus. 30610

Signiorina's concert. The public are respectfully informed that the Signiorina will give a miscellaneous concert, on Saturday evening, June 16, 1827, at the hall of the Musical Fund Society. [Philadelphia, Desilver? 1827] Bdsd. PPL. 30611

[Sigourney, Mrs. Lydia Howard (Huntley)] 1791-1865

Poems; by the author of "Moral pieces in prose & verse." Boston, S. G. Goodrich; Hartford, H. & F. J. Huntington, 1827. 228 p. CSmH; Ct; CtHT; ICU; IaU; MB; MBC; MH; MnU; NCH; NIC; NPV; NRU; NjP; OClWHi; PHi; PPL; PU; RPB; TxU. 30612

Simms, William Gilmore, 1806-1870

Early lays ... Charleston, A. E. Miller, 1827. 108 p. CSmH; MH; NIC; PPL; RPB; ScC. 30613

---- Lyrical and other poems. Charleston, Ellis & Neufville, 1827. 198, [6] p. CSmH; DLC; ICN; ICU; MB; MH; NIC; NN; NNPM; NcD; PHi; PPL; PU; RPB; BrMus. 30614

Simonde de Sismondi, Jean Charles Leonard, 1773-1842

Historical view of the literature of the south of Europe ...

Translated from the original, with notes, by Thomas Roscoe New York, Pr. by J. & J. Harper, for E. Duyckinck [etc.] 1827. 2 v. CtHT; CtW; GEU; ICM; In; KWiU; KyDC; LU; MH; MdBS; MeBaT; NCH; NNG; NSyU; NT; NjP; NjR; O; PPA; PPAmP; PRea; PU; RPB; ScNC; TxAuPT; UU; ViU; VtU. 30615

---- A review of the progress of religious opinions. From the French ... Boston, Bowles and Dearborn, Isaac R. Butts & Co., prs. 1827. 37 p. ICMe; MBC; MH; MWA; RPB. 30616

Sinclair, William

A sermon on universal charity: preached at the Maryland Institute ... Baltimore, Pr. by Benjamin Edes, 1827. 32 p. CSmH; MBAt; MWA; MdBE; MdHi; NjR; PHi; PPAmP; PPL. 30617

Single rail railway. [With lithograph plate by Pendleton. Boston, April 30th, 1827] 8 p. folded pl. DBRE; DLC; IU; MB; MCM; MWA; MiU-T; NN; NNC. 30618

Sir, As very erroneous impressions prevail. See Carey, Mathew.

Sir, On the 4th of May, I received a letter from Lewis Tappan. See Carey, Mathew.

Sir, The salutary bill. See Carey, Mathew.

Sir, the undersigned being a committee appointed by their fellow citizens of both political parties friendly to the state and national administrations call your attention to a meeting held at Faneuil Hall, on the 20th instant ... Boston, May 7th, 1827. Bdsd. MB. 30619

Sir, We have the honor to address you as a committee appointed by the citizens of Columbia and Richland, to carry into effect the following resolutions [on the woolen bills] Columbia, S. C. July 6, 1827. Bdsd. DLC. 30620

A sketch of the history of Framingham. See Ballard, William.

A sketch of the life and public services of John Quincy Adams, president of the United States, and commander in chief of the army and navy, &c. &c. [Signed] Plutarch. Fayette Co. July 31, 1827. 2 p. DLC. 30621

A sketch of the life and services of John Quincy Adams, president of the United States of America. 1827. 31 p. DLC; MH; PPL. 30622

Sketch of the life of John Quincy Adams. 1827. 11 p. DLC; MWA. 30623

A sketch of the politics, relations, and statistics of the Western world. See Chew, Benjamin.

Sketch of the resources of the city of New-York. See Dix, John Adams.

Sketches of Moravian missions; revived by the Committee of Publications of the American Sunday School Union. Philadelphia, American Sunday School Union, [1827] 179 p. ScCliTO; TxH. 30624

Skinner, Thomas H.

A discourse delivered June 10, 1827, in the Fifth Presbyterian Church of Philadelphia, commemorative of its dedication. Philadelphia, I. Ashmead, pr., 1827. 28 p. CSansS; CtHC; MAnP; MB; MBAt; MMeT-Hi; NcU; NjP; NjR; OO; PHi; PLT; PPPrHi. 30625

Slave labor. See Carey, Mathew.

Smellie, William
The philosophy of natural history, ... With an introduction and various additions ... By John Ware, M. D. 2d ed. Boston, Hilliard, Gray, Little and Wilkins [Cambridge, From the University press by Hilliard, Metcalf, & co.] 1827. viii, 322 p. ArCH; CtSoP; MB; MH; MNe; MSap; MiGr; NNNAM; NRU; PPC; RPB. 30626

Smiley, Thomas T.
An improved atlas, exhibiting the elevation of mountains, length of rivers, and population of cities from the best authorities; intended to accompany An easy introduction to the study of geography for the use of schools ... 5th ed. Philadelphia, J. Grigg's, 1827. Plates (maps). OMC; ScCleA. 30627

---- The new federal calendar, or Scholars' assistant ... for the use of schools and of counting-houses. Philadelphia, Pub. and for sale by J. Grigg, 1827. Griggs & Dickinson, prs., Whitehall. 180 p. ILebM; NcGw. 30628

[Smith, Francis Ormond Jonathan] 1806-1876
A dissertation on the nature and effects of lottery systems, and principles of public policy relating to them. By Civis [pseud.] Portland, Arthur Shirley, pr., 1827. 36 p. CtY; MH; MeBat; MeHi; NN; Nh; NjPT; OClWHi. 30629

Smith, Hannah Logan
From motives of deep interest in the beloved children and grandchildren of my dear departed husband ... [Philadelphia, 1827] 35 p. PPL. 30630

[Smith, Horatio]
Reuben Apsley. By the author of Brambletye house, The Tor hill, etc. ... Philadelphia, Carey, Lea & Carey, 1827. 2 v. DLC; GHi; InCW; LNHT; LU; MBAt; MBL; ScDuE. 30631

Smith, Hugh
Letters to married ladies ... To which is added, A letter on corsets, and copious notes, by an American physician. New-York, E. Bliss and E. White, and G. and C. Carvill [Sleight & George, Jamaica, L. I.] 1827. 283 p. MB; NJQ; NN; NjPT; BrMus. 30632

Smith, James
Sermon by the late Rev. James Smith, delivered in Light Street Church, Baltimore, June 12th, 1825. Taken in short hand, by M. T. C. Gould, stenographer. And revised by the author, a few days before his death. Philadelphia, Pub. by the Reporter. G. M. & W. Snider, prs., 1827. 24 p. MdHi; PPL; PSC-Hi. 30633

Smith, John Rubens
A compendium of picturesque anatomy, adapted to the arts of designing, painting, sculpture and engraving, on four folio lithographic plates ... Boston, Pub. by the author, 1827. 8 p., 4 pl. ICJ; MdBG. 30634

---- To the stockholders, or charter members and patrons, of the New York Academy of the Fine Arts ... [ca 1827] PPPM. 30635

Smith, Josiah P.
Who ever saw the like! A tragi-comedy, or rather a comico-tragedy; portraying the last elections of Knox County, with reference to the neighboring counties. Knoxville, T., Pr. at the "Enquirer Office," 1827. 46 p. MBAt. 30636

Smith, Roswell Chamberlain, 1797-1875
Practical and mental arithmetic on a new plan ... Boston, S. G. Goodrich [etc.] 1827. 196 p., 1 l. CtHT-W; CtSoP; DLC; MH; NNC; NbOM; OO; RPB. 30637

---- ---- 2nd ed. rev. and enl. Philadelphia, W. Marshall, 1827. 196 p. P. 30638

Smith, Samuel, 1752-1839
Speech of Mr. Smith, of Maryland, on the colonial trade: delivered in the Senate of the United States, Feb. 21, 1827. Washington, Pr. by Duff Green, 1827. 27 p. PPL. 30639

Smith, Samuel, b. 1792
Inside out; or, Roguery exposed; being the life, sufferings, and adventures of Samuel Smith, alias Samuel Corson, during a series of thirty-five years, now confined in Newgate prison in the state of Connecticut ... Hartford, Norton & Russell, prs. and pub., 1827. 48 p. CtHT-W; CtHi; Nh. 30640

Smith, Samuel Harrison, 1772-1845
Memoir of the life, character, and writings of Thomas Jefferson; delivered in the capitol, before the Columbian Institute, on the sixth of January, 1827 ... Washington, S. A. Elliot, pr., 1827. 38 p. DLC; ICHi; M; MBAt; MQ; MoSHi; MoSW; NCH; OCHP; PPL; ScU; ViU; WHi. 30641

[Smith, Southwood]
Use of the dead to the living. From the Westminster Review. Albany, Webster and Skinners, 1827. 40 p. MB; MWA; N; NBMS; NN; NNNAM; NjR; OC; PPL; RNR; BrMus. 30642

Smith, Stephen Rensselaer, 1788-1850
The teachings of Christ; addressed to the youth. Philadelphia, Pr. by Atkinson & Alexander, 1827. 12 p. NHi; PHi. 30643

Smith, William
Some remarks on the assassination of Julius Caesar ... Exeter, C. Norris, pr., 1827. 47 p. CSmH; CSt; CtSoP; ICN; MB; MBAt; MH; MiD-B; Nh-Hi; WHi; BrMus. 30644

Smithfield and Providence accommodation stage. Leaves Farnum's Hotel, [near Slaterville] every Tuesday, Thursday and Saturday at 6 o'clock A. M., and arrives in Providence, at 9 o'clock A. M. ... Chas. A Farnum, agent. Providence, June, 1827. Bdsd. Goodspeed's Cat. 172, 1928. 30645

Smollett, Tobias George, 1721-1771
Adventures of Roderick Random. Philadelphia, Pr. and pub. by J. Harding, 1827. 2 v. NcWsW; OClWHi. 30646

Snethen, Nicholas, 1769-1845
Salvation by grace through faith: a discourse delivered at a quarterly meeting of the German United Brethren ... Frederick [Md.] Pr. by John P. Thomson, 1827. 16 p. CSmH. 30647

Snow, Caleb Hopkins, 1796-1835
First principles of English spelling and reading ... Stereotyped at the Boston Type and Stereotype Foundry. Boston, Pub. by James Loring [1827] 72 p. MH. 30648

The snow drop. Philadelphia, American Sunday School Union, [1827] 16 p. NRAB. 30649

Snyder, Simon
Letters to the people of Penn-

sylvania, upon the subject of the presidential election ... Philadelphia, Pr. for the United States Gazette office, 1827. 32 p. DLC; IaU; MiD-B; OClWHi; PHi; PPL. 30650

Society for Promoting Religion and Learning in the State of New York.
Constitution of the Society for Promoting Religion and Learning in the State of New York, as finally adopted by the vestry of Trinity Church and said society, July 10, 1826. New York, Pr. by T. and J. Swords, 1827. 11 p. NBuU-M; PHi. 30651

Society for the Defence of the Catholic Religion
Constitution of the Society for the Defence of the Catholic Religion from calumny and abuse. Philadelphia, Pr. by Joseph R. A. Skerrett, 1827. 8 p. PPL. 30652

Society for the Encouragement of Faithful Domestic Servants, New York.
Second annual report of the managers of the Society for the Encouragement of Faithful Domestic Servants in New York. New York, Pr. by D. Fanshaw, at the American Tract Society's House, 1827. 32 p. M; NjR. 30653

Society for the Mutual Benefit of Female Domestics and Their Employers, Boston.
Constitution of the ... Instituted in Boston, April 11, 1827. [Boston, 1827] 8 p. MB; MHi; WHi. 30654

Society for the Promotion of Temperance, Ware Village, Mass.
Report of the managers of the Society for the Promotion of Temperance in Ware Village, presented at their quarterly meeting, November, 1827. Belchertown, Sentinel and Journal office, 1827. 8 p. CSmH; MBC. 30655

Society for the Reformation of Juvenile Delinquents in the City of New York.
Second annual report of the managers of the Society for the Reformation of Juvenile Delinquents in the City of New York. New York, Pr. by Mahlon Day, 1827. 62, [1] p. IU; M; MH; NNG; NjR; OClWHi; OO; PHi; PPAmP; PPC; PPL; PPPrHi; BrMus. 30656

Society for the Relief of Poor Aged and Distressed Masters of Ships, their Widows and Children, Philadelphia.
Act for incorporating the Society formed for the relief of poor aged & infirm masters of ships, their widows and children. Philadelphia, J. W. Allen, 1827. 32 p. PHi. 30657

Society for the Relief of the Destitute
Constitution of the Society for the Relief of the Destitute ... New York, Pr. at the Rutgers Press, by William A. Mercein, 1827. 23 p. DLC; MiD-B; NNC; NNNAM; NjR. 30658

Society of the Protestant Episcopal Church for the Advancement of Christianity in Pennsylvania. See Protestant Episcopal Church in the U. S. A. Pennsylvania (Diocese) Society for the Advancement of Christianity in Pennsylvania.

The Socinian. A narrative. Published by the Protestant Episcopal Tract Society. New-York, T. & J. Swords, 1827. 24 p. NNG. 30659

Some serious consideration. See Quandry, Christopher, pseud.

Sophia Morton. Boston, Pub. by

Bowles and Dearborn. Isaac R. Butts and Co., prs., 1827. 63 p. DLC; WHi. 30660

Soule, Joshua

Substance of a sermon preached in Augusta, Georgia, before the South Carolina conference, January 14, 1827. Baltimore, Pr. by John D. Toy, 1827. 24 p. GEU; GU-De; MB; MBC; MiD; MnHi; OMC; PPL; ScCMu; TxDaM; TxU. 30661

South, Robert, 1634-1716

Discourses on various subjects and occasions, selected from the complete English edition, with a sketch of his life and character. Boston, Pub. by Bowles & Dearborn, 1827. 455 p. CBPac; CSansS; CtHC; MA; MBC; MBNMHi; MH; MeBat; NCaS; NNUT; NcD; RP; OMC; OO; PU. 30662

South Carolina (State)

Acts and resolutions of the General Assembly of the state of South Carolina, passed in December, 1826. Columbia, D. & J. M. Faust, 1827. 46, 76, 4 p. IaU-L; In-SC; MdBB; Mi-L; Nb; Nj; Nv; W. 30663

---- Chancery cases argued and determined in the Court of Appeals of South Carolina, from January 1825 to May 1826, both inclusive. By D. J. M'Cord, state reporter. Vol. I. Philadelphia, Pub. by Carey, Lea & Carey, and sold by P. H. Nicklin [James Kay, Jun., pr.] 1827. 2 v. CSfBar; CU; Ct; F-SC; KyLxFL; MBS; MH-L; MdBB; MdUL; MoU; NCH; NN; NNC; NNLI; OClW; PPiAL; PU-L; RPL; TxDaM-L; WaPS; BrMus. 30664

---- Plan in form of a bill submitted by A. Blanding, Superintendent of Public Works, to the Legislature "for chartering joint stock companies, for the improvement of the roads of the state." [Columbia, 1827[16 p. NN 30665

---- Report of a special committee of the Senate, of South Carolina, on the resolution submitted by Mr. Ramsay, on the subject of state rights. Columbia, S. C., Pr. by Sweeny & Sims, state prs., 1827. 24 p. ICU; N; NN; NcU; PHi; PPAmP; RPB; ScHi; ScU; TNJ. 30666

---- Report of the Comptroller General Alexander Speer, to the Legislature of South Carolina on claims of the state against the United States on account of expenditure made during the last war. 1827. 7 p. NN. 30667

---- The report of the Superintendent of Public Works to the Legislature of South Carolina for the year 1827. Columbia, S. C., Pr. by Sweeny & Sims, at the Telescope Press, 1827. 18, 45, 6, 7, 8 p. NN. 30668

---- To the Honorable the President and others, members of the Senate of said State: The Committee appointed 20th December last, to report on the practicability of a code of the Statute and Common Law of the State and for other purposes beg leave to report as follows: [Pr. by D. & J. M. Faust, Columbia, S. C., Nov. 1827] 26 p. DLC; ICN; MB; MBAt; MH-L; MWA; NN; ScU. 30669

---- To the Honorable, the President and other members of the Senate of the said state. (Report of Thomas S. Grimke, appointed Chairman of the Committee on the part of the Senate to examine the Bank of the State.) [Columbia, D. & J. M. Faust, prs. 1827] 8 p. NN. 30670

South Carolina Society, Charleston.
General plan of education appointed for the South Carolina Society's Female Academy. With rules. Charleston, A. E. Miller, 1827. 4 p. CtY; MHi. 30671

---- General plan of education appointed for the South Carolina Society's Male Academy, July, 1827. Charleston, A. E. Miller, 1827. 8 p. CtY; MH; MHi; ScC. 30672

---- Rules of the South Carolina Society. Established at Charleston A. D. 1736. Chartered 17th May, 1751. 8th ed. rev. and altered. Ratified on the 11th Sept., 1827. Charleston, A. E. Miller, 1827. 73 p. CtY; MHi; ScC. 30673

The southern and western songster: being a choice collection of the most fashionable songs, many of which are original. 2d ed., greatly enl. Philadelphia, J. Grigg [Clark & Raser, prs.] 1827. 306 p. MB; OClWHi; RPB. 30674

Southey, Robert
A tale of Paraguay ... S. G. Goodrich. Boston, 1827. 10-209 p. AMob; CtHT; MA; MB; MBC; MFHi; MH; MNS; NCH; NNS; NR; NhPet; PPL; RPB. 30675

Southwick, Solomon, 1773-1839
A solemn warning against Free Masonry, addressed to the young men of the United States. With an appendix ... relating to the supposed murder of Mr. Murdock's father ... and several other interesting matters. Albany, Pr. by Geo. Galpin, Office of the National Observer, 1827. 140 p. CSmH; CtHT-W; MB; MBFM; NAl; NN; PPFM. 30676

Le souvenir, or Picturesque pocket diary for 1827 ... Philadelphia, A. R. Poole [etc., etc.] 1827. 68 p. PPL. 30677

Sparhaw, E. U., reporter
Report of trial, Circuit Court of the U. S. ... involving the claim of J. J. Astor to lands in Putnam county, with arguments of counsel and the charge of Judge Thompson. By E. U. Sparhaw, reporter to the New York American. New York, E. Bliss, 1827. 66 p. ICU; MH-L; NN. 30678

Sparks, Jared
An account of the manuscript papers of George Washington, which were left by him at Mount Vernon, with a plan for their publication. Boston, 1827. [1], 24 p. MB; MH; MHi. 30679

---- Washington's papers. An edition of these papers is preparing for publication under the following title; The works of George Washington ... [Cambridge, Mass., 1827] 24 p. CSmH. 30680

---- Der Charakter und Werth von Washingtons hinterlassenen Schriften, sowie der Plan zu deren herausgabe, erhellt aus dem folgenden Schreiben an Joseph Story. [1827] 22 p. MH. 30681

Speed, John
Fellow citizens of Jefferson and Oldham Counties. [Louisville, July 12-17, 1827] 8 p. KyBgW; KyLo. 30682

A spelling book written in the Chato language. See Wright, Alfred.

Spencer, Ezra
An antidote. Rev. E. Spencer's Defence and testimony against an egregious and butchering slander ... Cincinnati, Pr. by S. J. Browne, 1827. 54 p. CSmH. 30683

Spencer, John C.
Substance of the Hon. John C. Spencer's remarks in the Senate, on the bill to aid the contributions for certain Greeks ... on the 7th and 8th March, 1827. Albany, Pr. by Croswell & Van Benthuysen, 1827. 8 p. MB. 30684

Spicer, Tobias
Truth illustrated; being an attempt to explain several of the most difficult passages contained in the ninth chapter of St. Paul's epistles to the Romans ... J. Barber, pr., New Haven, Conn. 1827. 24 p. CtHi; DLC; MB. 30685

Spoliations of the French, prior to 1800. From the North American Review - July, 1827. 16 p. PPL. 30686

Sprague, Charles, 1791-1875
An address delivered before the Massachusetts Society for the Suppression of Intemperance, May 31, 1827. Boston, Bowles and Dearborn, Isaac R. Butts & Co., prs., 1827. 30 p. Ct; DLC; ICMe; ICN; ICU; KU; MB; MBAt; MH; MHi; MdBE; MdBJ; MdHi; MiD-B; MoSHi; NNUT; NjR; OClWHi; PHi; PPL; PPPrHi; RPB; WHi. 30687

---- ---- 2d ed. Boston, Bowles, and Dearborn, Isaac R. Butts & Co., prs. 1827. 24 p. CSmH; Ct; M; MB; MBAU; MH-AH; MMeT; MWA; MWHi; MeLB; MiD-B; MnHi; NIC; Nh; NjR; OClWHi; OO; PPL; WHi. 30688

Sprague, William Buell, 1795-1876
Character of Jesus Christ, a sermon delivered June 13, 1827, before the Hampden Association of Ministers and published at their request. Hartford, Goodwin, pr., 1827. 31 p. CSmH; Ct; CtHC; CtHT-W; CtHi; CtSoP; CtY; DLC; MB; MBAt; MHi; MPB; MiD-B; NcD; NjR; PHi; PPPrHi. 30689

---- The Gospel the wisdom of God. A sermon preached at Salem, February 14, 1827, at the ordination of the Rev. John P. Cleaveland, as pastor of the Tabernacle Church. Salem, Pub. by Whipple and Lawrence. T. R. Marvin, pr., Boston, 1827. 39, [1] p. CtHC; CtSoP; IaHi; MHi; MWA; MeBa; MeBaT; MeHi; NNC; Nh; PHi. 30690

---- Intemperance, a just cause for alarm and exertion. A sermon preached at West Springfield the day of the annual fast. Pr. by J. Seymour, New York, 1827. 26 p. CSmH; ICMe; MB; MBAt; MBC; MH; MHi; MPiB; MWA; MiD-B; PPPrHi; RPB; BrMus. 30691

---- Religious celebration of independence; a discourse delivered at Northampton, Fourth of July, 1827. Hartford, Goodwin, pr., 1827. 29 p. CBPac; Ct; CtY; DLC; IEG; LNHT; MBC; MH; MHi; MNF; MWA; MWiW; MiD-B; NN; NcD; PHi; PPL; PPPrHi. 30692

Spring, Gardiner
A dissertation on the means of regeneration. New-York, Pub. by John P. Haven, American Tract Society House [Pr. by Vanderpool & Cole, N. Y.] 1827. 50 p. CtHC; ICMe ICMcC; MBC; MWA; MeBa; MeBaT; MiD-B; NIC; NjR; OC; OClWHi; OO; PPPrHi. 30693

Spring Garden District, Philadelphia.
Report of the watering committee to the commissioners of the district of Spring Garden, January 22, 1827. Philadelphia, 1827. 12 p. PHi not loc., 1969. 30694

Springer, Moses, 1796-1870?
Songs of Zion; being a collection of hymns, for the use of the pious of all denominations. 5th ed. Hallowell, Pr. and sold by Glazier & Co.; sold also by M. Springer, Jun'r., Gardiner, 1827. 192 p. MeBaT; RPB. 30695

The spy. See Cooper, James Fenimore.

Squibb, Robert
The gardener's calendar for the states of North-Carolina, South-Carolina, and Georgia ... Charleston, S. C., P. Hoff, 1827. 176 p. CtW; DLC; GU-De; IaAS; MBHo; NHi; NcAS; NcD; ScC; ScHi; ScU. 30696

Stanton, Benjamin F.
The apostolic commission. A sermon delivered at the ordination of Rev. Daniel L. Carroll, Litchfield, Conn. Oct. 3, 1827. Pr. by S. S. Smith, Litchfield, 1827. 44 p. CSmH; CtSoP; CtY; DLC; In; MB; MBC; MWA; NjR; PLT; PPPrHi; RPB. 30697

A star of Virginia. See G., E. G.

State of Ohio agricultural almanac for 1828. By John Armstrong. Zanesville, William Davis [1827] 18 l. OHi. 30698

Statement and exposition of the title of John Jacob Astor to the lands purchased by him from the surviving children of Roger Morris and Mary his wife. New-York, 1827. 54 p. MH-L; MiD-B; NN. 30699

---- New-York, 1827. 60 p. CSmH. 30700

A statement of the facts and reasonings in support of the remonstrance against the consecration of the Rev. Henry U. Onderdonk ... Philadelphia, Pr. & pub. by William Stavely, 1827. 43 p. CtHT; DLC; NNG; PHi; PPL; TxDaM. 30701

Statement of facts, relating to the claim of Major Moses White upon the U. S. as executor of the late Gen. Moses Hazen including some consideration of its merits, and an exposition of the report of a committee on this subject, made 28th Feb., 1820. [Salem, 1827] 15 p. MH; MHi; ScU. 30702

Stearns, John Glazier, 1795-1874
An inquiry into the nature and tendency of speculative Free-Masonry. 2d ed., enl. Utica, Pr. for the author, 1827. 168, [1] p. IaCrM; MBFM; MWiW; PPFM. 30703

---- ---- 3d ed. Utica, Pr. by Northway & Bennett, 1827. 166 p. CSmH; DLC. 30704

Steele's Albany almanack for 1828. By Edwin E. Prentiss. Albany, Oliver Steele [1827] 12 l. CLU; DLC; MWA; NN; ViU. 30705

Stephens, D. S.
Views of the Reformer. Baltimore, Md., Pub. by W. J. C. Dulaney, 1827. 24 p. MdBBC not loc., 1969. 30706

Stephenson, Thomas
An oration delivered at Gloucester July 4, 1827, in commemoration of our national independence ... Gloucester, Pr. by Wm. E. P. Rogers, 1827. 24 p. MH; MHi; MiD-B; RPB. 30707

[Sterne, Laurence] 1713-1768
A sentimental journey through France and Italy. By Mr. Yorick ... New York, Pub. by James Gourlay, Samuel Marks, pr., 1827. [2], iv-viii, 10-144, [1] p. MH. 30708

[---] ---- Providence, Doyle & Hathaway, 1827. 160+ p. CtY. 30709

Steward, William
The first edition of Steward's Healing art, corrected and improved by the original hand. To which he has added, all his late improvements and new discoveries, both in physick and surgery, from the year 1812, to the year 1826, including his whole system upon physick and surgery. To which he has added a concise herbal, containing a full description of herbs, roots. Saco, Maine, Pr. by Putnam & Blake, 1827. 126, 40, 22 p. CSmH; MeBa; NhD; PPHa. 30710

Stewart, Dugald
Elements of the philosophy of the human mind. Volume third, to which are annexed additions to volume first. Philadelphia, Carey, Lea and Carey [Griggs & Dickinson, prs., Whitehall] 1827. 387 p. CtHC; MB; MPeaI; MWH; MsCliM; NjR; NmU; PMA; PPL; PWW; RKi; Vi; ViU. 30711

Stiles, Joseph Clay, 1795-1875
A sermon on predestination, preached in Milledgeville, August, 1826. 2d ed. Charleston, Pr. at the Office of the Charleston Observer, 1827. 60 p. CLU; CtHC; GDC; NN; NcU; PPPrHi. 30712

Stipp, George W.
The western miscellany, or accounts historical, biographical, and amusing. Xenia, O., Pr. for the compiler, 1827. 224 p. ICHi; InHi; KyHi; OCHP; OClWHi; WHi. 30713

Stockbridge, Mass. First Congregational Church
The confession, covenants, and standing rules of the church in Stockbridge ... Stockbridge, Pr. by Charles Webster, 1827. 8, 30, 13 p. MiD-B; NBLiHi. 30714

Stoddard, Solomon, 1643-1729
A guide to Christ, or, The way of directing souls that are under the work of conversion ... Princeton, N.J., Pub. by William D. Hart; D. A. Borrenstein, pr., 1827. 159 p. ICMcC; NN; NjP; PPLT. 30715

Stoddard's diary; or Columbia almanack for 1828. By Edwin E. Prentiss. Hudson, A. Stoddard [1827] 18 l. CtNhHi; DLC; MWA; NCooHi; NHi. 30716

Stone, John Augustus, 1800-1834
Tancred; or, The siege of Antioch. A drama in three acts. Philadelphia, Pub. by the prorietor, 1827. 45 p. MB; MH; MdHi; NN; PU. 30717

Storer, William, jr.
Questions adapted to Williams' History of the American revolution: for the use of schools ... Stonington [Conn.] Pr. by the author, 1827. 52 p. DLC; PHi. 30718

Stories from the Scriptures on an improved plan. Old Testament. Boston, Munroe and Francis, New York, Chas. S. Francis, 1827. 179 p. FTU; IObB; KU; MLanC; NICLA; ScCliTO. 30719

Storrs, Richard Salter, 1787-1873
The spirit of the Pilgrims. A sermon delivered at Plymouth, December the twenty-second, 1826. Plymouth [Mass.] Pr. by A. Danforth, 1827. 44 p. DLC; ICU; M; MH-AH; MHi; MWA; NCH; NN; PHi; RPB; WHi. 30720

[Story, Isaac]
Original and select poems, moral, religious and sentimental;

calculated to refine the taste, elevate the mind and attract the attention of the youth of both sexes. By the Stranger [pseud.] Albany, Pr. by Webster and Wood, 1827. 144 p. CSmH; DLC; IU; KSalW; MH; NN. 30721

Story of William and Ellen. Wendell, Mass., J. Metcalf, 1827. 8 l. PP. 30722

Stout, Z. Barton
An address, delivered before the Ontario Agricultural Society, at the town house, in Canandaigua, October 2, 1827. ... Canandaigua, Pr. by Bemis, Morse and Ward, 1827. 26 p. NCanHi; NRHi. 30723

Stow, Mass. Congregational Church
Order of exercises at the dedication of the meeting house in Stow, October 1, 1827. Concord [Mass.] Pr. by Allen & Atwill, 1827. 4 p. CSmH. 30724

Strang, Jesse, d. 1827
The authentic confession of Jesse Strang, executed at Albany, Friday, August 24, 1827, for the murder of John Whipple ... together with the account of his execution ... New York, E. M. Murden & A. Ming, 1827. 20 p. MH-L; PHi; PP; PPL. 30725

---- The confession of Jesse Strang, who was convicted of the murder of John Whipple, at a special court of oyer and termines, held in and for the county of Albany, on the fourth day of August, 1827 ... Made to C. Pepper, Esq., one his counsel. Albany, Pr. by J. B. Van Steinbergh, 1827. 35 p. CSfLaw; CSmH; DLC; MB; MBAt; MH-L; MdBB; MiD-B; MiGr; MoSM; MoU; NAl; NCH; NHi; NN; PHi; PP; PPAmP; RPB; BrMus. 30726

Stranger, pseud. See Story, Isaac.

A stranger's offering to infant minds, being a series of easy lessons on the Lord's prayer. New York, Pub. by N. Bangs and J. Emory, for the Methodist Episcopal Church, 1827. 24 p. DLC. 30727

Strong, James
An address on the necessity of education and the arts in a republican government, delivered before the Phi Sigma Nu Society of the University of Vermont at Burlington, August 7, A. D., 1827. Burlington, Pr. at the Free Press Office, 1827. 24 p. CSmH; MH; MdBP; MiD-B; MWA; NCH; Nh; Vt; VtU. 30728

[Strong, Titus] 1787-1855
Candid examination of the Episcopal Church, in two letters to a friend. 4th ed. To which is added, a Consideration of some popular objections to the Episcopal Church. Boston, R. P. & C. Williams [True & Greene, prs.] 1827. 71, [1] p. MBAt; MBC; MWA; NNG. 30729

---- The young scholar's manual; or Companion to the spelling-book ... 6th ed. Greenfield, Mass., Pr. and pub. by Ansel Phelps, 1827. 90 p. CtHT-W; MDeeP; MFiHi. 30730

Strong's almanack for 1828. By Uri Strong. New-Haven, Durrie & Peck; Herald Office Print [1827] 12 l. CtB; CtHi; CtY; DLC; MWA; N. 30731

Stroud, George McDowell, 1795-1875
A sketch of the laws relating to slavery in the several states of the United States of America. Philadelphia, Pub. by Kimber

and Sharpless, I. Ashmead, pr., 1827. 180 p. AB; CL; CSmH; CU; CtHT-W; CtW; DLC; GEU; ICMe; ICN; ICU; KU; MB; MBNMHi; MH; MHi; MWA; MdBE; MdBJ; MdHi; MeBa; MiD-B; MiU; MoSHi; NB; NIC; NNC; NR; NcMHi; NdU; Nh-Hi; NhD; OClWHi; OO; OkStA; PPAmP; PPF; PPL; PPPrHi; PSC-Hi; RPB; ScC; TNJ; TxH; TxU; Vi; WHi; BrMus. 30732

Stuart, Moses, 1780-1852
A commentary on the Epistle to the Hebrews. Andover, Pub. and for sale by Mark Newman. Codman press ... Flagg & Gould, 1827. 2 v. CtHC; CtW; IaDuU; ICT; IEG; KAStB; KyLoS; MA; MAnP; MBC; MH-AH; MW; MoSpD; NCH; NCaS; NbCrD; NhD; NjP; OClW; OkU; PLT; PPiW; RBr; ScC; TWcW; BrMus. 30733

---- A sermon delivered before His Excellency Levi Lincoln Esq., Governor, His Honor Thomas L. Winthrop, Lieutenant-Governor, the Hon. Council, the Senate, and House of Representatives of the Commonwealth of Massachusetts. May 30, 1827. Being the day of general election. Boston, True & Greene, state prs., 1827. 42 p. CBPac; CSansS; CSmH; Ct; CtHC; CtHT; CtSoP; CtY; DLC; GDC; ICMe; MA; MB; MBAt; MBC; MBNMHi; MH; MMeT-Hi; MNF; MNtcA; MWA; MWo; MeBat; MeHi; MiD-B; MnHi; MoSpD; NCH; NN; NNC; NHi; NNUT; NcU; Nh-Hi; NjR; OClWHi; PHi; PPPrHi; RPB; VtU; WHi; BrMus. 30734

Sturm, Christoph Christian, 1740-1786
Sturm's reflections on the works of God; and his providence throughout all nature. Philadelphia, J. J. Woodward, 1827. 2 v. ArCH; MB; MH; MHad; MMedHi; MoSU; NPla; NcCQ; OMC; TxSani; WNaE; WNaH; WStfSF. 30735

Suffolk County Bar
Rules of the bar of the County of Suffolk, as adopted June, 1819, with the subsequent amendments. Boston, T. R. Marvin, pr., Congress Street, 1827. 27 p. DLC; MH-L; MWA; MiD-B. 30736

Suggestions for the improvement of the commerce of the state of South-Carolina. As originally published in the Charleston Courier, the 27th October, 1827. Charleston, Pr. by J. S. Burges, 1827. 12 p. DLC; NHi; ScCC. 30737

Sullivan, John Langdon, 1777-1865
A description of the American marine rail-way as constructed at New York, by Mr. John Thomas, naval architect. With explanations of its principle, and manifestations of its safety for ships of war. To which is annexed the report of the committee of inventions of the Franklin Institute, to whom the above subject was referred ... Extracted from the Franklin Journal for February, 1827. Philadelphia, Jesper Harding, pr., 1827. 16 p. M; MB; NbO; NcD; Nh-Hi; PPAmP; PPi; PU. 30738

---- Mr. Sullivan's description of a cheap, durable rail road & certain routes in the states of New-York & New Jersey. [New York? 1827?] 22 p. MH; MH-BA; MiU-T; NHi; NN; PPL. 30739

---- Prospective economy in the future public works of the state of New-York, describing the savings and effects on the Otsego, Chenango, Cayuga, Chemung and Allegany routes, by the use of the durable wooden lock, and single elevated railway. With general remarks on the consequences of the Pennsylvania improvements. ... Albany, Pr. by Packard and Van Benthuysen, 1827. 30 p. DBRE; NHi. 30740

Sullivan, Thomas Russell, 1799-1862
A reply to Mr. Robinson's review of remarks upon his sermon, "Illustrating the human and official inferiority, and supreme divinity of Christ." Keene, N.H., Pr. by J. Prentiss, 1827. 78 p. CSmH; CtSoP; MBAU; MBAt; MH; Nh; Nh-Hi; BrMus. 30741

Summary notice concerning Bible societies in general, and those of France in particular. January, 1825. Translated by Jacob Porter. Northampton [Mass.] Pr. by Hiram Ferry, 1827. 16 p. CSmH; MB; MNF; NN; NNMr; PPL; BrMus. 30742

Sumter District, South Carolina
The memorial and resolutions adopted at the anti-tariff meeting held at Sumter district, South Carolina, on Monday the 3d of September, 1827. Charleston, Pr. by A. E. Miller, 1827. 16 p. NHi; Sc; ScU. 30743

The Sunday school hymn book. See American Sunday School Union.

A supplementary report of the committee appointed to ascertain the fate of Captain William Morgan. Rochester, Pr. for the committee by Edwin Scrantom, 1827. 10 p. IaCrM; NN; PHi. 30744

The surprising adventures of Baron Munchausen. See Munchausen.

[Surr, Thomas Skinner]
Richmond; or, Scenes in the life of a Bow Street officer, drawn up from his private memoranda ... New York, Pr. by J. & J. Harper, for Collins & Hannay, [etc.] 1827. 2 v. LU; NNS. 30745

Sutherland, Joel Barlow, 1791-1861
A manual of legislative practice and order of business in deliberative bodies. Philadelphia, Jacob Frick & Co., 1827. 8, 227 p. MH; MMeT; P. 30746

Swaim, William
The case of Nancy Linton, illustrative of the efficacy of Swaim's panacea. Philadelphia, Pr. by Clark & Raser, 1827. 12 p. PPL. 30747

---- Cases of cures performed by the use of Swaim's Panacea. Philadelphia, 1827. 84, [2] p. MBCo; PPL. 30748

Swain, Joseph
Redemption: A poem in eight books; by Joseph Swain. 1st Amer. from the 5th Edinburg ed. New York, G. & C. Carvill, J. P. Haven and E. Bliss, 1827. 177 p. MB; MiD; NN; NNUT; NcAS; NjR. 30749

Sweethearts and wives. See Kenney, James.

Swett, Samuel, 1782-1866
History of Bunker Hill battle. With a plan. 3d ed. with notes. Boston, Munroe, 1827. 58, 31-34 p. CSmH; CU; CtW; ICU; IaU; MB; MBNEH; MC; MH; MHi; MNF; Me; MiU-C; MnHi; NCH; NN; Nh; PHi; PPL; RP; RPB; TxU; Vi; WHi; BrMus. 30750

Swords's pocket almanack, Christian's calendar for 1828. New-York, T. & J. Swords [1827] 48 l. MBAt; MWA; NHi; NNG; NNS; NjR; PPL. 30751

T

T. V. Cuyler's Albany directory for 1827 ... Albany, Pr. by E. & E. Hosford, 1827. 100 p. MBNEH; N. 30752

Tacitus, Cornelius
Opera, ex recensione Io. Augusti Ernesti; denuo curavit J. J. Oberlinus, cum notis selectis. Boston, Wells and Lilly, 1827. 3 v. CoD; IJI. 30753

Take your choice! or, The A. B. C. regiment on parade. New York, Pub. by D. Felt, and Boston, D. Felt & Co., 1827. 13 l. DLC. 30754

Talbot, Charles S.
Captain Morgan; or, The conspiracy unveiled. A farce in two acts ... Rochester, Pr. for the author, 1827. 22 p. ICU; MH; NN; NRHi; NRU; PPFM; PU. 30755

---- Squire Hartley, a farce in two acts. Albany, Pr. by E. & E. Hosford, for the author, 1827. 35 p. MH; MWA; PU. 30756

Tales for Ellen. See Mant, Alicia Catherine.

Tales for leisure hours. See Phillips, Jonas B.

Tales of a voyager. See Gillies, Robert Pearse.

The tales of Peter Parley ... See Goodrich, Samuel Griswold.

Tales of the fireside. By a lady of Boston. ... Boston, Hilliard, Gray, Little and Wilkins, 1827. 225 p. CSmH; DLC; IU; MB; MH; MHi; RJa; RPB. 30757

Tales of the night. See Wood, Sally Sayword.

Tales of the O'Hara family. See Banim, John.

The talisman for MDCCCXXVIII ... Elam Bliss, Broadway, New-York, [J. Seymour, pr.] 1827. 288 p. CSmH; CSt; ICU; MB; MWA; MiU; NN; NNP; NjP; PU; WHi. 30758

Tamerlane. See Poe, Edgar Allan.

Tannehill, Wilkins
Sketches of the history of literature, from the earliest period to the revival of letters in the Fifteenth Century. Nashville, John S. Simpson, 1827. 344 p. CSmH; CtW; DLC; GU; ICU; IaDa; KyHi; KyLoF; MB; MH; MWA; MiU; MoSM; MsWJ; NN; NNC; NjP; OCHP; OCl; PPL; PPiU; PU; T; TKL; TMeC; TN; TNJ; TxU; WHi; BrMus. 30759

Tanner, Henry Schenck, 1786-1858
Map of Pennsylvania and New Jersey. Philadelphia, Tanner, 1827. PP. 30760

[Tayler, Charles Benjamin] 1797-1875
Is this religion? or, A page from the book of the world. By the author of "May you like it." 1st Amer. from the London ed. Georgetown, D. C., Pub. by Jas. Thomas, 1827. James C. Dunn, pr., 1827. 240 p. CSmH; DLC; DWP; OSW. 30761

Taylor, Mrs. Ann (Martin) 1757-1830
Familiar letters between a mother and her daughter at school. By Mrs. Taylor and Jane Taylor. Boston, Pub. and sold by James Loring, 1827. 114 p. DLC; MB. 30762

---- Original hymns for Sunday

Schools ... Philadelphia, American Sunday School Union, 1827. 48 p. PPAmS. 30763

---- Original poems for infant minds. By the Taylor family. Boston, Munroe and Francis, 1827. 180 p. MNBedfHi; NNC; ScCliTO. 30764

---- Reciprocal duties of parents and children. Boston, Pr. and sold by James Loring, 1827. 144 p. CSmH; MAub. 30765

Taylor, Isaac, 1759-1829
Scenes in Africa, for the amusement and instruction of little tarry-at-home travellers ... New York, W. B. Gilley, 1827. 126 p. PU;WGr. 30766

Taylor, James Dexter
Frederick Brainerd Bridgman, a modern pioneer missionary. [Boston, American Board of Commissioners for Foreign Missions, 1827] 34 p. NNMR. 30767

Taylor, Jane, 1783-1824
The contributions of Q.Q. to a periodical work: with some pieces not before published ... New-York, G. and C. Carvill, E. Bliss, and John P. Haven; Sleight & George, prs., Jamaica, L. I., 1827. 2 v. CSmH; ICMe; MBAt; MH; NN; NNC. 30768

---- Memoirs and poetical remains of the late Jane Taylor ... Philadelphia, J. J. Woodward, 1827. 330 p. CSmH; CtSoP; ICU; PMA; RPB. 30769

[----] Rural scenes; or, A peep into the country. Black Rock, Pr. by Smith H. Salibury, 1827. 64 p. DLC. 30770

Taylor, John
A history of ten Baptist Churches, of which the author has been alternately a member: in which will be seen something of a journal of the author's life for more than fifty years ... 2d ed. Bloomfield, Nelson County, Ky., Pr. by Will H. Holmes, 1827. 304 p. KyLoF; MoSM; NRAB; OMC; ViRU. 30771

Teackle, Littleton D.
Speech of Littleton D. Teackle, esquire, in the House of Delegates on the bill to regulate sales at public auction. Annapolis, Pr. by Wm. M'Neir, 1827. 12 p. MdBJ-G. 30772

Temascaltepec Mining Company, Baltimore
Documents laid before a meeting of the stockholders of the Temascaltepec Mining Company, of Baltimore, convened by public notice, August 24, 1827. Baltimore, Pr. by Thomas Murphy [1827?] 33 p. MdHi. 30773

Temple, Samuel
Temple's arithmetick [sic] A concise introduction to practical arithmetick [sic] 10th ed. Boston, Pr. and pub. by Lincoln & Edmands, 1827. 107 p. CtHT-W; MMhHi; MiU; BrMus. 30774

Templi carmina ... See Brown, Bartholomew.

The ten commandments. Philadelphia, American Sunday School Union, 1827. 16 p. MH. 30775

Tenderton, Francis
Wellesley Grey; an interesting history ... Boston, Pub. by Crocker & Brewster, 1827. 144 p. DLC; MVh. 30776

Tennessee (State)
Acts of a local or private nature, of the state of Tennessee, passed at the extra session, which was begun and held at Nashville, in Davidson County, on

Monday, the sixteenth day of October, one thousand eight hundred and twenty-six. [Knoxville? Heiskell & Brown? 1827?] 216, lviii p. DLC; IaU-L; In-SC; Ky; MH-L; Mi-L; NNB; NNLI; Nv; OCLaw; T. 30777

---- Acts passed at the extra session of the sixteenth General Assembly of the state of Tennessee. 1826. Heiskell & Brown & A. P. Maury, prs. to the state. "Knoxville Register" Office; Pr. by Heiskell & Brown, 1827. xiv, 59, xii p. DLC; In-SC; MH-L; MdBB; Mi-L; Mo; NNB; OCLaw; OrSC; RPL; TNJ. 30778

---- Acts passed at the stated session of the seventeenth General Assembly of the state of Tennessee, 1827. Hall & Fitzgerald and Heiskell & Brown, prs. to the state. Nashville, T., Pr. at the Office of the Nashville Republican and State Gazette, 1827. vii, xii, xxvi, 98, 245, xxx p. DLC; ICHi; In-SC; Ky; L; MH-L; Mi-L; Mo; NNB; NNLI; Nv; OCLaw; RPL; T; TU. 30779

---- Journal of the House of Representatives, of the state of Tennessee, at the seventeenth General Assembly; held at Nashville, from the seventeenth of September to the fifteenth of December, in the year eighteen hundred and twenty seven. Heiskell & Brown and Hall & Fitzgerald, prs. to the state. "Knoxville Register" Office; Heiskell & Brown, prs., 1827. 676 p. T; TNJ; WHi. 30780

---- Journal of the Senate, of the state of Tennessee, at the seventeenth General Assembly; held at Nashville, from the seventeenth of September to the fifteenth of December, in the year eighteen hundred and twenty seven. Heiskell & Brown and Hall & Fitzgerald, prs. to the state. "Knoxville Register" Office; Heiskell & Brown, prs., 1827. 520 p. CtY; CtY-L; THi; TMeC. 30781

---- Reports of cases argued and determined in the Supreme Court of Tennessee. Nashville, John S. Simpson, 1827. 446 p. ABCC; CSdCL; Ct; LNBA; MBS; MdBB; PPB; PPT-L; TN. 30782

---- Resolutions of the General Assembly of Tennessee; proposing to give the election of President directly to the people ... introduced by Mr. Brown, in the Senate, and adopted eighteen in the affirmative and two in the negative, and in the House of Representatives unanimously. Nashville, Pr. at the Office of the Nashville Republican & State Gazette, 1827. 8 p. PHi; TxU. 30783

Testimonies concerning the character and ministry of Mother Ann Lee. See Shakers.

Thacher, James, 1754-1844

A military journal during the American revolutionary war, from 1775 to 1783 ... 2d ed., rev. and cor. ... Boston, Cottons & Barnard, 1827. 487 p. C; CSmH; DLC; GU; IU; MB; MH; MWA; MdBJ; MiU-C; MoSW-M; NIC; NjP; NjR; OClWHi; PHi; PPC; PPL; RPJCB; ScC; TNJ; WHi; BrMus. 30784

The thatcher's wife. See Marks, Richard.

Thayer, Mrs. Caroline Matilda (Warren) d. 1844

Religion recommended to youth in a series of letters addressed to a young lady. To which are added poems on various occasions. 5th ed. New York, Pub. by N. Bangs and J. Emory, for the Methodist Episcopal Church. Azor

Hoyt, pr., 1827. 224 p. MiMu. 30785

Therese, the orphan of Geneva. See DuCange, Victor Henri Joseph Brahain.

Thinks I to myself. See Nares, Edward.

The third class book; comprising reading lessons, for young scholars. Boston, Hilliard, Gray, Little and Wilkins, 1827. iv, 211, [1] p. DLC. 30786

Third trial of Jacob Barker, for conspiracy. New York, Pr. by Clayton and Van Norden, 1827. 255 p. CSfLaw; MH-L; MNBedf; MoU; N-L; NBLiHi. 30787

---- New-York, Clayton and Van Norden, 1827. 8, 219 p. MH-BA; PP. 30788

This day is published, No. I of the Philosophical Library, containing the first part of Ecce Homo ... The Philosophical Library is published at the office of the Correspondent, 48 Pine-Street ... The Correspondent is published every Saturday at 48 Pine-Street. New-York, April, 1827. Bdsd. MBNEH. 30789

Tholuck, August, 1799-1877

Hints on the importance of the study of the Old Testament. Trans. from the German by R. B. Patton, professor of languages, Nassau Hall. Princeton, Pr. by D. A. Borrenstein, 1827. 58 p. CtY; DLC; ICMcC; MBC; MChi; NjP; PPPrHi; PPiPT; OCH; PPL. 30790

Thompson, John Samuel, b. 1787

The pastoral care: A discourse pronounced before the First Universalist Society, in Charlestown, Mass. and a number of the neighbouring clergy, on the evening of its author's installation. July 11, 1827. [Charlestown, 1827] 10 p. M; RPB. 30791

Thompson, Otis, 1776-1859

A sermon, preached at the funeral of George Washington Peck, Esq., who departed this life March 25th, 1827. Taunton, Pr. by Danforth and Thurber, 1827. 20 p. CSmH; CtSoP; MBC; MHi; MTaHi; MWA; NN. 30792

---- A sermon preached at the funeral of Mrs. Lucy Moulton, widow of the late Deacon Chase Moulton of Rehoboth; who departed this life, March 6, 1827, in the sixty-first year of her age. Providence, James B. Yerrington, pr., 1827. 17 p. MAtt; MBAt; MBC; MHi; MWA; NhHi; RPB; BrMus. 30793

Thompson, S.

Evidences of revealed religion, on a new and original plan: being an appeal to Deists on their own principles of argument. Philadelphia, Pub. by M'Carty and Davis, 1827. 130 p. MBGCT. 30794

Thomson, Samuel, 1769-1843

New guide to health; or Botanic family physician ... 3d ed. Columbus, Horton Howard, 1827. 115, [2] p. IU-M. 30795

Thorburn, G. & Son, firm.

Catalogue of kitchen garden, herb, flower, tree, and grass seeds ... sold by G. Thorburn and Son, 67 Liberty St. ... New York, Pr. at the Coke Law Press, 1827. 101, [2] p. MeBat. 30796

Thornton, I.

Examples of piety, in the lives of Richard Baxter, John Bunyan, Isaac Watts ... New York, Pr. for Oliver D. Cooke & Co., Hartford, 1827. 128 p. NNC; OClWHi. 30797

Thornton, J.
Die Busse erklärt und aubefohlen. Ein ernstlicher Ruf an das Gewissen eines jeden Menschen ... erste amerikanische Ausgabe- aus dem Englischen übusetzt, Hrsg. von Jacob Mayer, York Co. Harrisburg, Gedruckt bey Johann S. Wiestling, 1827. 256 p. PHi; PPL. 30798

Three letters. See De Lancey, William Heathcote, bp.

Three papers on rail-roads. 1. Rail road to New Orleans for transporting the mail. 2. Timber rail-ways--economical plan. 3. General remarks on rail-roads. With plates of reference. From the American farmer, n. p. [1827] 12 p. DBRE; DIC; M; MB; MH-BA; MWA. 30799

The thunderstorm. Philadelphia, American Sunday School Union. [Stereotyped by L. Johnson, I. Ashmead & Co., prs. 1827] 8 p. NPV. 30800

Tibbits, George
Essay on the expediency and practicability of improving or creating home markets for the sale of agricultural productions and raw materials, by the introduction or growth of artizans and manufacturers. Philadelphia, Pr. by J. R. A. Skerrett, 1827. 56 p. KU; MB; MH; MWA; MdHi; MiD-B; PPL; PU-W; ScCC; ViL. 30801

---- Memoir on the expediency and practicability of proving or creating home markets for the sale of agricultural productions and raw materials, by the introduction or growth of artizans and manufactures. 3d ed. To which are added four appendices. Philadelphia, Repr. by J. R. A. Skerrett, 1827. 48 p. ICU; IU; LU; MB; MBHo; MH; MH-BA; MWA; MPiB; MiD; MiGr; N; NcD; Nh; P; PHi; PPL; WHi. 30802

Tillinghast, Joseph Leonard, 1790-1844
Address delivered before the Rhode Island Society for the Encouragement of Domestic Industry at their anniversary, October 9, 1826. Providence, Smith and Paramenter, 1827. 26 p. MHi; NN; PPAmP; RP; RPB. 30803

Time's almanac for 1828. Baltimore, Armstrong & Plaskitt; R. J. Matchett, pr. [1827] PHi. (9 l.) 30804

To the citizens of Washington County. See National Republican Party. Pennsylvania.

To the freemen of the congressional district. See Barringer, Daniel Laurens.

To the Hon. John Thompson. Sir you have caused to be recently printed, circulated and published in the remote parts of this district a handbill address to "William Creighton, junr." your competitor for Congress, couched in terms which are highly indecorous and disrespectful, and which contains statements and allegations against that gentleman's private and public character which you and every other individual know are unfounded, false and slanderous ... [Signed] Anti- Cad-e-ous. [1827] 1 p. DLC. 30805

To the Hon. Lyttleton W. Tazewell. See Wallace, Cadwallader.

To the honourable the General Assembly of N. C. See Murphey, Archibald DeBow.

To the honorable the Legislature of Maryland. See Hepburn, John M.

To the honourable the Legislature of the state of New-York ... the petition of David Hosack, William James Macneven ... New York, Dec. 31, 1827. Bdsd. NjR. 30806

Second edition, Nov. 9, 1827. To the Honourable the Senate and House of Representatives of the United States, in Congress assembled - The Memorial of the subscribers, Citizens of the City and County of Philadelphia ... 12 p. MdHi. 30807

To the members of the Methodist Episcopal Church, in the city of Baltimore, who are opposed to a reform in the government of said church. [Philadelphia? 1827] 4 p. MdHi. 30808

To the people of the first congressional district, Ky. See Trimble, David.

To the people of the state of New York. See National Republican Party, Virginia.

To the people of the United States. [1827] 7 p. PPL. 30809

To the public. [Natchez? 1827?] Bdsd. Ms-Ar. 30810

To the publick. A third inquest having been held over the body found near the mouth of Oak Orchard Creek on the 7th ult., it is proper that some of the circumstances attending the inquest should be made public ... [Rochester, 1827] Bdsd. NRHi. 30811

To the thinking few. See Carey, Mathew.

To the yeomanry of York District. The time approaches when you will be called upon to exercise the dearest right of freedom, the right of suffrage ... At the approaching election for Representative to Congress you cannot mistake your true interest ... The ticket which bears the name of the Hon. Mark Dennett, has on this account, an advantage over the other ... A farmer. August, 1827. Bdsd. MeHi. 30812

To Thomas Scott. See Wallace, Cadwallader.

Todd, John, 1800-1873
Religious teachers tested: A sermon, delivered at the dedication of the Union meeting house, in Groton, Massachusetts, January 3, 1827 ... Published by the Union Church. Cambridge, Hilliard & Brown, Pr. by Hilliard, Metcalf & Co., 1827. 46 p. CBPac; DLC; ICN; M; MA; MB; MBAU; MBC; MH-AH; MHi; MNF; MWA; NN; NNUT; NcU; OClWHi; OO; RPB; BrMus. 30813

Todd, Lewis C.
An abridgement of English grammar: or A plain development of etymology and syntax ... 2d ed., enl. and imp. Fredonia [N. Y.] Pub. by Oliver Spafford; Hull and Snow, prs., 1827. 126 p. NNC. 30814

The token, a Christmas and New Year's present. Boston, S. G. Goodrich, [etc., Isaac R. Butts & Co., prs.] 1828 [i. e. 1827] 368 p. DLC; MB; MWA; NNC. 30815

A token for children. See Janeway, James.

Tommy Duff. New York, J. B. Jansen, 1827. [8] p. RPB. 30816

[Tonna, Mrs. Charlotte Elizabeth (Browne) Phelen] 1790-1846
Allen M'Leod, the Highland soldier, by Charlotte Elizabeth [pseud] Boston, Pub. by Crocker & Brewster, 1827. 107 p.

IObB; RNR. 30817

Torrey, John, 1796-1873
Account of a collection of plants from the Rocky Mountains and adjacent countries. New York, Pr. by J. Seymour, 1827. [160]-254 p., 3 plates. (From the Annals of the Lyceum of Natural History). AzFMu; CSmH; NNC; NNNBG; PPL. 30818

Town & country almanac for 1828. By Joseph Cramer. Philadelphia, D. & S. Neall [1827] 18 l. MWA; PP. 30819

---- ---- Philadelphia, D. & S. Neall [1827] 18 l. (Variant of 30819) CtY; MWA; PDoBHi; PHi. 30820

---- By Nathan Bassett. Baltimore, Cushing & Jewett; Wooddy, pr., [1827] 18 l. MdBE. 30821

Townsend, G.
Useful tables of scripture... including valuable harmonies of the scriptures. Boston, Pub. by Hilliard, Gray, Little ... Pr. at Treadwell's Power Press, 1827. 100 p. MB; MoSU. 30822

Tracts for the people; no. 1; the bargain and the sale; slander exposed [Mr. Buchanan's conduct toward Mr. Clay] Philadelphia, Daily News Office [1827] 12 p. CLU. 30823

Tracts, moral, historical, didactic and amusing: original and selected. Published in numbers convenient for common use and preservation. Cincinnati, Pr. at the office of the Western Tiller, 1827. 16 p. OCHP. 30824

Transylvania University. Medical Department
At a public commencement held in the chapel of the University, March 16th, 1827, the following gentlemen, alumni of the institution, received the degree of Doctor of Medicine. Lexington, Ky., March 16, 1827. 4 p. DLC; PU. 30825

Trcziyulny, Charles
Report of Charles Trcziyulny, appointed to explore the river Susquehanna, in pursuance of an act of the General Assembly, with a view to its improvement, from the New York to the Maryland line. Pr. for the Senate. Harrisburg, Cameron & Krause, 1827. 19 p. 1 fold. tab. MdHi; P; PPAmP. 30826

A treatise on the diseases most prevalent in the United States, with directions for medicine chests, designed for the use of families ... Philadelphia, Pr. by J. R. A. Skerrett, 1827. iv, 7-36 p. NNNAM. 30827

A treatise on the nature and effects of heat, light, electricity, and magnetism, as being only different developments of one element. Cambridge, Pub. by Hilliard and Brown, 1827. [4], 91 p. MWA; NNNAM; NjR; PPAmP. 30828

Trenck, Frederick, freiherr von den, 1726-1794
The life of Baron Frederick Trenck ... trans. from the German, by T. Holcroft. Philadelphia, F. Scott, 1827. 108 p. NjP. 30829

The trial, conviction and sentence of Jesse Strang, for the murder of John Whipple, at Albany, on the 7th of May, 1827. Containing all the evidence given on the very interesting trial, with the trial and acquittal of Mrs. Whipple, as an accomplice to the murder of her husband ... New York, Pub. by E. M. Murden, 1827. 40 p. DLC; MH-L; MWA; MoU; NTSC; NjR. 30830

Trial of Elsie D. Whipple, charged with being accessary to the murder of her husband, John Whipple, at a special court of Oyer and Terminer holden in Albany, July, 1827. [Albany? 1827] 11 p. NN. 30831

Trial of Jacob Barker, Thomas Vermilya, and Matthew L. Davis, for alleged conspiracy. Testimony as reported by Hugh Maxwell esq., district attorney. New York, Pr. at the Coke-Law press, Gould, pr., 1827. 328, iv p. C; Ct; DLC; ICLaw; MB; MH-BA; MSaEC; MiGr; NHi; NIC; NN; NNS. 30832

Trial of James Lackey, Isaac Evertson, Chauncey H. Coe, Holloway Howard, Hiram Hubbard, John Butterfield, James Ganson, Asa Knowlton, Harris Seymour, Henry Howard, Moses Roberts, for kidnapping Capt. William Morgan. At Ontario general session held at Canandaigua, Ontario, Aug. 22, 1827. New York, Pr. for pub., 1827. 24 p. DLC; IaCrM; MB; MH-L; MHi; MoU; N-L; NRU; PHi. 30833

Trial of Jesse Strang, for the murder of John Whipple, at a special court of oyer and terminer, holden in Albany in July, 1827. Albany, Pr. by D. M'Glashan, 1827. 35 p. CSfLaw; MBAt; MH-L; N-L; NCH; NN; NRAL; PP; PPB; PPL. 30834

The trial of Joshua Randell, by the New-England annual Conference of the Methodist Episcopal Church, on a charge of holding and disseminating doctrines which are contrary to our articles of religion. Hallowell, Pr. by Glazier & Co., No. 1, Kennebec Row, 1827. 18 p. MB; MeLB. 30835

Trial of Levi Kelley, for the murder of Abraham Spaford, on the evening of the 3d Sept., 1827. Before a special court of Oyer and Terminer, held at the court-house in the county of Otsego, in pursuance of a Commission for that purpose, on the 21st of November, 1827. Cooperstown, Pr. and sold at the office of the Journal, and at the office of the Watch-Tower, sold also by H. & E. Phinney, 1827. 22, [1] p. CSmH; N-L; NN; NUtHi. 30836

Trials of John Duncan White, alias Chas. Marchant, and Winslow, Curtis, alias Sylvester Colson, for murder on the high seas of Edward Selfredge and Thos. P. Jenkins, Capt. & mate of the schooner "Fairy" of Boston, held at Boston, Oct., 1826. Boston, Dutton & Wentworth, 1827. 176 p. C; ICLaw; In-SC; MB; MH; MNBedf; MdBB; MeHi; N-L; NIC-L; NjP; PP; PPL; RPL; BrMus. 30837

The trials of Margaret Lyndsay. See Wilson, John.

[Trimble, David]
To the people of the first congressional district, Ky. [Washington, Feb. 28th, 1827] 17 p. PPL; WStfSF. 30838

Trimmer, Mrs. Sarah
The robins; or Fabulous histories designed for the instruction of children respecting their treatment of animals. Boston, Munroe & Francis, 1827. 228 p. ScCliTO; BrMus. 30839

Trinity College. See Washington College Athenaeum.

Tripler, Charles Stuart, 1806-1866
Remarks on delirium tremens ... New-York, Pr. by J. Seymour, 1827. 22 p. DLC; NNNAM. 30840

Truair, John
An address delivered at Northampton, June 25, A. L. 5827 before Jerusalem Lodge on the anniversary festival of St. John the Baptist ... Northampton, Pr. by H. Ferry & Co., 1827. 15 p. MNF; N; NNFM. 30841

---- Sacred music; an address delivered at Westhampton, May 23, 1827. Northampton, Pr. by H. Ferry & Co., 1827. 14 p. MNF. 30842

True Reformed Dutch Church in the U. S. A.
The acts and proceedings of the general synod of the True Reformed Dutch Church, in the United States of America, at Wynant's and Poosten Kill, June 1827. New York, Pr. by Charles M'Devitt, 1827. 19 p. IaDuU-Sem; N; PPPrHi. 30843

[Trumbull, John] 1756-1843
Description of the four pictures, from subjects of the revolution, painted by order of the government of the United States, and now placed in the rotunda of the Capitol. 1827. New York, Pr. by W. A. Mercein, 1827. 25 p. DLC; ICN; MHi; NIC; NN; Nh; PPL; BrMus. 30844

---- Letters proposing a plan for the permanent encouragement of the fine arts, by the national government, addressed to the president of the United States. New York, Pr. by William Davis, Jr. 1827. 8 p. CtHi; KyLx; MWA; N; NBLiHi; NN; NNC; PPL; PPPM. 30845

Truth is no slander. See Clement, Samuel.

[Tucker, George] 1775-1861
A voyage to the moon: with some account of the manners and customs, science and philosophy, of the people of Morosofia, and other lunarians. By Joseph Atterley [pseud.] ... New York, E. Bliss, 1827. 264 p. CSmH; CtY; DLC; MB; MH; MWA; MnU; NGH; NNC; NNS; NcD; OMC; RPB. 30846

Tuckerman, Joseph
A letter on the principles of the missionary enterprise. 2d ed. Pr. for the American Unitarian Association. Boston, 1827. 40 p. GAGTh; MCon; MMeT-Hi; MNoanNP; N. 30847

---- Mr. Tuckerman's fourth quarterly, or First annual report addressed to the American Unitarian Association. Boston, Bowles and Dearborn, Press of I. R. Butts and Co., 1827. 15 p. DLC; NjR; PPL. 30848

---- Mr. Tuckerman's third quarterly report, addressed to the American Unitarian Association. Boston, Bowles and Dearborn, Isaac R. Butts & Co., prs., 1827. 16 p. PPL. 30849

Tufts, George A.
Address delivered before the Worcester Agricultural Society, October 12, 1825: being their seventh anniversary cattle show and exhibition of manufactures. Worcester, Charles Griffin, pr., 1827. [3], 16 p. DLC; M; MB; MH; MH-BA; MHi; MWA; MWH; MiD-B; NHi; OClWHi; RPB; BrMus. 30850

The tulip. See Selfridge, Thomas Oliver.

[Turnbull, Robert James] 1775-1833
The crisis: or, Essays on the usurpations of the federal government. By Brutus [pseud.] Charleston, Pr. by A. E. Miller, 1827. 166 p. A-Ar; AU; CSmH; DLC; GU-De; ICU; LU; MBAt; MH; NN;

NcD; NdU; PHi; PPL; PPAmP; RPB; ScC; ScHi; ScU; TxU; Vi. 30851

Turner, Edward
The substance of a discourse, delivered in the First Universalist meeting-house, in Portsmouth ... Portsmouth, N. H., Pr. by R. Foster, 1827. 24 p. NjR. 30852

The twinkling star. By the author of The shepherd and his flock... American Sunday School Union, Philadelphia, 1827. 35 p. MHa. 30853

The two friends; or Religion the best guide for youth. Revised by the committee of publication. Philadelphia, American Sunday School Union, 1827. 72 p. PP; PPPM. 30854

The two lambs. See Cameron, Mrs. Lucy Lyttleton (Butt).

Tyler, B. M.
Arithmetick, theoretically and practically illustrated. Middletown, Conn., E. & H. Clark, 1827. 300 p. CtHT-W; CtHi; DLC; PU. 30855

Tyler, Bennet, 1783-1858
A sermon, preached at Woodstock, Vt., November 28, 1827, at the ordination of the Rev. John Richards, as Pastor of the Congregational Church and Society in that place. Woodstock, Pr. by Rufus Colton, 1827. 17 p. GDC; ICN; InCW; MBC; MWA; NhHi; RPB; VtMiM. 30856

Tyson, Job Roberts, 1803-1858
Essay on the penal law of Pennsylvania. Philadelphia, Pub. by the Law Academy, Mifflin & Parry, prs., 1827. 69 p. DLC; MH-L; MWA; MiD-B; OCLaw; PHC; PHi; PPAmP; PPL. 30857

Tyson, John Shoemaker, 1797-1864
Speech delivered by John S. Tyson, in Concert Hall, Commerce street, in the city of Baltimore, in presence of a large concourse of the friends of the administration, on the ushering in of a new press called "The Marylander," devoted to the cause of the administration. [Baltimore, 1827] 8 p. DLC. 30858

Tytler, Alexander Fraser. See Woodhouslee, Alexander Fraser Tytler, lord.

U

Uncle Sam's almanack for 1828. By Joseph Cramer. Philadelphia, Griggs & Dickinson [1827] 18 l. MWA. 30859

---- ---- Philadelphia, Griggs & Dickinson, for Denny & Walker [1827] 18 l. DLC; MWA; PHi; WHi. 30860

Underhill, Daniel C.
Tables of arithmetic made easy. First stereotype from the 5th imp. ed. New-York, Pr. and sold by Mahlon Day, 1827. Stereotyped by James Conner, New York. 23 p. NNC. 30861

Uniacke, Crofton
A letter to the lord chancellor, on the necessity and practicability of forming a code of the laws of England: to which is annexed the new bankrupt law ... Boston, Hilliard, Gray, Little, and Wilkins, 1827. 52 p. CSmH; DLC; ICN; MBC; MH-L; MMeT; MWCL; N; NcD; Nh; OCLaw; BrMus. 30862

Union Canal Company
Annual report of the president and managers of the Union Canal Company of Pennsylvania to the stockholders. Nov. 20, 1827. Philadelphia, Pr. by Lydia R. Bailey, 1827. 19 p. NRom. 30863

Union College
Catalogue of the senior class ... 1826-27 [Schenectady, 1827] NSchU (According to Sabin 9774 note, but not now found in that library.) 30864

Union Society of Queen Ann's County
An address from the Union Society of Queen Ann's County, to the members of the Methodist Episcopal Church throughout the United States. Centreville, (E. S.) Md. Pr. and pub. at the office of the Times, 1827. 12 p. MdHi. 30865

---- Reply to the address of the male members of the Methodist Church in Baltimore. Centreville, (E. S.) Md., Pr. by John B. Spencer, at the Times Newspaper Office, 1827. 8 p. MdBP; MdHi. 30866

The Union spelling and reading book. See American Sunday School Union.

A Unitarian, pseud. See Upham, Charles Wentworth.

Unitarian Association of Philadelphia
Constitution of the Unitarian Association of Philadelphia, Auxiliary to the American Unitarian Association. Philadelphia, James Kay, Jun., pr., 1827. 8 p. ICMe. 30867

Unitarian Christians in Philadelphia
Charter of the First Congregational Society of the Unitarian Christians ... Philadelphia, James Kay, Jun., pr., 1827. 36 p. PHi. 30868

Unitarianism vindicated ... See Walker, James.

United States

Abigail Appleton. February 3, 1827. Mr. Bartlett, from the Committee on Naval Affairs, to which was referred the petition of Abigail Appleton, made the following report: [Washington, 1827] 2 p. (Rep. No. 69) DLC; NjP. 30869

---- Abstract of American seamen - 1826. Letter from the Secretary of State, transmitting an abstract of American seamen in the U. States, for the year 1826. Feb. 21, 1827. Read, and laid upon the table. Washington, Gales & Seaton, 1827. 19 p. (Doc. No. 128) DLC; NjP. 30870

---- An account of the receipts and expenditures of the United States for the year 1826. Washington, E. De Kraft, pr., 1827. PPL. 30871

---- An act authorizing certain persons to be placed on the Pension List of Revolutionary Pensioners. Feb. 5, 1827. [Washington, 1827] 3 p. (H. R. 315) DNA. 30872

---- An act authorizing the Secretary of the Treasury to exchange a stock of five per cent to the amount of sixteen millions of dollars, for certain stocks of six per cent, and to borrow a sum equal to any deficiency in the said amount authorized to be exchanged. Feb. 14, 1827. [Washington, 1827] 5 p. (H. R. 354) DNA. 30873

---- An act concerning Invalid Pensioners. Feb. 5, 1827. [Washington, 1827] 1 p. (H. R. 314) DNA. 30874

---- An act concerning lands in the Territories of the United States, belonging to non-residents. Feb. 5, 1827. [Washington, 1827] 1 p. (H. R. 300) DNA. 30875

---- An act for altering the times of holding the District Court of the United States for the Eastern District of Virginia, holden at Richmond. January 22, 1827. [Washington, 1827] 1 p. (H. R. 381) DNA. 30876

---- An act for increasing the compensation of the Marshal for the Eastern District of Virginia. January 22, 1827. Received. [Washington, 1827] 1 p. (H. R. 382) DNA. 30877

---- An act for the alteration of the acts imposing duties on imports. Feb. 12, 1827. [Washington, 1827] 1 p. (H. R. 362) DNA. 30878

---- An act for the preservation and repair of the Cumberland Road. Feb. 26, 1827. Received. [Washington, 1827] 1 p. (H. R. 290) DNA. 30879

---- An act for the relief of Isaac Delawder. Jan. 5, 1827. Received. [Washington, 1827] 1 p. (H. R. 335) DNA. 30880

---- An act for the relief of Marigny D'Auterive. Feb. 27, 1827. [Washington, 1827] 1 p. (H. R. 166) DNA. 30881

---- An act for the relief of Thomas Collins. Feb. 5, 1827. [Washington, 1827] 1 p. (H. R. 346) DNA. 30882

---- An act for the relief of William Thompson. Dec. 31, 1827. Received. [Washington, 1827] 1 p. (H. R. 6) DNA. 30883

---- An act making an appropriation for the purchase of books for the Library of Congress. Feb. 24, 1827. Received. [Washington, 1827] 1 p. (H. R. 440) DNA. 30884

---- An act making appropriations for certain fortifications of the United States, for the year eighteen hundred and twenty-seven. Feb. 23, 1827. Received. [Washington, 1827] 1 p. (H. R. 385) DNA. 30885

---- An act making appropriations for the erection and completion of certain barracks, store-houses, and hospitals, and for other purposes. Feb. 24, 1827. Received. [Washington, 1827] 1 p. (H. R. 394) DNA. 30886

---- An act making appropriations for the Indian Department for the year one thousand eight hundred and twenty-seven. Feb. 28, 1827. Received. [Washington, 1827] 1 p. (H. R. 368) DNA. 30887

---- An act making appropriations for the military service of the United States, for the year one thousand eight hundred and twenty-seven. Feb. 21, 1827. Received. [Washington, 1827] 1 p. (H. R. 372) DNA. 30888

---- An act making appropriations for the public buildings, and other objects. Feb. 24, 1827. Received. [Washington, 1827] 1 p. (H. R. 428) DNA. 30889

---- An act making appropriations for the support of government for the year one thousand eight hundred and twenty-seven. Feb. 16, 1827. [Washington, 1827] 17 p. (H. R. 367) DNA. 30890

---- An act making appropriations for the support of the Navy of the United States, for the year eighteen hundred and twenty-seven. Feb. 23, 1827. [Washington, 1827] 5 p. (H. R. 413) DNA. 30891

---- An act to alter the time of sitting of the courts of the sixth circuit required to be holden at Charleston, South Carolina, and Milledgeville, Georgia. Feb. 28, 1827. [Washington, 1827] 1 p. (H. R. 408) DNA. 30892

---- An act to amend an act entitled "An act for the better regulation of the Ordnance Department," approved Feb. 8, 1815. Feb. 5, 1827. [Washington, 1827] 1 p. (H. R. 399) DNA. 30893

---- An act to amend the act of incorporation of the Chesapeake and Ohio Canal Company. Feb. 8, 1827. Referred to the Committee of the Whole House to which is committed the "bill authorizing a subscription to the stock of the Chesapeake and Ohio Canal Company." Washington, Pr. by Gales & Seaton, 1827. 3 p. (Doc. No. 85) DLC; NjP. 30894

---- An act to authorize the building of lighthouses and beacons, and for other purposes. Feb. 28, 1827. [Washington, 1827] 5 p. (H. R. 403) DNA. 30895

---- An act to authorize the improving of certain harbors, the building of piers, and for other purposes. Feb. 28, 1827. [Washington, 1827] 3 p. (H. R. 438) DNA. 30896

---- An act to authorize the laying out and opening of certain roads in the Territory of Michigan. Jan. 2, 1827. [Washington, 1827] 1 p. (H. R. 293) DNA. 30897

---- An act to authorize the President of the United States to cause the reserved Salt Springs in the State of Missouri to be exposed to public sale. Jan. 8, 1827. Pr. by order of the House of Representatives. [Washington, 1827] 1 p. (S. 6) DNA. 30898

---- An act to authorize the Secretary of the Treasury to examine and confirm certain titles and claims to land in the Territory of Michigan. Feb. 27, 1827. [Washington, 1827] 2 p. (H. R. 100) DNA. 30899

---- An act to change the port of entry in the District of Pearl River, from Pearlington to Shieldsborough. Jan. 22, 1827. Received. [Washington, 1827] 1 p. (H. R. 244) DNA. 30900

---- An act to establish sundry post roads. Feb. 22, 1827. [Washington, 1827] 21 p. (H. R. 434) DNA. 30901

---- An act to make provision for the settlement of sundry claims under the Florida Treaty. Feb. 21, 1827. [Washington, 1827] 2 p. (H. R. 223) DNA. 30902

---- An act to provide for the completion of the road from a point opposite to Memphis, in the state of Tennessee, to Little Rock, in the Territory of Arkansas. Jan. 2, 1827. [Washington, 1827] 1 p. (H. R. 299) DNA. 30903

---- An act to provide for the confirmation and settlement of private land claims in East Florida, and for other purposes. Jan. 2, 1827. [Washington, 1827] 7 p. (H. R. 308) DNA. 30904

---- An act to provide for the confirmation and settlement of private land claims in East Florida, and for other purposes. Jan. 11, 1827. [Washington, 1827] 9 p. (H. R. 308 Repr.) DNA. 30905

---- An act to refund certain duties paid upon vessels belonging to citizens of Hamburg, and their er cargoes. Feb. 15, 1827. [Washington, 1827] 1 p. (H. R. 225) DNA. 30906

---- An act to regulate the commercial intercourse between the United States and the Colonies of Great Britain. Feb. 28, 1827. [Washington, 1827] 3 p. (S. 66) DNA. 30907

---- An act to secure the more effectual collection of the fees of the clerk of the district court for the District of Columbia, and of the circuit court of the said District, for the County of Alexandria. Jan. 27, 1827. Received. [Washington, 1827] 3 p. (H. R. 319) DNA. 30908

---- Alexander Hamilton's report on the subject of manufactures, made in his capacity of Secretary of the Treasury, on the fifth of December, 1791. 6th ed. To which are prefixed, two prefaces by the editor. Philadelphia, Pr. by W. Brown, 1827. 80 p. CSmH; Ct; DLC; MB; MH; OClWHi; PHi; PPL; RPJCB. 30909

---- Amend the Constitution. Resolutions of the Legislature of the state of Ohio upon the subject of amending the Constitution in relation to the election of President of the United States. February 20, 1827. Read, and laid upon the table. Washington, Pr. by Gales & Seaton, 1827. 4 p. (Doc. No. 109) DLC; NjP. 30910

---- Amendment intended to be proposed by Mr. Cambreleng, in Committee of the Whole, to the Bill for the alteration of the acts imposing duties on imports. January 23, 1827. [Washington, 1827] 1 p. (H. R. 362) DNA. 30911

---- Amendment intended to be proposed by Mr. Strong, to that intended to be proposed by Mr. Cambreleng. January 25, 1827. [Washington, 1827] 1 p. (H. R. 362) DNA. 30912

---- Amendment proposed by Mr. Verplanck, in Committee of the Whole on the state of the Union, to the bill to authorize the Secretary of the Treasury to exchange a stock, bearing an interest of five per cent. to the amount of sixteen millions of dollars, for certain stocks of six per cent. and to borrow a sum equal to any deficiency in the said amount authorized to be exchanged. January 29, 1827. [Washington, 1827] 3 p. (H. R. 354) DNA. 30913

---- American water rotted hemp. Letter from the Secretary of the Navy, transmitting the information required by a resolution of the House of Representatives, of 2d March, 1827, in relation to experiments on American water rotted hemp. Dec. 24, 1827. Referred to the Committee on Manufactures. Washington, Pr. by Gales & Seaton, 1827. 8 p. (Doc. No. 22) DLC; NjR. 30914

---- Andrew Turnbull's heirs. Dec. 20, 1827. Read, and laid upon the table. Mr. Shepperd, from the Committee on Private Land Claims, to which was referred the petition of the heirs and representatives of John Turnbull, made the following report: Washington, Gales & Seaton, 1827. 3 p. (Rep. No. 23) DLC; NjR. 30915

---- Andrew Westbrook. January 26, 1827. Mr. Buckner, from the Committee on Private Land Claims, to which was referred the petition of Andrew Westbrook, made the following report: [Washington, 1827] 2 p. (Rep. No. 58) DLC; NjP. 30916

---- ---- Dec. 19, 1827. Mr. Buckner, from the Committee on Private Land Claims, to which was referred the petition of Andrew Westbrook; made the following report: Washington, Gales & Seaton, 1827. 2 p. (Rep. No. 20) DLC; NjR. 30917

---- Annual report of the Commissioners of the Sinking Fund. February 7, 1827. Read, and laid upon the table. Washington, Pr. by Gales & Seaton, 1827. 18 p. (Doc. No. 84) DLC; NjP. 30918

---- Appropriation for the capitol. Estimate of money necessary for continuing the work upon the capitol, for the year 1827. Jan. 15, 1827. Laid before the H. R. and ordered to be printed. Washington, Gales & Seaton, 1827. 4 p. (Doc. No. 51) DLC; NjP. 30919

---- Appropriations - Second session, Nineteenth Congress. Statement of appropriations made during the second session of the Nineteenth Congress. Prepared in compliance with a resolution of the House of Representatives of the United States, of the 3d Mar., 1827. Mar. 3, 1827. Pr. by order of the House of Representatives. Washington, Gales & Seaton, 1827. 23 p. (Doc. No. 126) DLC; NjP. 30920

---- Archibald W. Hamilton. Feb. 2, 1827. Mr. Whittlesy, from the Committee of Claims, to which was referred the petition of Archibald W. Hamilton, made the following report: [Washington, 1827] 6 p. (Rep. No. 66) DLC; NjP. 30921

---- Arsenal at Watervliet. January 3, 1827. Mr. Ward, from the Committee on Military Affairs, to which had been referred the subject of purchasing additional land for the Arsenal at Watervliet, New York, made the following report: [Washington, 1827] 2 p. (Rep. No. 31) DLC; NjP. 30922

---- Asa Bulkley. Dec. 18, 1827. Read, and laid upon the table. Mr. McDuffie, from the Committee of Ways and Means, to which was referred the petition of Asa Bulkley and Luke Dewing, made the following report: Washington, Gales & Seaton, 1827. 1 p. (Rep. No. 14) DLC; NjR. 30923

---- Balances - Collectors of the customs and receivers of the land offices. Letter from the Comptroller of the Treasury, transmitting a list of balances on the books of the register, which appear to have remained unsettled by the collectors of the customs and others, for more than three years prior to 30th Sept. last, and a similar list in the case of receivers of public moneys for the sale of public lands. Jan. 23, 1827. Read, and laid upon the table. Washington, Gales & Seaton, 1827. 3 p., 5 bdsds. (Doc. No. 138) DLC; NjP. 30924

---- Balances on books of receipts and expenditures. Letter from the Comptroller of the Treasury, transmitting a report, by the register of the Treasury, of the balances on the books of receipts and expenditures, which appear to have remained due and unsettled more than three years prior to Sept. 30, 1826. Dec. 8, 1826. Read, and laid on the table. Washington, Gales & Seaton, 1827. 3 p., 7 bdsds. (Doc. No. 137) DLC; NjP. 30925

---- Balances on the books of fourth auditor. Letter from the Comptroller of the Treasury, transmitting an abstract of the balances on the books of the fourth auditor, which appear to have remained unsettled more than three years prior to 30th Sept. last. Feb. 3, 1827. Read, and laid upon the table. Washington, Gales & Seaton, 1827. 4 p., 15 bdsds. (Doc. No. 135) DLC; NjP. 30926

---- Balances on the books of fourth auditor. Letter from the Comptroller of the Treasury, transmitting an abstract of balances on the books of the fourth auditor of the Treasury, which have remained due and unsettled more than three years, prior to 30th Sept. last. Together with a list of officers who have failed to render their accounts according to law. Dec. 27, 1827. Read, and laid upon the table. Washington, Gales & Seaton, 1827. 4 p., 16 bdsds. (Doc. No. 25) DLC; NjR. 30927

---- Bank of Chilicothe. Jan. 19, 1827. Mr. Whittlesey, from the Committee of Claims, to whom was referred the petition of the president, directors and company of the Bank of Chilicothe, made the following report: [Washington, 1827] 3 p. (Rep. No. 48) DLC; NjP. 30928

---- Banks in the District of Columbia. Letter from the Secretary of the Treasury transmitting copies of the returns of the incorporated banks in the District of Columbia of the state of their affairs to the close of the year 1826. Feb. 24, 1827. Read, and laid upon the table. Washington, Pr. by Gales & Seaton, 1827. 13 p. (Doc. No. 118) DLC; NjP. 30929

---- Barracks, store houses, hospitals, &c. Letter from the Secretary of War, transmitting, to the chairman of the Military Committee, a report of the Quartermaster General, upon the subject of barracks, storehouses, hospitals, &c. Jan. 25, 1827. Laid before the House, by Chairman of the Military Committe, and ordered to be printed. Washington, Gales & Seaton, 1827. 8 p. (Doc. No. 61) DLC; NjP. 30930

---- A bill amendatory of the act regulating the Post Office Department. Jan. 30, 1827. Reported by the Committee on the Post Office and Post Roads. [Washington, 1827] 3 p. (H. R. 409) DNA. 30931

---- A bill authorizing a register to be issued for the brig Liberator, of Bath. Dec. 17, 1827. Reported by the Committee on Commerce. [Washington, 1827] 1 p. (H. R. 8) DNA. 30932

---- A bill authorizing a subscription to the stock of the Chesapeake and Ohio Canal Company. Jan. 30, 1827. Reported by the Committee on Roads and Canals. [Washington, 1827] 3 p. (H. R. 404) DNA. 30933

---- A bill authorizing certain persons to be placed on the list of Revolutionary pensioners. February 14, 1827. [Washington, 1827] 3 p. (H. R. 436) DNA. 30934

---- A bill authorizing paymasters to employ citizens to aid them in the discharge of their duties, in certain cases. January 4, 1827. Reported by the Committee on Military Affairs. [Washington, 1827] 1 p. (H. R. 342) DNA. 30935

---- A bill authorizing the Secretary of the Treasury to exchange a stock, of five per cent. to the amount of sixteen millions of dollars, for certain stocks of six per cent., and to borrow a sum equal to any deficiency in the said amount authorized to be exchanged. Jan. 9, 1827. Reported by the Committee of Ways and Means. [Washington, 1827] 1 p. (H. R. 354) DNA. 30936

---- A bill authorizing the completion and repair of certain roads in the Territory of Florida, and for other purposes. Jan. 4, 1827, Mr. Hendricks reported the following bill from the Select Committee on Roads and Canals; which was read and passed to a second reading. [Washington, 1827] 1 p. (S. 38) DNA. 30937

---- A bill authorizing the establishment of an arsenal in the town of Augusta, in Maine. January 16, 1827. Mr. Harrison, from the Committee on Military Affairs, reported the following bill; which was read and passed to a second reading: [Washington, 1827] 1 p. (S. 57) DNA. 30938

---- A bill authorizing the payment of interest to the state of Pennsylvania. Jan. 3, 1827. Agreeably to notice given, Mr. Marks asked and obtained leave to bring in the following bill; which was read twice, and referred to the Committee of Claims: [Washington, 1827] 1 p. (S. 36) DNA. 30939

---- A bill concerning appointments in the staff of the army. Reported by the Committee on Military Affairs. Feb. 22, 1826. Read twice, and committed to a Committee of the Whole House to-morrow. Dec. 18, 1826. Recommitted to the Committee on Military Affairs. Jan. 11, 1827. Reported with an amendment, and committed to a Committee of the Whole House to-morrow. [Washington, 1827] 1 p. (H. R. 117) DNA. 30940

---- A bill concerning free persons of color in the County of Washington, in the District of Columbia, and for other purposes. Jan. 11, 1827. Reported by the Committee for the District of Columbia. [Washington, 1827] 1 p. (H. R. 369) DNA. 30941

---- A bill concerning invalid pensioners, and the widows and children of certain officers and soldiers who died in the service of their country. Feb. 13, 1827. Reported by the Committee on Military Pensions. [Washington, 1827] 1 p. (H. R. 437) DNA. 30942

---- A bill concerning the entry of vessels at the port of Fairfield, in Connecticut. Feb. 6, 1827. Reported by the Committee on Commerce. [Washington, 1827] 1 p. (H. R. 423) DNA. 30943

---- A bill concerning the location of land reserved for the use of a seminary of learning in the state of Louisiana. Jan. 31, 1827. Reported by the Committee on the Public Lands. [Washington, 1827] 3 p. (H. R. 411) DNA. 30944

---- A bill concerning the government and discipline of the penitentiary in the District of Columbia. Jan. 12, 1827. Reported by the Committee for the District of Columbia. [Washington, 1827] 11 p. (H. R. 373) DNA. 30945

---- A bill declaring the assent of Congress to an act of the legislature of the state of Alabama. Feb. 13, 1827. Reported by the Committee on the Judiciary. [Washington, 1827] 1 p. (H. R. 432) DNA. 30946

---- A bill declaring the assent

of Congress to an act of the State of Alabama. Dec. 10, 1827. [Washington, 1827] 1 p. (S. 3) DNA. 30947

---- A bill directing the payment of the Georgia militia claims, for services rendered during the years one thousand seven hundred and ninety-two, three, and four. Jan. 12, 1827. [Washington, 1827] 1 p. (S. 51. N 2) DNA. 30948

---- A bill establishing a port of delivery at the town of Marshfield, in the District of Plymouth, and a port of delivery at Rhinebeck Landing, in the District of New York. Feb. 8, 1827. Reported by the Committee on Commerce. [Washington, 1827] 1 p. (H. R. 429) DNA. 30949

---- A bill explanatory of an act, entitled, "An act to reduce and fix the military peace establishment of the United States," passed March 2d, 1821. Feb. 6, 1827. [Washington, 1827] 1 p. (S. 87) DNA. 30950

---- A bill explanatory of an act, entitled "An act to reduce and fix the military peace establishment of the United States," passed March 2d, 1821. Dec. 11, 1827. [Washington, 1827] 1 p. (S. 4) DNA. 30951

---- A bill explanatory of, and supplementary to, an act, entitled "An act to reduce and fix the military peace establishment of the United States," passed second of March, eighteen hundred and twenty-one. Jan. 11, 1827. Reported by the Committee on Military Affairs. [Washington, 1827] 1 p. (H. R. 370) DNA. 30952

---- A bill extending the term within which merchandise may be exported with the benefit of drawback. Dec. 31, 1827. [Washington, 1827.] 1 p. (H. R. 28) DNA. 30953

---- A bill fixing the compensation of the surgeons and assistant surgeons in the Army. Jan. 12, 1827. Reported by the Committee on Military Affairs. [Washington, 1827] 1 p. (H. R. 374) DNA. 30954

---- A bill fixing the ratio of representation after the third day of March, eighteen hundred and thirty-three. Jan. 4, 1827. Reported by a Select Committee. [Washington, 1827] 1 p. (H. R. 341) DNA. 30955

---- A bill fixing the ratio of representation, after the third day of March, one thousand eight hundred and thirty-three. Dec. 12, 1827. [Washington, 1827] 1 p. (H. R. 1) DNA. 30956

---- A bill for improving the inland navigation between the St. Mary's River and the entrance of the River St. John's, in Florida. Feb. 3, 1827. [Washington, 1827] 1 p. (H. R. 421) DNA. 30957

---- A bill for improving the navigation of the Ohio River. Feb. 6, 1827. [Washington, 1827] 1 p. (S. 89) DNA. 30958

---- A bill for making a military road to facilitate the access to the military post of West Point, in the state of New York. Feb. 6, 1827. Reported by the Committee on Military Affairs. [Washington, 1827] 1 p. (H. R. 425) DNA. 30959

---- A bill for regulating processes in the courts of the United States, in States admitted into the Union since the twenty-ninth of September, one thousand seven hundred and eighty-nine. Feb. 2,

1827. [Washington, 1827] 1 p. (S. 81) DNA. 30960

---- ---- Dec. 13, 1827. [Washington, 1827] 3 p. (S. 11) DNA. 30961

---- A bill for the adjudication and liquidation of the claims for property taken away in violation of the fifth article of the Treaty of Ghent. Jan. 26, 1827. Reported by the Committee on Military Affairs. [Washington, 1827] 1 p. (H. R. 395) DNA. 30962

---- A bill for the alteration of the acts imposing duties on imports. Jan. 10, 1827. Reported by the Committee on Manufactures. [Washington, 1827] 1 p. (H. R. 362) DNA. 30963

---- ---- Jan. 23, 1827. Intended to be offered by Mr. Cambreleng as an amendment to the above-mentioned bill; and printed by order of the House of Representatives. [Washington, 1827] 1 p. (H. R. 362) DNA. 30964

---- The bill for the alteration of the acts imposing duties on imports being under consideration, Mr. Ingham submitted the following proposition; which was ordered to be printed by the House: Feb. 5, 1827. [Washington, 1827] 1 p. (H. R. 362) DNA. 30965

---- A bill a bill[sic] for the benefit of Andrew Westbrook. Jan. 26, 1827. Reported by the Committee on Private Land Claims. [Washington, 1827] 1 p. (H. R. 397) DNA. 30966

---- A bill for the benefit of Andrew Westbrook. Dec. 19, 1827. [Washington, 1827] 1 p. (H. R. 16) DNA. 30967

---- A bill for the benefit of Elijah L. Clarke, of Louisiana. Jan. 2, 1827. Reported by the Committee on Private Land Claims. [Washington, 1827] 1 p. (H. R. 330) DNA. 30968

---- A bill for the benefit of John B. Dupuis. Jan. 12, 1827. Reported by the Committee on Private Land Claims. [Washington, 1827] 1 p. (H. R. 375) DNA. 30969

---- A bill for the benefit of John Boardman. Jan. 26, 1827. [Washington, 1827] 1 p. (S. 76) DNA. 30970

---- A bill for the benefit of Samuel Sprigg, of the state of Virginia. Jan. 27, 1827. Reported by the Committee on Private Land Claims. [Washington, 1827] 1 p. (H. R. 402) DNA. 30971

---- A bill for the benefit of the heirs of the late Thomas Jefferson. Feb. 2, 1827. [Washington, 1827] 1 p. (S. 84) DNA. 30972

---- A bill for the better regulation of the fur trade. Jan. 17, 1827. [Washington, 1827] 1 p. (S. 61) DNA. 30973

---- A bill for the continuation of the Cumberland Road. Dec. 24, 1827. [Washington, 1827] 3 p. (S. 34) DNA. 30974

---- A bill for the erection of a marine hospital for the relief of sick and disabled seamen at or near Charleston, in South Carolina. Jan. 9, 1827. Reported by the Committee on Commerce. [Washington, 1827] 1 p. (H. R. 356) DNA. 30975

---- A bill for the gradual improvement of the Navy of the United States. Jan. 12, 1827. [Washington, 1827] 3 p. (S. 50) DNA. 30976

---- A bill for the improvement

of Pennsylvania Avenue, in the city of Washington. Feb. 12, 1827. [Washington, 1827] 1 p. (S. 97) DNA. 30977

---- A bill for the organization of the Corps of Topographical Engineers. Jan. 5, 1827. Reported by the Committee on Military Affairs. [Washington, 1827] 1 p. (H. R. 345) DNA. 30978

---- A bill for the preservation and repair of the Cumberland Road. Amendment intended to be offered by Mr. Buchanan to the above mentioned bill. Jan. 29, 1827. Pr. by order of the House of Representatives. [Washington, 1827] 1 p. (H. R. 290) DNA. 30979

---- A bill for the preservation and repair of the Cumberland Road. Dec. 12, 1827. [Washington, 1827] 6 p. (S. 6) DNA. 30980

---- A bill for the relief of Abigail Appleton, of Ipswich, in state of Massachusetts. Feb. 3, 1827. Reported by the Committee on Naval Affairs. [Washington, 1827] 1 p. (H. R. 420) DNA. 30981

---- A bill for the relief of Abraham Ogden, and others. Feb. 23, 1827. [Washington, 1827] 1 p. (S. 107) DNA. 30982

---- ---- Dec. 31, 1827. [Washington, 1827] 1 p. (S. 38) DNA. 30983

---- A bill for the relief of Alfred Flournoy. Jan. 17, 1827. [Washington, 1827] 1 p. (S. 60) DNA. 30984

---- A bill for the relief of Anna Dubord. Dec. 27, 1827. [Washington, 1827] 1 p. (S. 36) DNA. 30985

---- A bill for the relief of Archibald Bard and John Findlay, executors of the last will and testament of Doctor Robert Johnston. Jan. 5, 1827. Reported by the Committee of Ways and Means. [Washington, 1827] 1 p. (H. R. 343) DNA. 30986

---- A bill for the relief of Archibald W. Hamilton. Feb. 2, 1827. Reported by the Committee of Claims. [Washington, 1827] 1 p. (H. R. 418) DNA. 30987

---- A bill for the relief of Bar. J. V. Valkenburgh, Jan. 23, 1827. [Washington, 1827] 1 p. (S. 69) DNA. 30988

---- A bill for the relief of Catharine Stearns and George Blake. Dec. 14, 1827. Reported by the Committee of Claims. [Washington, 1827] 1 p. (H. R. 3) DNA. 30989

---- A bill for the relief of certain settlers on unconfirmed claims in the state of Missouri. Feb. 26, 1827. [Washington, 1827] 1 p. (S. 108) DNA. 30990

---- A bill for the relief of Chad Miller. Jan. 23, 1827. Reported by the Committee on Private Land Claims. [Washington, 1827] 1 p. (H. R. 391) DNA. 30991

---- A bill a bill [sic] for the relief of Charles A. Burnett. Jan. 23, 1827. Reported by the Committee of Expenditures on the Public Buildings. [Washington, 1827] 1 p. (H. R. 396) DNA. 30992

---- A bill for the relief of Elizabeth Shaw. Jan. 5, 1827. Reported by the Committee on Private Land Claims. [Washington, 1827] 1 p. (H. R. 349) DNA. 30993

---- A bill for the relief of Elvington Roberts, of Mississippi. Dec. 20, 1827. [Washington, 1827] 1 p. (S. 29) DNA. 30994

---- A bill for the relief of Francis Larche, of New Orleans. Dec. 31, 1827. [Washington, 1827] 1 p. (S. 37) DNA. 30995

---- A bill for the relief [!] Frederick Onstine. Jan. 5, 1827. Reported by the Committee on Private Land Claims. [Washington, 1827] 1 p. (H. R. 347) DNA. 30996

---- A bill for the relief of General Thomas Flournoy, of Georgia. Jan. 30, 1827. Reported by the Committee on the Judiciary. [Washington, 1827] 1 p. (H. R. 407) DNA. 30997

---- A bill for the relief of General Thomas Flournoy, of Georgia. Dec. 17, 1827. [Washington, 1827] 1 p. (H. R. 7) DNA. 30998

---- A bill for the relief of George Johnston, Jonathan W. Ford, Josiah Mason, and John English. Feb. 5, 1827. Reported by the Committee of Claims. [Washington, 1827] 1 p. (H. R. 422) DNA. 30999

---- A bill for the relief of George Wilson. Jan. 12, 1827. [Washington, 1827] 1 p. (S. 53 N. 2) DNA. 31000

---- A bill for the relief of Haley and Harris. Jan. 26, 1827. [Washington, 1827] 1 p. (S. 75) DNA. 31001

---- A bill for the relief of Hampton L. Boon. Dec. 24, 1827. [Washington, 1827] 1 p. (H. R. 25) DNA. 31002

---- A bill for the relief of Henry G. Rice. Jan. 3, 1827. Reported by the Committee of Ways and Means. [Washington, 1827] 1 p. (H. R. 334) DNA. 31003

---- ---- Dec. 18, 1827. [Washington, 1827] 1 p. (H. R. 10) DNA. 31004

---- A bill for the relief of J. S. Barney, administrator of George W. Evans, late Deputy Quarter Master General. Jan. 19, 1827. [Washington, 1827] 1 p. (S. 65) DNA. 31005

---- A bill for the relief of James Moore, of Mississippi, and the other heirs of Alexander Moore, deceased. Feb. 13, 1827. [Washington, 1827] 1 p. (S. 99) DNA. 31006

---- A bill for the relief of James Moore, of Mississippi, and the other heirs of Alexander Moore, deceased. Dec. 18, 1827. [Washington, 1827] 1 p. (S. 23) DNA. 31007

---- A bill for the relief of John Moffitt. Feb. 1, 1827. Reported by the Committee on Revolutionary Claims. [Washington, 1827] 1 p. (H. R. 417) DNA. 31008

---- A bill for the relief of John Rodriguez. Jan. 2, 1827. Reported by the Committee of Claims. [Washington, 1827] 1 p. (H. R. 329) DNA. 31009

---- A bill for the relief of John Rodriguez. Dec. 19, 1827. [Washington, 1827] 1 p. (H. R. 14) DNA. 31010

---- A bill for the relief of John Smith T. and Wilson P. Hunt. Dec. 18, 1827. [Washington, 1827] 1 p. (S. 24) DNA. 31011

---- A bill for the relief of Joseph Dunbar, receiver of the public moneys for the Land District West of Pearl river, in the state of Mississippi. Feb. 13, 1827. [Washington, 1827] 1 p. (S. 100) DNA. 31012

---- A bill for the relief of Joshua T. Chase, and others. Dec. 18, 1827. [Washington, 1827] 1 p. (H. R. 11) DNA. 31013

---- A bill for the relief of Luther Chapin. Feb. 7, 1827. Reported by the Committee of Claims. [Washington, 1827] 1 p. (H. R. 427) DNA. 31014

---- A bill for the relief of Marigny D'Anterive. Dec. 21, 1827. [Washington, 1827] 1 p. (H. R. 19) DNA. 31015

---- A bill for the relief of Marinus W. Gilbert. Jan. 8, 1827. Reported by the Committee of Claims. [Washington, 1827.] 1 p. (H. R. 353) DNA. 31016

---- ---- Dec. 21, 1827. [Washington, 1827] 1 p. (H. R. 20) DNA. 31017

---- A bill for the relief of N. Potts and Samuel Clement, assignees of Jacob Clement. Feb. 23, 1827. [Washington, 1827] 1 p. (S. 106) DNA. 31018

---- A bill for the relief of Nathaniel Patten. Dec. 18, 1827. [Washington, 1827] 1 p. (S. 25) DNA. 31019

---- A bill for the relief of Noah Noble, of Indiana. Jan. 17, 1827. [Washington, 1827] 1 p. (S. 62) DNA. 31020

---- A bill for the relief of Parke Walton. Jan. 16, 1827. [Washington, 1827] 1 p. (S. 56) DNA. 31021

---- A bill for the relief of Parker McCobb. Jan. 9, 1827. Reported by the Committee on Commerce. [Washington, 1827] 1 p. (H. R. 358) DNA. 31022

---- A bill for the relief of Pedro Miranda. Jan. 3, 1827. Reported by the Committee of Ways and Means. [Washington, 1827] 1 p. (H. R. 337) DNA. 31023

---- A bill for the relief of Polly Bell, alias Polly Collins. Jan. 15, 1827. [Washington, 1827] 1 p. (S. 54) DNA. 31024

---- A bill for the relief of purchasers of the public land, that have reverted for non-payment of the purchase money. Feb. 23, 1827. Reported by the Committee on Public Lands. [Washington, 1827] 1 p. (H. R. 442) DNA. 31025

---- A bill for the relief of purchasers of the public lands, that have reverted for non-payment of the purchase money. Dec. 19, 1827. [Washington, 1827] 3 p. (H. R. 13) DNA. 31026

---- A bill for the relief of Richard Harris and Nimrod Farrow. Feb. 14, 1827. Reported by the Committee of Claims. [Washington, 1827] 1 p. (H. R. 435) DNA. 31027

---- A bill for the relief of Robert Huston. Jan. 11, 1827. Reported by the Committee of Claims. [Washington, 1827] 1 p. (H. R. 379) DNA. 31028

---- A bill for the relief of Richard W. Steele. Feb. 2, 1827. Reported by the Committee of Claims. [Washington, 1827] 1 p. (H. R. 419) DNA. 31029

---- A bill for the relief of Samuel Chesnut. Jan. 10, 1827. Reported by the Committee of Claims. [Washington, 1827] 1 p. (H. R. 360) DNA. 31030

---- A bill for the relief of Samuel Gilbert. Jan. 18, 1827. [Washington, 1827] 1 p. (S. 63) DNA. 31031

---- A bill for the relief of Seth Knowles. Jan. 2, 1827. Reported by the Committee of Ways and Means. [Washington, 1827] 1 p. (H R. 333) DNA. 31032

---- A bill for the relief of Sewell, Williams & Co. Dec. 24, 1827. [Washington, 1827] 1 p. (H. R. 22) DNA. 31033

---- A bill for the relief of sundry citizens of Baltimore. Feb. 6, 1827. [Washington, 1827] 1 p. (S. 88) DNA. 31034

---- A bill for the relief of sundry citizens of the United States, who have lost property by the depredations of certain Indian tribes. Dec. 14, 1827. [Washington, 1827] 1 p. (S. 15) DNA. 31035

---- A bill for the relief of the administrator of the late Bloomfield M'Ilvaine, Esquire. Jan. 5, 1827. Reported by the Committee of Ways and Means. [Washington, 1827] 1 p. (H. R. 344) DNA. 31036

---- A bill for the relief of the Assignees, or Legal Representatives of Kendall and Butterfield. Feb. 2, 1827. [Washington, 1827] 1 p. (S. 80) DNA. 31037

---- A bill for the relief of the Columbian College, in the District of Columbia. Feb. 7, 1827. [Washington, 1827] 1 p. (S. 92) DNA. 31038

---- ---- Dec. 12, 1827. [Washington, 1827] 1 p. (S. 7) DNA. 31039

---- A bill for the relief of the heirs and legal representatives of Lewis Clarke, deceased. Jan. 2, 1827. Reported by the Committee on Private Land Claims. [Washington, 1827] 1 p. (H. R. 331) DNA. 31040

---- A bill for the relief of the heirs at law of Richard Livingston, a Canadian refugee. Feb. 15, 1827. Reported by the Committee on Revolutionary Claims. [Washington, 1827] 1 p. (H. R. 439) DNA. 31041

---- A bill for the relief of the heirs of Jeremiah Buckley, deceased. Feb. 21, 1827. Reported by the Committee on Private Land Claims. [Washington, 1827] 1 p. (H. R. 441) DNA. 31042

---- A bill for the relief of the indigent sufferers by fire in the city of Alexandria. Jan. 19, 1827. [Washington, 1827] 1 p. (H. R. 383) DNA. 31043

---- A bill for the relief of the legal representatives of Abraham Estes, an invalid pensioner, and for other purposes. Dec. 12, 1827. [Washington, 1827] 1 p. (S. 8) DNA. 31044

---- A bill for the relief of the legal representatives of Balthazar Kramar, and the legal representatives of Captain Richard Taylor. Jan. 31, 1827. [Washington, 1827] 1 p. (S. 79) DNA. 31045

---- A bill for the relief of the legal representatives of General William Hull. Jan. 31, 1827. Reported by the Committee of Claims. [Washington, 1827] 1 p. (H. R. 415) DNA. 31046

---- A bill for the relief of the legal representative of Giles Egerton. Jan. 18, 1827. [Washington, 1827] 1 p. (S. 64) DNA. 31047

---- A bill for the relief of the legal representatives of Joseph Jeans, deceased. Jan. 3, 1827. Reported by the Committee of Claims. [Washington, 1827] 1 p. (H. R. 339) DNA. 31048

---- A bill for the relief of the legal representatives of William Scott, deceased, citizens of the state of Mississippi. Feb. 15, 1827. [Washington, 1827] 1 p. (S. 104) DNA. 31049

---- A bill for the relief of the president, directors, and company, of the Bank of Chillicothe. Jan. 19, 1827. Reported by the Committee of Claims. [Washington, 1827] 1 p. (H. R. 386) DNA. 31050

---- A bill for the relief of the representatives of John P. Cox. Jan. 10, 1827. Reported by the Committee of Claims. [Washington, 1827] 1 p. (H. R. 361) DNA. 31051

---- A bill for the relief of the representatives of Patience Gordon, widow, deceased. Jan. 24, 1827. [Washington, 1827] 1 p. (S. 72) DNA. 31052

---- A bill for the relief of the surviving officers of the army of the Revolution. Jan. 22, 1827. [Washington, 1827] 1 p. (H. R. 33) DNA. 31053

---- A bill for the relief of Thomas Brown and Aaron Stanton, of the state of Indiana. Dec. 31, 1827. [Washington, 1827] 1 p. (S. 41) DNA. 31054

---- A bill for the relief of Thomas C. Withers. Jan. 24, 1827. Reported by the Committee of Claims. [Washington, 1827] 1 p. (H. R. 393) DNA. 31055

---- A bill for the relief of Thomas Constantine. Feb. 15, 1827. [Washington, 1827] 1 p. (S. 105) DNA. 31056

---- A bill for the relief of Thomas Gulledge. Jan. 15, 1827. [Washington, 1827] 1 p. (S. 55) DNA. 31057

---- A bill for the relief of Thomas S. Winthrop and others, directors of an association called the New England Mississippi Land Company. Dec. 31, 1827. [Washington, 1827] 1 p. (S. 40) DNA. 31058

---- A bill for the relief of Wilkins Tannehill. Jan. 23, 1827. [Washington, 1827] 1 p. (S. 67) DNA. 31059

---- ---- Dec. 13, 1827. [Washington, 1827] 1 p. (S. 14) DNA. 31060

---- A bill for the relief of William Cloyd. Dec. 17, 1827. Reported by the Committee of Claims. [Washington, 1827] 1 p. (H. R. 5) DNA. 31061

---- A bill for the relief of William Gentry, of Missouri. Dec. 17, 1827. [Washington, 1827] 1 p. (S. 20) DNA. 31062

---- A bill for the relief of William M. Sneed, and the executors of Stephen Sneed, senr. deceased. Jan. 23, 1827. [Washington, 1827] 1 p. (S. 70) DNA. 31063

---- A bill for the relief of William Morrisson. Jan. 31, 1827. Reported by the Committee of Claims. [Washington, 1827] 1 p. (H. R. 414) DNA. 31064

---- A bill for the relief of William Otis. Jan. 27, 1827. Reported by the Committee of Ways and Means. [Washington, 1827] 1 p. (H. R. 400) DNA. 31065

---- A bill for the relief of William Thompson. Jan. 5, 1827. Reported by the Committee of Claims. [Washington, 1827] 1 p. (H. R. 351) DNA. 31066

---- ---- Dec. 17, 1827. [Washington, 1827] 1 p. (H. R. 6)

DNA. 31067

---- A bill for the relief of Willie Blount. Jan. 3, 1827. Reported by a Select Committee. [Washington, 1827] 1 p. (H. R. 340) DNA. 31068

---- A bill for the restoration of Simeon Webster, a soldier of the Revolution, to the list of Revolutionary pensioners. Feb. 5, 1827. [Washington, 1827] 1 p. (S. 85) DNA. 31069

---- A bill further to amend "An act to establish the Judicial Courts of the United States, passed the twenty-fourth of September, seventeen hundred and eighty-nine. Jan. 10, 1827. [Washington, 1827] 3 p. (S. 51 N. 1) DNA. 31070

---- A bill further to amend the act, entitled "An act for regulating process in the courts of the United States. Jan. 5, 1827. [Washington, 1827] 1 p. (S. 43) DNA. 31071

---- A bill further to amend the judicial system of the United States. Jan. 11, 1827. Reported by the Committee on the Judiciary. [Washington, 1827] 1 p. (H. R. 366) DNA. 31072

---- ---- Feb. 9, 1827. [Washington, 1827] 1 p. (S. 95) DNA. 31073

---- A bill granting the right of preference, in the purchase of public lands, to certain settlers, in the St. Helena Land District, in the state of Louisiana. Dec. 24, 1827. Reported by the Committee on the Public Lands. [Washington, 1827] 1 p. (H. R. 21) DNA. 31074

---- A bill granting to the corporation of the city of Mobile, the right of preference in purchase of four sections of land, or a quantity equal to four sections, at or near Spring Hill, in the county of Mobile. Jan. 9, 1827. [Washington, 1827] 1 p. (S. 49) DNA. 31075

---- A bill in addition to an act, entitled "An act to amend the several acts imposing duties on imports." Jan. 26, 1827. Reported by the Committee of Ways and Means. [Washington, 1827] 1 p. (H. R. 398) DNA. 31076

---- A bill in addition to "An act to regulate and fix the compensation of the clerks in the different offices," Passed April, one thousand eight hundred and eighteen. Jan. 8, 1827. [Washington, 1827] 3 p. (S. 47) DNA. 31077

---- A bill in addition to the act, entitled "An act to provide for the sale of lands conveyed to the United States, in certain cases, and for other purposes," passed the twenty-sixth day of May, eighteen hundred and twenty-four. Dec. 12, 1827. [Washington, 1827] 1 p. (H. R. 4) DNA. 31078

---- A bill in favor of settlers and cultivators of the public lands. Feb. 18, 1827. [Washington, 1827] 1 p. (S. 102) DNA. 31079

---- A bill in relation to an act, entitled "An act to provide for the redemption of the public debt." Jan. 16, 1827. [Washington, 1827] 1 p. (S. 58) DNA. 31080

---- A bill making an appropriation for prize money due to Thomas Douty. Jan. 8, 1827. Reported by the Committee on Naval Affairs. [Washington, 1827] 1 p. (H. R. 359) DNA. 31081

---- A bill making an appropriation for removing the bar at the East pass of the mouth of Pascagoula River, and for improving the harbor thereof. Jan. 8, 1827. [Washington, 1827] 1 p. (S. 46) DNA. 31082

---- A bill making an appropriation for the construction of the Cumberland Road, from Bridgeport to Zanesville, in the state of Ohio, and for continuing and completing the surveys of the Cumberland Road, from Zanesville to the seat of government in the state of Missouri. Dec. 18, 1827. [Washington, 1827] 1 p. (S. 26) DNA. 31083

---- A bill making an appropriation for the erection of a breakwater near the mouth of Delaware Bay. Jan. 3, 1827. [Washington, 1827] 1 p. (S. 37) DNA. 31084

---- ---- Dec. 12, 1827. [Washington, 1827] 3 p. (S. 10) DNA. 31085

---- A bill making an appropriation for the purchase of books for the Library of Congress, and for an allowance to an assistant librarian. Feb. 16, 1827. Reported by the Committee of Ways and Means. [Washington, 1827] 1 p. (H. R. 440) DNA. 31086

---- A bill making appropriations for certain fortifications of the United States, for the year 1827. Jan. 19, 1827. Reported by the Committee of Ways and Means. [Washington, 1827] 1 p. (H. R. 385) DNA. 31087

---- A bill making appropriations for the erection and completion of certain barracks, store-houses, and hospitals, and for other purposes. Jan. 25, 1827. Reported by the Committee on Military Affairs. [Washington, 1827] 1 p. (H. R. 394) DNA. 31088

---- A bill making appropriations for the Indian Department, for the year one thousand eight hundred and twenty-seven. Jan. 11, 1827. Reported by the Committee of Ways and Means. [Washington, 1827] 1 p. (H. R. 368) DNA. 31089

---- A bill making appropriations for the military service of the United States, for the year one thousand eight hundred and twenty-seven. Jan. 12, 1827. Reported by the Committee of Ways and Means. [Washington, 1827] 1 p. (H. R. 372) DNA. 31090

---- A bill making appropriations for the public buildings, and other objects. Feb. 7, 1827. Reported by the Committee on the Public Buildings. [Washington, 1827] 1 p. (H. R. 428) DNA. 31091

---- A bill making appropriations for the support of government for the year one thousand eight hundred and twenty-seven. Jan. 11, 1827. Reported by the Committee of Ways and Means. [Washington, 1827] 17 p. (H. R. 367) DNA. 31092

---- A bill making appropriations for the support of the Navy of the United States, for the year eighteen hundred and twenty-seven. Jan. 31, 1827. Reported by the Committee of Ways and Means. [Washington, 1827] 1 p. (H. R. 413) DNA. 31093

---- A bill making appropriations to carry into effect certain Indian treaties. Feb. 26, 1827. Reported by the Committee of Ways and Means. [Washington, 1827] 3 p. (H. R. 444) DNA. 31094

---- A bill making compensation to Peter Hagner, Third Auditor of the Treasury Department, for extra services performed by him, under the act of Congress, passed the third day of March, eighteen hundred and twenty-five, entitled "An act further to amend the act authorizing payment for property lost, captured, or destroyed, by the enemy, while in the military service of the United States, and for other purposes, passed on the ninth April, one thousand eight hundred and sixteen." Feb. 14, 1827. [Washington, 1827] 1 p. (S. 103) DNA. 31095

---- A bill making further provision for the Military Academy at West Point, and for other purposes. Jan. 15, 1827. Reported by the Committee on Military Affairs. [Washington, 1827] 1 p. (H. R. 377) DNA. 31096

---- A bill making partial appropriations for the support of government during the year eighteen hundred and twenty-eight. Dec. 24, 1827. [Washington, 1827] 1 p. (H. R. 23) DNA. 31097

---- A bill more effectually to provide for the national defence, by establishing an uniform militia throughout the United States, and providing for the discipline thereof. Jan. 31, 1827. [Washington, 1827] 17 p. (S. 78) DNA. 31098

---- A bill prescribing the modes of commencing, prosecuting, and deciding controversies between states. Dec. 18, 1827. [Washington, 1827] 7 p. (S. 21) DNA. 31099

---- A bill providing for the gradual increase of the Corps of Engineers, and for other purposes. Jan. 10, 1827. Reported by the Committee on Military Affairs. [Washington, 1827] 1 p. (H. R. 365) DNA. 31100

---- A bill providing for the printing and binding sixty thousand copies of the Abstract of Infantry Tactics; including Exercises and Manoeuvres of Light Infantry and Riflemen, and for other purposes. Dec. 24, 1827. [Washington, 1827] 1 p. (S. 31) DNA. 31101

---- A bill repealing, in part, the duty on imported salt. Jan. 4, 1827. [Washington, 1827] 1 p. (S. 40) DNA. 31102

---- ---- Dec. 12, 1827. [Washington, 1827] 1 p. (S. 5) DNA. 31103

---- A bill supplementary to "An act for enrolling and licensing ships or vessels to be employed in the coasting trade and fisheries, and for regulating the same." Dec. 12, 1827. [Washington, 1827] 1 p. (S. 9) DNA. 31104

---- A bill supplementary to "An act further to establish the compensation of officers of the customs, and to alter certain collection Districts, and for other purposes." Feb. 8, 1827. [Washington, 1827] 1 p. (S. 93) DNA. 31105

---- A bill supplementary to an act intituled, "An act providing for the correction of errors in making entries of lands at the Land Offices, passed March 3, 1819. Dec. 24, 1827. [Washington, 1827] 1 p. (S. 32) DNA. 31106

---- A bill supplementary to, and in amendment of, the several acts for the punishment of crimes against the United States. Feb. 6, 1827. Reported by the Committee on the Judiciary. [Washington, 1827] 5 p. (H. R. 424) DNA. 31107

---- A bill supplementary to the act, entitled "An act for the gradual increase of the Navy of the United States." Jan. 5, 1827. Reported by the Committee on Naval Affairs. [Washington, 1827]

1 p. (H. R. 348) DNA. 31108

---- A bill to abolish imprisonment for debt. Jan. 3, 1827. [Washington, 1827] 9 p. (S. 2 Repr.) DNA. 31109

---- ---- Dec. 5, 1827. [Washington, 1827] 7 p. (S. 1) DNA. 31110

---- ---- Dec. 13, 1827. [Washington, 1827] 9 p. (S. 1) DNA. 31111

---- ---- Dec. 20, 1827. Re-printed as amended in Senate, and made the Order of the Day for Friday, the 28th inst. [Washington, 1827] 9 p. (S. 1) DNA. 31112

---- A bill to aid in making a canal to connect the Michigan Lake with the Illinois River. May 12, 1825. Read twice, and committed to a Committee of the Whole House to-morrow. Feb. 3, 1827. Re-printed by order of the House of Representatives. [Washington, 1827] 2 p. (H. R. 190) DNA. 31113

---- A bill to allow the citizens of the Territory of Michigan to elect the members of their Legislative Council, and for other purposes. Jan. 19, 1827. Engrossed for this day. [Washington, 1827] 1 p. (H. R. 384) DNA. 31114

---- A bill to alter and fix the time for the future annual meeting of Congress. Feb. 6, 1827. [Washington, 1827] 1 p. (S. 90) DNA. 31115

---- A bill to alter the time of holding the district court of the United States for the Southern District of Alabama, and for other purposes. Jan. 23, 1827. Reported by the Committee on the Judiciary. [Washington, 1827] 1 p. (H. R. 389) DNA. 31116

---- A bill to alter the time of holding the district courts of the United States, in the District of North Carolina. Dec. 24, 1827. [Washington, 1827] 1 p. (H. R. 26) DNA. 31117

---- A bill to alter the time of sitting of the courts of the Sixth Circuit, required to be holden at Charleston and Milledgeville, Georgia. Jan. 30, 1827. Reported by the Committee on the Judiciary. [Washington, 1827] 1 p. (H. R. 408) DNA. 31118

---- A bill to amend "An act authorizing the erection of a bridge over the River Potomac, within the District of Columbia." Jan. 30, 1827. Reported by the Committee on the District of Columbia. [Washington, 1827] 1 p. (H. R. 406) DNA. 31119

---- A bill to amend an act, entitled "An act to authorize the state of Tennessee to issue grants and perfect titles to certain lands therein described, and to settle the claims to the vacant and unappropriated lands within the same," passed the eighteenth day of April, one thousand eight hundred and six. Dec. 24, 1827. [Washington, 1827] 1 p. (H. R. 27) DNA. 31120

---- A bill to amend and explain an act entitled "An act confirming an act of the Legislature of Virginia, incorporating the Chesapeake and Ohio Canal Company, and an act of the state of Maryland, for the same purpose." Jan. 30, 1827. Reported by the Committee on Roads and Canals. [Washington, 1827] 1 p. (H. R. 405) DNA. 31121

---- A bill to authorize a subscription of stock, on the part of the United States, in the Columbus and Sandusky Turnpike Company. Jan. 12, 1827. [Washington, 1827] 1 p. (S. 52 N. 2) DNA. 31122

---- A bill to authorize the appointment of a surveyor for the Virginia Military District within the state of Ohio. Jan. 31, 1827. Reported by the Committee on the Public Lands. [Washington, 1827] 3 p. (H. R. 410) DNA. 31123

---- A bill to authorize the building of lighthouses and beacons, and for other purposes. Jan. 29, 1827. Reported by the Committee on Commerce. [Washington, 1827] 1 p. (H. R. 403) DNA. 31124

---- A bill to authorize the building of two schooners for the Naval service, and for rebuilding the schooner Nonsuch. Jan. 24, 1827. Reported by the Committee on Naval Affairs. [Washington, 1827] 1 p. (H. R. 392) DNA. 31125

---- A bill to authorize the cancelling of a certain bond therein mentioned. Dec. 20, 1827. [Washington, 1827] 1 p. (H. R. 17) DNA. 31126

---- A bill to authorize the cancelling of a certain bond, therein mentioned. Dec. 27, 1827. [Washington, 1827] 1 p. (S. 35) DNA. 31127

---- A bill to authorize the erection of military storehouses in New Orleans and the city of New York, for the use of the Army of the United States. Dec. 20, 1827. [Washington, 1827] 1 p. (H. R. 18) DNA. 31128

---- A bill to authorize the Governor and Legislative Council of Florida, to provide for holding additional terms of the superior courts therein. Feb. 1, 1827. Reported by the Committee on the Territories. [Washington, 1827] 1 p. (H. R. 416) DNA. 31129

---- A bill to authorize the improving of certain harbors, the building of piers, and for other purposes. Feb. 15, 1827. Reported by the Committee on Commerce, [Washington, 1827] 3 p. (H. R. 438) DNA. 31130

---- A bill to authorize the laying out and construction of a road from La Plaisance Harbor to the road leading from Detroit to Chicago, in the Territory of Michigan. Jan. 10, 1827. Reported by the Committee on Roads and Canals. [Washington, 1827] 1 p. (H. R. 364) DNA. 31131

---- A bill to authorize the Legislature of the state of Alabama to sell the lands heretofore appropriated for the use of schools in that state. Feb. 13, 1827. [Washington, 1827] 1 p. (S. 101) DNA. 31132

---- A bill to authorize the Legislature of the state of Illinois to sell and convey a part of the land reserved and granted to said state for the use of the Ohio Saline. Feb. 10, 1827. Reported by the Committee on Public Lands. [Washington, 1827] 1 p. (H. R. 430) DNA. 31133

---- A bill to authorize the Legislature of the state of Illinois to sell and convey part of the land reserved and granted to said state for the use of the Ohio Saline. Dec. 13, 1827. [Washington, 1827] 1 p. (S. 12) DNA. 31134

---- A bill to authorize the Legislature of the state of Indiana to sell the Lands heretofore appropriated for the use of schools in that state. Dec. 6, 1827. [Washington, 1827] 1 p. (S. 2)

DNA. 31135

---- A bill to authorize the licensing of ships and vessels, to be employed in the mackerel fishery. Feb. 24, 1827. [Washington, 1827] 1 p. (H. R. 443) DNA. 31136

---- A bill to authorize the occupation of the Oregon River. Dec. 18, 1827. [Washington, 1827] 3 p. (H. R. 12) DNA. 31137

---- A bill to authorize the President of the United States to ascertain and designate the northern boundary of the state of Indiana. Jan. 5, 1827. [Washington, 1827] 1 p. (S. 42) DNA. 31138

---- A bill to authorize the President of the United States to cause a road to be opened from Fort Smith, in Arkansas, to Nachitoches, in Louisiana. Jan. 4, 1827. [Washington, 1827] 1 p. (S. 39) DNA. 31139

---- A bill to authorize the President of the United States to cause the reserved lead mines, in the state of Missouri, to be exposed to public sale, and those on the Upper Mississippi to be leased. Dec. 14, 1827. [Washington, 1827] 1 p. (S. 17) DNA. 31140

---- A bill to authorize the President of the United States to cause the reserved salt springs in the state of Missouri to be exposed to public sale. Dec. 14, 1827. [Washington, 1827] 1 p. (S. 16) DNA. 31141

---- A bill to authorize the President of the United States to negotiate with the Chickasaw Indians, for a canal route to connect the waters of the Tennessee and Tombeckby Rivers. Jan. 13, 1827. Reported by the Committee on Indian Affairs. [Washington, 1827] 1 p. (H. R. 376) DNA. 31142

---- A bill to authorize the President of the United States to obtain from the Cherokee Indians a site for a canal to connect the western and southern waters. Jan. 2, 1827. Reported by the Committee on Indian Affairs. [Washington, 1827] 1 p. (H. R. 327) DNA. 31143

---- A bill to authorize the President of the United States to remove the land office in the District of Jackson, in the state of Mississippi. Jan. 10, 1827. Reported by the Committee on the Public Lands. [Washington, 1827] 1 p. (H. R. 363) DNA. 31144

---- A bill to authorize the President of the United States to run and mark a line, dividing the Territory of Arkansas from the state of Louisiana. Jan. 11, 1827. Reported by the Committee on the Judiciary. [Washington, 1827] 1 p. (H. R. 371) DNA. 31145

---- A bill to authorize the purchase of additional ground adjoining the arsenal at Watervliet, New York. Jan. 3, 1827. Reported by the Committee on Military Affairs. [Washington, 1827] 1 p. (H. R. 338) DNA. 31146

---- A bill to authorize the purchase of sites, and the erection of custom houses at Newport, in Rhode Island, and at Mobile, in Alabama. Feb. 7, 1827. Reported by the Committee on Commerce. [Washington, 1827] 1 p. (H. R. 426) DNA. 31147

---- A bill to authorize the purchase of sites, and the erection of custom-houses at Newport, in Rhode Island, and at Mobile, in Alabama, and to repair a building for a customhouse at Newburyport, Massachusetts. Dec. 31, 1827. [Washington, 1827] 1 p. (S. 39) DNA. 31148

---- A bill to authorize the sale of certain tracts of land in the state of Ohio, commonly called the Moravian land. Jan. 5, 1827. Reported by the Committee on Public Lands. [Washington, 1827] 1 p. (H. R. 350) DNA. 31149

---- A bill to authorize the selection of a quarter section of land, for the benefit of a seminary of learning, in the state of Alabama. Jan. 29, 1827. [Washington, 1827] 1 p. (S. 77) DNA. 31150

---- A bill to authorize the selection of lands for the benefit of a seminary of learning in the state of Alabama. Dec. 18, 1827. [Washington, 1827] 1 p. (S. 27) DNA. 31151

---- A bill to authorize the state of Indiana to locate and make a road therein named. Jan. 25, 1827. [Washington, 1827] 1 p. (S. 74) DNA. 31152

---- A bill to authorize those persons who have relinquished lands, under the provisions of the several acts for the relief of purchasers of public lands, to purchase the same, at private sale, at a fixed price. Jan. 15, 1827. [Washington, 1827] 5 p. (S. 3) DNA. 31153

---- ---- Dec. 14, 1827. [Washington, 1827] 5 p. (S. 18) DNA. 31154

---- A bill to carry into effect the grants of land made by the treaty of the 15th November, 1824, with the Quapaw Indians. Jan. 27, 1827. Reported by the Committee on Public Lands. [Washington, 1827] 2 p. (H. R. 401) DNA. 31155

---- A bill to change the place of holding the district court of Illinois. Feb. 2, 1827. [Washington, 1827] 1 p. (S. 82) DNA. 31156

---- A bill to change the port of entry in the District of Appalachicola. Jan. 31, 1827. [Washington, 1827] 1 p. (H. R. 412) DNA. 31157

---- A bill to compensate Susan Decatur, widow and representative of Captain Stephen Decatur, deceased, and others. Feb. 7, 1827. Amendments read, and bill laid on the table. As proposed to be amended by the Committee on Naval Affairs. [Washington, 1827] 3 p. (H. R. 70) DNA. 31158

---- A bill to confirm certain claims to land in the District of Opelousas, in Louisiana, and for other purposes. Jan. 17, 1827. Reported by the Committee on Public Lands. [Washington, 1827] 3 p. (H. R. 378) DNA. 31159

---- A bill to divide the District of Kentucky into two districts. Jan. 23, 1827. Reported by the Committee on the Judiciary. [Washington, 1827] 1 p. (H. R. 390) DNA. 31160

---- A bill to establish a Southern Judicial District in the Territory of Florida. Feb. 9, 1827. [Washington, 1827] 3 p. (S. 96) DNA. 31161

---- ---- Dec. 13, 1827. [Washington, 1827] 3 p. (S. 13) DNA. 31162

---- A bill to establish a uniform system of bankruptcy throughout the United States. Jan. 2, 1827. [Washington, 1827] 81 p. (H. R. 332) DNA. 31163

---- ---- Jan. 2, 1827. [Washington, 1827] 87 p. (S. 1. Repr.) DNA. 31164

---- A bill to establish certain collection districts in the states of Kentucky, Ohio, Indiana, Illinois, and Missouri. Jan. 4, 1827. [Washington, 1827] 11 p. (S. 41) DNA. 31165

---- A bill to establish certain post offices and post roads. Feb. 8, 1827. [Washington, 1827] 3 p. (S. 94) DNA. 31166

---- A bill to establish sundry post roads. Feb. 13, 1827. Reported by the Committee on the Post Office and Post Roads. [Washington, 1827] 17 p. (H. R. 434) DNA. 31167

---- A bill to exempt Swedish and Norwegian vessels, and the merchandise imported therein, from the payment of discriminating duties of tonnage and impost, for a limited time, and for other purposes. Jan. 5, 1827. Reported by the Committee on Commerce. [Washington, 1827] 1 p. (H. R. 352) DNA. 31168

---- A bill to extend the time of issuing and locating milary laitnd [sic] warrants to officers and soldiers of the Revolutionary Army. Feb. 7, 1827. [Washington, 1827] 1 p. (S. 91) DNA. 31169

---- A bill to extend the time within which goods, wares, and merchandise, may be exported for the benefit of a drawback of the duties thereon. Feb. 13, 1827. Reported by the Committee on Commerce. [Washington, 1827] 1 p. (H. R. 433) DNA. 31170

---- A bill to graduate the price of the public lands, to make donation thereof to actual settlers, and to cede the refuse to the states in which they lie. Dec. 24, 1827. [Washington, 1827] 3 p. (S. 33) DNA. 31171

---- A bill to grant a certain quantity of land to the state of Indiana, for the purpose of aiding said state in opening a canal to connect the waters of the Wabash river with those of Lake Erie. Jan. 23, 1827. [Washington, 1827] 1 p. (S. 71) DNA. 31172

---- A bill to grant a quantity of land to the state of Illinois, for the purpose of aiding in opening a canal to connect the waters of the Illinois river with those of Lake Michigan. Jan. 9, 1827. [Washington, 1827] 1 p. (S. 48) DNA. 31173

---- A bill to increase the pay of non-commissioned officers and privates, and to prevent desertion in the Army. Jan. 3, 1827. Reported by the Committee on Military Affairs. [Washington, 1827] 3 p. (H. R. 336) DNA. 31174

---- A bill to increase the pay of surgeons and surgeon's mates, in the Navy, whilst actually serving at sea and of Lieutenants, who shall have served as such ten years, or upwards; and of passed Midshipmen, who shall have served as such eight years, and upwards. Feb. 2, 1827. [Washington, 1827] 1 p. (S. 83) DNA. 31175

---- A bill to increase the salary of the Postmaster General. Jan. 11, 1827. [Washington, 1827] 1 p. (S. 53. N. 1) DNA. 31176

---- A bill to limit and restrain the jurisdiction of the courts of the United States, in certain cases. Jan. 5, 1827. [Washington, 1827] 1 p. (S. 45)

DNA. 31177

---- A bill to prevent desertion in the Army, and for other purposes. Dec. 19, 1827. [Washington, 1827] 1 p. (S. 28) DNA. 31178

---- A bill to provide for the adjustment of claims of persons entitled to indemnification, under the first article of the Treaty of Ghent, and for the distribution, among such claimants, of the sum paid, and to be paid, by the Government of Great Britain, under a Convention between the United States and his Britannic Majesty, concluded at London on the thirteenth of November, one thousand eight hundred and twenty-six. Jan. 23, 1827. [Washington, 1827] 3 p. (S. 68) DNA. 31179

---- A bill to provide for the distribution of a part of the revenues of the United States, among the several states of the Union. Dec. 17, 1827. [Washington, 1827] 1 p. (S. 19) DNA. 31180

---- A bill to provide for the purchase of certain copies of the Digest of the Laws of the United States, by Thomas F. Gordon. Feb. 5, 1827. [Washington, 1827] 1 p. (S. 86) DNA. 31181

---- A bill to provide for the settlement of the accounts of James W. Lent, deceased. Jan. 5, 1827. [Washington, 1827] 1 p. (S. 44) DNA. 31182

---- A bill to provide for the trial of claims to lands in the states of Missouri, Louisiana, Alabama, and Mississippi, and in the Territories of Arkansas and Florida, in the cases therein specified. Jan. 24, 1827. [Washington, 1827] 9 p. (S. 73) DNA. 31183

---- A bill to provide systems of cavalry, artillery, and infantry exercises, for the use of the militia of the United States. Feb. 10, 1827. Reported by the Committee on Military Affairs. [Washington, 1827] 1 p. (H. R. 431) DNA. 31184

---- A bill to reduce the duties heretofore levied on certain articles. Jan. 11, 1827. [Washington, 1827] 1 p. (S. 52 N. 1) DNA. 31185

---- A bill to reduce the duty on Greek and Latin Books printed previous to the year 1775. Dec. 24, 1827. [Washington, 1827] 1 p. (H. R. 24) DNA. 31186

---- A bill to reform the penal laws of the District of Columbia, and for other purposes. Jan. 11, 1827. Reported by the Committee on the District of Columbia. [Washington, 1827] 17 p. (H. R. 355) DNA. 31187

---- A bill to regulate the commercial intercourse between the United States and the colonies of Great Britain. Jan. 22, 1827. [Washington, 1827] 7 p. (S. 66) DNA. 31188

---- ---- Jan. 22, 1827. Reported by the Committee on Commerce. [Washington, 1827] 7 p. (H. R. 387) DNA. 31189

---- A bill to regulate the laying out and surveying a road, from the seat of government, in the city of Washington, to the eastern termination of the Cumberland road, at Cumberland, in the state of Maryland. Jan. 22, 1827. Reported by the Committee on Roads and Canals. [Washington, 1827] 1 p. (H. R. 388) DNA. 31190

---- A bill to regulate the salaries of certain officers in the

Indian Department. Jan. 17, 1827. [Washington, 1827] 1 p. (S. 59) DNA. 31191

---- A bill to repeal a part of the act, entitled "An act supplementary to, and to amend, an act, entitled 'An act to regulate the collection of duties on imports and tonnage,' passed the second of March, one thousand seven hundred and ninety-nine, and for other purposes." Feb. 13, 1827. [Washington, 1827] 1 p. (S. 98) DNA. 31192

---- ---- Dec. 18, 1827. [Washington, 1827] 1 p. (S. 22) DNA. 31193

---- ---- Feb. 27, 1827. Reported by the Committee on Commerce. [Washington, 1827] 1 p. (H. R. 446) DNA. 31194

---- A bill to revive and continue in force, "An act declaring the assent of Congress to a certain act of Maryland." Dec. 20, 1827. [Washington, 1827] 1 p. (S. 30) DNA. 31195

---- A bill to revive and continue in force the seventh section of an act, entitled "An act supplementary to the several acts for the adjustment of land claims, in the state of Louisiana, approved the eleventh of May, eighteen hundred and twenty. Jan. 2, 1827. Reported by the Committee on Public Lands. [Washington, 1827] 1 p. (H. R. 328) DNA. 31196

---- A bill to revive and continue in force the several acts making provision for the extinguishment of the debt due to the United States by the purchasers of the public lands. Dec. 14, 1827. Reported by the Committee on the Public Lands. [Washington, 1827] 1 p. (H. R. 2) DNA. 31197

---- A bill to secure to certain inhabitants in the Territory of Florida the right of voting at elections, and to alter the time of holding the Legislative Council therein. Feb. 27, 1827. Ordered to be engrossed for a third reading this day. [Washington, 1827] 1 p. (H. R. 445) DNA. 31198

---- Breakwater Delaware Bay. Statement, shewing values of vessels and their cargoes, bound into the Delaware, between 28th December 1826, and 15th January, 1827, which were compelled to go to sea, or to seek precarious shelter elsewhere. Jan. 29, 1827. Read, and laid upon the table. Washington, Gales & Seaton, 1827. 7 p. (Doc. No. 65) DLC; NjP. 31199

---- Brevet rank and pay. Letter from the Secretary of War, transmitting a report of the second and third auditors, and of the adjutant general, in relation to brevet rank conferred since 1821, and payments made to officers in consequence thereof. Jan. 8, 1827. Washington, Gales & Seaton, 1827. 99 p. 3 bdsd. (Doc. No. 41) DLC; NjP. 31200

---- Bulfinch on penitentiaries. Report of Charles Bulfinch on the subject of penitentiaries. Feb. 13, 1827, Pr. by order of the House of Representatives. Washington, Pr. by Gales & Seaton, 1827. 8 p. (Rep. No. 98) DLC; MH-L; NjP. 31201

---- Business to be acted upon. Feb. 15, 1827. Mr. Tomlinson, from the Joint Committee appointed to report what subjects it is necessary to act upon at the present session, and the order in which they shall be taken up, made the following report: [Washington, 1827] 4 p. (Rep. No. 82)

DLC; NjP. 31202

---- Business to be acted upon. Feb. 23, 1827. Mr. Tomlinson, from the Joint Committee of the two Houses of Congress, appointed to report what subjects it is necessary to act upon during the present session, and the order in which they should be taken up, reported further, in part: [Washington, 1827] 5 p. (Rep. No. 88) DLC; NjP. 31203

---- Cadwallader Wallace. Memorial of Cadwallader Wallace. Dec. 24, 1827. Referred to the Committee on the Public Lands. Washington, Pr. by Gales & Seaton, 1827. 31 p. (Doc. No. 19) DLC; NjR. 31204

---- Canal--Barnstable to Buzzard's Bay. Letter from the Secretary of War in reply to a resolution of the House of Representatives of the 2d of Jan. last, requiring an estimate of the expense of making a canal between Barnstable and Buzzard's Bay. Feb. 13, 1827. Read, and laid upon the table. Washington, Pr. by Gales & Seaton, 1827. 3 p. (Rep. No. 97) DLC; NjP. 31205

---- Canal--Lake Pontchartrain to the Mississippi. Letter from the Secretary of War, transmitting the information required by a resolution of the House of Representatives of the 13th Dec. last, in relation to a canal from Lake Pontchartrain to the Mississippi Rover. March 3, 1827. Read, and laid upon the table. Washington, Gales & Seaton, 1827. 18 p. 1 bdsd. (Doc. No. 133) DLC; NjP. 31206

---- Catharine Stearns and George Blake. Dec. 14, 1827. Mr. Whittlesey, from the Committee of Claims, to which was referred the petition of Catharine Stearns, and the account of George Blake, made the following report: Washington, Gales & Seaton, 1827. 10 p. (Rep. No. 2) DLC; NjR. 31207

---- Cavalry tactics. Letter from the Secretary of War, transmitting a system of cavalry tactics, or, rules for the exercises and maneuvres of the cavalry of the militia of the United States. Jan. 8, 1827. Read, and referred to the Committee on the Militia. Washington, Gales & Seaton, 1827. 142 p. (Doc. No. 57) DLC; NjP. 31208

---- Cephas L. Rockwood. Dec. 20, 1827. Read, and laid upon the table. Mr. Whittlesey, from the Committee of Claims, to which was referred the petition of Cephas L. Rockwood, made the following report: Washington, Gales & Seaton, 1827. 3 p. (Rep. No. 20) DLC; NjR. 31209

---- Chad Miller. Jan. 23, 1827. Mr. Markell, from the Committee on private land claims, to which was referred the petition of Chad Miller, made the following report: [Washington, 1827] 2 p. (Rep. No. 52) DLC; NjP. 31210

---- Charles A. Burnett. Jan. 26, 1827. Mr. Johnson of Virginia, from the Committee on the expenditures on the public buildings, to which was referred the petition of Charles A. Burnett, made the following report: [Washington, 1827] 1 p. (Rep. No. 57) DLC; NjP. 31211

---- Chesapeake and Ohio Canal. Jan. 30, 1827. Mr. Mercer, from the Committee on Roads and Canals, to which was referred the memorial of the Chesapeake and Ohio Canal Convention, made the following report: [Washington, 1827] 122 p. 2 bdsd. (Rep. No. 90) DLC; NjP. 31212

---- Clerks--Department of State. Letter from the Secretary of State transmitting a list of the names of the clerks employed in his office and in the Patent Office during the year 1826, and the compensation allowed to each. Feb. 9, 1827. Read, and referred to the Committee of Ways and Means. Washington, Pr. by Gales & Seaton, 1827. 3 p. (Doc. No. 89) DLC; NjP. 31213

---- Clerks--Department of War. Letter from the Secretary of War, transmitting a list of the clerks in the Department of War, during the year 1826, and the salary allowed to each. Jan. 10, 1827. Read, and laid upon the table. Washington, Gales & Seaton, 1827. 6 p. (Doc. No. 46) DLC; NjP. 31214

---- Clerks--Navy Department - 1826. Letter from the Secretary of the Navy, transmitting a report of the names of the clerks employed in the Navy Department, during the year 1826, and the compensation allowed to each. Jan. 3, 1827. Read, and laid upon the table. Washington, Gales & Seaton, 1827. 5 p. (Doc. No. 29) DLC; NjP. 31215

---- Clerks - Treasury Department, 1826. Letter from the Secretary of Treasury, transmitting a statement shewing the names of the clerks of the Treasury Department, during the year 1826, and the compensation allowed to each. Jan. 13, 1827. Read, and laid upon the table. Washington, Gales & Seaton, 1827. 13 p. (Doc. No. 48) DLC; NjP. 31216

---- Colonization of free people of colour. Mar. 3, 1827. Mr. Mercer, from the Select Committee appointed on the subject, made the following report: [Washington, 1827] 95 p. (Rep. No. 101) DLC; NjP. 31217

---- Communication across the Isthmus of Panama. Jan. 24th, 1827. Read, and with the bill, committed to a committee of the whole House to-morrow. Mr. Storrs, from the Committee on Naval Affairs, made the following report: [Washington, 1827] 7 p. (Rep. No. 56) DLC; NjP. 31218

---- Compensation to surveyor general, &c. Letter from the Secretary of the Treasury, transmitting a statement shewing the compensation to the Surveyor General, and other surveyors, &c. for the year 1824, 1825, and part of 1826. Jan. 17, 1827. Read, and laid upon the table. Washington, Gales & Seaton, 1827. 8 p. (Doc. No. 55) DLC; NjP. 31219

---- Construction of act to fix military peace establishment. Jan. 11, 1827. Mr. Drayton, from the Committee on Military Affairs, to which the subject had been referred, made the following report: [Washington, 1827] 5 p. (Rep. No. 40) DLC; NjP. 31220

---- Contingent expenses H. Representatives. Annual report of the clerk of the House of Representatives of the U. States, of the names of the clerks, messengers, &c. in the service of that House, and the expenditure of the contingent fund of 1827. Dec. 10, 1827. Read, and laid upon the table. Washington, Pr. by Gales & Seaton, 1827. 4 p. 1 bdsd. (Doc. No. 5) DLC; NjR. 31221

---- Contingent expenses - military - 1826. Letter from the

Secretary of War, transmitting a statement shewing the expenditures of the money appropriated for the contingent expenses of the military establishment, for the year 1826. Jan. 10, 1827. Read, and referred to the Committee of Ways and Means. Washington, Gales & Seaton, 1827. 3 p. 3 bdsd. (Doc. No. 43) DLC; NjP. 31222

---- Contingent expenses of the Navy - 1826. Letter from the Secretary of the Navy, transmitting an abstract of the expenditures on account of the contingent expenses of the Navy during the year ending Sept. 30, 1826. Jan. 3, 1827. Read, and laid upon the table. Washington, Gales & Seaton, 1827. 5 p. 5 bdsd. (Doc. No. 34) DLC; NjP. 31223

---- Contracts, Post Office Department, 1826. Letter from the Postmaster General, transmitting statements of contracts made by the Post Office Department, during the year 1826. Feb. 24, 1827. Read, and laid upon the table. Washington, Gales & Seaton, 1827. 22 p. (Doc. No. 121) DLC; NjP. 31224

---- Contracts - War Department - 1826. Letter from the Secretary of War, transmitting statement of contracts made by the War Department, in the year 1826. Feb. 22, 1827. Read, and laid upon the table. Washington, Gales & Seaton, 1827. 3 p. 18 bdsd. (Doc. No. 131) DLC; NjP. 31225

---- Convention with Great Britain. Message from the President of the United States, transmitting copies of a convention between the United States and Great Britain, signed on the 13th of Nov. last at London, providing for the payment of citizens of the U. States for claims arising under the First Article of the Treaty of Ghent. Jan. 16, 1827. Washington, Gales & Seaton, 1827. 8 p. (Doc. No. 53) DLC; NjP. 31226

---- Cumberland Road and domestic manufactures. Resolutions adopted at a meeting of inhabitants of Ohio County, in the state of Virginia, in relation to the Cumberland Road and the domestic manufactures of the county. Feb. 19, 1827. Read, and laid upon the table. Washington, Pr. by Gales & Seaton, 1827. 4 p. (Doc. No. 108) DLC; NjP. 31227

---- Destruction of Frigate Philadelphia. Feb. 7, 1827. Mr. Storrs, from the Committee on Naval Affairs, to which was recommitted the "bill to compensate Susan Decatur, widow and representative of Captain Stephen Decatur, and others," made the following report: [Washington, 1827] 23 p. (Rep. No. 74) DLC; NjP. 31228

---- Disbursements to the Indians - 1826. Letter from the Secretary of War, transmitting copies of accounts rendered by persons charged with the disbursement of money, goods, or effects for the benefit of the Indians, from 1st Sept. 1825 to 1st Sept., 1826. Feb. 24, 1827 ... Washington, Pr. by Gales & Seaton, 1827. 120 p. (Doc. No. 112) DLC; NjP. 31229

---- Discipline militia. Feb. 27, 1827. Mr. Metcalfe, from the Committee on the Militia, to which had been referred so much of the President's Message as relates to the organization and discipline of the militia of the United States, made the following report: [Washington, 1827] 18 p. (Rep. No. 92) DLC; NjP. 31230

---- Discriminating duties -

Government of the Netherlands. Message from the President of the United States, transmitting a report of the Secretary of State, with copies of a correspondence with the government of the Netherlands, relating to discrimination duties. Jan. 19, 1827. Referred to the Committee on Commerce. Washington, Gales & Seaton, 1827. 23 p. (Doc. No. 58) DLC; NjP. 31231

---- Discriminating duties - Sweden and Norway. Report of the Committee on Commerce, in relation to the imposition of discriminating duties on the vessels and cargoes of Sweden and Norway. January 5, 1827. Accompanied by a bill to exempt Swedish and Norwegian vessels, and the merchandise imported therein from the payment of discriminating duties of tonnage and impost, for a limited time, and for other purposes. [Washington, 1827] 3 p. (Rep. No. 36) DLC; NjP. 31232

---- S. 3. Documents accompanying the bill from the Senate. Feb. 28, 1827. Pr. by order of the House of Representatives. Washington, Gales & Seaton, 1827. 15 p. (Doc. No. 122) DLC; NjP. 31233

---- Documents accompanying the President's message to Congress, at the commencement of the first session of the twentieth Congress. Dec. 4, 1827. Referred to a Committee of the whole House on the state of the Union. Washington, Pr. by Gales & Seaton, 1827. [2], 19-37 p. (Doc. No. [2]) DLC. 31234

---- Documents furnished by the British government under the third article of the convention of St. Petersburg, of 30 June / 12 July 1822. and Bayly's list of slaves, and of public and private property, remaining on Tangier Island, and on board H. B. M. ships of war, after the ratification of the Treaty of Ghent. Washington, Pr. by Gales & Seaton, 1827. 2 p. l., 112 p. DLC. 31235

---- Drawback of duties. Dec. 31, 1827. Mr. Cambreleng, from the Committee on Commerce, to which the subject had been referred, made the following report: Washington, Gales & Seaton, 1827 3 p. (Rep. No. 39) DLC; NjR. 31236

---- Dry docks - Portsmouth, N. H., Charlestown, Mass., &c. Message from the President of the United States, transmitting a report of an examination and survey which has been made of a site for a dry dock at Portsmouth, N. H., Charlestown, Mass., Brooklyn, N. Y., and Gosport, Va. Jan. 10, 1827. Read, and referred to the Committee on Naval Affairs. Washington, Gales & Seaton, 1827. 46 p. (Doc. No. 125) DLC; NN; NjP. 31237

---- Dry dock--Portsmouth, New Hampshire. Memorial of the citizens of Portsmouth, N. H. respecting the construction of a dry dock at the Navy yard at that place. Feb. 12, 1827. Referred to the Committee on Naval Affairs. Washington, Pr. by Gales & Seaton, 1827. 5 p. (Doc. No. 92) DLC; NjP. 31238

---- Duff Green, Esq. - mail contract. Letter from the Postmaster General, transmitting the information required by a resolution of the House of Representatives, of 24th Feb. 1827, in relation to the transportation of the mail between the city of Washington and Vincennes, in the state of

Indiana. Feb. 28, 1827. Read, and laid upon the table. Washington, Gales & Seaton, 1827. 28 p. (Doc. No. 123) DLC; NjP. 31239

---- Duties on imports. Memorial of the Philadelphia Chamber of Commerce adverse to the passage of the bill imposing duties on imports. Feb. 22, 1827. Pr. by order of the Senate of the United States. Washington, Pr. by Gales & Seaton, 1827. 4 p. (Doc. No. 65) DLC; NjP. 31240

---- Duties on the inland frontier --northern. Letter from the Secretary of the Treasury transmitting the information required by a resolution of the House of Representatives of the 23rd ultimo in relation to duties collected for the three last years ending 30th September, 1826, in the states of Vermont, New York, Pennsylvania, and Ohio, on British manufactures and teas entered at the customhouses on our inland frontier. Feb. 3, 1827. Read, and laid upon the table. Washington, Pr. by Gales & Seaton, 1827. 8 p. (Doc. No. 75) DLC; NjP. 31241

---- Duties on woollen goods. Statements in relation to existing and proposed duties on woollen goods. Jan. 30, 1827. Pr. by order of the House of Representatives. Washington, Gales & Seaton, 1827. 1 p. 1 bdsd. (Doc. No. 66) DLC; NjP. 31242

---- Duty on imported salt. Remonstrance of inhabitants of Chatham, in the state of Massachusetts, against a repeal of the law imposing a duty on salt imported. Feb. 13, 1827. Referred to Committee of Ways and Means. Washington, Pr. by Gales & Seaton, 1827. 3 p. (Doc. No. 96) DLC; NjP. 31243

---- Duty on imported salt. Remonstrance of inhabitants of Provincetown, in the state of Massachusetts, against a repeal of the law imposing a duty on salt imported. Feb. 13, 1827. Referred to the Committee of Ways and Means. Washington, Pr. by Gales & Seaton, 1827. 4 p. (Doc. No. 95) DLC; NjP. 31244

---- Edward Wood--administrator of. Dec. 24, 1827. Read, and laid upon the table. Mr. Wolf, from the Committee on Revolutionary Claims, to which was referred the petition of James Wood, administrator and heir of Capt. Edward Wood, made the following report: Washington, Pr. by Gales & Seaton, 1827. 9 p. (Rep. No. 98) DLC; NjR. 31245

---- Elijah L. Clarke. Jan. 2, 1827. Mr. Buckner, from the Committee on Private Land Claims, to which was referred the petition of Elijah L. Clarke, made the following report: [Washington, 1827] 3 p. (Rep. No. 28) DLC; NjP. 31246

---- Elizabeth Shaw. Jan. 5, 1827. Mr. Varnum, from the Committee on Military Pensions, to which had been referred the petition of Elizabeth Shaw, made the following report: [Washington, 1827] 1 p. (Rep. No. 34) DLC; NjP. 31247

---- Emoluments of officers of the customs. Letter from the Secretary of the Treasury, transmitting an abstract of the official emoluments and expenditures of the officers of the customs, for the year 1826. Feb. 26, 1827. Read, and referred to the Committee of Ways and Means. Washington, Gales & Seaton, 1827. 7 p. 8 bdsd. (Doc. No. 134)

DLC; NjP. 31248

---- Encroachment on Choctaw lands. Letter from the Secretary of War, transmitting the information required by a resolution of the House of Representatives, in relation to encroachments by white men, upon the lands ceded to the Choctaw Indians, in the territory of Arkansas. Jan. 8, 1827. Read, and referred to the Committee on Indian Affairs. Washington, Gales & Seaton, 1827. 8 p. (Doc. No. 39) DLC; NjP. 31249

---- Estimates of appropriations for 1827. Report of the Secretary of the Treasury, of the estimates of appropriations necessary for the service of the year 1827. Jan. 4, 1827. Referred to the Committee of Ways and Means. Washington, Gales & Seaton, 1827. 57 p. (Doc. No. 36) DLC; NjP. 31250

---- Expenditure, artillery school of practice. Message from the President of the United States, transmitting the information required by a resolution of the H. R. of the 9th Jan. last, in relation to the expenditure, in any manner connected with the artillery school of practice, at Fortress Monroe, &c. &c. Feb. 28, 1827. Read, and laid upon the table. Washington, Gales & Seaton, 1827. 18 p. (Doc. No. 124) DLC; NjP. 31251

---- Expenditure--Naval appropriation 1826. Letter from the Secretary of the Navy transmitting a statement showing the appropriations for the Naval service, for the year 1826 and the expenditure of the same. Feb. 9, 1827. Read, and laid upon the table. Washington, Pr. by Gales & Seaton, 1827. 3 p. 2 bdsds. (Doc. No. 90) DLC; NjP. 31252

---- Expenditures at national armories. Letter from the Secretary of War transmitting a statement of the expenditures at the national armories, and the arms &c. made therein during the year 1826. Feb. 13, 1827. Read, and laid upon the table. Washington, Pr. by Gales & Seaton, 1827. 7 p. (Doc. No. 99) DLC; NjP. 31253

---- Expenditures on the public buildings. Feb. 16, 1827. Mr. Orr, from the Committee on Expenditures of the Public Buildings, made the following report: [Washington, 1827] 7 p. 1 bdsd. (Rep. No. 84) DLC; NjP. 31254

---- Florida Indians. Letter from the Secretary of War to the chairman of the Committee on Indian Affairs. Transmitting information in relation to the condition of the Indians in Florida. Feb. 7, 1827. Pr. by order of the House of Representatives. Washington, Pr. by Gales & Seaton, 1827. 7 p. (Doc. No. 82) DLC; NjP. 31255

---- Foreign commerce. Jan. 22, 1827. Mr. Tomlinson, from the Committee on Commerce, to which the subject had been referred, made the following report: [Washington, 1827] 22 p. 3 bdsds. (Rep. No. 50) DLC; NjP. 31256

---- Foreign commerce of the United States. Letter from the Secretary of the Treasury, transmitting statements of the commerce and navigation of the United States, during the year ending on the 30th of Sept., 1826. Feb. 26, 1827. Read, and laid upon the table. Washington, Gales & Seaton, 1827. 296 p. 3 bdsds. (Doc. No. 120) DLC; NjP. 31257

---- Foreign missions. Message from the President of the United

States transmitting the information required by a resolution of the House of Representatives of the 9th ultimo, relative to the appointment of Charges des Affaires, and to the commissions and salaries of the ministers and secretaries to the Panama Mission. Feb. 3, 1827. Read, and laid upon the table. Washington, Pr. by Gales & Seaton, 1827. 13 p. (Doc. No. 73) DLC; NjP. 31258

---- Foreign wool imported. Letter from the Secretary of the Treasury, transmitting the information required by a resolution of the House of Representatives, of the 12th ult. in relation to the quantity of foreign wool and woollen manufacturers imported during the last two years, &c. &c. &c. Feb. 3, 1827. Read, and laid upon the table. Washington, Gales & Seaton, 1827. 9 p. 3 bdsds. (Doc. No. 72) DLC; NjP. 31259

---- Fortifications--Pensacola Harbor. Letter from the Secretary of War transmitting a report from the engineer department in relation to the contemplated fortification of Pensacola Harbor. Feb. 9, 1827. Referred to the Committee of Ways and Means. Washington, Pr. by Gales & Seaton, 1827. 4 p. (Doc. No. 88) DLC; NjP. 31260

---- Fortifications for Pensacola. Letter from the Secretary of War, transmitting a report respecting plans and estimates of fortifications contemplated for Pensacola. Jan. 3, 1827. Read, and laid upon the table. Washington, Gales & Seaton, 1827. 6 p. (Doc. No. 30) DLC; NjP. 31261

---- Fortifications on Staten Island. Message from the President of the United States, with sundry documents, relating to a proposition by the state of New York, to sell to the government of the U. States, the fortifications erected by said state, on Staten Island. Jan. 15, 1827. Read, and referred to the Committee on Military Affairs. Washington, Gales & Seaton, 1827. 12 p. (Doc. No. 49) DLC; NjP. 31262

---- Francis Henderson, &c. Memorial and petition of Francis Henderson and Francis Henderson, Jun. On behalf of themselves and family, heirs and representatives of John Laurens, deceased. Dec. 19, 1827. Referred to the Committee on Revolutionary Claims. Washington, Pr. by Gales & Seaton, 1827. 26 p. 2 bdsd. (Doc. No. 18) DLC; NjR. 31263

---- Frederick Onstine. Jan. 5, 1827. Mr. Test, from the Committee on Private Land Claims, to which had been referred the petition of Frederick Onstine, made the following report: [Washington, 1827] 3 p. (Rep. No. 33) DLC; NjP. 31264

---- Free Negroes--District of Columbia. Jan. 11, 1827. Mr. Powell, from the Committee for the District of Columbia, to which the subject had been referred, made the following report: [Washington, 1827] 5 p. (Rep. No. 43) DLC; NjP. 31265

---- French and other spoliations. Memorial of merchants and others, of the state of Rhode Island, in relation to spoliations committed on the commerce of the United States, by the vessels of war of France and other European nations. Feb. 5, 1827. Referred to the Committee on Foreign Affairs. Washington, Pr. by Gales & Seaton, 1827. 4 p. (Doc. No. 78) DLC; NjP. 31266

---- ---- Petition of merchants of Baltimore upon the subject of spoliations on the commerce of the United States. Feb. 5, 1827. Referred to the Committee on Foreign Affairs. Washington, Pr. by Gales & Seaton, 1827. 6 p. (Doc. No. 77) DLC; NjP. 31267

---- Friendly Creek Indians. Letter from the Secretary of War on the resolutions of the Legislature of the state of Georgia, in relation to the suffering condition of the Friendly Creek Indians, &c. which had been referred to him by the House of Representatives to report thereupon. Feb. 6, 1827. Read, and referred to the Committee on Indian Affairs. Washington, Pr. by Gales & Seaton, 1827. 4 p. (Doc. No. 79) DLC; NjP. 31268

---- G. W. Perpall. Report of the Secretary of War on the petition of Gabriel W. Perpall. Dec. 10, 1827. Referred to the Committee on Indian Affairs. Washington, Pr. by Gales & Seaton, 1827. 12 p. (Doc. No. 6) DLC; NjR. 31269

---- General Thomas Flournoy. Dec. 17, 1827. Mr. P. P. Barbour, from the Committee on the Judiciary, to which was referred the petition of General Thomas Flournoy, made the following report: Washington, Gales & Seaton, 1827. 2 p. (Rep. No. 5) DLC; NjR. 31270

---- Georgia Militia claims. Feb. 10, 1827. Read, and referred to the Committee of the Whole House on the state of the Union. Mr. Vance, from the Committee on Military Affairs, to which the subject had been referred, made the following report: [Washington, 1827] 8 p. (Rep. No. 77) DLC; NjP. 31271

---- George Wilson. The Committee of Claims, to whom was referred the bill from the Senate entitled "An act for the relief of George Wilson" made the following report: Jan. 29, 1827. Read, and with the bill, committed to a Committee of the Whole House to-morrow. [Washington, 1827] 3 p. (Rep. No. 61) DLC; NjP. 31272

---- Giles Egerton. Feb. 14, 1827. Mr. Scott, from the Committee on the Public Lands, to which was referred the bill from the Senate for the relief of the legal representatives of Giles Egerton, made the following report: [Washington, 1827] 1 p. (Rep. No. 81) DLC; NjP. 31273

---- Grants of land under Quapaw Treaty. Jan. 27, 1827. Mr. Strong, from the Committee on the Public Lands, to which had been referred the petition of James Scull, & al. made the following report: [Washington, 1827] 4 p. (Rep. No. 60) DLC; NjP. 31274

---- Hampton L. Boon. Dec. 24, 1827. Mr. Whittlesey, from the Committee of Claims, to which was referred the petition of Hampton L. Boon, made the following report: Washington, Gales & Seaton, 1827. 1 p. (Rep. No. 30) DLC; NjR. 31275

---- Harris and Farrow. Feb. 14, 1827. Mr. Williams, from the Committee of Claims, to which had been referred the petition of Nimrod Farrow, for himself and Richard Harris, made the following report: [Washington, 1827] 7 p. (Rep. No. 80) DLC; NjP. 31276

---- Henry G. Rice. Jan. 3, 1827. Mr. Dwight, from the Committee of Ways and Means, to which had been referred the petition of Henry G. Rice, made the following report: [Washington, 1827] 1 p. (Rep. No. 32) DLC; NjP. 31277

---- ---- Dec. 18, 1827. Mr. McDuffie, from the Committee of Ways and Means, to which was referred the petition of Henry G. Rice, made the following report: Washington, Gales & Seaton, 1827. 1 p. (Rep. No. 7) DLC; NjR. 31278

---- History of America. Feb. 24, 1827. Mr. Everett, from the Committee of the Library, on the subject of procuring from the public offices, in England, copies of documents relative to the history of America, made the following report: [Washington, 1827] 16 p. (Rep. No. 91) DLC; NjP. 31279

---- House of Representatives United States, Jan. 2, 1827. Mr. Hamilton, of South Carolina, submitted the following preamble and resolution, which were read and laid upon the table. [Washington, 1827] 1 p. (Res. No. 4) DLC; NjP. 31280

---- Impressment of seamen from American vessels. Message from the President of the United States, transmitting a report from the Secretary of State, relating to the impressment of seamen from on board American vessels, since 18th Feb. 1815. Jan. 15, 1827. Read, and referred to the Committee on Foreign Affairs. Washington, Gales & Seaton, 1827. 12 p. (Doc. No. 50) DLC; NjP. 31281

---- Improvement in Hall of House of Reps. Letter from the Secretary of State transmitting a report of the Board of Inspection appointed 19th of May last, in relation to improvements of the Hall of the House of Representatives, U. S. &c. &c. Feb. 12, 1827. Referred to the Committee of the Public Buildings. Washington, Pr. by Gales & Seaton, 1827. 10 p. (Doc. No. 93) DLC; NjP. 31282

---- In Senate of the United States. Jan. 3, 1827. Mr. Woodbury, from the Committee on Commerce, to which the subject had been referred, made the following report: Washington, Gales & Seaton, 1827. 5 p. (Doc. No. 11) DLC; NjP. 31283

---- In Senate of the United States, Jan. 8, 1827. Mr. Hendricks, from the Select Committee on Roads and Canals, to whom was referred the memorial of the Legislature of the state of Mississippi, praying for an appropriation to aid in opening a passage for vessels over the bar, at the East pass of the mouth of Pascagoula river, made thereon the following report: Washington, Gales & Seaton, 1827. 2 p. (Doc. No. 13) DLC; NjP. 31284

---- In Senate of the United States. Jan. 9, 1827. The bill to graduate the price of the public lands, and to cede the refuse to the states in which they lie, being under consideration, Mr. Hendricks proposed the following amendment: [Washington, 1827] 1 p. (S. 5) DNA. 31285

---- In Senate of the United States. Jan. 11, 1827. Mr. Johnson, of Kentucky, made the following report: The Committee on the Post Office and Post Roads, to whom was referred the resolution of the Senate, instructing them to examine into the expediency of ... Washington, Gales & Seaton, 1827. 3 p. (Doc. No.

15) DLC; NjP. 31286

---- In Senate of the United States, Jan. 12, 1827. Mr. Cobb made the following report: The Committee of Claims, to whom was referred the petition of John Brunson. Washington, Gales & Seaton, 1827. 8 p. (Doc. No. 18) DLC; NjP. 31287

---- In Senate of the United States, Jan. 12, 1827. Mr. Van Buren made the following report: The Committee on the Judiciary upon the petition of George Wilson. Washington, Gales & Seaton, 1827. 1 p. (Doc. No. 19) DLC; NjP. 31288

---- In Senate of the United States, Jan. 15, 1827. Mr. Reed, from the Committee on Public Lands, to whom was referred the petition of Thomas Gulledge, of Pike County, in the state of Mississippi, made the following report: Washington, Gales & Seaton, 1827. 1 p. (Doc. No. 20) DLC; NjP. 31289

---- In Senate of the United States, Jan. 16, 1827. Mr. Smith, of Maryland, made the following report: The Committee of Finance, to which was referred the petition of Parke Walton, made the following report: Washington, Gales & Seaton, 1827. 2 p. (Doc. No. 22) DLC; NjP. 31290

---- In Senate of the United States, Jan. 18, 1827. Ordered to be printed. Documents relating to Senate Bill No. 63, for the relief of Samuel Gilbert. Washington, Gales & Seaton, 1827. 5 p. (Doc. No. 24) DLC; NjP. 31291

---- In Senate of the United States, Jan. 19, 1827. Mr. Johnson, of Ky. made the following report: The Committee on the Post Office and Post Roads, to whom was referred the bill for the relief of Nathaniel Patten, report: Washington, Gales & Seaton, 1827. 1 p. (Doc. No. 25) DLC; NjP. 31292

---- In Senate of the United States, Jan. 19, 1827. Mr. Marks made the following report: The Committee on Military Affairs, to whom was referred the petition of J. S. Barney, administrator of the late Colonel George W. Evans ... Washington, Gales & Seaton, 1827. 1 p. (Doc. No. 26) DLC; NjP. 31293

---- In Senate of the United States, Jan. 22, 1827. Mr. Johnson, of Louisiana, made the following report: The Committee on Commerce, to whom was referred so much of the President's message as relates to commerce, have had the same under consideration, and now beg leave to report: Washington, Gales & Seaton, 1827. 18 p. (Doc. No. 27) DLC; NjP. 31294

---- ---- Mr. Reed submitted the following motion: Washington, Gales & Seaton, 1827. 1 p. (Doc. No. 28) DLC; NjP. 31295

---- In Senate of the United States, Jan. 23, 1827. Mr. Benton made the following report: The Committee on Military Affairs, to which was referred the petition of William M. Sneed, Washington, Gales & Seaton, 1827. 4 p. (Doc. No. 30) DLC; NjP. 31296

---- ---- Mr. Hendricks, from the Select Committee on Roads and Canals to whom were referred a resolution of the Senate, and two memorials of the General Assembly of the state of Indiana... Washington, Gales & Seaton, 1827. 6 p. (Doc. No. 29) DLC; NjP. 31297

---- In Senate of the United States, Jan. 25, 1827. Mr. Hendricks made the following report: The Select Committee on Roads and Canals, to whom was referred the subject of a road from Lake Michigan, by the way of Indianapolis, to the Ohio river. Washington, Gales & Seaton, 1827. 2 p. (Doc. No. 31) DLC; NjP. 31298

---- ---- Mr. Smith, from the Committee on Private Land Claims, to which was referred "A bill for the relief of Elihu Hall Bay and others, confirming ... Washington, Gales & Seaton, 1827. 2 p. (Doc. No. 32) DLC; NjP. 31299

---- In Senate of the United States. Jan. 26, 1827. Documents relating to Senate bill 75, for the relief of Haley and Harris. Washington, Gales & Seaton, 1827. 3 p. (Doc. No. 33) DLC; NjP. 31300

---- ---- Mr. Cobb made the following report: The Committee of Claims, to whom was referred the petition of Hickman Johnson, guardian of Juliet Eliza Sollers. Washington, Gales & Seaton, 1827. 14 p. (Doc. No. 35) DLC; NjP. 31301

---- In Senate of the United States, Jan. 30, 1827. Mr. Smith, of Maryland, from the Committee on Finance, to which was referred the "Bill in addition to 'An act to regulate and fix the compensation of the clerks in the different offices,' passed April, 1818," reported the same with the following amendments: [Washington, 1827] 1 p. (S. 47) DNA. 31302

---- In Senate of the United States, Feb. 2, 1827. Mr. Johnson, of Ky. made the following report, which was concurred in by the Senate. Washington, Gales & Seaton, 1827. 2 p. (Doc. No. 41) DLC; NjP. 31303

---- ---- Mr. Johnson, of Louisiana, made the following report: The Committee of Commerce, to whom was referred the petition of the inhabitants of Wilmington, North Carolina, Washington, Gales & Seaton, 1827. 2 p. (Doc. No. 49) DLC; NjP. 31304

---- In Senate of the United States, Feb. 6, 1827. Mr. Benton made the following report: The Committee on Military Affairs, to which was referred so much of the President's message as relates to the non-execution, in part, of the act of ... Washington, Gales & Seaton, 1827. 3 p. (Doc. No. 44) DLC; NjP. 31305

---- In Senate of the United States, Feb. 7, 1827. Mr. Chambers made the following report: The Committee on the District of Columbia, to whom was assigned, by a resolution of the Senate, of the 15th ultimo, the duty of inquiring ... Washington, Gales & Seaton, 1827. 3 p. (Doc. No. 45) DLC; NjP. 31306

---- In Senate of the United States, Feb. 8, 1827. Mr. Holmes made the following report: The Select Committee, to whom was referred the petitions of Joseph Emerson ... Washington, Gales & Seaton, 1827. 19 p. 7 bdsd. (Doc. No. 48) DLC; NjP. 31307

---- In Senate of the United States, Feb. 12, 1827. Mr. Sanford made the following report: The Committee of Foreign Relations having considered the memorial of certain merchants of Portsmouth, in New Hampshire, the memorial of certain merchants of the city of New York ... submit their report: Washington, Pr. by Gales & Seaton, 1827. 1 p. (Doc. No. 52) DLC; NjP. 31308

---- In Senate of the United States, Feb. 13, 1827. Mr. Reed, from the Committee on Public Lands, to whom was referred the petition of James Moore, of Mississippi, made the following report: Washington, Pr. by Gales & Seaton, 1827. 1 p. (Doc. No. 55) DLC; NjP. 31309

---- ---- Mr. Reed, from the Committee on Public Lands, to which was referred the petition of Joseph Dunbar, Receiver of Public Money in the district west of Pearl River, state of Mississippi, made the following report: Washington, Pr. by Gales & Seaton, 1827. 1 p. (Doc. No. 56) DLC; NjP. 31310

---- In Senate of the United States, Feb. 14, 1827. Mr. Bateman made the following report: The Committee of Claims, to which has been referred the petition of Daniel Renner, report: Washington, Pr. by Gales & Seaton, 1827. 2 p. (Doc. No. 60) DLC; NjP. 31311

---- ---- Mr. Smith of Maryland made the following report: The Committee appointed by the Senate to join the Committee selected on the part of the House of Representatives, "To report what subjects it is necessary to act upon at the present session ..." Washington, Pr. by Gales & Seaton, 1827. 6 p. (Doc. No. 61) DLC; NjP. 31312

---- In Senate of the United States, Feb. 15, 1827. Mr. Reed, from the Committee on Public Lands, to which was referred the petition of the representatives of William Scott, deceased, with the accompanying documents, made the following report: Washington, Pr. by Gales & Seaton, 1827. 1 p. (Doc. No. 62) DLC; NjP. 31313

---- In Senate of the United States, Feb. 16, 1827. Mr. Eaton laid the following letter on the table, which was ordered to be printed. The undersigned, agent of the United States for defending the suits in ejectment, Duncan M'Arthur vs. John Reynolds, and the said M'Arthur vs. Henry Vanmetre ... Washington, Pr. by Gales & Seaton, 1827. 1 p. (Doc. No. 67) DLC; NjP. 31314

---- In Senate of the United States, Feb. 22, 1827. Mr. Smith, of Maryland, proposed to amend the bill to regulate the commercial intercourse between the United States and the Colonies of Great Britain, by striking out all after the enacting clause, and inserting the following: [Washington, 1827] 3 p. (S. 66) DNA. 31315

---- In Senate of the United States, Feb. 23, 1827. Mr. Johnston of Louisiana, made the following report: The Committee of Commerce, to whom was referred the petition of N. Potts and Samuel Clement, assignees of Jacob Clement, have had the same under consideration and report: Washington, Pr. by Gales & Seaton, 1827. 2 p. (Doc. No. 71) DLC; NjR. 31316

---- In Senate of the United States, Feb. 28, 1827. The Committee of Finance, to whom was referred the bill, entitled "An act making appropriations for the Indian Department for the year eighteen hundred and twenty-seven," report the same with the following amendment: [Washington, 1827] 1 p. (H. R. 368) DNA. 31317

---- In Senate of the United States, Mar. 1, 1827. The Committee to whom was referred the several messages of the President of the United States, of the 5th and 8th February, and a report and certain resolutions of the legislature of Georgia, ask leave to make the following report: Washington, Pr. by Gales & Seaton, 1827. 9 p. (Doc. No. 69) DLC; NjP. 31318

---- In Senate of the United States, Dec. 19, 1827. Ordered that the 29th and 37th sections of the act of Congress entitled "An act supplementary to, and to amend an act entitled 'An act to regulate the collection of duties on imports and tonnage,' passed 2d of March, 1799, and for other purposes," approved the 1st of March, 1823, to be printed for the use of the Senate. Washington, Pr. by Duff Green, 1827. 2 p. (Doc. No. 9) DLC; NjR. 31319

---- In Senate of the United States. Dec. 31, 1827. Mr. Woodbury made the following report: Washington, Pr. by Duff Green, 1827. 2 p. (Doc. No. 13) DLC; NjR. 31320

---- ---- Mr. Cobb made the following report: Washington, Pr. by Duff Green, 1827. 3 p. (Doc. No. 14) DLC; NjR. 31321

---- ---- The Committee on the Judiciary, to whom was referred the petition of Thos. S. Winthrop and others, adopt the following report ... Washington, Pr. by Duff Green, 1827. 8 p. (Doc. No. 15) DLC; NjR. 31322

---- In the district court of the U. S. of America for the Northern district of N. Y. James Jackson exdem. Martha Beadstreet vs Henry Huntington, Bill of exceptions. Albany, John B. Van Steenbergh, 1827. 41 p., 2 p. 1. WaU. 31323

---- Index to bills of the House of Representatives, second session, nineteenth Congress. [Note.--Bills which passed the Senate, and printed by order of the House of Representatives, are to be found at the end of the Bills of the House of Representatives; and the Joint Resolutions follow immediately, in order, after them.] [Washington, 1827?] 8 p. DNA. 31324

---- Index to printed resolutions and bills of the Senate of the United States, second session of the nineteenth Congress, 1826-7. Resolutions: [Washington, 1827] 9 p. DNA. 31325

---- Indian depredations in Missouri. Jan. 23, 1827. Read, and referred to the Committee of the Whole House, to which is committed the bill making appropriations for the Indian Department for the year 1827. Mr. McLean, of Ohio, from the Committee on Indian Affairs, to which was referred, on the 8th instant, the petition of inhabitants of Missouri, praying to be compensated for depredations committed by the Sacs, Fox, and Ioway tribes of Indians, made the following report: [Washington, 1827] 3 p. (Rep. No. 51) DLC; NjP. 31326

---- Inland channel--St. Mary's

to St. John's river. Feb. 3, 1827. Mr. Mercer, from the Committee on Roads and Canals, to which the subject had been referred, made the following report: [Washington, 1827] 11 p. (Rep. No. 70) DLC; NjP. 31327

---- Jacob Sights. Jan. 2, 1827. Read, and laid upon the table. Mr. Allen of Tennessee, from the Committee on Revolutionary Claims, to which had been referred the petition of Jacob Sights, made the following report: [Washington, 1827] 1 p. (Rep. No. 26) DLC; NjP. 31328

---- James Miller, James Robertson, Wm. H. Ellis, and Joshua Prentiss. Dec. 27, 1827. Read, and laid upon the table. Mr. Cambreleng, from the Committee on Commerce, to which had been referred petitions of James Miller, James Robertson, William H. Ellis, and Joshua Prentiss, made the following report: Washington, Gales & Seaton, 1827. 2 p. (Rep. No. 35) DLC; NjR. 31329

---- James Riley et al. Dec. 12, 1827. Referred to the Committee on Foreign Affairs. [Washington, Gales & Seaton] 1827. 4 p. (Pet. No. 1) DLC; NjR. 31330

---- James Wood. Jan. 23, 1827. Read, and committed to a Committee of the Whole House tomorrow. Mr. Allen of Tennessee, from the Committee on Revolutionary Claims, to which was referred the petition of James Wood, made the following report: [Washington, 1827] 3 p. (Rep. No. 53) DLC; NjP. 31331

---- Jan. 2, 1827. Read, and laid upon the table. Mr. Livingston submitted the following resolution: [Washington, 1827] 1 p. (Res. No. 5) DLC; NjP. 31332

---- Jeremiah Buckley - heirs of. Feb. 21, 1827. Mr. Moore, of Alabama, from the Committee on Private Land Claims, to which had been referred the petition of the heirs of Jeremiah Buckley, deceased, made the following report: [Washington, 1827] 11 p. (Rep. No. 85) DLC; NjP. 31333

---- John B. Lamaitre. Dec. 20, 1827. Read, and laid upon the table. Mr. McDuffie, from the Committee of Ways and Means, to which had been referred the petition of John B. Lamaitre, made the following report: Washington, Gales & Seaton, 1827. 1 p. (Rep. No. 24) DLC; NjR. 31334

---- John Burton and al. May 10, 1826. Jan. 3, 1827. Pr. by order of the House of Representatives. Mr. Dwight, from the Committee of Ways and Means, to which was referred the petition of John Burton and al. made the following report: [Washington, 1827] 6 p. (Rep. No. 30) DLC; NjP. 31335

---- John Dorr. Dec. 20, 1827. Read, and laid upon the table. Mr. McDuffie, from the Committee of Ways and Means, to which was referred the petition of John Dorr, made the following report: Washington, Gales & Seaton, 1827. 1 p. (Rep. No. 21) DLC; NjR. 31336

---- John Heard, assignee of A. Davis. Dec. 27, 1827. Read, and laid upon the table. Mr. McDuffie, from the Committee of Ways and Means to which was referred the petition of John Heard, assignee of Amos Davis, Jun., made the following report: Washington, Gales & Seaton, 1827. 1 p. (Rep. No. 37) DLC; NjR. 31337

---- John Jackson. Dec. 20, 1827. Read, and laid upon the table. Mr. Whittlesey, from the Committee of Claims, to which was referred the petition of John Jackson, made the following report: Washington, Gales & Seaton, 1827. 2 p. (Rep. No. 22) DLC; NjR. 31338

---- John Moffett. Feb. 1, 1827. Mr. Allen, from the Committee on Revolutionary Claims, to which was referred the case of John Moffett, made the following report: [Washington, 1827] 1 p. (Rep. No. 65) DLC; NjP. 31339

---- John Overall. Report of the Committee on Private Land Claims, on the petition of John Overall. Jan. 10, 1827. Read, and committed to a Committee of the Whole House to-morrow. [Washington, 1827] 11 p. (Rep. No. 42) DLC; NjP. 31340

---- John Rodriguez. Jan. 2, 1827. Mr. McCoy, from the Committee of Claims, to which had been referred the petition of John Rodriguez, made the following report: [Washington, 1827] 3 p. (Rep. No. 27) DLC; NjP. 31341

---- ---- Dec. 19, 1827. Mr. Clark, of New York, from the Committee of Claims, to which was referred the petition of John Rodriguez, made the following report: Washington, Gales & Seaton, 1827. 3 p. (Rep. No. 19) DLC; NjR. 31342

---- John Slavan. Dec. 24, 1827. Read, and laid upon the table. Dec. 27, 1827. Committed to a Committee of the Whole House to-morrow. Mr. Tucker, of S. C. from the Committee on Revolutionary Claims, to which was referred the petition of John Slavan, made the following report: Washington, Gales & Seaton, 1827. 1 p. (Rep. No. 38) DLC; NjR. 31343

---- John Stone. Dec. 24, 1827. Read, and laid upon the table. Mr. M'Duffie, from the Committee of Ways and Means, to which was referred the petition of John Stone, made the following report: Washington, Gales & Seaton, 1827. 1 p. (Rep. No. 29) DLC; NjR. 31344

---- John Willard. Dec. 14, 1827. Mr. Whittlesey from the Committee of Claims, to which was referred the petition of John Willard, made the following report: Washington, Gales & Seaton, 1827. 3 p. (Rep. No. 3) DLC; NjR. 31345

---- John Wilson against George Graham. Feb. 27, 1827. Mr. Whipple, from the Committee on the Public Lands, to which was referred sundry charges against George Graham, Commissioner of the General Land Office, by John Wilson, late Deputy Surveyor in the Southeastern District of the state of Louisiana, made the following report: [Washington, 1827] 86 p. (Rep. No. 94) DLC; NjP. 31346

---- Joint resolution directing experiments to be made to ascertain the length of a pendulum vibrating sixty times in a minute. Jan. 24, 1827. Read twice, and committed to a Committee of the Whole House on the state of the Union. [Washington, 1827] 1 p. DNA. 31347

---- Joint resolution directing the Secretary of War to cause to be inspected and appraised the fortifications erected on Staten Island, at the expense of the state of New York. Jan. 31, 1827.

Read twice, and referred to the Committee on Military Affairs. [Washington, 1827] 1 p. DNA. 31348

---- Joint resolution for the appointment of two extra clerks in the Patent Office, to record patents. Mar. 1, 1827. Read twice, and committed to the Committee of the Whole House on the state of the Union, to which is committed the bill from the Senate (No. 47), in addition to the act to regulate and fix the compensation of clerks in the different offices. [Washington, 1827] 1 p. DNA. 31349

---- Joint resolution for the purchase of a bust of Thomas Jefferson. Feb. 24, 1827. Read twice, and committed to a Committee of the Whole House on the state of the Union. [Washington, 1827] 1 p. DNA. 31350

---- Joint resolution to indemnify the Creek Indians for the land lying between the Chatahoochee River and the dividing line between Georgia and Alabama. Feb. 8, 1827. Read the first time, and laid upon the table. [Washington, 1827] 1 p. DNA. 31351

---- Joint resolutions providing for the distribution of certain public documents, and the removal of certain books from the Library. Jan. 25, 1827, received. Jan. 28, 1827, read. [Washington, 1827] 3 p. (H. R. 2) DNA. 31352

---- Jonathan Eastman - widow of. Dec. 18, 1827. Read, and laid upon the table. Mr. McDuffie from the Committee of Ways and Means, to which was referred the petition of sundry inhabitants of Detroit, in favor of the widow of Jonathan Eastman, deceased, made the following report: Washington, Gales & Seaton, 1827. 1 p. (Rep. No. 15) DLC; NjR. 31353

---- Joseph Smith--for J. B. Dupuis. Jan. 12, 1827. Mr. Buckner, from the Committee on Private Land Claims, to which was referred the petition of Joseph Smith, for John B. Dupuis, made the following report: [Washington, 1827] 2 p. (Rep. No. 44) DLC; NjP. 31354

---- Joshua Fults. Jan. 11, 1827. Read, and committed to a Committee of the Whole House tomorrow. Mr. Allen of Tennessee, from the Committee on Revolutionary Claims, to which was referred the petition of Joshua Fults, made the following report: [Washington, 1827] 10 p. (Rep. No. 41) DLC; NjP. 31355

---- Journal of the House of Representatives of the United States, being the second session of the 19th Congress ... Washington, Pr. by Gales & Seaton, 1826 [i. e. 1827] 494 p. DLC; NjP. 31356

---- Journal of the Senate of the United States of America; being the second session of the nineteenth Congress: begun and held at the city of Washington, December 4, 1826, and in the fifty-first year of the independence of the said United States. Washington, Gales & Seaton, 1826 [i. e. 1827] 384 p. DLC; NjP. 31357

---- La Plaisance Bay Harbor. Letter from the Secretary of War, transmitting a report of a survey of La Plaisance Bay Harbor in the territory of Michigan. Jan. 26, 1827. Read, and referred to the Committee on Commerce. Washington, Gales & Seaton, 1827. 10 p. (Doc. No. 142) DLC; NjP. 31358

---- Land claims in Opelousas.

Jan. 17, 1827. Mr. Scott, from the Committee on the Public Lands, to which the subject had been referred, made the following report: [Washington, 1827] 32 p. (Rep. No. 49) DLC; NjP. 31359

---- Lands reverted. Dec. 19, 1827. Mr. Vinton, from the Committee on the Public Lands, to which the subject had been referred, made the following report: Washington, Gales & Seaton, 1827. 2 p. (Rep. No. 2) DLC; NjR. 31360

---- Letter from G. Davis, surveyor of Mississippi, to Mr. Haile, of the House of Representatives. Feb. 8, 1827. Referred to the Committee on Public Lands. Washington, Pr. by Gales & Seaton, 1827. 8 p. (Doc. No. 102) DLC; NjP. 31361

---- Letter from Henry M. Shreve to the Hon. C. A. Wickliffe, upon the subject of the navigation of the Mississippi River. Dec. 14, 1827. Read, and referred to the Committee on Roads and Canals. Washington, Pr. by Gales & Seaton, 1827. 6 p. (Doc. No. 11) DLC; NjR. 31362

---- Letter from the Secretary of the Navy transmitting information respecting the cost of, and expenditures at the several navy yards; in compliance with a resolution of the Senate of January 17, February 12, 1827. Pr. by order of the Senate of the United States. Washington, Pr. by Gales & Seaton, 1827. 12 p. (Doc. No. 54) DLC; NjP. 31363

---- Letter from the Secretary of the Treasury transmitting information relative to the transactions of the mint of the United States. Feb. 26, 1827. Read, and laid upon the table. Washington, Pr. by Gales & Seaton, 1827. 3 p. 3 bdsds. (Doc. No. 119) DLC; NjP. 31364

---- Letter from the Secretary of the Treasury transmitting statements of the commerce and navigation of the United States during the year ending on the 30th day of September. February 26, 1827. Pr. by order of the Senate of the United States. Washington, Pr. by Gales & Seaton, 1827. 296 p. 3 bdsds. (Doc. No. 72) DLC; NjP. 31365

---- Letter from the Secretary of the Treasury transmitting the annual report of the state of the finances. Dec. 10, 1827. Pr. by order of the Senate of the United States. Washington, Pr. by Duff Green, 1827. 50 p. 5 bdsds. (Doc. No. 4) DLC; NjR. 31366

---- Letter from the Secretary of War, transmitting a report of the Commissioners appointed in pursuance of an act of the last session of Congress to hold treaties with the Choctaw and Chickasaw tribes of Indians, for the purpose of extinguishing their claims to lands within the state of Mississippi. Jan. 15, 1827. Pr. by order of the Senate of the United States. Washington, Gales & Seaton, 1827. 51 p. (Doc. No. 21) DLC; NjP. 31367

---- Letter from the Secretary of War transmitting information respecting the surveys of roads and canals, and of their relative importance. Feb. 19, 1827. Read, and laid upon the table. Washington, Pr. by Gales & Seaton, 1827. 4 p. 2 bdsds. (Doc. No. 106) DLC; NjP. 31368

---- Letter from the third auditor of the Treasury, transmitting, in obedience to a resolution of the Senate, passed on the 16th inst., a report of his proceedings in relation to payment for property lost, captured, or destroyed, while in the service of the U. States. Jan. 25, 1827. Pr. by order of the Senate of the United States. Washington, Gales & Seaton, 1827. 3 p. 12 bdsds. (Doc. No. 36) DLC; NjP. 31369

---- Letter from the Treasurer of the United States, transmitting copies of the general accounts of his office from 1st of April 1825, to 1st of April 1826. Feb. 9, 1827. Read, and referred to the Committee on public expenditures. Washington, Pr. by Gales & Seaton, 1827. 182 p. (Doc. 145) G. 31370

---- Lewis B. Willis. Dec. 18, 1827. Read, and ordered to lie upon the table. Mr. Whittlesey, from the Committee of Claims, to which was referred the petition of Lewis B. Willis, made the following report: Washington, Gales & Seaton, 1827. 1 p. (Rep. No. 9) DLC; NjR. 31371

---- Lewis Rouse. Feb. 2, 1827. Read, and laid upon the table. Mr. Martindale, from the Committee of Claims, to which had been referred the petition of Lewis Rouse, made the following report: [Washington, 1827] 16 p. (Rep. No. 68) DLC; NjP. 31372

---- Licenses to trade with the Indians. Letter from the Secretary of War transmitting an abstract of licenses granted to trade with the Indians. Feb. 8, 1827. Read, and laid upon the table. Washington, Pr. by Gales & Seaton, 1827. 3 p. 7 bdsds. (Doc. No. 86) DLC; NjP. 31373

---- A list of report to be made to the House of Representatives, at the first session of the twentieth Congress, by the Executive Departments. Prepared by the clerk, in obedience to a standing order of the House of Representatives. Dec. 3, 1827. Washington, Gales & Seaton, 1827. 15 p. (Doc. No. 1) DLC; NjR. 31374

---- Live oak timber. Letter from the Secretary of the Navy on the subject of live oak timber. Feb. 26, 1827. Read, and laid upon the table. Washington, Pr. by Gales & Seaton, 1827. 9 p. (Doc. No. 114) DLC; NjP. 31375

---- Luther Chapin. Feb. 7, 1827. Mr. Martindale, from the Committee of Claims, to which was referred the petition of Luther Chapin, made the following report: [Washington, 1827] 16 p. (Rep. No. 73) DLC; NjP. 31376

---- Madame Le Compte Piernes. Dec. 18, 1827. Read and laid upon the table. Mr. Whittlesey, from the Committee of Claims, to which had been referred the petition of Madame Le Compte Piernes, made the following report: Washington, Gales & Seaton, 1827. 1 p. (Rep. No. 8) DLC; NjR. 31377

---- Manuscripts and printed books in possession of Obadiah Rich, Esq. Dec. 27, 1827. Pr. by order of the House of Representatives. Mr. Everett, from the Committee on the Library, submitted the following list of manuscripts and printed books relating to America, in possession of Obadiah Rich, Esq. Consul of the United States at Valencia. Washington, Gales & Seaton, 1827. 24 p. (Rep. No. 57) DLC; NjR. 31378

---- Marigny D'Anterive. Dec. 21, 1827. Mr. Whittlesey, from the Committee of Claims, to which was referred the petition of Marigny D'Anterive, made the following report: Washington, Gales & Seaton, 1827. 2 p. (Rep. No. 21) DLC; NjR. 31379

---- Marine hospital - sick and disabled seamen. Letter from the Secretary of the Treasury, transmitting the information required by a resolution of the House of Representatives, of the 8th inst. in relation to the amount received and expended for the relief of sick and disabled seamen, from the year 1819 to the year 1826, &c. Jan. 29, 1827. Read, and referred to the Committee on Commerce. Washington, Gales & Seaton, 1827. 6 p. 2 bdsds. (Doc. No. 63) DLC; NjP. 31380

---- Marinus W. Gilbert. Jan. 8, 1827. Mr. Martindale, from the Committee of Claims, to which had been referred the petition of Marinus W. Gilbert, made the following report: [Washington, 1827] 5 p. (Rep. No. 38) DLC; NjP. 31381

---- ---- Dec. 21, 1827. Mr. McIntire, from the Committee of Claims, to which was referred the petition of Marinus W. Gilbert, made the following report: Washington, Gales & Seaton, 1827. 7 p. (Rep. No. 28) DLC; NjR. 31382

---- Mayor and council of George Town, D. C. Representation and resolution of the mayor and council of Georgetown, in the District of Columbia, upon the subject of a bill reported to the House of Representatives, entitled a bill concerning free people of color, in the county of Washington, in the District of Columbia. Feb. 1, 1827. Read, and referred to the Committee of the Whole House to which the above bill is committed. Washington, Gales & Seaton, 1827. 5 p. (Doc. No. 71) DLC; NjP. 31383

---- Memorial and petition of Francis Henderson and Francis Henderson, Jun. on behalf of themselves and family, heirs and representatives of John Laurens, deceased. Dec. 19, 1827. Pr. by order of the Senate of the United States. Washington, Pr. by Duff Green, 1827. 8 p. (Doc. No. 8) DLC; NjR. 31384

---- Memorial of Aaron Ogden and Alden Bradford, in behalf of the surviving officers of the Revolutionary army, praying for the benefit of the original promise of half-pay, or for a reasonable equivalent. Dec. 18, 1827. Pr. by order of the Senate of the United States. Washington, Pr. by Duff Green, 1827. 7 p. (Doc. No. 7) DLC; NjR. 31385

---- Memorial of citizens of Boston and its vicinity, against the contemplated increase of duty on certain woollen goods imported. Feb. 26, 1827. Read, and laid upon the table. Washington, Pr. by Gales & Seaton, 1827. 4 p. (Doc. No. 115) DLC; NjP. 31386

---- Memorial of citizens of Logan County in the state of Ohio. Feb. 12, 1827. Pr. by order of the Senate of the United States. Washington, Pr. by Gales & Seaton, 1827. 4 p. (Doc. No. 53) DLC; NjP. 31387

---- Memorial of delegates of St. Lawrence County, N. Y., praying countervailing measures, against the late acts of the British Parliament, regulating commercial intercourse, &c. Jan. 24, 1827. Pr. by order of the Senate of the United States. Washington, Gales & Seaton, 1827.

5 p. (Doc. No. 40) DLC; NjP. 31388

---- Memorial of inhabitants of Boston, and its vicinity, adverse to an increase of duty on imported woollen goods. Feb. 26, 1827. Pr. by order of the Senate of the United States. Washington, Pr. by Gales & Seaton, 1827. 3 p. (Doc. No. 68) DLC; NjR. 31389

---- ---- Dec. 17, 1827. Pr. by order of the Senate of the United States. Washington, Pr. by Duff Green, 1827. 15 p. (Doc. No. 6) DLC; NjR. 31390

---- Memorial of inhabitants of New Bedford, Dartmouth, &c. against reducing the duty on salt. Jan. 29, 1827. Referred to the Committee on Commerce. Feb. 6, 1827. Referred to the Committee of Ways and Means. Washington, Pr. by Gales & Seaton, 1827. 4 p. (Doc. No. 80) DLC; NjP. 31391

---- Memorial of merchants and traders of New York, in relation to spoliation on their commerce. Jan. 26, 1827. Pr. by order of the Senate of the United States. Washington, Gales & Seaton, 1827. 13 p. (Doc. No. 34) DLC; NjP. 31392

---- ---- Jan. 29, 1827. Read, and referred to the Committee on Foreign Affairs. Washington, Gales & Seaton, 1827. 13 p. (Doc. No. 62) DLC; NjP. 31393

---- Memorial of sundry citizens of Charleston, South Carolina, representing the necessity of passing a general bankrupt law. Jan. 4, 1827. Ordered to be printed. Washington, Gales & Seaton, 1827. 7 p. (Doc. No. 12) DLC; NjP. 31394

---- Memorial of sundry citizens of Portsmouth, N.H. on the subject of their claims against France for injuries sustained since A.D. 1806. Feb. 12, 1827. Pr. by order of the Senate of the United States. Washington, Pr. by Gales & Seaton, 1827. 4 p. (Doc. No. 51) DLC; NjP. 31395

---- Memorial of sundry inhabitants of Massachusetts praying that the duty on imported salt may not be repealed. Jan. 23, 1827. Read, and ordered to lie on the table. Washington, Pr. by Gales & Seaton, 1827. 4 p. (Doc. No. 91) DLC; NjP. 31396

---- Memorial of sundry merchants of the city of Philadelphia upon the subject of spoliations committed under the authority or decrees of the government of France. Jan. 8, 1827. Read, and referred to the Committee on Foreign Affairs. Washington, Gales & Seaton, 1827. 4 p. (Doc. No. 37) DLC; NjP. 31397

---- Memorial of the American Society for Colonizing the Free People of Color of the United States. Jan. 29, 1827. Referred to a select Committee. Washington, Gales & Seaton, 1827. 17 p. (Doc. No. 64) DLC; NjP. 31398

---- Memorial of the Baltimore Chamber of Commerce, against the proposed law increasing the duties on woollen goods imported from abroad. Feb. 22, 1827. Pr. by order of the Senate of the United States. Washington, Pr. by Gales & Seaton, 1827. 4 p. (Doc. No. 66) DLC; NjP. 31399

---- Memorial of the Chamber of Commerce of New York, adverse to the bill for altering the duties on imports. Feb. 19, 1827. Pr. by order of the Senate of the United States. Washington, Pr. by Gales & Seaton, 1827. 4 p. (Doc. No. 64) DLC; NjP. 31400

---- Memorial of the citizens of Portsmouth, N.H. respecting the construction of a dry dock, at the Navy yard at that place. Feb. 15, 1827. Pr. by order of the Senate of the United States. Washington, Pr. by Gales & Seaton, 1827. 5 p. (Doc. No. 57) DLC; NjP. 31401

---- Memorial of the city council of Charleston, S. Carolina, praying that a marine hospital be erected at that port for accommodation of sick and disabled seamen, &c. Jan. 18, 1826. Referred to the Committee on Commerce. Dec. 20, 1826. Referred to the Committee on Commerce. Jan. 9, 1827. Bill reported - No. 356. Washington, Gales & Seaton, 1827. 4 p. (Doc. No. 42) DLC; NjP. 31402

---- Memorial of the General Assembly of Missouri, relative to relief of inhabitants of New Madrid County, in that state, who suffered by earthquakes, &c. Jan. 29, 1827. Pr. by order of the House of Representatives. Washington, Gales & Seaton, 1827. 11 p. (Doc. No. 67) DLC; NjP. 31403

---- Memorial of the General Assembly of the state of Illinois, asking for a grant of land to aid the said state in opening a canal to connect the waters of Lake Michigan with the Illinois River. Feb. 7, 1827. Pr. by order of the Senate of the United States. Washington, Gales & Seaton, 1827. 4 p. (Doc. No. 46) DLC; NjP. 31404

---- Memorial of the General Assembly of the state of Illinois asking for a grant of land to aid said state in opening a canal to connect the waters of Lake Michigan with the Illinois River. Feb. 7, 1827. Referred to the Committee of the Whole House to which is committed the "bill to aid the state of Illinois in opening a canal to connect the waters of Lake Michigan with the Illinois River. Washington, Pr. by Gales & Seaton, 1827. 4 p. (Doc. No. 81) DLC; NjP. 31405

---- Memorial of the inhabitants of the state of Georgia, in relation to depredations committed by the Creek Indians prior to the year 1802. Feb. 1, 1827. Pr. by order of the Senate of the United States. Washington, Pr. by Gales & Seaton, 1827. 5 p. (Doc. No. 38) DLC; GU-De; NjP. 31406

---- Memorial of the Legislative Council of the Territory of Michigan, in behalf of the inhabitants who suffered by the destruction of property during the late war. Dec. 20, 1827. Referred to the Committee of Claims. Washington, Pr. by Gales & Seaton, 1827. 5 p. (Doc. No. 17) DLC; NjR. 31407

---- Memorial of the Legislature of Illinois, on the subject of the public lands in that state. Jan. 12, 1827. Pr. by order of the Senate of the United States. Washington, Gales & Seaton, 1827. 5 p. (Doc. No. 17) DLC; NjP. 31408

---- Memorial of the Legislature of Indiana in relation to the sale of the public lands. Jan. 29, 1827. Pr. by order of the Senate of the United States. Washington, Gales & Seaton, 1827. 4 p. (Doc. No. 37) DLC; NjP. 31409

---- Memorial of the Legislature of Missouri, on the subject of land titles in that state, derived from the French and Spanish government. Feb. 5, 1827. Pr. by order of the Senate of the United States. Washington, Gales & Seaton, 1827. 6 p. (Doc. No. 43)

DLC; NjP. 31410

---- Message from the President of the United States, in relation to the survey of Creek lands in Georgia, with accompanying documents. Feb. 5, 1827. Read, and ordered to lie on the table. Washington, Pr. by Gales & Seaton, 1827. 9 p. (Doc. No. 76) DLC; NjP. 31411

---- Message from the President of the United States, to both Houses of Congress, at the commencement of the first session of the Twentieth Congress. Dec. 4, 1827. Read, and committed to a Committee of the whole House on the state of the Union. Washington, Gales & Seaton, 1827. 260 p. 23 bdsd. (Doc. No. 2) DLC; NjR. 31412

---- Message from the President of the United States, to the two houses of Congress at the commencement of the first session of the Twentieth Congress, Dec. 4, 1827. Pr. by order of the Senate of the United States. Washington, Pr. by Duff Green, 1827. 265 p. 28 bdsds. (Doc. No. 1) DLC; NjR. 31413

---- ... Message from the President ... to the two houses of Congress, at the commencement of the first session of the Twentieth Congress. Dec. 4. 1827. Washington, Pr. by Duff Green, 1827. 38 p. CSmH. 31414

---- Message from the President of the United States, transmitting a detailed statement of the expenditures for the construction and repair of the Cumberland Road, in compliance with a resolution of the Senate of the 20th of May last. Jan. 10, 1827. Pr. by order of the Senate of the United States. Washington, Gales & Seaton, 1827. 7 p. (Doc. No. 14) DLC; NjP. 31415

---- Message from the President of the United States, transmitting a letter from the Governor of Georgia, with accompanying documents ... Washington, Pr. by Gales & Seaton, 1827. 14 p. TxFTC. 31416

---- Message from the President of the United States, transmitting a letter from the Governor of Georgia, with accompanying documents. Feb. 8, 1827. Pr. by order of the Senate of the United States. Washington, Gales & Seaton, 1827. 7 p. (Doc. No. 47) DLC; NjP. 31417

---- Message from the President of the United States, transmitting a letter from the Governor of Georgia (G. M. Troup), with accompanying documents, in relation to the proceedings of certain Indians in said state. Feb. 9, 1827 ... Washington, Pr. by Gales & Seaton, 1827. 7 p. (Doc. No. 87) GU-De. 31418

---- Message from the President of the United States transmitting a report from the Secretary of the Treasury in relation to the purchases and sales of the public lands since the Declaration of Independence. Feb. 16, 1827. Pr. by order of the Senate of the United States. Washington, Pr. by Gales & Seaton, 1827. 35 p. 4 bdsds. (Doc. No. 63) DLC; NjP. 31419

---- Message from the President of the United States transmitting a report from the Surveyor General of lands north-west of the Ohio, on the subject of the boundary line of the state of Indiana. Dec. 12, 1827. Pr. by order of the Senate of the United States. Washington, Pr. by Duff Green,

1827. 5 p. (Doc. No. 5) DLC; NjR. 31420

---- Message from the President of the United States, transmitting a report in relation to the execution of the Treaty of Oct. 18, 1820, with the Choctaw Nation of Indians. In compliance with a resolution of the Senate of the 18th ultimo. Feb. 2, 1827. Pr. by order of the Senate of the United States. Washington, Gales & Seaton, 1827. 4 p. (Doc. No. 42) DLC; NjP. 31421

---- Message from the President of the United States transmitting a report of the Commissioner of the General Land Office, relating to public lands in Missouri and Illinois, which are unfit for cultivation. In compliance with a resolution of the Senate of 4th April, 1826. Feb. 14, 1827. Pr. by order of the Senate of the United States. Washington, Pr. by Gales & Seaton, 1827. 10 p. 1 bdsd. (Doc. No. 59) DLC; NjP. 31422

---- Message from the President of the United States, transmitting a report relative to the result of an assay of foreign coins, in compliance with a resolution of the Senate. Jan. 18, 1827. Pr. by order of the Senate of the United States. Washington, Gales & Seaton, 1827. 16 p. 3 bdsds. (Doc. No. 23) DLC; NjP. 31423

---- Message from the President of the United States, transmitting (in compliance with a resolution of the Senate of 19th February last) a report from the Secretary of the Navy showing the expense annually incurred in carrying into effect the act of March 2, 1819, for prohibiting the slave trade. Dec. 6, 1827. Pr. by order of the Senate of the United States. Washington, Pr. by Duff Green, 1827. 11 p. 9 bdsds. (Doc. No. 3) DLC; NjR. 31424

---- Message from the President of the United States, transmitting copies of communications of the Governor of Georgia and Lieut. Vinton, to the Secretary of War. March 2, 1827. Referred to Select Committee on the Resolutions, &c. of the Legislature of Georgia. Washington, Gales & Seaton, 1827. 9 p. (Doc. No. 127) DLC; NjP. 31425

---- Military appropriations for 1826. Letter from the Secretary of War, transmitting a statement of appropriations for the service of the year 1826, showing the amount appropriated under each specified head, the amount expended under each, and the unexpended balance on 31st Dec. last. Feb. 3, 1827. Read, and laid upon the table. Washington, Gales & Seaton, 1827. 4 p. 6 bdsd. (Doc. No. 132) DLC; NjP. 31426

---- Military road--Fishkill Landing to Cold Spring. Feb. 6, 1827. Mr. Ward, from the Committee on Military Affairs, to which the subject had been referred, made the following report: [Washington, 1827] 4 p. (Rep. No. 72) DLC; NjP. 31427

---- Militia of the United States. Letter from the Secretary of War, transmitting an abstract of the general annual returns of the militia of the United States. Feb. 6, 1827. Read, and laid upon the table. Washington, Gales & Seaton, 1827. 3 p. 2 bdsd. (Doc. No. 130) DLC; NjP. 31428

---- Miscellaneous claims--contracts revenue service, sick seamen, and contracts for oil, lighthouses, &c. Letter from the Secretary of the Treasury transmitting statements shewing 1. Payments made at the Treasury during the year 1826 for the discharge of miscellaneous claims not otherwise provided for; 2. Contracts made for the revenue service during the year 1825; 3. Of expenditures on account of sick and disabled seamen; and 4. Of contracts made relative to oil, light-houses, light-vessels, beacons, buoys, &c. Feb. 13, 1827. Read, and laid upon the table. Washington, Pr. by Gales & Seaton, 1827. 13 p. 5 bdsds. (Doc. No. 101) DLC; NjP. 31429

---- Mr. Cocke, from the Committee on Indian Affairs, to which had been referred the estimate of appropriations for the service of the year 1827, so far as relates to certain Indian establishments, &c. made the following report: Feb. 22, 1827. [Washington, 1827] 1 p. (Rep. No. 86) DLC; NjP. 31430

---- Mr. Storrs, from the Committee on Naval Affairs, to which had been referred the bill from the Senate, (No. 50,) entitled "An act for the gradual improvement of the Navy of the United States," reported the same with amendments. Feb. 22, 1827. Read, and committed to a Committee of the Whole House on the state of the Union. [Washington, 1827] 3 p. (S. 50) DNA. 31431

---- Monthly statements bank U. States for 1826. Letter from the Secretary of the Treasury, transmitting the monthly statements of the bank of the United States, rendered in obedience to a resolution of the House of Representatives, of third instant. Jan. 9, 1827. Read, and laid upon the table. Washington, Gales & Seaton, 1827. 3 p. 12 bdsd. (Doc. No. 52) DLC; NjP. 31432

---- Nathaniel Hunt, et al. Dec. 18, 1827. Read, and laid upon the table. Mr. McDuffie, from the Committee of Ways and Means, to which was referred the petition of Nathaniel Hunt and others, made the following report: Washington, Gales & Seaton, 1827. 1 p. (Rep. No. 13) DLC; NjR. 31433

---- National Road--Wheeling to Missouri. Letter from the Secretary of War transmitting reports and drawings relative to the National Road, from Wheeling to the seat of government of the state of Missouri. Feb. 3, 1827. Read, and referred to the Committee on Roads and Canals. Washington, Pr. by Gales & Seaton, 1827. 26 p. (Doc. No. 74) DLC; NjP. 31434

---- Navigation of Red River. March 1, 1827. Mr. Mercer, from the Committee on Roads and Canals, to which was referred the memorial of the General Assembly of Arkansas, in relation to obstructions to the navigation of Red River, made the following report: [Washington, 1827] 8 p. (Rep. No. 96) DLC; NjP. 31435

---- Navy contracts for 1826. Letter from the Secretary of the Navy, transmitting a statement of contracts made by the department, during the year 1826. Jan. 3, 1827. Read, and laid upon the table. Washington, Gales & Seaton, 1827. 3 p. 6 bdsd. (Doc. No. 33) DLC; NjP. 31436

---- Navy hospitals. Report of the Commissioners of Naval hospitals, upon the state of their funds. Jan. 15, 1827. Referred to the Committee on Naval Affairs. Washington, Gales & Seaton, 1827. 15 p. (Doc. No. 54) DLC; NjP. 31437

---- Navy pension fund. Letter from the Secretary of the Navy, transmitting the annual report in relation to the navy pension fund. Prepared in compliance with the act of Congress, of 23d April, 1800. Jan. 12, 1827. Read, and laid upon the table. Washington, Gales & Seaton, 1827. 24 p. 2 bdsd. (Doc. No. 56) DLC; NjP. 31438

---- Old internal revenue and direct tax, and direct tax of 1815 & 1816. Letter from the Comptroller of the Treasury, transmitting lists of balances on the books of the register of the Treasury, on account of the old internal revenue and direct tax: also, an account of the direct tax of 1815 & 1816. Feb. 12, 1827. Read, and laid on the table. Washington, Gales & Seaton, 1827. 3 p. 7 bdsd. (Doc. No. 139) DLC; NjP. 31439

---- The opinion of Chief Justice Marshall, in the case of Garnett, ex'r of Brooke, v. Macon et al. ... Richmond, Pub. by Peter Cottom, and for sale at his law and miscellaneous book store, 1827. [Washington, 1827] 58+ p. CSmH. 31440

---- Orders of the day. Orders for Monday, Feb. 5th, 1827. [Washington, 1827] 6 p. DNA. 31441

---- ---- For Monday, Feb. 12th, 1827. [Washington, 1827] 5 p. DNA. 31442

---- ---- For Monday, Feb. 19th, 1827. [Washington, 1827] 7 p. DNA. 31443

---- ---- For Monday, Feb. 26th, 1827. [Washington, 1827] 8 p. DNA. 31444

---- Orleans Navigation Company. Feb. 24, 1827. Mr. Webster, from the Committee on the Judiciary, to which the subject had been referred, made the following report: [Washington, 1827] 20 p. (Rep. No. 88) DLC; NjP. 31445

---- Orson Sparks and John Watson. Dec. 21, 1827. Read, and laid upon the table. Dec. 24, 1827. Committed to a Committee of the whole House to-morrow. Washington, Gales & Seaton, 1827. 3 p. (Rep. No. 33) DLC; NjR. 31446

---- Passengers arriving in U. States - 1826. Letter from the Secretary of State, transmitting an abstract of passengers arriving in the U. States, from the 1st Oct. 1825, to 30th Sept. 1826. Feb. 24, 1827. Read, and laid upon the table. Washington, Gales & Seaton, 1827. 3 p. 24 bdsd. (Doc. No. 143) DLC; NjP. 31447

---- Patent office. Letter from the Secretary of State, transmitting the information required by a resolution of the House of Representatives of the 19th ult. upon the subject of the organization of the patent office. Jan. 13, 1827. Read, and laid upon the table. Washington, Gales & Seaton, 1827. 8 p. (Doc. No. 47) DLC; NjP. 31448

---- Patents for useful inventions in 1826. Letter from the Secretary of State transmitting a list of the names of persons to whom patents have been issued, for the invention of any new or useful art, or machine, manufacture or composition of matter, or any improvement thereon, from Jan. 1st 1826, to Jan. 1st 1827. Jan. 8, 1827. Read, and laid upon the table. Washington, Gales & Seaton, 1827. 21 p. (Doc. No. 27) DLC; NjP. 31449

---- Port entry--Penobscot River.

Feb. 10, 1827. Read, and commited to a committee of the whole House to-morrow. Mr. Tomlinson, from the Committee on Commerce, to which had been referred petition of inhabitants of the state of Maine, praying for the establishment of a collection district and port of entry on Penobscot river, made the following report: [Washington, 1827] 2 p. (Rep. No. 78) DLC; NjP. 31450

---- Post office clerks. Letter from the Postmaster General transmitting a statement of the number of clerks employed in the post office department during the year 1826, with their names and salaries. Jan. 3, 1827. Read, and referred to the Committee on the Post Office and Post Roads. Washington, Gales & Seaton, 1827. 4 p. (Doc. No. 32) DLC; NjP. 31451

---- Postage accruing in the U. S. - 1826. Letter from the Postmaster General, transmitting a statement of the nett amount of postage accruing at each post office, in each state and territory, for one year, ending 31st March, 1826. Jan. 3, 1827. Read, and laid upon the table. Washington, Gales & Seaton, 1827. 74 p. (Doc. No. 35) DLC; NjP. 31452

---- Pre-emption to actual settlers. Dec. 24, 1827. Mr. Isacks, from the Committee on the Public Lands, to which the subject had been referred made the following report: Washington, Gales & Seaton, 1827. 2 p. (Rep. No. 31) DLC; NjR. 31453

---- President's message. Martinsburg Gazette ... Extra. Thursday, Dec. 6, 1827. The President of the United States transmitted, this day, to both Houses of Congress, the following message ... John Quincy Adams. Washington, Dec. 4, 1827. Bdsd. Norona 891. 31454

---- ---- National intelligencer ... Extra. Tuesday, Dec. 4, 1827. [Washington, 1827] 1 p. DLC. 31455

---- Prohibition of the slave trade. Statement showing the expenditure of the appropriation for the prohibition of the slave trade, during the year 1826, and an estimate for 1827. Jan. 30, 1827. Pr. by order of the House of Representatives of the United States. Washington, Gales & Seaton, 1827. 4 p. (Doc. No. 69) DLC; NjP. 31456

---- The public and general statutes passed by the Congress of the United States of America ... published under the inspection of Joseph Story. Boston, Wells & Lilly, 1827-1828. 3 v. ICLaw; M; MBS; MH; MH-L; MS; MdAN; MsU; NPV; Nj; OM; ViU; BrMus. 31457

---- Public buildings. Feb. 7, 1827. Mr. Van Rensselaer, from the Committee on the Public Buildings, to which was referred so much of the President's message as relates to the progress of the public buildings, made the following report: [Washington, 1827] 8 p. (Rep. No. 75) DLC; NjP. 31458

---- Punishment of crimes. Feb. 6, 1827. Mr. Webster, from the Committee on the Judiciary, to which the subject had been referred, made the following report: [Washington, 1827] 3 p. (Rep. No. 71) DLC; NjP. 31459

---- Quapaw Indians. Letter from the Secretary of War, transmitting the information required by a resolution of the House of Representatives of the 18th ultimo, in relation to the present condition of the Quapaw Nation of Indians. Jan. 10, 1827. Read, and referred to the Committee on Indian Affairs. Washington, Gales & Seaton, 1827. 15 p. (Doc. No. 43) DLC; NjP. 31460

---- Ratio of representation under fifth census. Documents submitted by Mr. Peter Little of the House of Representatives. Feb. 17, 1827. Pr. by order of the House of Representatives. Washington, Pr. by Gales & Seaton, 1827. 7 p. 3 bdsds. (Doc. No. 104) DLC; NjP. 31461

---- ---- Dec. 12, 1827. Pr. by order of the House of Representatives. Washington, Pr. by Gales & Seaton, 1827. 32 p. 2 bdsds. (Doc. No. 12) DLC; NjR. 31462

---- Receipts and expenditures United States, 1825. Letter from the Secretary of the Treasury transmitting an account of the receipts and expenditures of the United States for the year 1825. Feb. 24, 1827. Read, and laid upon the table. Washington, Pr. by Gales & Seaton, 1827. 3 p. (Doc. No. 111) DLC; NjP. 31463

---- Receipts from the customs from 1815 to 1826. Letter from the Secretary of the Treasury transmitting the information required by a resolution of the House of Representatives of the 12th ultimo, being a statement of the annual receipts from the customs from the 30th December, 1815, to 30th September, 1826; and the annual amount of drawbacks from the same period. Feb. 20, 1827. Washington, Pr. by Gales & Seaton, 1827. 16 p. (Doc. No. 107) DLC; NjP. 31464

---- Removal of the Indians westward. Letter from the Secretary of War, transmitting, in obedience to a resolution of the House of Representatives, of the 20th Dec. last, information in relation to the disposition of the several tribes of Indians, to emigrate west of the Mississippi. Jan. 3, 1827. Read, and referred to the Committee on Indian Affairs. Washington, Gales & Seaton, 1827. 13 p. (Doc. No. 28) DLC; NjP. 31465

---- Report - Committee of accounts on contingent expenditures. Mar. 2, 1827. The Committee of Accounts, to whom was referred the resolution of the 19th inst. instructing them to inquire into the expediency of reducing the contingent expenses of this House, beg leave to report: [Washington, 1827] 1 p. (Rep. No. 97) DLC; NjP. 31466

---- Report--Director of the mint. Message from the President of the United States, transmitting a report from the director of the mint, and a statement of its operations during the year 1826. Feb. 24, 1827. Read, and laid upon the table. Washington, Pr. by Gales & Seaton, 1827. 6 p. 1 bdsd. (Doc. No. 113) DLC; NjP. 31467

---- Report and resolutions of the Legislature of Georgia, with accompanying documents. Jan. 23, 1827. Pr. by order of the House of Representatives. Washington, Gales & Seaton, 1827. 404 p. (Doc. No. 59) DLC; NjP. 31468

---- Report from the Secretary of the Senate showing the expenditure of the contingent fund of the Senate, for the year 1827. Dec. 5, 1827. Pr. by order of the Senate of the United States. Washington, Pr. by Duff Green, 1827. 7 p. (Doc. No. 2) DLC; NjR. 31469

---- Report from the Secretary of the Treasury (in obedience to a resolution of the Senate of the 14th inst.) showing the amount of revenue from imposts and tonnage in Florida, since its cession to the United States. Dec. 20, 1827. Pr. by order of the Senate of the United States. Washington, Pr. by Duff Green, 1827. 3 p. 1 bdsd. (Doc. No. 10) DLC; NjR. 31470

---- Report from the Secretary of War, with abstract of licenses granted by superintendents and agents of Indian affairs, to trade with the Indians during the year ending the first of September, 1827. Feb. 8, 1827. Pr. by order of the Senate of the United States. Washington, Pr. by Gales & Seaton, 1827. 3 p. 7 bdsds. (Doc. No. 58) DLC; NjP. 31471

---- Report of the Committee appointed on the 29th Dec., 1826, on a letter of John C. Calhoun, Vice-President of the United States asking an investigation of his conduct while Secretary of War, with accompanying documents. Feb. 13, 1827. Read, and ordered to lie on the table. Washington, Pr. by Gales & Seaton, 1827. 251 p. 2 bdsds. (Rep. No. 79) DLC; NjP. 31472

---- ... Report [of] the Committee on the public buildings, to whom was referred so much of the President's message, of December 8th, as relates to the progress of the public buildings ... Feb. 7, 1827. 4 p. DLC. 31473

---- Report of the Secretary of War, in relation to the number of white persons residing on Chickasaw and Choctaw lands. Rendered in compliance with a resolution of the Senate of the 25th ult. Feb. 1, 1827. Pr. by order of the Senate of the United States. Washington, Gales & Seaton, 1827. 5 p. (Doc. No. 39) DLC; NjP. 31474

---- Report of the Select Committee of the House of Representatives, to which were referred the messages of the President U. S. of the 5th and 8th February, and 2d March, 1827, with accompanying documents and a report and resolutions of the Legislature of Georgia. March 3, 1827. Washington, Pr. by Gales & Seaton, 1827. xi, 846 p. (Rep. No. 98) GU-De; NjP. 31475

---- Reports of cases argued and determined in the Circuit court of the United States for the second circuit [1810-1840] by Elijah Paine, Jun. New York, Donaldson, 1827-1856. [Geo. F. Hopkins, pr.] ArSC; C; CU-Law; DLC; F-SC; ICLaw; IaUL; In-SC; LNT-L; MBU-L; MSaEC; Md; MdBB; Me-LR; Mi-L; MoKB; NNLI; NUtSC; NbU-L; NcD; Nj; OClW; OrSC; PLL; PU-L; RPL; Sc-SC; ViU; TMeB. 31476

---- Reports of cases determined in the Circuit court of the United States, for the third circuit, comprising the districts of Pennsylvania and New Jersey, published from the manuscripts of the Honourable Bushrod Washington, one of the associate justices of the Supreme Court of the United States. Philadelphia, Philip H. Nicklin, Pr. by Lydia Bailey, 1827-29. 4 v. FU-L; L; MBU-L; Me-LR; Nj; NjHo; NjP. 31477

---- Representatives of Gen. Wm. Hull. Jan. 31, 1827. Mr. McCoy, from the Committee of Claims, to which was referred the petition of the widow and administrator of the late General William Hull, made the following report: [Washington, 1827] 2 p. (Rep. No. 63) DLC; NjP. 31478

---- Representatives of Joseph Jeans. Jan. 3, 1827. Mr. Whittlesey, from the Committee of Claims, to which had been referred the petition of the representatives of Joseph Jeans, made the following report: [Washington, 1827] 2 p. (Rep. No. 29) DLC; NjP. 31479

---- Resolution in Senate of the United States, Jan. 9, 1827. Received. [Washington, 1827] 1 p. DNA. (H. R.) 31480

---- Resolution. Mr. Hamilton submitted the following Resolution, which was read and ordered to lie on the table. Dec. 24, 1827. [Washington, 1827] 1 p. (H. R. 4) DNA. 31481

---- Resolution of the General Assembly of Indiana in relation to purchasers of public lands. Feb. 26, 1827. Referred to the Committee on Public Lands. Feb. 27, 1827. Pr. by order of the House of Representatives. Washington, Pr. by Gales & Seaton, 1827. 3 p. (Doc. No. 117) DLC; NjP. 31482

---- Resolution of the General Assembly of the state of Indiana upon the subject of the lands set far apart for the use of schools in said state. Feb. 27, 1827. Read, and laid upon the table. Washington, Pr. by Gales and Seaton, 1827. 3 p. (Doc. No. 116) DLC; NjP. 31483

---- Resolution of the Legislature of Georgia, on the subject of militia claims. Jan. 8, 1827. Referred to the Committee on Military Affairs. Washington, Gales & Seaton, 1827. 5 p. (Doc. No. 40) DLC; NjP. 31484

---- Resolution of the Legislature of Georgia, on the subject of militia claims. Jan. 11, 1827. Ordered to be printed. Washington, Gales & Seaton, 1827. 5 p. (Doc. No. 16) DLC; NjP. 31485

---- Resolution to amend the Constitution U. States. Mr. Mc Duffie submitted the following proposition to amend the Constitution of the United States: Dec. 19, 1827. Read, and committed to a Committee of the Whole House on the state of the Union. [Washington, 1827] 2 p. (H. R. 1) DNA. 31486

---- Resolution to amend the Constitution. Mr. Smyth, of Virginia, submitted the following Proposition to amend the Constitution of the United States. Dec. 19, 1827. Read, and committed to a Committee of the Whole House on the state of the Union. [Washington, 1827] 3 p. (H. R. 2) DNA. 31487

---- Resolutions and remonstrance of the Agricultural Society of St. Andrew's Parish, S. C. against any further increase of the duties on imports, &c. Dec. 14, 1827. Referred to the Committee on Manufactures. Washington, Pr. by Gales & Seaton, 1827. 4 p. (Doc. No. 13) DLC; NjR. 31488

---- Resolutions and remonstrance of the Agricultural Society of St. John's, Colleton, S. C. against any further increase of the duties on imports, &c. Dec. 14, 1827. Referred to the Committee on Manufactures. Washington, Pr. by Gales & Seaton, 1827. 4 p. (Doc. No. 14) DLC; NjR. 31489

---- Resolutions of the Legislature of Louisiana, in relation to a provision in lands for the disbanded officers of the late army of the United States. March 3, 1827. Pr. by order of the Senate of the United States. Washington, Pr. by Gales & Seaton, 1827. 3 p. (Doc. No. 70) DLC; NjP. 31490

---- Resolutions of the Legislature of the state of Ohio, upon the subject of amending the Constitution in relation to the election of President of the United States. Feb. 20, 1827. Read, and laid upon the table. Dec. 20, 1827. Referred to the Committee of the Whole House on the state of the Union. [Washington, 1827] 2 p. (H. R. 3) DNA. 31491

---- Resolutions of the state of Alabama in relation to the system for the disposal of the public lands. February 12, 1827. Pr. by order of the Senate of the United States. Washington, Pr. by Gales & Seaton, 1827. 3 p. (Doc. No. 50) DLC; NjP. 31492

---- Revenue of the United States. Statements exhibiting the revenue arising from duties on merchandise, tonnage, &c during the year ending on the 31st Dec., 1825; referred to in the annual report of the Secretary of the Treasury, upon the state of the finances of the 12th December, 1826. Dec. 13, 1826. Pr. by order of the House of Representatives. Washington, Pr. by Gales & Seaton, 1827. 19 p. 1 bdsd. (Rep. No. 146) DLC; NjP. 31493

---- Richard Livingston. Feb. 15, 1827. Mr. Hasbrouck, from the Committee on Revolutionary Claims, to which was referred the petition of Richard Livingston, made the following report: [Washington, 1827] 1 p. (Rep. No. 83) DLC; NjP. 31494

---- Richard W. Steele. Feb. 2, 1827. Mr. Whittlesey, from the Committee of Claims, to which was referred the petition of Richard W. Steele, made the following report: [Washington, 1827] 1 p. (Rep. No. 67) DLC; NjP. 31495

---- Road--Baltimore to Philadelphia. Letter from the Postmaster General transmitting a report of General Bernard, of surveys of routes for a post road from Baltimore to Philadelphia. Feb. 12, 1827. Read, and laid upon the table. Washington, Pr. by Gales & Seaton, 1827. 19 p. 7 bdsds. (Doc. No. 94) DLC; NjP. 31496

---- Road--La Plaisance Harbor, westward. Jan. 10, 1827. Mr. Mercer, from the Committee on Roads and Canals, to which the subject had been referred, made the following report: [Washington, 1827] 4 p. (Rep. No. 39) DLC; NjP. 31497

---- Road--Washington City to New Orleans. Feb. 22, 1827. Mr. Blair submitted the following, which he intends to offer as an amendment to the "Bill to regulate the laying out and making a road from the seat of government, in the city of Washington, to the city of New Orleans," &c. [Washington, 1827] 2 p. (H. R. 226) DNA. 31498

---- Road--Zanesville to Columbus. Letter from the Secretary of War, transmitting a report on the subject of the national road between Zanesville and Columbus. Jan. 3, 1827. Read, and referred to the Committee on Roads and Canals. Washington, Gales & Seaton, 1827. 7 p. (Doc. No. 31) DLC; NjP. 31499

---- Road from Washington City to Buffalo. Letter from the Secretary of War transmitting a report of surveys of proposed routes of a national road from the city of Washington to Buffalo in the state of New York. Feb. 17, 1827. Read, and referred to the Committee on Roads and Canals. Washington, Pr. by Gales & Seaton, 1827. 39 p. 3 bdsds. (Doc. No. 105) DLC; NN; NjP. 31500

---- Robert Davis. Dec. 18, 1827. Read, and laid upon the table. Mr. Whittlesey, from the Committee of Claims, to which was referred the petition of Robert Davis, made the following report: Washington, Gales & Seaton, 1827. 6 p. (Rep. No. 10) DLC; NjR. 31501

---- Robert Huston. Jan. 17, 1827. Mr. Whittlesey, from the Committee of Claims, to which was referred the petition of Robert Huston, made the following report: [Washington, 1827] 3 p. (Rep. No. 46) DLC; NjP. 31502

---- Salt springs in Illinois. Feb. 10, 1827. Mr. Scott, from the Committee on the Public Land to which was referred the memorial of the Legislature of the state of Illinois, upon the subject of lands reserved for the use of salt springs, made the following report: [Washington, 1827] 10 p. (Rep. No. 100) DLC; NjP. 31503

---- Samuel Sprigg. Jan. 27, 1827. Mr. Buckner, from the Committee on Private Land Claims, to which had been referred the petition of Samuel Sprigg, made the following report: [Washington, 1827] 2 p. (Rep. No. 58) DLC; NjP. 31504

---- Settlers on Choctaw lands. Feb. 27, 1827. Mr. Scott, from the Committee on the Public Lands to which the subject had been referred, made the following report. [Washington, 1827] 4 p. (Rep. No. 93) DLC; NjP. 31505

---- South Carolina - Abbeville District. Memorial of the citizens of Abbeville District, S. C. against an increase of duties on imported goods. Dec. 27, 1827. Read, and laid upon the table. Washington, Pr. by Gales & Seaton, 1827. 16 p. (Doc. No. 23) DLC; NjR. 31506

---- South Carolina - Edgefield District. Memorial of the citizens of Edgefield, against the woollens bill. Dec. 27, 1827. Read, and laid upon the table. Washington, Pr. by Gales and Seaton, 1827. 7 p. (Doc. No. 24) DLC; NjR. 31507

---- South Carolina. Memorial of the citizens of Columbia, S. C. praying a revision of the tariff, &c. Dec. 18, 1827. Referred to the Committee on Manufactures. Washington, Pr. by Gales & Seaton, 1827. 4 p. (Doc. No. 16) DLC; NjR. 31508

---- South Carolina. Memorial of the citizens of Orangeburg, S. C. against any increase of duties on woollen goods of foreign manufacture. Dec. 24, 1827. Referred to the Committee on Manufactures. Washington, Pr. by Gales & Seaton, 1827. 5 p. (Doc. No. 21) DLC; NjR. 31509

---- South Carolina. Memorial of the inhabitants of Barnwell District, in S. C. remonstrating against any additional duties on imported wool goods. Dec. 24, 1827. Referred to the Committee on Manufactures. Washington, Pr.

by Gales & Seaton, 1827. 4 p. (Doc. No. 20) DLC; NjR. 31510

---- South Carolina. Memorial of the inhabitants of Fairfield District, in South Carolina, praying a revision of the tariff, &c. Dec. 14, 1827. Referred to the Committee on Manufactures. Washington, Pr. by Gales & Seaton, 1827. 9 p. (Doc. No. 15) DLC; NjR. 31511

---- Spoliations on the commerce of the United States, by France, &c. Feb. 23, 1827. Mr. Everett, from the Committee on Foreign Affairs, to which the subject had been referred, made the following report: [Washington, 1827] 13 p. (Rep. No. 87) DLC; NjP. 31512

---- Spoliations on the commerce of the U. S. Letter from the Secretary of State, transmitting a schedule of claims of American citizens, for spoliations, by France and other European nations, since the year 1805. Jan. 31, 1827. Washington, Pr. by Gales & Seaton, 1827. (Doc. No. 68) 23 p., folding bdsds. DLC; NjP. 31513

---- State of the finances. Letter from the Secretary of the Treasury, transmitting the annual report on the state of the finances. Dec. 10, 1827. Referred to the Committee of Ways and Means. Washington, Gales & Seaton, 1827. 50 p. 2 bdsds. (Doc. No. 4) DLC; NjR. 31514

---- Stockbridge Indians. Extracts of letters upon the subject of the present condition of the Stockbridge Indians. Jan. 8, 1827. Laid before the House. Washington, Gales & Seaton, 1827. 4 p. (Doc. No. 38) DLC; NjP. 31515

---- A supplement to the Catalogue of the Library of Congress. Washington, Pr. by P. Force, 1827. 109 p. DLC; MBAt; MWiW; BrMus. 31516

---- Surgeons of the Navy. Jan. 17, 1827. Read, and ordered to lie on the table. Mr. Bartlett, from the Committee on Naval Affairs, to which the subject had been referred, made the following report: [Washington, 1827] 2 p. (Rep. No. 47) DLC; NjP. 31517

---- Survey of Kennebec River. Letter from the Secretary of War transmitting a report of a survey of Kennebec River in the state of Maine. Jan. 26, 1827. Referred to the Committee on Commerce. Washington, Pr. by Gales & Seaton, 1827. 6 p. (Doc. No. 103) DLC; NjP. 31518

---- Survey of Saugatuck Harbor and River. Letter from the Secretary of War transmitting a report and map of the survey of Saugatuck Harbor and River. Feb. 23, 1827. Read, and laid upon the table. Washington, Pr. by Gales & Seaton, 1827. 10 p. 1 bdsd. (Doc. No. 110) DLC; NjP. 31519

---- The survey of the Creek lands. Message from the President of the United States transmitting a letter from the Governor of Georgia with accompanying documents, in relation to the proceeding of certain Indians in said state. Feb. 9, 1827. Read, and referred to a Select Committee. Washington, Pr. by Gales & Seaton, 1827. 7 p. (Doc. No. 87) DLC; NjP. 31520

---- Surveys--roads and canals. Letter from the Secretary of War transmitting (to the chairman of the Committee on Roads and Canals) a statement exhibiting the number and designation of the examination and surveys, which have been made with a view to the construction of roads and canals. Feb. 7, 1827. Pr. by order of the House of Representatives. Washington, Pr. by Gales & Seaton, 1827. 4 p. 4 bdsds. (Doc. No. 83) DLC; NjP. 31521

---- Surveys harbor of Edgartown, Merrimack River, &c. Letter from the Secretary of War, transmitting reports of a survey of the flats on the northwest side of the harbor of Edgartown; a survey of the mouth of Merrimack River; also, a survey of the harbor of Hyannis, in the vineyard sound, with a map of each: rendered in obedience to a resolution of the House of Representatives of the fourth of last month. Feb. 9, 1827. Read, and referred to the Committee on Commerce. Washington, Gales & Seaton, 1827. 16 p. (Doc. No. 140) DLC; NjP. 31522

---- Surveys, with a view to making roads & canals. Mar. 2, 1827. Mr. Mercer, from the Committee on Roads and Canals, made the following report: [Washington, 1827] 31 p. (Rep. No. 102) DLC; NjP. 31523

---- Surviving Revolutionary officers. A memorial of Aaron Ogden and Alden Bradford, a committee in behalf of the surviving officers of the Revolutionary Army. Dec. 4, 1827, Referred to a Select Committee. Dec. 6, 1827, Pr. by order of the House of Representatives. Washington, Gales & Seaton, 1827. 13 p. (Doc. No. 3) DLC; NjR. 31524

---- System of accountability for clothing and camp equipage issued to the army of the United States. Washington, 1827. James C. Dunn, Pr., Georgetown, 22 p. DLC. 31525

---- Tennessee to issue grants, &c. Dec. 24, 1827. Mr. Polk, from the Select Committee, to which the subject had been referred, made the following report: Washington, Gales & Seaton, 1827. 6 p. (Rep. No. 32) DLC; NjR. 31526

---- Thaddeus Laughlin. Letter from the Secretary of the Treasury, transmitting the opinion of the Attorney General, in the case of Thaddeus Laughlin. Dec. 14, 1827. Read, and laid upon the table. Washington, Pr. by Gales & Seaton, 1827. 6 p. (Doc. No. 10) DLC; NjR. 31527

---- Thomas C. Withers. Jan. 24, 1827. Mr. Martindale, from the Committee of Claims, to which was referred the petition of Thomas C. Withers, made the following report: [Washington, 1827] 2 p. (Rep. No. 55) DLC; NjP. 31528

---- Thomas Flournoy. Jan. 30, 1827. Mr. Wright, from the Committee on the Judiciary, to which had been referred the petition, &c. of Thomas Flournoy, made the following report: [Washington, 1827] 2 p. (Rep. No. 62) DLC; NjP. 31529

---- Thomas Gulledge. Feb. 9, 1827. Read, and with the bill committed to a Committee of the whole House to-morrow. The Committee on Private Land Claims, upon the bill from the Senate for the relief of Thomas Gulledge, made the following report: [Washington, 1827] 2 p. (Rep. No. 76) DLC; NjP. 31530

---- Thomas McClanahan. Jan. 2, 1827. Read, and laid upon the table. Mr. Allen of Tennessee, from the Committee on Revolutionary Claims, to which was referred the petition of Thomas McClanahan, made the following report: [Washington, 1827] 1 p. (Rep. No. 25) DLC; NjP. 31531

---- Thomas Marsh and Joseph Yaw. Dec. 18, 1827. Read, and laid upon the table. Mr. McDuffie, from the Committee of Ways and Means, to which was referred the petition of Thomas Marsh and Joseph Yaw, made the following report: Washington, Gales & Seaton, 1827. 1 p. (Rep. No. 12) DLC; NjR. 31532

---- Tobias E. and Wm. Stansbury. Jan. 15, 1827. Read, and ordered that it lie on the table. Mr. Haile, from the Committee of Claims, made the following report: [Washington, 1827] 2 p. (Rep. No. 45) DLC; NjP. 31533

---- Tonnage of the United States--1825. Letter from the Secretary of the Treasury transmitting the annual statement of the district tonnage of the U. States, on the 31st December, 1825. Feb. 13, 1827. Read, and laid upon the table. Washington, Pr. by Gales & Seaton, 1827. 4 p. 6 bdsds. (Doc. No. 100) DLC; NjP. 31534

---- Trade with British American colonies. Letter from the Secretary of the Treasury transmitting statements exhibiting, annually, from the 30th Sept., 1815, to 30th Sept. 1826, the amount and description of merchandise exported to, and imported from, the British American colonies, embraced in the recent orders in council, and others, with the tonnage employed therein, &c. &c. February 24, 1827. Read, and laid upon the table. Washington, Pr. by Gales & Seaton, 1827. 423 p. 6 bdsds. (Rep. No. 144) DLC; NjP. 31535

---- Treasurer's accounts. Letter from the Treasurer of the United States, transmitting copies of the general accounts of his office, from 1st of April, 1825, to 1st of April, 1826. Feb. 19, 1827. Read, and referred to the Committee on Public Expenditures. Washington, Gales & Seaton, 1827. 182 p. (Doc. No. 145) DLC; NjP. 31536

---- Treaty between the United States and Sweden. Stockholm, 4th July, 1827. Confidential. [Washington? 1827?] 32 p. PPL. 31537

---- Treaty with Spain of 22d February, 1827. 9th article. Dec. 18, 1827. Read, and laid upon the table. Mr. Wickliffe, from the Committee on the Judiciary, to which the subject had been referred, made the following report: Washington, Gales & Seaton, 1827. 19 p. (Rep. No. 16) DLC; NjR. 31538

---- Two extra clerks - patent office. March 1, 1827. Mr. Trimble, from the Select Committee to which was referred a letter from the Secretary of State, upon the subject of the organization of the Patent Office, made the following report: [Washington, 1827] 8 p. 1 bdsd. (Rep. No. 99) DLC; NjP. 31539

---- Unproductive post roads - 1826. Letter from the Postmaster General, transmitting a list of unproductive post roads for the past year. Jan. 20, 1827. Read, and laid upon the table. Washington, Gales & Seaton, 1827. 54 p. (Doc. No. 129) DLC; NjP. 31540

---- Unsettled accounts. Letter from the first Comptroller of the

Treasury, transmitting a list of balances on the books of the second auditor. Dec. 11, 1826. Read, and laid upon the table. Washington, Gales & Seaton, 1827. 4 p. 2 bdsds. (Doc. No. 136) DLC; NjP. 31541

---- Unsettled accounts--Office of third auditor. Letter from the Comptroller of the Treasury, transmitting reports from the third auditor ... Dec. 13, 1826 ... Washington, Pr. by Gales & Seaton, 1827. 8 p., folding bdsds. (Doc. No. 141) DLC; NjP. 31542

---- Unsettled balances, book register of the Treasury. Letter from the Comptroller of the Treasury, transmitting a statement of accounts which appear to have been due and unsettled on the books of the Register of the Treasury more than three years prior to 30th September last. Dec. 12, 1827. Read, and laid upon the table. Washington, Pr. by Gales & Seaton, 1827. 3 p. 5 bdsds. (Doc. No. 9) DLC; NjR. 31543

---- Unsettled balances. Letter from the Comptroller of the Treasury, transmitting a statement of the names of officers who have not rendered their accounts within the year: an abstract of the moneys advanced prior to the 3d of March, 1809, not accounted for; and a statement of accounts on the books of the Third Auditor, which have been due and unsettled more than three years, prior to the 30th September, 1827. Dec. 5, 1827. Read, and laid upon the table. Washington, Gales & Seaton, 1827. 7 p. 84 bdsds. (Doc. No. 8) DLC; NjR. 31544

---- Unsettled balances 2d Auditor's office. Letter from the Comptroller of the Treasury, transmitting a statement of accounts which have remained unsettled, and upon which balances appear to have been due more than three years, prior to the 30th September last, on the books of the Second Auditor of the Treasury. Dec. 10, 1827. Read, and laid upon the table. Washington, Pr. by Gales & Seaton, 1827. 4 p. 2 bdsds. (Doc. No. 7) DLC; NjR. 31545

---- Vaccination. March 1, 1827. Mr. Condict, from the Select Committee appointed on the 27th ult. presented the following report: [Washington, 1827] 7 p. (Rep. No. 95) DLC; NjP. 31546

---- Washington medals. Feb. 27, 1827. Read, and laid upon the table. Mr. Everett, from the Committee on the Library, submitted the following resolution. [Washington, 1827] 1 p. (Res. No. 6) DLC; NjP. 31547

---- William and John Peirce. Dec. 20, 1827. Read, and laid upon the table. Mr. McIntire, from the Committee of Claims, to which was referred the petition of William and John Peirce, made the following report: Washington, Gales & Seaton, 1827. 1 p. (Rep. No. 25) DLC; NjR. 31548

---- William Bishop. Dec. 18, 1827. Read, and laid upon the table. Mr. Whittlesey, from the Committee of Claims, to which was referred the petition of William Bishop, made the following report: Washington, Gales & Seaton, 1827. 1 p. (Rep. No. 11) DLC; NjR. 31549

---- William Cloyd. Dec. 17, 1827. Mr. Whittlesey, from the Committee of Claims, to which was referred the petition of Wm. Cloyd, made the following report: Washington, Gales & Seaton,

1827. 2 p. (Rep. No. 4) DLC; NjR. 31550

---- William Hallaway and Westgate Watson. Jan. 23, 1827. Read, and laid upon the table. Mr. Wurts, from the Committee to which was referred the petition of Wm. Hallaway and Westgate Watson, made the following report: [Washington, 1827] 2 p. (Rep. No. 54) DLC; NjP. 31551

---- William Hull - representatives of. Dec. 19, 1827. Mr. Mc Coy, from the Committee of Claims, to which was referred the petition of the widow and administrator of the late General William Hull, made the following report: Washington, Gales & Seaton, 1827. 3 p. (Rep. No. 18) DLC; NjR. 31552

---- William Morrison. Jan. 31, 1827. Mr. Whittlesey, from the Committee of Claims, to which had been referred the petition of William Morrison, made the following report: [Washington, 1827] 22 p. (Rep. No. 64) DLC; NjP. 31553

---- William Schley, executor of J. G. Posner. Jan. 5, 1827. Mr. Whittlesey, from the Committee of Claims, to which had been referred the petition of William Schley, executor of J. G. Posner, made the following report, which was read, and laid upon the table. Jan. 6, 1827. Committed to a Committee of the whole House to-morrow. [Washington, 1827] 6 p. (Rep. No. 37) DLC; NjP. 31554

---- William Thompson. Jan. 5, 1827. Mr. Whittlesey, from the Committee of Claims, to which had been referred the petition of William Thompson, made the following report: [Washington, 1827] 2 p. (Rep. No. 35) DLC; NjP. 31555

---- William Thompson. Dec. 17, 1827. Mr. Whittlesey, from the Committee of Claims, to which was referred the petition of Wm. Thompson made the following report: Washington, Gales & Seaton, 1827. 2 p. (Rep. No. 6) DLC; NjR. 31556

---- Woollen manufactures. Letter from the Secretary of the Treasury, transmitting information in relation to woollen manufactures imported in the several years between the 30th September 1820, and the 30th September, 1826, &c. Jan. 25, 1827. Read, and laid upon the table. Washington, Gales & Seaton, 1827. 11 p. (Doc. No. 60) DLC; NjP. 31557

---- ---- Report of a committee of the House of Representatives of the state of Massachusetts, on the subject of woollen manufactures, &c. Feb. 1, 1827, Pr. by order of the House of Representatives. Washington, Gales & Seaton, 1827. 5 p. (Doc. No. 70) DLC; NjP. 31558

The United States' almanac [for 1828] By Seth Smith. Philadelphia, R. Desilver [1827] 28 l. CLU; CtY; DLC; InU; MB; MWA; P; PPL. 31559

---- ---- Philadelphia, R. Desilver; T. Desilver; John Grigg [1827] 28 l. DLC; IaU; MH; NBuHi; PPAmP. 31560

The United States Declaration of independence, the Constitution of the United States of America. The Constitution of the state of South Carolina, and General Washington's farewell address to the people of the United States. Charleston, S. C., Pr. and pub.

by C. C. Sebring, 1827. 67 p. ScU. 31561

United States Military Academy, West Point
Register of the officers and cadets of the U. S. Military Academy. June, 1827. 22 p. PPL. 31562

Universal almanac, for the year of our Lord 1828 ... Baltimore, Pub. by John Roach [1827] 35, [1] p. PPL. 31563

A universal biographical dictionary. See Baldwin, Charles N.

Universal emancipation. See Carey, Mathew.

The universal letter writer: containing a course of interesting letters on the most important and interesting subjects ... Auburn, Pub. by U. F. Doubleday, 1827. 96 p. MWA. 31564

Universalists. New York. Central Association.
Proceedings of the Central Association of Universalists, in the state of New-York, A. D. 1827. Utica, Pr. by Dauby & Maynard, 1827. 10 p. N. 31565

"Unlettered Mechanic," pseud. See Heighton, William.

[Upham, Charles Wentworth] 1802-1875
A letter to the editor of the Charleston Observer, concerning his treatment of Unitarians. (With some preliminary documents.) Charleston, Pr. for the Unitarian Book Society by James S. Burges, 1827. 40 p. CBPac; ICMe; MB; MBAU; ScC; TxU. 31566

---- Principles of the Reformation. A sermon preached at the dedication of the house of public worship of the First Congregational Society in Salem, Nov. 16, 1826. 2d ed. Salem, James R. Buffum, Pr. at the Gazette Office, 1827. 48 p. CSmH; DLC; MB; MHi; MWA; MiD-B; NN; Nh-Hi; PHi. 31567

[Upham, Thomas Cogswill] 1799-1872
Elements of intellectual philosophy: designed as a textbook. Portland, Pub. by Wm. Hyde. Jos. Griffin, pr., Brunswick, 1827. 504 p. DLC; MeHi; MeLB; MiU; NNC. 31568

Urcullu, José de
Gramatica inglesa, reducida a veinte y dos lecciones ... Nueva-York, La publican, Behr y Kahl, [en la imprenta de José Desnoues] 1827. 356 p. MB. 31569

Urrutia, José de, 1728-1800
Coleccion de ejercicios facultativos para la uniforme instruccion de la tropa del Real cuerpo de artillería. Formada por disposicion del Excmo. Sr. D. Joseph de Urrutia ... y aprobada por S. M. ... Filadelfia, 1827. 275 p. CU-B; DLC. 31570

Use of the dead to the living. See Smith, Southwood.

V

Valentine, Lawson
Wood for sale ... belonging to the estate of Samuel Valentine, Jr., of Hopkinton [Mass.] Boston, April 11, 1827. Bdsd. MHi. 31571

Valpy, Richard, 1754-1836
Delectus sententiarum graecarum, ad usum tironum accommodatus: cum notulis et lexico. Ed. americana 3. prioribus emendatior. Bostoniae, sumptibus Hilliard, Gray, Little et Wilkins, 1827. 103 p. CtW; CtY; DGU; IU; MB; MH; MeB; OCl. 31572

---- The elements of Greek grammar. 5th Amer. ed. Arranged on an improved plan, with extensive additions by Charles Anthon ... New-York, Collins & co., Collins & Hannay, and G. & C. Carvill, 1827. 322 p. ICMcC; ICU; KyBC; LShC; MBU; NjR; OSW; TxU-T; ViL. 31573

---- ---- 6th Amer. ed. Boston, Hilliard, Gray, Little and Wilkins, 1827. 265 p. CtW; MBC; MH; NGH; PHi. 31574

Van Buren, Martin, pres. U. S., 1782-1862
Speech of the Hon. Martin Van Buren, delivered at the capitol, in the city of Albany, before the Albany county meeting, held on the 10th July, 1827. Albany, Croswell & Van Benthuysen, 1827. 16 p. M; MH-BA; MWA; N; NN. 31575

Vance, David H.
American atlas. Sold by John Grigg, Philadelphia [1827] 15 colored maps. (Index, mounted on inside front cover, has imprint: Philadelphia published by Anthony Finley.) MH. 31576

Vanden Heuvel, J. A. See Van Heuvel, Jacob Adrien.

Van Deventer, Cornelius
The New Brunswick collection of sacred music; being a selection of tunes from the most approved authors in Europe and America ... 4th ed., enl. and imp. Morristown, Peter A. Johnson, 1827. [4], 136 p. NjMo. 31577

---- ---- 4th ed., enl. & imp. New-Brunswick (N. J.), Terhune & Letson, 1827. 124 p. NN. 31578

Van Heuvel, Jacob Adrien, 1787-1874
An oration, delivered at Ogdensburgh, New-York, on the fourth of July 1827, at the celebration of the fifty-first anniversary of American independence. Ogdensburgh [N. Y.] Pr.; New-York, Repr. by J. Seymour, 1827. 27 p. CSmH; DLC; MWA. 31579

Van Ness, Cornelius Peter, 1782-1852
To the publick. It is with great reluctance, etc. [Address on his political conduct.] [Burlington, Vt., 1827] 15 p. BrMus. 31580

[Van Ness, William Peter] 1778-1826
A concise narrative of General Jackson's first invasion of Florida, and of his immortal defence of New-Orleans: with remarks ... By Aristides [pseud.] New-York, February, 1827. 48 p. C; DLC; MB; MdHi; N; NBLiHi; NN; NjP; NjR; PHi; ScU; TxU; VtU; WHi; BrMus. 31581

[----] ---- Louisville, Pr. by S. Penn, jr., 1827. Photostat of t.-p. of C. P. Everitt copy. "From NN imp. catalogue, but not in NN." (1936) 31582

[----] ---- Pub. by order of the General committee of Republican young men of New-York. 2d ed., with additions. New York, Pr. by E. M. Murden & A. Ming, jr., 1827. 40 p. CSmH. 31583

Vans, William, b. 1763
An appeal to the Public, by William Vans, native citizen of Massachusetts, against the slanders circulated by Stephen Codman, executor of the wills of John and Richard Codman ... Salem, Pr. for William Vans, 1827. 116 p. CSmH; DLC; M; MBC; MBL; MH-BA; MHi; BrMus. 31584

Vanuxem, Lardner, 1792-1848
An essay on the ultimate principles of chemistry, natural philosophy, and physiology, deduced from the distribution of matter into two classes or kinds, and from other sources. Pt. 1. Philadelphia, Carey, Lea & Carey, J. Harding, pr., 1827. 91 p. CL; DLC; ICU; KU; NGH; PPAmP; PPC; PPL. 31585

Van Winkle, Cornelius S.
The printer's guide, or, An introduction to the art of printing: including an essay on punctuation and remarks on orthography. 2d ed., with additions and alterations. New York, Pub. by White, Gallaher, & White [C. S. Van Winkle, pr.] 1827. 240 p. IaDuMtC; Md; MdBP; NNC; OMC; P; TxU. 31586

Varlé, Charles
Candid considerations, respecting the canal between the Chesapeake and Delaware Bays. Whereby the impracticabilities of proceeding successfully with the same ... is demonstrably proved. Baltimore, The Author, 1827. 19 p. Title from Sabin (98628). 31587

Vaux, Roberts, 1786-1836
A discourse delivered before the Historical Society of the state of Pennsylvania, on New Year's day, 1827. Philadelphia, H. C. Carey & I. Lea, 1827. 51 p. CSmH; CU; DLC; ICU; MH; MdHi; MeHi; MiD-B; N; NjR; OClWHi; P; PHC; PP; PPAmP; PPPrHi; PPL. 31588

---- Anniversary discourse delivered before the Historical Society of the state of Pennsylvania, on January 1, 1827. Philadelphia, Carey, Lea & Carey, (Imprint verso t. p. [Phila.: Skerrett] 1827. 55 p. ICU; MB; MiU; PHi; PPFM. 31589

---- Letter on the penitentiary system of Pennsylvania. Addressed to William Roscoe. Philadelphia, Jesper Harding, 1827. 15 p. IU; MH; MiD-B; MiU; MHi; NcGu; NjR; P; PHC; PHi; PPAmP; PPL; PPPrHi; RPB; ScC; WHi; BrMus. 31590

---- Reply to two letters of William Roscoe, Esquire, of Liverpool, on the penitentiary system of Pennsylvania. Philadelphia, Jesper Harding, pr., 1827. 12 p. P; PHi; PPAmP; PPL; PPPrHi; PU; BrMus. 31591

Vedder, Nicholas I., comp.
A new and choice selection of psalms and hymns and spiritual songs. Designed for the Christian's companion through life. Selected from various authors, by Nicholas I. Vedder ... Cincinnati, U. P. James [1827] 218, [6] p. RPB. 31592

Velázquez de la Cadena, Mariano, 1778-1860
Elementos de la lengua castellana ... Tercera edición. Nueva-York, Impr. de E. Grattan, 1827. 112, [2] p. DLC; BrMus. 31593

Vergilius Maro, Publius
P. Virgilii Maronis Opera; illustravit Carolius Ruaeus, 11th stereotype American ed. Philadelphia, H. C. Carey & I. Lea, Pub., 1827. 667 p. NSyU. 31594

---- ---- With copious notes ... in English. New-York, White, Gallaher & White, Clayton & Van Norden, prs., 1827. xvi, 619 p. CSfCW; ICN; MDeeP; MtBu; PHi; PPA; PPF; RPB; TxAuPT; ViRU; BrMus. 31595

Veritas, pseud. See Plumer, William.

Vermont (State)
An act to provide for the suppost of common schools. [1827] 11 p. MB; MH. 31596

---- Acts passed by the Legislature of the state of Vermont, at their October session, 1827. Woodstock, Pr. by David Watson [1827] 102 p. CSmH; IaU; In-SC; Ky; MdBB; MSaEC; Mi; NNLI; Nb; Nj; Nv; R; TxU. 31597

---- Governor's speech. Gentlemen of the Council and Gentlemen of the House of Representatives ... Oct. 12, 1827. Bdsd. MB. 31598

---- Journal of the General Assembly of the state of Vermont, at their session, begun and held at Montpelier, Washington County, on Thursday, 12th October, 1826. Rutland, Pr. for the state by William Fay, 1827. 209 p. Mi. 31599

---- Journal of the General Assembly of the state of Vermont, at their session begun and held at Montpelier, Washington County, on Thursday, 11th October, 1827. Woodstock, Pr. by Rufus Colton [1827] 259 p. Mi. 31600

---- ... A proclamation ... I have thought it fit to appoint, and hereby do appoint, Wednesday, the fourth day of April next, to be observed as a day of humiliation and prayer, throughout the state of Vermont... Given under my hand, at Waterbury this twenty-fourth day of February, in the year of our Lord one thousand eight hundred and twenty-seven ... Bdsd. DLC. 31601

---- Reports of cases argued and determined in the Supreme Court of the state of Vermont. Prepared and published in pursuance of a statute law of the State. By Asa Aikens. Vol. I. Windsor, Pub. for the reporter, by Simeon Ide, 1827. vii, [8] 432 p. CU-Law; Ct; DLC; ICLaw; Ia; In-SC; M; MBS; MBU-L; MH-L; MSaEC; MdBB; MiD-B; Mn; MoKB; NCH; NNLI; Nv; OClW; ODaL; PPiAL; PPT-L; PU-L; RPL; TMeB; W; Wy. 31602

---- Unanimous address of the Council of Censors to the freemen of Vermont; with articles of amendment to the Constitution-sections of the present Constitution which will be altered or superseded by the adoption of the Amendments, and an ordinance, calling a convention. Montpelier, Watchman Office, 1827. 15 p. MWA; NN; NhD. 31603

Vermont Bible Society
Fifteenth report of the Vermont Bible Society, communicated at their annual meeting at Montpelier, Oct. 17, 1827. Montpelier, Pr. by E. P. Walton, Watchman Office, 1827. 17 p. IEG. 31604

Vermont Colonization Society
Eighth report of the Vermont Colonization Society, communicated at the annual meeting, at Montpelier, Oct. 17, 1827. Montpelier, Pr. by E. P. Walton, Watchman Office, 1827. 11 p. MBC. 31605

Vermont Domestic Missionary Society
Annual report of the Vermont Domestic Missionary Society, presented at Montpelier, Sept. 13, 1827. Windsor, Enos Folsom [1827] 23 p. MH; Nh; OCHP. 31606

Vermont Sabbath School Union
Second annual report of the Vermont Sabbath-School Union: presented at Montpelier, Sept. 12, 1827. Rutland, Pr. by William Fay, 1827. 16 p. VtU. 31607

Vermont. University.
Laws of the University of Vermont. Burlington, Pr. by E. & T. Mills, 1827. 22 p. MH; MHi; MWA; NN; Nh; OO; RPB; VtU. 31608

---- University of Vermont. Commencement, Aug. 8, 1827. Order of Exercises. [Burlington] Free Press Office Print. [1827] Bdsd. VtU. 31609

Vermont. University. Society for Religious Inquiry.
Constitution and laws of the Society for Religious Inquiry, of the University of Vermont, as amended, revised and adopted. Oct. 18, 1827. Burlington, Pr. by E. & T. Mills, 1827. 14 p. NN. 31610

The vicar's garden; or, The Greek medal: by an American Lady. 5th ed. American Sunday School Union, Philadelphia, 1827. 32 p. BrMus. 31611

A view of South America and Mexico. See Niles, John Milton.

A view of the claim of Alex. Nisbet, A. D. B. N. of Thomas Cockey Deye, containing an examination of the report of the treasurer of the state, made to the last General Assembly, together with all the proceedings of the Legislature on the subject. Baltimore, Pr. by John D. Toy, 1827. 41 p. Md; MdHi. 31612

The village harmony ... Newburyport, Pub. by Little and Co., 1827. C. Norris and Co., prs. 320 p. MNoboroHi. 31613

... The village in the mountains. New York, American Tract Society [1827?] 20 p. DLC; NN. 31614

Village reformed, or the Sunday School. Revised by the Committee of Publication. Philadelphia, American Sunday School Union, 1827. 16 p. LNHT. 31615

The village school ... Boston, Pub. and sold by James Loring, 1827. 35 p. NNC. 31616

Village tales. See Potts, Stacy Gardner.

Vindication of Mr. E. C. Genet's Memorial. See Genet, Edmond Charles.

A vindication of the recent and prevailing policy of the state of Georgia. See Clayton, Augustin Smith.

The vine. Philadelphia, American Sunday School Union, 1827. 16 p. CtY; DCU; RPB; BrMus. 31617

Virginia (State)
Acts passed at a General Assembly of the commonwealth of Virginia, begun and held at the capitol, in the city of Richmond, on Monday, the fourth day of December, in the year of our Lord one thousand eight hundred and twenty-six. Richmond, Pr. by Thomas Ritchie, pr. for the commonwealth, 1827. 155 p. Mi; Vi. 31618

---- Journal of the Convention of Virginia; held in the city of Richmond, on the first Monday in June, in the year of our Lord one thousand seven hundred and eighty-eight. Richmond, Pr. by T. W. White, 1827. 39 p. DLC; MH; PPL; Vi. 31619

---- Journal of the House of Delegates of the commonwealth of Virginia, begun and held at the capitol, in the city of Richmond, on Monday, the fourth day of December, one thousand eight hundred and twenty-six. Richmond, Pr.

by Thomas Ritchie, pr. for the commonwealth, 1826 [i. e. 1827] 211 p. Vi. 31620

---- Journal of the Senate of the commonwealth of Virginia, begun and held at the capitol in the city of Richmond, on Monday the fourth day of December, in the year one thousand eight hundred and twenty-six. Richmond, Pr. by John Warrock, pr. to the Senate, 1826 [i. e. 1827] 155, [1] p. Vi. 31621

---- Journal of the House of Delegates of the commonwealth of Virginia; begun and held at the capitol, in the city of Williamsburg, on Monday, the fifth day of May, in the year of our Lord one thousand seven hundred and seventy seven [- one thousand seven hundred and seventy nine] Richmond, Pr. by Thomas W. White, 1827. v. p., separate titles for each session of the House. Vi. 31622

No entry 31623

---- Journal of the House of Delegates of the commonwealth of Virginia, begun and held in the town of Richmond, in the county of Henrico, on Monday, the first day of May, in the year of our Lord one thousand seven hundred and eighty [-28 December 1790] Richmond, Pr. by Thomas W. White, 1827-1828. v. p., separate titles for each session of the House. Vi. 31624

---- Journal of the House of Delegates of the commonwealth of Virginia, begun and held in the town of Richmond, in the county of Henrico, on 28th of December, 1790. Richmond, Pr. by Thos. W. White, 1827-1828. v. p.

No entry 31625

---- Journal of the Senate of the commonwealth of Virginia, begun and held in the city of Richmond, on Monday the 17th day of October, in the year of our Lord Christ, 1785 [-29 December, 1790] Richmond, Printed by Thomas W. White, 1827-1828. v. p., separate titles for each session of the Senate. DLC; Vi. 31626

No entry. 31627

---- Report of the Joint Committee appointed to examine into the state of the penitentiary institution, and accompanying documents. Richmond, Pr. by Thos. Ritchie, 1827. 31 p. PPL. 31628

---- Sketch of the laws of the General Assembly of Virginia, passed during the session of 1826-7. 2 p. DLC. 31629

Virginia. University

Enactments by the rector and visitors of the University of Virginia, for constituting, governing & conducting that institution. For the use of the university. [Charlottesville] Pr. by C. P. M'Kennie, 1827. 56 p. CtY; MH; NP; ViU; ViW. 31630

---- Report of the rector and visitors exhibiting the results of an examination into the progress of students, etc. [1826] Richmond, Ritchie, 1827. 27 p. MB. 31631

---- Report of the rector and visitors of the University of Virginia, to the president and directors of the Literary Fund, July 19th, 1827. Richmond, Pr. by Thomas Ritchie, pr. for the Commonwealth, 1827. 32 p. Vi. 31632

Virginia and North Carolina almanack for 1828. By David Richardson. Richmond, John Warrock [1827] 18 l. MWA. 31633

Visit for a week. See Peacock, Lucy.

Visits to a cottage. Boston, Pub. and sold by James Loring, 1827. 35 p. NNC. 31634

Vivian Grey. See Beaconsfield, Benjamin Disraeli, 1st earl of.

Der Volksfreund und Haggerstauner Calender auf 1828. von Carl F. Egelmann. Hagerstaun, J. Gruber und D. May [1827] 15 l. InU; MWA; MdBE; PHi; PPeSchw; PYHi. 31635

Vose, John, 1766-1840
A system of astronomy, on the principles of Copernicus ... Concord, [N. H.] J. B. Moore, 1827. 252 p. CU; DLC; GU; InCW; MA; MB; MBC; MH; MeHi; MoSpD; NCH; Nh; Nh-Hi; NhD; RP; TNJ. 31636

W

Wainwright, Jonathan Mayhew, bp. 1793-1854
A sermon preached in St. Thomas's Church, New York, on ... August 26, 1827, being the Sunday after the decease of the Rev. Cornelius R. Duffie. ... New York, T. & J. Swords, 1827. CtHT; MBC; MH; N; NGH; NNG; PHi; RPB; WHi; BrMus. 31637

Walden, Hiram
A guide to the true knowledge of Christian baptism. Haverhill, Pr. by A. W. Thayer, 1827. 32 p. DLC; MBNMHi. 31638

Walker, Charles
The believers rest. A sermon, delivered at New Ipswich, N. H. on Lord's Day, June 10, 1827, occasioned by the death of widow May Appleton, relict of Dea. Isaac Appleton, who deceased May 22, 1827, aged 85 years. New Ipswich, Pr. by S. Wilder, 1827. 16 p. MWA; N; Nh; Nh-Hi. 31639

Walker, James, 1794-1874
The exclusive system. A discourse delivered in Groton, Massachusetts, at the installation of Rev. Charles Robinson, Nov. 1, 1826. Boston, Bowles and Dearborn ... Stephen Foster, pr., 1827. 56 p. CBPac; CSmH; ICMe; MB; MH; MiD-B; N; OClWHi; PPL; RPB. 31640

[----] 1st series. No. 11 Unitarianism vindicated against the charge of not going far enough. Pr. for The American Unitarian Association. Boston, Bowles & Dearborn [Isaac R. Butts and Co., prs.] 1827. 24 p. CBPac; GAGTh; ICMe; MA; MBAU; MBC; MH; MHing; MMeT; MNBedf; MNF; MeB; NNS; OClWHi; PPL; BrMus. 31641

Walker, John, 1732-1807
Cobb's abridgment of J. Walker's critical pronouncing dictionary & expositor of the English language ... Philadelphia, E. C. Markley & Son, Charles Desilver, [1827?] 440 p. PU. 31642

---- A critical pronouncing dictionary and expositor of the English language ... Boston, N. H. Whitaker, 1827. 336 p. GMWa; Nh. 31643

---- Walker's critical pronouncing dictionary and expositor of the English language. Abridged. By the Rev. Thomas Smith, London ... Cooperstown, Stereotyped and pr. by H. & E. Phinney ... 1827. 400 p. CSmH; MiU. 31644

---- ---- 1st pocket ed. Hartford, S. Andrus, 1827. 325 p. CtY; IaDmD; LNHT; MiU. 31645

---- ---- 1st pocket ed. Hartford, Pub. by Silas Andrus, 1827. 336 p. CtHi. 31646

---- ---- To which are prefixed principles of English pronunciation. New York, Collins and Hannay, 1827. 71, 609, 8, [8]-11, [13]-103 p. Ct; CtHT-W; IEN-H; KyBgW; MB; MS; MoS; MoSpD; NNC; NRU; NT; NcAS; NcD; NhD; NjN; OClWHi; PHi; PU. 31647

---- ---- Philadelphia, Pr. and pub. by Griggs & Dickinson, 1827. 413 p. DLC; MB; PHi. 31648

Walker, Sarah

Succinct account of the case, Sarah Walker, vs. John Martin, in which the system of spunging and fraud is exposed; with an appendix. Providence, 1827. 47 p. RHi; RPB. 31649

A walking gentleman. See Grattan, Thomas Colley.

[Wallace, Cadwallader]

To the Hon. Lyttleton W. Tazewell of the Senate and to Hon. John Randolph of the House of Representatives of the Congress of the United States. Chillicothe, Oct. 1st, 1827. [Chillicothe? 1827?] 14 p. OClWHi. 31650

[----] To Thomas Scott, Esq. of Chillicothe, and John Alexander, Esq. of Xenia. Chillicothe, June 1st, 1827. [Chillicothe? 1827?] 11, 4 p. NN. 31651

Waln, Robert

Life of the Marquis De Lafayette; Major General in the service of the United States of America in the war of the Revolution ... 4th ed. Philadelphia, Pub. by J. P. Ayres, 1827. xii, 507 p. AB; CtW; In; KyLoF; MNe; MoSU; MoSW; TN; WHi. 31652

Walsh, Hatton

A sermon preached in St. Patrick's Cathedral, New York, on Sunday, Sept. 2nd, 1827; in aid of the funds of the Ladies Roman Catholic Benevolent Society. New York, Pr. by William Van Norden, 1827. 22 p. DGU; MChB. 31653

Waltham, Mass. Trinitarian Congregational Church.

The articles of faith and covenant of the Trinitarian Congregational Church in Waltham. As revised July 5, 1826. Boston, T. R. Marvin, pr., 1827. 12 p. MB. 31654

Walton's Vermont register and farmer's almanack for 1828. By Zadock Thompson. Montpelier, E. P. Walton [1827] 63 l. CLU; DLC; InU; MB; MHi; MWA; NHi; NNC; Nh; Nh-Hi; OO; P; VtU. 31655

Wanderer in Washington. See Watterston, George.

Wanostrocht, Nicolas

A grammar of the French language, with practical exercises. 9th Amer. from the last London ed. Boston, Pub. by Richardson & Lord, Pr. by J. H. A. Frost, 1827. xi, [1], 482, [2] p. GDC; IaDuMtC; LNStM; MB; MH; NNC; NNG; P; PPL. 31656

Ward, Minus

Remarks, propositions and calculations, relative to a railroad and locomotive engines to be used upon the same, from Baltimore to the Ohio River. Baltimore, Pr. by J. D. Toy, 1827. 50 p. DBRE; DLC; MCM; MH-BA; MdHi; MdToH; NN; NRom; PHi; WU. 31657

[Ward, Robert Plumer]
De Vere; or, The man of independence. By the author of Tremaine ... Philadelphia, Carey, Lea and Carey, 1827. 3 v. DeWI; LU; MB; MH; PPL; PU. 31658

Warden, W.
The pleasant walk in spring, including the story of the poor old soldier and the history of Orphan Henry. New York, Pub. by S. King, 1827. [24] p. MiD-B. 31659

Ware, Ashur, 1782-1873
A discourse pronounced before the Phi Beta Kappa Society, at Brunswick, on the anniversary celebration, September 6, 1827. Portland, Pr. at the Argus Office, by Thomas Todd, 1827. 36 p. CSmH; MHi; MeHi; NCH; RPB. 31660

Ware, Henry, 1794-1843
Scriptural reasons for disbelieving the doctrine of the Trinity. Extracted from an address delivered at Kennebunk, Oct. 24, 1827. [Belfast, Pr. for the Unitarian Society for the Diffusion of Christian Knowledge, 1827] 4 p. MH. 31661

---- A sermon on small sins. Boston, Nathaniel S. Simpkins & Co., 1827. 12 p. CBPac; CSansS; CSmH; CtHC; CtSoP; ICMe; MB; MBAU; MBAt; MBC; MH; MMeT; MNF; MiD-B; OClWHi; OO; PPL; RPB; BrMus. 31662

Warfield, Charles
Sacred books of New Testament, expounded. Baltimore, Pr. by William Wooddy, 1827. 148 p. MdBS; MdHi. 31663

Warning and example to the young; or The story of Mrs. Neville and her grandchildren ... New York, 1827. 144 p. MHi. 31664

Warren, William
Proposals of Messrs. Warren and Wood for the erection of a new theatre in the city of Philadelphia ... Philadelphia, Pr. by T. Desilver, 1827. 22 p. PHi. 31665

Warren County administration meeting. See National Republican Party, Ohio.

Washburn, Emory, 1800-1877
Address delivered before the Worcester Agricultural Society, Oct. 11, 1826: Being their eighth anniversary cattle show and exhibition of manufactures. Worcester, Charles Griffin, pr., 1827. 20 p. CSmH; DLC; M; MB; MBAt; MH; MHi; MW; MWA; MWHi; MiD-B; NN; OClWHi; RPB; BrMus. 31666

Washington, George, pres. U.S., 1732-1799
Washington's farewell address, the Constitution of the United States, and the Declaration of independence, Boston, 1827. 71 p. CSmH; DLC; MB; MBAt; MH; MWA. 31667

Washington, William
An address delivered in Charleston, before the Agricultural Society of South Carolina, at its anniversary meeting, on the 21st of August, 1827 ... Charleston, Pr. by A. E. Miller, 1827. 20 p. NcD; NcU; ScC. 31668

Washington, D. C.
Laws of the corporation of the city of Washington passed by the twenty-fifth council, printed by order of the council. Washington, Pr. by Way and Gideon, 1827. 74 p. In-SC. 31669

Washington College Athenaeum
First exhibition of the Washington College Athenaeum. Wednesday, Dec. 19, 1827. [Hartford,

1827] Bdsd. NcU. 31670

The Washington directory, showing the name, occupation, and residence, of each head of a family & person in business, together with other useful information. City of Washington, S. A. Elliot [1827]-30. 2 v. DLC; DWP; MWA. 31671

Washington Literary, Scientific and Military Gymnasium, Washington, D. C.
Laws of the Washington Literary, Scientific & Military Gymnasium. Georgetown, D. C., J. C. Dunn, pr., 1827. 24 p. DLC. 31672

Waterman, Jesse
A plain, comprehensive, practical English grammar, in two parts ... 3d ed., imp. Philadelphia, The author, 1827. 215 p. DLC; MB; NNC. 31673

Waters, Francis
A letter in review of the proceedings and address of the meeting of Methodists, held in the city of Baltimore, on the 5th August last. Addressed to the members of that meeting. [Baltimore? 1827] 16 p. MdBP; MdHi. 31674

Watson, Richard, 1781-1833
The religious instruction of the slaves in the West India colonies, advocated and defended ... 1st Amer. ed. Philadelphia, J. Clarke, 1827. 32 p. PHC; PHi; RPB. 31675

[Watterston, George] 1783-1854
Wanderer in Washington. Washington, Pr. at the Washington Press, by J. Elliot, jr., and sold by P. Thompson, 1827. 226 p. DLC; MH; MWA; NN; NcU; PPL. 31676

Watts, Isaac, 1674-1748
Caniadau sion, sef casgliad o hymnau a salmau. Yr hymnau, gan mwyof, o waith y parch. William Williams, gynt o bant y celyn, a Dr. Isaac Watts: a'r salmau gan Edmund Prys, gynt arch-diacon meirionydd. Utica, Argraffwyd gan William Williams. 1827. 343, [1] p. NUt. 31677

---- Divine & moral songs for children. Philadelphia, American Sunday School Union, 1827. 48, 48 p. PPAmS. 31678

---- ... Divine songs for children. New York, American Tract Society [1827?] 20 p. DLC. 31679

---- Dr. Watts's divine songs, suited to the capacities of children ... New York, Pub. by N. Bangs and J. Emory for the Methodist Episcopal Church; Azor Hoyt, pr., 1827. 32 p. DLC. 31680

---- Dr. Watts' plain and easy catechism for children. To which is added, some verses and short prayers for children. Canandaigua, Pr. by Bemis, Morse & Ward, 1827. 32 p. DLC. 31681

---- Hymns and spiritual songs. In three books. New York, Pub. by White, Gallaher & White, 1827. 274 p. NIC; OO. 31682

---- ---- A new ed., corrected. Princeton, N. J., Borrenstein, 1827. 278 p. NNUT; NjP; PPPrHi; WS. 31683

---- The psalms and hymns of Dr. Watts, arranged by Dr. Rippon; with Dr. Rippon's Selection. In one vol. With improved indexes. Stereotyped by L. Johnson, Philadelphia. Philadelphia, Pub. and for sale by David Clark, 1827. xxxv. 906 p. IJI; KyLoS; NjP; PPAmS; PPL; PPLT;

PU. 31684

---- The psalms, hymns, and spiritual songs ... Boston, S. T. Armstrong & Crocker, Brewster, 1827. 496, 156 p. MBC; MDeeP; NNUT; NRU; RPB. 31685

The way to divine knowledge. See H., B. D.

Wayland, Francis, 1796-1865
The moral dignity of the missionary enterprise. A sermon delivered before the Boston Baptist Foreign Mission Society on the evening of Oct. 26, and before the Salem Bible Translation Society on the evening of Nov. 4, 1823. 7th ed. Boston, 1827. 44 p. CtHC; CtHT; CtSoP; IaDuU; MH; MNtcA; NRAB; NjR; RHi; RPB. 31686

Wayne, Anthony
To the freemen of Maryland. Read, pause, and reflect. Facts! stubborn facts! An aged man, who has been a silent spectator of the presidential contest, thus far, has been compelled, from a sense of duty to the public, to state a few facts ... [1827?] Bdsd. MH. 31687

Webb, James Watson
To the officers of the army ... [Trial of Col. John McNeil.] [New York, Sept. 10, 1827] 22 p. MB. 31688

Webster, James, 1803-1854
A card, During the last winter, Dr. John Eberle published a certain pamphlet ... [Philadelphia, 1827] 8 p. MB; PPL. 31689

Webster, Noah, 1758-1843
The American spelling book ... The revised impression, with the latest corr. Stereotyped by C. N. Baldwin, New-York. Baltimore, Pub. by Cushing and Jewett, 1827. 168 p. MdHi; NNC. 31690

---- ---- The revised impression, with the latest corr. Brattleboro, Holbrook & Fessenden [1827?] 8-168 p. CSt; CtHT-W; MDeeP; MH; MWA; OClWHi; NN; NNC. 31691

---- ---- The revised impression stereotyped by E. & J. White, New-York. Canandaigua, Pr. by Bemis, Morse & Ward, 1827. 168 p. MiU; NCanHi. 31692

---- ---- Cincinnati, Pub. by N. & G. Guilford. Stereotyped by J. Howe, Philadelphia, 1827. W. M. & O Farnsworth, Jr., prs. 160 p. Collection of Harlow Lindley, Columbus, O. 31693

---- ---- Concord, N. H., Pub. by Manahan, Hoag & Co. [1827?] 168 p. MH. 31694

---- ---- Middletown, Conn., Pub. by Wm. H. Niles, stereotyped by A. Chandler, 1827. 168 p. CtHi. 31695

---- The prompter; or, A commentary on common sayings and subjects which are full of common sense--the best sense in the world. Windsor, Pr. by Simeon Ide, 1827. 96 p. MB; MH; MWA; NN; VtU; BrMus. 31696

Webster's calendar: or the Albany almanack for 1828. Albany, Websters & Skinners [1827] 18 l. InU; MWA; MiU-C; MnU; N; NHi; NN; PHi; WHi. 31697

---- Albany, Websters & Skinners [1827] 18 l. DLC; MWA; N; NN; PHi. 31698

Weeks, William Raymond, 1783-1848
The doctrine of the universal agency of Good, the proper source of consolation under affliction. A sermon, preached at

the funeral of Mrs. Millicent E. Peirce, the wife of Rev. John D. Peirce, at Sangerfield, N. Y., Feb. 1, 1827 ... Utica, Pr. by Ariel Works, 1827. 32 p. CBPac; CSmH; MBNEH; MWA; NN; PPPrHi. 31699

Weems, Mason Locke
The drunkard's looking glass ... 7th ed. greatly imp. Philadelphia, Pub. by Joseph Allen. Sold by John Grigg, 1827. 120 p. DGU. 31700

---- God's revenge against duelling: or, The duellist's looking-glass ... 3d ed. Philadelphia, Pub. by Joseph Allen, 1827. 96 p. NNG. 31701

Welch, Oliver
The American arithmetic, adapted to the currency of the United States; to which is added a concise treatise on the mensuration of planes and solids. Compiled for the use of the common schools in the United States, to which is annexed a short system of book-keeping. 6th ed., revised, corr., imp. and enl. Portland, 1827. Williamson: 10,448. 31702

The well-spent hour. No. V. Boston, Pub. by Wait, Green & Co., [c 1827] 15 p. DLC. 31703

Wells, Elnathan
An improved chronological summary of the history of the United States of America from its discovery in the year 1492 to the present, 1827. Pr. and sold by Nichols & Seely, Brooklyn, 1827. 31 p. CtY; DLC; MB; N; NBLiHi; NJQ; NN; NNC; NcU; NjR; WHi. 31704

Wells, J. T.
To the public. [1827] 8 p. DLC. 31705

Wells, O. and H.
A specimen of printing type, from the foundry of O. & H. Wells, Walnut, between Third & Fourth streets, Cincinnati, 1827. [186] p. NNC. 31706

[Wells, William]
Excerpta quaedame scriptoribus Latinis probatioribus, notis illustrata. Boston, Wells et Lilly, 1827. 406 p. CtW; IaHi; IaK; ICMcC; MB; MH; MWA; MWiW; OUrC; PLFM; PPL; PU; RPB. 31707

Wesley, John
Sermons on several occasions. From the last London ed. New York, Pr. by J. & J. Harper, 1827. 3 v. CLSU; MB; MBr; MeBat; MsJPED; NjMD; PPi. 31708

---- ---- New-York, Pub. by N. Bangs and J. Emory, Azor Hoyt, pr., 1827-28. 2 v. GAuP; GAuY; ILebM; MPiB; NNMHi; OClW; ODaB; TxAuPT. 31709

Wesleyan Academy. See Wilbraham Academy.

Western almanack for 1828. By Oliver Loud. Rochester, Marshall & Dean [1827] 12 l. N; NRHi; NRMA; NRU. 31710

---- ---- Cleaveland [sic] Henry Bolles [1827] 18 l. OClWHi. 31711

---- ---- Buffalo, Day, Follett & Haskins [1827] 18 l. NBuHi; WHi. 31712

Western almanack, for the year of our Lord 1828: ... Calculated for the meridian of Rochester ... and will serve for any part of the western counties of the state, or the province of Upper Canada, or eastern part of Ohio. Rochester, N. Y., Pr. and sold by E. Peck & Co., [1827] 18 l. N; NRHi; NRM. 31713

---- Rochester, N. Y., Pr. and sold by E. Peck & Co. [1827] 18 l. (Variant of 31713) CSmH; ICU. 31714

Western Auxiliary Foreign Mission Society of Rockingham Co.
Second annual meeting of the Western Auxiliary Foreign Mission Society of Rockingham County, New Hampshire at Candia, June 20-1827. Miller & Brewster, prs., Portsmouth, 1827. 8 p. MBC; MLow; Nh-Hi. 31715

Western Domestic Missionary Society, New York
The first report of the Western Domestic Missionary Society of the state of New-York, auxiliary to the American Home Missionary Society: submitted by the executive committee at the anniversary meeting in Utica, May 3, 1827. Utica, Pr. by Hastings & Tracy. 1827. 28 p. N. 31716

The western farmer's almanac for 1828. Auburn, Oliphant & Skinner [1827] OClWHi (missing from shelves). 31717

---- By Rev. John Taylor. Pittsburgh, H. Holdship & Son; D. and M. Maclean, prs. [1827] 18 l. CLU; OHi; PPL; PPiHi. 31718

---- ---- Pittsburgh, H. Holdship & Son; D. and M. Maclean, prs. [1827] Issue with added "Magazine." 36 l. MWA; NN; OMC; PHi; PPPrHi. 31719

---- By Samuel Burr. Louisville, J. P. Morton; W. W. Worsley, pr. [1827] 12 l. DLC; KyLo; KyU; OClWHi. 31720

Western Pennsylvania Emigrant Society
To all those who may be desirous of emigrating to the Western country... Meadville, Pa., Aug. 31, 1827. Bdsd. NN. 31721

Western Sunday School Union. New York
The second report of the Western Sunday School Union of the state of New-York, auxiliary to the American Sunday School Union. Presented at the annual meeting in Utica, Sept. 23, 1827. Utica, Western Sunday School Union; J. Colwell, pr., 1827. 40 p. NUt; OO; WHi. 31722

Der Westliche Menschenfreund u. SchellsburgerCalender auf 1828. Von Carl F. Egelmann. Schellsburg, Friedrich Goeb [1827] 18 l. DLC; NjR; PPL; WHi. 31723

Westminster Assembly of Divines.
The larger catechism, agreed upon by the Assembly of Divines at Westminster, with the assistances of commissioners from the Church of Scotland as received by the Associate Reformed Church in North-America, with the proofs from the scripture. Salem, N. Y., Pr. and sold by Dodd & Stevenson, 1827. 193 p. CtHT-W; NcMHi. 31724

Wharton, Thomas Isaac, 1791-1856
An oration delivered on the 4th of July, 1827, in the State house ... [Philadelphia? 1827] 16 p. DLC; PPL. 31725

Wheeler, Jacob D.
An introductory lecture upon criminal jurisprudence, delivered in Rutger's College the fifth of March, 1827. New-York, Pr. and pub. by C. S. Van Winkle, 1827. 33 p. DLC; MBAt; MH-L; NNNAM; PHi; PPL. 31726

When a Christian may be said to have done his duty to the heathen. [Boston, 1827] 32 p. N. 31727

Whipple, P. L.
A Masonic address, delivered at Herkimer ... June 25, 1827. Herkimer, N.Y., Seymour & Carpenter, 1827. 11 p. MB; NN (not loc.) 31728

White, Elipha, 1795-1849
The claims of seamen. A sermon preached before the Port Society of Charleston, South Carolina July 1, 1827. Charleston, Pr. by C. C. Sebring, 1827. 20 p. MAnP; MBC; MiD-B; ScC. 31729

White, Henry Kirke
The beauties of Henry Kirk White, consisting of selections from his poetry and prose. By Alfred Howard esq. Boston, Pub. by N. H. Whitaker [Stereotyped by David Hills] 1827. 214 p. CPa; IEG; MB; NjP; NjR; PU. 31730

White, Joseph, 1789-1836
A sermon delivered at Sandwich, New-Hampshire, on Lord's Day, June 11, 1826, before the yearly meeting of the Free-Will Baptist connexion. Limerick. W. Burr, pr., 1827. 23 p. CSmH; MeHi; RP; RPB. 31731

White, Joseph Blanco, 1775-1841
The poor man's preservative against popery: addressed to the lower classes of Great Britain & Ireland. 1st Amer., from the 3d London ed. Georgetown, D. C., J. C. Dunn, 1827. 116 p. DLC; DWP; PPPrHi. 31732

White, William, bp. 1748-1836
An address delivered at the commencement of the General Theological Seminary of the Protestant Episcopal Church in the United States held in St. John's Chapel, in the city of New York, on the 29th day of June, 1827. New York, T. & J. Swords, 1827. 16 p. MB; MBD; N; NGH; NIC; NNG; RPB; WHi. 31733

White, William, 1783-1831
A history of Belfast, with introductory remarks on Acadia. Belfast [Me.] Pub. by E. Fellows, 1827. 119, [1] p. CSmH; CtSoP; DLC; ICN; M; MB; MBNEH; MH; Me; MeBa; MeHi; OClWHi; PPPrHi; RPJCB; WHi. 31734

[Whitehead, David]
An oration, delivered at Potter's Field; on the Fourth of July, 1826--by the first adopted, by the thirteen mothers of the union, whose seal is union, and secretary is truth. Also, an oration delivered on the Fourth of July, 1827 in the park, in the city of New-York. Pub. at 61, Thompson-street, in the 66th year, 10th month, and 6th day of David [1827] 19 p. NHi; NN. 31735

Whitehead, George
A gospel salutation in true Christian love; recommended to Friends who believe in the name of the Son of God ... London, J. Sowle, 1719; repr. in Philadelphia, for B. & T. Kite, 1827. 24p. MBAt; MH; MiD-B; N; NjR; WHi. 31736

Whitelock, Samuel
An address to the citizens of the United States, on the effects of war and peace, and the means of prosperity. Rutland, Pr. by William Fay for the author, 1827. 15 p. MBAt; BrMus. 31737

Whiting, John
An address delivered before the Berkshire Association for the Promotion of Agriculture and Manufactures, at Pittsfield, Oct. 5, 1826. Pittsfield, Pr. by Phinehas Allen, 1827. 23 p. M; MPiB. 31738

Whitman, Bernard
A discourse on denying the Lord Jesus. 2d ed. Boston, Pr. by Isaac R. Butts & Co., 1827.

47 p. ICN; MB; MH-AH; MMeT; NCH; BrMus. 31739

---- ---- Boston, Bowles and Dearborn, Isaac R. Butts & Co., prs., 1827. 47 p. CSmH; ICMe; IaHi; M; MBAU; MBC; MLexHi; MWal; MiD-B; NjR; RPB; BrMus. 31740

---- ---- 3d ed. Boston, Bowles & Dearborn, 1827. 47 p. CtHC; MBAt; OClWHi. 31741

---- ---- 4th ed. Boston, Bowles & Dearborn, Isaac R. Butts & Co., prs., 1827. 47 p. CSmH; MDovC; OClWHi. 31742

Whitney, George

Some account of the early history and present state of the town of Quincy, in the commonwealth of Massachusetts ... [Boston] Christian register office, S. B. Manning, pr. [1827] 64 p. CSmH; DLC; ICN; MB; MBAt; MH; MQ; MWA; MdBJ; MiD-B; NHi; NN; RPB; WHi; BrMus. 31743

Whitridge, J. B.

Remarks on fractures, embracing a description of an improved apparatus for their treatment ... Boston, Wells & Lilly, 1827. 21 p. NNNAM. 31744

Whittemore, Benjamin

A sermon delivered in Scituate, Mass., March 7, 1827. Boston, Pub. by Henry Bowen, 1827. 16 p. MScitHi; MiD-B; PPL; BrMus. 31745

[Whittemore, Thomas?] 1801-1861?

A dialogue between parent and child, concerning John V. 28, 29. For the instruction of children and youth ... Boston, Pub. by Henry Bowen, 1827. 24 p. MB. 31746

Whiuemore, T. See Whittemore, Thomas.

Wickliffe, C. A.

To the citizens of Jefferson, Oldham, Nelson & Bullitt Counties. C. A. Wickliffe, July 16, 1827. 8 p. KyLoF. 31747

Wickliffe, Robert, 1775-1859

Address of Robert Wickliffe, Esq. to his constituents. [Lexington, March, 1827] 16 p. DLC; ICU; KyLoF; MH; PHi; PPAmP. 31748

Wilbraham Academy

Catalogue of the officers and students of the Wesleyan Academy, Wilbraham, Mass. Fall term, Oct. 1827. [Springfield? S. Bowles? 1827] 8 p. MB. 31749

Wild flowers; or, The May day walk. Written for the American Sunday School Union ... Philadelphia, American Sunday School Union, 1827. 122 p. DLC; KU; MHa; ScCliTO; BrMus. 31750

Wilhelm, Benjamin

The ready reckoner, at rate percentage, in a compendium of federal money: or Traders' convenient assistant, in buying or selling all sorts of commodities, either wholesale or retail ... Dayton, O., Pr. by J. Regans, 1827. 132 p. OClWHi; ODa; OTifH. 31751

Willard, Emma (Hart) 1787-1870

Ancient geography as connected with chronology and preparatory to the study of ancient history; accompanied with an atlas; to which are added problems on the globes, and rules for the construction of maps. 2d ed., imp. Hartford, O. D. Cooke, pub., J. & J. Harper, prs., New York, 1827. viii, 96 p. illus., maps and atlas. MH; MiD-B; NTEW; NjP; OCL; OClWHi. 31752

[Willard, Samuel] 1776-1859

Secondary lessons, or The improved reader; intended as a sequel to the Franklin primer ... Greenfield, Mass., Phelps & Clark, 1827. 197, [1] p. DLC; ICHi; MB; MDeeP; MNF; NNT. 31753

William Cooper and his family; or, Christian principle exemplified ... Boston, Wait, Greene and co., 1827. 24 p. DLC; MBAt. 31754

Williams, Rev. C.
Masonry inseparable from religion. A sermon preached before the Grand Lodge of Maryland, at the dedication of Ashler Lodge, No. 85, held at the Savage factory, Anne Arundel County, Maryland, on the 4th day of July, 1827. Baltimore, Pr. by John D. Toy, 1827. 26 p. N; NNG; PPFM; WHi. 31755

Williams, James R.
Defence against the charges exhibited by his prosecutors in Baltimore city station. Baltimore, Pr. by John D. Toy, 1827. 16 p. MdBBC; MdBP. 31756

[Williams, John]
Dr. J. W.'s last legacy, or the useful family herbal. Middlebury, 1827. 32 p. BrMus. 31757

---- Dr. John Williams' last legacy, and useful family guide. New-York, Pr. for O. Taylor & Co. 1826. New-Ipswich, N. H., Repr. by S. Wilder, 1827. 24 p. MWA. 31758

---- ---- [New York, 1827?] 22 p. NNNAM. 31759

Williams, John Lee
A view of West Florida, embracing its geography, topography, &c ... Philadelphia, Pr. for H. S. Tanner and the author, L. R. Bailey, pr., 1827. 178 p. A-GS; C; DLC; F; FJ; FTaSC; FWpR; GEU; ICN; IaK; MB; MH; MiU-C; MoSM; MsJs; NNA; NNNBG; NjP; OCl; OFH; OMC; PPAmP; PPL; RPA; RPB; WHi; WM; BrMus. 31760

Williams, Nathaniel West, 1784-1853
The reign of Jesus Christ. A sermon, delivered at Concord, before His Excellency the Governor, the honorable Council, and both branches of the legislature of the state of New-Hampshire, June 7, 1827. Concord, Pr. by J. B. Moore, for the state, 1827. 23 p. CSmH; DLC; MBC; MH; NhD; PHi; BrMus. 31761

Williams, Samuel, 1743-1817
A history of the American revolution: intended as a reading-book for schools. 3d stereotype ed. Stonington [Conn.] W. Storer, jun., 1827. 204 p. DLC; MiU-C. 31762

Williams, Samuel Porter
Sermons on various subjects, chiefly practical. Salem, Pr. at the Essex Register Office, 1827. Pr. by W. Palfray, Jr. and J. Chapman, Salem. xx, 306 p. CtSoP; ICU; IEG; InCW; MA; MB; MBC; MH-AH; MFiHi; MNe; MNF; MShM; MeBat; MoSpD; NcMHi; OO; PPPrHi. 31763

Williams' calendar, or the Utica almanack for 1828. By Edwin E. Prentiss. Utica, William Williams. [1827] 18 l. ICN; MWA; MiD-B; N; NHi; NUt; WHi. 31764

---- ---- Utica, William Williams; Watertown: Knowlton and Rice [1827] 18 l. NHC; NWattHi. 31765

Williams College
Catalogue of the officers and students of Williams College, and the Berkshire Medical Institution, connected with it. 1827. [Williamstown, R. Bannister? 1827] 20 p.

MBC; MWiW; NNNAM. 31766

---- Commencement. Williams College, September 5, 1827. [Williamstown, R. Bannister? 1827] 4 p. MWiW. 31767

---- Junior exhibition. Williams College, May 15, 1827. [Williamstown, R. Bannister? 1827] Bdsd. MWiW. 31768

---- Senior exhibition. Williams College, January 1, 1828. [Williamstown, R. Bannister? 1827] 2 l. MWiW. 31769

---- Adelphic Union
Exhibition of the Adelphic Union Society. Williams College, August 1, 1827. [Williamstown, R. Bannister? 1827] 2 l. MWiW. 31770

Willis, Nathaniel Parker, 1806-1867
Sketches ... Boston, S. G. Goodrich, MDCCCXXVII. 96 p. CSf; CSmH; CU; GDC; ICMe; ICN; IU; Ia; IaU; In; MA; MB; MBAt; MH; MHi; MNS; MWH; MdBP; MdW; MiD-B; MnU; NN; NPV; NT; Nh-Hi; NjMo; NjP; OClW; PPL; PU; ScC; TxU; ViU; WvC. 31771

Willison, John
The afflicted man's companion, or A directory for persons and families afflicted with sickness or any other distress. New York, American Tract Society, 1827. 343 p. NSyHi. 31772

Williston, Ebenezer Bancroft, 1801-1836
Eloquence of the United States ... Middletown, Conn., E. & H. Clark, 1827. 5 v. CSmH; DLC; MA; MB; MH; MWiW; PPL. 31773

Williston, Seth, 1770-1851
A sermon on revivals of religion; containing a caution to the church, in the nineteenth century, to beware of Satan in corrupting them. New York, Pr. by D. Fanshaw, 1827. 40 p. ICT; IEG; MAnP; MBC; MMeT-Hi; NN; NjR; OO; PLT; PPPrHi; RPB; TxH. 31774

Wilmingtonian
Address of the carriers of the Wilmingtonian, to their patrons, on the commencement of the new year 1827. Bdsd. DeHi. 31775

Wilson, A. & H.
Fellow citizens read this. Sept. 7, 1827. We do hereby certify, that several propositions have been made to us by the partisans of General Jackson to obtain the possession, or the control, of the American Watchman newspaper establishment ... If necessary, we stand ready to make public the names of those persons implicated in this statement. A. & H. Wilson ... [Dover, Del. 1827] 1 p. DLC. 31776

[Wilson, James Patriot]
An essay, on the probation of fallen men; or, The scheme of salvation, founded in sovereignty, and demonstrative of justice ... Philadelphia, Pr. by William F. Geddes, 1827. 111, [1] p. CSansS; DeWI; ICMcC; MBC; MiU; MnSM; MoSU; NCH; NNUT; OCl; OMC; PHi; PMA; PPPrHi; PU. 31777

[Wilson, John] 1785-1854
Lights and shadows of Scottish life. A selection from the papers of the late Arthur Austin. Exeter, N. H., Pub. by J. C. Gerrish, & L. A. Tyler, J. C. Gerrish, pr., 1827. 291 p. MBev; NOy. 31778

[----] ---- New York, Dixon and Sickels, 1827. 266 p. MFai; NcAS; OC; ViU. 31779

[----] The trials of Margaret Lyndsay by the author of Lights

and Shadows, &c. Pub. by Tyler & Conner, Exeter, N. H., 1827. 235 p. Nh-Hi; RPB. 31780

Wilson, John Lyde
Codification. Speech of the Hon. John L. Wilson, senator in the Legislature of South Carolina, on the propriety and expediency of reducing the laws of the state into a code: to which is added a codification of the law of carriers. New-York, Pr. by Gray and Bunce, 1827. 44 p. MH-L; NN; NcD; NcU; PU-L; ScCC. 31781

Wilson, Joshua Lacy, 1774-1846
The testimony of three who bear witness in earth, on the fact and mode of purification: a sermon ... in Lebanon, Ohio, August 19, 1827 ... Cincinnati, Pr. by Morgan, Fisher, and L'Hommendieu, 1827. 14 p. CSmH; OCHP; PPPrHi. 31782

[Wilson, Mrs. Lucy Sarah (Atkins)]
Fruits of enterprize exhibited in the travels of Belzoni in Egypt and Nubia ... By the author of the "India Cabinet." Boston, Pub. by Munroe and Francis, New York, Charles S. Francis, 1827. 248, 4 p. KyBC; MH; NNS; NT; OC; PU; RP; ViNew. 31783

Wilson, Thomas, bp.
Christians daily companion; family and private devotions from the prayers of Bishops Wilson and Andrewes. Added, a compilation from Palmer's and Cotterhill's formularies. By William Meade, later bp. of Virginia. 2d ed. Georgetown, D. C., 1827. 292 p. MCET. 31784

---- ... The private meditations and prayers of the Rt. Rev. Thos. Wilson, D. D. ... 4th New-York ed. New-York, Pr. and sold by T. and J. Swords, 1827. 171 p. NNS; VtMiS. 31785

Wilson's Tennessee farmer's almanac for 1828. Nashville, George Wilson [1827] 18 l. MWA. 31786

Winebrenner, John, 1797-1860
Prayer meeting and revival hymn book; or, A selection of the best "Psalms and hymns and spiritual songs," from various authors, for the use of social prayer meetings and revivals of religion ... 3d ed. Harrisburg, Pr. by John S. Wiestling, 1827. 360, 14 p. OO. 31787

Winwright, John
Funeral invitation. Yourself and family are respectfully invited to attend the funeral of Maria Louisa, infant daughter of Mr. John Winwright, this morning at 10 o'clock, from his residence on Sycamore between Fourth and Fifth Streets. Cincinnati, July 14th, 1827. Bdsd. DLC. 31788

Wisner, Benjamin Blydenburg, 1794-1835
A sermon occasioned by the death of the Hon. William Phillips, preached on the third day of June, 1827 ... [Cambridge... University Press] - Hilliard, Metcalf & Co. Boston, Hilliard, Gray, Little and Wilkins, 1827. 52 p. CtHT; ICMe; ICN; ICU; M; MB; MBAt; MBB; MBC; MBNEH; MH-AH; MHi; MWA; MeBat; NBLiHi; NCH; Nh-Hi; NjR; OClWHi; PHi; RPB; WHi; BrMus. 31789

Wistar, Caspar, 1761-1818
A system of anatomy for the use of students of medicine ... 4th ed. Philadelphia, Carey, Lea & Carey, 1827. 2 v. ICJ; ICU-R; KCoU; KyLxT; MnRM; MoInRC; MoKJM; MoSMed; NBMS; NNC-M; NNNAM; OCGHM; PAtM; PPC; PPiAM; ScCMe; TxU; WaSK. 31790

The witty exploits of George Buchanan, commonly called the king's fool ... to which is added, Paddy from Cork, with his coat buttoned behind; being an elegant conference between English Tom, and Irish Teague. Philadelphia, F. Scott, 1827. 72 p. PHC. 31791

Woburn, Mass., Baptist Church
Summary declaration of the faith and practice of the Baptist Church of Christ in Woburn, which was adopted by the church when constituted at West Cambridge, 1781. ... Boston, Jonathan Howe, pr., 1827. 15 p. MWo; MiD-B. 31792

Woburn, Mass. First Congregational Church
Rules and regulations of the First Congregational Church in Woburn, Ms. Together with the covenant of said church, and a list of the names of existing members. [Boston, Pr. by Crocker & Brewster, 1827?] 12 p. MA; MWo. 31793

Wolfe, Charles, 1791-1823
Remains of the late Rev. Charles Wolfe ... curate of Donoughmore, Diocese of Armagh; with a brief memoir of his life ... Hartford, H. and F. J. Huntington, pub., 1827. 294 p. NUtHi. 31794

[Wood, Sally Sayward (Barrell) Keating] 1759-1855
Tales of the night. By a lady of Maine, author of Julia, The speculator, The old man's story, &c. Portland, Pr. and pub. by Thomas Todd, 1827. 74, 90 p. DLC. 31795

Woodbridge, William
A letter to the Hon. Abraham Edwards, president of the legislative council of the Territory of Michigan. Detroit, April 14, 1827. 16 p. MiD-B; OClWHi. 31796

---- Lettre a l'Honorable Abraham Edwards, president du conseil legislatif du Territoire du Michigan. [Detroit, 1827] 16 p. MiD-B; NN; OClWHi. 31797

Woodbridge, William Channing, 1794-1845
A system of universal geography, on the principles of comparison and classification. 2d ed. Hartford, O. D. Cooke, J. and J. Harper, prs., New York, 1827. xxxi, 336, 4 p. Ct; DLC; ICU; MDeeP; MH; MHad; MNF; MNHi; MiD-B; NTEW; NhD; NjR. 31798

[Woodhouslee, Alexander Fraser Tytler, Lord]
Elements of general history, ancient and modern. By Alexander Fraser Tytler ... With a continuation, terminating at the demise of King George III, 1820. By Rev. Edward Nares, D. D. Stereotyped by T. H. Carter and co., Boston. Pr. and pub. by Manahan, Hoag and co., Concord, N. H., 1827. 527, [3], 44 p. IU; MH; MiDU; NjP; NjR; OMC; PHi; TC; TNJ; TxDaM; TxU; ViAlTh. 31799

Woodland, Miss
Bear and forbear: or, The history of Julia Marchmont. New-York, W. B. Gilley, 1827. 142 p. DLC; MH. 31800

---- Matilda Mortimer; or, False pride. New York, Pub. by W. B. Gilley, 1827. 108 p. MAbD. 31801

---- Rose and Agnes: or, The dangers of partiality. New York, Gilley [W. E. Dean, pr.] 1827. 108 p. KU. 31802

---- A tale of warning: or, The victims of indolence. New York, W. B. Gilley, 1827. 94 p. DLC. 31803

Woodman Sandbornton Academy
Catalogue of the officers and students of Woodman Sanbornton Academy, Fall Term, November, 1827. Concord, Pr. by Luther Roby, 1827. Nh-Hi. 31804

Woods, Leonard
Duties of the rich. A sermon delivered in Newburyport. Feb. 18, 1827, on occasion of the death of Moses Brown, Esq. Andover, Pr. by Flagg & Gould, 1827. 39 p. CSmH; CtSoP; ICMe; M; MAnHi; MB; MBC; MH; MNe; MWA; MiD-B; Nh; PPL; PPPrHi; RHi; RPB; WHi; BrMus. 31805

Wood's almanac for 1828. By Joshua Sharp. New York, Samuel Wood & Sons [1827] 18 l. DLC; MWA; NHi; NNA. 31806

Worcester, Joseph Emerson, 1784-1865
Elements of geography, ancient and modern: with an atlas. Stereotype ed. Boston, Hilliard, Gray, Little & Wilkins, 1827. 293, [1] p. CtHT-W; KyLo; MH; NjR; RPB; TxU-T. 31807

---- Elements of history, ancient and modern. 3d ed. Boston, Pub. by Hilliard, Gray, Little & Wilkins, 1827. 338 p. ICU; MB; MH; MMhHi;OO. 31808

---- An historical atlas, containing the following charts ... A new ed. Boston, Hilliard, Gray, Little and Wilkins, 1827. 1 p. l., 9 charts. DLC; MCM; TxU. 31809

Worcester, Noah, 1758-1837
The doctrine of pronouns applied to Christ's testimony of himself. Pr. for the American Unitarian Association. Boston, Bowles & Dearborn, 1827. 24 p. CBPac; DLC; ICMe; KyHi; MBAt; MBC; MMeT; MNF; MW; Nh-Hi; PPWe; RPB; ScCC. 31810

[----] The peace catechism, on Christian principles. By Philo Pacificus, author of the "Friend of Peace." Rochester, Pr. by Marshall & Dean, 1827. 35 p. CSmH. 31811

Worcester, Samuel
First lessons in English grammar. Gloucester [Mass.] William M. H. Copeland, 1827. 36 p. MH; NNC. 31812

---- The importance of divine knowledge: a sermon preached at the ordination of the Rev. David Jewett, ... in Gloucester, Oct. 30, 1805. 2d ed. New York, Pr. by Vanderpool and Cole, for Cornelius Davis, 1827. 24 p. MBC; MeBat; NNC; NjR; OO; PPPrHi; BrMus. 31813

Worcester Central Association. Auxiliary Foreign Mission Society.
Proceedings ... at their third annual meeting, at Shrewsbury, Oct. 17, 1827. Worcester, William Manning, pr. [1827] 20 p. MWA. 31814

Worcester Female Samaritan Society
Constitution of the Worcester Female Samaritan Society. Worcester, Griffin and Morrill, prs. 1827. 8 p. MWA. 31815

A word to those whom it concerns, on the impropriety of using and selling spirituous liquors ... New-London [Conn.] Pr. by J. B. Clapp, 1827. 16 p. CSmH. 31816

Words of the duetts and songs, sung at Mrs. Knight's second grand concert. New York, J. Booth & sons [1827?] 10 l. RPB. 31817

Worshipper at St. Mary's. See An address to the pewholders...

Worsley, W. W.
Conduct of General Jackson to the Kentucky troops at New-Orleans. Compiled from public documents by Worsley & Buchanan, editors of the Focus, Louisville, Ky. [Louisville, W. W. Worsley, pr., 1827] 20 p. CSmH. 31818

Worthington, Erastus, 1779-1842
The history of Dedham, from the beginning of its settlement, in September, 1635, to May 1827. Boston, Dutton and Wentworth, prs., 1827. 146 p. CBPac; Ct; ICN; ICU; IaGG; IaHA; M; MA; MB; MBC; MC; MDed; MH; MNBedf; MWC; MWiW; MdBJ; MeHi; MiD-B; MiU; NNC; Nh; NhD; OO; PHi; PPi; RP; RNR; WHi; BrMus. 31819

The wreath; a collection of poems from celebrated English authors. Hartford, S. Andrus, publisher, 1827. vii, 252 p. ICMe; Ia-L; MB; MWA; MnSST; NNG; NcA-S. 31820

[Wright, Alfred]
Chahta holisso a tukla, or The second Chahta book: containing translations of portions of the scriptures, biographical notices of Henry Obokiah and Catharine Brown, a catechism, and dissertations on religious subjects. Cincinnati, Pr. by Morgan, Lodge and Fisher, 1827. 144 p. MBAt; OCHP. 31821

[----] A spelling book written in the Chato language with an English translation. 2d ed., revised. Cincinnati, Pr. by Morgan, Lodge, and Fisher, 1827. 160 p. MBAt; OkHi; PPAmP; PU. 31822

Wright, Frances
Deed of the lands of Nashoba, West Tennessee. by Frances Wright. Dated Nashoba, 1st Feb. 1827. [3] p. DLC. 31823

Wright, John Crafts, 1783-1861
Speeches of Mr. Wright, of Ohio, on the resolution calling on the Secretary of State for information relative to the selection of newspapers for the publication of the laws. Washington, 1827. 36 p. CSmH; DLC; MH; PPL; WHi. 31824

Wyatt, William Edward
Christian offices for the use of families and individuals, compiled from the liturgy of the Protestant Episcopal Church ... Baltimore, Edward J. Coale [J. D. Toy, pr.] 1827. 424 p. ICU; IObB; KWiU; MBC; MdHi; MiOC; NNG. 31825

X-Y-Z

Yale, Calvin, 1789-1882
A sermon, delivered before the Vermont Colonization Society at Montpelier, Oct. 17, 1827. Montpelier, Pr. by E. P. Walton, 1827. 15 p. CSmH; MiD-B; NNF; OClWHi; VtHi; VtMiM; WHi; BrMus. 31826

Yale, Cyrus, 1786-1854
An address, delivered before the Adelphic Union Society, of Williams College, on the evening before commencement, Sept. 4, 1827. Williamstown, Pr. by Ridley Bannister, 1827. 20 p. FK; MH; MWiW; NCH; NN; NNUT; PPLT; TNJ. 31827

---- A sermon preached at Torringford, Conn., Jan. 24, 1827, on occasion of the death of Miss Sophia Eliza Hawley, daughter of Dr. Orestos K. Hawley, of Austinburgh, Ohio. Hartford, Goodwin, pr., 1827. 24 p. Ct; NjR; OClWHi; OO; RPB. 31828

Yale University
Catalogue of the graduates of

Yale College ... 1702-1827; the names alphabetically arranged with the year of graduating prefixed to each ... New Haven, H. Howe, 1827. 98 p. CtY; M; MB; MH; MHi; MWA; RPB; ScCC. 31829

---- Catalogue of the officers and students in Yale College, Nov. 1827. New Haven, [Treadway and Adams, prs.] 1827. 31 p. CtY; MeB; NCH. 31830

---- Order of exercises at the exhibition of the junior class in Yale College, April 30, 1827. New Haven, Treadway & Adams, prs., 1827. 4 p. Ct. 31831

---- Divinity School.
Yale College, The theological department of this institution, it is well known, sustained a loss of nearly all its productive fund by the failure of the Eagle Bank ... Many individuals in this city have expressed their readiness to contribute a small sum annually ... and have recommended a meeting of the friends of the Theological School, to devise means for continuing it in existence ... July 27, 1827. [New Haven, 1827] 1 l. CtY. 31832

---- Society of the Alumni
Constitution of the Society of the Alumni of Yale College. [New Haven? 1827] [2] p. CtY. 31833

A Yankee, pseud. See A glance at the times.

The yankee. The farmer's almanack and annual register for 1828. By Thomas Spofford. Boston, David Felt & Co. [1827] 18 l. CLU; DLC; MHi; MWA; MiD-B; N; WHi. 31834

Yates, J. B.
Statement of the objections to the passage of the bill entitled "An act to regulate the sale of lottery tickets," submitted to the consideration of the Hon. the Legislature of the state of New-York. Albany, March, 1827. Albany, Pr. by Packard and Van Benthuysen, 1827. 20 p. C; DLC; N; NN. 31835

Yearly messenger or New town and country almanac for the year of our Lord 1828. Baltimore, Pr. & sold by John T. Hanzsche [1827] 32 p. MWA; NcU. 31836

Yeats, J. of Boston, U. S. A.
An address to the parents ... of the youth of Boston ... on the nature and importance of a good education etc. Boston (U. S.), 1827. BrMus. 31837

Yorick, Mr., pseud. See Sterne, Laurence.

Young, Alexander
Young against Chipman. Narrative of the case, and a concise statement of the trial at the Circuit Court before Judges Smith Thompson, and Elijah Paine, on the fourth October, 1826, at Rutland. Verdict for the plaintiff: damages $8, 927 51. [Mottoes.] [Published by the plaintiff. Pr. by Gamaliel Small, Vergennes, Vermont, 1827] 176 p. MH-L; VtMiS; VtU. 31838

The young child's prayer book. 2d ed. Boston, Bowles and Dearborn, I. R. Butts and Co., prs., 1827. 27 p. MHingHi. 31839

The young Jewess: a narrative illustrative of the Polish and English Jews of the present century, exhibiting the superior moral influence of Christianity. From the London ed. Boston, Pub. by James Loring, 1827. 180 p. PPL; RPB. 31840

Young Ladies' High School, Boston.
[Circular] Boston, 1827. 1 p. DLC. 31841

Young Men's Bible Society of Brooklyn
Constitution of the Young Men's Bible Society, of Brooklyn. Instituted 7th August, 1827. Brooklyn, Pr. by A. Spooner, 1827. 8, [1] p. CSmH. 31842

Young Men's Education Society of New-York City
The second report of the ... December 12, 1826. New-York, Pr. by John M. Danforth, 1827. 7, [1] p. MWA. 31843

Young Men's Unitarian Book and Pamphlet Society
Constitution of the Young Men's Unitarian Book and Pamphlet Society, formed August, 1827. Boston, Dutton & Wentworth, prs. 1827. 8 p. ICMe; MDovC. 31844

The young philosopher. By a lady ... Boston, Bowles & Dearborn, J.H. Eastburn, pr., 1827. 60 p. DLC; MH; NTEW. 31845

The young rifleman's comrade. See Mämpel, Johann Christian.

The youth and manhood of Cyril Thornton. See Hamilton, Thomas.

The youth's prayer book. See Palfrey, John Gorham.

Zeisberger, David, 1721-1808
Grammar of the language of the Lenni Lenape or Delaware Indians. Trans. from the German manuscript of the author by Peter Stephen Du Ponceau. Philadelphia, Pr. by J. Kay, jun., 1827. 188 p., 1 l. CtW; DLC; MB; MiD-B; NIC; PP; PU. 31846

Zollickoffer, William
A materia medica, of the United States, systematically arranged ... 2d ed., with emendations, &c. Baltimore, J. Lovegrove, 1827. Wm. Wooddy, pr. 245 p., 1 l. IaU; MdBM; MdHi; PPC; PU; RPB; WU-M. 31847

Alvarez, José Maria, 1777-1820
Instituciones de derecho real de Castilla y de Indias ... 2d. ed. Nuevament aumentada, revista y corregida. Tono III. Nueva York. En casa de Lanuza. Mendia y c. Impresores Liberos, 1827. Vol. III only. C-S. 31848

Baptists, Maine. Baptist Convention of the State of Maine
Minutes of the Maine Baptist Convention, held in Thomaston, Oct. 10 & 11, 1827. Hallowell, Pr. by Spaulding & Livermore, 1827. 24 p. MeB. 31849

Belleville Seminary
Catalogue instructors and pupils. Belleville Seminary, Spring term, 1827. Newburyport, Pr. at the office of the Newburyport Herald, 1827. Bdsd. MNe (not verified, 1970) 31850

Brewer, Samuel N.
Circular, announcing his partnership as druggist. [Boston, 1827?] Bdsd. MHi (not loc., 1970) 31851

Carey, Henry Charles and I. Lea, firm
Valuable works, now preparing, and speedily to be published, by H. C. Carey & I. Lea, Philadelphia. [Philadelphia] 1827. 12 p. DeGE. 31852

Cochin, Jacques Denis, 1726-1783
Platicas, ó Instrucciones familiares sobre las oraciones y ceremonias del santo sacrificio de la misa. Re-impresso en Fildadelfia, 1827. 2 v. C-S. 31853

Colombia
Esposicion de los sentimientos de los funcionarios publicos, asi nacionales como departamentales y municipales, presentada al Libertador. New York, re-imp. 1827. 26 p. Sabin 14585; MHi, not loc., 1970. 31854

Freemasons. Pennsylvania. Grand Encampment
By laws of holy and undivided trinity encampment held at Harrisburg, Pennsylvania under the jurisdiction of the grand encampment of the United States, 1827. Harrisburg, Pr. by companion Simon Cameron, 1827. 8 p. OCM; not verified, 1970. 31855

Graham & Mandeville, Philadelphia
Catalogue of teas, imported in the ship New Jersey, from Canton, to be sold at the auction store, corner of Front and Chesnut [!] streets, on Friday morning, August 10th, at 11 o'clock, by Graham & Mandeville, auct'rs. [Philadelphia, 1827?] 4 p. DeGE. 31856

McDuffie, George, 1790-1851
Speech of Mr. McDuffie, of S. C. in the House of Representatives of the U. S. on the woollens' bill. February 7, 1827. Washington, Pr. by Gales & Seaton, 1827. 19 p. DeGE. 31857

New York (State)
An act concerning religious and other corporations (Chapter

XVIII of the first part) [Albany, Pr. by Croswell & Van Benthuysen, 1827] 36 p. NNB. 31858

---- Amendments proposed by the select committee to Articles two and three, of Chapter XVI. [Albany, Pr. by Croswell & Van Benthuysen, 1827] 11 p. NNB. 31859

---- Amendments to Chapter VI. As proposed by the Committee. [Albany, Pr. by Croswell and Van Benthuysen, 1827] [1], 8 p. NNB. 31860

---- Amendments to the Second chapter of the report of the revisers. Proposed in Senate, March 1, 1827. [Albany, Croswell and Van Benthuysen, 1827] 3 p. NNB. 31861

---- Analysis and contents of Chapter X of the first part of the proposed revision of the statute laws of this state. Albany, Pr. by Croswell and Van Benthuysen, 1827. xviii p. NNB. 31862

---- Chapter V. Of the Second part of the proposed revision of the statute laws of the state of New-York. Albany, Pr. by Croswell & Van Benthuysen, 1827. [4], 77 p. NNB. 31863

---- Chapter VI. Of the first part of the proposed revision of the statute laws of the state of New-York. As amended and passed by the Senate. Albany, Pr. by Croswell and Van Benthuysen, 1827. 35 p. NNB. 31864

---- Chapter XI. Of the first part of the proposed revision of the statute laws of the state of New-York. As passed by the Senate. Albany, Pr. by Croswell and Van Benthuysen, 1827. 39 p. NNB. 31865

---- In Assembly, Sept. 21, 1827. Second meeting. Amendments to Chapter IX. Proposed by the Joint Committee. [Albany, Pr. by Croswell and Van Benthuysen, 1827] 19 p. NNB. 31866

---- In Assembly, Oct. 23, 1827. - Second meeting. Chapter XIII. Title IV. Regulations concerning the assessment of taxes on incorporated companies and the commutation or collection thereof. [Albany, Pr. by Croswell and Van Benthuysen, 1827] 10 p. NNB. 31867

---- In Senate. November 17, 1827. - Third meeting. Amendment of the committee of the whole, to chapter VI. Title IV. With note. [Albany, Pr. by Croswell & Van Benthuysen, 1827] 3 p. NNB. 31868

---- In Senate, Nov. 28, 1827. Third meeting. Amendment to Chapter II, Part two, sections 22-24. [Albany, Pr. by Croswell & Van Benthuysen, 1827] [1] p. NNB. 31869

North American Coal Company

A brief sketch of the property belonging to the North American Coal Company; with some general remarks on the subject of coal and coal mines. New York, Pr. by G. F. Hopkins, 1827. 23 p. DeGE. 31870

Pennsylvania Society for the Promotion of Manufactures and the Mechanic Arts

Members of the Pennsylvania Society for the Promotion of Manufactures and the Mechanic Arts. [Philadelphia, 1827] [2] l. DeGE. 31871

Sherwood, Mrs. Mary Martha (Butt), 1775-1851

Lady of the manor, being a series of conversations on the subject of the confirmation. Intended for the use of the middle and higher ranks of young females. Baltimore, 1827. MDeeP (not verified, 1970). 31872

Something new; or, A budget of Calvinism. By a friend of truth and fair dealing. Haverhill, 1827. MHi (not loc., 1970) 31873

Stewart, Andrew, 1791-1872
Mr. Stewart's speech on the bill for the protection of wool and woollen manufactures, in the House of Representatives, February 1, 1827. [Washington, E. Bellamy, pr., 1827] 16 p. DeGE. 31874